N 0096517 0

ENCYCLOPEDIA
OF BIBLICAL THEOLOGY
Volume 1

Bauer Encyclopedia of Biblical Theology

edited by Johannes B. Bauer

Volume 1

Abraham – Hour

SHEED AND WARD · LONDON AND SYDNEY

Sheed and Ward Ltd, 33 Maiden Lane, London WC2, and
Sheed and Ward Pty Ltd, 204 Clarence Street, Sydney

First published 1970

Originally published as *Bibeltheologisches Wörterbuch*, Verlag Styria, Graz-Vienna-Cologne (1959). This translation is made from the third enlarged and revised edition of 1967.

SBN 7220 0620 9
Made and printed in Great Britain by
William Clowes and Sons, Limited, London and Beccles
This book is set in 11/13½ pt. Baskerville

Nihil obstat: Nicholas J. Tranter, S.T.L, Censor
Imprimatur: + Patrick Casey, Vic. Gen.
Westminster, 17 October 1969

CONTENTS

Volume 1

Volume 3

Contributors

Nikolaus Adler, Mainz-Gonsenheim
Paul Asveld, Graz
Albert Auer, Flüeli
Johannes B. Bauer, Graz
Wolfgang Beilner, Salzburg
Peter Bläser, Paderborn
Josef Blinzler, Passau
G. Johannes Botterweck, Bonn
Norbert Brox, Salzburg
Henri Cazelles, Paris
Jean Daniélou, Paris
Alfons Deissler, Freiburg
Josef Dey, Hofheim
Walter Dürig, Munich
Jean de Fraine†, Louvain
Johannes Gabriel†, Vienna
Johann Gamberoni, Brixen
Heinrich Gross, Trier
Odilo Kaiser, Freiburg
Robert Koch, Rome
Elisabeth Koffmahn, Vienna
Walter Kornfeld, Vienna
Johannes Kosnetter, Vienna
Elmar M. Kredel, Munich
Johannes Kürzinger, Eichstätt
Johann Michl, Munich
Georg Molin, Graz
Franz Mussner, Regensburg
Paul Neuenzeit, Würzburg
Friedrich Nötscher†, Bonn
Jakob Obersteiner, Gurk
Elpidius Pax, Jerusalem
Rudolf Pesch, Freiburg
Wilhelm Pesch, Hennef
Myriam Prager, Pertlstein
Karl Prümm, Rome
Josef Scharbert, Freising
Karl Hermann Schelkle, Tübingen
Johannes Schildenberger, Beuron
Othmar Schilling, Bochum
Josef Schmid, Munich
Ernst Schmitt, Bamberg
Rudolf Schnackenburg, Würzburg
Suitbert H. Siedl, Salzburg
Ceslaus Spicq, Fribourg
F. L. R. Stachowiak, Lodz
Meinrad Stenzel†, München-Freising
Alois Stöger, Rome
Gerhard Trenkler, Graz
Anton Vögtle, Freiburg
Viktor Warnach, Salzburg
Georg Ziener, Hünfeld bei Fulda
Heinrich Zimmermann, Bochum

TRANSLATORS

Joseph Blenkinsopp
David J. Bourke
N. D. Smith
Walter P. van Stigt

ABBREVIATIONS

1. *Biblical: Old Testament, New Testament, and Apocrypha*

Acts	Acts of the Apostles	2 Kings	2 Kings
Amos	Amos	Lam	Lamentations
Bar	Baruch	Lev	Leviticus
1 Chron	1 Chronicles	Lk	Luke
2 Chron	2 Chronicles	1 Macc	1 Maccabees
Col	Colossians	2 Macc	2 Maccabees
1 Cor	1 Corinthians	Mal	Malachi
2 Cor	2 Corinthians	Mic	Micah
Dan	Daniel	Mk	Mark
Deut	Deuteronomy	Mt	Matthew
Eccles	Ecclesiastes	Nahum	Nahum
Eph	Ephesians	Neh	Nehemiah
Esther	Esther	Num	Numbers
Ex	Exodus	Obad	Obadiah
Ezek	Ezekiel	1 Pet	1 Peter
Ezra	Ezra	2 Pet	2 Peter
Gal	Galatians	Phil	Philippians
Gen	Genesis	Philem	Philemon
Hab	Habakkuk	Prov	Proverbs
Hag	Haggai	Ps	Psalms
Heb	Hebrews	Rev	Revelation
Hos	Hosea	Rom	Romans
Is	Isaiah	Ruth	Ruth
Jas	James	1 Sam	1 Samuel
Jer	Jeremiah	2 Sam	2 Samuel
Jn	John	Sir	Sirach (Ecclesiasticus)
1 Jn	1 John	Song	Song of Songs
2 Jn	2 John	1 Thess	1 Thessalonians
3 Jn	3 John	2 Thess	2 Thessalonians
Job	Job	1 Tim	1 Timothy
Joel	Joel	2 Tim	2 Timothy
Jon	Jonah	Tit	Titus
Josh	Joshua	Tob	Tobit
Jude	Jude	Wis	Wisdom
Judg	Judges	Zech	Zechariah
Judith	Judith	Zeph	Zephaniah
1 Kings	1 Kings		

2. *Non-biblical: Talmudic, apocalyptic, and other apocryphal writings*

ActAndr	Acts of Andrew	Keth	Kethuboth (Talm.)
ActJn	Acts of John	3 Macc	3 Maccabees
ActPaul	Acts of Paul	4 Macc	4 Maccabees
ActPet	Acts of Peter	MartIs	Martyrdom of Isaiah
ApocAbr	Apocalypse of Abraham	Men	Menahoth (Talm.)
		MidrSong	Midrash to the Song of Songs (etc.)
ApocElij	Apocalypse of Elijah		
ApocMos	Apocalypse of Moses	PsSol	Psalms of Solomon
ApocPet	Apocalypse of Peter	Sib	Sibylline Oracles
AssMos	Assumption of Moses	TestXII	Testaments of the Twelve Patriarchs
Bar (Gr)	Apocalypse of Baruch (Greek)	TestAsh	Testament of Asher, etc: Benj(amin); Iss(achar); Jos(eph); Jud(ah); Levi; Naph(tali); Reub(en); Sim(eon); Zeb(ulun)
(Syr)	(Syriac)		
Ber	Berakoth (Talm.)		
Did	Didache		
EpBarn	Epistle of Barnabas		
Enoch (Eth)	Enoch (Ethiopic)		
(Gr)	(Greek)		
(Heb)	(Hebrew)		
(Slav)	(Slavonic)	TestAbr	Testament of Abraham
GosPet	Gospel of Peter		
Jub	Book of Jubilees	Zeb	Zebahim (Talm.)

In abbreviations of the Qumran texts, the symbol Q (=Qumran) is preceded by a number indicating the cave of the find, and in the case of biblical books followed by the usual abbreviations (a, b, c, etc in smaller type is used when several copies of the same text have been found in the same cave). For other texts the accepted Hebrew abbreviation is used, and in the case of bible-commentaries this is preceded by p (=*peser*, explanation). Thus 1 QIs[a] = the first Isaiah-scroll found in the first cave at Qumran; 1 QpHab = the commentary on the Book of Habbakkuk from the first cave; 1 QS = *Serek hayaḥad*, the Manual of Discipline, found in the first cave; QM = *Milhamoth bne or*, the War Rule; QH = *Hodayoth*, the Thanksgiving Psalms. The Damascus Rule is CD (=Cairo Document), the corresponding texts found in Qumran 4QD and 6QD. Translations of the Qumran writings are readily available in G. Vermes, *The Dead Sea Scrolls in English*, Harmondsworth 1962.

3. *Books and periodicals*

AA	*Alttestamentliche Abhandlungen*, ed. A. Schultz, Münster 1908ff
AAS	*Acta Apostolicae Sedis*, Rome 1909ff
AfO	*Archiv für Orientforschung*, Berlin 1926ff
Allmen	J.-J. von Allmen (ed.), *Vocabulary of the Bible*, London 1958 (translation of *Vocabulaire biblique*, Neuchatel 1956²)
ALW	*Archiv für Liturgiewissenschaft*, Regensburg 1950ff
AOT	*Altorientalische Texte zum AT*, ed. H. Gressmann, Berlin 1926²
ARW	*Archiv für Religionswissenschaft*, Leipzig 1898ff
ATR	*Anglican Theological Review*, Evanston (Ill.) 1918ff
AV	Authorised Version of the Bible
BASOR	*Bulletin of the American Schools of Oriental Research*, New Haven (Conn.) 1919ff
BBB	*Bonner Biblischer Beiträge*, Bonn 1950ff
Bbl	*Biblica*, Rome 1920ff
BHHW	*Biblisch-historisches Handwörterbuch*, ed. B. Reicke and L. Rost, Göttingen 1962
BJRL	*Bulletin of the John Rylands Library*, Manchester 1903ff
BK	*Bibel in Kirche*
BKW	*Bible Key Words* (fourteen volumes), London 1949–65 (translations of some major articles in *TWNT*, q.v.)
BL	*Bibel und Liturgie*
BM	*Benediktinische Monatshefte*, Beuron 1919ff
Bousset-Gressmann	W. Bousset and H. Gressmann, *Die Religion des Judentums im späthellenistischen Zeitalter*, Tübingen 1926³
BRL	*Biblisches Reallexikon*, ed. K. Galling, Tübingen 1937
BTHW	*Biblisch-theologisches Handwörterbuch*, ed. E. Osterloh and H. Engelland, Göttingen 1954
Bultmann	R. Bultmann, *Theology of the New Testament* I, London 1965²; and II, London 1965² (translation of *Theologie des NT* [one volume], Tübingen 1954²)
BWANT	*Beiträge zur Wissenschaft vom A* (*und N*) *T*, Leipzig 1908ff and Stuttgart 1926ff
BZ	*Biblische Zeitschrift*, Paderborn 1957ff (n.s.)
BZAW	*Beiheft zur ZAW* (q.v.)
BZF	*Biblische Zeitfragen*, ed. P. Heinisch and F. W. Maier, Münster 1908ff
BZNW	*Beiheft zur ZNW* (q.v.)
CBQ	*Catholic Biblical Quarterly*, Washington 1939ff
CC	*La Civiltà Cattolica*, Rome 1850ff

CCSL — *Corpus Christianorum, Series Latina*, ed. E. Dekkers, Turnhout 1953ff
CIC — *Codex Iuris Canonici*, Rome 1918
CIG — *Corpus Inscriptionum Graecarum*, ed. Boeckh and others
CSEL — *Corpus Scriptorum Ecclesiasticorum Latinorum*, Vienna 1866ff
Cullmann — O. Cullmann, *The Christology of the New Testament*, London 1962[2] (translation of *Christologie des*[2] *NT*, Tübingen 1957)
CV — *Communio Viatorum*

DACL — *Dictionnaire de l'Archéologie chrétienne et Liturgie*, ed. F. Cabrol and H. Leclerq, Paris 1924ff
DB, DB(S) — *Dictionnaire de la Bible* (*Supplément*), ed. L. Pirot and others, Paris 1928ff
DB, DS — H. Denzinger, *Enchiridion Symbolorum, Definitionum, et Declarationum de Rebus Fidei et Morum*, ed. C. Bannwart and others, Freiburg 1908ff; ed. A. Schönmetzer, Freiburg 1963ff (with revised numeration)
DBT — *Dictionary of Biblical Theology*, ed. X. Léon-Dufour, London and New York 1967 (translation of *Vocabulaire de théologie biblique*, Paris 1962)
DEB — *Dictionnaire encyclopédique de la Bible*, Paris-Turnhout 1960
de Vaux — R. de Vaux, *Ancient Israel: Its Life and Institutions*, London and New York 1961 (translation of *Les Institutions de l'AT* [two volumes] Paris 1958–60)
Diels — H. Diels and W. Kranz (ed.), *Die Fragmente der Vorsokratiker* (three volumes), Berlin-Neukölln 1954[7]
DV — *Dieu Vivant*, Paris 1954ff

Eichrodt — W. Eichrodt, *Theology of the Old Testament* I, London and Philadelphia 1960; and II, London and Philadelphia 1967; and *Theologie des AT* III, Stuttgart and Göttingen 1939 (1961[2])
EKL — *Evangelisches Kirchenlexikon*, Göttingen 1958
ET — *Evangelische Theologie*, Munich 1934ff
ETL — *Ephemerides Theologicae Lovanienses*, Bruges 1924ff

Feine — P. Feine, *Theologie des NT*, Berlin 1951[8]
FRLANT — *Forschungen zur Religion und Literatur des A und NT*, Göttingen 1903ff

GL — *Geist und Leben*, Würzburg 1947ff
Greg — *Gregorianum*, Rome 1920ff

Haag — H. Haag (ed.), *Bibellexikon*, Einsiedeln 1951
Heinisch — P. Heinisch, *Theology of the Old Testament*, Collegeville (Minn.) 1955 (translation of *Theologie des AT*, Bonn 1940)

HTG	*Handbuch theologischer Grundbegriffe*, ed. H. Fries, Munich 1962–3
HTR	*Harvard Theological Review*, Cambridge (Mass.) 1908ff
HUCA	*Hebrew Union College Annual*, Cincinnati (Ohio) 1914ff
IEJ	*Israel Exploration Journal*, Jerusalem 1950ff
Imschoot	P. van Imschoot, *Theology of the Old Testament* I, New York 1965; and *Theologie de l'AT* II, Tournai 1956
ITQ	*Irish Theological Quarterly*, Dublin 1951ff (n.s.)
Jacob	E. Jacob, *Theology of the Old Testament*, New York 1958 (translation of *Théologie de l'AT*, Neuchatel 1956)
JBL	*Journal of Biblical Literature*, Boston (Mass.) 1881ff
JEH	*Journal of Ecclesiastical History*, London 1950ff
JPOS	*Journal of the Palestine Oriental Society*, Leipzig-Jerusalem 1920ff
JSS	*Journal of Semitic Studies*, 1956ff
JTS	*Journal of Theological Studies*, London 1899ff
KD	*Kerygma und Dogma*
Köhler	L. Köhler, *Old Testament Theology*, Philadelphia (Pa.) 1958 (translation of *Theologie des AT*, Tübingen 1953[3])
LM	*Liturgie und Mönchtum*, Maria Laach 1948ff
LTK	*Lexikon für Theologie und Kirche* (ten volumes), ed. J. Höfer and K. Rahner, Freiburg 1957–65[2]
LV	*Lumière et Vie*, Lyons 1951ff
LXX	Septuagint
Mansi	J. Mansi and others (ed.), *Sacrorum Conciliorum Nova et Amplissima Collectio*, Florence 1759ff and Paris-Leipzig 1901–27
MAOG	*Mitteilungen der Altorientalischen Gesellschaft*, Leipzig 1925ff
MD	*La Maison-Dieu*, Paris 1945ff
Meinertz	M. Meinertz, *Theologie des NT* (two volumes), Bonn 1950
MTZ	*Münchener theologische Zeitschrift*, Munich 1950ff
MVAG	*Mitteilungen der vorderasiatisch(ägyptisch)en Gesellschaft*, Leipzig 1896ff
NA	*Neutestamentliche Abhandlungen*, ed. M. Meinertz, Münster 1909ff
NKS	*Nederlandse Katholieke Stemmen*, Zwolle 1901ff
NKZ	*Neue kirchliche Zeitschrift*, Leipzig 1890ff
NRT	*Nouvelle Revue théologique*, Tournai-Louvain 1879ff
NTS	*New Testament Studies*, Cambridge 1954ff
NTT	*Norsk Teologisk Tidsskrift*
NvT	*Novum Testamentum*, Leiden 1956ff

OS	*L'Orient Syrien*, Paris 1956ff
OTS	*Oudtestamentische Studien*, Leiden 1942ff
PG	*Patrologiae Cursus completus, Series Graeca*, ed. J. P. Migne, Paris 1857ff
PL	*Patrologiae Cursus completus, Series Latina*, ed. J. P. Migne, Paris 1844ff
Proksch	O. Proksch, *Theologie des AT*, Gütersloh 1950
RAC	*Reallexikon für Antike und Christentum*, ed. T. Klauser, Stuttgart 1950[2]ff
RB	*Revue biblique*, Paris 1892ff
RGG	*Religion in Geschichte und Gegenwart*, ed. K. Galling, Tübingen 1956[3]ff
RHE	*Revue d'Histoire ecclésiastique*, Louvain 1900ff
RHPR	*Revue d'Histoire et Philosophie religieuses*, Strasbourg-Paris 1921ff
RHR	*Revue de l'Histoire des Religions*, Paris 1880ff
RNT	*Regensburger Neues Testament*, ed. A. Wikenhauser and O. Kuss, Regensburg 1956[3]ff
RQ	*Revue de Qumran*, Paris 1959ff
RSPT	*Revue des Sciences philosophiques et théologiques*, Paris 1907ff
RSR	*Recherches de Science religieuse*, Paris 1910ff
RSV	Revised Standard Version of the Bible
RT	*Revue thomiste*, Brussels 1893ff
RTP	*Revue de Théologie et Philosophie*, Lausanne 1951ff (n.s.)
SB	H. Strack and P. Billerbeck, *Kommentar zum NT aus Talmud und Midrasch* (five volumes), Munich 1922–8 and 1956[2]
Schnackenburg	R. Schnackenburg, *The Moral Teaching of the New Testament*, London and New York 1968 (translation of *Die sittliche Bottschaft des NT*, Munich 1954)
SE	*Sciences ecclésiastiques*
SEA	*Svensk exegetisk årsbok*, Uppsala 1936ff
SJT	*Scottish Journal of Theology*, Edinburgh
SKZ	*Schweitzerische Kirchenzeitung*
SNTSB	*Studiorum NT Societas Bulletin*
SP	*Sacra Pagina*, Paris-Gembloux 1959ff
ST	*Studia Theologica*, Lund 1948ff
Stauffer	E. Stauffer, *Theology of the New Testament*, London 1963[2] (translation of *Theologie des NT*, Gütersloh 1948[5])
SZ	*Stimmen der Zeit*, Freiburg 1871ff
TB	*Theologische Blätter*, Leipzig 1922ff

TDNT	*Theological Dictionary of the New Testament* I–VI, ed. G. Kittel and G. Friedrichs, Grand Rapids (Mich.), 1964–7 (translation of *TWNT* [q.v.] I–VI, Stuttgart 1930ff)
TG	*Theologie und Glaube*, Paderborn 1909ff
TLZ	*Theologische Literaturzeitung*, Leipzig 1878ff
TPQ	*Theologisch-praktische Quartalschrift*, Linz 1848ff
TQ	*Theologische Quartalschrift*, Tübingen 1819ff
TR	*Theologische Rundschau*, Tübingen 1897ff
TS	*Theological Studies*, Baltimore 1940ff
TSK	*Theologische Studien und Kritiken*, Gotha 1828ff
TT	*Tijdschrift voor Theologie*, Wageningen
TTK	*Tidsskrift for Teologi og Kirke*
TTZ	*Trierer theologische Zeitschrift*, Trier 1888ff
TU	*Texte und Untersuchungen zur Geschichte der altchristlichen Literatur*, Leipzig 1882ff
TWNT	*Theologisches Wörterbuch zum NT* VII–VIII, ed. G. Friedrich, Stuttgart 1954ff (earlier volumes translated as *TDNT*, q.v.)
TZ	*Theologische Zeitschrift*, Basle 1945ff
VC	*Vigiliae Christianae: A Review for Early Life and Language*, Amsterdam 1947ff
VD	*Verbum Domini*, Rome 1921ff
von Rad	G. von Rad, *Old Testament Theology* I, Edinburgh-London and New York 1962; and II, Edinburgh-London and New York 1965 (translation of *Theologie des AT* [two volumes], Munich 1957–60)
Vriezen	T. C. Vriezen, *Outline of Old Testament Theology*, Oxford and Newton Centre 1958 (translation of *Hoofdlijnen der Theologie van het OT*, Wageningen 1960[2])
VS	*La Vie Spirituelle*, Paris 1869ff
VT	*Vetus Testamentum*, Leiden 1951ff
WW	*Wissenschaft und Weisheit*, Düsseldorf 1934ff
WZKM	*Wiener Zeitschrift für die Kunde des Morgenländes*, Vienna 1887ff
ZAW	*Zeitschrift für die alttestamentliche Wissenschaft*, Berlin 1881ff
ZDMG	*Zeitschrift der deutschen morgenländischen Gesellschaft*, Leipzig 1847ff
ZDPV	*Zeitschrift des deutschen Palästina-Vereins*, Leipzig 1878ff
ZEE	*Zeitschrift für evangelische Ethik*, Gütersloh 1957ff
ZKG	*Zeitschrift für Kirchengeschichte*, Gotha-Stuttgart 1876ff
ZKT	*Zeitschrift für katholische Theologie*, Innsbruck 1877ff
ZNW	*Zeitschrift für die neutestamentliche Wissenschaft und die Kunde der älteren Kirche*, Giessen-Berlin 1900ff

ZRG	*Zeitschrift für Religions- und Geistesgeschichte*, Marburg 1948ff
ZST	*Zeitschrift für systematische Theologie*, Berlin 1923ff
ZTK	*Zeitschrift für Theologie und Kirche*, Tübingen 1891ff

TRANSLITERATION

1. *Transcription of Hebrew characters*

Aleph	ʾ	Pe	p
Beth	b	Tsade	ts
Gimel	g	Qoph	q
Daleth	d	Res	r
He	h	Sin	ś
Waw	w	Šin	š
Zayin	z	Taw	t (th)
Heth	ḥ	Qames	ā
Teth	ṭ	Pathah	a
Yod	y	Tsere	ê or ē
Kaph	k	Seghol	e
Lamed	l	Hireq	î, i
Mem	m	Holem	ô, ō
Nun	n	Sureq	û
Samech	s	Qibbuts	u
Ayin	ʿ	Šewas	a e o

2. *Transcription of Greek characters*

Alpha	a	Ksi	ks
Beta	b	Omicron	o
Gamma	g (n before g, or k)	Pi	p
Delta	d	Rho	r
Epsilon	e	Sigma	s
Zeta	z	Tau	t
Eta	ē	Upsilon	u
Theta	th	Phi	ph
Iota	i	Psi	ps
Iota subscript	(i)	Khi	kh
Kappa	k	Omega	ō
Lambda	l	Digamma	(w)
Mu	m	Aspirate (rough	
Nu	n	breathing)	h

Preface to the first German edition

Biblical theology

The diversity of views about biblical theology makes it necessary to begin with a brief account of them. In this way, by seeing what biblical theology is not, we may more clearly see what it is, and what is its status, its nature, and its justification.

Biblical theology may, in the first place, be viewed as that part of theology which supplies all the many doctrinal theses with their bases in scripture. This may be useful, but it contains many dangers. In this view the usual starting point is from the classifications and categories of modern theology, and these can all too easily be imported back into scriptural revelation itself, thereby causing shifts of emphasis and changes of proportion. But of course, if the identity of the doctrinal structure is to be preserved, all that is essential must remain essential and all that is accidental merely accidental. For example, the resurrection of Christ does not play a prominent part in the soteriology of Anselm—but it does in the soteriologies of Paul or John. This should be borne in mind. Again, particular points of doctrine may disappear altogether because they are no longer fully or properly discussed in later theology and so are not found in our contemporary handbooks of dogmatics. Take, for example, the cosmic significance of the redemption—a theme which is certainly mentioned by Paul (in Rom 8 and in the captivity epistles) and which finds expression in the liturgy: 'Unda manat et cruor; terra, pontus, astra, mundus, quo lavantur flumine' (see Aquinas, *Summa contra Gentiles* IV, last chapter).[1]

The alternative method does not start from modern categories of thought but from the sacred texts themselves; nor is it concerned with apologetics or with proving or disproving theses. The aim is to reveal, where possible, the categories, the modes of thought, of the biblical writers themselves—to show the world in which Christ, the apostles, and the early christians lived, their views and ideas, the images they used. In this way biblical theology is an attempt to arrive at a complete understanding of christian doctrine; it does not proceed from some preconceived system or in terms alien to its subject-matter, but uses modes of thought peculiar to the scriptures, trying to go to the very heart and real background of revelation.[2]

We must bear in mind that, since the time of Christ and the apostles, further development has taken place in christian doctrine, and above all that christian

[1] S. Lyonnet, 'La valeur sotériologique de la résurrection du Christ selon S. Paul', *Greg* 39 (1958), 295–318; J. B. Bauer, 'Um die ganze Lehre', *Der Seelsorger* 24 (1954), 373–6; and J. B. Bauer, 'In doctrina integritatem', *Oberrhein. Pastoralblatt* 55 (1954), 214–16.

[2] V. Warnach, 'Gedanken zur ntl. Theologie', *Gloria Dei* 7 (1952), 72.

doctrine has been presented in terms of certain philosophical systems, so that our present concepts and views have necessarily been influenced by—and are dependent on—this development. No wonder that a marked difference can be seen between the concept of *caritas Dei*, of God's love, as employed by the Council of Trent[1] in referring to Rom 5:5 and Paul's views as actually expressed in this passage, where he speaks, not of sanctifying grace through which God dwells in us, but of God's love towards man. The Council has quoted this text rightly only if it can be proved from the text that man, supernaturally reborn, does indeed possess the new life, the divine life, of the blessed Trinity.

Moreover, revelation was completed with the death of the last apostle, but not before. Up until then there was, for a period of about half a century, not only a kind of further elaboration—as afterwards—but a real development. It is evident from the writings of the evangelists that even Christ revealed himself by stages and still left a great deal to the Holy Spirit who was to teach his disciples—not because there was no more for him to reveal, but because the disciples were incapable of grasping any more at the time (see Irenaeus, *Adv. Haer.* IV, 38, 1ff). That is the reason why even the New Testament authors differ and diverge from each other in certain respects: eg Mark's christology is not necessarily identical with John's or Paul's. This may strike non-catholic readers as a contradiction, but anyone who really believes in the divine inspiration of the whole of the bible cannot view this development within revelation as anything but homogeneous. Indeed, in virtue of this homogeneity, a deeper understanding of Christ's own words may be obtained in the light of later revelation (as in the case of Paul)—an even deeper understanding than can be ascribed to the evangelist who actually heard these words and wrote them down. These different stages must always be in the foreground of our minds. It is the task of biblical theology to map out this 'history of revelation'.[2]

The significance of biblical theology

Dogmatic theology cannot be reduced to biblical theology. It arises out of tradition, although tradition can never be considered independently of the bible, any more than the bible can be fully understood independently of tradition. All the same, the importance of biblical theology for dogmatic theology can hardly be overestimated. It assists dogmatic theologians in their work and acts as a safeguard against the losing sight of those truths which receive less emphasis—a safeguard, too, against the shifting of emphasis and the change of relative importance as between the various different elements. Biblical theology will be of special use in the business of providing biblical proof which will no longer consist, like some fleshless skeleton, of texts taken out of their contexts. Rather, it will exhibit the development of a given doctrine in relation to other doctrines; it will enable us to form an idea of the place one particular truth occupies within the whole framework of revelation, and of the different forms in which this truth has been repre-

[1] *Decretum de justificatione* (DS 1530 [=DB 800]).
[2] P. Benoit, *RB* 54 (1947), 611f.

sented during the different periods of revelation—and this in turn will bring about a better preparation for the 'ministry of the word', the preaching of the faith.[1] Experience has shown that biblical theology is exactly what appeals to our contemporaries, and this alone should be enough to evoke our interest in it. It is not mere coincidence that the theology of the apostolic fathers had and still has such vital influence—our predigested, systematised handbooks, weighed down with speculation, were not available to them. They had to build up their own theology, and in their preaching they had to draw on their own resources. Their theology was always the result of personal study of the original sources—of the scriptures and the living tradition of teaching in the church. 'That is why the study of these hallowed sources gives the sacred sciences a kind of perpetual youth: evade the labour of probing deeper and deeper yet into the sacred deposit, and your speculations—experience shows it—grow barren', as Pope Pius XII put it, and one feels that he must have had some bitter experience in the matter himself.[2]

The study of biblical theology also demands collaboration with our separated brethren. Biblical theology is to them what dogmatic theology is to us Roman Catholics, since the bible is their only norm and they have to consult it to a correspondingly greater degree. One of the most prominent protestant scholars remarked a few years ago: 'Let us state once and for all what is really needed if we are to ascertain the facts about the early church: a merciless attitude towards one's own dogmatics. In the study of biblical theology one has to be prepared to cut one's own dogmatics to the bone without hesitation.'[3]

Moreover, biblical theology clearly shows the independence of catholic dogma from any system of philosophy. Provided the substantial identity of the various dogmas is preserved, no harm can be done by an explanation in terms of Platonism, Aristotelianism, or Indian and Chinese systems of philosophy. On the contrary, such attempts are to be desired since, if this is the case, the pearl of the gospel will always preserve its supernatural and manifest splendour and never be mistaken for the setting in which man has enclosed it—which will always be cramping, however beautiful it may be.[4]

The question remains whether biblical theology deserves the name 'theology'. Is it not really a history of christian doctrine? By no means. Unlike the historian, the biblical theologian does not approach pauline or johannine teaching with a purely historical interest, but because of the extent to which it reveals what the teaching of the Catholic Church was at that time. He regards this doctrine as a phase, an aspect, of the present teaching of the church, not independent of its present state. Such a view, which takes account of the later explication of revelation, enables us to assume what has not yet been fully worked out—without,

[1] A. Bea, *Greg* 33 (1952), 85–105; see also *BL* 19 (1952), 262ff.

[2] *Humani Generis*, 21: 'Quapropter sacrorum fontium studio sacrae doctrinae semper iuvenescunt, dum contra speculatio, quae ulteriorem sacri depositi inquisitionem neglegit, ut experiundo novimus sterilis evadit'.

[3] A. Oepke, *TLZ* 79 (1954), 103.

[4] P. Benoit, *RB* 54 (1947), 543–72.

however, importing our modern categories of thought into our interpretation. In this way the function of faith will be made clearer. Biblical theology, in fact, is simply 'the teaching of the New Testament or of one of the authors of the biblical books as shown in the light of faith' (Braun).[1]

The purpose of the Encyclopedia of Biblical Theology

In French there are about five different expressions corresponding to the English word *speech* (viz. *parole*, *discours*, *langage*, *langue*, *propos*): that is, the English word *speech* has such a wide range of meanings that it can be used to express any of these French words. We find something similar in translating Hebrew expressions in the bible. A word in one particular context can very often only be rendered by an entirely different word in our modern languages, although people have tried to construct new and unusual words and sum up in them all the meanings included in the Hebrew stem (eg the AV rendering 'loving kindness' and RSV rendering 'steadfast love' for the Hebrew *ḥešed*). But when, as is usually the case, a comprehensive Hebrew term is translated by a much more restricted English word or phrase—however justified this may be in the particular case—it will inevitably lose some of its original vigour and depth. Moreover, the wide span of the one comprehensive word has been broken. Instead of one comprehensive idea we have several more restricted ideas without the obvious underlying coherence which existed in the original text. Another drawback is the fact that our modern expressions, apart from being narrower than their Hebrew equivalents, are often saddled with other more or less clear-cut concepts or nuances. Take, for example, words like *justice*, *truth*, *peace*, etc. And what can be said of the Hebrew words of the Old Testament applies equally to the Greek words of the New Testament. There is a strong temptation, here more than anywhere else, to take these Greek words and expressions simply in their Greek sense. But again, recent investigations have shown how very much more the Greek New Testament is rooted in Old Testament judaism than in hellenism. True to the tradition of the LXX translation, the Greek expressions in the New Testament frequently have the same wide range of meanings and nuances as their Hebrew-Aramaic equivalents, and have to be interpreted accordingly.

Needless to say, in this encyclopedia it is mainly the theologically important words that are discussed, though no claim is made for completeness. Nevertheless, the encyclopedia offers much more than a mere dictionary: as far as possible, we have tried to indicate the essential lines of development of any given concept. Only occasionally is an attempt made to explain non-biblical words by reference to the bible (eg 'asceticism'). Anything purely historical, biographical, or archaeological had, of course, to be omitted altogether.

[1] For general reading, see the introductions to the various biblical theologies. See also: C. Spicq, *RSPT* (1951), 561–74; F. M. Braun, *RT* (1953), 221–53; W. Hillmann, *WW* 14 (1951), 56–67 and 200–11; V. Warnach, *Gloria Dei* 7 (1952); S. Lyonnet, *VD* 34 (1956), 142–53; H. Schlier, *BZ* 1 (1957), 6–23; J. Michl, *BZ* 2 (1958), 1–14; M. Meinertz, *Theol. Rev.* 54 (1958), 1ff; V. Hamp and H. Schlier, *LTK* II², 439–49; R. Schnackenburg, *Neutestamentliche Theologie*, Munich 1963, 11–24; W. Beilner, *Dienst an der Lehre* (Festschrift F. König), Vienna 1965, 145–65.

This encyclopedia does not present a general survey of the whole field of biblical theology. The biblical texts themselves would admit of more than one opinion about how to make such a survey and more than one attempt at doing it. Rather, this work has been designed to provide one clear and straightforward service: wherever an approach is made towards God's word in the bible, whenever people begin to read the bible (prompted, often, by the liturgy), there is need of a companion such as this to explain and reveal in its full splendour each expression replete with meaning and with God's Spirit.

In order to encourage private reading of the scriptures and to help enrich the preaching of the word of God, in order to help reveal the source of divine revelation more purely and clearly, the contributors to this encyclopedia have unanimously and generously given their services, sparing themselves no efforts, in the hope that many may drink of the water given by the Lord, which shall quench their thirst and 'become in them a spring of water welling up to eternal life' (Jn 4:14).

Johannes B. Bauer

Foreword to the English Edition

It is fair to say that Prof J. B. Bauer's encyclopedia represents one of the finest fruits of the renewal in Roman Catholic biblical scholarship, comprising as it does important original articles by the outstanding German, Austrian, Swiss, and French biblical theologians of the present day. In the German-speaking world this fact was immediately recognised, and the first two German editions quickly sold out. In preparing the third German edition—from which this English translation has been made—Prof Bauer took the opportunity to add a further thirty-four articles and to revise many of the earlier articles and bibliographies, so that the English-speaking world first meets the encyclopedia in a thoroughly up-to-date and more comprehensive form.

As Prof Bauer's preface makes clear, the encyclopedia was conceived, written, and edited to provide a service to professional and amateur students of the bible alike—to act as a companion and aid to biblical scholars in their work, to parochial clergy in the preparation of sermons and addresses, and indeed to all christians who regard serious and regular scripture study as an essential part of their own spiritual growth. Both these concerns, the 'academic' and the 'pastoral', have been kept very much in mind throughout the preparation of this English edition, and the manner in which we have attempted to maintain a proper balance between them calls for additional comment in four particular respects:

1. *Translation.* The greater part of the translation has been carried out by the English biblical scholars, Mr Joseph Blenkinsopp and Mr David J. Bourke, though Mr N. D. Smith and Mr Walter P. van Stigt have also each translated a number of articles. Bible references and quotations are according to the Revised Standard Version (RSV). Its advantages are well known. Originally sponsored by the National Council of the Churches of Christ in the USA, it has been subsequently officially approved—in its complete form, including the deuterocanonical as well as canonical books—by the Roman Catholic Church. It is familiar to both British and American christians, and has won general acceptance among scholars. One further point on translation: for the benefit of readers who do not know Hebrew or Greek, all words and phrases quoted in these languages are literally translated into English wherever their meaning is not immediately apparent from the context.

2. *Bibliographies.* The bibliographies which appear at the end of each article have been transferred in their entirety from the third German edition, despite the fact that German-language books and articles predominate. (This preponderance reflects, of course, not merely the German authorship of the majority of articles and bibliographies here, but the general pre-eminence of German scholarship in the fields of biblical exegesis and theology.) The retention of these

bibliographies is, we believe, essential if the encyclopedia is to be of real service to professional scholars and students: often they will have cause to follow up the references given, but in any case they will always need to know what secondary sources were available to or used by the author of a particular article. Nevertheless, every effort has been made to ensure that the bibliographies are also of the greatest possible use to readers who either have no knowledge of German or have no ready access to German books and periodicals. For these last we would point out that: (a) after German-language works, English-language books and periodicals are the most frequently cited in the German edition of the encyclopedia, and all these are of course retained in the English edition; (b) wherever they are available, English translations of German (or other foreign) works are substituted for the original works in the bibliographies here (in these cases, page references are to the English editions); (c) we have added recent English-language titles to some of the bibliographies where they seemed appropriate (such additions are marked by an asterisk); and (d) many more English-language works are included in the supplementary bibliography at the end of volume 2, which has been specially provided by Prof Bauer for this English edition. Above all, it should be noted that no less than thirteen major works frequently cited in the bibliographies are now wholly or substantially available in the following English translations:

Allmen, J.-J. von (ed.), *Vocabulary of the Bible*, London, Lutterworth Press, 1958; and *Companion to the Bible*, New York, OUP, 1958.

Bultmann, Rudolf, *Theology of the New Testament* I and II, London, SCM Press, 1952 (1965[2]); and New York, Scribner, 1951.

Cullmann, Oscar, *The Christology of the New Testament*, London, SCM Press, 1959 (1962[2]); and Philadelphia, Westminster Press, 1959.

de Vaux, Roland, *Ancient Israel: Its Life and Institutions*, London, Darton, Longman and Todd, 1961; and New York, McGraw-Hill, 1961.

Eichrodt, Walther, *Theology of the Old Testament* I and II,* London, SCM Press, 1961 and 1967; and Philadelphia, Westminster Press, 1961 and 1967.

Heinisch, Paul, *Theology of the Old Testament*, Collegeville, Liturgical Press, 1955.

Imschoot, Paul van, *Theology of the Old Testament* I,† New York, Desclee, 1965.

Jacob, Edmund, *Theology of the Old Testament*, London, Hodder and Stoughton, 1958; and New York, Harper and Row, 1958.

Kittel, Gerhard, and G. Friedrich (eds.), *Theological Dictionary of the New Testament* I–VI,‡ Grand Rapids (Mich.), Wm. B. Eerdmans, 1964–9.

* Volume III of Eichrodt's *Theologie des AT* is not yet published in English translation.

† Volume II of Imschoot's *Théologie de l'AT* is not yet published in English translation.

‡ All eight volumes of Kittel's *Theologisches Wörterbuch zum NT* have now been published in German. Six of these have already appeared in English translation (see further the entries *TDNT* and *TWNT* in section 3 of the list of abbreviations, p. xxi above). Moreover, some of the most important articles are also available in English translation in the *Bible Key Words* series published by A. & C. Black, London, 1949–65 (see further the entry *BKW*, p. xvii above).

LEON-DUFOUR, Xavier (ed.), *Dictionary of Biblical Theology*, London, Geoffrey Chapman, 1967.

SCHNACKENBURG, Rudolf, *The Moral Teaching of the New Testament*, London, Burns and Oates, 1968; and New York, Herder and Herder, 1968.

STAUFFER, Ethelbert, *Theology of the New Testament*, London, SCM Press, 1955 (1963[2]).

VON RAD, Gerhard, *Old Testament Theology* I and II, Edinburgh and London, Oliver and Boyd, 1962 and 1965; and New York, Harper and Row, 1962 and 1965.

3. *Tables and indexes.* Several tables and indexes have been specially compiled or adapted for the English edition. Thus, the analytical index of articles and cross-references not only incorporates all the cross-references between articles of the German edition, but also includes many additional references to articles from synonyms and from theological themes which, though not given separate treatment, are covered in one or more of the articles. This table should provide readers with quick access to the subject in which they are currently interested, as well as enabling them to make the fullest possible use of the encyclopedia. The index of biblical references—an innovation in the English edition—is designed to serve two purposes. First, it will provide readers who are using the encyclopedia as a companion to their study of the bible or of a bible commentary with direct access to what the encyclopedia has to say about any given scriptural (or apocryphal) passage. Secondly, it will provide priests with a handy tool for using the encyclopedia in the preparation of their sermons, and it is for their especial benefit that parallel passages in the synoptic gospels—which in the text are referred to in the form 'Mt 3:1–12 and parallels'—are listed under Mark and Luke as well as Matthew.

4. *Transliteration.* The decision to transliterate Hebrew and Greek words by Roman characters was not taken lightly. We are well aware that readers who understand Hebrew or Greek will find this irritating, but we ask their indulgence for the sake of the far greater number who do not understand these classical languages. Hebrew and Greek words are invariably quoted in this encyclopedia for theological rather than for philological reasons, and so the transliteration makes it possible for readers who do not understand Hebrew or Greek to follow fully the theological argument of the writer.

Volume I

Abraham – Hour

Abraham

A. *Old Testament.* Abraham's name may have a different etymological explanation from the one which occurs in Gen 17:5, and the short form *'abrām* and the longer form *'abrāhām* may in fact be identical (that is, 'the father is exalted', or 'he is exalted with regard to his father'). In either case, the interpretation of the name cannot diminish its theological significance, since P (the priestly source) posits assonance with the word *hamon* (=surging multitude) in order to express, in the name itself, the position Abraham occupies in the history of salvation. 'Father of the multitude' implies not only a great number of descendants, but also an abundance of blessings on those descendants (see Gen 12:2f).

Abraham's position is based on the call he received from God (Gen 12:1–3) and on the covenant established between him and God (Gen 17:7). His role is accomplished in the faith and obedience with which he responded to God and which was counted as justice in his favour (Gen 15:6). As a result of this Abraham was regarded, in the whole of the biblical tradition, and in a very real sense, as the bearer of revelation and of salvation, and was given the titles 'prophet' (Gen 20:7), 'friend of God' (Is 41:8), and 'servant of God' (Ps 105:6). Yahweh is the God of Abraham (Gen 26:24, etc) and Abraham is the father of Israel, the rock from which the people is hewn (Is 51:1f).

While it is necessary for us to avoid looking on revelation as a process similar to that of a *deus ex machina*—as taking place without the concurrence of the viewpoints of people living in a determined period of history—at the same time, revelation must not be confused with a process of development conceived as, for example, the building of a house or the crystallisation of a chemical element, a process which comes about inexorably following a geometrical pattern. We have, moreover, to think of Abraham as a real human being who lived in the full light of history and in an age of spiritual awareness — whether we date him around 1800 BC with Professor A. Parrot or follow C. Gordon's more recent suggestion of a date around 1400 BC. This is shown by the testimony of archaeology with reference to either the early civilisation of Sumer-Akkad (the city of Ur) or that of the kingdom of Mari (the city of Haran).

Particularly revealing is the 'object' of his faith. God did not ask Abraham either to square the circle or to come to grips with towering speculations in the realm of the supernatural. What he promised him was pasture land and a posterity—precisely what any other Bedouin sheik longed for—and expected him to accept this in faith and be convinced that in this way the foundation for the salvation of the nations was being laid. The simplicity of this agreement (↗ Covenant), the form in which it was given, so perfectly consonant with contemporary conditions, the rich promise which at the same time it held out for the future, could not have been invented but must have been copied from reality.

The alliance with Abraham is the immediate prerequisite for the Sinaitic alliance. In addition, however, this latter must be understood against the background of the account of original sin and the *protoevangelium*. This is, in fact, 'the meaning of the first chapters of the bible: it is impossible to understand Israel correctly . . . unless everything is seen with God's creation of the world in the background' (Von Rad). It is thus obvious that Abraham represents the final stage in the ideal historical sequence which extends back by way of the lists of the descendants of Shem and Adam to Adam himself, and which can show clearly the divine work of selection within the history of salvation which leads up to the Semites and to Israel. The figures given for Abraham's age—his migration at 75, the birth of his promised son at 100, his death at 175—are ideal rather than chronological, and, with Isaac's birth in Abraham's hundredth year, conclude the remarkable interchange of generation-numbers between 100, 70, and 30 which appear in the genealogy of Shem.

It must therefore be stated plainly that the history of religion would have taken a very different course if Abraham had not believed. His faith was a condition *sine qua non* for the history of salvation, both in its factual origins in Israel and in its fulfilment in Jesus of Nazareth. The condition is, admittedly, not an absolute one, but it is certainly applicable within the limits of that human freedom which is recognised by God.

The key position which Abraham held introduces for the first time into the history of salvation (↗ mediation) both the fact and the potentiality of God's saving ways; in other words, that it is not God's method to reveal himself to each individual man, but only to one who is to pass on what is revealed to the rest of the community and who, in this manner, assumes responsibility for all members of the community.

One further law in the history of salvation can be clearly recognised in the life of Abraham. His position is not entirely free from a certain dialectic. On the one hand, the numerous offspring promised to him (Gen 13:16) can be taken in the literal sense to signify that the means of salvation and the results of those who bring salvation are to be seen as closely related to Abraham's biological lineage. On the other hand, the exclusion of Ishmael from the line of salvation and the continued preferment of Isaac, the promised son, show that Abraham's vocation did not come about because of racial considerations, but that God left himself freedom of choice in the biological issue, and further that the basis, extent, and significance of Abraham's vocation are not to be understood in a biological but in a theological sense. In Hagar-Ishmael, as the representative of the merely biological element, and Sarah-Isaac, representing God's free choice, the points were already changed which would lead the Pauline interpretation of salvation away from that of the Pharisees. In this manner, 'justification by faith', as treated in the New Testament (Rom 3:28), finds its basis in the Old Testament.

B. *New Testament*. From the New

Testament we can discover one possible outcome of the attitude of the Jewish people towards Abraham, and from that we can deduce the teaching of Christ and the apostles concerning him. The Jewish people saw the basis of salvation in Abraham's biological lineage, and even though his 'merit' was not entirely disregarded, it was interpreted in many different ways (see Mt 3:8f and PsSol 9:17; 3 Macc 6:3; also Philo, *De Abr.*). From the theological point of view, the apocryphal books presented the writers of the New Testament with no material for a representation of Abraham; the Book of Jubilees simply provides a repetition of the story contained in Genesis, while the ApocAbr and TestAbr get hopelessly lost in fantasy and heavenly journeyings.

The Jewish obsession with the biological lineage of Abraham was bound to provoke the opposition of Christ and the apostles, and thus the figure of Abraham makes the essential law of redemption and salvation all the more intelligible: in the eyes of God the descendants of Abraham are worthless unless they also follow in his footsteps (Jn 8:39; Jas 2:21). God is thus able to bring forth children of Abraham 'from the stones' (Mt 3:9), that is, without recourse to the normal biological process, so that the spiritual children of Abraham as well as his physical children will sit down with him at table (Mt 8:11f). 'Father Abraham' cannot, then, even save 'his son', the rich glutton, from Gehenna (Lk 16:25f), whereas Lazarus, the poor beggar, is able to rest in 'Abraham's bosom' (Lk 16:22)—that is, Lazarus is permitted to recline with Abraham on the couch at the feast of the blessed (see Jn 13:25).

In accordance with his normal theological method of meditation and presentation, Paul made the figure of Abraham his criterion in his dispute with the Jews. Paul appreciated the meaning of the antithesis between Hagar/Ishmael and Sarah/Isaac, and fully exploited all the aspects of the question of ↗ justification; in this way he succeeded in exposing the underlying significance of this episode, namely, that the origins of the history of salvation in Abraham are, despite their association with Abraham's lineage in the purely biological sense, directly traceable to the freedom of God's grace. (Gal 4:28ff; Rom 9:7.)

Just as God's freedom of choice within sacred history was delineated in the figures of the ancestral women taken as types, so Paul illustrates, in the light of Abraham's attitude to faith, the 'works' of Abraham, which are an indispensible qualification for redemption, both for Abraham himself and for everyone. Abraham lived in the time before the proclamation of the law and he was not dependent on the law for his justification (Rom 4:3f). In his case, faith alone was sufficient (Rom 4:13).

As a consequence of this we find in Paul that, although the fact that Abraham is also the 'father of the circumcised' is clearly recognised (Rom 4:12), he is considered as 'father of the multitude' only with regard to his descendants in the faith (Rom 4:16ff). Just as each one of us is bound to prove himself by means of his faith before Abraham who is the 'father of our faith', so Abraham, in his turn assumed responsibility for all of us. That is why Abraham's faith is counted in his favour, not only out of personal consideration to him, but also—and even more particularly—with regard to the many who were to find faith through him (Rom 4:22ff).

Paul also interprets the blessing that was to pass, so to speak, in a kind of chain-reaction of salvation through Abraham to the nations. Paul regards the promise of Christ, which had been held out to Abraham for his offspring (Gal 3:16f; see Jn 8:56), as fulfilled in its true messianic perspective, even if the grammatical implication of collectivity in the statement 'thy seed' is discounted (Gen 12:7 and elsewhere).

Bibliography: H. H. Rowley, 'Discovery and the Patriarchal Age', *BJRL* 32 (1949); N. S. Schneider, 'Patriarchennamen in zeitgenössischen Keilschrifturkunden', *Bbl* 33 (1952), 516–22; H. Gordon, *Geschichtliche Grundlage des Alten Testaments*, Einsiedeln 1956; S. Moscati, *I Predecessori d'Israele*, Rome 1956; A. Parrot, *Babylon and the Old Testament*, London 1958; O. Schmitz, 'Abraham im Spätjudentum und im Christentum', *Festschrift A. Schlatter* 1922, 99–123; J. Jeremias, *TDNT* I, 8–9; M. Colacci, 'Il Semen Abrahae alla luce del V e NT', *Bbl* 21 (1940), 1–27; O. Kuss, *Der Römerbrief* I, Regensburg 1957, 178–95.

Othmar Schilling

Adam

A. *Old Testament*. 'Adam' is the generic name for 'man'—its etymology is uncertain—and also the name of the first man (in J, Gen 4:5 and elsewhere; 1 Chron 1:1). Although the use of the article renders it grammatically quite unambiguous, the representation underlying the concept is fluid in the chapters dealing with the creation. (Is it 'man' or 'Adam' who calls his wife the 'mother of the living'?) The usually accepted connection with '*adāmâh*' (=field) (Gen 2:5 etc) would point to the meaning of 'human existence' in the name itself (see Gen 3:19).

The history of the first man in Gen 1–5 serves, in accordance with the salvation-theology presentation of the bible and within the framework of the selected traditions related to the history of salvation, like a splendid theological aetiology, in that everything of importance in the theological sense, for all mankind in general and also for Israel in particular, is exemplified in the first man. It was not uncommitted speculation which determined the narratives about Adam, but uniquely an interpretation of his being viewed from the standpoint of his relationship with God. In view of this, details of the natural sciences were considered of secondary importance, and so were omitted from the biblical record, thus being left open as far as revelation is concerned. The two essential aspects of Adam which emerge most clearly are his relationship with God and his relationship with himself and his environment.

1. *Adam's relationship with God*. The bible recognises the evidence in this connection as among the most decisive and important of all. Adam's development is traced back to God's creation (Gen 1:26ff; 2:7). It can be affirmed that, apart from the basic human state of being a creature, the first man became a living being only by the inbreathing of the divine spirit. His exceptional position in creation is a visible expression of the doctrine that

man is made in God's image (according to P, Gen 1:26; 5:1).

Corresponding to man's origin in God, there should be a communion with God lasting for the whole of life. The essential characteristic of the state of living in paradise is an intimate acquaintanceship with God. If it is affirmed (in P, Gen 5:1) that the quality of being made in God's image was transmitted to Seth and was, over the generations, passed on through Noah and Shem to Abraham, it becomes apparent how Israel saw itself from its very origins to be in a close alliance with God.

In the other documents which give an account of the creation, this succession of 'being made in the same image' (deriving from P) has, however, taken on another precise shade of meaning. The negative aspect of the first man's relationship with God is also brought into prominence with particular clarity and meaning in the form of an aetiology of salvation, in Adam's sin, his punishment, culminating in the threat of death, and God's curse on the land (Gen 3:17ff). Adam's wife nonetheless remains the 'mother of all living' (Gen 3:20), and the curse on the serpent offers to both of them the hope of salvation.

In this way it becomes evident that the position of Israel is the result of election, since Adam's sin was carried on in his sons and in the generation which perished in the flood. God's call to Israel to become one in his ↗ covenant is therefore a further call to mankind to fellowship with him.

2. *Adam's relationship with himself and his environment.* Adam's essential characteristics are expressed quite clearly, although only incidentally, as a result of this interpretation of his personality, which can be understood in the sense that God's covenant with Israel is ever present in the history of salvation. Two distinct elements which go to make up his being may be deduced from Adam's formation from the dust and the divine breath. That man is powerless to exist and that he is, in his substance, worthless, is typified above all by the dust, which forms the material part of his being. The divine breath, on the other hand, is not a part, but is in fact the element of perfection in man and of his vivification through God. Life is grace! In connection with the subject of creation and man's likeness to God, Jesus, the son of Sirach, speaks in clear terms of Adam's spiritual and volitional endowments (Sir 17:1–7), just as in the Book of Wisdom creation and man's likeness to God are regarded as the basis of the first man's immortality (Wis 2:23).

Adam's relationship with his environment is in the same way outlined quite clearly. Adam was given a counterpart, Eve, who was in substance equal to himself and to whom he was bound in a monogamous union (↗ Marriage). Thus he became the progenitor of the entire human race.

Adam's position of authority, which is derived from his having been made in God's image, and the superiority he demonstrates over the animals in giving them their names, that is to say, in interpreting their nature, indicate that he has been placed only 'a little less than God' (Ps 8).

And so the Old Testament, though in an awkward literary style, expresses itself on the subject of the formation and worth, the nature and dignity of the first man so uniquely that, in the whole of the world's literature, there exists nothing which can be placed on the same level.

A biblical expression of this presentation of Adam living in communion with God as we read in Genesis can be found in the final sentence of Ben Sirach's song in praise of the great men of the past: 'Shem and Seth were honoured among men, and Adam above every living being in the creation' (Sir 49:16).

B. *New Testament.* That Adam was the first man for the New Testament writers emerges clearly from the genealogy of Christ (Lk 3:38) and from the fact that Paul establishes the position of man and woman in the community by means of a scriptural argument drawn from the original creation of Adam and the original seduction by Eve (1 Tim 2:13f).

The genealogy given in Luke is the christological continuation of a line which began in Gen 5:1ff, and thus places Christ in a striking relationship with Adam, who was 'of God'.

Paul, who designates Adam as *tupos mellontos* (Rom 5:14), completes in various ways this already suggestive Adam typology. As in the passages first quoted, it is the Old Testament, in the light of advanced christological studies, which might have provided the point of departure for the further development of this typology, and not the speculation of later judaism on the subject of the primordial Man, who was identified with the Messiah (thus *TDNT* 1, 142f). An example of this is that the 'Son of Man' in Enoch 1 (48:6; 62:7) is not called Adam, and Paul's 'Son of Man' applies neither to Adam nor to Christ, though both would have come very close to this title, both from the point of view of linguistic usage and from Christ's own custom of referring to himself as the 'Son of Man'. The 'firstborn of all creation', who is the 'image of the invisible God' (Col 1:15), is without doubt an allusion to Wis 7:26 (↗ Likeness). In addition, the conception of the 'first' and the 'second' Adam in Philo (*Leg. All.* 1, 31; 2, 13; *De Conf. Ling.* 146) does not correspond to that of Paul; if it did, the 'second' or 'last' Adam would have to be identical with the Adam of Genesis. For Paul, even though he calls him 'the firstborn', Christ is the 'second' Adam. Paul has at least transformed the principal elements in the light of the christological data, since what is of first importance for him is not lengthy speculation on pre-existence, but the divine ascendancy of the second Adam over the first, on which the work of salvation of the new covenant is based, and the fact that it was precisely this work which was made necessary by the history of the first Adam. There does not seem to have been any speculation on Adam in Qumran, apart from occasional allusions to the first men (*CD* 4:21–5:1).

In accordance with the custom of employing the conceptual distinctions of *nepheš/rûah* and *psukhē/pneuma* in antithesis for earthly/natural and heavenly/supernatural (1 Cor 2:14) Paul sees in the assertion that Adam was created to become a 'living soul' (as the over-literal translation of Gen 2:7 reads) an expression of the first Adam's earthly, 'natural' state, which was to be overcome and exalted by the 'life-giving *pneuma*' of the second Adam, so that thereby the condition was established, among other things, for the christian hope of resurrection (1 Cor 15:45ff).

The Adam/Christ typology has been set out in classic terms by Paul for the new 'hereditary succession' in the history of salvation: 'For as by one man's disobedience many were made sinners, so by one man's obedience, many will be made righteous' (Rom 5:19). This statement 'evidently means that mankind in the line of Adam as well as mankind in the line of Christ "was placed in a certain situation" as a result of the action of our first parents, by reason of God's judgement. . . . Many were in fact made "sinners" by Adam's deed, and through Christ many were made "righteous"' (Kuss). Paul has thus made use of typology in order to clarify the doctrine of original sin and grace which so deeply affects the history of our salvation.

In accordance with this doctrine, Paul also refers to a matter of which the Jews were not ignorant—that of the existence of an inherited death since Adam (↗ Original Sin). He sets against this, however, the efficacy of Christ's resurrection for all men (1 Cor. 15:21)

The church as the new mother of the living is to some extent on the same footing as Christ, the progenitor of the new life, so that not only is a new line of inheritance established in the history of salvation, but also a new depth is achieved in the relationship between man and woman, which goes beyond that indicated in Gen 2:23ff (Eph 5:21–33).

Bibliography: J. Jeremias, *TDNT* I, 141–3; Haag 27; *LTK* I², 125–30; J. Feldmann, *Paradies und Sündenfall* (*AA* 4), Münster 1913; J. Freundorfer, *Erbsünde und Erbtod beim Apostel Paulus*, Münster 1927; J. Daniélou, *From Shadows to Reality: Studies in the Biblical Typology of the Fathers*, London 1960; O. Kuss, *Der Römerbrief*, Regensburg 1957; H. Renckens, *Urgeschichte und Heilsgeschichte*, Mainz 1959; P. Morant, *Die Anfänge der Menschheit*, Lucerne 1960; J. de Fraine, *Adam und seine Nachkommen*, Cologne 1962; O. Schilling, *Das Mysterium lunae die Erschaffung der Frau nach Gen 2:21f*, Paderborn 1963; P. de Haes, *Die Schöpfung als Heilsmysterium*, Mainz 1964.

Othmar Schilling

Adoration

A. *Old Testament. Hištahawâh*, together with *sogud*, are the usual expressions to describe adoration or worship. In the first place they denote a physical bowing down, and this meaning is clarified by such additions as 'to the ground' (Gen 18:2; 33:3, etc). By *qādad*—always used in conjunction with *hištahawâh*—is meant casting oneself down on one's knees. In most places, this 'proskynesis' (the Greek bible translates the Hebrew by *proskunein*) implies not only a public act of worship, above all of the true God (Gen 22:5; Ex 4:31; Deut 26:10; Ps 5:7; etc), but also homage paid to idols and false gods (Ex 20:5; Deut 4:19; 1 Kings 22:53; 2 Kings 5:18; Is 2:8; etc). Proskynesis is clearly perceptible in a song of praise and homage such as Ps 99 (v 2): 'The Lord is great in Sion: and high [*rām*] above all people'. In order that God's high position should be acknowledged, the cry is made: 'Exalt ye [*rômᶜmû*] the Lord our God, and "adore" at his footstool' (v 5; see also v 9: 'at his holy mountain'). The 'and' is explanatory in character, and might conceivably be translated 'while ye are adoring him'. Thus the 'exaltation' of the Lord in praise is carried out both outwardly and inwardly by bowing down in adoration and homage. Vv 6 and 8 connect petition and the certainty of a hearing directly with the paying of homage. This is not by accident: on the contrary, the petition takes place, especially if it is performed with particular emphasis, in the attitude of proskynesis. In this sense of making an urgent request, Elijah bows down on the summit of Mount Carmel and lays his head between his knees, in order to implore God to send the longed-for rain (1 Kings 18:42), and the Rabbi Hanina ben Dosa entreats God in the same attitude to cure the son of the Rabbi Johanan ben Zakkai (see J. B. Bauer, 'Inter Genua Deposito Capite', *Hermes* 87 [1959], 383f).

The act of 'homage' is often accompanied by sacrificial acts (Deut 26:10; 1 Sam 1:3), music and the singing of psalms (2 Chron 29:28; Sir 50:16–18) and by prophetic exhortations to ↗ conversion (Ps 95).

Whenever homage is rendered to men, as in the case of Abraham to the children of Heth (Gen 23:7, 12), it is seldom done in a purely orthodox manner, and it was in fact later expressly forbidden (Esther 3:2, 5). It is customary to give due honour and to pay due homage to kings (1 Sam 24:8; 1 Kings 1:16, 23, 31), prophets (1 Sam 28:14; 2 Kings 2:15; 4:37) and to God's angels (Num 22:31; Gen 18:2; 19:1), because the power and authority which these hold and exercise comes from God.

Viewed in the light of prophecy and eschatology, Yahweh's universal dominion and sovereignty will be recognised by all mankind. All nations will come and, falling down before him, will pay homage to him and adore him (Is 2:3f; 24:15; Ps 22:27; 66:4; 86:9).

Bibliography: see under B.

Johannes B. Bauer

B. *New Testament*. 1. In the New Testament, the expression used in LXX—*proskunein*—is generally employed for 'adore', and the New Testament range of meaning does not to any great extent exceed the limits of the Old Testament meaning. Devotion is due to God alone (Mt 4:10; Lk 4:8; see also 1 Cor 14:25; Heb 11:21; Rev 4:10; 5:14; 7:11; 11:1, 16; 14:7; 15:4; 19:4, 10; 22:9), although false claims to devotion are made by idols, false gods, and demons, and indeed by Satan himself. Conversely, men sacrilegiously accord devotion to them (Mt 4:9; Lk 4:7; see also Acts 7:43; Rev 13:4, 8, 12, 15; 14:11; 16:2; 19:20). That is why angels, such as the Angel of the Apocalypse (Rev 19:10; 22:9), and men, such as Peter (Acts 10:26), refuse adoration, which is due to God alone. The instance of the church at Philadelphia (Rev 3:9), to whom it is promised that the Jews who are persecuting them will fall down in adoration at their feet, is apparently inconsistent with this conclusion. It must be noted, however, that this harks back to Is 45:14; 49:23; 60:14. If it is promised in these passages that the heathens will render proskynesis to God's people of the old covenant, then the promise is also made that the Jews will fall at the feet of God's people of the new covenant. This promise further holds good in the eschatological sense for the entire community of those included in the work of salvation and, finally, for the exalted Christ himself.

2. *Proskunein* in the New Testament corresponds exactly to the Old Testament reading in that adoration is to be given to a God who is personal and actually present. That is why the physical movement of falling down always accompanies *proskunein*, as is shown by the frequent association of *piptein* (=fall) with *proskunein* (Mt 2:11; 4:9; 18:26; Acts 10:25; 1 Cor 14:25; Rev 4:10, 5:14; 7:11; 11:16; 19:4, 10; 22:8). It is also why the place in which God's presence is manifested in a particular way is also important for the act of true adoration (see MidrPs 91 § 7 [200b]: 'Whoever prays in Jerusalem is as one who prays before the throne of glory, for there is the gate of heaven and the open door for his prayer to enter' [SB II, 437]). In this way *proskunein* can be used in the New Testament simply as a technical term for the pilgrimage to Jerusalem (Jn 12:20; Acts 8:27; 24:11; see Jn 4:20ff). In the new covenant, christian public worship is the 'place' in which God's presence is manifested (1 Cor 14:25).

3. The reading of *proskunein* in the New Testament stands in contrast to that in the Old Testament, as well as to that found in later Jewish usage, in that it admits of adoration—in the sense of *latreia*—of Christ, who has been elevated to God's right hand, to the extent that what is applicable to God within the framework of the Old Testament is now taken to relate to Christ too. This can be seen quite clearly in the hymn to Christ contained in the Letter to the Philippians (2:6–11). The words of Isaiah, which Paul uses at the conclusion of the hymn—'To me every knee shall bow, every tongue shall swear' (Is 45:23)—are found in Paul's epistle in the form: 'At the name of Jesus every knee should bow . . . and every tongue should confess' (Phil 2:10f). In Isaiah, as the content of an adoring confession, we find: 'only in the Lord . . . have I righteousness and strength' (Is 45:24); similarly, Paul has: 'Jesus Christ is Lord' (Phil 2:11). This is also the case in Heb 1:6, where Ps 97:7 (LXX) is referred to Christ. The passage in the psalm referring to God—'adore him, all you his angels'—may be compared with Heb 1:6, a passage referring to Christ: 'Let all God's angels worship him' (see also Deut 32:43). In the same way this 'proskynesis' applies also to the risen Lord (Mt 28:9, 17; see also Lk 24:52), and Thomas falls down in worship before him with the words: 'My Lord and my God' (Jn 20:28).

4. The distribution of the word *proskunein* between the various books of the New Testament is as follows: Mt, thirteen times; Mk, twice; Lk, twice; John, eleven times; Acts, four times; Paul, once only (1 Cor 14:25); Heb, twice; and Rev, twenty-four times. From this it is clear that the verb occurs with greater frequency in the gospels of Mt and Jn than in all but one other book of the New Testament, and that it occurs with entirely disproportionate frequency in Rev. For this reason it will be useful to discuss these last three books separately.

a. Matthew's gospel. *Proskunein* has a special connotation in Mt: it is 'obviously one of his favourite words' (H. J. Held, *Matthäus als Interpret der Wundergeschichten*, Neukirchen 1960, 217). This emerges clearly from a comparison of Mt with the other synoptic gospels.

(1) in comparison with Mk and Lk:

Mt 8:2 *lepros proselthōn prosekunei autō(i)*
Mk 1:40 *lepros parakalōn auton kai gonupetōn*
Lk 5:12 *pesōn epi prosōpon edeēthē autou*
Mt 9:18 (of Jairus) *prosekunei autō(i)*
Mk 5:22 *piptei pros tous podas autou*
Lk 8:41 *pesōn para tous podas Iēsou*

(2) in comparison with Mk:

Mt 14:33 *hoi de en tō(i) ploiō(i) prosekunēsan autō(i) legontes alēthōs theou huios ei*
Mk 6:51 *kai lian ek perissou en heautois existanto*
Mt 15:25 (of the Canaanite woman) *hē de elthousa prosekunei autō(i) legousa*
Mk 7:25 *elthousa prosepesen pros tous podas autou*
Mt 20:20 (of the mother of the sons of Zebedee) *prosekunousa kai aitousa ti par' autou*
Mk 10:35 *prosporeuontai autō(i) . . . legontes*

(3) in comparison with Lk:

Mt 4:9 *ean pesōn proskunēsēis moi*
Lk 4:7 *ean prokunēsēis enōpion emou*
Mt 4:10 *kurion ton theon sou proskunēseis kai autō(i) monō(i) latreuseis* (Deut 6:13)
Lk 4:8 *proskunēseis kurion ton theon sou kai autō(i) monō(i) latreuseis* (Deut 6:13)

With the exception of the last-mentioned, the account of the temptation in the desert, Luke uses the word only in 24:52, where, however, the reading is not certain. Here it is a question of adoring the ascended Lord. Matthew has, in no less than five places, altered or expanded the text of Mark, 'in order to describe the gesture of those who approach Jesus explicitly as proskynesis' (H. Greeven, *TDNT* VI, 763). On the other hand, he has cut the word out completely in the account of the mocking of Jesus, while Mark preserves it, because in this instance there is no expression of true proskynesis. This suggests a highly conscious use of the word on Matthew's part and leads to the assumption that *proskunein* is, for the writer of the first gospel, 'a theological concept' (W. Trilling, *Das wahre Israel: Studien zur Theologie des Matthäusevangeliums*, Leipzig 1959, 148) which he wants to be understood in the sense of a genuine adoration of Jesus. At the same time he realises himself to be tied so strongly to the tradition that has been passed on to him that he introduces the word only in places where Mark uses a phrase that can be interpreted in the sense of *proskunein*.

The use of *proskunein* in exceptional cases in Matthew's gospel is in line with these general conclusions. The case, in Mt 28:9, 17, of proskynesis of the risen Christ, can be accepted unhesitatingly as a reasonable one. Nor does Mt 18:26 constitute an exception, for, if in this parable of the wicked servant it is said: *pesōn oun ho doulos prosekunei autō(i) legōn*, then it is probable that, as the connection with the 'household of God' (Mt 18) suggests, the Lord of the community is to be seen behind the *kurios* of the parable, especially as the falling down of the 'fellow-servant' is not to be interpreted as proskynesis. Finally, the proskynesis of the Magi must also be interpreted, in Matthew's view, as an adoring homage paid to the new-born King (Mt 2:11; see 2:8). This does not contradict the fact that proskynesis can also be seen in this case as 'the oriental expression of respect and subjection (see Gen 19:1; 42:6), and especially of homage paid to a king' (J. Schmid, *Das Evangelium nach Matthäus*, Regensburg 1956, 48). There is also no reason to fear that the idea of the proskynesis of the Magi, in the sense previously indicated, should 'cause either the meaning of the account to be misconstrued or its historicity to be sacrificed' (Schmid, 48).

b. John's gospel. If we disregard the technical term for the pilgrimage to Jerusalem mentioned above (Jn 12:20), there is an occurrence of the verb *proskunein* in the episode recounted in Jn 9:38 where the man whose sight Jesus had restored fell down and adored Jesus after his self-revelation and confessed his faith. Apart from this, the occurrence of the word is concentrated in the conversation with the Samaritan woman at the well of Jacob (4:20–24). This conversation with the Samaritan woman about worship arises from the question of the proper place for the adoration of God, a controversial issue between the Jews and the Samaritans. Whereas the Samaritans regarded Gerizim as the place where God desired to be worshipped, the Jews believed that the only place of worship was the temple in Jerusalem (4:20). This demonstrates, on the one hand, how strongly a people can regard adoration as being tied to a particular place and, on the other hand, how much value the old order places on the temple in Jerusalem as the proper place of worship. In v 23, however, a new kind of adoration is mentioned: 'But the hour cometh, and now is, when the true worshippers will worship the Father in spirit and in truth.' This adoration is new by reason of the fact that it corresponds to the new order which is to dawn with the eschatological hour. (It is to this dawning that the phrase 'the hour is coming, and now is', points [see 5:25].) But how is this new form of worship 'in spirit and truth' to be understood? Does it imply a spiritualised, inner adoration which, in contrast to the customary form of Jewish worship, is no longer tied to any particular posture or to any particular place? Or is the practice of worship to be transformed from an outward act on the part of the worshipper into something which happens within him, as Schlatter seems to imply:

> Now the practice of worship no longer remains a mere gesture, but takes place interiorly, within the worshipper. It is not simply an outward appearance to impress the onlooker, but is something offered to God. [A. Schlatter, *Der Evangelist Johannes*, Stuttgart 1948, 126.]

But this is clearly incorrect. The true interpretation is, in fact, rather more subtle, for in this context ↗ 'spirit' does not mean the spirit or soul of man, nor does ↗ 'truth' mean the truthfulness of man. The 'true worshippers' are not, therefore, those who worship God in 'truthfulness' rather than in 'hypocrisy' (↗ Hypocrite), in which the only thing that counts is outward appearance:

> The prophets too demanded a spiritual worship of God (Is 1:11–20; 29:13; Joel 2:13; Amos 5:21–6; Mic 6:6–8; Ps 40:6; 50:7–23; 51:18f). Both the Jews and the heathens of that period recognised that the prophets transcended the purely formal aspect of worship. [A. Wikenhauser, *Das Evangelium nach Johannes*, Regensburg 1957, 109.]

In this context, the 'new' kind of adoration which is to dawn with the eschatological hour has no place; rather are the 'spirit' and 'truth' of the new adoration to take their character not from man but from God himself. That is also postulated in v 24: 'God is spirit; and [therefore] those who worship him must worship him in spirit and truth'. The sentence: 'God is spirit', is not intended to be in any way a definition of God, but sets out to paraphrase God's being as the sphere of the divine in contrast to the sphere of the *sarx* = ↗ flesh (see Jn 3:6–8; 'The term *pneuma* being appropriated to Deity as such', C. H. Dodd, *The Interpretation of the Fourth Gospel*, Cambridge 1963, 226). God's being is, however, revealed through Jesus Christ, and the divinity of God has become, through him, a visible reality. That is what John means when he speaks of the *alētheia* (= truth): if the 'place' of worship is, so to speak, designated by *en pneumati* (= in the spirit), then *en alētheiā(i)* (= in the truth) infers that this 'place' has become a present reality in Jesus Christ. Adoration 'in spirit and truth' thus means adoring God in a manner which has become possible and real for men in the revelation of Jesus Christ in the eschatological hour. He is the 'new temple' (see Jn 2:19–22), in which God may be worshipped in the way which is fitting to him alone. It can thus be seen that neither the 'place' nor the 'posture' of *proskunein* is preserved in the designation 'spirit' and 'truth', and that the link between these is permanently maintained in the revealed person of God.

c. Revelation to John. In Revelation, the word *proskunein* frequently occurs in connection with descriptions of heavenly worship (4:10; 5:14; 7:11; 11:16; 19:4), and, wherever *proskunein* occurs, the gesture of falling down before God and the Lamb is always expressly mentioned, and at the same time associated with a hymn of praise. It has been pointed out with some justification that the description of heavenly worship in Revelation is to be understood as a reflection of christian public worship on earth. Just as the heavenly beings fall down in adoration before God and Christ with hymns and songs of praise, so the christians on earth should have adored God and their risen Lord with the same, or at least with similar, words in their acts of public worship (see 4:8; 5:9f; 7:12; 11:17; 15:3f; 19:1–3). But the fact that the visionary only describes heavenly proskynesis in this way must be taken, as it were, as an image set in contrast to the situation on earth. For there another kind of proskynesis exists, a perverted public worship, as adoration is offered to the Dragon and the Beast, and all men, with the exception of those whom God has chosen, fall down in adoration of the power of Satan (13:4, 8, 12, 15; see also 14:9, 11; 16:2; 19:20; 20:4). True, christians on earth are styled *proskunountes* = adorers (11:1), and indeed the church of Philadelphia is given the promise that the Jews will come and be made to adore before it (3:9); from the Angel the summons goes forth to all the inhabitants of the earth that they are to worship God (14:6, 7). In the strict sense, however, adoration exists only in heaven: it will not become a reality for all the elect in the new creation until 'the Lord God Almighty is the temple thereof and the Lamb' (21:22).

Bibliography: ↗ Prayer; see further: A. Frövig, 'Die Anbetung Christi im NT' *Tidskr. for Teol. og Kirke* I (1930), 26–44; J. Horst, *Proskynein*, Gütersloh 1932 (with bibliography); H. Greeven, *TDNT* VI, 758–66; E. Mussner, *LTK* I², 498–500 (with bibliography).

Heinrich Zimmermann

Agapē

A. ↗ Love.

B. *Love-feast*. Apart from the unlikely reading *agapais* in 2 Pet 2:13, there is in the New Testament only one instance (Jude 12) where *agapē* is used as 'brotherly feast' or 'love-feast'. In this epistle, written against the libertinistic heretics (gnostics?), it says: 'These are blemishes in your love-feasts, as they fare sumptuously at your side, shepherds that feed themselves without scruple'. From a certain, authentic custom (Tertullian, *Apologeticum* 39) dating from the end of the second century, we may infer that it was a liturgical, communal meal, during which the presiding bishop or elder spoke the words of blessing over the bread while the same was done over the wine by each member taking part. Otherwise nobody besides the bishop was allowed to speak unless he was called upon. It cannot be stated with absolute certainty whether the *agapē* was a feast independent from the Lord's Supper or, as implied in 1 Cor 11:17–34, was combined with it in one common action, or preceded it. It is also doubtful whether the breaking of bread in Acts 2:42–6; 20:7–11, refers to these feasts (↗ Eucharist).

In spite of its liturgical character this love-feast does not seem to have obtained a real sacramental function. Its indisputable importance was to express and foster the brotherly union founded by baptism and eucharist, and also to help the needy members of the community (compare the daily ministration of the widows in Acts 6:1). In comparative theology, *agapē* may be related to the Jewish ritual meals, as they were common practice mainly among the late Jewish sects, the Essenes (Flavius Josephus, *Bell. Jud.* II 8, 5) and the congregation of Qumran (*Book of Laws* 1 QS CI 4). This custom, however, also corresponds with the general view among the ancient peoples and especially in the Hellenistic cultural world that ritual meals have the power of forming communal solidarity.

Bibliography: H. Leclercq, *DACL* I, 775–848; L. Thomas, *DB(S)* I, 134–53; P. Battifol, *Etudes d'Historie et de Théologie Positive*, Paris 1926², 283–325; E. Baumgartner, *Eucharistie und Agape im Urchristentum*, Solothurn 1909; R. L. Cole, *Love Feasts: A History of the Christian Agape*, London 1916; H. Lietzmann, *Mass and the Lord's Supper*, Leiden 1934; K. Völker, *Mysterium und Agape*, Gotha 1927; W. Goossens,

Les Origines de l'Eucharistie, Paris 1931, 127-46; D. Tombolleo, *Le Agapi*, Rome 1931; Bo Reicke, *Diakonie, Festfreude und Zelos in Verbindung mit altchristlichen Agapefeiern*, Uppsala-Wiesbaden 1951; J. A. Jungmann, 'Agape II', *LTK* I², 218f; F. Bammel, *Das heilige Mahl im Glauben der Völker*, Gütersloh 1950, 90–107; V. Warnach, *HTG* II, 54–75.

Viktor Warnach

Almsgiving

The stipulations of the law at various levels in favour of widows, orphans, strangers, and levites with regard to the harvest, tithes, mortgages, years of remission, jubilee, and so on (see especially Ex 22:21–7; 23; Lev 25; Deut 15; Sir 29:1ff) concern various contributions and benefits. However, it is not possible to regulate individual acts of almsgiving along legal lines, since these consist of free, personal gifts bestowed without any claim to a return or to compensation from the one in need. Such stipulations can nevertheless foster and stimulate further voluntary material help, or alms, especially if the motives are religious and of a broad and even universal character—the will of Yahweh (eg Lev 19:15–18); an unmerited act of deliverance by God leading the people to exercise a similar generosity (Lev 19:34; 25:35–8; Deut 24:18, 22; 15:15); God as the true possessor of the land and the fruits of the land, for which reason those in need have an immediate claim on their brethren (Lev 25:23; Job 31:15–22).

Throughout the entire eastern world of those times, ↗ justice was, in contrast to that of the West, not simply a question of a relationship between man and his fellow-men, but between the powerful and the rich on the one hand and the weak and the poor on the other. *Tsᵉdāqâh* (righteousness) is almost identical with mercy (Prov 21:21; 29:7, 4; Jer 22:16). Doubtless under the influence of the Aramaic, and because of the alarming spread of want and distress during and after the Exile, it also incorporates the meaning of actual alms. In LXX it is translated, in an apparently arbitrary way, sometimes by *eleēmosunē* (=pity, mercy) and sometimes by *dikaiosunē* (= righteousness): both are frequently placed side by side (see especially Tobit 12:9 BA; 14:11 BA; 14:9 S; etc). Moreover, 'alms' is often expressed synonymously, and so it is hardly possible to define any clear boundary between almsgiving and other negative or positive demands of justice and charity. (Compare the similar lack of clear distinction between alms and wages or reward: Lk 10:7; Mt 10:10b; 1 Tim 5:17f; 1 Cor 9:1–14; 2 Cor 12:14f; Gal 6:6—Bolkestein, *Wohltätigkeit*, 420–30.)

Almsgiving became more important in proportion as prophets and sapiential writers pondered over it and preached about it. For them, true morality, piety, and justice in the widest sense are inconceivable without almsgiving (Ezek 18:7, 16; Tobit 14:2 BA). It is spoken of in the same breath as fasting and prayer (Tob 12:8 BA; compare Mt 6:2, 16; against this, the Coptic *Gospel of Thomas*, Logion 14 [Leipoldt]). It is meritorious and brings about forgiveness of sins (Prov 11:4; 19:17–22; Tob 4:7–11; 12:9; Ps 41:1ff; Dan 4:27; Sir 3:30). It is a condition of salvation (Is 58:6–12). It is considered to be on the same level as sacrifice (Tob 4:11; Sir 35:2; see Heb 13:16).

In the sapiential literature there is, among countless commendatory phrases, no lack of references to the advantages of almsgiving (Prov 28:27) and to the disadvantages and disgrace of 'wicked and foolish' conduct and avarice (Sir 14:3–10; 20:10–17; 41:21; Prov 28:8; Job 27:13–17). These books also abound in exhortations to prudence (Sir 12:1–6; see *Didache* 1, 5–6). Where the poor are concerned, God is involved, their champion (Prov 14:31; 17:5; 19:17; Sir 4:6, 10). So much attention has been paid to the ethical aspect that the friendly word which accompanies the giving is regarded as more important than the gift itself (Sir 18:15–18; 4:1–6). The Jewish people allowed usury to be practised by private initiative to such an extent that almsgiving eventually came to count as the fulfilment of the whole law (SB IV, 536–41; Eichrodt III³, 61 and 131).

In the *New Testament* the practice and high esteem of almsgiving still continue (Jn 13:29; Lk 16:19–31; Acts 3:2; 6:1–6; 10:2–31; 1 Cor 16:15–17; see also 1 Tim 5:16; 1 Cor 11:20–22)—a fact borne out by the frequent use of Old Testament texts. On the other hand, it is not possible to detect any influence of the hellenistic environment here (Bolkenstein, *RAC* I, 302). In the same way, the fact that Jesus bases this practice on ↗ love is not by any means entirely new: his commandment to love is undoubtedly linked to that of the Old Testament (Deut 6:4; Lev 19:18; see also Sir 4:2; 18:15ff;). But his chief commandment equates the love of God with the love of one's neighbour (Mt 22:34–40; Lk 10:25–8; Mk 12:28–31; see also 1 Jn 3:14–22; 4:7f). This love has exclusive claims over every other consideration (Mt 7:12; Lk 6:31). It transcends all barriers or bonds between individuals and groups (Lk 6:27; 10:29–37; Mt 5:43–8; Mk 7:27–8; Rom 12:20; Jas 2:1–4, 8f, 15f)—transcends, too, every restriction or calculation, since God has the only valid claim to consideration (Mk 6:33–7; Lk 6:34–8; Mt 18:33; Jas 2:13). The christian acts in the knowledge that what is done to the poor is done to the Master (Mt 25:31–46; see Mt 10:40; 18:5). Almsgiving serves as a standard at the judgement (see Mt 18:23–5), and Christ is the ultimate reason for true beneficence (Mt 25:40, 45; 10:40–42; Jn 12:44f). The only standard which matters is that set by God. It is not the calculable value of the gift which counts, but the unselfish love which occasions the act of giving. The decisive factor is not the outward performance of the deed but the sentiment behind it (Mk 12:41–4; Lk 18:9–14; 19:1–10; 21:1–4; 1 Cor 13:3; 2 Cor 8:12; see 12:15). Alms thus bestowed are a store laid up in heaven (Lk 12:33; see Mt 6:19–21; 2 Cor 9:9f). Jesus also commends almsgiving as a means of making oneself free to follow him and thus of becoming perfect (Mt 19:21; Mk 10:21; Lk 18:22). Almsgiving can overcome the danger of riches (1 Tim 6:17–19; see Mt 19:23f; Mk 10:25; Lk 16:1–13, 19–31; 18:25). Jesus, however, takes sides with the woman who is said to have 'wasted' a fortune of ointment on his feet, and against the apostles—who, it is true, are thinking of the poor, but not from equally unselfish love (Mt 26:6–13; Mk 14:3–9; Jn 12:1–8).

The disposition of the primitive

church in Jerusalem (Acts 2:44f; 4:32–5), and, even more strikingly, the collections of Paul (Gal 2:10; 1 Cor 16:1–3; Rom 15:15–27, 31; 2 Cor 8, 9; see 1 Cor 11:20–22) cater, among other things, for the organised collection of alms—that is to say, in a social setting and with a social aim in view, arising from the situation within the church at any given moment (see Allo, *RB* 45 [1936], 529–37). Paul is on his guard against everything extravagant (2 Cor 8:12–13). He upholds, in a particularly realistic way, the first, though by no means exclusive, claim of those who belong to the household of the faith (Gal 6:10), and aims to restrain abuses (1 Thes 4:11; 2 Thes 3:6–15; 1 Tim 5:16; see Jude 12–16). The act of giving can, and should, take into account certain physical, moral, or social limitations and regulations (see 2 Cor 8:13; *Didache* 1, 5–6; E. Peterson, *Frühkirche*, 147–8; for a different view, Audet, *La Didachè*, 275–80). It is not, however, possible to impose limitations on the disposition to give alms. The right disposition can be maintained even where personal sacrifice is involved (Eph 4:28; see 1 Thes 4:11; 1 Cor 4:12; 2 Cor 8:2; Acts 20:35). The act of giving should be made in simplicity (Rom 12:8; 2 Cor 8:2; 9:11–13), that is to say, it should be performed with God in mind (see Mt 6:21; Lk 12:14). For that reason, the act is of its nature liberal, impulsive, and cordial (2 Cor 9:5, 7–9; Rom 12:8; Bacht, *GL* 29 [1956], 424–6). Only what is given from the heart has any real value (2 Cor 9:7), not what is given out of covetousness (2 Cor 9:5, 7; see 1 Tim 6:10). There is, to be sure, an 'equality' (*isotēs* 2 Cor 8:13f), but not as an adjustment of relations here on earth, but rather as *koinōnia*, a solidarity in sharing and participation (Rom 15:26f; 2 Cor 8:4; 9:13) in everything which can be of service (*diakonia* Rom 15:25, 31; 2 Cor 8:4, 19, 20; 9:1, 12, 13) to others. This follows naturally from, and expresses in a concrete way, the religious fellowship founded by Christ (Hauck, *TDNT* III, 804–9). Everything is *kharis* (=love, charity), applied in different ways, beginning with the poverty of Christ which causes grace to operate (2 Cor 8:9) and ending with the money distributed by christians among each other for the love of Christ (1 Cor 16:3; see 2 Cor 8, 9). No word of thanks is due to men. Everything is done from God-given love, with the result that the recipients are fortified in faith and charity and give thanks and praise to God (2 Cor 9:8–15; see Phil 2:13–15; 2 Cor 8:5).

Christian almsgiving is not to be thought of as a continuous or general relief of a distress which is always present (Mt 26:11; Mk 14:7; see Deut 15:11), but as the affirmation of a charity which arises from the prevailing circumstances. That is why, in the New Testament, there is relatively little explicit or exclusive discussion of almsgiving as such. Whatever discussion one finds is aimed at an immediately attainable end, as in the case of Paul's collections. For Jesus, it is a question of the general prevalence of charity, whether it happens to be in polemics directed against a ritualistic scrupulosity that is devoid of love (Lk 11:39–42; see Mt 23:25f), or in the application or illustration of the consequences of charity (Lk 12:33f; Mt

6:1–4, 19–21). The giving of alms shares in the nobility of charity.

Bibliography: E. B. Allo, 'La portée de la collecte pour Jérusalem dans les plans de S. Paul', *RB* 45 (1936), 529–37; J.-P. Audet, *La Didachè, Instructions des Apôtres*, Paris 1958; H. Bacht SJ, 'Einfalt des Herzens—eine vergessene Tugend?, *Geist und Leben* 29 (1956), 416–526; Bammel, *TDNT* VI, 885–915; J. Bauer, 'Ut quid perditio ista? Zu Mk 14:4f und parr.', *Novum Testamentum* 3 (1959), 54–6; Beyer, *TDNT* II, 81–93; R. Bloch, 'Valeur religieuse de la Justice dans le Bible', *Cahiers Sioniens* (Paris) 6 (1952), 17–32; H. Bolkenstein and W. Schwer, *RAC* I, 301-07; H. Bolkenstein, *Wohltätigheit und Armenpflege im vorchristlichen Altertum*, Utrecht 1939; R. Bultmann, *TDNT* II, 477–87; A. Descamps, *Les Justes et la Justice dans les évangiles et le christianisme primitif hormis la doctrine proprement paulinienne*, Louvain 1950; A. Descamps, *DB(S)* IV, 1443–4; Hauck, *TDNT* III, 804–9; J. Hempel, 'Das Ethos des AT', *BZAW* 67 (1938); J. Nikel, *Das Alte Testament und die Nächstenliebe*, Münster 1913; R. North, 'Sociology of the biblical Jubilee', *Analecta Biblica* 4 (1954); Erik Peterson, *Frühkirche, Judentum und Gnosis*, Freiburg and Rome 1959; SB IV, 536–610; A. Wikenhauser, 'Die Liebeswerke in dem Gerichtsgemälde Mat 25:31–46', *BZ* 20 (1932), 366–77; W. Nagel, 'Gerechtigkeit—oder Almosen? (Mt 6:1)', *VC* 15 (1961), 141–5; V. Balogh, '"Selig die Barmherzigen". Dic christliche Barmherzigkeit bei Matthäus im allgemeinen und in der 5. Seligpreisung im besonderen im Lichte des AT', Rome 1959 (dissertation).

Johann Gamberoni

Amen

A. *Old Testament.* Derived from the root *'mn* (= to be secure, firm, valid, or certain; ↗ truth), *'âmēn* is generally rendered in LXX by *genoito* (= so be it). In the Old Testament and in later judaism the word was never used simply to endorse a statement, but exclusively as a sign of agreement with what another affirmed. In 1 Kings 1:36; Jer 11:5; 28:6, assent is given to a command; in Num 5:22; Deut 27:15–26; Neh 5:13, a curse or a threat is submitted to; in Ps 41:13; 72:19; 89:52; etc, *'âmēn* is pronounced after a benediction or a eulogy.

An acclamation with *'âmēn* is the usual way of concluding a previously expressed aspiration in prayer with a personal affirmation. This custom is to be found since time immemorial in the liturgy, and numerous examples from later Jewish public worship can be quoted in support of it. At Qumran, benedictions and maledictions are assented to in this way when a covenant is entered into (1 QS 1:20; 2:10, 18).

B. *Jesus* uses *'âmēn* in quite a singular sense at the beginning of his own utterances in order to reinforce them: 'Amen, I say to you'. In John's gospel the word is always repeated, as in liturgical usage. This usage of Jesus can be rendered in English with a fair degree of accuracy as: 'I say to you in all seriousness', 'I say to you once and for all'. In this fashion the Lord expresses his claim to authority and the fact that his words have power absolutely to bind the conscience. There is no example in later Jewish literature which can be compared with this application of the word *'âmēn* on the part of Jesus, and for this reason it can be regarded as a characteristic of the *ipsissima vox* of Jesus, his very own manner of speaking (see Mt 5:18, 26; 6:2, 5; etc; Jn 1:51; 3:3, 5; etc). This *'âmēn* is also occasionally translated by *nai* (= yes) (Mt 11:9; Lk 7:26; etc) or, in the case of Lk 9:27; 12:44; 21:3, by *alēthōs* (= truly), and in Lk 4:25 by *ep' alētheias* (= in truth).

Elsewhere in the New Testament, *'âmēn* occurs in the usual way as a liturgical acclamation (1 Cor 14:16; Rev 5:14; 7:12; etc), or in order to reinforce an aspiration made in prayer or a eulogy (Rom 15:33; Gal 6:18). In certain cases the use of *'âmēn* cannot, from the point of view of textual criticism, be satisfactorily testified, and is then generally the addition of a copyist. Such cases include the use of *'âmēn* at the end of epistles (1 Cor 16:24; 2 Cor 13:14; etc) and other books (Mt 28:20; Mk 16:20; Lk 24:53; Jn 21:25; Acts 28:31; 1 Jn 5:21; 2 Jn 13; 3 Jn 15; see also Tob 14:15 LXX).

In Rev 22:20 the church replies to the divine promise with *'âmēn*. In 2 Cor 1:20 the community gives the answer *'âmēn* to God's 'Yes' that he has uttered through Christ and in which all promises have been realised. In Rev 3:14 Christ himself is called 'Amen' as the 'faithful and true witness' of divine revelation.

Bibliography: J. Jeremias, 'Kennzeichen der ipsissima vox Jesu', *Festschrift A. Wikenhauser*, Munich 1953, 86–93; J. Schmid, *LTK* I[2] (1957), 432f; A. Stuiber, *Jahrbuch für Antike und Christentum* 1 (1958), 153–9.

Johannes B. Bauer

Angel

A. *Word and meaning*—The English word *angel*, like its equivalent in most modern languages, is derived through the Latin word *angelus* from the Greek word *angelos* (= messenger). In christian usage, developed during the Middle Ages after a start in early christian times, it stands for supernatural spirits; in the bible not so much because of their nature, as in present-day usage (in that sense they are usually referred to as 'spirits', 'powers', etc), but because of their function in the service of God or the devil (Augustine: 'Angelus enim officii nomen est non naturae' [*Sermo* VII 3]). Although the belief in spirits and angel-like intermediary beings between God and man may be found in many religions, the conception of 'angels' is characteristic of the Jewish and christian beliefs and of those religions that have been influenced by them (eg old Syncretism, Islam).

B. *Angels in the Old Testament*

a. *Early period*. There are beings between God and man which are sometimes called 'angels' according to their function (*mal'kîm* [originally: 'messengers'], *angeloi* [Gen 19:1; 28:12; 32:1; Ps 103:20]), in other places 'men' according to their outward appearance (Gen 18:2, 16; 19:10, 12), or according to their relation to God, 'host of Jahweh' (Jos 5:14), of 'the army of heaven' (1 Kings 22:19). God consequently is called 'God of hosts' (Hos 12:5; Amos 3:13; 6:14) or 'Yahweh of hosts' (1 Sam 1:3, 11; Ps 24:10; 46:7, 11). The angels very often have a warlike appearance (Gen 32:1ff; Jos 5:13; Judg 5:20). They are with God in heaven (Gen 21:17; 22:11) and there form his heavenly household (1 Kings 22:19), but, according to an old tradition, they also live on earth (Gen 32:2). The angels come to man as messengers of God (Gen 16:7ff; 19:1ff; 21:17; 22:15; Num 22:22ff; Judg 2:1; 6:11; 13:3; 1 Kings 13:18; 2 Kings 1:3); they protect man (Gen 24:7, 40; 48:16; Ex 23:20–23; Ps 91:11), but occasionally they also pass divine judgement on him (2 Sam 24:16; 19:35; Ps 78:49). People generally pictured angels as beings in human form, as is evident from many apparitions (cf the epithet 'men') and therefore without wings.

The Angel of Yahweh. Among the angels, special prominence is given to the 'Angel of Yahweh' (Gen 16:7, 9; 22:11, 15; 31:11; Ex 3:2, 4; Judg 2:1; 6:11ff; see Gen 18f; Acts 7:30–5) or the 'Angel of God' (Gen 21:17; Judg 13:6, 9). God reveals himself through him in such a way that the text speaks directly of God and not of his angel (Gen 16:10, 13; 22:10–18; 31:11–13; 48:15f; Ex 3:1ff); but on the other hand this angel appears quite distinct from God (Gen 24:7; Ex 33:1f; 2 Sam 24:16). The relation of this angel towards God, which up to today has never been satisfactorily explained, has given rise to different attempts at explanation. The 'Representation-theory' sees in the Angel of Yahweh an angel-like creature acting on the authority of God (Jerome, Augustine). According to the 'Identity-theory' he is God himself, who, though in himself invisible, shows himself as visibly present and active in certain situations. The 'Logos-theory' (now obsolete) regards him as a revelation of the Logos, ie, of the pre-existing Son of God (early christian writers). According to the 'Interpolation-theory' (many modern exegetes) it is an indication of later theological convictions; ever since the period of an absolutely transcendental concept of God, the old stories of God's direct intercourse with man had become objectionable and therefore 'God's Angel' took the place of God himself. The figure of the Angel of Yahweh comes very close to that of the 'Angel of the Covenant' (Mal 3:1).

Cherubim and Seraphim. Mention is made occasionally of 'Cherubim' (*kᵉrûbîm*: probably related to the Accadian word *karibu* or *kuribu*, a deity of lower order mediating between man and the higher gods originally represented in human form and later with wings and the characteristics of the eagle, the lion, or the bull. This may have been influenced by the usual representation of Egyptian goddesses or genii by the Assyrian winged Colossi with bodies of lions or bulls and human heads standing at the entrances of temples and palaces). They guard ↗ paradise beside the flaming sword so that the first human couple could not again enter this garden of Eden from which they had been expelled (Gen 3:24). They were furthermore thought of as 'Bearers of God' (2 Sam 22:11; Ps 18:10), and as such they had very realistically been placed on either side of the cover of the ark (Ex 25:19f; cp the cherubs in the Holy of Holies of Solomon's Temple, which were of a related but quite different form, 1 Kings 6:23–8; 2 Chron 3:10–13), so that God was said to be 'sitting upon the cherubim' (1 Sam 4:4; Ps 99:1). This idea found its full and impressive expression in Ezekiel's vision, where four cherubs of a fiery nature with the faces respectively of a man, a lion, a bull, and an eagle were drawing God's chariot with their hands, feet, and wings (Ezek 1:10). The Tabernacle (Ex 26:1, 31; 36:8, 35) and the Temple of Solomon (1 Kings 6:29, 32; 2 Chron 3:14) were decorated with the woven and carved figures of cherubs.

In the glorious vision of Isaiah

(6:2–6) mention is made of 'Seraphs', beings with six wings, with hands, feet, and human faces, standing before God's Throne (*śᵉrāphîm*, originally: 'the burning ones'; other meanings of the word are: 'poisonous serpent' [Num 21:6, 8] or 'flying serpent' [Is 14:29; 30:6], which suggests an original connection of seraphs with snakes).

Cherubs and seraphs are not angels in the original sense of the word and are, therefore, never referred to as such in earlier times. But during the later Jewish period they are classed under those beings which are now called 'angels', for which reason they can safely be indicated as angels in the modern sense of the word.

b. *Later period.* The Jewish conception of angel and its representation became increasingly more elaborate and rich during the Persian and Greco-Roman period, especially in the so-called Apocryphal writings (*Pseudepigrapha*), eg the Books of Henoch, the Book of Jubilees, the Syrian Apocalypse of Baruch, etc, and to a certain extent also in the canonical writings of this period, eg Job, Daniel, and Tobit. The main reason for this development is the stronger emphasis on God's transcendence during this time as opposed to the preceding period, which again gave greater prominence to the part played by angels as intermediaries between God and the world. Other factors may have contributed, although there is not sufficient certainty as to their details (introduction of popular conceptions into the Jewish religion, contact with the religious ideas of the pagan countries where the Jews stayed). An especially fertile ground for this development is the apocalyptic literature which was coming into fashion with the Book of Daniel. From this time onwards, new names are chosen for the angels. According to their relation to God, they are called 'sons of God' in the sense of 'beings closely related to God' (Job 1:6; 2:1; 38:7; Wis 5:5; see also LXX-suppl. Deut 32:43); 'holy ones' (Job 5:1; 15:15; Ps 89:5, 7; Dan 4:13, 17, 23; 8:13; Zech 14:5; Sir 42:17; Wis 5:5; Jub 17:11; 31:14; 33:12; Enoch [Eth] 1:9f; TestLev 3:3; 1 QS 11:8; 1 QM 12:1, 4; 1 QH 3:22; 4:25; 10:35); 'holy angels' (Tob 11:14; 12:15; Enoch [Eth] 71:8f; 1 QM 7:6); 'divine beings' (*'êlîm*: 1 QM 1:10f; 14:15; 17:7; 1 QH 7:28; 10:8); or, according to their function, 'watchers' (Dan 4:13, 17, 23; 8:13; Jub 4:15, 22; 7:21; 8:3; 10:5; Enoch [Eth] 1:5 etc; Enoch [Slav] 18:1, 3; 35:2; TestRub 5:6; TestNaph 3:5; CD 2:18); 'they who never sleep' (Enoch [Eth] 39:12f; 40:2); 'princes' (Dan 10:13, 20f; 12:1; 1 QS 3:20; 1 QM 13:10, 14); and, according to their nature, 'spirits' (Jub 15:31; Enoch [Eth] 15:4, 6, 8, 10; 1 QM 12:9; 13:11f; 1 QH 1:11; 11:13; 13:8; see also 1 Kings 22:21; Wis 7:23); and 'majestic beings' (1 QH 10:8; Enoch [Slav] 21:1, 3). According to their nature all angels and angel-like beings are called 'spirits', so that God is then referred to as 'Lord of spirits' (LXX Num 16:22; 27:16; 2 Macc 3:24; the constant expression used in the similitudes of Enoch [Eth] 37:2, 4ff; see also Ps 104:4; Sir 39:33). He is 'Prince of divine beings, King of majestic beings, and Lord of all spirits' (1 QH 10:8).

LXX mentions an angel in many places where, according to the Hebrew text, God acts himself (eg Ex 4:24;

Job 20:15); also 'the angels' instead of God himself (Ps 8:5). Also the phrase 'Son of God' is replaced by 'Angel' (Job 1:6) and 'gods' by 'angels' (Ps 97:7; 138:1; see also Dan 2:11 Theodotion).

During this period God no longer speaks directly to the prophet or apocalyptist as in the older prophecies; rather, an angel is sent to him to present and explain God's revelations, first in Ezekiel (40:3f; 43:6; 47:3–6), where he is simply referred to as 'a man', later, in a particular way, in Zechariah (1:8–14; 2:1, 7; 4:1–6 etc), where 'the angel of Jahweh' performs this function; also in Daniel (8:16–26; 9:21–27), where it is seen to by Gabriel, and in the Apocrypha (eg, Uriel in Hen [Eth] 10:1; 19:1f; 2 Esdras 4:1f).

Angels are disembodied spirits (Hen [Eth] 15:6; Philo, *De Sacrificiis Abelis et Caini*, 5; ApocAbr 19:6), of fiery essence (Bar [Syr] 21:6; 59:11; ApocAbr 19:6; Enoch [Slav] 1:4f; 20:1; 29:1, 3; 30:1), whom God has created (Jub 2:2: 'on the first day'; Bar [Syr] 21:6: 'right from eternity')—created, however, as immortal beings (Enoch [Eth] 15:4, 6). In accordance with their nature their food was not of an earthly or material kind (Tob 12:19; see also Judg 13:16 and the older, opposite view in Gen 18:8); it was, on the contrary, a heavenly manna (LXX Ps 78:25; Wis 16:20; 4 Esdras 1:19; see also Tob 12:19). They are visible on earth only as apparitions, not in material bodies. (Tob 12:19.) The angel appears in the form of a man (Dan 8:15; 10:5, 16; Tob 5:4f; Enoch [Slav] 1:4; see also Gen 19:5), as a young man (2 Macc 3:26), in glory (Dan 10:5f; Enoch [Slav] 1:5); his face is like lightning (Dan 10:6). He is clothed in linen (Ezek 9:2f, 11; 10:2, 6f; Dan 10:5; 12:6f), in a beautiful garment (2 Macc 3:26), in white (TestLevi 8:2; see also 2 Macc 11:8; Enoch [Eth] 87:2; 90:21, 31). His belongings are made of gold (2 Macc 3:25) or fire (Enoch [Slav] 29:3; Joseph and Asenath 17:8). In the vision he speaks with a loud voice (Dan 10:6). The apparition of an angel confounds a man (Dan 10:9 [strictly speaking, the confusion here is resolved by the words of the angel]; Tob 12:16; 3 Macc 6:18f; Enoch [Slav] 1:7; see also Esther 5:2a LXX [=15:16 Vulg]), but the angel lifts him up again (Dan 10:10; Tob 12:17; Enoch [Slav] 1:8). Men hide themselves from the sight of an angel (1 Chron 21:20). The movement of angels is generally represented as flying, even when wings are not mentioned (Dan 9:21; ApocAbr 12:9; see also Dan 14:36, 38).

The number of angels is beyond reckoning (Job 33:23; Dan 7:10; Enoch [Eth] 1:9f; Enoch [Slav] 11:4; 18:1; 1 QM 12:1, 4; 4 Esdras 6:3; Bar [Syr] 21:6f; see also Deut 33:2; Ps 68:17). They form God's council, along the lines of similar bodies at earthly courts, although, of course, God's sole and exclusive dominion is always preserved and the angels do not share his supreme rule (Job 1:6–12; 2:1–7; 15:8; Ps 89:7; see also 1 Kings 22:19–21; Dan 4:17). They stand before God as he sits on his throne (Dan 7:10; Enoch [Eth] 71:8; Bar [Syr] 21:6; 48:10; 4 Esdras 8:21). They praise him for ever more (Enoch [Eth] 39:13; Enoch [Slav] 8:8; 17:22–3; 42:4; TestLevi 3:8 (here it is a question of the 'thrones' and 'powers'), with one voice (Enoch [Eth] 61:11; Enoch [Slav] 19:6), with beautiful song (Enoch [Slav] 8:8, 17), with soft and gentle voices (Enoch [Slav] 20:4; see also 21:1). They form the 'host of heaven' (Neh 9:6; for angels and hosts of heaven side by side see Ps 103:2Lf; 148:2), the 'eternal army' (1 QH 11:13), which is equipped to fight for God's cause (Enoch [Eth] 60:1; 61:10; TestLevi 3:3; 1 QM 12:1, 4; 1 QH 3:35f; 11:13 etc; see also 2 Macc 3:25f). They are the 'angels of heaven' (Enoch [Eth] 97:2; see also 71:8; 104:1), who have their station in the different zones of heaven (TestLevi 3:2f, 5–8).

Angels come to men as bearers of divine messages (Tob 3:17; Dan 14:34), give him an unparalleled insight (LXX Dan Susanna 45), give him orders (1 Chron 21:18), and make known what God wants him to do (Job 33:23). They speak to God on behalf of men. (Job 33:23f) and present their prayers to God (Tob 12:15; Enoch [Eth] 99:3; TestDan 6:2; see also TestLevi 3, 7). The angels protect men (Dan 3:23 (26, 28), 25; LXX Sus 45; Vulg Jud 13:20; 2 Macc 11:6; 15:22f; Enoch [Eth] 100:5; 1 QM 9, 15f; 13:10; TestJud 3:10; TestDan 6:5; TestJos 6:7 etc), rescue them from danger (Dan 3:23 (26), 25; 6:23; Tob 3:17; 2 Macc 15:23; see also 2 Kings 19:35; Is 37:36), and help them in various ways (Tob 5:6; 12:3, 14; 3 Macc 6:18f; 4 Macc 4:10; see also 2 Macc 3:25). They transport them through the air to places they have never seen before (Dan 14:34–39); they have power over demons (Tob 8:3; Jub 10:7, 11). Individual men are under the protection of particular angels (1 QS 4:15f); two spirits, one of truth and the other of unrighteousness, are given to men (1 QS 3:18f; see also TestJud 20:1; 1 QH 1:17; 17:17). Each man has an angel allotted to him by God. (Bar [Greek] 12:3; 13:1; Enoch [Slav] 19:4.)

Holy men of God are occasionally called 'angels' when they act as mediators between God and man in a role similar to that of the angels (eg the priest in Mal 2:7 and Moses in AssMos 11:17). A similar parallel is sometimes drawn between the king and an angel (Esther 5:2a, LXX [=15:16 Vulg]; even earlier in 1 Sam 29:9; 2 Sam 14:17, 20; 19:27; see also Zech 12:8).

Every nation has its own angel (Dan 10:13, 20f; Jub 15:31f; Enoch [Eth] 89:59; 90:22, 25; see also LXX Deut 32:8; Dan 12:1; LXX Sir 17:17.) The angel of Israel is Michael (Dan 10:13, 21; 12:1; Enoch [Eth] 20:5); but according to another point of view Israel does not come under any angel, but directly under God (Jub 15:32; see also LXX Deut 32:8f).

There are angels in charge of created things, as an angel of the firmament (Esdras 6:41), of the stars (Enoch [Eth] 72:1, 3; 74:2f; Enoch [Slav] 4; 19:2, where the stars themselves are not regarded as animated, angelic beings: Enoch [Eth] 18:13–16; 21:3–6; Philo, *De Opificio Mundi*, 73; *De Gigantibus*, 8), of the natural elements such as the wind, thunder and lightning, rain, and the like (Jub 2:2; Enoch [Eth] 60:11–21); also of the seasons (Jub 2:2; Enoch [Slav] 19:4; see also Hen [Eth] 82:11–20); water (Enoch [Eth] 61:10; 66:2; 69:22; Enoch [Slav] 19:4); fruit (Enoch [Slav] 19:4); and metals (Enoch [Eth] 65:8).

God passes judgement on man through his angels. (1 Chron 21:12, 15f, 27; 1 Macc 7:41; Bar [Syr] 6:4ff; Joseph and Asenath 25:6; see also 2 Macc 3:24–6.)

Groups of angels are formed, eg, a group of seven angelic princes or archangels (Tob 12:15) Enoch [Greek] 20:2–7; Enoch [Eth] 81:5; 90:21; Jerusalem Targum I ad Gen 11:7; see also TestLevi 8:2–10). Elsewhere, however, only six are given (Enoch [Eth] 20:1; Jerusalem Targum I ad Deut 34:6), or four (Enoch [Eth] 9:1; 10; 40:2–10f; Sib II 215). Besides these, seven orders of angels are known (TestLevi 3:2–8), or also ten (Enoch [Eth] 61:10; Enoch [Slav] 20:1; including in both cases the cherubim and seraphim). Names are also given to certain angels, such as Michael (Dan 10:13; 12:1; Enoch [Eth] 9:1; 10:11; 20:5; 1 QM 9:15f; Bar [Gr] 11:8; ApocMos 1:40; Sib II 215; JerTargum I ad Deut 34:6, etc); Gabriel (Dan 8:16; 9:21; Enoch [Eth] 9:1; 10:9; 20:7; 1 QM 9:15f; ApocMos 40; Sib II 215; JerTargum *loc. cit.*, etc); Raphael (Tob 3:17; 5:4; 9:1, 5; 12:15; Enoch [Eth] 9:1; 10:4; 20:3; 1 QM 9:15; ApocMos 40; Sib II 215; JerTargum *loc. cit.* etc); as well as Uriel in extracanonical writings (Enoch [Eth] 9:1; 10:9; 20:2; ApocMos 40; 2 Esdras 4:1; 5:20; 10:28; Sib II 215; JerTargum *loc. cit.* etc) together with a great number of often fantastic names.

The angels are not represented as being free from the possibility of sin in the eyes of God (Job 4:18; 15:15), but the canonical books of the Old Testament do not speak of a given sin committed by the angels; nevertheless, they are subject to God's judgement (Job 21:22; see also Is 24:21–23). The extracanonical literature, on the other hand, infers such a sin from Gen 6:2, 4: a section of the angels—those, namely, who are referred to in that text as 'sons of God' at one time left heaven, took the daughters of men to wife and by them engendered giants; for which, as a punishment, these angels were, for a time, chained in the underworld, to be thence cast into eternal fire at the judgement (Jub 4:22; 5:1; 6:10; 7:21; 10:5; Enoch [Eth] 6f; 10:4–13; 12:4; 15; 54:3–6f; TestRub 5:6; TestNeph 3:5; Bar [Syr] 56:12f; Philo, *De Gigantibus*, 6; Josephus, *Ant. Iud.*, 1, 3, 1 [73]; see also CD 3, 4 (Riessler) (=2, 17f [Schechter]). See also ↗ Demon.

While the Essenes were greatly exercised with angels (see Josephus, *Bell. Iud.*, 2, 8, 7, 142), popular belief went no further than can be seen from the extant texts, while the Sadducees, according to Acts 23:8, refused to accept such representations (cf. Hippolytus, *Refutatio Omnium Haeresium*, 9, 30, 4). Rabbinical Judaism, which grew out of Pharisaism, left plenty of freedom in the matter of belief in angels, but opposed exaggerations and attempted to bring this belief into a right relationship with belief in God, in keeping with Old-Testament conceptions.

3. *Angels in the New Testament.* The conception of angel in the New Testament is based on that of the late Jewish period as found in the so-called late Jewish apocrypha and related writings, rather than on the earlier canonical books of the Old Testament. In the New Testament, however, this conception is more subdued. Angels function

as messengers sent from God to man (Mt 1:20; 2:13, 19; Lk 1:11, 26; 2:9f; Acts 8:26; 10:3; 27:23; see also Gal 1:8). They appear to him in dreams (Mt 1:20; 2:13, 19), but also when they are fully awake (Mk 16:5; Lk 24:4f; Jn 20:12); in a vision (Acts 10:3), and resembling young men in shining white robes (Mk 16:5; Mt 28:3; Lk 24:4; Jn 20:12; Acts 1:10; 10:30; Rev 15:6; 19:14). People are frightened at the sight of angels (Lk 1:12; 2:9; see also Mk 16:5, 8); but the angels sent them at ease (Lk 1:13; 2:10; see also Mk 16:6; Mt 28:5.

There are a great many angels (Mt 26:53; Heb 12:22; Rev 5:11); they are spirits (Heb 1:14; see also Rev 1:4); they have been created in Christ (Col 1:16) and, like all other things they have been reconciled with God through his blood (Col 1:20). They form the legions of God (Mt 26:53) and represent the heavenly world (Mt 22:30; Lk 12:8f; Eph 3:15; 1 Tim 5:21; Heb 12:22; 1 Pet 3:22). The New Testament mentions various groups of heavenly beings (similar to the Apocrypha of the late-Jewish periods: Hen [Eth] 61:10; Hen [Slav] 20:1; TestLev 3:2–8): eg 'virtues' (*dunameis* Rom 8:38; 1 Cor 15:24; Eph 1:21; 1 Pet 3:22; see also 2 Thess 1:7); 'powers' (*exousiai* 1 Cor 15:24; Eph 1:21; 3:10; 6:12; Col 1:16; 2:10, 15; 1 Pet 3:22); 'principalities' (*arkhai* Rom 8:38; 1 Cor 15:24; Eph 1:21; 3:10; 6:12; Col 1:16; 2:10, 15); 'dominations' (*kuriotētes* Eph 1:21; Col 1:16); 'thrones' (*thronoi* Col 1:16), although the difference between these choirs of blessed spirits is not disclosed. The law of the old covenant was given to man by angels (Acts 7:53; Gal 3:19; Heb 2:2). They serve Christ (Mt 4:11; Lk 22:43) and his disciples (Acts 5:19; 12:7–10; Heb 1:14). They rejoice in the proven integrity of the just and in the conversion of the sinner (Lk 15:10; see also 15:7). Children have their angels in heaven (Mt 18:10), and—at least in popular belief—everybody has his own angel (resembling him) (Acts 12:15). Angels guide the dead into eternity (Lk 16:22). In the resurrection of the dead, men will be like angels (Mk 12:25 and parallel passages); but even now the face of a witness of Christ, full of the Holy Ghost, may resemble that of an angel (Acts 6:15). Christ will come for his last judgement with his angels (Mt 16:27; 24:31).

Being the Son of God, Christ is superior to all angels, both before his incarnation and when he will be the God-man raised to the right hand of God (Mk 13:27 and parallel passages; Eph 1:20f; Col 1:16f; 2:10; Heb 1:5–14; 2:1–9; 1 Pet 3:22). Through his death and resurrection Christ has despoiled the principalities and powers (Col 2:15). The faithful will share Christ's restoration to power and will even judge the angels in the last judgement (1 Cor 6:3). God's intentions regarding the salvation of man will be made known to the angels through the church (Eph 3:10; 1 Tim 3:16); and learning of God's wise doings will be a joy to the angels (1 Pet 1:12).

The New Testament also uses the expression 'the Angel of the Lord' corresponding to the old expression 'the Angel of Yahweh', or 'the Angel of God' (Mt 1:20; 2:13; 28:2; Lk 1:11; 2:9; Acts 5:19; 8:26; 12:7 and many other instances) when referring to the angel sent from God with a special message. Only two angels have been given names, Gabriel (Lk 1:19, 26) and Michael (Jude 9; Rev 12:7), the latter once (Jude 9) being referred to as 'archangel' (*arkhangelos*, a Jewish-hellenistic word formation first used in Enoch [Gr] 20:7). The worshipping of angels is rejected (Col 2:18; see also Rev 19:10; 22:8f). Beside the angels of God there are the angels of the devil (Mt 25:41; 2 Cor 12:7; Rev 12:7, 9). Occasionally (Jude 6; 2 Pet 2:4) mention is made of a fall of certain angels and their punishment (in accordance with a widespread late-Jewish legend, eg in the Book of Jubilees 4:22; 5:1; 7:21; 10:5; Enoch (Eth] 6f). Neither angels nor principalities nor virtues are able to separate the christian from the love of God (Rom 8:38f), but he has to struggle against these principalities and powers, these rulers of the world of darkness (Eph 6:12). But when the time of the eternal Kingdom of God has come, principalities, powers, and virtues will lose the power they wield in this present world (1 Cor 15:24). Consequently, many of these beings have something demoniacal about them, are in league with the devil and 'spirits of wickedness' (Eph 6:12; see also 6:11).

Angels are most frequently mentioned in the Revelation to John in whose visions angels perform various functions. An angel sent from God conveys the revelations to the Seer (1:1; see also 19:10; 22:6, 8f). The Seer writes to the 'angels' of seven churches in Asia (1:20; 2f; it is very clear that real angels are referred to, not bishops or other officials of these churches). The traditional cherubs and seraphs have merged into a group of four 'living creatures' (4:6–8 and other instances) round the throne of God. And also before him stand the equally traditional seven angel-princes (Rev 8f), also simply referred to as 'seven spirits' (1:4; 3:1; 4:5; 5:6). There also appear the angels of the four winds (7:1f), the angel-prince of the demoniac locusts of the bottomless pit called Abaddon (=Destroyer; 9:11), the angels of the malicious horsemen (9:14), an angel with power over fire (14:18), another with power over the waters (16:5), and seven angels with vials full of the wrath of God (Rev 15f). See also ↗ Principalities and powers.

D. *Theological value of biblical statements concerning angels.* In the theological appreciation of biblical evidence concerning angels, we must above all be mindful of the literary nature of the text; whether we are confronted with a simple account of facts or a free narrative in which more popular notions have been assimilated (eg Tobit), whether they represent a view strongly connected with the ancient conception of the world (the classification of angels in Paul), or whether they must be regarded as symbolic visions whose real meaning can only be found after lifting the veil of symbolism (eg the Book of Revelation). The church holds in accordance with the bible that apart from our visible world God created a world of pure, invisible spirits, serving God and man; also that that part of this host of angels has turned from God and is pitted against him in eternal enmity (see IV Lateran Council, DS 800 [DB 428]). The doctrine of the guardian angel for every human being is based on the bible and has always been held in the church, although it has not been formally pronounced as a dogma.

Bibliography: W. Grundmann, G. von Rad, and G. Kittel, *TDNT* I, 74–87; K. Prümm, *Der christliche Glaube und die altheidnische Welt* I, Leipzig 1935, 137–56; L. S. Chafer, 'Angelology', *Bibliotheca Sacra* 98 (1941), 389–420; 99 (1942), 6–25; Haag, 390–98; M. Ziegler, *Engel und Dämon im Lichte der Bible*, Zürich 1957; A. Winklhofer, *Die Welt der Engel*, Ettal 1958; J. Michl and R. Haubst, *LTK* III², 863–72; J. Michl, *RAC* v, 53–258; J. Michl, 'Engel', *HTG* I, 269–81.
On Section B: S. Landersdorfer, 'Zur Lehre von den Schutzengeln im AT' *Katholik* 98 (1918), 2 and 114–20; J. Felten, *Neutestamentliche Zeitgeschichte*, II, Regensburg 1925³, 107–41; P. Dhorme and L. H. Vincent, 'Les Chérubins', *RB* 35 (1926), 328–58 and 481–95; W. Bousset and H. Gressmann, 320–31; G. H. Dix, 'The Seven Archangels and the Seven Spirits', *JTS* 28 (1927), 233–50; C. Kaplan, 'Angels in the Book of Enoch', *ATR* 12 (1930), 423–37; J. Rybinski, *Der Mal'akh Jahwe*, Paderborn 1930; F. Stier, *Gott und sein Engel im AT*, Münster 1934; P. Volz, *Die Eschatologie der jüdischen Gemeinde im ntl. Zeitalter*, Tübingen 1934² (under 'Engel'); F. König, *Die Amesha Spentas des Avesta und die Erzengel im AT*, Melk 1935; E. Langton, *The Ministries of the Angelic Powers according to the Old Testament and later Jewish Literature*, London 1937; B. Stein, 'Der Engel des Auszugs', *Bbl* 19 (1938), 286–307; H. B. Kuhn, 'The Angelology of the Non-Canonical Jewish Apocalypses', *JBL* 67 (1948), 217–232; G. Heidt, *Angelology of the Old Testament: A Study in Biblical Theology*, Washington 1949; A. Dupont-Sommer, 'L'Instruction sur les deux Esprits dans le "Manuel de Discipline"', *RHR* 142 (1952), 5–35; A. Kolaska, 'Gottessöhne und Engel in den vorexilischen Büchern des AT und in der Ras-Schamra-Mythologie im Lichte des biblischen Monotheismus', Vienna 1953 (dissertation); B. Otzen, 'Die neugefundenen hebräischen Sektenschriften und die Testamente der zwölf Patriarchen', *ST* 7 (1953/4), 125–57; F. Nötscher, *Geist und Geister in den Texten von Qumran*, Paris 1957, 305–15; V. Hamp, *LTK* III², 879; H. Gross, 'Der Engel im AT', *ALW* VI, I (1959), 28–42; W. Herrmann, 'Die Göttersöhne', *ZRG* 12 (1960), 242–51.
On section C: M. Dibelius, *Die Geisterwelt im Glauben des Paulus*, Göttingen 1909; G. Kurze, *Der Engels- und Teufelsglaube des Apostels Paulus*, Freiburg 1915; J. Michl, *Die Engelvorstellungen in der Apokalypse des hl. Johannes* I, Munich 1937; E. Langton, *The Angel Teaching of the New Testament*, London 1937; K. L. Schmidt, 'Die Natur- und Geistkräfte im paulinischen Erkennen und Glauben', *Eranos-Jahrbuch 1946*, vol. 14 (1947), 87–143; H. Bietenhard, *Die himmlische Welt im Urchristentum und Spätjudentum*, Tübingen 1951; C. Spicq, *L'Épitre aux Hébreux* II, Paris 1953, 50–61; G. H. C. Macgregor, 'Principalities and Powers: The Cosmic Background of St Paul's Thought', *NTS* I (1954/5), 17–28; G. B. Caird, *Principalities and Powers: A Study of Pauline Theology*, Oxford 1956; H. Schlier, *Principalities and Powers in the New Testament*, London 1961; H. Schlier, 'Die Engel nach dem NT', *Arch. für Liturgiewissenschaft* VI, I (1959), 43–56.

Johann Michl

Antichrist

Antichrist (*antikhristos*) is a word-formation used for the first time in 1 and 2 Jn, and occurs only here in the whole of the New Testament—one which belongs certainly to Greek-speaking christians. It means 'against Christ', and thus stands for the antagonist, the rival of Christ (1 Jn 2:18; 4:3). Scripture contains no formal declaration about the Antichrist; there is only occasional reference to him from which, however, some characteristics of this figure may be known.

A. *Prehistory*. The expectation of an Antichrist to come has its roots in the late Jewish period. The so-called history-of-religion exegetical school (represented by W. Bousset, H. Gunkel, R. Reitzenstein, and others) thought in terms of a background which was originally mythological—namely, either the primordial or final struggle of a god against a being hostile to him which he conquers. Thus, in Babylonia, we have the primordial victory of Marduk over

Tiamat, dragon of Chaos, and, in Persia, the final annihilation of the evil spirit Ahra Manju by Ahura Mazda. It would, however, be better to seek an explanation much nearer at hand than such a remote and entirely foreign conception, the development of which cannot be traced through judaism down to the figure of the Antichrist. Painful experiences in the past and the present gave the Jews reason to fear that also in the future heathen nations and their rulers would oppress Israel. In particular, it was expected that there would come in the last days a potentate of unprecedented power and cruelty.

Ezekiel (38f) already knows of such a prince and gives him the enigmatic name 'Gog', evoking thoughts of terror and brutality (Ezek 38:2f, 14, 16, 18; 39:1, 11, 15). Daniel speaks in prophecy of the 'Contemptible One', whom he beheld as a small horn which blasphemed against God, oppressed his people and eradicated his worship (7:8, 11, 20f, 24–26; 8:9–12, 23–25; 11:21–45). This was Antiochus IV Epiphanes (176–164 BC). The mysterious description is, however, intended to lead one to look beyond this Syrian king to a terrible figure belonging to the last days, of whom Antiochus is but the precursor. In the Book of Judith (6:2) Nebuchadnezzar, king of Babylon, who is fighting against Israel, is characterised as an anti-Yahweh.

The compilers of the late-Jewish apocryphal writings were powerfully stimulated by such material in the Old Testament. In the Ethiopian Book of Enoch (90:16) it is the Hellenistic nations, in the Jewish Sibylline Oracles (III 663–668) the kings of the heathen nations, who make war upon Israel. In 2 Esdras (13:33–8) the nations of the earth make a concerted assault on the Messiah who punishes them on this account with annihilation. (Cf also 5:6.) More detailed descriptions can be found in the Syrian Apocalypse of Baruch (36–60) and in the Testament (Assumption) of Moses (8); a particularly powerful and dangerous ruler, who exceeds all his predecessors in evil, makes his appearance on the very threshold of the messianic age, in this case before the general judgement, and crushes and persecutes the religion of the true God. This future transgressor does not as yet bear any definite name indicative of his nature. He is known simply as 'ruler' (BarSyr 40, 1) or 'potentate' (AssMos 8, 1). In keeping with the politically coloured messianic expectation of late judaism this assault was seen in a predominantly political light, as a struggle waged by a hostile army under the command of several, or, in the last resort, one leader against the people of God. At the same time, it was also believed that definite religious persecution would take place, a belief which emerges most strongly in the Testament of Moses.

The spiritual world of Qumran may well have made some contribution to the idea of an Antichrist; we find there, at any rate, mention of 'the Man of Lies' (1 Qp Hab 2, 1f), 'the Wicked Priest' (idem 8, 8), 'the Mocker' who deceives Israel and leads her astray. (*CD* 1, 10 [Riessler] = 1, 14f [Schechter]; cf 9, 39 [Riessler] = 20, 15 [Schechter].)

B. *New Testament.* These expectations were given a decisive turn by primitive christianity, though the way had admittedly been prepared already in late judaism. As it is now no longer a question of a blood-relationship with the people of Israel, but of belief in Christ, the coming fiend is seen as a tempter who tries to make the faithful apostatise and to put obstacles in the way of those who have not yet come to believe. The picture conjured up is of a gigantic levy, with its own means of recruiting and political machinery, in the service of these ends.

1. *General considerations*. Jesus himself spoke of false christs and false prophets who were to come and who would perplex his church and lead his people away from the true faith (Mk 13:22; Mt 24:24). The fear for the future was that false teachers would appear (Acts 20:29f), with particular reference to the last days. (1 Tim 4:1–3; 2 Tim 3:1–8; Jude 18; 2 Pet 3:3f.) This is known through a communication of the spirit (1 Tim 4:1), or is referred back to the prediction of the apostles (Jude 17f) or, alternatively, the prophets and apostles (2 Pet 3:2). Finally, the 'abomination of desolation' (Mk 13:14; Mt 24:15) is mentioned in Jesus' eschatological discourse with reference to Daniel (9:27; 11:31; 12:11). Many commentators have, right from the earliest times (Irenaeus, *Adv. Haereses*, V, 25, 2,5; Origen, *Contra Celsum* VI, 46 etc) referred this to the Antichrist.

2. *Paul* knows of 'the Man of Sin', 'the Lawless One', 'the Son of Perdition who opposes and exalts himself against every so-called god or object of worship'. The 'mystery of lawlessness' is already at work, but the evildoer is not yet in full control, since his coming is, for the time being, prevented by a power which stands in his way. As soon as he does make his appearance, however, he will set himself up, in the strength of the devil, against God in an attitude of self-deification, spread false teaching and find an audience among those who refuse the christian message and embrace error. Christ will eventually destroy this adversary at his second coming (2 Thess 2:3–12).

3. *John* also knows of a fiend who is to come, whom he refers to simply as 'Antichrist'. (1 John 2:18.) This title, however, also covers the false teachers who are at work destroying the church's teaching about Christ by their divergent interpretations (1 John 2:18, 22; 2 Jn 7; see also 1 Jn 4:3). They are, in fact, heralds of the seducer who is to come. If John calls a false teacher 'Antichrist' and sees in him the spirit of the Antichrist at work (1 Jn 4:3), it follows that, just as all the hostility and violent opposition of Israel's adversaries added up, in earlier Jewish representations, to the one oppressor of the last days, so the Antichrist is the sum total of all the opposition to Christ, the denials of christian doctrine, the surrender of the christian life. The Antichrist is thus, quite simply, the false teacher who tempts people away from loyalty to the Lord. Although, however, John allows only this aspect to emerge in the passages in which he mentions the Antichrist, we need not limit his conception just to this. On this assumption, then, the Antichrist of 1 Jn appears as the same figure as that of 2 Thess, even if the two descriptions differ in many respects.

4. A relevant parallel to the fiend that was to come can be found in the two beasts of the *Revelation*, the beast that came up from the sea and its

companion, the beast that came out of the earth. The first (Rev 13) appears like a leopard with the feet of a bear and mouth like a lion, with ten horns crowned with diadems and seven heads inscribed with blasphemous names (vv 1f). It has the strength of the dragon, who is the devil, and possesses its throne (v 2), makes men adore it (vv 4, 8; cf emperor-worship), blasphemes God (vv 5f), and persecutes the christians (v 7; see also v 15). Its name, which is not given, corresponds to the number 666 (v 18). In Chapter 17 this beast that comes from the sea bears the Whore of Babylon on its back (vv 3–6), the 'great city' (v 18). The seven heads of the beast refer to seven mountains upon which the city is built, likewise to seven kings, the seventh of whom is ruling at the time of the apocalyptic vision (vv 9f). The beast itself will come as the eighth and last of the kings, and together with it ten other kings will reign for a short time; these are symbolised by the ten horns (v 12). In Rev 11:7 this same beast rises up out of the abyss and slays the two witnesses of God. In 19:19f it joins battle with Christ and his warriors, but is vanquished and cast into a sea of fire. The beast that comes out of the earth resembles a lamb, has two horns but talks like the dragon (or devil, Rev 13:11). It performs wonders and leads men astray, causing them to worship the first beast or its image (13:12–15). Whoever refuses to do this is slain (13:15). It is the 'false prophet' (Rev 16:13; 19:20; 20:10; see also Mk 13:22f and parallels) who, together with the other beast, is cast into the sea of fire (19:20). The figure of the first beast forms a clear link with Daniel 7 and can be taken to symbolise, if not a demon, certainly a very powerful, godless ruler of the last days who claims divine worship for himself and persecutes those christians who do not give him it. The second beast, who also can hardly be taken for a demon, is the symbolical figure, standing for the bearer of a false religion, which encourages the divine honours paid to that ruler.

C. *Post-biblical, early christian literature.* The idea of the Antichrist plays an important part here. In the *Didache* (16:4) we find the expectation that 'the Tempter of the world' will appear in the last days, will come like the Son of God, rule over the earth, perform miracles and perpetrate hitherto unheard-of atrocities. In the Apocalypse of Peter (2) he is also 'the Tempter' who performs miracles and slays those who do not follow him. In a christian section of the Sibylline Oracles (III 63–74), he is given the name 'Belial' (see 2 Cor 6:15), which is the usual name for the devil in late judaism, but is not yet attested for the Antichrist. This can probably be best understood with reference to the *Ascensio Isaiae* (4:1–16) in which Belial, that is, the devil, appears in person on the earth 'in human form' and goes about his unholy business. We find references to 'the Man of Lawlessness' as late as Justin (*Dialogue with Trypho*, 32,3f), but thereafter as from the time of Irenaeus (*Adv.Haereses*, 1, 13,1; 3, 6,5; 7,2; 23,7; 5, 30,3f; 35,1) and Tertullian (*Scorpiace*, 12,10; *De Praescriptione*, 4,5; *De Monogamia*, 16,5) the title 'Antichrist' takes the place of this expression with reference to the tyrant, evidently influenced by the Johannine usage.

D. *Theological weight of the biblical evidence.* The Antichrist is the great tempter away from Christ, the oppressor of christians and a tool of the devil, though never the devil himself, since he is clearly distinguished from him (we meet the opposite view of the identity of both for the first time in the *Ascensio Isaiae*). The 'Antichrist' in John and the corresponding figure in Paul can be understood, in accordance with the statements which both writers make and in the light of the messianic expectation of late judaism, hardly otherwise than as a person, a human being, not just as an embodiment of tendencies and forces hostile to God or a group of false teachers. At the same time, John does know of other antichrists already at work in his own day (namely, teachers of false doctrine) apart from the Antichrist to come. The seer of the Revelation distinguishes between the political potentate and the religious seducer, who both together bring about the period of oppression connected with 'Antichrist'. This means at least that the 'Antichrist-like' attitude of spirit is found in several men, not only in one determined individual of the last days, and that in consequence the 'Antichrist-like' movement must not be attributed to one single person.

Paul, moreover, depicts the evildoer to come in a way peculiar to his own day, so that we cannot expect his representation will be fulfilled in every detail—literally as it is. It is legitimate, therefore, to ask whether the figure of the evildoer himself (although he is presented as an individual according to the conceptions peculiar to a certain age) may not nevertheless be interpreted in a collective sense of those rulers and seducers who oppose Christ. This would involve the expectation, not just of one, but of many 'Antichrists'. This problem cannot be settled with full certainty, but the evidence of scripture, and not just of 2 Thess, but also of the Johannine epistles and Revelation (even if these latter speak less clearly) would seem rather to indicate a definite person corresponding to the single person who is Christ—therefore an 'Antichrist' in the strict sense of the word who, however, has his precursors as history draws to an end.

Bibliography: commentaries on 2 Thess, 1 and 2 Jn, and Revelation; B. Rigaux, *L'Antéchrist et l'opposition au royaume messianique dans L'Ancien et le Nouveau Testament*, Paris 1932; A. Arrighini, *L'Anticristo*, Turin 1945; E. Stauffer, *New Testament Theology*, London 1955, 213–15; J. Schmid, 'Die Antichrist und die hemmende Macht', *TQ* 129 (1949), 323–43; E. Lohmeyer, *RAC* I, 450–57; Haag 72–4; P. Althaus, *Die letzen Dinge*, Gütersloh 1955, 282–97; H. Schlier, *Vom Antichrist, Zum 13 Kapitel der Offenbarung Johannis: Die Zeit der Kirche*, Freiburg 1956, 16–29; R. Schnackenburg and K. Rahner, *LTK* I², 634–6; M. Brunec, 'De "Homine Peccati" in 2 Thess 2:1–12', *VD* 35 (1957), 3–33; B. Rigaux, '*bdelugma tēs erēmōseōs*', *Bbl* 40 (1959), 675–83; V. Maag, 'Der Antichrist als Symbol des Bösen', *Das Böse*, Zurich 1961, 63–89; O. Betz, 'Der Katechon', *NTS* 9 (1962/3), 276–91; L. Sirard, 'La Parousie de l'Antéchrist: 2 Thess 2:3–9', *Studiorum Paulinorum Congressus* II, Rome 1963, 89–100; F. Mussner, 'Das Buch Judith und die ntl. Antichristidee', *TTZ* 72 (1963), 242–4.

Johann Michl

Apostle

A. *The word 'apostle' in general.* Neither the Greek nor the Aramaic speaking world of early christianity knew the word 'apostle' in the sense of the New Testament. Christianity itself has created this idea and the institution itself for the first holders of this office.

The word *apostolos*, however, is already used in prechristian literature. In classical Greek it means 'naval expedition', and in the papyri 'receipt' or 'passport'. LXX does not know the word at all (the Codex Alexandrinus uses it once [1 Kings 14:6], but this may have been taken from Aquila). Only Herodotus uses it twice in a meaning related to that of the New Testament (messenger, ambassador). It is therefore quite possible that Herodotus has adopted a colloquial idiom which, although not found in literature, may have been familiar to the authors of the New Testament. Nevertheless, from the choice of the word in this—to say the least—very unusual meaning, we may conclude that the more usual Greek words of related meaning seemed unsuitable to the early christians to describe the office held by the Apostles.

Neither is it a matter of the word *apostolos* being a translation of a usual Aramaic word. The Semitic equivalent of the Greek *apostolos* is used for the first time in the second century, and it is hard to believe that there were Jewish apostles before AD 70.

Nevertheless, the word 'apostle' points in its meaning to the world of the Semitic languages. It is closely related to the Hebrew verb *šālaḥ*. The meaning of *šālaḥ* is not fully covered by the English verb 'to send'; it means *to send with authority, to delegate*. In the Jewish legal system after the Babylonian captivity there was a kind of delegation through which people could act legally by proxy (eg contract a marriage). The person so empowered (*šālûaḥ*) was by law the representative of the one commissioning. Here applies the old rabbinic principle deeply rooted in judaism; 'the representative is equal to the person who has sent him' (Ber 5:5; see also Jn 13:16). In this context we must also remember the old Semitic laws of delegation which in point of fact are closely related. The ambassador of the king was the lawful and personal representative of his distant master, which explains why the insult offered to David's ambassadors by the Ammonites was the immediate cause of a destructive war (2 Sam 10). This was also the reason why Abigail washed the feet of David's servants (1 Sam 25:40f). In spite of his high rank, the ambassador of the king remained, of course, the servant of his master as before (1 Sam 25:41).

But when Jesus sent some of his disciples on a similar mission (Mk 6:7) he did not send them simply as messengers or as missionaries (late-Jewish missionaries are never called *šelûḥîm*; Cynic-Stoic itinerant preachers are never called *apostoloi*) or as heralds who had only to announce messages officially. Neither were they prophets (even prophets in the late-Jewish period were never called *šeluḥim*); even the idea of eye-witness is absent in the original concept of an apostle. Apostles were rather his personal and lawful representatives. This much can be derived from linguistic data. The purpose and duration of the mission are not indicated in this conception.

B. *The apostolic mission before the resurrection.* The men in Jesus' company are referred to in the gospels in three different ways. Jesus called ↗ *disciples* to follow him; from these he selected '*the twelve*' (↗ Disciple); he gave full powers to the *apostles*.

A future mission for the realisation and propagation of Christ's work is already mentioned in the individual call to the disciples. Christ was sent into the world to call all men to the kingdom of God. Simon and Andrew would one day undertake this task as 'fishers of men' (Mk 1:17). In the election of the twelve (Mk 3:13–19) the prospect of a future mission is even more clearly indicated. Certainly, Christ did not choose the twelve only in view of a future authorisation, 'He appointed twelve to be with him' (Mk 3:14). The very number *twelve* points to a quite different purpose (↗ Disciple). Nevertheless, it is also an election for the future function of apostle; 'He appointed twelve . . . to be sent out to preach [the joyful tidings] and have authority to cast out demons' (Mk 3:14). The proclamation of the kingdom of God (see Lk 4:18–21) and the defeat of the prince of this world (see Lk 11:20) were the object of Christ's mission, and it was Christ's will that his apostles should share this mission (compare also Mt 10:1 and Lk 9:1). Their task was to propagate his messianic mission especially where he could not go himself. Christ expressed very clearly how greatly he wanted the apostles to be his legal and personal representatives: 'He who receives me receives him who sent me' (Mt 10:40–11:1; compare also Jn 13:20), and: 'He who hears you hears me; and he who rejects you rejects me, and he who rejects me rejects him who sent me' (Lk 10:16; compare also Heb 3:1, where Christ himself is called an apostle). The city which does not accept the apostles shall suffer a fate worse than that of Sodom and Gomorrha (Mt 10:15). The person authorised is equal to the one who conferred the authority. Therefore, the mission of the twelve before the resurrection remained within the limits set to Christ. Like Christ himself, who was sent only 'to the lost sheep of the house of Israel', his apostles were to go 'nowhere among the Gentiles and enter no town of the Samaritans' (Mt 10:5f). Returning from their temporary mission the apostles were once again disciples of Jesus as before (Mk 6:30f).

C. *The definitive authorisation.* As early as the period of Christ's public life, some disciples were at certain times entrusted with the mission to represent the Messiah. The careful and extensive training of the disciples for their apostolic mission, as well as certain promises (see Mt 16:19; 18:18) show clearly that these temporary apostolic activities could not be the full realisation of Christ's plans for the apostles. He did not want to leave his flock behind after his departure 'like sheep without a shepherd' (see Mt 9:36; Jn 21:15–17). He therefore promised his disciples the power to bind and loose. Their decisions in the church would be the decisions of the Lord in heaven (Mt 16:18; 18:18). This power, unlimited in time and space, was given by the risen Lord (Mt 28:18f). From this time forward, Christ is sent not only to the lost sheep of Israel, but to all nations, which are subject to his power; and therefore he entrusted his authorised representatives with the pastoral care of all nations. Only when the Lord comes again will this representation of the Good Shepherd become superfluous, and end. This leads inevitably to the conclusion that power of representing Christ must be propagated throughout the history of the church, for it would surely be unthinkable that certainty of forgiveness of sins was only given to the first generation of the church. This divine power, which so much astounded the Jews (see Mt 9:8), Christ delegated to his apostles (Jn 20:21), so that this gift of grace should remain in this world even after the day of his ascension, and until his second coming.

Finally, Jn 21:15–17 shows (as already in Mt 16:18f) the special position of Peter as the first among those endowed with authority. In creating this prerogative, Christ established the hierarchical principle and gave a certain inner structure to the group of apostles. Multiplicity itself necessarily demands some kind of subordination.

D. *The apostolate in the early church.* The election of Matthias in place of Judas, which took place before Pentecost, is an event unique in the history of the church (Acts 1:15–26). It indicates above all the significance of 'the twelve' and is less important to the concept of 'apostle'. Of far greater importance is the fact that the apostolate can by no means be regarded as identical with 'the twelve'. Apart from the twelve, other apostles are mentioned who did not have to fulfil the conditions required for membership of 'the twelve' (Acts 1:21f). First of all we might mention Barnabas, who is called an apostle in Acts and in order of enumeration is mentioned before Paul (14:4, 14). He introduced Paul into the community of the early church (Acts 9:27) and brought him from Tarsus to Antioch to join the missionary work there (Acts 11:25f). After the laying on of hands at Antioch, they were both sent out on their missionary travels. It is not quite certain that Acts 13:3 refers to their full authorisation as apostles; but at all events, Barnabas was an apostle in name and in function just like Paul (compare also Gal 2:9, and especially 1 Cor 9:4–6). The greater degree of gratitude and reverence in the church which Paul was to experience later on was not due to high rank or office but to other reasons. Whether Andronicus and Junias (Rom 16:7) were apostles cannot be definitely ascertained, but we must take into account the possibility. The fact that Paul mentions 'great apostles' (2 Cor 11:5; 12:11) and 'pseudo-apostles' (2 Cor 11:13) in his second epistle to the Corinthians may point to a considerable number of apostles. On the other hand, 2 Cor 8:23 and Phil 2:25 seem to refer not to apostles of Jesus Christ, but to delegates of the congregations who represented their communities to Paul. It is quite possible that at the time these two epistles were written, the word 'apostle', though created to express representation of Christ, was also used to indicate different but related functions. However, there is certainly at this time no question of its hardening into a term of special distinction reserved for a few persons only.

E. *The apostolate of Paul.* For the later church and especially for the western church, Paul became the apostle *par excellence.* This is understandable enough, since he rendered a prominent service to the western church through his missionary work, and he is the only one of whom we know details concerning his life and work. His epistles form the most extensive part of the canon of the New Testament. We should not, however, be tempted to derive our idea of what an apostle was solely from the apostolate of Paul. Paul worked as a missionary, but this does not imply that missionary work is an essential element in the conception of apostle: whether the apostle represented Christ in the metropolis or in the diaspora is of no importance in defining the essence of apostolate. Paul knew himself to be primarily intended for the ↗ preaching of the gospel (1 Cor 1:17), but it does not necessarily follow that the apostle is essentially a preacher. Paul also set great store by the fact that the risen Lord was also seen by him (1 Cor 9:1; 15:8); but, again, it does not follow that it is essential that an apostle should have seen the risen Lord and be one of the eye-witnesses of his resurrection.

It is quite clear from the epistles of Paul that the function of an apostle is essentially a function of an ambassador: 'So we are ambassadors for Christ, God making his appeal through us. We beseech you, on behalf of Christ, be reconciled to God' (2 Cor 5:20). Paul's ambassadorial activities, however, are not restricted to entreating in Christ's name. This is apparent from 1 Cor 2:4 and especially 2 Cor 2:4. The apostle is fully aware of his solidarity with Christ. We can clearly perceive here the echo of Christ's words: 'He who hears you, hears me, and he who rejects you rejects him who sent me' (Lk 10:16). But he also knows well that as an apostle he is even more a servant of the Lord who has sent him, and that he is nothing but an 'earthen vessel' which God has filled with the precious treasure of his grace (2 Cor 4:7) for the blessing of christendom.

F. *The twelve apostles*. Difficulties in the daily administration of charitable relief were undoubtedly only the immediate motive for the institution of the *seven* (Acts 6:1–7). Their solemn investiture and activities, fully recorded in Acts (Philip and Stephen), show the seven as the apostolic assistants of the twelve. Here we can see how the twelve communicated their apostolic power. At the same time it is quite clear that this power was not necessarily to be transferred wholly and completely, but that certain limitations are possible (see Acts 8:14–25). But although the seven had the apostolic mission of representing Christ, Acts never refers to them as 'apostles'. Philip is only referred to as 'the evangelist' (Acts 21:8). The same applied to those who assisted Paul in his missionary work. They were men entrusted with apostolic power (cf the pastoral epistles) but are never referred to as 'apostles'. Occasionally they are also called Evangelists (2 Tim 4:5). We can even go further: Paul passionately defended his title of 'apostle' in his Epistles to the Corinthians, which, however, did not prevent later periods from not regarding him any longer as an apostle. Luke calls him an apostle only once (Acts 14:14), and this only together with Barnabas (Luke obviously uses an old source here); elsewhere he speaks only of the twelve apostles. The same applies to Revelation (see 18:20; 21:14). We find the same tendency even in the Epistle to the Ephesians (see 2:20; 3:5). The office of apostle remained; the power to represent Christ has been handed down. Even by the time that the books of the New Testament were written the title of apostle had become restricted to the twelve. The twelve who, as such, held a unique and fundamental office in the church (↗ Disciple) were certainly also representatives of Christ. These two functions, however, should be clearly distinguished. The one is limited to the twelve and cannot be handed down; the other will continue to exist till the second coming of the Good Shepherd, even though those who possess this apostolic authority later are no longer called apostles.

Bibliography: A. Verheul, 'De moderne exegese over *apostolos*', *Sacris Erudiri* (1948), 380–96; A. Wikenhauser, *RAC* I (1950), 553–5; P. Gaechter, 'Die Sieben', *ZKT* 74 (1952), 129–66; E. M. Kredel, 'Der Apostelbegriff in der neueren Exegese', *ZKT* 78 (1956), 169–93 and 257–305 (references to the older literature are also given); J. Dupont, 'Le nom d'apôtres a-t-il été donné aux Douze par Jésus?', *OS* I (1956), 266–90 and 425–44; H. Reisenfeld, *RGG* I (1957), 497–9; K. H. Schelkle, *Discipleship and Priesthood*, London and New York 1966; P. Gaechter, *Petrus und seine Zeit*, 1958; K. H. Rengstorf, *TDNT* I, 407–47 (=*Apostleship* [*BKW* VI], London 1952); K. H. Rengstorf, *Apostolat und Predigtamt*, 1954²; A. M. Farrer, *The Ministry in the New Testament: the Apostolic Ministry*, London 1947; H. von Campenhausen, 'Der urchristliche Apostelbegriff', *ST* I (1948), 96–130; H. von Campenhausen, *Kirchliches Amt und geistliche Vollmacht in den ersten drei Jahrhunderten*, 1953; A. Fridrichsen, *The Apostle and his Message*, Uppsala 1947; P. H. Menoud, *L'Eglise et les ministères*, 1949; H. Mosbech, '*Apostolos* in the New Testament', *ST* II (1950), 166–200; J. Munck, 'Paul, the Apostles, and the Twelve', *ST* III (1950), 96–110; O. Cullmann, *Peter: Disciple, Apostle, Martyr*, London 1962; E. Lohse, 'Ursprung und Prägung des christlichen Apostolats', *TZ* 9 (1953), 259–75; A. Ehrhardt, *The Apostolic Succession in the First Two Centuries of the Church*, 1953; G. Klein, *Die zwölf Apostel: Ursprung und Gehalt einer Idee*, 1961; W. Schmithals, *Das christliche Apostelamt: Einer historische Untersuchung*, 1961; B. Gerhardsson, 'Die Boten Gottes und die Apostel Christi', *SEA* 27 (1962), 89–131; E. M. Kredel, 'Apostel', *HTG* I, 61–7; P. Bläser, 'Zum Problem des urchristlichen Apostolats', *Unio Christianorum* (1962), 92–107; *S. Freyne, *The Twelve: Disciples and Apostles. A Study in the Theology of the First Three Gospels*, London 1968 (with extensive bibliography).

Elmar M. Kredel

Ascension

I. *Textual findings*. 1. Luke is the only evangelist who mentions the 'ascension' in the conventionally accepted sense—as an event in the history of salvation which occurred in a given place and at a given time. This reference is to be found at the end of his first book and at the beginning of his second. According to Lk 24:50f, it would appear that Jesus ascended into heaven on Easter Sunday; in the second narrative, which is connected without a break to Jesus' words of farewell to his apostles, Luke reiterates what he has already said (Acts 1:9–12; see 1:2f): after the 'last appearance', forty days after his resurrection (Acts 1:3), the Lord was 'taken up into heaven' (Acts 1:2, 11: the aorist passive of *analambanō* = 'take up' [lacking in the 'western' text]), and 'as they were looking on, he was lifted up' (Acts 1:9: aorist passive of *hupolambanō* = 'take up', 'lift up'). As in the instances where God appeared of old (see Ex 13:21f; 24:15–18; 40:34–8), and in Jesus' transfiguration before his disciples (Mt 17:5; Mk 9:7; Lk 9:34f), the 'cloud' appears as a sign of God's presence; 'A cloud took him out of their sight' (Acts 1:9). As two angels in shining apparel announce Jesus' resurrection in Lk 24:4, so here two *angeli interpretes* promise the glorious second coming of the Lord in the same manner—that is, 'in a cloud' (Acts 1;11: see also Dan 7:13; Mt 24:30; 1 Thess 4:17; Rev 1:7; 14:14–16). Following their Lord's example, the two witnesses will also ascend 'in a cloud' into heaven (Rev 11:12), and those who are still alive when the Lord comes again will be taken up 'in the clouds' (1 Thess 4:17). According to the account given in Acts, Jesus did not 'ascend into heaven' on his own initiative, but was taken up into heaven by the Father through the Holy Spirit (see also Rom 6:4).

The bodily ascension of Christ is also the subject-matter of the (canonical) 'long ending' of Mark's gospel (Mk 16:9–20), but this summarises the account given by Luke and cannot be considered as a valid independent testimony.

2. Side by side with this visible ascension of Christ, which is reported only by Luke, the various books of the New Testament invariably speak only of the resurrection and exaltation of Christ. We touch here on the very heart of the apostolic work of preaching the gospel: it is a striking feature of the early missionary sermons that the *apostles* bear witness exclusively to the resurrection (Acts 1:21f; 2:32; 3:15, 26; 4:10, 33; 10:40f; 13:30–37; 17:18–31; 22:15; 26:16); to Jesus' 'exaltation at the right hand of God' (Acts 2:33–6; 5:30–32; 7:55f; see also Mt 22:44; 26:64; Mk 12:36; 13:26; 16:19; Lk 20:42; 22:69); and, finally, to his glorious second coming (Acts 3:20f; 1:7, 11). The subject of an ascension which was perceptible to the senses played no further part in the early church's preaching of the work of God.

Paul uses the same manner of speaking in his epistles. He emphasises again and again the close connection between the resurrection and exaltation of the Lord, without troubling greatly about the way in which Christ penetrated into this world of heavenly transfiguration. After the Easter-event, Christ inhabits heaven, where he is seated 'at the right hand of God' (Rom 8:34; 1 Cor 15:25; Eph 1:20; Col 3:1–3; Heb 1:3, 13; 2:7–9; 8:1; 10:12; 12:2) until he comes again at the end of time in power and in glory (1 Thess 1:10; 4:16; 2 Thess 1:7; 1 Cor 4:5; Phil 3:20; Col 3:4; 1 Tim 6:14), to judge the living and the dead (2 Tim 4:1, 8; Tit 2:13) and to take the faithful up into the eternal paschal glory (1 Thess 4:16; 2 Cor 4:14; 5:1–10).

The *catholic epistles* also allude to the glorification of Christ inaugurated by his resurrection (1 Pet 1:3f, 21; 1 Jn 2:1) and in due course to be crowned by his glorious second coming (Jas 5:7f; 1 Pet 1:7, 13, 21; 4:13; 5:1, 4, 6, 10; 1 Jn 2:28; 3:2), and by the transformation of mankind and all creation (2 Pet 3). It is self-evident that this exaltation presupposes an 'ascension', but for the most part such an ascension is implied only.

True, several texts allude to an 'ascension', but without reference to a particular time or place. In Eph 4:8–10 the ascent of the Lord above all the heavens is contrasted in a very general way with his descent into the lower parts of the earth and the underworld. In this instance, as in the case of the liturgical hymn in 1 Tim 3:16, the 'taking up in glory' is clearly more a matter of theological assertion, or confession of faith, than of a statement of fact concerning an actual experience. In the Epistle to the Hebrews, the mysterious journey of Christ to the right hand of God is compared with the entry of the high priest into the Holy of Holies (Heb 4:14; 6:19f; 9:11f, 24): just as once every year the high priest took the blood of calves and goats, passed through the tabernacle, and entered the Holy of Holies to sprinkle the top of the ark of the covenant with the blood (Heb 4:14; 6:19f; 9:24), so, in the same way, Christ passed, with his own blood, through a more perfect tabernacle and entered the innermost sanctuary. In other words, after his death as a sacrificial offering of the flesh, Christ penetrated the tabernacle of his own body (see 2 Cor 5:4; 2 Pet 1:13) and entered once and for all the sanctuary, the Holy of Holies of the Godhead, when he entered into glory (Heb 2:9f), appeared before the face of God (Heb 9:24), and took his place at God's right hand. We could express this another way by saying that, through his sacrifice, Christ gained—in a very real sense—a joint share in the Godhead. Whenever the text goes on to allude to the body as well, the intention is not to describe an event which can be perceived by the senses, but merely to stress a particular theological doctrine such as that contained in Eph 4:8–10. According to 1 Pet 3:21f, 'Jesus Christ . . . has gone into heaven and is at the right hand of God, with angels, authorities, and powers subject to him': in this instance, too, his 'ascension' is doubtless conceived as a fact of dogma which eludes the experience of the senses.

John goes more deeply and thoroughly into the original proclamation of the apostles concerning Christ's exaltation. On the morning of Easter Sunday, the risen Christ appeared to the faithful disciple Mary Magdalene: 'Do not hold me, for I have not yet ascended to the Father; . . . to my Father and your Father, to my God and your God' (Jn 20:17). Here the text refers to the ascension of the Lord to his Father *on Easter Sunday itself*—an ascension which eludes all possibility of apprehension by the senses. This mysterious event, this 'Easter ascension', therefore preceded the various appearances accorded to the disciples (see Jn 14:28; Mk 16:9–14).

Revelation celebrates the heavenly Christ in his triumph (Rev 1:13–18), sitting at the right hand of the Father (3:21; 5:6–14; 7:17), on a cloud (14:14) and in the new Jerusalem (3:12). But we are not told how he came there.

II. *The twofold 'ascension'*. It is clear that the texts quoted so far cannot be harmonised with each other. They appear to envisage a twofold 'ascension'.

1. The oldest tradition places chief stress on the real and essential taking up of the Lord into glory at the right hand of God on Easter Sunday itself. According to the evidence given in *Acts*, the missionary sermons of Peter (Acts 2:14–39; 3:12–26; 4:8–12; 5:29–32; 10:34–43) and Paul (Acts 13:16–41; 17:22–31; 22:1–22; 26:1–29; 28:17–28)—which Luke presents in a highly stylised form—continue to proclaim only the risen Lord who sits at the right hand of the Father, without

mentioning a visible ascension. *Paul*, too, sees the resurrection from the tomb, and the exaltation to the right hand of God above all heavens and the thrones of angels, as being very closely related to each other. Resurrection and exaltation form one, single paschal mystery of Christ's victory over sin, death, and hell. Even in the texts where the word 'ascension' is used (Eph 4:8–10; 1 Tim 3:16; Heb 4:14; 6:19f; 9:24; 1 Pet 3:21f) it is largely a question of a theological assertion without intended narrative content. The evangelist *John* construes this paschal transfiguration of the Lord as a return to the Father (Jn 8:14, 21; 13:33; 14:2, 12, 28; 16:5, 16, 28) which took place before his visible ascension, on the morning of Easter Sunday itself. If this return to the Father in heaven had coincided with a visible taking up, John would probably not have neglected to mention this in his narrative.

It seems clear that this 'ascension' of the Lord to the Father on the morning of Easter Day must be taken to exist on a higher plane. No human eye witnessed this exaltation and transfiguration: it was only because of Christ's own revelation of this invisible glorification that the apostles learned of it. With his resurrection Jesus adopted a different physical mode of being, into which the existence of the 'heavenly Adam' (1 Cor 15:42–50), penetrated and dominated by the Holy Spirit, had been assumed. It is with this 'invisible ascension' that we come into contact with the innermost heart of the mystery of the ascension. The risen Christ has, with this incursion into the world of the divine, penetrated all at once into the central core of the mystery of salvation. Even if Christ the Lord had not been taken up bodily into heaven while his disciples were looking on, their belief in this 'ascension' would have lost very little by it. Even if Mary Magdalene and the apostles did not actually see the risen Lord enter into glory, such an entry into glory did nevertheless take place, and all the ancient creeds containing the phrase: 'ascended into heaven', pick up from the various confessional formulae in the New Testament and refer to this 'essential ascension'.

2. The *visible ascension* from the Mount of Olives (Lk 24:51f; Acts 1:2f, 9–12) is mentioned only by Luke. The paschal sermons of the early christian period are silent on the matter; similarly, the apostolic fathers—such as Clement of Rome, Ignatius, and Polycarp—make no mention of it. Some who do mention it place it eighteen months or even twelve years after the first Easter. Certain fathers—eg Tertullian and Jerome—sometimes refer to Christ's ascension as taking place on the twelfth day of his resurrection, but at other times as taking place after forty days.

Some critics conclude from these facts, often taken together with an explicit or implicit denial of a physical resurrection of Jesus, that the story of his ascension is a 'later legend'. Their reasoning takes the following form: in the view of the early christians, it was only the soul of Jesus which was taken up immediately into heaven after the death on the cross, and this victory of the soul was from time to time referred to by the term 'ascension'. With the passage of time this triumph was made to serve the cause of christian apologetics and extended to the body. In this way, the legends of Christ's appearances and of the empty tomb, and finally of the visible ascension of Christ's body into heaven, are said to have originated. We can make the following comment on this theory: no one who was by birth a Jew would have been able to make anything of the idea of an ascension of Christ's soul without his body, for—in the Old Testament view—the soul was not freed from the 'shackles of the body' at the moment of death. That was a purely Greek conception. On the contrary, it was held in the Old Testament view that body and soul were torn violently apart as a punishment for sin (see Gen 3:19; Wis 1:13), and so the triumph over death began in Jesus' case with his *bodily* resurrection, and will be completed with the 'resurrection of the flesh' on our Lord's second coming (see 1 Cor 15:3–5). Hence, from the very beginning, the various accounts of the Easter events are always given with reference to Jesus' body as well as his soul. This explains why Luke is so precise in his statements regarding the place ('the mount called Olivet', Acts 1:12; 'as far as Bethany', Lk 24:50) and the time ('during forty days', Acts 1:3) of the ascension. In Acts 1:9–11 he mentions the ascension 'into heaven' four times (though the second reference in v 11 does not appear in D, it is demanded by BSA as well as by Nestlé and Merk), and this would seem to be because he wants to give an account of a historical occurrence. Moreover, it is not as if Christ 'goes up' into heaven of his own free will, like the heroes of certain myths: on the contrary, his transfigured body is 'taken up' into heaven.

Luke, who knows the main theme of the early christian *preaching* on the resurrection and exaltation of Jesus very well indeed, cannot, as a painstaking compiler of narrative (see Lk 1:1–3), prevent himself from including the ancient tradition of the visible ascension in his *account*. According to his testimony, Christ appeared after his resurrection in transfigured corporeality to the two pilgrims on the way to Emmaus on the afternoon of Easter Sunday (Lk 24:13–35; see also Mk 16:12f), and to the disciples assembled in the room the same evening (Lk 24:36–43; Mk 16:14; see also 1 Cor 15:5–7). The last time that he appeared to his disciples was on the Mount of Olives ('the mount called Olivet'), forty days after his resurrection (this is, of course, in round figures: compare Deut 9:18, 25; 1 Kings 19:8; Mt 4:2 and parallels), with the purpose of taking his final leave from them on this earth until he comes again on the clouds of heaven. This farewell appearance of Christ to his disciples on the Mount of Olives was a concession to the frailty of men, men who are tied to their senses. This visible ascension while they were looking on was, however, something enacted on the mere fringe—as it were—of the Easter mystery. For this reason no more than secondary importance can be attached to this 'last appearance' of the risen Christ. Luke, the only real historian in the New Testament, does not see in it any new glorification or exaltation of the Lord, but, when he reports it, he has in view the connection between the risen Lord and the disciples remaining behind on earth.

The church has always, and from the

earliest times, celebrated the festival of the risen and exalted Lord—the very centre of the Easter mystery, the invisible and as it were 'background' ascension (see section 1, above). The feast of the Lord's ascension as we understand it does not appear in the liturgy until the fourth century, and serves then to convey to us one aspect of the whole paschal mystery, namely, that of the 'essential ascension of Jesus' in the terms of Luke's account of the 'taking up of Jesus into heaven after forty days'. This feast ought not to be allowed to obscure the essential exaltation of Easter Sunday: on the contrary, it should underline this very exaltation yet once more and in a special respect, that of the Lord's being 'seated at the right hand of God'. This can only be grasped by faith, of course, but it gives the deepest and fullest meaning to the mystery of Easter, and its effects will be fully realised only when the Lord comes again in his glory.

Bibliography: among various commentaries on Acts, see in particular: A. Wikenhauser, *Die Apostelgeschichte* (*RNT* 5), 1956, 28–32; E. Haenchen, *Die Apostelgeschichte*, Göttingen 1959, 115–19. See further: E. Nestlé, 'Zu Acta 1:12', *ZNW* 3 (1902), 247–9; B. W. Bacon, 'The Ascension in Luke and Acts', *The Expositor* (1909), 254–61; F. X. Steinmetzer, *TPQ* 77 (1924), 82–92 and 224–41; W. Michaelis, *TB* 4 (1925), 101–09; E. Fascher, *ZNW* 27 (1926), 1–26; G. Bertram, in *Festgabe A. Deissmann*, Tübingen 1927, 187–217; A. Friedrichsen, *TB* 6 (1927), 337–41; M. S. Enslin, *JBL* 47 (1928), 60–73; D. Plooij, Amsterdam 1929; U. Holzmeister, *ZKT* 55 (1931), 44–82; K. Lake, 'The Ascension' and 'The Mount of Olives and Bethany', *The Beginnings of Christianity* v, ed. K. Lake and H. J. Cadbury, London 1933, 16–22 and 475f; M. Goguel, *La foi et la resurrection de Jesus dans le christianisme primitif*, Paris 1933; S. M. Creed, *JTS* 35 (1934), 176–82; V. Larrañaga, *L'Ascension de Notre-Seigneur dans le NT*, Rome 1938; A. Oepke, *Luthertum* (1939), 161–86; A. N. Wilder, *JBL* 62 (1943), 307–18; W. Michaelis, *Die Erscheinungen des Auferstandenen*, Basle 1944; E. Flicoteaux, *VS* 76 (1947), 664–75; J. Leclerc, *VS* 72 (1945), 289–300; P. Benoit, *RB* 55, (1949), 161–203; P. Benoit, in Haag, 714–19; A. M. Ramsay, *SNTSB* 2 (1951), 43–50; H. Bietenhard, *Die himmlische Welt im Urchristentum und Spätjudentum*, Tübingen 1951; J. Daniélou, *The Bible and the Liturgy*, London 1960; P. H. Menoud, *Ntl. Studien für R. Bultmann* (*BZNW* 21), Berlin 1954, 148–56; G. Kretschmar, *ZKG* 66 (1954/5), 209–53; J. A. M. Weterman, *NKS* 50 (1954), 129–37; A. W. Argyle, *Expository Times*, 66 (1955), 240–42; J. Haroutunian, *Interpretation* 10 (1956), 270–81; P. Bonnard, Allmen 25–6; O. Cullmann, *The Christology of the New Testament*, London 1959; H. Kremers, *EKL* II, Göttingen 1958, 159–61; W. G. Kümmel, *RGG* III³, Tübingen 1959, 335; P. A. van Stempvoort, *NTS* 5 (1958/9), 30–42; R. Koch, *SKZ* 127 (1959), 493–4; M. Brändle, *Der grosse Entschluss* 14 (1959), 345–7; H. Conzelmann, *The Theology of St Luke*, London 1960, 187–206; J. Heuschen, *DEB*, 143–9.

Robert Koch

Asceticism

Askēsis (=exercise) is usually understood as the systematic training of human passions for a moral and religious purpose. Since this is hardly possible without abstaining from worldly goods it often stands for abstinence itself. In catholic theology, however, *askēsis* has a wider and more positive meaning; it is the systematic striving after christian perfection as far as this depends on human endeavour. Asceticism is not a biblical idea, and the bible can therefore hardly be consulted on this particular point. An *askēsis* not motivated by religion (a mere training of the will or a purely natural pursuit of virtue) is unknown to the biblical writers. Neither do we find a unanimous answer to the question as to how far man should seek union with God and his holy will through his own endeavour and renunciation. Nevertheless, much can be learned from the bible, and Christ's words and example give us guidance for a sound and beneficial asceticism or *askēsis*.

There is no tendency towards *askēsis* in the religious practice of the Old Testament when God's blessing consisted in earthly goods, conjugal bliss, and a long life (see the promises made to Abraham, Gen 12:1–3; 13:14–17 etc; Jacob's blessing, Gen 49; Job's rehabilitation, Job 42:10–16), unless one wants to see a certain form of asceticism in the unquestioning obedience to God's will (see the sacrifice of Isaac, Gen 22). The Semitic conception of man was of one undivided being of which the body was no inconsiderable 'part'. The bodily impulses reason to resist the passions and bodily instincts; a sumptuous dish (Ps 23:5), enjoyment of wine (Ps 104:15), a happy married life and fertility (Ps 128) are highly valued. Only religious reverence and fear of the holy prescribes in certain conditions abstinence from sexual intercourse (the people at mount Sinai, Ex 19:15; over the eating of holy bread, 1 Sam. 21:5f; at the holy war, 2 Sam 11:11) and from wine (priests in the holy tent of meeting, Lev 10:9 ↗ Wine). But a certain asceticism motivated by religion may be found in the penitential fasting practised by all the people on special occasions (1 Sam 7:6; Jer 36:6; Joel 1:13f; 2:12), on the Feast of Expiation (Lev 16:29f) and later too on the days of Phurim (Esther 9:31), and also by some people individually after a grave offence (David, 2 Sam 12:16f; Ahab, 1 Kings 21:27) in order to avert God's wrath. The Nazirites bound themselves by a vow of abstinence to a special service of God (Num 6:1–7; see also Judg 13:4f; Amos 2:11; 1 Macc 3:49), and similar vows for religious reasons were not infrequent in Israel (Num 30). The Rechabites, in accordance with an ancestral law, did not grow vineyards and abstained from wine, and they were praised for their faithfulness (Jer 35). This, however, hardly alters the general picture of the religious practices in ancient Israel in which joy in created things played such a central part.

It is only in the *later Jewish periods*, when through suffering and exile people had become more conscious of their own guilt and that of their ancestors, that we find a growing sense of abstinence and penance. At the same time stronger emphasis on the moral law, good works, and merit advanced the development of religious practices such as prayers at certain times, almsgiving, and fasting (Tob 12:8; see also Mt 6:1–18). The righteous freely imposed chastisement on themselves even for their errors (Ps Sol 3:9), and there were pious people who did not hanker after gold, silver, exquisite food and worldly honour, but 'who valued heaven higher than life in this world' (1 Enoch 108:7–8; see also 4 Ezr 7:125). This attitude, however, never became widespread; by the time of the New Testament many of these pious men had again become prosperous and practised fasting (twice a week, Lk 18:12) and almsgiving only as meritorious works, often for their own glory rather than for the love of God or from a sense of true remorse and contrition, a sanctimonious attitude severely castigated by Christ. The spirit of real asceticism was alive only among certain sections of the Jewish community (the Therapeutai in Egypt, the Essenes, the 'League of God' at Damascus, and the community of Qumran, all more or less related sects; see also the Testaments of the Twelve Patriarchs); voluntary poverty (community of goods), celibacy, severe labour, vigilance, and strict obedience were highly valued and to some extent realised, even in their absolute demands. The motive behind all this was the will to study intensively the law of God and put it into practice. Moreover, they were full of ardent eschatological expectation; the (Essene) community of Qumran wanted to be the 'holy remnant' of Israel at the end of time, priests as well as laymen 'who had been faithful to the covenant with God and had stood firm in the midst of general wickedness and had therefore propitiated for all the people' (*Supplement to the Manual of Discipline* [1 QSa], beginning). This resulted in their secession from the rest of the people and the foundation of monastic settlements in the desert, where the ideal of religion and moral purity could be fully realised.

A different form of asceticism is to be found in the New Testament, to a certain extent in the life and words of John the Baptist, the great preacher of penance, and even more in the life and words of Jesus himself. John the Baptist certainly lived a life of complete self-denial, but this mainly to add force to his prophetic message as the one crying 'in the wilderness' (Is 40:3). He does not demand flight from the world but an inner conversion and 'fruits that befits repentance' from everybody in every state of life or profession (see Mt 3:7–10; Lk 3:10–14). His baptism of repentance (as distinct from the immersion practised by the Essenes) was received only once and was intended for all Israel for the cleansing of sins against the coming day of judgement. Jesus proclaimed the happiness and joy of the messianic times and therefore waived special acts of penance (see Mk 2:19); he took part in banquets (Jn 2:1–11; Mk 2:15; Lk 7:36 etc; see also Mt 11:19), and allowed women of substance to provide for him (Lk 8:3). Nevertheless, his life, in accordance with his messianic mission, was hard and full of adversities (Lk 9:58). All those who wanted to 'follow' him and share his itinerant life had to adopt a similar attitude, a serene acceptance of what was offered to them as preachers, and yet frugality too (Lk 10:7; see also 22:35). But most fundamental was the renunciation of possessions, home, and family (cp Lk 9:57–62; 14:26–33). This form of asceticism founded by Christ demanded more than a few mere practical acts of temperance; it demanded, first from his immediate companions and apostles but fundamentally from all who believed in him, open profession of their belief in him and willingness to take up his cross and even give their lives for him (Mt 10:34–38 and parallels). The actual demand might be different for different individuals; not everyone was called to unrestricted renunciation of possession (eg the rich young man, Mk 10:21ff and parallels) or to celibacy 'for the kingdom of heaven' (Mt 19:12). The hard struggle, however, to enter the kingdom of heaven ('the narrow gate', Mt 7:13) was common to all.

The *early church* accepted Christ's

demands and, mindful of his cross, came to an even deeper understanding of these demands. Paul considers the christian after baptism as 'crucified with Christ' (Rom 6:6; Gal 2:20), not only free from the 'sinful body' but also called to do the works of the spirit: he should 'crucify the flesh with its passions and desires' (Gal 5:24), 'not yield [his] members to sin as instruments of wickedness' (Rom 6:13), and 'put to death what is earthly in him' (Col 3:5). This requires abstinence and discipline as it does of competitors who run in the stadium (1 Cor 9:24–27, the classic quotation for *askēsis* as a systematic training). But christian asceticism in its fullest and deepest sense is revealed only in 'the inward struggle in suffering' (Phil 1:27–30), the free and conscious acceptance of the sufferings in the service of Christ. For the sufferings of those in union with Christ are part of 'the present evil age', this still continuing but doomed world from which they have been freed in principle (Gal 1:4), but in which they are still held by their mortal existence. Those who have been baptised have already become 'a new creation [in Christ]' (2 Cor 5:17); they have become citizens of the heavenly city of God (Phil 3:20; see also Gal 4:26) and should therefore 'not be conformed to this world' (Rom 12:2), nor be utterly devoted to the world, 'for the form of this world is passing away' (see 1 Cor 7:29–31). In contrast with the riotous joys and pleasures of the heathen we hear Paul's advice 'to conduct ourselves becomingly as in the day' (Rom 13:11–14; 1 Thess 5:1–11; 1 Pet 1:13), 'as sons of light' (1 Thess. 5:5; Eph 5:8f), and 'pray constantly' (1 Thess. 5:17; 1 Pet 4:7; 5:8f; see also Mk 14:38). As is shown in all these passages, aversion from the world is designed not as an escape from the duties of this world: no, the world is rather to be shunned as something dangerous and seductive (see Jas 1:27; 4:4; 1 Jn 2:15–17; 2 Pet 1:4; 2:20), especially in the expectation of the coming 'day of the Lord' (↗ Parousia and ↗ Judgement) (1 Thess 5:2; see also Rom 13:12; Phil 4:4f) for which all shall be 'prepared and guiltless' (1 Cor 1:8; Phil 1:10; 1 Thess 5:23).

This struggle against the evil desires of the flesh (1 Pet 2:11; 2 Pet 2:18) and the warning against 'the lust of the flesh and the lust of the eyes and the pride of life' (1 Jn 2:16) are not to be mistaken for rigorism and false asceticism. The early church had soon to make a stand against certain (gnostic) views according to which all that is corporeal or material should be regarded as sinful in itself, and any contact with it as a pollution of the spirit (see Tit 1:15f). Paul defends christian freedom against those who through rigorous and petty legislation try to reintroduce the old slavery of the law (Col 2:21f; see also Gal 4:9f). He permits the use of meat and wine, contradicting the scruples of over-delicate minds, but demands consideration for the weaker brother—charity first! (Rom 14). The pastoral epistles condemn those heretics who forbid marriage and the use of certain kinds of food (1 Tim 4:1–5; Tit 1:14f). Christian asceticism should be practised freely, in union with Christ and in accordance with his special call. The early church, and especially the Book of Revelation, regard martyrdom as the highest form of *askēsis*, designed only for those chosen by God. Whatever has been predestined, whether imprisonment or death, we have to accept in 'the endurance and faith of the saints' (Rev 13:10). But 'the new song before the throne' of God is the privilege of those 144,000 ransomed from the earth, those 'who have not defiled themselves with women, for they are chaste' (in the literal or the metaphorical sense?); 'it is these who follow the Lamb wherever he goes' (Rev 14:4).

Bibliography: F. Martinez, *L'ascétisme chrétien pendant les trois premiers siècles de l'église*, Paris 1913; F. Tillmann, *Der Idee der Nachfolge Christi*, Düsseldorf 1949[2], 227–41; R. Schnackenburg, *The Moral Teaching of the New Testament*, London 1965; C. Feckes, *Die Lehre vom christlichen Vollkommenheitsstreben*, Freiburg 1953[2]; K. Rahner, *Theological Investigations* III, London 1967; A. Steinmann, *St John the Baptist and the Desert Tradition*, London 1958; L. Bouvet, *L'ascèse de S. Paul*, Lyons 1936; A. Penna, 'L'ascetismo dei Qumranici', *Rivista Biblica* 6 (1958), 3–22; R. Völkl, *Christ und Welt nach dem NT*, Würzburg 1961; E. Neuhäusler, *Anspruch und Antwort Gottes*, Düsseldorf 1962; A.-M. Denis, 'Ascèse et vie chrétienne', *RSPT* 47 (1963), 606–18. See further: H. Strathmann, *Geschichte der frühchristl. Askese bis zur Entstehung des Mönschstums*, Leipzig 1914; H. Strathmann, *RAC* I, 749–53, 758–63, and 794f; A. Köberle, 'Der asket. Klang in der urchristl. Botschaft', *Festschrift für A. Wurm*, 1948, 67–82; H. von Campenhausen, *Die Askese im Urchristentum*, Tübingen 1949; H. Braun, *Spätjüdisch-häretischer und frühchristlicher Radikalismus* (two vols.), Tübingen 1957; G. Kretschmar, 'Ein Beitrag zur Frage nach dem Ursprung frühchristlicher Askese', *ZKT* 61 (1964), 27–67.

Rudolf Schnackenburg

Assurance of salvation

The question of the assurance of salvation—which has been discussed with special interest since the reformation in connection with the doctrine of justification—is essentially connected with the understanding of christian salvation in general. As presented in the New Testament this consists of that deliverance from sin and death and summons to the ↗glory of God (Rom 3:23) which has been achieved by the redemptive work of Jesus Christ, and graciously offered to mankind. It finds a basis already in this present life in the bestowal of the Holy Spirit, and the 'sonship of God' thereby given (Rom 8:14) will only achieve its full effect at the ↗*parousia* of the Lord. Man obtains access to this grace of salvation by being justified by faith in Christ Jesus (Rom 3:21ff; 5:2), and by ↗baptism in him (Rom 6). Does the christian, then, receive this salvation already on this earth as his inalienable possession, so that he appropriates it to himself with the utmost certainty, and is able to look forward to the fullness of salvation with complete and unwavering certainty? According to the particular point of view which is adopted it is possible to speak not only of 'the assurance of salvation', but of 'the assurance of grace' or 'the certainty of faith' as well.

In discussing this question we shall abstract from the problem (always obscure) of how the election or rejection of men (see Rom 9:6–29) are based upon the absolute freedom of God. Doubtless this problem also has a connection with our question, but we shall focus our attention upon the christians who are admitted to the community of salvation in the sense intended by Paul in the situation he depicts in Rom 8:29ff.

The New Testament has no direct answer to give to the question of the assurance of salvation, unless we are prepared to take particular sentences in isolation and to interpret them without regard to their context. All that we can establish is that we have two contrasted groups of statements which can only be related theologically to each other by having regard to revelation as a whole.

The first and most significant statement is found in all the passages in which christian salvation is proclaimed as being purely the work of God revealing himself in an act of ineffable love; in this way it is asserted to be a grace in the fullest sense of the term. Evidently these statements, in which the optimistic attitude towards salvation is strongly emphasised throughout, can of their nature provide a basis for an assurance of salvation in a high degree. We may call to mind words of Jesus such as, for example, the beatitudes in the Sermon on the Mount (Mt 5:3–12; Lk 6:20–23), the promises that prayers offered in a spirit of trust will be answered (Mt 7:7–11; Lk 11:5–13), his revelations concerning the powerful support of the Holy Spirit (Mt 10:19; 28:20; Lk 24:49; Jn 14:15ff; 16:13ff; Acts 1:8), and above all the strong emphasis that is placed upon the power and invincibility of ↗faith (Mt 8:13, 26; 9:22, 29; 17:20; 21:21f; Mk 16:16; Jn 1:12; 3:16ff: '. . . that whoever believes in him should not perish but have eternal life . . . He who believes in him is not condemned'; (Jn 11:25: 'He who believes in me, though he die yet shall he live, and whoever lives and believes in me shall never die'; see also Jn 10:28: 'I give them eternal life and they shall never perish, and no one shall snatch them out of my hand'). We find the same message in the farewell discourse in Jn 14–16, with its powerful themes of confident faith and the security of Christ's disciples which is based upon this faith.

Paul spoke with special emphasis of the assurance of salvation which is attained in faith. In the last analysis the underlying purpose of the first eight chapters of the Epistle to the Romans is simply to arouse an unshakeable consciousness of salvation—see Rom 5:2ff: 'We rejoice in our hope of sharing the glory of God . . . and hope does not disappoint us, because God's love has been poured into our hearts through the Holy Spirit who has been given to us'. The↗Adam–Christ antithesis (Rom 5:12–21) is likewise intended to support and strengthen this confidence. Rom 6 shows, in the accumulation of terms which are formed in Greek with the prefix *sun*—(= with, together with), the special basis for this confidence of salvation in the oneness of life with the risen Lord which is achieved sacramentally in the christian through baptism. Rom 8 brings these themes to a climax which is movingly expressed in the passage beginning at 8:31: 'If God is for us who is against us? . . . Who shall separate us from the love of Christ? . . . Neither death nor life . . . will be able to separate us from the love of God in Christ Jesus'. Similar statements of how God graciously intervenes with his almighty power on behalf of those who believe in him are to be found also in the rest of the Pauline epistles: see 1 Cor 1:18, 21; 2:9, 12; 15:2; 2 Cor 2:15; 4:14; 5:1, 5 (with a phrase which has an important bearing upon our question, namely the 'guarantee of the Spirit'; see also 1:22; Rom 8:23); Gal 1:4; 3:9, 29; Eph 1:4, 14; 2:6, 18; Phil 1:6; Col 1:13; 3:4; 1 Thess 1:10; 2 Thess 2:13f; 2 Tim 1:14; Tit 3:4ff. We encounter the same great confidence in salvation in 1 Pet 1:3ff; 2 Pet 1:11; 1 Jn 5:4; Jude 24; Rev 7:15; 12:11; 21:3f; 22:4f, 17.

While these statements appear to provide an adequate basis for full certainty of salvation on the part of the christian, they stand in sharp contrast to the second group of passages—many of which are closely woven into the pattern of the text—which warn us against adopting such an attitude of certainty in any absolute sense. To this second group belong all those passages in which, in conformity with the basic law of redemption, salvation appears to be connected not only with the working of God's grace, but also, as is stated very plainly and emphatically, on the co-operation of man and his perseverance through testing circumstances. Moreover, even the man who has been received into the grace of Christ is still exposed to peril from the attacks of the powers of evil, and is called to watchfulness and care in defence of the ↗ salvation with which he is initially entrusted as the 'guarantee of the Spirit'. Only in this way can any understanding be achieved of the numerous exhortations and warnings which are addressed to the redeemed in all the New Testament writings. What we are confronted with here is that same law we encounter in the story of the first sin, the original cause of our fallen state, as set forth in the narrative of Gen 3, inasmuch as when man had been created by God and endowed with his grace he lost his salvation by the misuse of the freewill which had been given to him. In the New Testament, however, this law is applied in an inverse manner. For all the pre-eminence of the element of grace in his election, the christian is called upon to stand prepared to contribute his personal decision to receive this grace, and to work out his own salvation.

In the *gospels*, therefore, the possibility of losing salvation even after having received it is made clear by means of various images. For example, the saying about the 'salt of the earth' (Mt 5:13; Mk 9:50; Lk 14:34f), the exhortation to inner faithfulness (Mt 7:21ff, 24ff). The relevant themes in the parable of the sower (Mt 13:1–23; Mk 4:1–20; Lk 8:4–15), the saying about the sinning 'brother' (Mt 18:15–20; Lk 17:3), the warning against being led astray and allowing one's love to grow cold (Mt 24:4, 10, 12f, 22), together with the exhortation to constant watchfulness (Mt 24:42–51; 25:1–13) and preparedness (Mt 25:14–30; Lk 19:11–27), and the solemn warning against all falling back into sin (Lk 11:24ff). Again the fate of the apostle who betrayed Jesus is an illustration of this idea. The farewell discourse in Jn 17 should also be noted, for here Jesus prays (referring explicitly to Judas) that his apostles may be guarded against sin, and prays likewise for all who believe in him. We encounter the same theme in Lk 22:32: 'But I have prayed for you that your faith may not fail'.

Again the idea that the grace of salvation once received has to be maintained through the testing conditions of life is implicit in the idea of men being judged according to their works, to which Jesus often explicitly adverts (Mt 25:31–46; Mk 8:34f; Lk 6:37f; 8:17f; 12:5, 48; 19:26; 21:34f).

From these statements in the gospel it can already be seen that one called by God to salvation has a contribution to make towards it, and that the ultimate achievement of salvation in its fullness is closely connected with the fulfilment of this responsibility. This impression, already gained from the gospels, does not, however, make its full impact upon us until we turn to *Paul.* It is precisely in the writings of Paul, the man who might be regarded as the preacher of the assurance of salvation in its full and uncompromising sense, that the requirement that man shall take some of the responsibility upon himself is impressed upon us with the greatest possible urgency. Hence the close connection between the indicative and the imperative of salvation in Paul. It must be observed, however, that this imperative is related to the indicative not as an external and concomitant factor, but rather follows as an integral consequence from the fact that the grace of salvation has been bestowed. For in this bestowal it is not merely the subject's awareness of having been raised to a state of salvation that is awakened, in the sense that he then feels himself obliged to act in conformity with that state; it is the actual state of salvation in itself that is presented as a prior condition, in that it makes it possible for man to act in this way. As a result, faith in the apostle's sense is the opposite of Jewish legalism in that it is, of its very nature, applicable also to the sphere of action and morality. Union of life with the risen Lord in the *pneuma khristo* (=spirit of Christ, Rom 8:9) creates an essentially new prior condition for right action and for the process of testing and purifying which is necessary for salvation to achieve its fullness. On the basis of this, the concept of ↗ hope, to which Paul accords such prominence and importance (see Rom 5:2ff; 8:16, 19–25) acquires a content which comes very near to the 'assurance of salvation', even though this is not to be understood in an absolute sense.

But for all his emphasis on this confidence of salvation we can see how vividly the apostle is aware of the possibility of not persisting to the end from passages such as Rom 2:6f; admittedly, he is thinking here primarily of the Jews, but so far as the idea of judgement according to works is concerned what he says has universal application; or again, there is 1 Cor 9:27: '. . . lest after preaching to others I myself should be disqualified'. The same solicitude for salvation is also expressed in Phil 3:12: 'Not that I have already obtained this or am already perfect; but I press on to make it my own, because Christ Jesus has made me his own'. On the basis of the insight which the apostle offers us here we can understand his exhortation: 'Work out your own salvation with ↗ fear and trembling' (Phil 2:12), though here it must be admitted that the sentence immediately following is once more important for the Pauline understanding of salvation: 'For God is at work in you, both to will and to work for his good pleasure' (Phil 2:13). On this tension between the grace of and the responsibility for salvation

Rom 6 is extremely instructive, inasmuch as we find here a close interpenetration of the two ideas, that of consciousness of salvation on the one hand, and at the same time also the demand for 'the obedience leading to righteousness'—the two ideas being connected together and formulated in a manner strongly suggestive of juridical concepts.

It will be observed, too, that the apostle draws attention again and again in his epistles to the significance of entreaty (↗ prayer) for salvation (Eph 1:17; 6:18; Phil 1:3 with the connected sentence in 1:6: 'I am sure that he who began a good work in you will bring it to completion at the day of Jesus Christ'; see also 1:9 with its similar theme; 4:6; Col 1:9f etc). The apostle's references to the seriousness with which we ought to regard our state of salvation, and the possibility of our losing it (see 1 Cor 10:1–13; 2 Cor 7:1; 13:5; Gal 5:4; 6:7f; Phil 2:16; 3:18f; Col 1:23; 1 Thess 4:8; Heb 3:12; 6:4; 10:26f) are also important for our question, as are the catholic epistles and the Book of Revelation, which abound with demands for perseverance and with concern lest perseverance should be wanting (see the Seven Letters, Rev 2:1–3:22 with their emphatic summons to stand firm).

To conclude, this interplay between the assurance of salvation and the presence of continual threats to salvation can only be explained on the basis of the eschatological situation in which man is placed, and of the basic law for the final fulfilment of salvation—that is, the law by which man with his active co-operation is subsumed into the work of the ↗ grace of God. It should not be overlooked that in the message of salvation as presented in the gospels and Paul alike the main accent falls upon the redemptive work of Jesus Christ, and the assurance of salvation for the christian which is based upon him. From this we may conclude that it is possible to speak of an extremely high degree of assurance of salvation, amounting to certainty, which if not to be taken absolutely, is at any rate a moral and practical certainty, for the man who entrusts himself to this grace with a lively faith 'to the end' (Mt 10:22; Rev 2:26).

Bibliography: the articles on ↗ faith, ↗ grace, ↗ judgement, ↗ justification, ↗ salvation, etc are all relevant here. See in particular: R. Schnackenburg, *The Moral Teaching of the New Testament*, London 1965; R. Schnackenburg, *LTK* v², 157f; O. Kuss, *Der Römerbrief* (two parts), Regensburg 1959, 396–430 ('Heilsbesitz und Bewährung' with copious bibliography); L. Cerfaux, *The Christian in the Theology of St Paul*, London 1967.

J. Kürzinger

Atonement

A. *Old Testament*. The Hebrew verb *kippēr* means 'to purify', through a priest, from things which defile (Lev 16:16, 33, the sanctuary; Ezek 45:20, the temple); or, when the subject is God, 'to forgive sins' (Num 35:33; Deut 21:8; 1 Sam 3:14; Ps 65:3; 78:38; Ezek 16:63). The Greek *hilaskomai* renders, besides other underlying Hebrew words, the idea of 'purifying' (Ezek 43:20, 22), of 'forgiving', 'being merciful' (Ex 32:12, 14; 2 Kings 5:18; Dan 9:9; Sir 5:5f), and so throws some light on the meaning of *kipper*. *Hilaskomai* never has God for object: Mal 1:9 is an intended irony—as if God could be 'placated' like any heathen idol! Zech 7:2 speaks of heathens who want to apply their own religious practices to the God of Israel, and 8:21f is likewise spoken by heathens and probably uses *kipper/hilaskomai* in a different sense, namely, 'to pray', 'to beseech'. In Greek religion, as in that of the Assyrians, Hittites, and Canaanites, God is always 'placated'—with sacrifices and the like; but against this conception stand texts like Ps 50:9; 51:17 (↗ Sacrifice).

B. *New Testament. Hilaskomai* is in no way used in the New Testament in the hellenistic sense, but must be connected with the Old Testament usage (as is the case, for that matter, with the Qumran use of *kipper*. See 1 QM 2:5; 1 QS 3:4; 5:6. The community practised virtue in order to win atonement and forgiveness for all men of good will; they made atonement for the world polluted by transgressors, but could not do so for the transgressors themselves as these were destined to be annihilated: 1 QS 8:6; see also 1 QS 8:10; 1 QSa 1:3). In Heb 2:17 the true high priest blots out sin, as in the Old Testament; the same is said in 1 Jn 2:2 of Jesus the righteous, whom the Father has sent for the expiation of our sins (1 Jn 4:10). The same is true of Rom 3:25, where Paul evidently wants to bring to our mind the Old Testament rite of atonement which consisted in sprinkling ↗ blood on the 'mercy seat' and offering sacrifices for sins on the Day of Atonement.

In LXX *hilastērion* translates *kappōreth*, the golden cover of the ark of the covenant which supported the cherubim, or at other times *ᶜᵃzārâh*, the pedestal of the altar in Ezekiel's temple (Ex 25:17–22; 26:34; 30:6; 31:7; 35:12 etc; Ezek 43:14, 17, 20; 45:19; Sir 50:11). This 'mercy seat' or *propitiatorium* (Jerome's term—Luther calls it the 'throne of grace') is the really essential thing in the Holy of Holies (1 Chron 28:11), the throne of God (hence the phrase 'enthroned on the cherubim': 1 Sam 4:4; Ps 80:1; 99:1) where revelation and the word of God are made immediately present (Jerome has *oraculum*, Ex 25:19, 20; Num 7:89)—compare Heb 1:2: 'In these last days he has *spoken* to us by a Son'. It was here that the sin of the whole people—not that of any individual—was expiated through the sprinkling of blood (Lev 16:14f: on the great Day of Atonement, except on occasions when it was not permitted to enter before the 'mercy seat', in which case the sevenfold sprinkling took place before the veil [Lev 4:13–21]). In Rom 3:25 we have 'type' and 'antitype': Christ on the cross makes expiation 'by his own blood' (see also 1 Pet 1:18f), no longer in secret since the veil has been rent (Mt 27:51; Mk 15:38; Lk 23:45), but openly manifested (*proetheto* = put forward) to all, so that 'God was in Christ reconciling the world to himself, not counting their trespasses against them' (2 Cor 5:19). ↗ Reconciliation.

Bibliography: A. Médebielle, *DB(S)* 3, 1–262; J. Hermann and F. Büchsel, *TDNT* III, 300–23; F. Büchsel, *TDNT* I, 251–9; J. Dupont, *La Réconciliation dans la Théologie de S. Paul*, Louvain 1953; L. Moraldi, *Espiazione sacrificiale e riti espiatori nell' ambiente biblico e nell'Antico Testamento*, Rome 1956; L. Moraldi, *Dict. de Spiritualité* 4 (1960), 2026–45; L. Moraldi, 'Espiazione nell'Antico e Nuovo Testamento', *Rivista Biblica* 9 (1961), 289–304 and 10 (1962), 3–17; Imschoot II, 314–38; S. Lyonnet, *Theologia Biblica Novi Testamenti*,

Rome 1954, 103ff; L. Morris, *NTS* 2 (1955), 33–43; O. Kuss, *Der Römerbrief* 1, Regensburg 1957, 155–61; L. De Lorenzi, *Rivista Biblica* 5 (1957), 237–43.↗ Redemption.

Johannes B. Bauer

Authority

The concept of 'authority' in the context of biblical theology (in Greek *exousia*, for which there is no term in Hebrew or Aramaic which corresponds exactly) is a complex one as indeed it is in extra-biblical usage where it can mean possibility, right, freedom, power to perform some specific task, even arbitrariness; also used of office and the one who holds it.

A. *The Old Testament.* The reality itself is of course there from the beginning (cf the expression 'to fall into someone's hands'—2 Sam 24:14; 1 Chron 29:12; 2 Chron 20:6; Job 10:7 etc), but as a well-defined concept 'authority' appears only in the later books, which is hardly surprising since the idea is connected with the Greek. It signifies the power and sovereignty of God (Esther 13:9, 'the universe is in thy power'; Dan 4:17, 'the most High rules the kingdom of men, and gives it to whom he will'; Sir 10:4, 'the government of the earth is in the hands of the Lord', etc; cf also Dan 2:21f; 4:25, 34f; 6:26f). But God has also given authority over the earth to men (Sir 17:2). Such authority befits the king but he can subdelegate it (Dan 5:7). Through the 'law' God gave to the Israelites authority to perform specific actions (Tob 2:13; 'We have no authority to eat anything stolen'). Everlasting authority will be given to the 'Son of Man' (Dan 7:13)—and much of what the New Testament has to say about the authority which appears in Christ rests on this consideration.

B. *The New Testament* contains the concept of 'authority' in the fullness of its meaning. As in the Old Testament, we find the idea expressed that authority belongs essentially to God himself. He has the power to cast into hell (Lk 12:5). The Father has placed in his own power the decisive *kairoi* (Acts 1:7). The potter has the right or authority to make what use he sees fit of his vessels (Rom 9:21). Authority is one of the most essential characteristics of God and is attributed to him in hymns of praise (Jude 25).

Similarly the New Testament knows, as does the Old, that God entrusts this power to others in different degrees. It is a general postulate that any kind of power or authority exists only because it has its origin in God (Jn 19:11; Rom 13:1).

Such power committed to men by God comes to light also in the New Testament in the state. This 'power' is an essential element in the state and is distributed among individual holders of office: eg, 'power over ten cities', Lk 19:17; Herod (Lk 23:7); Pilate (Jn 19:10f) have power but are themselves, like the centurion (Mt 8:9 and parallels), set under human power and authority. This power and authority can be used either for good or for evil (Acts 9:14; 26:10, 12); Saul has authority from the Supreme Council to persecute the christians; Pilate condemned Christ who was in his power—in fact Christ was to be maliciously handed over to this power even earlier, on the occasion of the question about the tribute money (Lk 20:20). Since, however, all power comes from God (Rom 13:1) it must be respected (Rom 13:2; see also Titus 3:1). To be sure, Paul is here evidently referring to the state which has come by its power by fair means and uses it well—see Rom 13:3! It is quite another question with the manifestations of power exercised for evil and which have to be endured, such as are indicated in the Book of Revelation (see below).

The veil a woman wears is a sign of the authority which a man has over her (1 Cor 11:10—taking account of all the uncertainty involved in the explanation of this text!). The authority of the man, given by Moses and reaching so far as to enable him even to leave his wife (Mt 19:3—'for any cause?') is, however, brought back again into line with the true purpose of God by the Lord (Mk 10:9 and parallels; 1 Cor 7:10f).

'Authority', however, does not just signify power over another—even over inanimate objects (see Acts 5:4)—but can also express *dominion over oneself*. He who has control over himself—meaning his sexual desires—may keep 'his virgin' as she is, intact (1 Cor 7:37). He does well to do so; for it is now the last days (1 Cor 7:29), so that man and woman can give their attention wholly to the Lord (1 Cor 7:32–34).

The special kind of authority which Jesus has can be seen in everything he does. The people recognise this unique authority in and from what he teaches (Mk 1:22, 27; Mt 7:29; Lk 4:32). Jesus shows his authority when he casts out demons (Mk 1:27; Lk 4:36). That he stakes the claim for himself even to be able to forgive sins on earth (Mt 9:6 and parallels) is only the other side of this inclusive power of Christ. Jesus gave continual offence to the influential circles of the scribes and Pharisees with his continually asserted particular and unique authority; a good example of which would be the discussion about his authority after the entry into the city on Palm Sunday and the cleansing of the Temple (Mt 21:23, 24, 27 and parallels). But this offence is present in the whole opposition of Christ to the religious leaders of his people. He does not conform to current interpretations of the law (see Mt 12:2 and parallels; Mt 9:14 and parallels; Lk 13:10–17; 14:1–6). His opponents notice this and know that with this attitude Jesus arrogates to himself a unique authority. He does not enquire whether he may perform a certain action as in accord with the law: his own will is the norm of law. When his opponents take offence at his conduct his only answer is to renew his claim to unique authority: with him God's appointed time of salvation and joy has broken into the present (Mt 9:15 and parallels). He is Lord of the sabbath, and therefore not just of a particular interpretation of the law (Mt 12:8 and parallels). His achievement signified that Satan had been bound (Mt 12:29) and that therefore the rule of God, his kingdom, had come (Mt 12:28).

In his usual way, John gives a presentation of the whole question in just a few texts which, however, are full of meaning. The Son of Man has authority to hold judgement (5:27). Christ has the power (=freedom) to lay down his life and to take it up again (10:18). He has received from his Father authority over all flesh (17:2). We have to bear in mind both aspects of this: namely, that his authority is conferred on him by his Father and that it is, at the same time, a limitless authority. This is precisely what the risen Lord says to his disciples, according to Matthew: 'All authority in heaven and on earth has been given to me' (28:18).

The spirit world, too, participates in the divine authority. With the texts which speak of this participation we must also enumerate those others which speak of the powers which God makes use of in putting into operation his plan for the world. This motif is continually in evidence in Revelation: Death and Hades (6:8); the locusts (9:3, 10); the horses (9:19); in a certain sense also the two witnesses (11:6); the angel in charge of the fire (14:18); another angel (18:1). It is not just the spirits who submit themselves absolutely to God who are bearers of his power; God has entrusted, given over, such authority also to the fallen spirits. Consequently 'powers' is a specific proper name for a spiritual being in general which has received such authority from God. They, all together, have been created in Christ (Col 1:16); he is the Head (Col 2:10, see also 1 Pet 3:22). The powers must recognise the manifold wisdom of God (Eph 3:10) which operates in him whom it has raised above all powers (Eph 1:21). The battle against the prince of the power of the air (Eph 2:2), against the powers of darkness in general (Eph 6:12) is left to man, even man who has been redeemed. They have already really been overcome by him who has freed us from the power of darkness (Col 1:13), but it is also true that he has to win this victory first (1 Cor 15:24). Satan, who is able to pass on the authority left to him by God (see Rev 13:2, the dragon gives the beast great authority; 17:12f, the ten kings pass on their authority to the beast) tries by means of this authority conferred on him to tempt all the kingdoms of the world (see Jn 12:31) and even Christ himself (Lk 4:6). Christ, who is the Lord and Head, victor over the powers of darkness, himself at the appointed time falls into their power (Lk 22:53). The fearful strength of these powers of darkness (for which see Rev 13:7: 'to make war on the saints and to conquer them') is given to them by God for a determined time only (see also Rev 13:5: 'forty-two months') and must co-operate in its turn in bringing to fulfilment 'that which has to come about'.

The authority of the Redeemer is not restricted to his own person, for he passes it on, in some measure, to his disciples and the faithful in general. As an essential element, he transfers to his disciples power over demons (Mt 10:1; Mk 3:15; 6:7; 'over all demons', Lk 9:1) and their wiles (Lk 10:19: 'to tread upon serpents . . . and over all the power of the enemy'). Through the participated power of Christ, the apostles are able to communicate the Holy Spirit (Acts 8:19). The authority given to the apostles by the Lord must contribute to the 'edification' of the faithful (2 Cor 10:8; see also 13:10). But the apostolic authority is not just a means of serving the church; it also confers rights with regard to the members of the church, even of a material kind. The apostle has the 'authority' (=right) to eat and drink, to be accompanied by a 'sister' as a wife, to be exempt from working for a living (1 Cor 9:4–6; for the last see also 2 Thess 3:9). These rights, however, give way before the service of the Gospel (1 Cor 9:18).

Those who believe in Christ have the power to become children of God (Jn 1:12). As members of the church, they have the authority to partake of the altar from which the Jews who have not believed may not eat (Heb 13:10). The knowledge proper to a believer allows him to eat of the so-called meat offered to idols (1 Cor 8:9), although charity dictates consideration for the 'weak brethren' (see on this point 1 Cor 6:12: 'All things are lawful for me, but not all things are helpful'). In the case of the victor in the epistle to the church of Thyatira to whom is promised authority over the heathens (Rev 2:26) the reference is to a share in the authority of Christ over the demons hostile to God. He who will share in the 'first resurrection' will not be subject to the power (authority) of the 'second death' (Rev. 20:6). Finally, there stands as a great promise to the faithful the Word which assures fulfilment for the deepest longing of man right from the beginning: 'Blessed are they who wash their robes, that they may have the right [authority] to the tree of life!' (Rev 22:14).

Bibliography: W. Foerster, *TDNT* II, 560–75 with corresponding bibliography (down to 1935); Bultmann I, 230, 257, 337; II, 95ff; H. Schlier, *Principalities and Powers in the New Testament*, London and New York 1961; W. Beilner, *Christus und die Pharisäer*, Vienna 1959, esp. 242–5. On particular questions: W. F. Arndt and F. W. Gingrich, *A Greek–English Lexikon of the New Testament and other Early Christian Literature*, 1957; *R. Murray, 'Authority and the Spirit in the NT', *Authority in a Changing Church*, J. Dalrymple and others, London 1968. Among recent commentaries: R. Bultmann, *Johannes-Evangelium*, 1941, 36; V. Taylor, *The Gospel according to St Mark*, London 1955, 173 and 469.

Wolfgang Beilner

Ban

The corresponding Hebrew word *ḥērem* (from the verb *ḥāram*=separate, cf *hārem*=an enclosure set aside for women) signifies separation from the profane sphere and deliverance into the power of God. It can be translated either 'ban' or 'interdict'.

The ban is connected in the first place with the practice of war. The Assyrians also imposed the ban on their enemies (see 2 Kings 19:11=Is 37:11), and Mesha king of Moab boasted that he had annihilated the city of Nebo with its 7,000 inhabitants, thus dedicating it to his god Kemosh (see the Moabite stone lines 14–17). In the Old Testament the ban is always regarded as a religious punishment. The religious motivation behind this idea of annihilating everything pagan can at least be clearly perceived in that the inheritance of the surrounding nations is made to serve the religion of Yahweh (cf Num 21:2; Josh 6:18f; 7:15ff; 10:28–42; Judg 21:11; 1 Sam 15:3; see also ↗War).

The operation of the ban is not, however, limited to time of war. In Ex 22:20 we learn that 'whoever sacrifices to any god, save to the Lord only, shall be utterly destroyed', with which can be compared the ordinances in Deut 13:12–19 threatening the ban against Israelites not against pagans. As can be seen by comparing Gen 38:24 with Lev 21:9 there was also a private curse comparable to the ban. The same seems to be presupposed by Lev 27:28f, which speaks of the punishment which had to be meted out to a member of a family for some flagrant violation of law. In this case the possessions of this person, his cattle for example, could not be redeemed with money but became the property of the sanctuary and the priests, though they could be made use of only after a ritual of purification. In keeping with this the gold, silver, and bronze instruments taken from the interdicted city of Jericho were 'consecrated' to the Israelite cult.

In 1 Sam 15:20–22 a clear distinction is drawn between the ban and sacrifice. The *ḥērem* of Jephthah, Judg 11:30ff, is not a ↗ sacrifice in the strict sense of the word.

In LXX *ḥērem* is generally translated by *anathema*. In the New Testament also *anathema* generally corresponds to *ḥērem*, with the exception of Lk 21:5, where it refers to consecrated offerings in keeping with Hellenistic usage. In later judaism *ḥērem* also applies to the ban imposed by the synagogue, a kind of excommunication. Something similar to this is found in 1 Cor 5:3–5 and 1 Tim 1:20. But there is really nothing in the New Testament comparable to the practice of the ban in later judaism with the well-defined degrees by which it was implemented, though it is worth while comparing this latter with the statements found in the Qumran community rule (1 QS VI, 24–VII, 25). In the New Testament a curse is pronounced on anyone who preaches a different gospel (Gal 1:8f) or does not love the Lord (1 Cor 16:22). This can also be a self-imposed curse for those who do not fulfil a duty which is incumbent on them (Acts 23:14). Rom 9:3 provides a difficulty: 'I could wish that I myself [Paul] were accursed and cut off from Christ for the sake of my brethren'. It should be interpreted in much the same way as the prayer of Moses in Ex 32:32, and in line with Gal 3:13 (which follows the principle laid down in Gen 18:23–32): the unrighteous and guilty will be saved with the righteous and the innocent for the sake of the community as a whole. In all of these New Testament texts *anathema* can hardly refer exclusively to separation from the community of salvation. In keeping with the Old Testament use of the word *ḥērem* it must also mean to be subject to the anger of God and to be delivered over to divine judgement. Both of these elements are stressed in Ezra 10:8 which brings out clearly the transition from the first to the second sense.

According to Zech 14:11 and Rev 22:3 the ban will cease to exist after the eschatological victory and the definitive overthrow of the powers which are opposed to God, since by then it will have no more reason to exist.

Bibliography: SB IV, 293–333 on the practice of the synagogue with relation to the ban: J. Döller, *ZKT* 37 (1913), 1–24; A. Fernandez, *Bbl* 5 (1924), 3–25; J. Behm, *TDNT* I, 353–6; H. Junker, *TTZ* 75 (1950), 227–30; Haag 153f; S. Cavaletti, *Festschrift Millás Vallicrosa*, Barcelona 1954, 347–50; C. H. Hunzinger, *Die jüdische Bannpraxis im neutestamentliche Zeitalter*, Göttingen 1954 (dissertation in typescript); W. Doskocil, *Der Bann in der Urkirche*,

Munich 1957; H. Gross, *LTK* 1², 1225–7; C. H. W. Brekelmans, *De cherem in het OT*, Nijmegen 1959.

Johannes B. Bauer

Baptism

A. *The origin of christian baptism.* From the middle of the second century BC until AD 300 there was in Palestine and Syria widespread practice of baptism among many sects of various beliefs (see J. Thomas, *Le mouvement baptiste en Palestine et Syrie*). A prominent place in this movement is held by John, the son of Zechariah during the period immediately preceding Christ's public appearance, so that his contemporaries gave him the significant title 'the Baptist'. His baptism, to which even Jesus submitted himself, is distinguished from the Jewish (and Essenic) baptismal immersion in various respects: 1. It is received *only once*. 2. It is designed *for all the Jewish people* (not for the 'unclean' and 'sinners' only, or for proselytes). 3. It is received in order *to escape the coming judgement through repentance* (confession of sins). 4. The recipients did not administer this baptism to themselves, but *were baptised by the Baptist*, the eschatological prophet sent by God, or by one of his disciples. 5. It therefore had an *eschatological significance*: the creation of a holy people for God at the end of time, for the 'one mightier', the Messiah is soon to come for his final judgement and salvation. The early church regarded this baptism of John as preliminary to its own baptism and claimed that its baptism as distinct from that of John was 'a Baptism with the Holy Ghost' (see Mk 1:8 and parallels; Acts 1:5; 11:16). Scientific criticism may consider John to be more than only 'the precursor' of Jesus and 'witness' of the Messiah (see Jn 1:7, 33–5), the more so since the later disciples of John formed an independent group and entered into competition with the christian community (see Acts 18:25; 19:1–7; Pseudo-Clementines), but the peculiar characteristics of his baptism are indisputable. Both christian baptism and that of John were administered by others and could not be repeated; they both shared the prospect of an eschatological salvation (although this was certainly different after the coming of Christ). Christian baptism can hardly be related to the Jewish baptism of proselytes, which, although an act of incorporation into a supernatural community and received only once, was only an initiatory ceremony producing effects of a purely liturgical (purification from 'uncleanness') and legal nature. Even its age has not been satisfactorily ascertained. If the primitive church has administered and demanded baptism from its very foundation (Acts 2:38), even though the eschatological gift of the Holy Spirit may seem to be communicated without the actual ceremony with water (Whitsun; see also Acts 10:44; 11:15ff), it can only be based on a special command of Christ himself. True, we first hear it from the lips of the risen Lord (Mt 28:19; see also Mk 16:16), but not until then did it obtain its full significance, for the Spirit would only be released after Christ's exaltation (see Jn 7:39) and fill, guide, and build up the congregation, orphaned through Christ's departure. The far-seeing conversation of Jesus with Nicodemus reveals the deep significance of the necessity of baptism and its full meaning. It is impossible to explain baptism as an institution introduced by the primitive church, as a kind ceremony of admission resembling the Jewish baptism of proselytes, or a means of forgiving sins before the receiving of the Holy Spirit. Neither can the baptism of Jesus administered by John, which has its own unique messianic-christological significance, have been the cause and prototype of the early christian baptism. The references in Acts bear no relation to Christ's baptism and death (O. Cullmann has interpreted Christ's death as a kind of 'general baptism' of all christians: see Mk 10:38; Lk 12:50).

B. *Baptism in the early christian community.* The baptism administered by the apostles after the coming of the Holy Spirit is explained in Acts in the following ways. 1. It is an expression of the inner ↗ 'conversion' working (sacramentally) the *forgiveness of sins* (see 2:38; 3:19; 5:31; 11:18; 22:16; 26:20). 'Conversion' means a complete turning away from one's past life, detestation of ↗ sin (see 5:31 referring to the Jews; 11:18; 17:30 referring to the Gentiles), but also abandonment of an adverse attitude towards the Messiah (see 3:17, 19). The conditions for baptism are faith in Christ as the divine bringer of salvation and acceptance of the christian message of salvation ('the word' or 'the word of God': see 2:41; 4:4; 8:4f, 12f; 10:43; 16:30–3; 18:8). The forgiveness of sins is the beginning of salvation, the first eschatological act of God leading up to life everlasting (see 11:18; 13:46, 8). 2. Baptism is administered '*in the name of the Lord Jesus Christ*' (see 22:16; also 9:14, 21), which means surrender to Christ as the Lord and Saviour, the only mediator of salvation (4:12) and author of life (3:15). 3. Baptism is the (normal) occasion of the *pouring out of the Spirit.* Only those who have been baptised in the name of Jesus Christ (see 19:2–7) will receive 'this gift of the Holy Ghost' (2:38), the eschatological pledge of God (see 2:17–21, 33). Although the Holy Ghost is (usually) 'poured out' after baptism (through the imposition of hands 19:6), baptism is not merely an occasion but the real cause and medium of this communication. The dissociation of the receiving of the Holy Spirit from baptism is probably due to the extraordinary effects of the coming of the Holy Spirit at that time (gift of tongues, prophecy). 4. Baptism is the *incorporation into the community of Jesus Christ.* Through this baptism God adds new members to the primitive church, and so the church grows outwardly and visibly (see 2:41, 47; 5:14; 11:24–6:7; 9:31; 11:21). Outside this community of God there is no salvation, and the church is charged with the world wide mission to bring salvation to the whole world. Therefore, all the essential elements of the doctrine of baptism can already be found in the primitive church, although theological development and penetration was yet to come.

C. *Paul's doctrine of baptism.* Paul is the first to give real impetus to the development of the theology of baptism in the primitive church. Although in his theology he places ↗ faith as the sole means of salvation, contrary to the Jewish doctrine of salvation and justification through the law, and although he regards the preaching of the gospel and not the administration of baptism as his own personal task (1 Cor 1:17), he accepts baptism as a matter of course and gives it a firm place in the construction of his theology. Faith and baptism are not mutually exclusive but stand in need of each other. There is no baptism without faith—not a purely spiritual faith, but a faith together with the external profession of faith in the act of baptism (see Rom 10:8–10). The ceremony of baptism, which consisted in an immersion in water, is explained by Paul in various ways: 1. Being a rite of washing in water, baptism is a '*washing off the stain of sin*' (see the remission of sins in Acts), and at the same time a sanctification and justification of the former sinner (1 Cor 6:11). 2. He who is baptised is baptised *in the name of Jesus Christ* and is therefore subordinate to his Lord and belongs to him (see 1 Cor 1:13; 3:23; 15:23; Gal 3:29; 5:24 and other instances where possession is indicated by the use of the genitive; see again Acts). This, however, is not a purely external subordination but a sharing in one common life (often expressed as 'being in Christ'). 3. Compared to the initiatory ceremony of the chosen people in the Old Testament, baptism is called a '*circumcision in Christ*', which however does not consist in the removal of a small part of the human body but in a burial of the old man full of sin (Col 2:11; see Rom 6:6). 4. Positively speaking, baptism is '*putting on Christ*' (Gal 3:27), ie, he who is baptised is clothed with Christ, absorbed in him, so that he becomes 'a new man in Christ' (see Eph 4:24; Col 3:10), a 'rebirth' (2 Cor 5:17; Gal 6:15). This idea presupposes that Christ possesses a new, glorified life since his resurrection and ascension, a 'pneumatic' existence, through which the closest conceivable union of Christ with those baptised was made possible ('mystical union with Christ'). They receive a *new existence* 'in Christ', in which all previously valid sexual, racial, and social characteristics are transcended (Gal 3:28; Col 3:11), an *eschatological* existence in as much as those baptised already participate in the life of the risen Lord ('the Spirit'; see 1 Cor 15:44f) and this infused life points towards a bodily resurrection as the ultimate object (see Rom 6:5, 8; 8:11). 5. The sacramental union with Christ can also be described as a 'being crucified with him', 'buried with Christ', 'rising with him', and being 'restored to life' with him, so that those baptised will undergo all that happened to him (see Rom 6:4–8; Gal 2:19f; Eph 2:5f; Col 2:12–20; 3:1). These expressions are difficult to interpret and have in fact been interpreted in various ways but they have their main theological foundation in the Adam–Christ parallelism (Rom 5:12–21; 1 Cor 15:20–2, 45–9): Christ is the progenitor of a new, redeemed human race and—as the first who is raised from the dead, 'the first fruits of those who have fallen asleep' (1 Cor 15:20; see Col 1:18), the 'first born among many brethren' (Rom 8:29)—continually incorporates new members through this baptism. On their behalf he accepted his cross and death (see 2 Cor 5:14–21; Gal 3:13), but they accept and share his fate in complete union with him, first of all sacramentally in receiving baptism in which they are 'buried . . . with him' (Rom 6:4, probably referring to the rite of immersion), then morally by 'dying to sin' and 'living for God' (Rom 6:4, 6; Gal 5:24; 6:14; Col 3:5, and other instances), but also by suffering and dying with him daily in the strength and hope of resurrection (mysterious significance of suffering; see Rom 8:17; 2 Cor 4:10–14; Phil 3:10f; 2 Tim 2:11f). 6. Since all christians in baptism experience the same and are filled with the same divine spirit (*pneuma*), baptism has another relation to the *community*: everybody, Jews and Greeks, slaves and freemen, men and women, will be 'all one in Christ Jesus' (Gal 3:28), one single body by the power of one Spirit (1 Cor 12:13; see Eph 4:4f); the body of Christ (1 Cor 12:27; Rom 12:5). Bearing this in mind one will certainly come to a better and deeper understanding of the ↗ church (see Eph 1:23; 2:16–22; 4:12–16; 5:23, 30; Col 1:18; 2:19; 3:11, 15). 7. Starting from this view of baptism, Paul built up his moral theology stating the serious effects that baptism should have on the christian way of life in this world. A clear understanding of baptism precludes abuse of God's abundant grace (Rom 6), demands a continuous and hard struggle against our sinful desires and passions (Rom 6:12–14, 19; Gal 5:24; and other instances), requires that the community should be kept pure (1 Cor 5:6–8), and supplies many motives for a moral struggle in this world surrounded by evil (Eph 5:6–14; Phil 2:15f; Col 3:12–17; 1 Thess 4:3–8; and other instances).

D. *Other views on baptism in the New Testament.* It is hardly possible to improve on Paul's theology of baptism, which was centred on Christ. But in his later Epistle to Titus he used an expression which would be of great influence in the period that followed: 'the washing of regeneration' (Tit 3:5; see ↗ Rebirth). This is reminiscent of an idea which formed the final object of the initiation in the Greek mysteries (↗ Mystery) and in Hellenistic mysticism (see the 'Mithraic Liturgy', *Corpus Herm.* XIII), a kind of transformation through contemplation, a deification of man. But the idea of being raised to a divine level, a deification and ecstatic vision of God in the fashion of the Greek mysteries, is completely absent in the pastoral epistle. Paul speaks in a biblical way of a pouring forth of the Holy Spirit (Tit 3:6) and of a 'renewal' being worked in us by the recreating Holy Spirit (see also the texts of Qumran). This eschatological promise is fulfilled sacramentally in the communication of grace worked by the baptismal washing, which therefore becomes a source of life, recreating us and enabling us to participate in eternal life. A similar idea is to be found in our Lord's conversation with Nicodemus (Jn 3); the 'old man', bodily and earthborn, cannot see the kingdom of God unless he is born anew (Jn 3:3), without a re-conception and re-birth in water and the Holy Ghost (v 5). Nicodemus' misinterpretation of this rebirth (v 4) made Christ expound his analogy with natural human conception and birth. This can also be found in 1 Pet, an epistle full of references to baptism, regarded by many as a sermon for newly baptised and by others even as an early christian baptismal liturgy. By God's 'great mercy we have been born anew to a living hope' (1 Pet 1:3); christians are reconceived (or 'reborn'), 'not of perishable seed but of imperishable, through the living and abiding word of God' (1:23). The analogy of baptism and our 'first birth' (ie, our natural birth) and their difference was even further extended in the second century by Justin (*Apol.* 6:10). Other expressions of Paul, 'God . . . has put his seal upon us and given us his Spirit' (2 Cor 1:22; Eph 1:13; 4:30) and 'seeing the light' (see 2 Cor 4:4, 6; Eph 1:18—and even stronger in Heb 6:4; 10:32) have gradually since the second century been interpreted as references to baptism.

Other texts complete and confirm this doctrine of baptism in the New Testament. It is referred to as the cleansing and sanctifying laver prepared by Christ for his church, so that it may be presented to him, a glorious church, not having spot or wrinkle or any such thing (Eph 5:26—often thought of as a kind of ritual bridal bath). It is the great means of salvation through which we, like Noah in his ark, are saved by passing through the water, and which does not wash off any external contamination but gives us the assurance of a good conscience (1 Pet 3:20f—several themes converge here). There is also a deep relationship between the baptismal water and the ↗blood of Christ, for the former derives its power from the latter. Through the blood of Christ we enter the heavenly sanctuary; this way lies open to us by having 'our hearts sprinkled clean from an evil conscience and our bodies washed with pure water' (Heb 10:22; see 19). Also the stream of water and blood flowing from Christ's side (Jn 19:34) has, in the eyes of the fourth evangelist, a deeper meaning and refers to the sacraments of the eucharist and baptism. A similar reference is almost certain in 1 Jn 5:7ff where 'the Spirit, the water, and the blood' are the three who give testimony, because in this passage the author does not only look back on Christ's historical coming into this world for our redemption but sees his continued presence in the present dispensation of grace: Christ's redeeming actions are also effective for later periods through the sacraments and the co-operation of the Holy Spirit—a profound view of John on the relation of the sacraments and Christ's work of salvation and his continued activity in the Holy Ghost.

To many questions concerning the external aspect of baptism there is no clear answer in the New Testament; we know little about the rite except that it was an immersion. The administration of baptism with the words 'in the name of our Lord Jesus Christ' (Acts) seems to contradict the traditional trinitarian formula as given in Mt 28:19; but both versions can be found side by side in the *Didache* (7:1–3 [trinitarian formula], 9:5 'those baptised in the name of our Lord') and need not be mutually exclusive. The question of the baptism of children in the primitive church, which has been passionately discussed for the last few years among protestants, cannot be answered from the New Testament with absolute certainty. As in many other cases, the New Testament finds complementary clarification in the teaching tradition and practice of the church in the following period, but the fundamental theology of baptism in the New Testament is an inexhaustible source which can inspire theology and devotion of any time.

Bibliography: *General*. J. Coppens, 'Baptême', *DB(S)* I, 852–924; A. Oepke, *TDNT* I, 529–46; H. Schlier, 'Zur kirchlichen Lehre von der Taufe', *TLZ* 72 (1947), 321–36; B. Neunheuser, *Taufe und Firmung*, Freiburg 1956; J. Crehan, 'Ten Years' Work on Baptism and Confirmation', *TS* 17 (1956), 494–515; J. Duplacy, J. Giblet, Y. B. Tremel, and M. E. Boismard, *LV* 27 (1956); J. Ysebaert, *Greek Baptismal Terminology*, Nijmegen 1962. See also: H. G. Marsh, *The Origin and Significance of NT Baptism*, Manchester 1941; F. J. Leenhardt, *Le bapteme chretien, son origine, sa signification*, Neuchatel-Paris 1946; W. F. Flemington, *The NT Doctrine of Baptism*, London 1948; O. Cullman, *Baptism in the New Testament*, London 1950; J. H. Crehan, *Early Christian Baptism and the Creed*, London 1950; G. W. K. Lampe, *The Seal of the Spirit*, London 1951; M. Barth, *Die Taufe ein Sakrament?*, Zollikon-Zurich 1951; J. Schneider, *Die Taufe im NT*, Stuttgart 1952; G. Delling, *Die Zueignung des Heils in der Taufe*, Berlin 1961; G. Delling, *Die Taufe im NT*, Berlin 1963; G. R. Beasley-Murray, *Baptism in the New Testament*, London 1962.

On A. J. Thomas, *Le mouvement baptiste en Palestine et Syrie*, Gembloux 1935; O. Kuss, 'Zur Frage einer vorpaulinischen Todestaufe', *MTZ* 4 (1953), 1–17; O. Betz, 'Die Proselytentaufe der Qumran-Sekte und die Taufe im NT', *Revue de Qumran* 1 (1958/9), 123–234; J. Gnilka, 'Die essenischen Tauchbäder und die Johannestaufe', *Revue de Qumran* 3 (1961), 187–207. See also: J. Leipoldt, *Die urchristliche Taufe im Lichte der Religionsgeschichte*, Leipzig 1928; R. Reitzenstein, *Die Vorgeschichte der christlichen Taufe*, Leipzig 1929; N. A. Dahl, 'The Origin of Baptism', *Festschrift for S. Mowinckel*, Oslo 1955, 36–52.

On B. J. Gewiess, *Die urapostolische Heilsverkündigung nach der Apg.*, Breslau 1939; N. Adler, *Taufe und Handauflegung*, Münster 1951; O. Heggelbacher, *Die christl. Taufe als Rechtsakt nach dem Zeugnis der frühen Christenheit*, Fribourg 1953. See also: H. Mentz, *Taufe und Kirche in ihrem ursprüngl. Zusammenhang*, Munich 1960; D. G. Molenaar, *De doop met de Heil. Geest*, Kampen 1963.

On C. R. Schnackenburg, *Baptism in the Thought of St Paul*, Oxford 1964 (with bibliography); R. Schnackenburg, 'Todes- und Lebensgemeinschaft mit Christus—Neue Studien zu Rom 6:1–11', *MTZ* 6 (1955), 32–53; V. Warnach, 'Taufe und Christusgeschehen nach Rom 6', *ALW* 3 (1954), 284–366; V. Warnach, 'Die Tauflehre des Römerbriefes in der neueren theologischen Diskussion', *ALW* 5 (1958), 274–332; H. Schlier, *Die Taufe nach Rom 6: Die Zeit der Kirche*, Freiburg 1956, 47–56; O. Kuss, *Der Römerbrief* I, Regensburg 1957, 307–19; V. Warnach, *Taufwirklichkeit und Taufbewusstsein im Eph*, V. Warnach, 'Taufwirklichkeit und Taufbewusstsein im Eph', *LM* 33 (1963), 49–74. See also: G. Bornkamm, *Das Ende des Gesetzes*, Munich 1961[3], 34–50; G. Braumann, *Vorpaulinische christl. Taufverkündigung bei Paulus*, Stuttgart 1961; G. Wagner, *Das religionsgeschichtl. Problem von Rom 6: 1–11*, Zurich 1962.

On D. J. Dey, *Palingenesia*, Münster 1937; F. M. Braun, 'Le baptême d'après le quatrième év.', *RT* 48 (1948), 358ff; I. de la Potterie, '"Naître de l'eau et naître de l'Esprit"', *SE* 14 (1962), 417–43; M. E. Boismard, 'Une Liturgie baptismale dans la Prima Petri', *RB* 63 (1956), 182–208 and 64 (1957), 161–83; M. E. Boismard, *Quatres hymnes baptismales dans la première Ep. de Pierre*, Paris 1961. See also: W. Nauck, *Die Tradition und der Charakter des 1 Jn*, Tübingen 1957.—On infant baptism: K. Barth, *The Teaching of the Church regarding Baptism*, London 1948; J. Jeremias, *Infant Baptism in the First Four Centuries*, London 1960 (with bibliography); K. Aland, *Did the Early Church Baptise Infants?*, London 1963; J. Jeremias, Nochmals: *Die Anfänge der Kindertaufe*, Munich 1962; G. R. Beasley-Murray, *Baptism in the NT*, London 1962, 306–86; *C. Davis, *The Making of a Christian*, London 1964.

Rudolf Schnackenburg

Baptism of Jesus

All three of the synoptic gospels contain accounts of the baptism of Jesus (Mk 1:9–11; Mt 3:13–17; Lk 3:21f), whereas John contains only a brief mention of the episode (1:32–34), and Acts contains a bare reference to it (10:38). A fuller apocryphal account is to be found in the Gospel of the Ebionites (preserved by Epiphanius, *Haer.* 30, 13, 7f), while a shorter one is to be found in the Gospel according to the Hebrews (in Jerome, *Commentary on Isaiah* IV, on Is 11:2). A distinction must be drawn between the baptism of Jesus itself and the theophanic episode which follows it.

A. *It can be accounted historically certain that Jesus was baptised by John the Baptist*, for already in the early church the difficulties which this episode raises were being felt. The fact that Jesus took over the 'baptism of repentance for the forgiveness of sins' (Mk 1:4) seemed difficult to reconcile with his personal sinlessness (cf the omission of the words 'For the forgiveness of sins' by Matthew). In the Gospel according to the Hebrews Jesus explicitly puts the question: 'What sin have I committed that I should go and be baptised by him?'

Moreover such a proceeding could be interpreted as implying that Jesus was subordinate to John the Baptist. In the fourth gospel the difficulties are circumvented by omitting any real account of the episode of Jesus' baptism as such. With regard to the second point of difficulty, Luke mitigates this by omitting any reference to the Baptist in his narrative, which only touches in passing on the baptism of Jesus, while Matthew achieves a similar effect by interpolating the dialogue between John and Jesus in 3:14f (elaborated upon in the Gospel of the Ebionites: 'John fell at his feet and said: I beseech thee, Lord, do thou baptise me'). We should probably regard this dialogue as representing the answer of early christian apologetics to objections which had actually been put, although this is not to rule out the fact that the saying contained in v 15 represents a genuine saying of Jesus uttered on some other occasion (Descamps). If Jesus was aware of his role as Servant of God even before his baptism, then his motive in undergoing it would have been to manifest himself as him who was to take the sins of the 'many' upon himself (Mk 10:45 and parallels; 14:24 and parallels; Jn 1:29), and to make himself one with the sinners (see Mk 2:5, 16f etc). In any case we must assume that Jesus was conscious of the fact that when he took over the rite of baptism he was fulfilling the will of God. Mk 1:9 and parallels (together with Mt 11:7–15 = Lk 7:24–8 and Mt 21:32) bears witness to the fact that Jesus recognised the Baptist as a prophet, and his baptism and preaching of repentance as coming 'from heaven' (Mk 11:30); in other words his mission constituted a fulfilment of God's will and more immediately in the concrete a preparation for his own messianic work.

B. *The motive of the synoptic writers in including an account of the baptism of Jesus at all is to be found in the ensuing theophanic scene*. All of them agree in including three phenomena in their accounts: the opening of the heavens, the descent of the Spirit, and the voice issuing from heaven. The Gospel of the Ebionites and other witnesses also refer to an illumination (on this see W. Bauer, *Leben Jesu im Zeitalter der neutestamentliche Apokryphen*, Tübingen 1909, 110–41; A. d'Alès, *SDB* 1, col 855f).

1. The opening of the heavens is primarily a prelude to the second phenomenon, but at the same time it has a significance of its own as a sign of the inauguration of the eschatological age of grace (see Is 64:1). The descent of the (Holy) Spirit in the form of a dove upon Jesus is likewise an eschatological sign (see also Jn 1:32f) by which visible expression is given to the

fact that Jesus is now equipped with the power of the Spirit (his 'anointing' by God 'with the Holy Spirit and with power', Acts 10:38) so that he can take upon himself the task imposed by God (see Judg 3:10; 6:34; 11:29; 1 Sam 10:6; 11:6). There is an unmistakable reference here to Is 11:2 ('The Spirit of the Lord shall rest upon him'; see also Jn 1:32f), and also to Is 42:1. This indicates that it is the role of the messianic servant of God that Jesus is here assuming (on the messiah as the bearer of the Spirit, see also PsSol 17:37; Enoch [Eth] 49:3; 62:2; TestLev 18:7; TestJud 24:2). The dove as a symbol of the Spirit only appears at a late date in Jewish writings (Targum on Song 2:8). But the Spirit is not infrequently compared with a dove (instances in *TDNT* VI, 67f). The original form of the message uttered by the voice from heaven is that recorded in Mark and Luke. In other words it is couched in the second person singular. The suggestion that the words 'My Son' are derived from *pais mon* in Is 42:1 is hardly tenable, for already in the Q version of the temptation narrative reference is made to the designation of Jesus as 'Son of God' *huios tou theou* in the voice from heaven at the baptism (Mt 4:3, 6; Lk 4:3, 9: 'If you are the Son of God . . .'). The words 'beloved' (=only) and 'in thee I am well pleased' refer back to the opening words of the first Servant poem (Is 42:1; see also Mt 12:18). The latter words have the force of 'I have chosen you' (see 1 Macc 10:47; Ps 151:5 LXX), that is as messianic Servant of God. Even if, in accordance with apocalyptic and rabbinical ideas, we take these words as referring to a decree of election already formulated before the world began, in their existing context they are equivalent to a directive to execute that decree by assuming the role of the messianic Servant of God. In Lk 3:22 D these words are amplified by the phrase 'today I have begotten thee'. This would have been tantamount to saying that Jesus has now been exalted to the position of Son of God. But this reading is certainly secondary, formulated with the aim of completing what was assumed to be an incomplete quotation from Ps 2:7. In reality Ps 2:7 is not being quoted here at all, and even if there were any allusion to this verse, one would have to conclude from the fact that the closing words of the verse have been omitted that the idea of adoption and initiation into sonship now taking place for the first time is quite foreign to the author's intention. 'Sonship' as predicated of Jesus here was certainly understood by the community from whom the tradition derives in the same sense as in those other passages in which Jesus speaks of himself as ↗ Son of God and of God as his Father (Mt 11:27=Lk 10:22; Mt 17:25f; Mk 13:32; see also Mt 7:21 etc). In other words it was understood, not as a messianic title, but rather as the expression of the unique personal 'Father-Son' relationship between Jesus and God. It is to this relationship that the voice from heaven refers, because it constitutes the basis for the election of Jesus and for the fact that he is entrusted with the role of messiah.

2. On the character and meaning of the theophanic scene opinions have been, and still continue to be widely

divided. According to the earliest account, that of Mark, it is an experience personal to Jesus himself that is in question: Mk 1:10 (=Mt 3:16): 'He [Jesus] saw . . .'; Mk 1:11 (=Lk 3:22): 'You are . . .'. It is only in the other two synoptic authors that a tendency manifests itself to give the episode the character of a formal theophany (Mt 3:17: 'This is . . .' =17:5 parallel; Lk 3:22: 'In bodily form'). According to Jn 1:32–4 the Baptist at any rate witnessed the descent of the Spirit, though admittedly here it is clearly implied that others were excluded from the vision. It is nowhere stated that he actually heard the voice from heaven. (For an appraisal of Jn 1:32–4 see A. Vögtle, 631.) Whether the experience of Jesus consisted in an objective vision and audition, as most interpreters have assumed, or in a purely interior experience, as is sometimes concluded nowadays, can hardly be determined on the basis of the narratives alone. Probably the most unforced interpretation of the theophanic scene is that which envisages a divine directive to Jesus to commence his mission as messianic Servant of God. The descent of the Spirit is not merely a sign that this eschatological role has been laid upon him, but at the same time a sign that he is equipped for that role (Acts 10:38; Mk 1:8 and parallels; 1:12 and parallels; Lk 4:14, 18; 10:21; Mt 12:18, 28). The divine utterance solemnly recognises Jesus and confirms him in his role, just as Jesus himself has declared his submission to God's will by his gesture in undergoing baptism. The words uttered by God constitute an acknowledgment of Jesus as his Son, and characterise his status as Son as the basis of his election for the role of messianic Servant of God. Hence the solemn 'You are my Son' instead of the mere form of address 'My Son' (see, for instance, Mt 21:28). It has sometimes been suggested that it was not until this point that Jesus became aware either of his status as Son of God or of his messianic mission. But there are no real grounds for supposing this. This interpretation, and probably every other one which, like it, is based on the assumption that the account of the baptismal theophany is historical, is fraught with difficulties. For this reason the question has recently been raised of whether this account does not simply have the purpose of conveying to the early christian hearer or reader of the gospel in clear and vivid terms 'Who and what Jesus really is despite the fact that he was baptised by John and therefore seemed to be subordinate to him' (Vögtle, 664f). Another theory is that this account constitutes a mere didactic poem, the author of which has taken as his model Is 63:7–19 and/or TestJud 24 or TestLevi 18 (see Maurer, *TWNT* VII, 962 A. 17). But this theory too does not provide any convincing basis for our understanding of the account, although it is evident that numerous parallel motifs are to be found in these passages (Is 64:1; the dividing of the heavens; v 8, the voice of God and the acknowledging of his sons; vv 11, 14, the promise of the Spirit. TestJud 24:2: 'The heavens open over him and pour down the Spirit, the holy blessing of the Father'; v 4: 'This is the shoot of the most high God' [this verse, however, is probably a gloss]; TestLevi 18:6: 'The heavens open and holiness descends upon him from the shrine of glory, together with the voice of the Father like that of Abraham to Isaac'; v 7: 'The glory of the Most High is surely promised to him, and a Spirit of understanding will rest upon him, as also the Spirit of holiness [in the water]'; v 11: 'Then the Spirit of holiness rests upon them'; v 13: 'The Lord rejoices in his children, and has been well pleased in his loved ones for ever').

Bibliography: J. Kosnetter, *Die Taufe Jesu*, Vienna 1936 (with bibliography); J. Dupont, '"Filius meus es tu": l'interprétation de Ps. II, 7 dans le N.T.', *RSR* 35 (1948), 522–43; W. F. Flemington, *The NT Doctrine of Baptism*, London 1948; C. K. Barrett, *The Holy Spirit and the Gospel Tradition*, London 1948; H. Sahlin, *Studien zum dritten Kapitel des Lk-Ev*, Uppsala 1949; J. Dupont, 'Jésus, Messie et Seigneur dans la foi des premiers chrétiens', *VS* 83 (1950), 385–416; A. Descamps, *Les justes et la justice dans les évangiles*, Louvain 1950; G. W. H. Lampe, *The Seal of the Spirit*, London 1951; J. Bieneck, *Sohn Gottes als Christusbezeichnung des Synoptiker*, Zurich 1951; A. Robert, 'Considérations sur le Messianisme du Ps. II', *RSR* 39 (1951/2), 88–98; J. Schneider, *Die Taufe im NT*, Berlin 1952; J. A. T. Robinson, 'The Baptism as a Category of NT Soteriology', *SJT* 6 (1953), 257–74; V. Subilia, *Gésu nella più antica tradizione cristiana*, Torre Pellice 1954; C. E. B. Cranfield, 'The Baptism of our Lord', *SJT* 8 (1955), 53–63; M. E. Boismard, 'La révélation de l'Ésprit Saint', *RT* 63 (1955), 5–21; M. Dutheil, 'Le baptême de Jésus', *Stud. Bibl. Franc. Liver Annuus 6* (1955/6), 85–124; M. E. Boismard, *Du baptême à Cana*, Paris 1956; J. M. Robinson, *The Problem of History in Mark*, London, 1962; M. Karnetzki, 'Textgeschichte als Überlieferungsgeschichte', *ZNW* 47 (1956), 170–80; E. E. Fabbri, 'El bautismo de Jesús en el Evangelio de los Hebreos y en el de los Ebionites', *Rev. de Teologia* 22 (La Plata 1956), 36–56; I. Buse, 'The Markan Account of the Baptism of Jesus and Is. LXIII', *JTS* 7 (1956), 74f; H. Bouman, 'The Baptism of Christ with Special Reference to the Gift of the Spirit', *Concordia Theol. Monthly* 28 (1957), 1–14; J. E. Menard, '"Pais Theou" as Messianic Title in the Book of Acts', *CBQ* 19 (1957), 83–92; F. Gils, *Jésus prophète d'après les évangiles synoptiques*, Louvain, 1957; Cullmann, *The Christology of the New Testament*, London 1959; J. A. T. Robinson, 'The Baptism of John and the Qumran Community', *HTR* 50 (1957), 183–87; G. W. H. Lampe, 'The Holy Spirit in the Writings of St Luke', *Studies in the Gospels* (*Essays in Memory of R. H. Lightfoot*), ed. D. E. Nineham, Oxford 1957, 159–200; I. de la Potterie, 'L'onction du Christ', *NRT* 80 (1958), 225–52; M. A. Chevallier, *L'Ésprit et le Messie dans le Bas-Judaïsme et le NT*, Paris 1958; A. Feuillet, 'Le symbolisme de la colombe dans les récits évangéliques du Baptême', *RSR* 32 (1958), 524–44; A. Feuillet, 'Le baptême de Jésus d'après l'évangile selon Saint Marc', *CBQ* 21 (1959), 468–90; M. Smith, '"God's Begetting the Messiah" in 1 QSa', *NTS* 5 (1959), 218–24; J. Lamarié, 'Le baptême du Seigneur dans le Jourdain d'après les textes scripturaires en usage dans les églises', *MD* 59 (1959), 85–102; G. H. P. Thompson, 'Called-Proved-Obedient: a Study in the Baptism and Temptation Narratives of Mt and Lk', *JTS* 11 (1960), 1–12; J. Knackstedt, 'Manifestatio SS. Trinitatis in Baptismo Domini?', *VD* 38 (1960), 76–91; A. Nisin, *Histoire de Jésus*, Paris 1960; E. Lövestam, *Son and Saviour*, Lund/Copenhagen 1961; R. Siebeneck, 'The Dove as Epiphany', *Worship* 35 (1961), 97–102; J. Dutheil, *Le baptême de Jésus au Jourdain* Strasbourg 1961 (dissertation); A. Legault, 'Le baptême de Jésus et la doctrine du Serviteur souffrant', *SE* 12 (1961), 160–6; B. M. F. van Iersel, *'Der Sohn' in den synopt. Jesusworten*, Leiden 1961; T. de Kruijf, *Der Sohn des Lebendigen Gottes*, Rome 1962; H. Braun, 'Entscheidende Motive in den Berichten über die Taufe Jesu von Mk bis Justin', *Gesamm. Studien zum NT und seiner Umwelt*, Tübingen 1962, 168–72; M. Sabbe, 'Het verhaal va n Jezus' doopsel', *Coll. Brug. et Gand.* 8 (1962), 456–74, 9 (1963), 211–30, 333–65; J. H. Eybers, 'Die doop van Johannes die Doper', *Nederduitse Geref. Teol. Tydskrif* 4 (1963), 184–92; M. E. Boismard, 'Les traditions johanniques concernant le baptiste', *RB* 70 (1963), 5–42; F. Hahn, *Christologische Hoheitstitel*, Göttingen 1963; O. Kuss, 'Zur vorpaulin. Tauflehre im NT', *Auslegung und Verkündigung* I, Regensburg 1963, 98–120; A. Vögtle, 'Exegetische Erwägungen über das Wissen und Selbstbewusstsein Jesu', *Gott in Welt* (*Festg. K. Rahner*), Freiburg i. Br. 1964, 608–67; C. H. Lindijer, 'Jezus' doop in de Jordan', *TT* 18 (1963/4), 177–92; A. Feuillet, 'Le Baptême de Jésus', *RB* 71 (1964), 321–52.

Josef Blinzler

Binding and loosing

Besides 'to bind' (*deō*) in its literal sense ('bind', 'bind together', 'fetter') there is also a figurative sense which refers to the marriage bond (Rom 7:2; 1 Cor 7:27, 39) and to a supernatural bond (with Satan, Luke 13:16; Satan being 'bound', Rev 20:2).

'To loose' (*luō*) in its figurative sense, either with or without the analogy of the demolition of a building (Jn 2:19; Eph 2:14), denotes the abrogation of a law, a repeal (Mt 5:19; Jn 7:23; 10:35; Jn 5:18 with reference to the Sabbath).

'To bind' and 'to loose' are the usual translations of the Hebrew *ʾāsar* and *pittah* respectively, or the Aramaic *asar* and *sera*, as used by the rabbis; here they mean 'to declare a thing either forbidden or licit by means of a scholastic pronouncement, removal or imposition of an obligation'. Occasionally these two words refer to the infliction or removal of a ban. It is not certain whether Mt 16:19 and 18:18 use these words in one of these two meanings (a third meaning, based on Greek and rabbinical parallels, 'a binding and loosing by means of magic', certainly need not be considered). There exists in the semitic languages—and also in others—the peculiarity of expressing a totality by means of two contrary concepts (as heaven and hell, old and young, great and small, good and evil, etc). One must go to the context in order to know what the totality is which is so expressed. Peter is given the power of the keys (Mt 16:19) and this without restriction, as a totality! It appears from the change from singular to plural that Mt 18:18 is an addition to the original text which makes an exact interpretation rather difficult. The most obvious one, in view of the context as we have it, would be the above-mentioned *power of admitting into and excluding from the community which is the church in a way valid in the eyes of God.* This interpretation is generally accepted in defining the powers given to Peter (Mt 16:19).

Bibliography: SB I, 738–47; F. Büchsel, *TDNT* II, 60–61; IV, 335–7; G. Lambert, 'Lier—Délier', *Vivre et Penser* 3 (1943/4), 91–103; see also for expression by contraries: A. M. Honeyman, *JBL* 71 (1952), 11–18; P. Boccaccio, *Bbl* 33 (1952), 173–90; A. Massart, *Mélanges Robert*, Paris (1957), 38–46; O. Michel, *RAC* II, 374–80; C. H. Dodd, *NTS* 2 (1955/6), 85f; A. Vögtle, *LTK* II (1958²), 480–2.

Johannes B. Bauer

Blasphemy

A. *Terminology.* There are several terms in Hebrew for 'slander': *gādap*, *nāʾats* (in Piel), *ḥārap*, *lāʿag*, *qillēl* (in Piel), *qābab*, *nāqab*. The object of these verbs can be either men or God. In LXX and the New Testament the corresponding terms are *oneidizein*, *paroxunein*, and *blasphēmein*; this last has only God, persons chosen by God, or holy things or institutions for object.

B. *Old Testament.* 1. In the Old Testament blasphemy is a contempt of, an insulting of God or his name. (↗ Curse.) He blasphemes against God who makes use of the name of God for evil ends (magic, unlawful cursing of his fellow-men; Ex 20:7; Deut 5:11); who, being one of God's chosen (king or priest) commits a transgression, thus bringing his sacred office into discredit

(1 Sam 3:13; 2 Sam 12:14); who opposes one of God's chosen (Num 16:30); who breaks the covenant with Yahweh (Deut 31:20; Is 1:4); who despises the word of God (Jer 23:17) or doubts of the power of Yahweh to punish (Is 5:24) or to help (Num 14:11, 23; 20:10, 12). Job, stricken with suffering, is expected by Satan and by his own wife to 'curse God to his face' (in the Hebrew we find the euphemism 'to bless God to his face')—meaning, to doubt his help and thus to blaspheme against him. (Job 1:11; 2:5, 9.) The worst form of blasphemy is when a man, by comparing him with the mighty gods of the heathens, represents the God of Israel as a pitiable, helpless figure from whom nothing can be expected. (2 Kings 18:30–35; 19:4, 6, 22; 2 Chron 32:13ff; Is 10:8–11; 36:18ff; 37:10–13; Judith 6:1–4; probably also Lev 24:11, 14f, 23.) But also anyone who mocks at or opposes Israel as Yahweh's own people blasphemes against God. (Is 52:5; Ezek 35:12f; 1 Macc 2:6; 2 Macc 8:4; 10:34; 12:14; 15:24.) In general, the heathens are considered as blasphemers (2 Macc 10:4).

2. Blasphemy is a transgression which deserves death, and is punished either by human judges (Lev 24:10–16; 1 Kings 21:13) or by God himself with the most severe penalties (burning, extermination) (see Ex 20:7; Num 16:30; Deut 5:11; 1 Sam 4:11; 2 Kings 19:7; 2 Chron 32:21; Is 37:36ff; 2 Macc 9:4, 12, 28).

3. Though the self-righteous friends of Job consider objections against God as blasphemy (Job 15:2–6; 34:35ff), in fact God reacts against the at times daring reproaches of the just against him in a strikingly mild way or even does not object at all (eg, Ex 5:22; Num 11:11ff; Josh 7:7; Is 38:13; Jer 12:1–5; 15:16–21; 20:7–10; Lam 3:10f; Job 9:12–20; 19:6–21; 30:18–23; 38:2; 40:2, 8). In these cases, there is no question of what the Old Testament means by blasphemy, that is, there is no 'making small' of Yahweh, no mockery. Quite the contrary: God appears here to these just men tried by suffering as incomparably mighty, as the Lord who rules with absolute freedom, whom man cannot call to account.

C. *New Testament.* 1. The Jews in Jesus' day, in accordance with the Old Testament, regarded as blasphemers those who claimed rights and powers which can be ascribed to God only (see SB I, 1007–19); in particular, the power to forgive sins (Mt 9:3; Mk 2:7; Lk 5:21; Jn 5:18f; 10:33–36). It was on this score that Jesus was accused of blasphemy (Mt 26:64ff; Mk 14:62ff).

2. The New Testament considers as blasphemy words and ways of acting which injure the holiness, majesty and honour of God. These can be directed either immediately against God (Acts 6:11; Rev 13:6; 16:11, 21), against his name (Rom 2:24; 1 Tim 6:1; Rev 16:9), his word (Tit 2:5), his law (Acts 6:11) or his angels (2 Pet 2:10ff; cf Jude 8–10).

3. They also commit blasphemy who deride Jesus' claim to messianic status and divine sonship (Mt 27:39; Mk 15:29; Lk 22:64f; 23:39). He also is guilty of blasphemy who falls away from his faith (Acts 26:11; 1 Tim 1:20) and spreads erroneous teaching (Rom 3:8; 2 Pet 2:2). The whole emergence of the apocalyptic enemies of God who

oppose him is one great blasphemy (Rev 13:1, 5f; 17:3, 5f). But christians also, through lack of charity and by leading a bad life, can be the occasions of others blaspheming (Rom 2:24; 1 Tim 6:1; Tit 2:5; Jas 2:7).

4. Just as the Jews and heathens have blasphemed against Christ, so will they against the disciples of Christ; therefore, it is the lot of the Church and its members to be the object of blasphemous talk (1 Cor 4:13; 1 Pet 4:4, 14; Rev 2:9). It is blasphemy when the Jews mock at and oppose Paul and his teaching (Acts 13:45; 18:6); Paul himself had been at one time a blasphemer, when he persecuted the christians (1 Tim 1:13). Even christians themselves can be guilty of 'blasphemy' when they hate and are angry with one another (Mt 15:19; Mk 7:22; Eph 4:31; Col 3:8; 1 Tim 6:4; 2 Tim 3:2; Tit 3:2).

5. According to Mt 12:31f; Mk 3:28f; Lk 12:10, any blasphemy can be forgiven except 'blasphemy against the Holy Spirit'. The exact meaning of this expression is disputed. Perhaps we should understand it this way: to blaspheme against the Holy Spirit means, maliciously and against one's better judgement, to ascribe the miracles of Jesus worked through the power of the Holy Spirit to the devil (Mt 12:24–28; Lk 11:19f); an attitude of this kind reveals a hardness and blindness of heart which stands in the way of conversion, which is a necessary condition for forgiveness.

Bibliography: H. W. Beyer, *TDNT* I, 621–5; SB I, 1006–20; J. Blinzler, *LTK* IV², 1117ff; J. Blinzler, *Der Prozess Jesu*, Regensburg 1960³, 108–15 and 129–37; J. Scharbert, '"Fluchen" und "Segnen" im AT', *Bbl* 39 (1958), 1–26 (esp. 8f and 13f); S. H. Blank, 'Men against God', *JBL* 72 (1953), 1–13; S. H. Blank, 'The Curse, the Blasphemy, the Spell, and the Oath', *HUCA* 23 (1950/1), 73–95.

Josef Scharbert

Blessing

A. *Terminology*. The Hebrew root *bārak* with its verbal and substantival formations has a far wider meaning than the English 'blessing'. The Arabic *baraka* is the innate gift of good fortune which some people have, which enables them to be successful in every enterprise, and which they can pass on to others; but it also stands for fertility, abundance, wealth of camels, water which is so longed for in the desert. Also in the Old Testament we can detect a connection between *bārak* and fertility of human beings, animals, and the fields. (See Gen 1:22, 28; 9:1; 12:2; 22:17; 24:60; 49:25; Ex 23:25ff; Deut 7:13f; 28:3ff; Ezek 34:26; Ps 84:4; 107:38; Prov 5:18.)

In Piel, *barak* means the opposite of *qillēl* (see ↗ Curse A), therefore 'to praise someone as great, successful, mighty, happy'; when the king is the object, 'to honour' or the like (Gen 47:7–10; 2 Sam 14:22; 1 Kings 1:47); when it is God or his name, 'to praise' (Gen 24:48; Deut 8:10; Judges 5:2–9; Neh 8:6; 9:5; very often in the Psalms; the passive participle *bārūk* means therefore 'praised', Gen 9:26; 14:20; 24:27; Ps 41:13; 89:52; etc); when it is any person of merit 'to praise (with thanks)' or the like (Deut 24:13; Judg 5:24; Ruth 2:19f; 2 Sam 2:5; Neh 11:2; Job 31:20; Ps 72:15; Prov 10:7). When it is a question of one who has won a battle, *b^e^rākâh* refers to the recognition of his might and claims (2 Kings 18:31; Is 36:16). The godless, of course, do not bless their wickedness, but 'boast' of it (Deut 29:19; Ps 10:3; 49:6; Is 66:3).

As with a ↗ curse, so with a blessing people were convinced that it really brought about the good fortune of which it spoke. This explains why in Babylonian 'blessing' is simply called 'the good word'. With such a 'good word' Ps 45:2 addresses the royal bride and bridegroom convinced that the effect will follow. Whence the real meaning of *bārak* (in Piel) is 'to address a good word to someone' or, at times, 'to speak well of someone'. It thus acquires the meaning of 'to wish well', 'to bless'. Good wishes, which imply at the same time blessing, are addressed to the king when he ascends the throne (1 Kings 1:47), to a friendly ruler on the occasion of a victory (2 Sam 8:10; 1 Chron 18:10), to the owner of a flock on the occasion of sheep-shearing (1 Sam 25:5f; 2 Sam 13:23–5), to newly-weds (Gen 24:60; Ruth 4:11f; Tob 8:17; 11:16f), to one who is departing before beginning his journey (Gen 28:1; 31:55; Tob 5:16). Since in Israel every greeting was a form of blessing, however, *bārak* in Piel can mean also simply 'to greet' (1 Sam 13:10; 2 Kings 4:29; 10:15; Ps 129:8). A present which is given on such an occasion is called *b^e^rākâh*, namely, a 'blessing' in visible form; we might say 'a greetings present' (Gen 33:11; 1 Sam 25:27; 30:26), a 'wedding present' (Josh 15:19; Judg 1:15), an honorarium (2 Kings 5:15). The meaning 'to bless', 'blessing' occurs particularly when it is a question of fathers blessing their sons, priests blessing those taking part in the service and the promises of God in favour of mankind (see B below). In the ritual instructions of Num 6:22–27; Deut 11:26–30 it is a question of well-established liturgical formulae.

There are certain turns of phrase the meaning of which is not at once apparent: *bārak* in Piel with *b^e^* referring to things means evidently 'to bless with goods' or the like (Gen 24:1; Deut 16:15; 23:20; 24:19; Ps 29:11)—which, however, is precisely the same as the granting of the goods in question. When used in Piel, Niphal, or Hithpael with *b^e^* referring to persons the meaning is very disputed. Gen 48:20 could give us a clue to the meaning: when other people pronounce a blessing they will say 'God make you as Ephraim and as Manasseh!' Gen 12:3; 18:18; 22:18; 26:4; 28:14 could be made to give a similar meaning, namely, 'to bless oneself with reference to the happiness of a certain person'. We must give the same meaning to the phrase 'to be a blessing', 'to be made a blessing', that is, the person named is a blessing insofar as his happiness, good estate, has become proverbial, and as such is mentioned in wishing a blessing when another person desires for the one to be blessed a similar great happiness (Gen 12:2; Is 19:24; Ezek 34:26; Zech 8:13; Ps 37:26). Many commentators prefer to translate *bārak* in Niphal or Hithpael when followed by *b^e^* referring to persons as 'to be blessed by means of a certain person', but this interpretation hardly corresponds to the Old Testament way of thinking. As far as the sense is concerned, this meaning is in any case contained in the interpretation given above; the naming of the person in question implies an avowal to him, a recognition of his happiness as God-given, and—since the pronouncing of a blessing was regarded as efficacious —the blessing comes about indirectly through the person named. Finally, the combination Piel with *b^e* referring to God means 'to bless with the invocation of God's name' (Ps 129:8; Is 65:16).

Corresponding to the Hebrew *barak* in LXX and the New Testament we usually find the Greek *eulogein* (=to bless) and *eulogia* (=a blessing), with much the same meanings.

B. *Blessing in the Old Testament.* Both blessing and ↗ curse are forces which bring about what the words signify. One possesses a blessing (Gen 27:38), but it can be taken away (Gen 27:35f). One can be 'filled with' a blessing (Deut 33:23); a blessing can be 'set before' a person (Deut 11:26; 30:19), can be 'on a house' (Ezek 44:30) or 'laid on a place' (Deut 11:29) or can be 'poured out' (Is 44:3). The power of the blessing is transferred through the laying on of hands (Gen 48:14–17) or pronunciation of the formula of blessing (Gen 27:27ff; 49:28) to the one to be blessed. The blessing of the pious man benefits the town where he lives (Prov 11:11) and 'establishes its roots' (Sir 3:9). The blessing, once pronounced, releases a force which is no longer under the control of the one who has said it (Gen 27:33–5; see Num 22:6).

The source of all blessings in the Old Testament is always God himself even if he is not actually mentioned. God 'puts forth his blessing' (Lev 25:21; Deut 28:8; Ps 133:3); he blesses his creatures (Gen 1:22), the first human beings (Gen 1:28; 5:2; 9:1), the patriarchs and their wives (Gen 12:2; 17:16; 22:17; 24:1, 34f; 25:11; 26:12–24; 35:9; 48:3; Is 51:2), that they may be fruitful and multiply. Yahweh also blesses individuals who play a part in salvation history (Judg 13:24; 2 Sam 6:11f; 1 Chron 26:5) and the pious in general (Ps 5:12; 67:1; 115:13; 134:3; Is 61:9; Jer 17:7) together with their children and their 'house', namely, their whole offspring (Gen 17:20; Deut 7:13; 2 Sam 6:11; 7:29; Ps 112:2; 147:13; see also Ps 128:2ff). The object of the divine blessing is, in the first place, the people of Israel, as long as they keep the covenant with Yahweh (Ex 20:24; Deut 2:7; 7:13; 14:24, 29; 15:4–18; 16:10; 26:15; 30:16; 2 Chron 31:10; Ps 28:9; 29:11; 115:12). In the messianic age, however, the heathens too would receive a blessing from Yahweh (Is 19:25). The man who is chosen to serve Yahweh in a special capacity or on whom he showers his special gifts of good fortune is called 'blessed of Yahweh' (Gen 14:19; 24:31; 26:29; Judg 17:2; 1 Sam 15:13; 23:21; 2 Sam 2:5; Ruth 2:20; 3:10; Ps 115:15; Is 65:23).

Not just persons but things too can be the object of the divine blessing insofar as they belong to people who are worthy of a blessing. Thus fields (Gen 27:27; Jer 31:23; Ps 65:10), the produce of labour and the undertakings of the pious (Deut 28:12; 33:11; Job 1:10), food (Ex 23:25), 'the fruit of the womb and of the ground' (Deut 7:13), and, in general, all the possessions of the pious man (Ex 23:25; Deut 28:3–6; Prov 3:33).

From the point of view of theology and the history of salvation, it is particularly significant that Yahweh will bless all those who unite in friendship with his friends and chosen ones and give proof of their solidarity with them (Gen 12:3; Num 24:9). He who gives a friend of Yahweh hospitality will meet with his blessing. (Gen 30:27–30; 39:5.) Those who are blessed by Yahweh cannot be harmed by the curse of man. (Ps 109:28.)

God also dispenses his blessing through the medium of man. Certain men, in a particular way, receive a call to bestow blessing and are given power to do so. Such a blessing which is spoken by or mediated through a man will be all the more powerful in proportion as the one blessing has a closer relation to Yahweh, for which the fact of belonging to Israel is not an indispensable prerequisite. Thus Yahweh orders the heathen seer Balaam to bless Israel, although he had in fact been called on by his human overlord to curse her (Num 22–4). According to the Old Testament view, not everyone is *ipso facto* able to bless—if we prescind from the greeting which is, in point of fact, also a form of blessing (see above, under A). In the Old Testament, people who enjoy special authority pronounce a blessing in the real sense of the word: the patriarchs over their sons and descendants (Gen 9:26f; 27:23–9; 48:9–20; 49); fathers over their children (Sir 3:9); the great mediators of the covenant—Moses, Aaron, Joshua—over the people (Ex 39:43; Lev 9:23; Deut 33; Josh 14:13; 22:7). Also in liturgy the giving of blessing is the duty of particular persons. Thus, the king blesses the people at the dedication of the Temple or at the conclusion of a liturgical reform (2 Sam 6:18; 1 Kings 8:14, 55f; 1 Chron 16:2; 2 Chron 6:3). The priests bless individual people who come to the sanctuary with their particular petitions (1 Sam 2:20; cf also Gen 14:19), pilgrims just arrived or about to depart (Ps 118:26; 134:3), the whole people gathered together for a liturgical celebration (Lev 9:22; 2 Chron 30:27). A particularly festive blessing is that reserved to the priests alone and called 'the blessing of Aaron' (Num 6:23–6). According to Deut 21:5 (see also 1 Chron 23:13) it would appear that only the priests are able to bless, but in Deut 10:8 the Levites may too. Only in a very special case do the people, gathered together as a unity, bless the king after the latter has blessed them (1 Kings 8:66). According to Ex 12:32, the Pharaoh asks Moses and Aaron for a blessing when they carry out their liturgical celebration in the wilderness which they were planning to do, but this is certainly not to be conceived of as a blessing which the people will pronounce but a prayer of intercession; apart from this case the Old Testament is familiar with sacrifices and prayers for the high kings of the heathens (Ezra 6:10). Whereas we today are familiar with liturgical blessings of devotional objects, cattle, houses, and other things, it does not appear that Israelite liturgy used blessings for things. Only in 1 Sam 9:13 do we find the isolated case of Samuel blessing the sacrificial victim.

As with the curse on the breakers of the law, so the blessing on those who observe it was the sanction of the great legal corpora (Lev 26; Deut 28). On the occasion of covenant renewal the Levites pronounced curse and blessing formulae and the assembled people confirmed them by their 'Amen' (Deut 11:26–30; 27:12–26; Josh 8:33). Curse and blessing were two juxtaposed powers laid upon the whole land and brought into effect in accordance with the people's attitude to the covenant of Yahweh.

The fact that *barak* in Piel often has God for its object has led many exegetes to the conclusion, on the grounds of parallels taken from the history of religions among primitive peoples, that Yahweh also could be blessed. This blessing would have the purpose of increasing the power, might, and happiness of God. This interpretation, however, is certainly false since *barak* (Piel) here means nothing more than 'to glorify', 'to praise' or the like (see above, under A). A case which requires a similar interpretation would be '... who do not bless their mothers' parallel with '... who curse their fathers' (Prov 30:11), where *barak* (Piel) is used over against all (Piel), since in no other case do subordinates pronounce a real blessing over people in authority, or children over their parents; and so here it is not a case of a blessing on the mother but only of speaking respectfully of her.

Even if the unusual constructions with Niphal and Hithpael as well as the phrase 'to be a blessing' are interpreted differently, as we have already noticed under A, the texts in question still tell us that the patriarchs and their 'seed' (Gen 12:2f; 18:18; 22:18; 26:4; 28:14), meaning the whole people of Israel (Jer 4:2; Zech 8:13) and even, in the messianic age, the converted heathen nations of Assyria and Egypt together with Israel (Is 19:24), and finally the Messiah as representative of the messianic people of God (Ps 72:17), will be the means of blessing for all peoples and races. This is to be understood in the sense that they will induce all nations, by means of the gift of salvation which Yahweh has given them, to acknowledge them and their God and to desire this same gift for themselves.

The net result of all this is that blessing in the Old Testament has nothing to do with magic. It is always either a petition addressed to Yahweh or an avowal to those chosen by Yahweh or a decision arrived at by Yahweh himself. It has its effect only when the person in question, in whose benefit the blessing is pronounced, is worthy of it by reason of his fidelity to God and his law or when, in spite of his unworthiness, Yahweh grants him a blessing purely out of his grace. As with a curse, a blessing is not irrevocable; for even if man cannot take it back (Gen 27:33, 35; Num 22:6) God can render it null and void; he can change a blessing into a curse (Mal 2:2; see also 1 Sam 2:30).

C. *Blessing in the New Testament.* In the Jewish temple liturgy at the time of Christ the officiating priests pronounced the blessing of Aaron (Num 6:22ff) at the daily morning service. This blessing was also in use in the synagogues and was there likewise reserved to the priests. Apart from this, the rabbinical writings know of the blessing of children by those learned in the law (Sopherim 18:5), of pupils by their teachers (Ber 28b, Meg 28a), of children by their fathers (GnR 16d ad Gen 26; *Siddur Sephat Emet*, ed. Rodelsheim, 1886, 44). The tractate Berakoth in the Mishna,

Tosefta, and the Talmud regulate the various blessing formulae in which it is a question of the praise of God. In Qumran, blessings as well as curses play a part in the covenant renewal and the ceremony of admission (1 QS II, 1–4). In the text 1 Q 28b there is contained a whole ritual for a blessing on the faithful, on the high-priest, on other priests, and on the head of the community.

The New Testament takes over, for the most part, the Old Testament and Jewish views on blessing as well as the practice. The Epistle to the Hebrews mentions the blessing of Melchizedek on Abraham (7:6f) and that of Isaac on Jacob (11:20; cf 12:17); these blessings were fulfilled because those blessed trusted in the divine promises. According to Gal 3:8f (cf Heb 6:14) faith is a necessary condition for the blessing of Abraham to be fulfilled in regard to those who believe, and this irrespective of descent by blood. Thoroughly in accord with the Old Testament where, as a rule, the formal blessing belongs to those who exercise authority over others, the author of the Epistle to the Hebrews deduces the superiority of Melchizedek over Levi, who was as yet 'in Abraham's loins', from the fact that Melchizedek blessed Abraham and not vice versa, since 'it is beyond dispute that the inferior is blessed by the superior' (Heb 7:6f).

Jesus blesses children as do those learned in the law (Mk 10:16); he also blesses his disciples (Lk 24:50). Peter sums up the mission of Jesus in the words: God has sent his son 'to bless you' (Acts 3:26). In contrast, however, to the old law, where the blessing had for its object material goods, the blessing which goes out from Jesus is a *eulogia pneumatikē* (='spiritual blessing', Eph 1:3) which will be fully realised only when the Lord at his second coming will say to his faithful: 'Come O blessed of my Father, inherit the kingdom prepared for you from the foundation of the world' (Mt 25:34).

Natural man curses as easily as he blesses (Jas 3:9f); but the supernatural man, the christian who has been called to inherit a blessing, does not curse but blesses only (1 Pet 3:9). Jesus demands from his disciples: 'Bless those who curse you' (Lk 6:28). Paul demands the same from those to whom he writes (Rom 12:14) and himself acts accordingly (1 Cor 4:12).

In the New Testament the following only are mentioned as 'blessed'= *eulogēmenoi*: the Messiah (Mt 21:9; 23:39; Mk 11:9; Lk 13:35; 19:38; Jn 12:13); his kingdom (Mk 11:10); his mother (Lk 1:42); and his redeemed disciples, when he welcomes them into the kingdom of his Father (Mt 25:34).

Whereas in LXX there are men who are called *eulogētoi* (eg, Gen 12:2; 26:29; Judg 17:2), in the New Testament *eulogētos* refers only to God (Mk 14:61; Lk 1:68; Rom 1:25; 9:5; 2 Cor 1:3; 11:31; Eph 1:3; 1 Pet 1:3).

In connection with meals *eulogein* or *eulogia*, in accordance with Jewish usage, do not mean 'to bless', 'a blessing', but rather refers to the prayer said at table in which thanksgiving and praise is offered to God (Mk 6:41; 8:7; 14:22; Mt 26:26). Only in 1 Cor 10:16 do we hear of 'the cup of blessing which we bless' in connection with the eucharist. Here the praise and thanksgiving concern the eucharistic meal itself as the pledge of our fellowship with Christ.

Bibliography: B. Landsberger, 'Das "gute Wort"', *MAOG* 4 (1929), 294–321; F. Horst, 'Segen und Segenshandlungen in der Bibel', *ET* (1947), 23–37; H. Junker, 'Segen als heilsgeschichtliches Motivwort', *SP* I (Gembloux 1959), 548–58; A. Murtonen, 'The Use and Meaning of the Words *lebarek* and *berakah* in the OT', *VT* 9 (1959), 158–77 and 330; T. Schäfer, 'Eucharistia', *BM* 36 (1960), 251–8; S. H. Blank, 'Some Observations concerning Biblical Prayer', *HUCA* 32 (1961), 75–90; E. J. Bickerman, 'Bénédiction et prière', *RB* 69 (1962), 524–32; J. Schreiner, 'Segen für die Völker', *BZ* 6 (1962), 1–31; H. W. Beyer, *TDNT* II, 754–65. ↗ Curse.

Josef Scharbert

Blood

A. *Terminology*. The Hebrew term for 'blood' is *dām* in the Old Testament; in the plural it refers to a deed of blood or blood-guilt. An *ʾîs dāmîm* is a man who has burdened himself with blood-guilt on account of having committed a murder or been guilty of some other transgression punishable by death. The *gōʾēl haddām* is the blood-avenger (Num 35:19, 21, 24f; Deut 19:6, 12; Josh 20:3, 5, 9; 2 Sam 14:11). LXX translates *dam* by *haima*, but also uses *phonos* (= murder, bloodshed) when it is a question of blood-guilt (Ex 22:3; Deut 22:8; etc); *aitia phonou* (= cause of bloodshed, Prov 28:17) and other expressions are also found. The 'man of blood' is *anēr haimatōn metokhos* (Prov 29:10).

The Israelites, in common with neighbouring peoples, regarded blood as the bearer of life (Lev 17:11) even to the extent of identifying the two (Gen 9:5; Lev 17:14; Deut 12:23). 'To shed blood' and 'to seek after a person's blood' meant the same as to take someone's life or to seek after someone's life respectively (Lev 19:16; Deut 27:25; Prov 1:16; Sir 11:32; Acts 22:20; Rom 3:15). David refused to drink the blood of his heroes, namely, he refused to drink the water which they had obtained at the risk of their lives (2 Sam 23:17). According to Lk 22:44 great fear can force blood with sweat out of the pores.

Only in the hellenistic period does 'blood' together with 'flesh' become a plastic expression for all that is transitory and mortal (Sir 14:18; 17:31; Enoch 14:4; for rabbinical usage see SB I, 730f). In the New Testament 'flesh and blood' is synonymous with the material and natural element in man in contrast with the supernatural (Mt 16:17; Jn 1:13; 1 Cor 15:50 etc). The Hebrew language has no term corresponding to 'blood-relationship', but expresses this idea by the phrase 'to be one bone and one flesh', etc (Gen 29:14; Judg 9:2; 2 Sam 5:1). Blood is used for the first time to express relationship in Judith 9:4. According to Wis 7:2 life in the maternal womb comes about through the semen causing the mother's blood to clot, but Jn 1:13 implies that the blood of the father mixes with that of the mother. The idea that the blood of the father of the race flows on through his descendents is testified only in some important manuscript readings of Acts 17:26, but elsewhere in this kind of context it is always a question of semen.

B. *Human blood in biblical theology*. Since life is located in the blood according to the Israelite view, or even is regarded as identical with it and both as the property of God alone, God protects human life insofar as he forbids the shedding of innocent blood (Gen 9:6). God defends the life of the just since 'precious is their blood in his sight' (Ps 72:14). He who sheds innocent blood encroaches on God's supreme rights and is therefore guilty of a monstrous crime especially should it happen in the precincts of the sanctuary (Gen 37:22; 2 Sam 12:5–12; 1 Macc 1:37; 7:17; 2 Macc 1:8; Mt 23:30, 35; 27:4). This crime can be expiated only with the blood of the murderer (Gen 9:5f; Ex 21:12, 23; Lev 24:17, 21; Num 35:19ff; Deut 19:11ff). The blood of a murdered person 'cries' for vengeance (Gen 4:10; 2 Macc 8:3; Rev 6:10; see also Heb 12:24), especially when it has not been covered up with earth (Is 26:21; Ezek 24:7f; Job 16:18). The murderer is 'a man of blood' (2 Sam 16:7f; Ps 5:6; 26:9; 55:23); he is defiled with blood (Jer 2:34; Lam 4:14), has blood 'on his hands' that he cannot thereafter wash off (Is 1:15; 59:3; Ezek 23:37, 45) and that gives him no rest (Gen 4:12–16; Prov 28:17; Lam 4:14f). The shedding of innocent blood represents a constant threat that it will come back upon the murderer, 'upon his head', thus destroying him (Deut 19:10; Joshua 2:19; Judges 9:24; 1 Sam 25:26, 33; 2 Sam 1:16; 1 Kings 2:33; Jer 26:15; Ezek 35:6; Hos 12:14). The blood of murdered prophets and martyrs brings judgement upon their persecutors (Mt 23:30–5; Lk 11:50f; Rev 6:10f; 16:5f; 18:21–4). The enemies of Jesus in their blindness go so far as to call down upon themselves and their descendants the blood of him who though innocent was condemned to death, thus bringing down divine judgement upon themselves (Mt 27:25; see also Acts 5:28).

The blood of the murdered man threatens not only his murderer but also the murderer's family (Deut 22:8; 2 Sam 21:1) and even him who is responsible for the vengeance of blood if he does not do his duty (1 Kings 2:31). It can pollute a city and the whole land and bring them disaster (2 Sam 21:2; Ps 106:38; Jer 26:15; Ezek 7:23; 22:3; 24:6ff; Mic 3:10; Nahum 3:1; Hab 2:12). The soil which has received the blood of a murdered man remains sterile (Gen 4:11f) and has to be freed from this condition by the blood of the murderer (Num 35:33; Deut 19:13). If the murderer is not found, it is the duty of the community to dissociate itself from the deed of blood by a rite of purification (Deut 21:1–9).

Vengeance of blood was considered as a normal legal procedure and even enjoyed divine sanction in the Old Testament during the period when the maintenance of law was still very deficient and before a centralised political authority had taken over (↗ Vengeance). For this reason God himself sometimes interfered by inflicting a national catastrophe in order to encourage those responsible for avenging blood, whenever circumstances permitted, to carry out their duty (2 Sam 21). Even down to the monarchy, the actual execution of the murderer was not the competence of the public authority but was reserved for the next of kin of the murdered man. The king or other public authorities limited themselves to conducting an enquiry and handing over the murderer to the 'avenger of blood' (Num 35:19, 21; Deut 19:11f; 2 Sam 21:8f). If no human avenger could be found God himself took over the duty of the blood-avenger (Deut 32:43; 2 Kings 9:7; Ps 9:12; 79:10). In war it is allowed and even, all things being equal, commanded to shed blood, but even then the stain of blood attaches to the king so that he is not capable of certain religious functions (1 Kings 5:3; 1 Chron 22:8; 28:3).

There are other crimes apart from murder which can burden the guilty one with 'blood' and which, in the same way, can be atoned for only with the blood of the offender (Lev 17:4; 20:9–27). God demands the blood of those warriors who, through a too hasty surrender, jeopardise the very existence of the people (Judith 8:21), and of those guards who do not warn the population in time of a danger which threatens. This last image is also applied to prophets who do not warn the people of the divine judgement which threatens (Ezek 3:18, 20; 33:4–8). Paul, too, fears to make himself guilty of the blood of his hearers by not preaching repentance and conversion to them (Acts 20:26).

In this way blood becomes *a symbol of divine judgement.* Thus, the changing of water into blood throughout the land stood as a warning for the Egyptians (Ex 4:9; 7:14–21; Ps 78:44; 105:29). On the Day of Judgement the blood of God's enemies will flow in streams (Is 15:9; Ezek 14:19; 21:32; 32:6; Zeph 1:17; Ps 58:10; 68:23), like the blood of animals in a sacrificial feast, a feast of the slaughter (Is 34:3, 6; Ezek 39:17). It will stain the garments of the divine Judge and his assistants like the juice of grapes that stains the clothes of him that treads the winepress (Is 63:1–6; Lam 1:15; Rev 14:19f; 19:13ff). On that day the moon will turn to blood (Joel 2:31f; Acts 2:20; Rev 6:12).

C. *Blood in the cult or sacrificial system.* Since blood is the bearer of life, and God is the only lord of life, the eating of meat with the blood was forbidden in the Old Testament under pain of exclusion from the community (Gen 9:4; Lev 3:17; 7:26f; 17:10–14; Deut 12:16, 23ff; 15:23; Ezek 18:11). This prohibition was taken and continues to be taken very seriously in judaism, and its observance was accepted as a sign of belonging to the people of the covenant (see SB II 734–9). According to Lev 17:11, God has reserved the blood to himself, but has presented it to his people in another form, namely, as the means of expiation.

The New Testament repealed this prohibition of the eating of flesh with the blood as it did other stipulations of the Old Testament cultic legislation. The profoundly modified view of ↗ life which we owe to New Testament revelation superseded this identification of blood and life, and, in the same way, the statement about what blood is for in Lev 17:11 is surpassed through the atoning death of Christ. Thus, the whole purpose of the prohibition collapsed. Only in the apostolic decree, Acts 15:20–29; 21:25, does it have value as a disciplinary regulation, with the purpose of facilitating the living together of Jewish christians and those converted from paganism; and, in any case, the prohibition of eating flesh with the blood seems to have had hardly any place in practice in the communities founded by Paul.

Blood plays a great part in the *sacrificial liturgy* of the Old Testament. According to Lev 17:11 God, in his mercy, has put into the hands of his people Israel a means of freeing themselves from the guilt of sin. Life is in the blood, and therefore it contains a force which opposes death, a force which has its origin in God. According to God's disposition, therefore, blood produces its effect in the sacrificial liturgy by opposing sin and the forces hostile to salvation in general. It is from this point that we can understand the Old Testament expiation rites. But that blood itself was ever considered as an offering or that the blood of animals was ever considered as a substitute for human blood cannot be proved from the Old Testament.

In the *consecration of persons* (priests) *and things* (altar, sanctuary) daubing with blood had a consecratory significance. It removed the person or thing in question from the sphere of the profane and furnished them with a consecration which brought them into a close relationship with God (Ex 29:15–26; Lev 8; Ezek 43:20–7).

The blood which was sometimes sprinkled, sometimes daubed, on men, the altar, the curtain, or the ark of the covenant on the occasion of a *sacrifice of purification* or *guilt-offering*, as well as on the Day of Atonement, removed the pollution incurred by sin, purified persons, the community, the temple, altar, and land, and established once again the fellowship between God and man which had been destroyed by sin (Lev 4:5; 14:16; Num 19:4).

The *blood of the paschal lamb* (Ex 12:13–27) and perhaps also *the blood of circumcision* in Ex 4:24ff marks out the friends and chosen ones of God and exempts them from the effects of God's anger.

The ritual of the sprinkling of blood on the altar and people on the occasion of the making of the covenant is not quite clear (Ex 24:4–8). At any rate, the covenant came into force in this way and the contracting parties (God and the people) were bound together in fellowship. The blood ritual could, however, be similar to what we find at the conclusion of other contracts in the ancient Near East, a kind of oath-taking ceremony which says in effect: if the covenant is broken, the blood of the guilty party will be shed just as the blood of this animal here. Since the Sinaitic Covenant came into force through blood, Yahweh remembers the 'blood of the covenant' while Israel was in exile and has mercy on his people 'because of the blood of my covenant' (Zech 9:11).

At the time of Christ, judaism understood by the 'blood of the covenant' either the blood shed at the covenant-making on Sinai according to Ex 24:4–8 (Targum Onkelos and Jerusalem Targum *ad loc.*) or the blood of circumcision (pJeb 8:9a, 5). The rabbinical axiom 'without blood no expiation' (Zeb 6a; Joma 5a; Men 93b) implies at least that Jewish theology knows of no expiation without blood-rites, but this maxim probably refers only to expiation by means of a sacrificial rite—meaning that a sacrifice can have expiatory force only when the liturgical action includes the shedding of blood. At any rate, the rabbis know of other means of expiating: intercession, penance, 'chastisement'. This has to be taken into account in the interpretation of Heb 9:22.

In the New Testament only the Epistle to the Hebrews comments on the blood-rites of the Old Testament. The author does not deny that these rites have a deep meaning; they have sanctified such as are defiled 'for the purification of the flesh', that is, they have enabled these to take part in the cult and thus to approach God (9:13), and have 'purified almost everything' (9:22) (↗ Clean and unclean). The Sinaitic Covenant came into force through blood (9:18ff) and the blood of the paschal lamb prevented the entry of 'the Destroyer of the first-born' (11:28). But these rites brought about a purely cultic purity; they did not purify on the moral and existential plane. Sin remained and its power was not broken; on the contrary, these rites even made man's consciousness of sin stronger and showed up the hopelessness of his position, for 'it is impossible that the blood of bulls and goats should take away sins' (10:3f).

The Old Testament knows already of an expiatory death of the just for the salvation of God's people (Is 53; Zech 12:10–14; 2 Macc 7:38; ↗ Sin; ↗ People of God), but it is in the extra-canonical texts that, for the first time, the salvation of Israel is ascribed in particular to *the blood of the martyrs* (4 Macc 17:21f). The New Testament teaches that such *expiatory force can be ascribed only to the ↗ blood of Christ*, and that this is for the benefit of all mankind (Rom 3:25; 5:9; Heb 9:14; 10:19, 29; 13:12; 1 Pet 1:19; 1 Jn 1:7; Rev 1:5).

Bibliography: J. Behm, *TDNT* I, 172–7; SB II, 734–9; *LTK* II², 538–41; O. Schmitz, *Die Opferanschauungen des späteren Judentums und die Opferaussagen des NT*, Tübingen 1910; E. Bischof, *Das Blut im jüdischen Brauch*, Leipzig 1929; C. Vriezen, 'Hizza: Lustration and Consecration', *OTS* 7 (1950), 201–35; L. Morris, 'The Biblical Use of the Term "Blood"', *JTS* 3 (1952), 216–27 and 6 (1955/6), 77–82; T. L. Dewar, 'The Biblical Use of the Term "Blood"', *JTS* 4 (1953), 204–8; L. Moraldi, *Espiazione sacrificale e riti espiatori*, Rome 1956; A. Charbel, 'Virtus sanguinis non expiatoria in sacrificio *šelamîm*', *SP* I (Gembloux 1959), 366–76; J. E. Steinmueller, 'Sacrificial Blood in the Bible', *Bbl* 40 (1959), 556–67; H. Graf Reventlow, '"Sein Blut komme über sein Haupt"', *VT* 10 (1960), 310–27; S. Lyonnet, 'De munere sacrificali sanguinis', *VD* 39 (1961), 18–38; K. Koch, 'Der Spruch "Sein Blut bleibe auf seinem Haupt"', *VT* 12 (1962), 396–416; T. Canaan, 'Das Blut in den Sitten und im Aberglauben der palästinens. Araber', *ZDPV* 79 (1963), 8–23; N. Füglister, *Die Heilsbedeutung des Pascha*, Munich 1963, 77–105; L. Sabourin, 'Nefesh, sang et expiation', *SE* 18 (1966), 25–46.

Josef Scharbert

Blood of Christ

The blood of Christ is frequently (more than thirty times) mentioned in the New Testament. This was not a mere emphasis on the bloody character of Christ's death. Neither was the blood of Christ ever thought of as an entity separate from the person of Christ from which a new 'blood-theory' developed. It is rather a phrase which is used to refer to Christ's death in relation to our salvation, and this in a comprehensive manner. In the background lies the Old Testament idea that ↗ blood is the principle of life and that giving up life works expiation (Lev 17:11) and also that Christ is the 'servant of the Lord' who has given his life for many (Mk 10:45). That this phrase was used before Paul can be proved not only from his account of the institution of the eucharist where he cites from tradition (1 Cor 11:25 = Lk 22:20; Mk 14:20): those passages where Paul mentions the blood of Christ sound rather formal, and may therefore not have been coined by him. Christ through his blood has made propitiation for the sins of man (Rom 3:24f; Rev 1:5), and we being now justified by his blood shall be saved from wrath through him (Rom 5:9); 'in him we have redemption through his blood, the forgiveness of our trespasses' (Eph 1:7). God has reconciled all things through the blood of Christ's cross (Col 1:20). Christ has redeemed us through his blood (1 Pet 1:19; see also 1 Cor 6:11; 7:23); he has redeemed all christians out of every tribe and nation (Rev 5:9), and won for himself the congregation of God (Acts 20:28). Even the heathens who, far from Israel's *politeia* (= state), were once without hope in the world 'have been brought near' (Eph 2:13). This blood cleanses us from all sin (1 Jn 1:7), its force enables all christians to conquer the satanic accuser (Rev 12:11) and the martyrs to complete their martyrdom (Rev 7:14). As the old covenant became operative through blood (Ex 24:8) so the new, eternal covenant, the perfect covenant promised in Jer 31:31f, the new divine dispensation has been founded by Christ's blood (Lk 22:20 = 1 Cor 11:25). This blood is therefore called 'the blood of the [new] covenant' (Mk 14:24; Heb 9:18–22; 10:29; 13:20). What could not be effected by the sacrifices of the Old Testament—the remission of sins, the purification of conscience from the works of death, and the entry into the heavenly sanctuary—this was worked by Christ, the true eternal High Priest, through shedding his own blood (Heb 10). The sanctifying power of this blood is applied in the Supper of the Lord (1 Cor 10:16). Redemption through his blood imposes on the christians the obligation of a renewed way of life (1 Pet 1:13ff; Heb 10:19ff). The idea of Christ's blood working salvation is almost completely absent in the Johannine writings (see 1 Jn 1:7; 2:2; 4:10). John presents Christ's death more as the beginning of his exaltation ('being lifted up': see the double meaning of *hupsōthēnai* = 'exalt', 'lifts up [on the cross]', 3:14; 8:28; 12:32, 34) and of his glory (7:39; 12:16–23; 13:31ff; 17:1–5). When the Baptist refers to Christ as the Lamb that takes away the sins of the world, the word *airei* (= take away) is used (as in 1 Jn 3:5), which means 'carry away' and not 'take upon oneself' or 'shoulder'. Even if he uses the image of the Lamb of God when referring to Christ as the 'servant of the Lord' of Is 53, the evangelist was not necessarily thinking of Christ's death rather than of the whole of his life-work. Neither is there any reference (at least not expressly mentioned) to his death on the cross in 6:53–6 where Jesus offers his own flesh and blood as a food for man which gives eternal life. In 1 Jn 5:6 ('came by water and blood') water and blood in the anti-gnostic polemic only refer to the beginning and the end (Baptism and Death) of Christ's life-work.

Bibliography: H. Windisch, *Hebräerbrief*, 1931², 82–92; C. Spicq, *L'Épître aux Hébreux*, Paris 1953, 271–85; E. Lohse, *Märtyrer und Gottesknecht*, Göttingen 1964²; L. Morris, *JTS* (1952), 216–27 and (1953) 204–08; E. H. Withley,

JTS (1957), 240–55; *RGG* 1^3, 1329; R. Schnackenburg, *The Gospel of St. John*, London 1968; P. Neuenzeit, *Das Herrenmahl*, Munich 1960.

Josef Schmid

Body

A. *In the Old Testament and judaism.* Just as God fashioned Adam's body out of earth and transformed it into a living human being by means of his breath (Gen 2:7), so, in the same way, he co-operates in the formation of each human body (Gen 2:21f; Ps 103:14; 139:13ff; Wis 7:1f). Historical and biological theories and hypotheses of modern science ought not to be inconsistent with these theological statements in the Old Testament, as they exist on different levels. According to the Old Testament, the body returns to dust at death (Gen 3:19; Ps 90:3; 146:4; Job 4:19f; 10:9; Eccles 3:19f; Wis 2:3; cf 1 Sam 17:44), whereas the living spirit returns to God (Ps 146:4; Job 34:14; Eccles 12:7). A life which followed after death was an unfamiliar notion in the Old Testament. Any anxiety about such a life was for the most part left without a second thought in God's hands, or else life after death was lamented as a shadowy existence, as an end or a downfall (↗ Death). It is only more recent texts which refer to a continuation of life after death (↗ Life), and in these texts mention is frequently made of a resurrection, which betokens a 'reanimation of the body' (↗ Resurrection; see Is 25:8; 26:19; Dan 12:1–3; 2 Macc 7:9, 11, 14, 36; Ezek 37:1–14).

The body, in the Old Testament view, is an essential part of man and the vehicle of his personality (Job 14:22; Ps 44:25), and as such also pertains essentially to the true image or likeness of God (↗ Likeness; Gen 1:26f; 9:6). All expressions of human life, including those which are spiritual, are at the same time inevitably 'bodily'.

Such an evaluation of the role of the body has exerted a great influence in the Old Testament over the answers given to many questions about life. With this in mind it becomes easier to understand why happiness and good fortune in this world, and especially good health (Sir 30:14–16), the blessing of many children (Ps 128) and of long life (Prov 3:16; Eccles 9:4) are valued so highly in the world of the Old Testament (↗ Blessing, ↗ Riches). This is also the reason why those phenomena which were later known as self-denial and ascesis were absent in those days. The Old Testament takes a positive view of physical impulses and desires and demands that they should be satisfied (↗ Asceticism). The feelings of affection that each individual had for those related to him—that is, for his family, tribe and race—gained powerful stimuli from this evaluation of the part played by the body. Genealogies were in this case more than mere proofs of birth and descent. Sometimes they offered prospects of happiness and good fortune, at other times they made it easier to accept and understand ill fortune (↗ People of God). The participation of the individual in religious services or in the liturgy was unthinkable without physical attendance (↗ Prayer, ↗ Sacrifice). There was also an important connection between the body and sin. Although sin admittedly does not reside in man's body, but in his ↗ heart (Gen 6:5; Sir 9:9), it is nevertheless committed with the body and leaves its effects behind in the body. Illness and disease were for this reason given a theological rather than a medical explanation, and the merciful God was regarded as the only reliable physician (2 Kings 20:2, 5; Sir 38:9–11). Every time any physical harm was caused to a pious man, the question of theodicy was raised (but see also Is 50:6; 52:13–53:12; ↗ Suffering). Finally, the concern expressed in the Old Testament for a fitting interment of the body (Gen 23 etc; Deut 32:50; Judg 2:9; 1 Kings 2:10), and that there should be no desecration of the dead, must be borne in mind, as these things were of great consequence (Is 14:19f; Jer 8:1ff; 22:19; Ezek 32:23). 'To bury the dead' developed into a very important work of mercy and thereby into a special application of the Old Testament idea of wisdom (Tob 1:17ff; 2:3–9; 4:3f; 12:13; Sir 38:16; 44:14).

It is not until the last period of the Old Testament and in late judaism that a dichotomy or even a trichotomy seems to arise under the influence of various trends, in particular hellenistic and perhaps also Parsee. In 2 Macc and in Wis, the soul can be regarded as a life-spirit dwelling in man, and the body is correspondingly the house of the soul (Wis 8:19f; see also Sir 47:19; Wis 1:4; 2:22f; 3:1f; 4:14f) or even the prison of the soul (Wis 9:15).

In 4 Macc and in Philo of Alexandria, such thoughts are modelled on the lines of Plato and the Platonic school and are brought into harmony with biblical data. In this respect, Gen 6:3 and Job 10:4 had an important part to play. The members of the Qumran Community taught in theory and in practice that the body and its influence were evil and opposed to God and that it stood, as a result of this, in need of discipline and was the cause of constant temptation to man (see also Test Dan 1; Test Gad 4). The Palestinian rabbis, however, attributed wickedness to the evil inclination which dwelt in man's heart (↗ Concupiscence) and thus remained faithful to the ancient inheritance. They seldom regarded the body as inferior and never subscribed to the harsh hellenistic view.

B. *New Testament.* In contrast to the contemporary spirit of judaism, and to that of later theologians, the New Testament never concerns itself with a precise determination of the essence and functions of the body. The Greek word *sōma* (=body) has in the New Testament, besides the meaning of 'corpse' (Mk 15:43ff and parallels; Lk 17:37; Acts 9:40; Jn 19:38; 20:12; Rev 11:8f), that of 'a body visible, tangible and entire' (Mt 5:29f; 6:22; Mk 5:29; 14:8 and parallels; Lk 11:34; Jn 2:21; Rom 1:24; 1 Cor 6:18). It is frequently found in conjunction with *pneuma* (=spirit; Rom 8:10, 13; 1 Cor 5:3; 7:34; Jas 2:26) and with *psukhē* (=soul; Mt 6:25; 10:28; Lk 12:22f) or even in conjunction with both together (1 Thess 5:23). This 'body' is systematically constructed and has organs and members (Mt 5:29f; Rom 12:4f; 1 Cor 12:12, 14–26; Jas 3:6) as well as possessing various physiological functions (Rom 12:1; 1 Cor 6:20; 2 Cor 4:10; Gal 6:17; Phil 1:20), among which Paul, for topical reasons, stresses sexual activity in particular

(Rom 1:24; 4:19; 1 Cor 6:12–20; 7:4).

Because of the controversies of the period, several passages in the New Testament sound an almost dualistic note, especially in those places where the body appears as a garment or as a tabernacle for man (2 Cor 5:1–10; 2 Pet 1:13f; cf 2 Cor 12:2–4; Phil 1:23). Other passages contain suggestions that the body and its functions are inferior (1 Pet 2:11; 2 Pet 2:18; 1 John 2:16) and the ↗ asceticism which was gradually beginning to gain importance and has been accounted for in various ways also played a part in this view. In Paul this comes especially to the fore in his treatment of ↗ marriage, which he designated as a necessary evil (1 Cor 7:1–11). It would, however, be wrong to lift these isolated passages, whose interpretation is the subject of much controversy, out of the whole doctrine of the New Testament, or to infer any exact anthropology from such observations made in passing (↗ Man). The conclusion of the speech on the Areopagus and the negative response of the Greeks to the doctrine of the resurrection gives a clear proof of how consciously the christians of the time would have felt this to be diametrically opposed to the Greek way of thinking (Acts 17:32). It cannot be denied that the concept of the 'body' which is found in the New Testament is equivocal, but it is clear that the origins of this concept are in the Old Testament.

This evaluation which places the soul on a higher plane than the body is not found in the synoptic texts (according to Schmid). The call to conversion, the conclusion that everyone is sinful and thus dependent upon God, and the message that salvation has been conferred upon sinful man, are all applicable to the body also, since the body is nothing else but man himself in one aspect of human existence. Even in Mk 14:38 ('The spirit indeed is willing, but the flesh is weak') it is not a question of the body being more sinful than the soul, but of man himself being prone to weakness. 'The evil in man is not the body, as a kind of inferior ego which somehow drags the superior part down to its level. It is, on the contrary, man's will which is evil. It is man's heart which makes him good or bad and not his body' (Schmid on Mk 7:20–23). The demand is made of the christian that he should have absolute trust in the Father (Mt 6:25–34), follow Jesus without looking back (Lk 9:57–62), and lead a new life of faith and charity (Mk 9:43–8). This demand means that all considerations of physical wellbeing must take second place, whatever the consequences may be (Mk 8:34–8). The early church reiterated this demand in many different forms (see 1 Cor 9:27; 13:3; Phil 1:20).

The teaching of Paul is of especial significance here, as being, in all essential points, a culmination of the teachings of the Old Testament. In Paul the word 'body' expresses the more popular concept already mentioned, but is also used as a precise term for the whole person, the man himself (↗ Man). It would be wrong, in such cases, to place any special emphasis on the use of the word 'body', as though it were only the body which christians present as a living sacrifice (Rom 12:1), the body over which man and wife have reciprocal control (1 Cor 7:4) and in which Christ is to be glorified (Phil 1:20).

The idea of the body as an influence which is hostile to God and prone to sin (↗ Flesh) is also found in Paul (see Rom 6:6 and 8:3), in particular where he refers to the body of unredeemed man (Rom 7:14–24). Such a man's deeds (Rom 8:13) and desires (Rom 6:12) are bad, since man himself, and not only his body, comes under the influence of the flesh, which is hostile to God and prone to sin. The language which Paul uses in many cases also serves the purpose of determining the existence of the christian between the infinitive of salvation itself and the imperative of the working out of his salvation. The body of the christian remains weak and is never proof against temptation. The christian's heart is, in other words, inclined towards evil (1 Cor 2:14; 2 Cor 4:7–18; 12:7–10; 1 Thess 5:23). That is why the christian must subject himself voluntarily, or be subjected against his will, to sacrifice (1 Cor 9:27; Gal 6:17; see also 1 Cor 13:3).

Paul draws a distinction between the body on this earth and the body after the resurrection. Elsewhere his ideas of the body and the flesh merge into one another, but here the distinction is precise. The flesh is the old man who will perish (see Gal 5:24; Col 3:9f) by virtue of the grace of ↗ baptism (Rom 8:9f), and finally pass away for ever at the ↗ resurrection (1 Cor 15:50). Christians must, however, possess the body in sanctification and honour (1 Thess 4:4; 1 Cor 6:13), since baptism has made it a temple of the Holy Ghost (1 Cor 3:16f; 6:19). At the resurrection of the dead it will be completely transformed and made into a 'heavenly body' (1 Cor 15:44–9), refashioned by the glory of God (Phil 3:21; see also 2 Cor 3:18) on the model and in the power of the reanimated and glorified body of Jesus (Col 1:18; cf Acts 3:15; 5:31; 26:23; Rev 1:5).

The New Testament contains several different references to the body of Jesus and to the reality of his incarnation (Rom 8:3; Phil 2:7; Col 1:22; Eph 2:15; 1 Tim 3:16; and especially Jn 1:13; 1 Jn 4:2; 2 Jn 7), in particular in connection with his vicarious death (Mk 15:43–5 and parallels; Mt 26:12; Jn 19:38ff; Rom 7:4; Heb 10:5, 10; 1 Pet 2:24), the resurrection (Lk 24:3, 23; Jn 20:12; see also Jn 2:21) and the Last Supper (↗ Eucharist; Mk 14:22 and parallels; 1 Cor 10:16; 11:24, 27, 29). In the figurative sense the christian community is characterised as the body of Christ (↗ Church).

Bibliography: ↗ Concupiscence, ↗ Death, ↗ Flesh, ↗ Life, ↗ Man.—Bultmann I, 192–203; Jacob, Mehl, and Koehnlein, Allmen 247–53; J. Schmid, *LTK* I², 603–15; Schweitzer, Baumgärtel, and Meyer, *TWNT* VII, 98–151 (with bibliography); W. G. Kümmel, *Das Bild des Menschen im NT*, Zurich 1948; W. Eichrodt, *Das Menschverständnis des AT*, Basle 1951²; J. A. T. Robinson, *The Body*, London 1952; J. Jerwell, *Imago Dei*, Göttingen 1960 (with bibliography). See also: E. Dhorme, *L'emploi métaphorique des noms de corps en hébreu et en akkadien*, Paris 1923; E. Käsemann, *Leib und Leib Christi*, Tübingen 1933; W. Gutbrod, *Die paulinische Anthropologie*, Stuttgart and Berlin 1934; W. L. Knox, 'Parallels to the NT use of *sōma*', *JTS* 39 (1938), 243–6; O. Kuss, 'Das Fleisch', *Der Römerbrief* II, Regensburg 1959, 506–40.

Wilhelm Pesch

Book

The idea that there are heavenly books was widespread and is of theological importance. In this connection it is possible to divide such books into three types: a. the so-called 'Book of Destiny'; b. 'books of judgement', in which men's works as well as their sins are recorded; and c. the 'Book of Life'.

a. According to the Babylonian view, 'tablets of destiny' were already in existence at the time of creation. Acting on the instructions of Marduk, in whose power destiny lies, Nebo noted down before all else the destinies of men. 'Records of human destiny' are to be found in Egypt, and are not unknown even in the Greco-Roman world (an Athenian epitaph refers to the Fates as writers, *CIG* 3, 2, 1337; see also Ovid, *Metam.* 15, 809ff; Martial 10, 44, 5f; etc).

The notion of a book of fate is met with here and there in the biblical and apocryphal writings (↗ Predestination): 'Thy eyes beheld my unformed substance; in thy book were written, every one of them, the days that were formed for me' (Ps 139:16).

In Jude 4 and similarly in Enoch 106:19; 108:7, evil-doers already have sentence passed on them by virtue of God's fore-knowledge, and this is set down in writing. The book with the seven seals may also possibly belong here (Rev 5:1ff). In this book are contained God's hidden decrees and judgements which powerfully determine the destinies of men and penetrate to the very end of history: see 1 QH 1, 23f: 'Everything is engraved for you with the stylus of memory for the duration of all time'—that is to say, engraved on heavenly tablets. (See also SB II, 173–6).

b. In Egypt the works of men were recorded for the judgement of souls by the God Thoth. In the Old Testament it is in Dan 7:10 that reference to such books of judgement is found, see Is 65:6; Jer 22:30, or Mal 3:16 and CD 20, 19, where a 'note-book' is referred to. In Bar (Syr) 24, 1, the writer recognises that sins are recorded in this book, and this idea is taken for granted when the suppliant prays for his sins to be rubbed out (as in Ps 51:1, 9 etc). The prayer *Abinu Malkenu*, which was used by Rabbi Akiba, contains the petition: 'In thy great mercy obliterate all [written] records of our debts', and the *kheirographōn* (=handwriting) of Col 2:14 can also be understood in this light as a setting down in writing of our sins. In Rev 20:12, 'the books [are] opened' and the dead are judged 'according to their works' (see also Rev 14:13; Ps 56:8) and these works are recorded in the books. (But note that the dead are also judged according to their good works and not only according to their sins—in this the spirit of the New Testament is discernible.)

c. A 'Book of Life' is referred to only in biblical writings. The first mention is in Ex 32:32f, in which Moses offers the Lord his life for his people (as Paul does later, Rom 9:3), and God replies that he will erase only the name of the sinner from this book. For the 'blotting out' of the name of the evildoer from the 'Book of Life', see also Ps 69:28, Rev 3:5 and Enoch 108, 3. Further references are found in Ps 56:8; 87:6; 139:16; Is 4:3; 56:5; Ezek 13:9; Dan 12:1; Lk 10:20; Phil 4:3; Heb 12:23; and especially Rev 3:5; 13:8; 17:8; 20:12, 15; 21:27 and the many texts in the apocryphal books, such as Enoch 47:3; 104:1; Jub 19:9, etc. The 'Book of Life' does not appear in the Dead Sea texts.

A similar idea emerges from the 'bundle of the living' found in 1 Sam 25:29; 1 QH 2:20. A. Marmorstein (*ZAW* 43 [1925], 119–24) is inclined to think of this as a magic spell, but it is possible to draw a parallel between this and the 'Book of Life', and to regard *tsᵉrôr* (= bundle) as the linen or leather outer cover in which the book, that is to say, the scroll, is placed, bound with cords and possibly even sealed (see also Job 14:17). ↗ Assurance of salvation, ↗ Seal. Eissfeldt shows, with reference to the Nuzi texts, that a herd of cattle was counted and a tally made by putting pebbles into a bag.

Bibliography: G. Schrenk, *TDNT* 1, 615–20; L. Koep, 'Das himmlische Buch in Antike und Christentum', *Theophaneia* 8 (1952); L. Koep, *RAC* 2, 725–31; J. Leipoldt and S. Morenz, *Heilige Schriften*, Leipzig 1953; G. Rinaldi, *Bbl* 40 (1959), 282ff; O. Eissfeldt, 'Der Beutel der Lebendigen', *Verh. Sächs. Akad. Phil. Hist.* 105/6 (Berlin 1960); T. Holtz, 'Die Christologie der Apokalypse des Johannes', *TU* 85 (Berlin 1962), 31–6.

Johannes B. Bauer

Brethren of Jesus

Brothers and sisters of Jesus are referred to in the New Testament (Jn 2:12; Mk 3:31–5; Mt 12:26–50; Lk 8:19–21; Mk 6:3; Mt 13:55f; Jn 7:3–5, 9f; Acts 1:14; Gal 1:19; 1 Cor 9:5). Four brothers are mentioned, in fact, and their names are given as James, Joses (a form existing side by side with Joseph, see Mt 13:55), Judas, and Simon. We are not told the number or the names of Jesus' sisters, though we may infer from Mt 13:56, where 'all his sisters' are referred to, that there are at least three.

It is of some importance to examine the word *adelphos* (= brother) and ascertain the full extent of its meaning, in order to establish the precise degree of relationship in which these 'brethren' stood to Jesus. In Greek the word is generally used to denote one's full brother or at least one's half-brother. There are, however, many exceptions to this (Marcus Aurelius, 1, 14, 1, as well as numerous Egyptian papyrus texts). In LXX, too, first cousins and even second, third, and more distant cousins are referred to as 'brothers' and 'sisters'. LXX arrived at this extension of the original meaning of the Greek word as a consequence of the lack of any native Hebrew or Aramaic word for 'cousin'. In these languages, 'cousin' is simply known as 'brother' (ʾāḥ) in order to avoid more lengthy circumlocutions. The carelessness of the writers of the New Testament in the use of the Greek word *adelphos* can be explained on the one hand by this usage in LXX and on the other hand by the fact that they are themselves Semites and do not correct the inexactitudes of their native language even in the Greek version, although they would have had the chance to do so here, by using the word *anepsios* (= cousin). An analogous case is found in Latin, where the very precise terms *avunculus/patruus* and *amita/matertera* clearly differentiate between uncles and aunts as, on the one hand, brothers or sisters of the father and, on the other, as brothers or sisters of the mother: this precision of meaning was lost in the Romance languages, in which the words *patruus* and *matertera* failed to survive.

The following evidence shows that the term 'brother' must have had this wider meaning in the New Testament passages under question. Two of Jesus' brethren were certainly sons of a Mary different from Mary the mother of Jesus. According to Mk 15:40 (see Mt 27:56), 'Mary the mother of James the younger and of Joses' was at Golgotha beside Mary Magdalen, Salome, and the other women. The evangelist has hitherto not named this Mary, although he has already (Mk 6:3) introduced her sons as the Lord's brethren, and the unusual form of the name Joses (for Joseph) in both places proves that Mark has the same brothers in mind in 15:40. Mark calls this Mary in 16:1 (see Lk 24:10) simply 'Mary, the mother of James', whereas Matthew in both instances refers to 'the other Mary' (27:61; 28:1). The mother of Jesus is named as 'his mother' in addition to the above, once in Mk (3:31), eight times in Matthew and John, five times in Luke, and once in Acts.

Similarly, Jesus' act, when he was at the point of death, of giving his mother into the beloved disciple's keeping, must remain inexplicable if Jesus had had brothers or sisters. It emerges clearly from the emphatic use of the article in the designation of Jesus as '*the* son of Mary' (Mk 6:3) that he is Mary's only child, and this is borne out by the fact that Jesus is named as the son of Mary and Joseph (Lk 3:23) and that in the whole of the New Testament sons, daughters, or children of Mary or Joseph never appear. Furthermore, according to Lk 2:7, Jesus was Mary's firstborn. According to Lk 2:41–52, Mary takes part in the pilgrimage to Jerusalem at the time of the Passover, and this would be difficult to understand if she had left little children at home for the fourteen days of the pilgrimage. If Mary had had other children after this pilgrimage, these would not have reached the age of twenty by the time Jesus began his public life and would never have been able to behave towards their elder brother in such a free and easy manner as is outlined in Mk 3:21, 31–5 and Jn 7:2–5, in which texts they appear to treat him almost as a guardian treats his ward.

What emerges from all this is that Mary had no other children apart from Jesus.

This fact is not contradicted by the naming of Jesus in Lk 2:7 as the 'firstborn', as every firstborn child bore this title in the Jewish world, whether succeeded by other brothers or sisters or not (Ex 13:2; Num 3:12). It is probable, moreover, that Luke used this expression to emphasise the ↗ virgin birth, and certainly not to contrast Jesus with any other children Mary might have had later (see W. Michaelis, *TWNT* VI, 877, 14ff). Again, we cannot understand Mt 1:25 to mean that Joseph lived a normal married life with Mary after the birth of Jesus, for the translation (RSV and others): 'but [he] knew her not until she had borne a son', is philologically wrong. The true meaning of this passage must be: 'but although he knew her not, behold, nonetheless she bore him a son' (on this point, and on the general tendency of Mt, see M. Krämer, *Bbl* 45 [1964], 1–50).

Any attempt at a more accurate definition of the various degrees of relationship is bound to fail because of the paucity of information given by the New Testament and ancient tradition. It is possible to regard the Lord's brothers as cousins (Blinzler), yet the possibility must also remain that they were Joseph's sons as a result of a previous marriage (Stauffer). This view is supported by the fact that in the oldest christian tradition they are never given the name of 'nephews' (*anepsioi*)—it is even possible that the phrase 'Lord's brother' may very well have been used as a mark of distinction—and that whenever they appear it is almost always in close association with Mary (see Mk 3:31ff; the family list in Mk 6:3; Jn 2:12; Acts 1:14), and finally that the position of authority over Jesus to which they presume as older half-brothers can thus quite easily be justified.

Bibliography: Abundant material and a detailed bibliography in J. Blinzler, 'Simon der Apostel, Simon der Herrenbruder, und Bischof Symeon von Jerusalem', *Passauer Studien (Festschrift Bischof Simon Landersdorfer)* 1953, 25–55; J. Blinzler, 'Zum Problem der Brüder des Herrn', *TTZ* 67 (1958), 129–45 and 224–46; J. Blinzler, *LTK* II², 714–17 and *Lexikon der Marienkunde*, pts 5 and 6, Regensburg 1960, 959–69; E. Stauffer, 'Begegnung der Christen', *Festschrift Otto Karrer*, Frankfurt 1960², 367f (esp. *n* 46).

Johannes B. Bauer

Brother

A. The Hebrew word *ʾāḥ* means in the first place 'brother', but it is also used for other male relatives, like its Akkadian and Ugaritic equivalents. The Greek word *adelphos*, used to translate *ʾaḥ*, has sometimes, under the influence of the more flexible Semitic usage, acquired the wider meaning of this latter, although etymologically it means 'son of the same mother' (*a*-copulative; *delphus* = womb).

In the Old Testament, 'brother' is the word used for those who are of the same race (Lev 10:4; Deut 15:3, 12 etc). Especially in Lev 19:18 (↗ Neighbour) it is contrasted with the alien who happens to live in the land (*gêr*, Deut 1:16) and foreigners just passing through (*nākrî*, Deut 15:3).

For the rest *ʾāḥ* divides up the field of meaning in relationship with *rēᶜa* (↗ Neighbour A), extending not only to fellow countryman but even further, eg, friend (2 Sam 1:26; Prov 17:17), colleague (2 Chron 31:15; Ezra 3:8; 6:20 etc), one who shares the same ideas or the same fate (Gen 49:5; Job 30:29; Prov 18:9) or just any other person at all (see Jer 9:4; Ps 49:7; Ezek 4:17; etc). While in the later history of Israel only *rēᶜa* is used in the wider sense, *ʾāḥ*, on the other hand, is used in the strict sense (or is even further narrowed down, as with the members of the Qumran sect, who called themselves 'brothers'). The common brotherhood of Israelites is founded in their father Abraham (Jn 8:39) who was 'called' by God. Thus brother has a double meaning: 'fellow countryman' and 'fellow believer'; and the double commandment of love—of God and of the neighbour, that is, the brother—has its correspondents in the worshipping community and the civic community. The whole history of Israel is played out within these two concentric circles. Brotherhood in Israel is confined by nation and worship; in the New Testament, however, brotherhood is limited but is at the same time universal.

B. The distinction in the later period of Israel's history between a civic and religious community became fully manifest in the New Testament: 'Do not presume to say to yourselves, "We have Abraham as our father"; for I tell you, God is able from these stones to raise up children to Abraham' (Mt 3:9). Instead of a brotherhood based on *natural birth* there appears one which has its origin in a *rebirth*. Natural brotherhood had, literally, received its death-blow in the history of Cain and Abel; true brotherly love is therefore a sure sign that we are children of God (1 Jn 3:11ff). The brotherhood founded in Jesus Christ is the fulfilment and completion of that founded in Abraham; the true sons of Abraham are those who believe in Christ (Gal 3:7, 29; Rom 4:11f). The beginnings of this usage can already be found in the synoptic tradition, as Mk 3:31–5 shows. In Mk 10:30, the 'brothers and sisters and mothers' clearly refers to the christian brotherhood of the community. The distinction in Acts 14:2 is unmistakable: 'Jews . . . Gentiles . . . brethren'. This true brotherhood, however, was not founded and made possible by Christ's teaching and example, but only by his atoning death (Eph 2:11–18).

This christian brotherhood, therefore, does not come about as the result of an idealist theory of unity among men of good will nor just through the imitation of Christ's example, but through membership of a visible redeemed community. Christ is the first cause and the last end of this brotherhood; but its essence and its outward manifestation are ↗ love, for it is by our love for the brethren that we know we are reborn (1 Pet 1:22ff). This love unites the brother not to another man but to God. The adjective most frequently attached to *adelphos* is *agapētos* or *ēgapēmenos* (=beloved), which is further defined in 1 Thess 1:4 as 'brethren beloved by God'.

We must bear with the weakness of our brethren (Rom 15:1) if we are not to sin against Christ (1 Cor 8:12). There are, however, limits, and the division can run through the visible community: there are false brethren (Gal 2:4; 2 Cor 11:26) and brethren only in name (1 Cor 5:11). Brotherhood is the privilege of those who are reborn, to such an extent that it does not necessarily apply to all the organised community, not even to all the Twelve (Jn 6:70).

Characteristics of the brotherhood. The brotherhood is never impersonal; it is always realised in some concrete form. It is a personal fellowship with the brethren in Christ; it flourishes wherever visible and tangible relations with the brethren are possible (Acts 28:15); it is life in communion with the children of God (the daily assembly of the faithful). This brotherhood is universal and yet circumscribed in time and place—the unity of the church as the body of Christ, the mystery of unity in diversity and diversity in unity (Groenewald). Scherffig is of the opinion that brotherhood is not to be identified with just unity of mind and spirit since it is founded in Christ only, that it does not depend on the extent to which it has been put into practice, and that it is not a community based on tradition and confined within the limits of a certain creed ('that which can have its origin only in Christ would be mistaken for the acceptance of specific theological propositions'). But reading Mt 18:15–17; Tit 3:10ff; 2 Tim 2:25ff, we are led to the conclusion that this view can be accepted only with the strongest reservations. There are 'false teachers' among the brethren according to 2 Pet 2:1, and if there are brethren in the visible community of God who are not true brothers the question arises whether, according to the New Testament, true brotherhood could be realised outside the church. This question in all its implications was never actually dealt with in the New Testament, any more than were the questions of schism and heresy (see M. Meinertz, *BZ* [1957], 114–8).

The relationship between 'brother' and 'neighbour' is almost like that of two circles, a smaller enclosed in a larger. The 'neighbour', as is clear from the parable of the Good Samaritan (↗ Neighbour B), is not only our brother in faith but anyone whom we 'assist' or help because we happen to be on the spot. Paul speaks of the smaller circle (Gal 6:10), and 2 Pet 1:7 (see also 1 Thess 3:12) shows clearly that love of the brotherhood (*philadelphia*) is a special and privileged form of love (*agapē*) in general (see Spicq).

Bibliography: H. von Soden, *TDNT* I, 144–6; F. Zorell, *Lexikon hebraicum*, 29f; W. Bauer, *A Greek–English Lexikon of the NT and other Early Christian Literature*, ed. W. F. Arndt and F. W. Gingrich, Cambridge and Chicago 1957; Bartelink, 75f; D. J. Georgacas, *Glotta* 36 (1957), 106–8 (etymology); K. H. Schelkle, *RAC* II, 631–40; W. Scherffig, *ET* 9 (1949/50), 49–65; E. P. Groenewald, 'Die christelike Broederskap volgens die Heilige Skrif', *Arcana Revelata*, Kampen 1951, 23–32; C. Spicq, 'La charité fraternelle selon 1 Thess 4:9', *Festschrift A. Robert*, Paris 1957, 507–11; H. Schürmann, *Gemeinde als Bruderschaft im Lichte des NT, Diaspora, Gabe, und Ausgabe*, Paderborn 1955, 21–31; J. Ratzinger, *Christian Brotherhood*, London and New York 1966; A. Andrewes, 'Phratries in Homer', *Hermes* 89 (1961), 129–40; C. Brady, *Brotherly Love: A Study of the Word 'Philadelphia' and its Contribution to the Biblical Theology of Brotherly Love*, Fribourg 1961 (dissertation); J. Gonda, *Mnemosyne* 15 (1962), 290ff; B. Lifshitz, *Aegyptus* 42 (1962), 241–56.

Johannes B. Bauer

Building up

The Greek word under consideration here is *oikodomein*, the Hebrew *bānâh*. In secular writing, besides its obvious literal meaning of 'build',' construct' (walls, houses, temples, etc), the word often has a figurative sense: eg, Cicero, *De Orat.* III, 152: 'quid ipse aedificet orator, . . . id esse nobis quaerendum atque explicandum' ('the question we have to ask and answer is: What does the orator "construct"?'); Seneca, *Ep.* 88, 23: 'mathematica . . . in alieno aedificat' ('mathematics "builds" on other things'); Xenophon, *Kyrop.* VIII, 7, 15: '*epi tauta euthus oikodomeite alla philika erga*' ('on these friendly actions at once "build" more'). (Further examples can be found in Vielhauer, *Oikodome*, 25f; Schelkle, *RAC* I, 1265f.)

In the *Old Testament*, God himself 'built' Eve out of Adam's rib (Gen 2:22); the restless fugitive Cain built a city in order to have a settled abode (Gen 4:17); Noah built an altar of sacrifice (Gen 8:20) for the worship of God, and similarly Solomon built his splendid temple (1 Kings 6:1–6). He built a throne-room for himself, in which he sat to pronounce judgement (1 Kings 7:7), and a palace or house for his wife (7:8). Later, unfortunately, he also built places of sacrifice for the idols Chemosh and Molech (1 Kings 11:7). Ahab built a Temple of Baal in Samaria (1 Kings 16:32) and allowed Jericho to be rebuilt (16:34). While still in captivity, Tobit blessed those who were to rebuild the destroyed city of Jerusalem, and even dreamed that the gates of the city would be built of sapphire and emerald (Tob 13:16). This splendid vision is mentioned again in the description of the heavenly Jerusalem (Rev 21:19ff; see also Is 54:11f).

God gives 'commissions to build', in the best sense of the word, to many prophets, and one of the most noteworthy of these is Jeremiah, whose task is first and foremost to uproot and pull down, but then to build up and plant again (Jer 1:10; Sir 49:7).

A difficult problem is always raised when sinful men wish to erect a shrine to the infinite God; hence the question which Yahweh puts to the Jews in Is 66:1f: 'Heaven is my throne, and the earth is my footstool; What is the house which you would build for me, . . . But this is the man to whom I will look, he that is contrite and humble in spirit'. The builder is also often Yahweh himself. According to Jer 33:7, he will build up the house of Israel again, and in Jer 31:4, the 'virgin' of Israel. The ruined tabernacle of David (Amos 9:11) and the shrine on Mount Sion (Ps 102:16) are also to be reconstructed. In all this God does not, however, dispense with the cooperation of man. When the Jews spent their time exclusively on the reconstruction of their own houses after their return from the Babylonian captivity, God had to send bad harvests and drought to compel them eventually to set about the rebuilding of the temple (see Hag 1:2–15). Even the 'wicked neighbouring peoples' were incorporated into this work of reconstruction—that is to say, they were able to share in the benefits of salvation, provided that they were converted to the worship of the true God (see Jer 12:14ff). God spoke, through Jeremiah, to the disheartened Jewish warriors who were afraid of the vengeance of Babylon and wished to flee: 'If you will remain in this land, then I will build you up and not pull you down; I will plant you, and not pluck you up' (Jer 42:10). God also comforted the Jews in their Babylonian captivity with the assurance that their homeland that had been laid waste would one day again be made as beautiful as the Garden of Eden (Ezek 36:35), and went on to promise them: 'The nations that are left round about you shall know that I, the Lord, have rebuilt the ruined places and replanted that which was desolate'. Wisdom, which can be interpreted as divine wisdom, has also built a house for herself and repeatedly invites men to her banquet (Prov 9:1ff). A perfectly ideal transition to the New Testament and the spiritual rebuilding of the temple by the Messiah (see Jn 2:19) is to be found in Zech 6:12: 'Behold the man whose name is the Branch [LXX: *anatolē* =rise, rising]: for he shall grow up in his place, and he shall build the Temple of the Lord'.

In the *Rabbinical writings*, the image of 'building' also occurs quite frequently. Here it is God who is the master-builder of the world (see SB 1, 732). The 'architect's plan' from which he constructs his edifice is often the

Torah (SB II, 357: 'Who advised him when he created the world? It was only the Torah that he consulted)'. The pupils of the Hebrew scholars or rabbis are occasionally named as builders (SB I, 876; III, 379), since, by studying the Torah (b. Schabb. 144a) they build the world and add to the peace of the world (see Ber 64a, with reference to Is 54:13). A similar comparison made by Elisha ben Abuja automatically calls to mind the conclusion of the Sermon on the Mount: 'A man who has performed many good works and has learnt much of the Torah, with whom can he be compared? With a man who ... builds with stones and then with bricks' (SB I, 469). In one midrash it is expected that the heavenly city will be completely rebuilt in the last days for the coming of the Messiah: 'Then Jerusalem, perfectly rebuilt, will come down from heaven with 72 pearls which will gleam from one end of the world to the other' (SB III, 796). In 4 Esdras 10:27, too, there is a vision of the rebuilt Jerusalem which aims to console the Jews of AD 70 and later.

There is an interesting example of the figurative use of the word under consideration in Ber 63a (Goldschmidt, I, 286f). In the passage in question, the high priest has been reviling two scribes and accusing them of lying, after having bestowed high praise on them only a short while before. Their reply to him is: 'Thou hast already built up and canst not pull down again. Thou has already fenced in and canst no more break through that fence.'

According to Philo, *Leg. Alleg.* II, 3, 6, the heart of a man is created first and the rest of the human body is built on the heart (*oikodomeitai to allo sōma* = the rest of the body is built [on it]), just as a ship is built up on the keel. Implanting virtues in the soul and building them up is, of course, a concern of God himself: *prepei tōi theōi phuteuein kai oikodomein en psukhēi tas aretas* ('it belongs to God to implant and build up virtues in the soul'; *Leg. Alleg.* I, 15, 48). Philo, the philosopher, must naturally regret the way fools build their doctrine without foundation, like a tower: *dogma adokimon oikodomountes eis hupsos hoia purgon* ('building bad doctrine up on high like a tower'; *De Somn.* II, 284)—a tower which God is bound to destroy as he once destroyed the Tower of Babel. (Further references in *TDNT* V, 137f and in H. Leisegang, *Philo-Index*.)

The idea of a building or construction, the foundation of a wall, a tower, and so on, which stand for God's protection and powerful aid, is found in the Qumran texts and denotes both the entire community and the individual pious man. One example of this usage is: 'Thou settest me up as a strong tower, as a lofty wall; thou placest my building firmly on a rock and givest me eternal foundations' (1 QH VIII, 8f). In QH VII, 4, the fear of wicked men is clearly expressed by the author of the hymn: 'The foundations of my building [ie, body] are breaking to pieces, my frame is collapsing, my innermost heart is pitching and tossing like a ship in a raging storm'. The Community Rule of the Dead Sea sect has this to say with regard to the approaching judgement: 'Then, with his truth, God will sift and examine all the works of man and clear out his building [ie, body], so as to drive all evil spirits out of his flesh (1 QS IV, 20). In the Damascus text which follows, it is not certain whether the word 'house' refers to the Temple or perhaps to the community of the faithful (by analogy with Enoch 53:6; 89:36; 1 Tim 3:15; Heb 3:6; 1 Pet 4:17): 'He built them a safe house in Israel, like none other than has ever existed from times of old until the present' (CD III, 19). In QS VIII, the latter is certainly the case, for the 'men of the community' are described as 'a holy house for Israel and a dwelling of the Most Holy One for Aaron'. In the fragment of a commentary on Ps 37, the teacher (is this the Teacher of Righteousness?) has been appointed by God to build a community for him (4 Qp Ps 37, II, 16). (For these passages and further examples of the same kind, reference can be made to G. Vermes, *The Dead Sea Scrolls in English*, London 1962.)

The well known phrase 'builder of walls' (*bōnê haḥayits*) has no commendatory connotation but is, on the contrary, equated in CD VIII 2 with house-painters who cover all (moral) damage with a coat of limewash (see also Ezek 13:10). The name is applied to those half-hearted and impenitent members of the chosen people who are hated by God (CD VIII, 18). According to Nötscher 57, the word refers to the adherents of the preacher of lies and probably to the Pharisees as well, who, acting against God's express command (Gen 1:27; 2:24), permitted polygamy (see *CD* IV, 19ff). A. S. van der Woude, among others, is of the opinion that the word refers to the Pharisees (*Die messianische Vorstellungen der Gemeinde von Qumran*, Assen 1957, 240). The bitter allusion to Mic 7:11: 'The wall is built, but the law is remote. In all these years Belial will be let loose against Israel' (CD III, 12), confirms the unfavourable meaning mentioned above.

In the *New Testament*, the word 'build' is mainly used in its literal sense. A man builds a house (Mt 7:24 and parallels) or a tower (Mk 12:1 and parallels) in order to have a better view over his vineyard, although the expenditure must be carefully calculated in advance (Lk 14:28). The stupid farmer wishes to build new and bigger barns (Lk 12:18), the Jews build tombs and memorials for the prophets (Lk 11:47), and the centurion, who was a gentile, even built a synagogue (Lk 7:5). There are many other examples. Buying and selling, planting and building, have formed an essential part of the ordinary language of human civilisation since the time of Lot (see Lk 17:28).

Those who build, or, in the figurative sense, 'edify', include God himself (Acts 20:32); Christ (Mt 16:18); the apostles, acting in Christ's name and receiving their commission from him (Rom 15:20), and—among the apostles —especially Paul (1 Cor 3:10, 12; 2 Cor 10:8; 13:10); many men who have been liberally endowed with grace (1 Cor 14:3–5); and, finally, every christian (Rom 15:2), either by his kind words of comfort (1 Thess 5:11; Eph 4:29) or else by foregoing some pleasure, which is in itself permitted, for his 'weaker' brother's sake (1 Cor 8:1; 10:23). Above all, fitting communal worship contributes a great deal to the edification of those who take part in it (1 Cor 14:26). The use of 'build up', in Gal 2:18, is completely out of place in this connection, as it refers to the old law and the 'wall of partition' which Christ fortunately did away with. It is in this instance 'quite unusual and not at all characteristic' of Paul (Vielhauer, 89).

If there are many different builders, there can be many different buildings too: a. The basis of our redemption and our faith must always be the Easter event, when *Christ's dead body*, the temple 'not made with hands', was 'built up' again 'in three days' (Mk 14:28: *oikodomēsō* ['I will build'] = Jn 2:19 *egerō* ['I will wake up, raise up']). b. Furthermore, the church was built on the rock of Peter (Mt 16:18), and this did not come about by an 'eschatological act on the part of Christ' on the Lord's day, as O. Michel (*TDNT* v, 139, 5f and 12f) seems to regard as possible. This building of the church is, on the contrary, clearly an immediate consequence of the resurrection of Jesus. The same Peter was solemnly entrusted with the duty of feeding Christ's entire flock only a short time after the resurrection (Jn 21:15ff). Despite the controversy surrounding the authorship of Chap. 21, R. Bultmann (*Johannes-Evangelium*, 1964, 552) maintains along with others that these three verses are derived from ancient tradition, since the risen Christ must somehow or other have adopted a definite attitude towards Peter's 'fall', as ultimately he had to keep his solemn promise to build his church on the rock of Peter. Vielhauer (76) calls the passage in Mt 16:18 an 'erratic block', by which he means that this is the only place in the New Testament in which Christ is named as a builder of the community. But it is permissible, in this connection to ask, with Karl Barth (716), who would then have built the church other than the one whom the church always calls her 'Lord'. After many setbacks, such as the death of Stephen, for example, a new era of peaceful 'construction' or 'edification' dawned when Paul, now converted to christianity, had left Palestine (Acts 9:31).

Paul brings a new vision and fresh points of interest to bear on the character of this mysterious building up of the church. It is built up on the foundation of the apostles and the New Testament prophets, and its cornerstone is Jesus Christ (Eph 2:20), who had already described himself as such in Ps 118:22f (Mk 12:10 and parallels). It stands to reason that the gentiles and the heathen who had recently been converted are incorporated into this building (Eph 2:22). But just as the ancient temples and, in the course of time, also the Gothic cathedrals of a later age, were in constant need of 'building', that is, of restoration and preservation (see A. Deissmann, *Paul: A Study in Social and Religious History*, New York 1957[2], 212), so also was the church itself. Indeed, the structure 'grows into a holy temple in the Lord' (Eph 2:21) and 'upbuilds itself in love' (Eph 4:16), since it is not a dead body but—in a mysterious way—the living body of Christ (Col 1:18, 24; Eph 1:22). 'It is precisely this complex picture of the "growing edifice" which does full justice to the historical character of the church in all its many aspects' (V. Warnach, *Die Kirche im Epheserbrief*, 1949, 34). The ↗ head of this body is Christ (Eph 4:16; Col 1:18). The baptised, however, are the 'body of Christ' (1 Cor 12:27), or the 'members of his body' (Eph 5:30). Everyone, including the apostles, the prophets, and the evangelists, must assist in the 'edification' of this body of Christ (Eph 4:12), until the time when perfect unity in faith—'the measure of the stature of the fullness of Christ' (Eph 4:13)—is attained.

H. Schlier claims that 'this intermingling of body and building is also a kind of gnostic building-allegory' (*Der Brief an die Epheser*, 1963, 143). Today there are other catholic exegetes, too, who regard it as quite possible that Paul was influenced by (prechristian) gnosticism at least as far as the precise wording and linguistic imagery of his thought was concerned (see Pfammatter, 107–14). However, this double image of body and building can be clearly traced back to Christ himself. Mention has already been made of the fact that Christ refers to himself as the cornerstone which the builders (ie, the powers-that-be in Israel) have rejected (Mt 21:42 and parallels). Jn 2:21 would seem to be decisive in this respect: 'But he spoke of the temple of his body'. This must certainly have been familiar to the oldest synoptic tradition (on this see A. Wikenhauser, *Johannes-Evangelium*, 1957, 81). In this connection, too, 1 Pet 2:5 invites christians to be 'like living stones . . . built into a spiritual house'. Paul, needless to say, is concerned not only with the church as a whole, but also with the 'edification' of each individual community, as, for example, the church at Corinth (2 Cor 12:19). Out of loyalty, he certainly does not wish to build up on foundations laid by others (Rom 15:20), despite the constant appeal that a preaching mission to the christians in Rome must have had for him, anxious as he was to evangelise the populations of the great cities (Rom 1:13ff).

One last question remains to be answered: c. Is it possible, in accordance with New Testament teaching, for the individual christian as such to be 'edified', or is edification intended only for the christian community as a whole? Karl Barth (*Church Dogmatics* IV/2, Edinburgh 1958, sections 67f) comes down very strongly in support of the latter thesis, but F. Niebergall takes the opposite view and claims (*RGG* II [1928], 213): 'The first and foremost aim is not the edification of the christian community as a whole, but . . . of the individual in his christian life.' Both these views are onesided and fail to take all the scriptural data into consideration. If a christian who has the gift of tongues (which, after all, is meant to be a means of religious stimulation and advancement for all) 'edifies himself' only (1 Cor 14:4), then that is a result which the apostle certainly represents as of small account. Apart, however, from worship in common, the christian is recommended to 'build [himself] up' by prayer (Jude 20). This is made explicit in 1 Thess 5:11: 'Therefore encourage one another [*allēlous*] and build one another [*heis ton hena*] up'; and in Rom 15:2 Paul exhorts every christian to serve his neighbour 'to edify him'. It is also possible for the individual conscience to be edified (1 Cor 8:1). For these reasons the claim is made, in *TDNT* v, 144, 4f, that the notion of 'building' or 'edification' is applicable both to the christian community or church and to the spiritual growth of the individual christian. With this can be compared Schoenen's statement ('Aedificatio', 21): all building up of the church, both as a whole and in its individual members, can therefore be regarded as the essential fructification of Christ's ↗ cross. This condition occurs when grace and faith come into contact with each other.

Although Luther translated the word in question, wherever it is used in the figurative sense (Rom 15:2; 1 Cor 8:1; 10:23; 2 Cor 10:8; 12:19 etc), by 'reform' or 'reformation' and thus succeeded in emphasising the 'grave, temperate quality and the vigorous ethical tone of the word' (Laasch, 1113), at the same time he deprived it of a great deal of its particular and venerable lustre. The word later acquired, with the pietists, a strong flavour of sentimentality and a meaning charged with a cheap emotionalism. Some indication of the depths to which this word—used so often by the Old Testament writers and by Paul—has sunk in the protestant church, is given by Doerne (*RGG* 2 [1958], 539): 'The word is worn out beyond repair. It has become alien to the linguistic and conceptual terminology of the christian religion and is an annoying, even blasphemous, word. It could hardly now be restored to its original dignity.' And yet, as we have seen, 'build' is used on the first pages of the bible, to describe a divine activity, and the church which has stood until the present day can thus stand only because she is, in fact, 'God's building' (1 Cor 3:9). This is why the christian must regain an understanding of the full import of this word, so full of meaning, as it is used in the bible, as there can surely be no more worthwhile and important task for the christian than to 'build up' or 'edify'—in other words, to strengthen in faith—both the church, caught up as she is today in such a desperate struggle, and each one of his hard-pressed fellow christians. Above all, the pastor will feel himself, more than ever nowadays, bound to the principle of the Good Shepherd (Mt 12:20; Lk 15:4), which was so clearly formulated by Paul in the statement: *eis oikodomēn humōn kai ouk eis kathairesin humōn* ('for building you up and not for destroying you' 2 Cor 10:8; see also 13:10).

Bibliography: H. Bassermann, 'Über den Begriff "Erbauung"', *Zt. prot. Theol.* 4 (1882), 1–22; H. M. Scott, 'The Place of *oikodomē* in NT Worship', *The Princeton Theol. Rev.* 2 (1904), 402–24; P. C. Trossen, 'Erbauen', *TG* (1914), 804–12; W. Straub, *Die Bildersprache des Apostels Paulus*, 1937, 36, 85ff, and 93f; P. Vielhauer, *Oikodome. Das Bild vom Bau in der christl. Lit. vom NT bis Clem. Alex.*, 1939; K. L. Schmidt, *Die Erbauung der Kirche mit ihren Gliedern als den Fremdlingen und Beisassen auf Erden*, 1947; P. Bonnard, *Jésus-Christ édifiant son Eglise*, Neuchâtel-Paris 1948; T. Schneider (K. H. Schelkle), *RAC* I (1950), 1265–78; K. Barth, *Church Dogmatics* IV/2, Edinburgh 1958, 614–76; T. Laasch, *Evang. Kirchenlexikon* I (1956), 1112–3; A. Schoenen, 'Aedificatio. Zum Verständnis eines Glaubenswortes in Kult und Schrift', *Enkainia*, ed. H. Edmonds 1956, 14–29; W. Bauer, *A Greek–English Lexikon of the NT and other Early Christian Literature*, ed. W. F. Arndt and F. W. Gingrich, Cambridge and Chicago 1957, 560–62; M. Doerne, *RGG* 2 (1958), 538–40; H. Schlier, *LTK* III² (1959), 959–61; H. Kosmala, *Hebräer-Essener-Christen*, Leiden 1959, 363–78; J. Pfammatter, *Die Kirche als Bau*, Rome 1960; H. Pohlmann, *RAC* v (1962), 1043–70.

Johannes Kosnetter

Charisma

The Greek word *kharisma* (=free gift of grace) was coined by Paul in order to reduce a whole series of striking manifestations of the emotive state induced by faith in the first christian communities founded by him (especially in Corinth) to a common denominator. He laid down specific rules to govern these manifestations.

A. *Meaning of the term.* By 'charisma' we are to understand, in the majority of cases, a *supernatural and actual grace* which is given for the advancement of the mystical body of Christ and which comes from the Holy Spirit. Three conclusions can be drawn from this:

a. A charisma is a gift which has its origin in the *kharis* (=↗ Grace), the favour or goodwill of God. Of his own free will (1 Cor 12:11) God portions out these 'gifts' or 'services' or 'manifestations' of power (1 Cor 12:4–6), but in doing so takes into account the needs of the church as a whole and the talents and capacities of the individual.

b. These gifts are such that the whole community may profit by them, that is, they are allotted, in the first place, 'for the common good' (1 Cor 12:7), and not for the spiritual benefit of the person so endowed. Scholasticism expresses this as *gratia gratis data* as distinct from a *gratia gratum faciens.* They are embodied in the most manifold 'services' or 'functions' which God raises up and presides over for the advancement and growth of the church, for the preservation of unity of faith and purity of doctrine (see Eph 4:7–16).

c. They are to be attributed to the Holy Spirit who was given to the disciples after the resurrection and ascension of Christ (see Eph 4:7–11 and Jn 7:39). Already during the lifetime of Jesus we meet with some extraordinary manifestations of the Spirit, but these are not described as 'charismatic gifts' but as 'miraculous signs' (Mt 17:19; Mk 16:17f; Lk 21:15). The chosen people had witnessed, especially in times of need, mighty miracles such as the display of supernatural forces, heroic courage in war, the predictions of the prophets, and ecstasy. These same were foreseen as a part of the messianic age (Deut 28:49; Is 29:11f; Joel 3:1–3; ↗ Spirit A).

B. *Different kinds of charisma.* Paul enumerates a series of charismatic gifts without pretending to be exhaustive. Some of these are a constant feature of the life of the church, while others are conditioned by particular circumstances at a given time, as, for example, 'the gift of tongues' in the communities founded by the apostle of the gentiles. They are embodied in various 'services' connected with the life of the church (see 1 Cor 12:14; Rom 12:3–8; Eph 4:7–16; 1 Pet 4:10f).

1. *Charismata and the service of teaching.* Most 'gifts of the Spirit' play a major role in the worship and liturgy of the early church (see Acts 2:42).

a. The charismatic 'gift of tongues', otherwise known as 'glossolalia' or—better—'ecstatic utterance', was held in the highest honour at the liturgical gatherings of the faithful of Corinth (1 Cor 12:10; 14:1, 5, 6, 18; see also 13:1; 2 Cor 12:4). This gift was connected with the service of the word of God which was a preparation for the celebration of the eucharistic sacrifice. On the first occasion, the apostles probably spoke, as a result of the coming down of the Holy Spirit, 'in strange tongues' (not 'in foreign tongues'—compare the distinction in French between *langues étranges* and *langues étrangères*), implying that they were quite beside themselves with the exultation and joy of the Holy Spirit (Acts 2:4, 11, 15; see also 10:46; 11:15; 19:6). Those who had been seized by the Spirit emitted inarticulate, unintelligible sounds and expressions, disjointed and meaningless, which 'no one understands' (1 Cor 14:2, 6, 7–12, 16). They should therefore pray for the grace (14:13) to understand this 'ecstatic utterance' themselves or to be able to do so through someone else (12:10; 14:5, 27f). Only in this way can those who take part in the liturgical service draw spiritual profit (14:16, 26).

b. Paul gives a higher place to the service of teaching than to 'the gift of tongues'. The Holy Spirit takes part with power in the instruction of converted Jews and heathens by means of numerous charismatic manifestations which it is not always possible for us to distinguish and differentiate exactly. Particularly in 1 Cor 12:14 the apostle deals with these *ex professo*. The gift of *wisdom* endows the charismatic person with an amazing knowledge and a masterly command of the art of exposition with regard to the christian mystery in all its height and depth (see 1 Cor 2:6–16; Eph 1:2–23; Heb 6:1). The '*utterance of knowledge*' is shown in an intelligent presentation of the common, indispensable truths, 'the elementary doctrines of Christ' (Heb 6:1). The gift of '*prophecy*' has a foremost place (see Acts 11:27; 13:1; 15:32; 21:9f); it bestows the gift of reading the secrets of the heart (1 Cor 14:24f; see also 1 Tim 1:18; 4:14), predicting the future (Acts 11:28; 21:10f), and serves for 'upbuilding and encouragement and consolation' (1 Cor 14:3; see also Acts 4:36; 11:23f). The most important task of the 'prophets' is, however, to interpret under the influence of the Holy Spirit the messianic oracles in a christological sense (1 Pet 1:10–12), and so to reveal the 'mystery' of the divine economy of salvation in Christ (1 Cor 13:2; Eph 3:5 Rom 16:25). The gift of *the discernment of spirits* permits the identity of a 'prophet' to be established beyond the possibility of doubt—whether he is such according to the Spirit of God or according to a 'lying spirit' (1 Cor 14:29; 1 Tim 4:1; 1 Jn 4:1). Distinct from the 'prophets' who give utterance during the liturgical celebration as a result of spontaneous inspiration, the '*teachers*' speak *ex officio* (Rom 12:7; 1 Cor 12:2–28; Acts 13:1; Eph 4:11–14). They are entrusted with the task of expounding the Holy Scriptures, that is, the Old Testament, and of giving moral instruction. The charismatic gift of *exhortation* puts in the mouth of the pastor of souls the admonishing and consoling word.

All the charismatic gifts so far named refer to teaching and instruction addressed to brethren in the faith in the context of the church, a teaching which, endorsed as it is by the Holy Spirit, is endowed with irresistible force.

2. *Charismata and the service of the missions*. When we read, in 1 Cor 12, that God had designated some as ↗ *apostles* (vv 28, 30; see also Eph 4:11–14), we have to take it in a fairly wide sense. They are *sent* to the heathens in order to bring them the word of God about Jesus Christ which has power to win them over. The charismatic gift of *apostolate*, which includes both ministers

and laypeople, will continue until the end of the world (Mt 28:20).

a. This gift of the Spirit equips its bearers with supernatural strength in order to proclaim to the nations the glad tidings of the glorified Lord and of his return with all confidence (↗ Word, ↗ Witness). Paul does not base the preaching of the message of salvation on human wisdom, but on the Holy Spirit and the strength which comes from him (1 Cor 2:4–5, 13; see also Rom 1:9; 1 Thess 1:5). This charismatic gift of proclamation has never been absent in the church's history. Thus, to take just one example, right in the middle of the shallow period of the Enlightenment, Blessed Clement Maria Hofbauer, the apostle of Vienna, raised the challenge: 'Today the Gospel must be proclaimed anew!' The return to the fountainhead in the bible, the liturgy and ancient tradition can be taken, to use an expression of Pius XII, as 'a sign of God's providence in regard to the present age, the breath of the Holy Spirit in his Church'. This providential return gives to missionary preaching a more biblical, liturgical, paschal and eschatological accent.

b. The Holy Spirit inspires and directs also the manifold *apostolic undertakings* which gave to life in the church at that time the kind of stamp which comes in our day from Catholic Action, the apostolate of the laity, the Legion of Mary, the Mission de France, the worker priests, etc.

The function of teaching and of missionary work in the early church was given firm support by the *gift of healing* and the *power of working miracles*, which made a great impression on 'those without' and provided a spectacular proof of the truth of the christian message (1 Cor 12:9f, 28ff; see also Acts 4:30). Paul exults of 'what Christ has wrought through me to win obedience from the Gentiles, by word and deed, by the power of signs and wonders, by the power of the Holy Spirit' (Rom 15:18f; see also Gal 3:5).

3. *Charisma and the service of love.* The Spirit of God leads on irresistibly to deeds of charity. He gives the grace of 'solicitous charity' (*diakonia*), of loving service (Rom 12:7), so that this can stand as a shining sign of the love of Christ among men (see Jn 21:15–17; 1 Pet 5:1, 4).

a. At the birth of every great charitable work of the church there is present the charismatic gift of *assistance*. The Holy Spirit himself *appoints* certain people for the foundation of charitable institutions suited to the needs of the church at different times. The apostles appointed for the service of tables 'seven men of good repute, full of the Spirit and of wisdom' by means of the laying on of hands and of prayer (Acts 6:1–6; see also Rom 16:11). This gift of *diakonia* has never been extinguished in the church of God, and today it is as strong as ever: we have only to think of the ragpickers of Emmaus of Abbé Pierre, of Père Pire's villages for displaced persons, of the large-scale work of assistance organised by Fr van Straaten, etc.

b. Under the influence of this gift which comes from the Spirit, its bearers laid down with a sure touch the norms and the rhythm for an orderly development of this service of love.

c. This charismatic gift makes fruitful the labour of love of christian men and women who do not shrink back from the colossal difficulties and do not lay down their arms in view of the miserable means at their disposal. Just as the word of God possesses irresistible power, so is the work of God fruitful to an unsuspected, a supernatural degree.

4. *Charisma and hierarchy*. How are the charismatic gifts and the hierarchy related? Those who possess the gift of the Spirit go to work, as a rule, with great energy in every sector of church life, for the establishment of the kingship of Jesus Christ, while ecclesiastical rulers prefer to bide their time and weigh everything carefully. From this situation there arise tensions which sometimes deeply affect the parties concerned, but which are resolved in due time through the Holy Spirit. For, in the last analysis, it is the Holy Spirit who appoints to positions of leadership in the church (see the gift of 'administration', 1 Cor 12:28) and who governs the church through his representatives (see Acts 10:19; 11:28; 20:23; 21:4). It is the Holy Spirit who in particular gives to those in authority in the church the gift of 'differentiating' so that they can separate the weeds from the good wheat. It is the Holy Spirit who equips the successors of Peter with the charismatic gift of infallibility (according to the first Vatican Council; DS 3074), and by so doing unites in one person office and Spirit-given gift. These precious Spirit-given gifts can enrich the church as a blessing only when their bearers submit to the final decision of ecclesiastical authority.

C. *Order of importance of the charismata.* The charismatic gifts are not all of equal value. Paul admonishes his christians to strive after the most perfect gifts of the Spirit, by which he meant the offices of apostle, prophet, and teacher (1 Cor 12:28, 30), since it is these which most advance the good of the church (1 Cor 14:4, 6).

But even the greatest and the most precious gifts of the Spirit are eclipsed by ↗ love. It is for this reason that the hymn to charity (love) (1 Cor 13) has such a dominant position between Chaps. 12 and 14, which contain an exposition of the charismatic gifts. In the Epistle to the Romans, the explanation of the gifts of the Spirit is crowned by the commandment of love (Rom 12). Even if the charismatic gifts do not belong to the essence of the church, they make a valuable contribution as building material for the construction of the mystical body of the Lord; and so the words of Peter still have their value today: 'As each has received a gift (*kharisma*), employ it for one another, as good stewards of God's varied grace: whoever speaks, as one who utters oracles of God; whoever renders service, as one who renders it by the strength which God supplies; in order that in everything God may be glorified through Jesus Christ. To him belong glory and dominion for ever and ever. Amen' (1 Pet 4:10–11).

Bibliography: F. Grau, *Der ntl. Begriff 'charisma', seine Geschichte und seine Theologie*, Tübingen 1947 (dissertation); E. Schweitzer, *Das Leben des Herrn in der Gemeinde und in ihren Diensten*, Basle-Zurich 1946; J. Brosch, *Charismen und Ämter in der Urkirche*, Bonn 1951; H. von Campenhausen, *Kirchliches Amt und geistliche Vollmacht in den ersten drei Jahrhunderten*, Tübingen 1953; G. von Rad I, 93–102; A. Lemmonyer, *DB(S)* I, 1233–43; J. V. M. Pollet, *Catholicisme* 2 (1949), 956–9; X. Ducros, *Dict. de Spiritualité* 2 (1953), 503–7; *LTK* II[2], 1025–36; J. Behm, *TDNT* I, 719–26; Haag, 540f; *BTHW*, 1631; E. Käsemann, *RGG* II[2], 1272–9; A. George and P. Grelot, *DBT*, 55–7. See also the commentaries on 1 Cor and other NT epistles mentioned, in particular E. B. Allo, *Première Epître aux Corinthiens*, Paris 1934, 317–86; K. Rahner, *The Dynamic Element in the Church*, London 1969; *K. Rahner, *Mission and Grace* II, London 1964, 26–34; G. Murphy, *Charisma and Church Renewal*, Rome 1965.

Robert Koch

Church

In opposition to the institutional vision of the church which up to now has been dominant, recent exegesis is bringing more strongly to the foreground a view of the church seen within the context of salvation history. This does not of course imply that the former view has become marginal or even superfluous; but when compared with the question of the foundation and structure of the church as a socio-religious corporation, the more important question of its position and function in the whole context of the redemptive operation brought to its completion by God through Christ is seen as more urgent. That this view corresponds with New Testament findings is established by a review of this material under the relevant headings.

A. *Terminology and concept*. What we mean by 'church' (derived from the late Greek *kuriakon* [*dōma*] = [house] of the Lord) can be established from the New Testament chiefly by means of the term *ekklēsia* (=assembly called together), which is derived from the verb *ek-kalein* (=to call [someone] out of). The word is also found in the New Testament with the secular meaning, which goes back to the period of classical Greek, of 'popular assembly' (Acts 19:39; see also 19:32, 41—'a gathering of men'), but in general it has a specifically religious or theological range of meaning. This is also the case in LXX, where it occurs almost a hundred times, mostly (seventy-two times) as translating the Hebrew *qāhāl* (=assembly), but sometimes with the more specific meaning of *qâhâl Yahweh* (=*ekklēsia kuriou* = assembly of the Lord: Deut 23:1–3, 8; 1 Chron 28:8; see also Num 16:3: *sunagōgē kuriou* = assembly, congregation of the Lord) or *ekklēsia theou* (=assembly of God: Neh 13:1), indicating the people of Israel as the gathered cultic or redeemed community of Yahweh. In the same way, in the New Testament writings—particularly in Acts and Paul—*ekklēsia* refers to the redeemed community of the new covenant or, at times, is used to characterise the sum total of men redeemed through Christ (eg, Mt 16:18; 1 Cor 12:28; Eph 1:22; 3:10, 21; 5:23–7, 29, 32; Phil 3:6; Col 1:18, 24), occurring quite often as *ekklēsia tou theou* (1 Cor 10:32; 11:16; 15:9; Gal 1:13; 1 Tim 3:15; in the plural: 1 Thess 2:14; 2 Thess 1:4; 1 Tim 3:5) or *ekklēsia tou khristou* (Rom 16:16). Very often *ekklēsia* means the particular community in a specified place (apart from references in the opening address of the epistles: see, eg, Acts 8:1; 11:22; 14:27; 15:41; 1 Cor 7:17; Gal 1:22; Phil 4:15; Rev 2:1, 8 etc) or also the 'house-church' (Rom 16:5; Col 4:15; Philem 2), in particular, however, the community gathered together for worship (1 Cor 11:18; 14:4f, 19, 28, 34f; see also Acts 15:22). The distinction between the local community and the church as a whole accepted by most exegetes is not, however, carried through with any great emphasis in the terminology used in the New Testament (eg, Acts 5:11; 8:3; 9:31; 12:1; 1 Cor 4:17; 6:4; 1 Tim 5:16), which fits in well with the idea of the universal church as realised in a concrete way in the local community (see under C2).

There is another distinction in the use of *ekklēsia* which is more relevant theologically. In many texts this term possesses a greater depth of meaning which is not exhaustively expressed in terms such as 'the church as a whole', or 'the universal church'; this is especially true in the epistles of the captivity (we might quote Eph 1:22f; 3:10, 21; Col 1:18). It can hardly be a question simply of the empirical church as realised here below in history; rather does it assume in these expressions a dimension which takes us beyond history and indeed beyond the cosmos. In this sense we could justly designate it as 'mystery' in the pauline sense, a point we shall establish more exactly under C1. In this sense it refers to the work of God with regard to men within history leading either to salvation or to judgement. We have now to distinguish (but not separate!) from this concept of the church in terms of mystery the more historical and concrete view according to which the church is the community of those who believe in Christ, a community at one and the same time visible and invisible since supernatural, whether used in the universal or local sense. The church as a redeemed community (*congregatio fidelium*) is in one sense the result, the historical manifestation or incarnation, of the church as mystery. Both concepts refer to the one and the same existent reality of the church as seen from different points of view.

Apart from the term *ekklēsia*, the New Testament uses other expressions for the existing reality which we call 'the church'. Significantly, *sunagōgē* is used only once of the christian community (Jas 2:2, but see also 5:14), since this word was then applied to Jewish communities (eg, Acts 17:1). More frequently the church is referred to as *laos* (=people: Tit 2:14; Heb 2:17; 13:12; 1 Pet 2:9 [Ex 19:6]), more specifically as *laos theou* (=people of God: Rom 9:24ff [Hos 2:23; 1:10]; 2 Cor 6:16 [Lev 26:12]; Heb 4:9; 8:10 [Jer 31:33]; 1 Pet 2:10; Rev 18:4; 21:3). Numerous other expressions have a more or less plastic character, and can only be explained in terms of typological interpretation of the Old Testament, which means that we have to look into this first, since the New Testament—and not just Hebrews and Revelation, but also the synoptic gospels, John, and by no means least Paul (Gal 4:21–31; 1 Cor 10:1–11; Eph 5:31f)—make clear and explicit use of these figures.

B. *The church in Old Testament typology and New Testament imagery.* We find traces of such figures from the very first pages of the Old Testament writings; their deep roots and the wide-ranging ramifications of their prehistory takes us back to the time of the patriarchs and even as far as the Garden of Eden, since, according to Eph 5:31f, the mystery of Christ and the church is already announced in the matrimonial community of our first parents. The various covenants which we meet with in the course of Old Testament salvation history are likewise so many stages in the preparation for the new and eternal covenant which takes on living form in the church. In particular, the Old Testament people of the covenant, which passed under Moses' leadership through the Red Sea and the desert into the land of promise is, in its concrete destiny, a 'type' (1 Cor 10:6; cf 10:1–11) of the true 'Israel of God' (Gal 6:16; cf Rom 9:6), and even of the whole of mankind which is set free from the slavery of sin and death through the blood of Christ and which has already entered into the 'Sabbath rest' of God (Heb 4:9f) on the strength of rebirth by the water of baptism and may taste of 'the heavenly gift' (Heb 6:4). On the grounds of the contrast with 'the Israel according to the flesh' (Gal 4:22ff) we may conclude that the christian people is 'the Israel according to the Spirit' (see Eph 2:12; Heb 8:8–10; Rev 7:4; 21:12) to whom the promises first made to the patriarchs are transferred (Eph 3:6; see also Gal 3:22f, 29). Likewise, in contrast with the *politeia tou Israēl* (=commonwealth of Israel) from which the heathens were excluded there stands the church as the true theocratic commonwealth to which all heathens as well as Jews are admitted, thus forming *sumpolitai tōn hagiōn* (=fellow citizens of the saints) and even *oikeioi tou theou* (=members of God's household)—in short, the intimate community and family of God (Eph 2:12–19).

The metaphor of a 'flock' is often tied up in the Old Testament with the concept of a 'people', as in Ps 95:7; 100:3; etc. Just as Israel was the flock pastured by Yahweh (Ps 80:1; Is 40:11; Jer 13:17; 23:1–4; 31:10; Ezek 34; Mic 7:14; Zech 10:2f)—a metaphor which is used at times particularly of the 'remnant' of the people of God (Mic 2:12f), but at others admits of a certain universality (Sir 18:13)—so is the church, as the new people of God, compared with a flock (Mt 26:31; Lk 12:32; Acts 20:28f; 1 Pet 5:2f; Jn 10:1–16; see also 21:15–17), whose 'true shepherd' is Christ (Jn 10:11–16; Heb 13:20; 1 Pet 2:25; 5:4), but Christ as Messiah (Jer 23:4; Ezek 34:23f; see also Mt 25:32; 26:31). And just as Israel is described as the *vineyard* of Jahweh (Ps 80:8ff; Is 5:1–7; Jer 2:21; 12:10), so our Lord himself describes the plan of salvation and therefore the church as a vineyard into which the workers, that is, the prophets and apostles (and in reality all christians) are sent in order to cultivate it (Mt 20:1–16; see also Mk 12:1–12 and parallels; Rev 14:17–20). Further, he describes himself as the 'true Vine' from which we as the vine-branches take into ourselves the life of grace and love (Jn 15:1–6; see also Sir 24:17).

From another point of view the *city of God*, Sion (=Jerusalem), despite its dignity and glory, is only a shadowy model for the Jerusalem which is 'above' or which comes 'from above', and which is no longer a simple maiden but a lady and mother of the free, that is, of those who have been set free through Christ who gives true freedom (Gal 4:21–31 referring to Is 54:1; see also Is 26:1ff; 27:13; 40:1f, 9–11; 51:17; 52:1–10; 60; 62:10–12). This is seen in that we 'have come to Mount Sion and to the city of the living God, the heavenly Jerusalem, and to innumerable angels in festal gathering, and to the assembly of the first-born' (Heb 12:22f). The church is therefore the 'new' city of God (Rev 3:12) which the author of Revelation sees in a vision coming down from heaven as the 'holy city, the new Jerusalem, prepared as a bride adorned for her husband' (21:2). She is 'the dwelling of God with men' in which he himself dwells among them so that they may be truly 'his people' (21:3). She is also 'the Bride, the wife of the Lamb' (21:9) adorned with divine glory (21:11). In the last resort, these are all eschatological expressions; but they refer to the church on earth which is, in essence, one with that in heaven, which can be shown—to quote but one example—by the use of the perfect tense *proselēluthate* (=you have come [already]) in Heb 12:22.

The metaphor of a *city* is closely allied with that of a *house* or the 'house of God' (*oikos tou theou*); this is how the 'church of the living God' is designated in 1 Tim 3:15 (see Heb 3:6; 8:8ff [quoting Jer 31:31ff]; 10:21; 1 Pet 4:17). This metaphor is likewise rooted in Old Testament representations, such as 'the house of Jacob' (Is 2:2–6) or 'the house of Israel' (Is 5:7 and *passim*) or also 'the house of Wisdom' (Prov 9:1; see also 'the house of the Thorah' in the Damascus Document, 20:13). That it is a question of a 'spiritual edifice' is expressly stated and emphasised in 1 Pet 2:5. Its foundation-stone or corner-stone is Christ (1 Pet 2:6 [Is 28:16]; see also Mk 12:10 and parallels [Ps 118:22]; Acts 4:11; Eph 2:20), upon whom the faithful are built up 'like living stones' (1 Pet 2:4f; see also Eph 2:19–22). In 1 Tim 3:15 the church is further described as 'pillar and bulwark of the truth', by which is indicated one of her most important functions, namely, the preservation of true or 'sound' doctrine (Tit 1:9). What is most specific in the idea of the church is represented even more forcefully in the metaphor of 'temple' (*naos*). Thus, according to Paul, the faithful are referred to as 'God's temple' in which 'God's Spirit dwells' (1 Cor 3:16f; see also 2 Cor 6:16f; Rev 11:1ff; 21:3).

If, as we have seen, the new Jerusalem, the church, is identified in Rev 21:2 and even more clearly in 21:9 as 'the bride, the wife of the Lamb' (see also 19:7ff; 22:17), this is explained by and corresponds to the common oriental way of designating a city as female. It is on this basis that we have to understand some typical Old Testament motifs. It was in fact precisely in this way that the prophets conceived of the relation between Yahweh and Israel: of bridegroom and bride (Jer 2:2, 32; see also 31:1–6; Is 49:18; 61:10); husband and wife (Hos 2:16–22; Is 50:1; 54:5f; 62:4f; Ezek 16:1–14; see also 23:4); even as lover and courtesan (Hos 2:4–15; Jer 2:20–25; see also 3:12f; 9:1; Ezek 16:15–63). The image of the community as the bride of Christ occurs in Paul at all events, for example 2 Cor 11:2, and particularly in the passage on matrimony in Eph 5:22–33 in which the relation between the Lord and the church, which he has made holy and cleansed from all stain through his living self-offering (5:25–7) and which he nourishes and cherishes as the bride entrusted to his care (5:29—referring to the eucharist), stands as a type of christian matrimony which, in its turn, becomes the actualisation of the 'great mystery' of the community of love between Christ and the *ekklēsia*

(5:32). How far, both here and in general in the later writings of the New Testament, we have to take into account gnostic speculations about the 'union' of the Saviour with the 'Wisdom-assembly' (*Sophia-Ekklēsia*) is not quite clear or unambiguous according to the latest research, though the possibility of some such connection cannot be absolutely excluded.

Of greater importance for the Pauline concept of the church is the motif of the *body* as a community, which is already suggested in the Old Testament (eg, 2 Sam 19:13f; 1 Chron 11:1) and which is connected with the image of the church as a bride insofar as the woman is, as it were the 'body' of the man (Eph 5:28f). Behind this idea there stands the ancient understanding of the body as an element making for community, not just a means of intercourse, and, above all, the ancient semitic principle of solidarity. It cannot now be called into doubt that when Paul uses expressions with *sōma* (= body) the reference is first and foremost to a metaphor by means of which the church is described as a living organism in which a great variety of different kinds of members and organs (which, however, are related one to the other) are bound together in an organic and functional unity—as, for example, in 1 Cor 12:12, 14–26; Rom 12:4f; see also Eph 4:16. This is patterned on the 'diatribe' of popular philosophy, in particular of the Stoics. It would appear from the context that the use of this figure had the purpose of inculcating church unity despite the manifold nature of the several gifts given to each and in opposition to different schismatic groups and charismatic excesses. There are, however, certain texts, beginning in the major epistles, which cannot be understood in a purely metaphorical sense. For instance, 1 Cor 10:16f reads 'The bread which we break, is it not a participation in the body of Christ (*koinōnia tou sōmatos tou khristou*)? Because there is one bread, we who are many are one body, for we all partake of the one bread'—here it is hardly adequate to take the collective *sōma* of v 17 in a purely metaphysical sense if we at the same time interpret *sōma* in v 16 realistically, since there is an internal (and originally intended) connection between the two phrases. There should be no reason for doubting that *sōma tou khristou* in v 16 is not metaphorical, whether one refers it directly to the eucharistic body of Christ (with the majority of exegetes) or to the crucified but now glorified body which is present to us sacramentally in the eucharist and socially in the church. No more is it possible to interpret 1 Cor 12:12f in a purely metaphorical or figurative sense.

While in the major epistles Paul has in view in a special way the relation of the members one to another and their unity in Christ (Rom 12:5: *hen sōma en khristō(i)* =one body in Christ), in the captivity epistles the relation of Christ as 'head' to the church as 'body' (ie, the 'body of Christ' *sōma tou khristou*; Eph 1:22f; 4:15f; Col 1:18) occupies the foreground, a fact which emphasises the 'bride' motif (Eph 5:23–33) closely related to it. In the passages which predicate *sōma* of the church, the purely metaphorical (as distinct from the realistic) content falls more and more into the background. Thus it cannot be just metaphor when Paul says that Christ has reconciled both Jew and heathen 'to God in one body (*en heni sōmati*)' (Eph 2:16; see also 4:4; Col 1:22). The statement about the church in Eph 1:22f sounds like a definition: *tē(i) ekklēsiā(i), hētis estin to sōma autou* (=for the church, which is his, ie Christ's, body). The expression in Col 1:24 has a similar function—in it Paul speaks of his sufferings for the sake of Christ's body *ho estin hē ekklēsia* (=that is the church). Similarly, in Col 1:18 the words 'the church' (*tēs ekklēsias*) appear in apposition to the phrase 'he [ie, Christ] is the head of the body' (*autos estin hē kephalē tou sōmatos*) (see also Eph 4:12). The context of these formulations within the history of religions, and in particular against the background of gnosticism, has not yet been sufficiently elucidated, but they are certainly statements about realities, and so they bring us at once into the field—indeed, into the centre—of biblical theology.

Before we go any further one general comprehensive point should be made: the metaphors which we have been reviewing can be divided into two groups according to the point of view which prevails in each. The one group refers to the church rather as redeemed community, the other more in its relation to Christ (the church as mystery):

Church as redeemed community:
Flock—shepherd
People, political entity
City, new Jerusalem
House, temple of God

Church as Mystery:
Vineyard or vine—vine branches
Covenant (marriage)—partner
Bride—bridegroom
Body—head

In the last resort, however, both aspects are mutually inclusive; thus, for example, the image of the city implies its spiritual origin 'from above', and therefore from Christ, and the image of the body illustrates the mutual belonging together of the members. It is a question here rather of a difference in the incidence of emphasis or of perspective.

C. *The theology of the church in the New Testament.* While the biblical images teach us much about the nature of the church, there are a good number of positive statements which speak directly of this even more clearly, though of course we shall never be able to grasp in its entirety what is, after all, a divine mystery.

1. *The church as mystery.* If we approach the question from the angle of the history of salvation, we have first to discuss, among the many deep and complex aspects of the idea of the church in the New Testament, the concept of the church as mystery in the sense explained above (see under A). That the church is in the real sense of the word *mustērion* can be deduced from the great parenthesis in Eph 3; for here the 'mystery of Christ' (3:4) is described as coextensive with the community of Jew and gentile in the one church, since in it the gentiles 'are fellow heirs, members of the same body [*sussōma*], and partakers of the promise [to the Jews] in Christ Jesus through the gospel' (3:6). Hence the *ekklēsia* belongs essentially to the mystery of Christ; indeed she is herself, as being in community with the Lord her bridegroom, a true 'mystery' (5:32),

and therefore a reality which originates in God. Since in Pauline usage *mustērion* refers principally to the eternal counsel and decision of God and the concrete revelation and actualisation of this counsel in the history of created reality as a whole and salvation history in particular, the church in its character as mystery is characterised as an essential factor in the carrying out of this counsel and decision which is itself the primordial mystery. The church is therefore related to the total history of the world and consequently to the work of creation and exists in view of 'the final restoration of all things in Christ as head' at the end of the world. In this *oikonomia* (=plan; Eph 1:10; 3:2, 9) the church has an inalienable and indeed a cosmic function. This is proved by Eph 1:22f, where Paul says that God has made Christ 'the head over all things for the church which is his body, the fullness of him who fills all in all' (see also Col 1:15–20 especially 1:18). The cosmic task of the church appears precisely in this, that here she is characterised not just as the body but also as the 'fullness' (*plērōma*) of Christ —and this *plērōma*, as we have shown elsewhere ('Die Kirche im Epheserbrief', 12–14, see bibliog.) is used with the twofold meaning of 'fulfilled' and 'fulfilling'.

This comes through even more forcefully in Eph 3:9–11, insofar as it is precisely by means of the church that 'the manifold wisdom of God might now be made known to the principalities and powers in the heavenly places' who have their part to play through Christ and the church in the working out of the primordial mystery which is 'the design prepared for the ages'. In view of this one can very well speak, with *Didache* 11:11, of the *mustērion kosmikon ekklēsias* (=universal mystery of the church). Nevertheless, the soteriological function of the church remains for Paul in the foreground, as it is presented, for example, in Eph 2:13–22; 3:12; 4:12–16; Col 1:18–23. The church is, first and foremost, the 'mystery of salvation'. It is its essential purpose to transform mankind split into two hostile groups (Jew and gentile) and man himself divided within himself (*sarx/pneuma* = flesh/spirit) into the 'one new man' through the body of Christ on the cross immolated for the atonement of all (see Eph 2:15f with 4:23 and Col 1:20–2 with 3:9–15).

Considered as mystery, the church is a reality which is beyond history, eschatological and supernatural or 'pneumatic'. According to Eph 3:9f, the church—together with the 'principalities and powers' (*tais arkhais kai tais exousiais*), is 'in the heavenly places' (*en tois epouraniois*); she is the 'heavenly Jerusalem' (Heb 12:22) or 'the Jerusalem above (*anō*)' (Gal 4:26), and so in herself a reality from 'beyond' which nevertheless 'comes down' into this world (Rev 21:2, 10) and is 'incarnated' in space and time. This follows from the essence of the mystery, according to Paul, by which God and man, eternity and temporality, come together in a concrete symbol. On the basis of its spiritual ('pneumatic') existence, the church is therefore 'from above', a reality which has its origin in God and therefore, like everything spiritual, is in a certain sense pre-existent. This pre-existence implies that the church existed before the world (Eph 1:22f; see also 5:25), an understanding which is attested in an impressive way by ancient christian tradition starting from 2 Clement 14 and the *Shepherd* of Hermas, 2nd Vision, 4, 1 (see my 'Die Kirche im Epheserbrief' 33; 75–7) and does not in any way deny its created character. One must view it in relation to the created *sophia* (=wisdom) of the sapiential literature (Prov 8:22–31; Wis 7:22–8; Sir 1:1–10; 24:3–22) when thinking of its cosmic function. The *origin* of the church in the context of salvation history, however, has to be sought without a doubt in the sacrificial death of Christ (Col 1:20–2; Eph 2:13–16; 5:25ff; cf Jn 19:26f), since she originated as the 'new' or 'true' Eve out of the side of the second Adam asleep on the cross, as theologians since Tertullian (*De Anima*, 43), with reference to Jn 19:34, have almost unanimously taught. Finally, her historical manifestation before the peoples of the world took place in the Pentecost event, when the Lord, exalted to the Father, sent down the Holy Spirit on the primitive community gathered together around the apostles and the mother of Jesus (Acts 2:1–5, 33).

The intimate connection existing between the church and the Spirit (*pneuma*) is expressed by Paul by means of the co-ordination of *hen sōma* (=one body) with *hen pneuma* (=one Spirit) (Eph 4:4; see also 2:16: *en heni sōmati* = 'in one body' alongside 2:18: *en heni pneumati* = 'in one Spirit'). The *pneuma* of Christ is the intrinsic, organic principle which gives growth and structure to the church considered as the 'pneumatic' body of the Lord (1 Cor 12:3–11; Eph 2:22; see also Rom 8:4–16, 27; etc).

It is by bearing in mind the origin of the church in the mystery of the cross that we can have an exact understanding of Paul's statements about the church as *body* in their peculiar theological connotation, statements which are of such central importance for Paul's ecclesiology. The church is certainly not identical with the physical body of Jesus in his earthly sojourn, since he has once and for all renounced his 'body of flesh' (*sōma tēs sarkos*: Col 1:22; 2:11) on the cross. And yet it is with particular emphasis that Paul calls the church to *sōma tou khristou* or *to sōma autou* (1 Cor 12:27; Eph 1:23; 4:12; 5:30; see also Rom 7:4; Col 2:17; Heb 10:10, 19f). For him the church is, in a mysterious way, 'the [true] body of *Christ*', understood certainly in a particular mode of existence or presentation. According to the New Testament, and in particular Paul, the body cannot simply be identified with the material body (*sarx* = flesh)—on the contrary, the visible here-and-now phenomenon taken normally as connected with a body corresponds to an inner, hidden, mostly personal reality. For this reason the church as the body of Christ is the social (collective?) modality of existence of the spiritual Lord living on and operative here below, somewhat similar to the way Christ takes on a sacramental modality of existence in the eucharist. For just as we cannot suppose—assuming the doctrine of the real presence—that the 'bread which we bless' at the Lord's Supper is a different 'body of Christ' from his crucified body now glorified in heaven (1 Cor 10:16; see also 11:27), so the church, if she is really to be the 'body of Christ', cannot be any other than this, the more so because it is precisely here (10:17) that the underlying unity of the eucharistic and ecclesiological body of the Lord is expressly stated. That the ecclesiological or 'mystical' body of Christ is in some way one with his material body can be deduced by comparing Col 1:22 with Eph 2:16, where both the crucified 'body of flesh' of the Lord and the 'one body' of the church are given as means of reconciliation with God. We might also refer to Rom 7:4 and to the Lord's word about his body as a 'temple' which he would build up again in three days (Jn 2:19–21; also Mk 14:58 and parallels). The one body of Christ, therefore, has several different forms and modalities of existence: physical and material during the historical life of Jesus, heavenly and glorified after his 'passing over' to the Father, sacramental — eucharistic — and social-ecclesiological. Behind these different modalities of existence there exists, however, a unity analogous to and based on the real unity of the personal body of Christ.

By means of the Pauline *sōma*-terminology the relation between *Christ and the church* in particular is illustrated. As mystery or, more precisely, as the 'body of Christ', the church is an objective, supra-personal reality in relation to different individual men but united in the most intrinsic way with Christ. She is the 'one new man' *to* (*eis*!) whom Christ through his creative activity had reduced a divided humanity (Eph 2:15), and this 'one new man' is in its turn none other than Christ himself, but 'the whole Christ' with head and body (see 1 Cor 12:12: *ho khristos*) or 'the complete man' into whom we all have to grow up (Eph 4:13) just as we all, through baptism, 'put on Christ' so becoming 'one person [*heis*!] in Christ' (Gal 3:27f).

Christ and the church, therefore, are together one 'person', not of course in the individual sense, but in a higher 'mystical' but real unity through which the personal independence of the individual members of this body and of the head is in no way attacked, since it is not a question of a material fusion but of spiritual liberation and fulfilment. In any case, Christ remains as the 'head' in whom the 'whole *plērōma*' or the 'fullness of the Godhead' dwells (Col 1:18f; 2:9), established before and above the church. He is the source as he is the last end of all our being and existence; the *gratia corporis* is always a participation in the *gratia capitis*. There goes out from him who is the head that *pneuma* which gives life to all the members (see 1 Cor 15:45; 2 Cor 3:17f), producing in them an abundance of services and gifts of the Spirit (1 Cor 12:4–11; Eph 4:7–12, 16; Col 2:19; see under C 2). The whole body 'grows up' into him in order to fulfil itself in him 'the perfect man', 'to the measure of the stature of the fullness of Christ' (Eph 4:13, 15).

2. *The church as redeemed community.* As we saw, the church considered as mystery and even more as 'body' has also an external, visible, and concrete aspect and, indeed, the spiritual body of the Lord takes on in her the form of the community of men redeemed through the saving deed of Christ, which has to be brought into existence within history and which has, in fact, already been partially realised. She is not a pure 'church of the spirit'; on

the contrary, she has a particular sociological structure peculiar to herself which on the one hand puts her in relation with other human social structures and on the other distinguishes her from them.

In the church there are Jews and gentiles who, having accepted faith in the crucified Christ, are one in the true *people of God*, the 'Israel according to the Spirit'. It is of this new people of God that 1 Pet 2:9f speaks: 'But you are a chosen race, a royal priesthood, a holy nation, God's own people, that you may declare the wonderful deeds of him who called you out of darkness into his marvellous light. Once you were no people but now you are God's people; once you had not received mercy but now you have received mercy.' This text refers to practically all the stages which are relevant for the constitution of the church. In the first place, only election and call from God's side can lead to the church (1 Thess 1:4; Eph 1:4; 4:1, 4; 2 Pet 1:10; see also Rom 8:29f; 11:28). Consequently christians are known as *eklektoi* (=those who are chosen, the elect; Rom 8:33) and *klētoi* (=those who are called; Rom 1:6). The community finds its highest fulfilment and greatest honour in priestly service (1 Pet 2:5; Rev 1:6; 5:10), that is, in the liturgical worship; and so the church is conscious of itself as a cultic community (Eph 3:21; Heb 12:22f), since she is a 'holy' people, one, namely, set aside by God and consecrated to him—precisely that people which he acquired for himself in his merciful love by snatching it from the power of darkness and transferring it into the kingdom of light, the kingdom of his Son (Col 1:13).

Through this predominant history of salvation perspective the church is brought into close relationship with the ↗ *kingdom of God*. There is, however, no straightforward identity between the two realities, especially if we look at the church as a social and historical-contingent structure to which sinners also belong. Rather should we consider her as the *basileia* of Christ, the rule of *Christ* and the area where that rule obtains (Eph 5:5; see also 2 Pet 1:11; Jn 18:36; Rev 11:15), being, as it were, the prelude and preparation for the kingdom of God which is realised only at the end of time (1 Cor 15:24). The earthly church is still on the way towards the eternal 'kingdom of Heaven', yet the kingdom is in her by anticipation, it has already broken in (Rom 14:17; 1 Cor 4:20; see also 2 Tim 4:1; 2 Pet 1:11f; Rev 1:9; 5:10; also Mk 1:15 and parallels; Mt 12:28 and parallels; Lk 17:20f; etc). At the ↗ parousia of the Lord the church will be made one with the completed *basileia tou theou* (=kingdom of God) and, in consequence, her character as mystery will be annulled or 'fulfilled'.

As a community of the redeemed, the church is the new *politeia* (=commonwealth), that is, the 'state' and even the 'family' of God to which also the converted gentiles belong as 'members of the household' (Eph 2:19). The bond of ↗ *love* (*agapē*) unites all in the 'unity of the Spirit' (Col 3:14f; Eph 4:2f, 15f) as a true ↗ brotherhood (*adelphotēs*, 1 Pet 2:17; 5:9) in which no difference of race, social condition, or even sex is of decisive importance (Gal 3:28; 1 Cor 12:13; Rom 10:12; Col 3:11), since here all are fundamentally the same in the eyes of God (Acts 10:34;

Rom 2:11; see also 2 Cor 5:10; Eph 6:9). At the same time, it should not be considered merely as church bound together by love; it also has a juridical structure proper to itself. As a community actualised in the course of history, the church cannot exist without a social arrangement and a hierarchical order. Whence, according to 1 Cor 12:4–11, the Spirit effects in her the differentiated functions and charisms (see 12:14–25; Rom 12:3–8), though these are to be attributed to the glorified Christ, according to Eph 4:7–11, which really comes to the same thing, since the Spirit which is operative in the church is the divine power mediated through the Lord (Acts 2:33). Among those who serve the church under God or Christ, the ↗ apostles take the first place (1 Cor 12:28: *prōton* = first); then follow the ↗ prophets and teachers (*didaskaloi*) or the evangelists and pastors of the community (1 Cor 12:28; see also Eph 4:11), and finally the different 'ministries' among which we are to consider as not least in importance the various works of mercy (1 Cor 12:4–11; see also Acts 6:1). Already, therefore, in the New Testament period, the principal grades of the hierarchy had been set up, in particular the office of community leader (*prebuteros* = 'elder', Acts 11:30; 14:23; etc; or *episkopos* = 'overseer, bishop', Phil 1:1; 1 Tim 3:2; both identical in Acts 20:17, 28; Tit 1:5–7). The hierarchical (juridical) primacy of Peter (and his successors) can be deduced from the Lord's words in Mt 16:18f and is corroborated by other texts (eg, Lk 22:31f; Jn 21:15–17). The infallible power of the keys and of teaching possessed by the church is referred to in Mt 18:17f and Lk 10:16 (see also 1 Cor 5:3–13; Jn 20:23; 1 Jn 2:24; 4:6).

The most important ministry entrusted to the church is the ministry of the word (*diakonia tou logou*, Acts 6:4) and the administration of the sacraments. ↗ Preaching (*kērugma*, eg 1 Cor 2:4) constitutes a decisive ecclesiological function which has the purpose of awakening the faith (Rom 10:14f) which leads to conversion (*metanoia*) and *baptism* (Acts 2:38). Through baptism the individual believers are 'aggregated' (*prostithenai* = 'add', Acts 2:41, 47; 5:14; 11:24; see also 13:36) to the community of God—that is, are made members of or 'one body with' the church as the 'body of Christ' (see 1 Cor 12:13; Gal 3:27f). In the Lord's Supper, on the other hand, the church experiences itself as a sacrificial and living fellowship with and in Christ, since all those who eat 'of one bread' share in the one (immolated) body of the Lord and are therefore also in the deepest possible way united with one another (1 Cor 10:16f), a fact expressed in a particularly striking way in the ↗ *agapē* or love-feast, the celebration of which was often connected with the eucharist.

Church and sacrament have, therefore, a real relation one to the other, a fact already apparent in our consideration of the church as the body of Christ. Baptism has more the function of establishing (1 Cor 12:13), while the other sacraments, in particular the eucharist, have rather the function of building up and deepening (in addition to 1 Cor 10:16f, see Eph 5:29 with 2:20–22 and 4:15f). In the sacramental mystery which, like every true symbol, includes the outward sign and the reality indicated by the sign (*res*), the inner unity of the church as mystery of salvation and of fellowship is realised and experienced in a concrete way.

In this respect, moreover, the biblical *principle of solidarity* is of particular relevance and can be applied in two ways. The church is not just the body of the 'last Adam' (see 1 Cor 15:45); rather, she comes into existence and grows in proportion as the faithful, who are made members of this body, really co-operate in fulfilling the redemptive destiny of Christ. This ontological fellowship in destiny with the Lord is now made possible principally through the sacraments. Thus, we die with Christ in baptism, are 'crucified with him' in it and are 'buried with him into death' so that, rising with him, we may be able to walk in 'newness of life' (Rom 6:3–6; Col 2:12). When, however, we celebrate the Lord's Supper, which according to 1 Cor 10:16–21 (see also 11:24f) possesses a sacrificial character, by uniting our oblation to his we enter into the once-and-for-all sacrificial death of Christ and, in this way, 'proclaim', through the cultic commemoration implied in the action, this one saving death until the Lord comes again (11:26). Also in the everyday living of this mystical life of christians, the sacramental action in union with Christ is continued in the form of the following of Christ by carrying one's cross (Mk 8:34 and parallels; Rom 8:17; etc). It will reach its complete fulfilment one day in our physical death—the 'last mystery'—as the most real participation in the 'passing over' of Christ (see 1 Thess 4:14; 1 Cor 15:12–22, 51–57). The church is therefore, in its essential nature, a fellowship of destiny or an existential fellowship with Christ and of each member with the others in Christ (1 Cor 12:26; Rom 12:13, 15f), as is demonstrated by the relation existing between the apostle Paul and his communities, with whom he knew himself to be united 'in dying together and in living together' (2 Cor 7:3; see also 6:11–13; 11:28; 1 Pet 5:1, 9).

As regards the relationship of the *church as a whole*, in which the mystery of the church is primarily embodied, to the *local communities*, the latter can be considered as concrete reproductions or configurations derived from the former, as, for example, when it is a question of the church 'which is in Jerusalem' (Acts 11:22; see also 8:1; 13:1; 1 Cor 1:2; 14:23 (in the singular!); 1 Cor 10:32; 11:22; 1 Tim 3:15). These local communities, however, retain the ability to express this truth only as long as they remain in union with the church as a whole and the doctrine it believes, for there can be *only one legitimate historical collective embodiment* of the church of Jesus Christ considered as mystery, and the signs of this legitimate status are in the first place unity of teaching and continuity of function (the apostolic succession).

Unity is therefore the first mark of the church. This is by nature a spiritual thing (Eph 4:3f; see also 4:13), but in her outward aspect too she admits of no divisions (*skhismata*), as Paul in particular emphasises (1 Cor 12:25; see also 1:10; 11:18). The *holiness* of the church (Eph 5:26f; Heb 13:12; see also 2:11; 10:10, 14; 1 Thess 5:23; 1 Cor 1:2; 6:11; Acts 20:32; 26:18) does not just mean in the negative sense a separation from the profane, but a positive dedication to God (see Jn 17:19). Its *catholicity* leaves no room for racial or class distinction (*diastolē*, Rom 10:12; see also 3:22; Gal 3:28; 1 Cor 12:13), on account of the 'one Lord' whom she serves. Its *apostolicity* (Eph 2:20; 3:5) rests above all on the preservation of the apostolic tradition (*paradosis*, 2 Thess 2:15; 3:6; 1 Cor 11:2; see also 2 Pet 3:2; Jude 17) and succession imparted through the laying on of hands (Acts 13:3; 1 Tim 4:14; 5:22; 2 Tim 1:6; see also Acts 14:23).

The *eschatological* orientation which was brought to our attention in dealing with the relation between the church and the kingdom of God is especially important for the 'pilgrim' church (1 Pet 2:11; see also Heb 11:13–16; 13:14), but for the most part here, as elsewhere in the New Testament, it is a question of a 'realised eschatology'. Certainly, the church understands herself as the redeemed 'remnant' of the last days (Rom 9:24–9; 11:5; see also 1 Cor 10:11; 1 Pet 4:7; 1 Jn 2:18), but certainly not as an esoteric community like the Essene sects or that of Qumran. She knows that she has been 'called out' from the world (see Jn 15:19) and that her true 'commonwealth' (*politeuma*) is in heaven (Phil 3:20), and that therefore she is not 'of' this world (Jn 17:14, 16). But she retains the consciousness that she has been placed 'in' this world in order to be tested through faith and in patience (Jn 16:33; 17:11, 15, 18; see also Phil 2:15; 1 Pet 5:9).

The church consequently has a *task in the world*, not a profane and merely cultural one but religious, namely, the proclamation of the gospel (*euangelion*, Mt 28:19; Mk 16:15) and the rescue of the things of the world from the demonic powers by a consecration to God accompanied by thanksgiving through the powerful grace which Christ gives (sacramentals; see 1 Cor 10:23–33 and, especially, 1 Tim 4:4f). She therefore cannot indulge in a spiritualism which does not take seriously God's creation and the incarnation of Christ, but at the same time cannot conform to the world in the manner of the false messianic expectation of the Jews who wanted to set up the kingdom of God on this earth and therefore thought of the cross as a 'scandal' (1 Cor 1:23; see also Gal 6:12; Phil 3:18). Rather would the church's slogan be: 'Freedom from the world and freedom for God' (1 Cor 2:12; 7:29–34; Jas 1:27; 4:4; 1 Jn 2:15–17; see also Gal 6:14; Col 2:8; 2 Tim 2:4). The real mission of the church in the world is to co-operate in the redemption and return of the creation to God, the last end and native home of all being, by means of the grace measured out to her (Rom 8:19–22; 1 Cor 3:21ff; 2 Cor 10:5). Thus, in addition to her more urgent soteriological task, the church has also a *cosmological* one which will be completed only in the eschatological transformation and fulfilment, when the church on earth, united with the church in heaven and with the cosmos renewed through Christ, enters into the eternal kingdom of God. Then will she be in truth, as the perfected body of Christ, 'the fullness of him who fills all in all' (Eph 1:22f).

Bibliography: Older studies in O. Linton, *Das Problem der Urkirche in der neueren Forschung*,

Frankfurt 1957[2]; and A. Médebielle, *DB(S)* II (1934), 687–91.

Terminology and concept: H. Koehnlein, 'La Notion de l'Eglise chez l'Apôtre Paul', *RHPR* 17 (1937), 357–77; K. L. Schmidt, *TDNT* III, 501–36; N. A. Dahl, *Das Volk Gottes. Eine Untersuchung zum Kirchenbewusstsein des Urchristentums*, Oslo 1941; J. C. Fenton, 'NT Designations of the Catholic Church and of its Members', *CBQ* 9 (1947), 127–46 and 275–306; S. Giuliani, 'La nomenclatura paolina interno alla Chiesa', *Sap.* 3 (1950), 195–219; O. Moe, 'Um den ntl. Ekklesia-Begriff', *TTK* 23 (1952), 26–30; E. Schweitzer, 'The NT Idea of the Church', *Theology Today* 13 (1956), 471–83; P. Alonso, 'Idea de comunidad del pueblo de Dios en la Biblia', *Liturgia* 13 (1958), 76–89; P. S. Minear, *Images of the Church in the NT*, Philadelphia 1960; H. Schlier, 'Zu den Namen der Kirche in den paulinischen Briefen', *Besinnung auf das NT*, Freiburg 1964, 294–306; L. Cerfaux, 'Die Bilder für die Kirche im NT', *De Ecclesia* I, ed. G. Baraúna, Freiburg 1966, 220–35.

Church and OT: L. Rost, *Die Vorstufen von Kirche und Synagoge im AT*, Stuttgart 1938; H. W. Herzberg, *Werdende Kirche im AT*, Munich 1950; P. H. Menoud, *L'Eglise naissante et le Judaisme*, Montpellier 1952; J. D. W. Kritzinger, *Qehal Jahwe. Wat dit is en wie daaraan mag behoort*, Kampen 1957 (with a summary in English); O. Linton, 'Ecclesia I', *RAC* 4 (1959), 905–21; K. Thieme, 'Das Mysterium der Kirche in der christlichen Sicht des Alten Bundesvolkes', *Mysterium Kirche* I, Salzburg 1962, 37–87; H. Gross, 'Der Sinai-Bund als Lebensform des auserwählten Volkes im AT', *Ekklesia*, Trier 1962, 1–15; H. Junker, 'Sancta Civitas, Jerusalem Nova (Is 2)', *Ekklesia*, 17–33; J. Schreiner, *Sion-Jerusalem, Jahwes Königssitz*, Munich 1963.

Jesus and the church: K. Pieper, *Jesus und die Kirche*, Paderborn 1932; R. N. Flew, *Jesus and his Church*, London 1938; P. Nepper-Christensen, *Wer hat die Kirche gestiftet?*, Lund 1950; R. L. Hicks, 'Jesus and His Church', *ATR* 34 (1952), 85–93; W. G. Kümmel, 'Jesus und die Anfänge der Kirche', *ST* 7 (1953), 1–27; A. Nygren, *Christus und seine Kirche*, Göttingen 1955; O. Kuss, 'Bemerkungen zu dem Fragenkreis: Jesus und die Kirche', *TQ* 135 (1955), 28–55 and 150–83; E. Finke and A. Vögtle, 'Jesus und die Kirche', *Begegnung der Christen*, ed. M. Roesle and O. Cullmann, Frankfurt-Stuttgart 1960[2], 35–54 and 54–81.

The church in the individual NT writings: S. Cipriani, 'La dottrina della Chiesa in S. Matteo', *Riv. bibl. it.* 3 (1955), 1–31; W. Trilling, *Das wahre Israel*, Leipzig 1949; J. Gnilka, 'Die Kirche des Matthäus und die Gemeinde von Qumran', *BZ* 7 (1963), 43–63; E. Schweizer, *Der Kirchengedanke im Evangelium und den Briefen des Johannes*, Berlin 1959, 363–81; A. Corell, *Consummatum est: Eschatology and Church in the Gospel of John*, New York 1959; L. Cerfaux, *La communauté apostolique*, Paris 1953[2]; J. Schmitt, 'L'Eglise de Jérusalem ou la "Restauration" d'Israel d'apres Actes 1–5', *RSR* 27 (1953), 209–18; C. Charlier, 'De la communauté de Jérusalem aux églises pauliniennes (Actes 1–12)', *Bibl. et Vie chrét.* 1 (1953), 72–93; F. Mussner, 'Die Bedeutung des Apostelkonzils für die Kirche', *Ekklesia*, 35–46; H. Schürmann, 'Das Testament des Paulus für die Kirche (Acts 20:18–35)', *Unio Christianorum*, Paderborn 1962, 108–46; K. Pieper, *Paulus und die Kirche*, Paderborn 1932; W. L. Knox, *St Paul and the Church of the Gentiles*, Cambridge 1939; G. Sciaretta, *La Croce e la Chiesa nella Teologia di S. Paolo*, Rome 1952; C. T. Craig, 'The Church in Paul', *Rel. in Life* 22 (1953), 538–50; G. Bornkamm, 'Herrenmahl und Kirche bei Paulus', *ZTK* 53 (1956), 312–48; L. Cerfaux, *L'Eglise des Corinthiens*, Paris 1946; H. Schlier and V. Warnach, *Die Kirche im Epheserbrief*, Münster 1949; F. Mussner, *Christus, das All und die Kirche. Studien zur Theologie des Epheserbriefes*, Trier 1955; A. Feuillet, 'L'Eglise plérôme du Christ d'après Eph 1:23', *NRT* 78 (1956), 449–72 and 593–610; H. Schlier, 'Die Kirche als das Geheimnis Christi nach dem Eph', *Zeit der Kirche*, Freiburg 1962[3], 293–307; N. A. Dahl, 'Das Geheimnis der Kirche nach Eph 3:8–10', *Zur Auferbauung des Leibes Christi*, Kassel 1965, 63–75; T. da Castel S. Pietro, *La Chiesa nella lettera agli Ebrei*, Turin-Rome 1945; A. Kassing, *Die Kirche und Maria. Ihr Verhältnis im 12 Kapitel der Apokalypse*, Düsseldorf 1958; K. Stendhal, 'Kirche im Urchristentum', *RGG* III[3] (1959), 1297–1304; *Y. Congar, 'The Council as an Assembly and the Church as Essentially Conciliar', *One, Holy, Catholic, and Apostolic*, ed. H. Vorgrimler, London 1968, 44–88 (with an anthology of texts based on Mt 18:20).

Theology of the church: A. Médebielle, *DB(S)* II, 487–687; O. Michel, *Das Zeugnis des NT von der Gemeinde*, Göttingen 1941; Y. Congar, *The Mystery of the Church*, London 1960; F. M. Braun, *Aspects nouveaux du problème de L'Eglise*, Fribourg 1941; J. Daniélou, *Le signe du Temple ou la Présence de Dieu*, Paris 1942; G. Johnston, *The Doctrine of the Church in the NT*, Cambridge 1943; L. Cerfaux, *The Church in the Theology of St Paul*, London 1959; H. de Lubac, *The Splendour of the Church*, London 1956; W. H. Robinson, *The Biblical Doctrine of the Church*, St Louis 1949; T. W. Manson, 'The NT Basis of the Doctrine of the Church', *JEH* 1 (1950), 1–11; E. Sjöberg, 'Kirche und Kultus im NT',

Ein Buch von der Kirche, Berlin 1950, 85–109; Meinertz I, 69–79 and 231–7; II, 155–84, 254, 260, 309–12, and 326–9; V. Warnach, *Agape*, Düsseldorf 1951, 550–81; E. Schweizer, *Geist und Gemeinde im NT*, Munich 1952; K. L. Schmidt, 'The Church', *Theol. Today* 9 (1952), 39–54; E. Peterson, 'L'Eglise', *DV* 25 (1953), 99–112; J. F. Walvoord, 'Premillenarianism and the Church as a Mystery', *Bibl Sacr.* 111 (1954), 1–10 and 97–104; J. Lonke, 'Credo Ecclesiam Christi Apostolicam', *Coll. Brug.* 50 (1954), 23–32 and 318–27 (against Cullmann); A. Orbe, 'Cristo y la Iglesia', *Est. Ecl.* 29 (1955), 299–344; O. Cullmann, *The Early Church, Historical and Theological Studies*, London 1956; N. A. Dahl, 'Christ, Creation and the Church', *The Background of the NT and its Eschatology*, Cambridge 1956, 422–43; J. Schneider, *Taufe und Gemeinde im NT*, Kassel 1956; H. Schlier, *Die Zeit der Kirche*, Freiburg 1958²; R. Grosche, *Et intra et extra*, Düsseldorf 1958; P. Carrington, *The Early Christian Church*, Cambridge 1958; E. Peterson, *Il mistero degli Ebrei e dei Gentili nella Chiesa*, Milan 1960²; J. Pfammatter, *Die Kirche als Bau*, Rome 1960; R. Schnackenburg, *LTK* VI² (1961), 167–72; R. Schnackenburg, *The Church in the New Testament*, London 1965; E. Heible, 'Die Kirche als Wirklichkeit Christi im NT', *TTZ* 72 (1963), 65–83; F. Mussner, '"Volk Gottes" im NT', *TTZ* 72 (1963), 169–78; B. Rigaux, 'Das Mysterium der Kirche im Lichte der Schrift', *De Ecclesia* I, ed. G. Baraúna, Freiburg 1966, 197–219; *R. Schnackenburg, 'Church and Parousia', *One, Holy, Catholic, and Apostolic*, ed. H. Vorgrimler, London 1968, 91–134.

The church as the body of Christ: E. Mersch, *The Whole Christ*, London 1949; E. Käsemann, *Leib und Leib Christi*, Tübingen 1933; E. Mura, *Le corps mystique du Christ. Sa nature et sa vie divine d'après S. Paul et la théologie*, Paris 1937² (two vols.); S. Tromp, *Corpus Christi quod est Ecclesia*, Rome 1946²; A. Wikenhauser, *Die Kirche als der mystische Leib Christi nach dem Apostel Paulus*, Münster 1940²; E. Percy, *Der Leib Christi in den paulin. homologumena und Antilegomena*, Lund-Leipzig 1942; E. Mersch, *La théologie du Corps mystique*, Paris-Bruges 1944; L. Malevez, 'L'Eglise, corps du Christ. Sens et provenance de l'expression chez S. Paul', *RSR* 30 (1944,) 27–94; W. Goossens, *L'Eglise, corps du Christ d'après S. Paul*, Paris 1949; T. Soiron, *Die Kirche als der Leib Christi*, Düsseldorf 1951; P. Michalon, 'Eglise, Corps mystique du Christ glorieux', *NRT* 74 (1952), 673–87; E. Sauras, *El cuerpo mistico de Cristo*, Madrid 1952; E. L. Mascall, *Corpus Christi: Essays on the Church and the Eucharist*, London 1953; H. Holstein and D. Boumard, *L'Eglise, Corps vivant du Christ*, Paris 1953; A. Oepke, 'Leib Christi oder Volk Gottes bei Paulus', *TLZ* 79 (1954), 363–8; E. Best, *One Body in Christ: A Study in the Relationship of the Church to Christ in the Epistles of the Apostle Paul*, London 1955; P. Benoit, 'Corps, Tête et Plérome dans les épîtres de la Captivité', *RB* 63 (1956), 5–44; J. I. Meuzelaar, *Der Leib des Messias*, Assen 1961.

Church unity: S. Hanson, *The Unity of the Church in the NT: Colossians and Ephesians*, Uppsala-Copenhagen 1946; F. Puzo, 'La unidad de la Iglesia en función de la Eucaristía', *Greg* 34 (1953), 145–86; C. T. Craig, *The One Church in the Light of the NT*, New York 1951 and London 1953; P. A. van Stempvoort, 'Paulus und die Spaltungen zu Korinth', *Begegnung der Christen*, 83–98; H. Schlier, 'Die Einheit der Kirche nach dem Apostel Paulus', *Begegnung der Christen*, 98–113; H. Schlier, 'Die Einheit der Kirche nach dem NT', *Besinnung auf das NT*, Freiburg 1964, 176–92; P. Benoit, 'L'unité de l'église selon l'épître aux Ephésiens', *Anal. bibl.* (Rome 1963), 57–77.

The church and the kingdom of God: E. Sommerlath, 'Kirche und Reich Gottes', *ZST* 16 (1940), 562–575; O. Cullmann, *Königsherrschaft Christi und Kirche im NT*, Zollikon-Zurich 1950³; D. M. Stanley, 'Kingdom to Church: The Structural Development of Apostolic Christianity in the NT', *TS* 16 (1955), 1–21; T. F. Torrance, *Kingdom and Church*, London 1956; J. Bright, *The Kingdom of God in the Bible and the Church*, London 1956; R. Schnackenburg, *God's Rule and Kingdom*, London 1963.

Church and world: M. A. Wagenführer, *Die Bedeutung Christi für Welt und Kirche*, Leipzig 1941; V. Warnach, 'Kirche und Kosmos', *Enkainia*, Düsseldorf 1956, 170–205; I. J. du Plessis, *Christus als Hoof van Kerk en Kosmos*, Groningen 1962.

Church and state: K. L. Schmidt, *Die Polis in Kirche und Welt*, Basle 1939; W. Bieder, *Ekklesia und Polis im NT und in der alten Kirche*, 1941; K. H. Schelkle, 'Staat und Kirche in der patrist. Auslegung von Rom 13:1–7', *ZNW* 44 (1953), 223–36; O. Kuss, 'Paulus über die staatl. Gewalt', *TG* 45 (1955), 321–34; A. Weithaas, 'Kirche und Staat in paulin. Sicht', *TG* 45 (1955), 433–41.

Life and constitution of the early church: G. Sass, *Apostelamt und Kirche*, Munich 1939; C. Journet, *L'Eglise du Verbe Incarné*, Paris 1942/51 (two vols.); P. H. Menoud, *L'Eglise et les ministères selon le NT*, Neuchâtel-Paris 1948; P. H. Menoud, *La vie de l'église naissante*, Neuchâtel-Paris 1952; J. Schniewind, 'Aufbau und Ordnung der Ekklesia nach dem NT', *Festschrift R. Bultmann*, Stuttgart-Cologne 1949, 202–8; H. von Campenhausen, *Kirchliche Amt* *und geistliche Vollmacht in der ersten drei Jahrhunderten*, Tübingen 1953; J. Gewiess, 'Die ntl. Grundlagen der kirchllichen Hierarchie', *Hist. Jahrb.* 72 (1953), 1–24; B. Reicke, *Glaube und Leben der Urgemeinde*, Zurich 1957; R. V. Clearwaters, *The Local Church of the NT*, Chicago 1954; B. C. Butler, *The Church and Infallibility*, London 1969²; F. W. Beare, 'The Ministry in the NT Church: Practice and Theory', *ATR* 37 (1955), 3–18; G. Dix, *Le ministère dans l'église ancienne*, Neuchâtel 1955; J. Daniélou, 'La communauté de Qumrân et l'organisation de l'église ancienne', *RHPR* 35 (1955), 104–15; J. Colson, *Les fonctions ecclésiales aux deux premiers siècles*, Bruges 1956; K. H. Schelkle, *Discipleship and Priesthood*, New York 1965 and London 1966; E. Schweitzer, *Church Order in the NT*, London 1962; K. H. Schelkle, 'Kirche als Elite und Elite in der Kirche nach dem NT', *TQ* 142 (1962), 257–82; O. Kuss, 'Kirchliches Amt und freie geistliche Vollmacht', *Auslegung und Verkündigung* 1, Regensburg 1963, 271–80; *J.-P. Audet, *Structures of Christian Priesthood: Home, Marriage, and Celibacy in the Pastoral Service of the Church*, London and New York 1967.

Viktor Warnach

Circumcision

Circumcision refers to the removal of the foreskin and took place on the eighth day after birth (Gen 17:12; 21:4; Lev 12:3). The fact that circumcision was first carried out with a flint (Ex 4:25; Josh 5:2f) is indicative of the antiquity of this custom. In more remote times it was carried out by the father of the child (Gen 21:4)—there is only one case where the mother does it (Ex 4:25)—and later by a specialist (1 Macc 1:61), but never by a priest in a sanctuary. In order to take part in the passover, which was *the* Israelite community festival, non-Israelite slaves and aliens also had to be circumcised (Ex 12:43–9). According to the view found in the most recent strand of the Pentateuch, which comes from priestly circles, circumcision was imposed on Abraham's family by God as a sign of the covenant (Gen 17:9ff; ↗ covenant). It was practised by the patriarchs and probably kept up during the sojourn in Egypt (Gen 34:13ff; Josh 5:4f). From the fact that Moses was uncircumcised (Ex 4:24–6) we may suppose that it gradually fell into desuetude and was taken up once again after the conquest of Canaan (Josh 5:4–9).

Ethnological studies have shown us that circumcision was practised by many African tribes, but we cannot be certain that it was widespread in the ancient Near East. It seems that priests had to be circumcised in ancient Egypt. As far back as the third millennium BC we find representations of circumcision being carried out on stone reliefs. Ancient texts refer to it, as does Herodotus, yet on the other hand there are mummies which show no trace of circumcision. Nor does the Old Testament provide unambiguous evidence for the widespread practice of circumcision by the mere fact that it describes Egyptians, Edomites, Ammonites, Moabites, and Arabs as uncircumcised (Jer 9:25f), and places the uncircumcised Egyptians, Assyrians, Elamites, Edomites, and Sidonians in Sheol (Ezek 32). According to the testimony of Herodotus the Phoenicians and Syrians were circumcised. The Arabs of antiquity were too, since the Romans attempted to prohibit circumcision in Arabia. After the conquest the Israelites came into immediate contact with the Philistines who were certainly uncircumcised (Judg 14:3; 15:18; 1 Sam 14:6; 17:26, 36; 18:25–7; 31:4) and with the Canaanites whom they never branded as uncircumcised. We must conclude, then, that circumcision could never have been a unique individuating factor of the Israelites *vis-à-vis* other groups in Palestine. On the contrary, the people of Old Testament times must have learned of this practice for the first time in Canaan and begun to practise it there (Gen 17:9–14, 23–27; Josh 5:2ff). But as was the case with so many other practices taken over by Yahwism, circumcision in Israel was given an entirely new and specifically religious sense.

Among the customs most widespread among the peoples of the world belong what are called *rites de passage*, that is, rites which are connected with birth, arrival at sexual maturity, marriage, and death. The initiation rituals which qualified a candidate for married life and life as a full member of the community demanded of him some proof of valour and courage (eg killing a man, chopping off a finger, pulling out an incisor, etc). Circumcision took place at the time of puberty as an initiation ritual—as it does among primitive tribes today—and this significance probably attached to it also in the ancient Near East. The Arabic verb *ḫatana* (to circumcise) corresponds to the Hebrew *ḥōtēn* (father-in-law, see Ex 3:1), *ḥ^{a}tan* (son-in-law, see Gen 19:12) and *ḥ^{a}tunnâh* (marriage, see Song 3:11). The story of the Shechemites (Gen 34) and of the 'bridegroom of blood' (Ex 4:24–6) associate circumcision expressly with marriage. Even the metaphorical reference to circumcision points to its original character as an initiation ritual. An 'uncircumcised heart' cannot understand (Jer 9:25; Deut 10:16; 30:6), an 'uncircumcised ear' cannot hear (Jer 6:10), and 'uncircumcised lips' cannot speak (Ex 6:12, 30).

When circumcision began to be practised shortly after birth its significance as a ritual of initiation naturally ceased and it acquired a new meaning as a necessary qualification for life as a member of the chosen people (Gen 34:14–16; Ex 12:47f). It also became a sign of the covenant which God had made with Abraham and his descendants (Gen 17:9–14, from P). But this religious view of circumcision took a long time to establish itself. It is given only incidental mention in the law in connection with the stipulations concerning the passover (Ex 12:44, 48), the purification of a woman who has just given birth (Lev 12:3), and in comparison with the first-fruits of trees (Lev 19:23 ↗ Firstfruits). It was only during the Exile that circumcision became the characteristic of one who belonged to the covenant-people, since the peoples of Mesopotamia were uncircumcised and those of Palestine had already given it up (cf Ezek 32:19ff; Judg 14:3). At all events, Flavius Josephus notes that in his day—that is, in the first century AD—the Jews were the only people living in Palestine who practised circumcision. It was therefore demanded of those gentiles who wished to embrace the Jewish faith, since it was the sign of the covenant (Esther 8:17). With the advance of hellenism Antiochus Epiphanes, then ruler of Palestine, prohibited circumcision under the most severe penalties (1 Macc 1:60f; 2 Macc 6:10). Jews who were weak in faith attempted to remove any sign of circumcision (1 Macc 1:15; cf 1 Cor 7:18).

As we know from Jn 7:22f, circumcision was carried out at the time of Jesus on the sabbath. But for those who were part of the new covenant it had lost its significance since it was a sign of the old covenant (Acts 15; Rom 4; Gal 2).

Bibliography: A. van Gennep, *Les Rites de passage*, 1909; A. E. Jensen, *Beschneidung und Reife-zeremonien bei Naturvölkern*, 1933; J. G. Schur, *Wesen und Motive der Beschneidung im Lichte der alttestamentlichen Quellen und der Völkerkunde*, 1937; A. Allwohn, 'Die Interpretation der religiösen Symbole erläutern an der Beschneidung', *ZRGG* VIII (1956), 32–40; F. R. Lehmann, 'Bemerkungen zu einer neuen Begrundung der Beschneidung', *Sociologus* VII (1957), 57–74; de Vaux, 46–8.

Walter Kornfeld

Clean and unclean

A. *Concept and Terminology*. The idea of *cultic* (as distinct from moral) cleanness and uncleanness is found both in the primitive religions and among the Greeks, and also in the world of the ancient Near East in general which constitutes the background to the bible. Intercourse with the divinity requires that man shall be free from everything which is hostile to that divinity: from contamination by 'common' or everyday things, which were regarded as causing uncleanness. Examples of this are manifestations of the sexual functions, birth, sickness, death. All these entail cultic uncleanness. The biblical terms covering this department are *ṭâhôr* or *katharos* (=clean), and *ṭāmēʾ* and *ṭumʾāh*, or *akathartos* (=unclean).

B. In the *Old Testament*, where special emphasis seems to be laid upon the holiness of God, the contrast between clean and unclean is drawn particularly sharply. The category of the unclean applies *above all* to everything which is in any way associated with *pagan cults*. It is prohibited to eat various kinds of 'unclean' animals. Now on closer examination it turns out that the animals covered by this prohibition are those which have some sort of cultic or religious significance in the religions of Israel's neighbours (Lev 11, Deut 14). Again land belonging to Gentile peoples is 'unclean land' (Amos 7:17). Palestine alone, as belonging to Yahweh himself, is clean. A further factor, associated with this uncleanness of the territory of the Gentiles, is the ↗ ban which is pronounced upon it (Josh 6:24–7:26). These ideas are carried so far that it is even prohibited to partake of the fruits of the land of Canaan in the first three harvests after the conquest. Those of the fourth year have to be offered to Yahweh, and it is not until the fifth year comes that the Israelites are allowed to take the fruits of the harvest for their own use, 'For I, Yahweh, am your God' (Lev 19:23). For similar reasons it was also prohibited to partake of meat offered to idols (1 Macc 1:62f).

For the rest an idea which Israel had in common with the surrounding peoples of her world was that contact with corpses or with the phenomena connected with sex brought about uncleanness (for examples of this see Num 19:11 or Lev 12:5; 1 Sam 21:5; 2 Sam 11:4). The same applies to blood and diseases (probably the so-called 'leprosy' referred to is in reality a curable skin-disease, and not leprosy in the modern sense: see L. Köhler, *ZAW* 67 [1955/1956], 290f). The case of uncleanness incurred through contact with corpses enables us to realise how little the concept of uncleanness here has to do with *morality*. To bury the dead is actually a duty, or at least a praiseworthy deed (Lev 21:1–3; Tob 1:18; 2:9; 12:12).

Nevertheless—and this is characteristic for the Old Testament—uncleanness of this cultic kind does exclude the subject in some sense from communion with Yahweh. The priest who has incurred uncleanness is thereby disqualified from the normal priestly activities (Lev 21f), while the layman who is in this condition must not partake of sacred meals or enter the temple or take part in the holy war (Lev 7:20f; 12:4; Deut 23:9–14 etc).

The means of cleansing which is employed is water (or less frequently blood as well) applied in the form of sprinkling, washing, or bathing. In addition certain prescribed periods have to be observed during which the state of uncleanness continues.

The specialists are divided in their opinions as to what precisely constitutes the original basis for believing that corpses, various kinds of animals, blood, etc, cause uncleanness. We do not possess any texts which could throw light upon this problem for us. In the case of the Old Testament at least all these matters have been brought under a common heading by acquiring a specific reference to Yahweh. The religion of Yahweh has taken over the heritage of earlier times and customs, and placed it at its own service. Whatever the earlier significance of these purificatory rites may have been, henceforward their function is to protect Israel from believing in idols and idolatrous practices, or to rid them of such practices where they are already in existence. Admittedly, when the idea of cleanness is over-emphasised it does lead, in the last analysis, to a ludicrous degree of formalism, and this had in fact already taken place even before the time of Jesus.

It is against this kind of formalism that the prophets inveigh when they urge the claims of interior purity of mind and heart. For many had come to neglect this in favour of a wholly external and ritual purity (Hos 6:6; Amos 4:1–5; 5:21–5; Is 1:10–17; above all Is 6:5, Jer 13:27 etc). Morals, and not an externalist idea of purity, must be accorded the first place, a morals consisting in acknowledgement of God, obedience to his will, and especially practical love of one's neighbour. It is this that is truly demanded (see also Ps 15; 40:7–9; 50:16; etc).

C. In the *New Testament* the idea of ritual cleanness or uncleanness is presented as inadequate and destined to disappear. In its place, and in continuation of the message of the prophets, *inner purity* is demanded. In his controversies with his opponents on the subject of clean and unclean (Mk 7:1–23; Mt 15:1–20) Jesus has spoken the last word on this subject. In these controversies Jesus first defines his position with regard to the concept of the tradition of the elders, and then goes on to treat of various particular cases. In Mk 7:14ff and Mt 15:19f he touches upon our subject in particular. He provides a definition of the idea of cleanness which is fundamentally new. The death blow is dealt to the old view of ritual cleanness and uncleanness, but in its place the basic principle of all morality, of morality as such, is defined: it is on the basis of what comes from the ↗ heart of man (ie, from his disposition, his attitude), his words, therefore, and his deeds, that he can be pronounced truly clean or unclean. The primitive church had, of course, still much to do before this radical decision could be put into effect with all its implications. Something which had been rooted so deeply and so long in the customs and habits of men could not be abolished overnight. Jesus himself was fully aware of this, if we may take Mt 23:23ff as representative in this sense (see also Acts 10:10–16; ↗ Three A; 15:20f, 28f; Gal 2:11ff etc). The procedure of the early church was, in fact, comprehensible not only from the standpoint of Jewish Old Testament tradition, but also from that of its own teaching. So long as the observance of the prescriptions of purity did not constitute an obstacle to that which was essential in the christian message there was no need to insist upon its abolition. But whenever this did become desirable the church did not hesitate so to insist.

The effect of this was that attention came to be concentrated exclusively upon one particular aspect of cleanness, one which was certainly also present in contemporary Judaism (under the influence of the prophets), namely cleanness in the inner man (R. Meyer, 426f). Jesus declares that those who are 'clean of heart' are blessed, and promises them that they will ↗ see God and share in the ↗ kingdom of God (Mt 5:8; see also Ps 24:4; 73:1). Again in 1 Tim 1:5; 3:9 and 2 Tim 1:3; 2:22 we find references in the same sense to the 'pure heart' and 'clear conscience' (the two are synonymous). Again in John strong emphasis is laid upon purity. The disciples of Jesus are 'clean' through his word (15:3). The betrayer is 'unclean' (13:11). It can be deduced from this that uncleanness is sin in all its aspects (see 1 Jn 1:7, 9). According to 1 Pet 1:22 purification is achieved through obedience to the ↗ truth. In Eph 5:26 (see Heb 9:13f) it is the blood of Christ which 'cleanses' us through the conferring of baptism. It is always a question of purification, a liberation from sin of every kind. This purification is achieved essentially through the sacramental act of ↗ baptism, in which the salvific work of Christ is applied to the individual. But the obedience of man in faith is also an indispensable contributory factor (as Jn 15:3 and 1 Pet 1:22 likewise show).

D. The *restriction* of 'cleanness' in the moral sense (inner purity) to the *sexual sphere* is foreign to the New Testament. Uncleanness as conceived of among pagans, on the other hand, consists primarily in avarice and unchastity. It is precisely uncleanness and excesses in the sexual sphere, 'burning the candle at both ends', which is felt as 'uncleanness' (*akatharsia*: see Gal 5:19; Rom 1:24–32; 2 Cor 12:21; etc). The idea that relationships *even in marriage* may cause uncleanness in the moral sense (ie, may have an element of sinfulness in them) is utterly foreign to the bible. Ideas of this sort, remotely derived from those of the bible, were put forward by certain fathers of the church. But they are the outcome of, and at the same time characterised by, a certain intermingling of the two originally distinct concepts of 'cultic' and 'moral' uncleanness, and at the same time of a fresh incursion of the ancient Jewish ceremonial law as an influence upon the theology of the church. Thus the prohibition of servile works (*opera servilia*) as an act of sanctification of the sabbath entered once more into christian moral theology on the basis of the principle: 'Si Judaei quanto magis Christiani' ('if the Jews did it, how much more should christians do it too'). In the same way too the church's concept of celibacy was arrived at on the basis of the same principle (see Lev 22:2ff and 15:18; and, on the principle itself, see Ex 19:15). Further examples are that it was forbidden to come to church or receive communion after married intercourse or *pollutio nocturna* (='nocturnal emission of semen': thus, *ne polluantur corpora*='that [our] bodies may not be defiled' in the hymn of compline). Further examples still might be adduced. Not the least important result of all this was that it paved the way for the disastrous process by which all the emphasis in moral teaching was exaggeratedly laid on sexual morality.

Bibliography: F. Hauck and R. Meyer, *TDNT* III, 413–31; P. van Imschoot in Haag, cols 1420–3; Imschoot II, 204–16; von Rad I, 272–9; D. Lys and M. Carrez in Allmen, 59–63; J. Schmid, *RNT* on Mk 7:1–23 with Excursus; Schnackenburg, 35f; W. H. Gipsen, *OTS* I (1948), 190–6; A. Penna, *Riv. Bibl. It.* 6 (1958), 15f; a thorough treatment of the individual passages is provided especially by J. Döller, 'Die Reinheits- und Speisegesetze des At', *AA* 7/2f (1917). On D: F. Pettirsch, *ZKT* 69 (1947), 257–327, 417–44 (esp. 430, *n.* 196, and 439); H. Doms, *Vom & Sinn des Zölibats*, Regensberg-Münster 1954; A. Adam, *Der Primat der Liebe*, Kevelaer 1954[6]; L. Moulinier, *Le pur et l'impur dans la pensée des Grecqs*, Paris 1952; O. W. Buchanan, 'The Role of Purity in the Structure of the Essene Sect', *RQ* 15/4/3, 397–406.

Johannes B. Bauer

Confession

Confession or avowal corresponds to ↗ preaching, as can be seen from Rom 10:8–9: 'The word is near you . . . the word of faith which we preach (*kērussein*); because, if you confess (*homologein*) with your lips that Jesus is Lord and believe in your heart that God raised him from the dead, you will be saved'. In other words, if what you say with your lips agrees with what you say in your heart, if the *same word* comes from both in agreement with the word of the preacher (*homo-*=the same, *logos*=word) you will reach salvation. The original sense of the word, therefore, implies expressing what the heart receives in faith. Faith and avowal are intimately associated; both together they constitute the response to the preached word or kerygma. In this way the kerygma is enlarged through the confession or avowal of faith—an idea which, though rooted in the Old Testament, only reaches its complete development in the New.

A. *The Old Testament*. The verb 'to avow' occurs thirteen times in LXX with the sense of acknowledging, being in agreement, confessing. The texts are as follows: Job 40:9[14] corresponding to Hebrew *yādaᶜ*; Wis 18:13; 2 Macc 6:6; 4 Macc 6:34; 9:16; 13:5; Esther 1:10; in 1 Macc 6:61; Jer 51(44):25 the sense is 'to swear by' or 'vow' ('avow') corresponding to Hebrew *nādar*; the phrase 'confess (avow) one's sins' occurs in Sir 4:26; Dan 13:14 (Vulg: with which see 1 QS I, 18–III); in Ezra 4:60; 5:58 (see also 1 QH) it occurs with the sense of 'praise'.

The noun *homologia* (=confession, avowal) occurs seven times. It can refer to a vow (Hebrew: *nēder*) in Lev 22:18; Jer 51(44):25; a 'goodwill offering' in Dt 12:6, 17; Ezek 46:12; Am 4:5; and in one case (Ezra 9:8) has the meaning 'praise'.

As in classical Greek the compound verb *exhomologeisthai*, more rarely *anthomologeisthai*, can have the meaning 'to make open profession or confession' (eg of sins). In LXX the connotation 'praise, thank' is original, a genuinely new sense which has no doubt been influenced by the Hebrew verb *yāda*[c] meaning 'know' or 'confess openly'.

In this connection we have to take into account the old Testament liturgy of thanksgiving sacrifices (*tôdâh*) which included a series of short, hymnic utterances dealing with the high deeds of Yahweh in leading his people. The greatest of these was of course his taking them out of Egypt, usually expressed in the classical formula: 'Yahweh who has led Israel out of Egypt' (eg Ex 20:2; Lev 11:45; 25:38; Num 15:41; 23:22; 24:8; Dt 5:6; 8:14; Mic 6:4; Ps 81:10; 136:11 etc), 'with a mighty hand' (Dt 6:21; 7:8) or 'with a mighty hand and an outstretched arm' (Dt 4:34; 26:8; Ps 136:12; see also Ex 6:6).

This is the primitive confession of faith and all others are in some way connected with it: the promise to the fathers, the leading of the people through the wilderness, the revelation on Sinai, 'the entry into the cultivated land of Canaan' (M. Noth). The *Sitz im Leben* of all these individual confessions is to be sought in the cult.

The confessional character of the Old Testament also finds expression in the wider historical presentations as, for example, in Josh 24:2–15, Jud 5:6–21 and Ps 105, 136; etc.

In the last resort all of these confessional formulations, whether short or long (as Dt 26:5–9), are to be understood on the basis of covenant theology. They constitute the response of the people to the wondrous movement of God in their direction. This comes through in the classical covenant formula: 'Yahweh is our God' (eg Ex 6:7; 24:3, 7; 29:46; Dt 4:7, 35) which is expressed with greater theological profundity in Dt 5–6; 10:17; Josh 3:10; 24:24; 1 Kings 18:21; 2 Kings 19:15; and elsewhere.

All of these confessional forms in the Old Testament refer not to abstract truths but always to events which have taken place within the history of salvation or, more precisely, to the God who guides this history, the God who is acknowledged and praised in the 'historical credo' (von Rad) of Dt 26:6–9; 6:21–5 and Josh 24.

B. *The New Testament.* In the New Testament the verb *homologein* occurs twenty-six times. In most cases it has the meaning 'to acknowledge': Mt 7:23; 10:32 (twice) = Lk 12:8 (twice); Jn 1:20 (twice); 9:22; 12:42; Acts 23:8; 24:14; Rom 10:9, 10; 1 Tim 6:12; Tit 1:16; Heb 11:13; 13:15; 1 Jn 2:23; 4:2, 3, 15; 2 Jn 7; Rev 3:5. In addition to these twenty-three texts we find the verb once with the meaning 'to confess sins' (1 Jn 1:9) and twice with the meaning 'to swear, to promise with an oath' (Mt 14:7; Acts 7:17). The noun *homologia* is used six times and refers rather to the content of what is professed in faith than the act of confessing or avowing (2 Cor 9:13; 1 Tim 6:12–13; Heb 3:1; 4:14; 10:23).

The compound verb *exhomologein* which occurs ten times, means 'to confess' (Phil 2:11) and more especially 'to praise', the latter under the influence of LXX usage Mt 11:25 = Lk 10:21; Rom 14:11; 15:9. The meaning 'to confess sins' is also found (Mt 3:6 = Mk 1:5; Acts 19:18; Jas 5:16), and in one case 'to promise, agree' (Lk 22:6).

Homologein and *homologia*, as well as other forms which do not use this technical expression, always refer to a confession or avowal by which one makes a public decision for Christ. The New Testament use of this term always therefore contains strongly christological connotations (Rom 10:8–10; Phil 2:11; 1 Tim 6:12, 13; 1 Jn 4:2, 3).

I. *The form of confession or acknowledgement.* 1. *The synoptic gospels.* a. Peter was no doubt the first to give public expression to his faith: 'You are the Messiah (the Christ)' (Mk 8:29). Matthew enlarged this by the addition of 'the Son of God' (Mt 16:16), while Luke has 'the Messiah of God' (Lk 9:20). The title 'Christ' has a striking part to play throughout the passion narratives. So, for example, the high priest asks Jesus: 'Are you the Christ, the Son of the Blessed?' (Mk 14:61; Mt 26:63; Lk 22:67 cf Mt 27:17, 22; Mk 15:32; Lk 23:35, 39).

b. 'Son of God' is also found as a confessional formula in the synoptics. It occurs at the baptism of Jesus (Mt 3:17; Mk 1:11; Lk 3:22), in the temptation scene (Mt 4:3, 6; Lk 4:3, 9), the transfiguration (Mt 17:5; Mk 9:7; Lk 9:35); is used by the unclean spirits (Mk 3:11; 5:7; Lk 4:41), by Peter after the storm at sea in the Matthean tradition (Mt 14:33) and at Caesarea Philippi (only in Mt 16:16), during the hearing before the Sanhedrin (Mt 26:63; Mk 14:61), and the mocking on the cross (Mt 27:40, 43), and by the Roman centurion (Mt 27:54; Mk 15:39).

c. The three earliest gospels have also handed down another title, that of Son of David. This was attributed to Jesus by the people (Mt 12:23; 21:9 cf Mk 11:10; Mt 22:41–5 = Mk 12:35–7; Lk 20:41–4) and by the unclean spirits speaking through the mouths of the sick: 'have mercy on us (me), Son of David' (Mt 9:27; 15:22; Mt 20:30, 31 = Mk 10:47, 48; Lk 18:38, 39).

2. In *Acts* the word *homologia* does not occur and *homologein* only in the sense of 'promising' (7:17) and 'acknowledging' something (23:8; 24:14). But in the preaching of the apostles we meet with a whole series of christological titles.

a. The most common of these is 'Jesus is the Messiah' as, for example, on the lips of the apostles in Jerusalem (5:42: *euangelizomenoi ton khriston Iēsoun* = 'preaching Jesus as the Christ'. Taking in the preceding *didaskontes* = 'teaching' we should translate: 'teaching and preaching that Jesus is the Messiah'). It is also used by Paul in the synagogues of Damascus (9:20, 22), Thessalonika (17:2–3), and Corinth (18:5, 28), and by Apollos in Ephesus (18:28).

b. The classical formula 'Jesus is the Lord' occurs several times. The Hellenistic Christians from Cyprus and Cyrenaica preach the good news (*euangelizomenoi*) of the Lord Jesus or, paraphrasing, 'they preach: Jesus is the Lord' (11 :20). The Lord-ship of Jesus is the nucleus of the message as presented to the Gentiles, as is clear from Pauline theology. It is grounded on the resurrection of Jesus: 'God has made both Lord and Christ this Jesus whom you crucified' (2:36). Peter puts it the same way to the Gentile Cornelius: 'He [Christ] is lord of all' (10:36), of Jews and Gentiles. Although the Kyrios-formula seldom occurs expressly in Acts and almost always as addressed to Gentiles, it reflects the faith in the exalted Lord as held and expressed at the time the book was written.

c. Acts also testifies to Jesus under another confessional title as 'judge of the living and the dead' (10:42) whom God has appointed 'to judge the world' (17:31). That this is really a confessional formula can be seen in the use of the introductory particle *hoti* (=[to the effect] that); see also (17:31; 9:20, 22) or the infinitive with indirect speech (18:28).

d. In addition to these christological formulae made up of one clause or member there are also others with two which refer to the death and resurrection of Christ. In these cases the formulaic character of the confessional statements is apparent in the use of the *hoti* which introduces the formula (4:10). In the first half of Acts we find many different ways of avoiding a dichotomy between crucifixion and resurrection, as can be seen in 2:22–4; 2:36; 3:15; 5:30–1 cf 10:39–40; 17:2–3; 26:23 (*ei*='whether' instead of *hoti*).

3. *The Pauline epistles*. Just as the formula 'Jesus is the Messiah' predominates in the synoptics and Acts, so does 'Jesus is the Lord' in Paul. Both confessional formulae reflect the different spatial and temporal situations of Jewish and Gentile christianity respectively.

a. The short form of this formula is introduced by *homologein* in Rom 10:9 (with introductory *hoti* in Codex B) and by *exhomologein* in Phil 2:11. We have here a formula in current use at the time of Paul and one which must have made a deep impression on the communities to which he writes. In most cases, however, it does not occur with the verb *homologein*, eg 1 Cor 8:6; 12:3; Heb 13:20.

b. At a slightly later stage a two-part formula developed from this: Jesus is the Lord whom God has raised from the dead. Here the verb occurs twelve times in the active voice (Rom 4:24; 8:11, 11; 10:9; 1 Cor 6:14; 15:15, 15; 2 Cor 4:14; Gal 1:1; Eph 1:20; Col 2:12; 1 Thess 1:10) and thirteen times in the passive (he who has been raised by God) Rom 4:25; 6:4, 9; 7:4; 8:34; 1 Cor 15:4, 12, 13, 14, 16, 17, 20; 2 Cor 5:15).

When the emphasis is on *God* who has raised Jesus the direct object is *Jesus* (Rom 8:11; 1 Thess 1:10), *the Lord* (1 Cor 6:14), *the Christ* (1 Cor 15:15; Eph 1:20; Col 2:12), *Jesus the Lord*, or *the Lord Jesus* (Rom 4:24; 10:9; 2 Cor 4:14). When, however, the verb is in the passive, *Christ* is always the subject (except Rom 4:25), even in Rom 8:34 (following B, D, Koine and Syr.). We may therefore conclude that even if in the christology of Paul the emphasis has passed from Messiah to Lord the original Messiah-motif appears still in the titles 'Jesus Christ' (sixty-five times) or 'Christ Jesus' (sixty-three times).

c. As a result of theological reflection these christological formulae are given a deeper and broader connotation and expressed dialectically in the opposites: 'died—raised from the dead' (Rom 8:34; see also Rom 4:24, 25; 1 Cor 15:3–5; 2 Cor 13:4; 1 Thess. 4:14; Rom. 14:9), 'descended—ascended' (Eph 4:8–10; see also Rom 10:6–13; Phil 2:6–11), 'descended from David according to the flesh—designated Son of God' (Rom 1:3, 4 and, dependent on this, 2 Tim 2:8), 'according to the flesh—according to the Spirit' (Rom 1:3, 4; compare 'crucified in weakness—living by the power of God', 2 Cor 13:4), 'put to death in the flesh—made alive in the Spirit' (1 Pet 3:18).

d. In the pastoral epistles Jesus himself is represented as the exemplar of confession or avowal during his trial before Pilate. In the presence of the Roman ruler he made 'the good confession' (1 Tim 6:13) by stating that he was the Messiah (cf Mk 15:2).

4. *The Johannine writings.* The confessional character of these writings can be clearly discerned in the frequent use of *hoti* as an introductory formula (Jn 1:20; 1 Jn 4:15), the double accusative (Jn 9:22; 1 Jn 4:2; 2 Jn 7; see also Rom. 10:9), and the infinitive (Jn 9:22 in D and e; 1 Jn 4:2 in B; see also Tit 1:16).

a. The primitive confessional formula 'Jesus is the Christ' is found also in the Johannine writings (Jn 1:20, 41; 3:28; 4:25, 29; 7:26, 27, 41; 9:22; 10:24; 11:27; 12:34; 20:31; 1 Jn 2:22; cf v 23; 4:15; 5:1; 2 Jn 7).

b. The closely related form 'Jesus is the Son of God' is often met with in the fourth gospel and the Johannine epistles (eg Jn 1:34, 49; 6:69; 10:36; 1 Jn 4:15; 5:5) and is practically identical with 'Jesus is Christ (Messiah)' (see 1 Jn 2:22 with v 23; 1 Jn 4:15 with 5:1; 5:5 with v 6). Reference to Jesus as Christ and as Son can also be found together, as in Jn 11:27 and 20:31: 'Jesus is the Christ, the Son of God'.

c. The expression: 'Jesus Christ has come in the flesh' (1 Jn 4:2; 2 Jn 7 cf 1 Jn 5:6) provides a further interpretation of the original confession of faith: 'Every spirit which confesses (*homologein*) that Jesus Christ has come in the flesh' (1 Jn 4:2 and 2 Jn 7). Referring back to 1 Jn 4:3 and Johannine christology as a whole, Jesus and Christ are put together to form one accusative. In 1 Jn 5:6 the author spells out further the christological formula: 'Jesus Christ . . . is hc who came by water and blood'. His intention in putting it this way is to stress the humanity of Jesus.

II. *The Word.* Jesus stands at the centre of the confession of faith as we find it in the New Testament. It is he who, through the mouth of the apostles, announces the good news of eschatological salvation and demands the response of faith and confession of his name. Faith and confession or avowal are therefore intimately related. The *proclaimed word* awakens *faith* in the heart and *confession* on the lips (see Rom 10:8–9; 2 Cor 4:13). All of the christological formulae found in the New Testament are not only doctrinal but confessional—above all, confessional. They are originally and remain preponderantly of a pure christological character. The whole thought-world of the early church centres on Jesus Christ whose incomparable prerogatives are expressed compendiously by the sacred writers, interpreted and deepened by theological reflection, and then acknowledged and praised openly before the world by the early Christian communities.

1. According to the witness of *the synoptic gospels and Acts*, the expression 'Jesus is the Christ' forms the most original and basic confession of faith first proclaimed by Peter at Caesarea Philippi (Mk 8:29). The *Sitz im Leben* of this confession has to be sought in the earthly life of Jesus and in that of the early church at a time when the messianic question played a prominent part in the polemic with official judaism. The decisive question for the contemporaries of Jesus and convert judaeo-christians in Palestine and in the diaspora was precisely this: is Jesus really the promised Messiah who has come as king of Israel to free his chosen people from their enemies? (See Jn 1:41; 4:29; 7:26f, 41f; 9:22; 12:34; 20:31; Mk 14:61; 15:2; Acts 1:6.) The significance which Jesus attached to the messianic idea after the confession of Peter (Mk 8:29), according to which the Son of Man was to suffer, die, and be raised from the dead (Mk 8:31 cf 9:31; 10:33f), was filled out after Pentecost by the inspired writers with reference to the relevant Old Testament texts. The intention of the apostles in their preaching was to show that, in accordance with the scriptures, Jesus had to die and be raised and thus establish himself as the promised messiah (see Lk 24:25–7; Acts 2:22–4; 3:15; 4:10; 5:30; 10:40; 13:29f, 34; 17:2f; 18:28).

The belief that Jesus had appeared as the promised Messiah (see Acts 4:10; Rom 8:34) entered so deeply into Paul that he made a proper name out of the christological formula: Jesus Christ or Christ Jesus.

For the early church the title 'Christ' was not a jaded formula as it has come to be for so many today. It awakened in their minds the figure of the suffering, dying, and risen Jesus in keeping with the representation of the Son of Man in the way Jesus himself had interpreted it. In its liturgy the early church acknowledged and praised Jesus the 'Christ' as the one who suffered, died, and was raised for the salvation of the world.

We conclude therefore that the formula 'Jesus is the Christ' preceded the avowal of his sonship and lordship both logically and chronologically.

2. The formula 'Jesus is the Lord' forms the kernel of *Pauline* christology. For the first christian communities it at once recalled the easter-event. Jesus, who had lived and died in a given place and at a given point of history, had been designated by God as *lord* (*kurios*) by the resurrection from the dead. This brief confessional formula was in use principally in the gentile-christian communities (see Acts 11:20 with 11:19). It evoked the figure of Jesus Christ as raised to the right hand of God (Rom 10:9; 1 Cor 12:3) at the resurrection (1 Cor 15:3–8), having subdued the powers and principalities (Phil 2:10f; 1 Pet 3:22), as present in the community and one day to return in glory (1 Cor 16:22: *marana tha*—our lord, come!).

Here we come to the very centre of the early church's life. Dedicated entirely as it was to the risen and glorified lord, it could not start out with the enunciation of timeless truths. Hearing the title *kurios*, christians of Jewish extraction would think automatically of Yahweh the God of the fathers, translated *kurios* in LXX. Gentile christians would praise Jesus as the one and only *kurios* as against the official cult of Caesar and the gods. *All* Christians would acknowledge him as the risen and glorified lord, the *kurios* of the life and death of his followers and servants, the lord of the church and of the entire creation.

In the two-part christological formulae the avowal 'Jesus is the Lord' is expanded by reference to God the Father who had raised Jesus from the dead; but the reference to Jesus as *kurios* is antecedent to mention of God the Father (as in Eph 4:5f; 1 Jn 2:23f; 4:15), not vice versa (as in 1 Cor 8:6; 1 Pet 1:3).

In the three-part formulae a reference to the Holy Spirit is added (Rom 15:30; 2 Cor 13:14).

In this way the reference to Jesus as *kurios* is expanded by a confession of faith in God the Father who had glorified Jesus and strengthened by reference to the Holy Spirit through whom he is present to his community.

3. The christological title 'Son of God' is encountered chiefly in the *gospel and epistles of John*, but we find it also in the Pauline epistles and in the synoptics (see above).

We should take note of the fact that, according to the synoptic tradition, Jesus never refers to himself expressly as 'Son of God', despite the fact that he was conscious of being such in a unique manner, as can be seen from the way he addressed God as father and spoke of him as *his* father in a way different from other people. It is quite another question, however, whether the apostles arrived at an understanding of this title in all its significance during the lifetime of Jesus. If we take in the various stages of the gospel tradition it will be clear that they understood it in full significance only after the resurrection and *in the light of* the resurrection. After the descent of the Holy Spirit they were able to recognise that Ps 2:7 (see Acts 13:33; Rom 1:3f; Heb 1:5) and the promise to David in particular (Mt 22:41–6) had been fulfilled in Jesus. He was truly the messianic king and Son of God.

This post-resurrection acknowledgement of the unique and inalienable divine sonship of Jesus is confirmed in the christology of Paul. In such important, and in some cases, ancient confessional formulae as 1 Cor 15:3–8, 1 Tim 3:16, 2 Tim 4:1, and 1 Pet 3:18–22 the resurrection is mentioned but Jesus is not referred to as 'Son of God' as is the case elsewhere (eg Rom 1:3; Heb 1:5). We may conclude from this that the resurrection and exaltation of Jesus were not deduced as consequences of the divine sonship of Jesus previously recognised and accepted. On the contrary, the great event of the resurrection and glorification of Jesus led directly to belief in his divine origin and nature.

By using this most recent of the christological formulae 'Jesus is Son of God', therefore, the early church expressed and professed its unshakeable faith in the divine sonship of Jesus and read it back into his earthly life, his birth and miraculous conception (Mt 1:20–23; Lk 1:34f), and from it deduced his pre-existence (Phil 2:6–11; Col 2:9; Rom 9:5; Tit 2:13).

Nowhere more strongly does this title appear than in the Johannine gospel and epistles which represent Jesus in the light of his 'glory as of the only Son from the Father' (Jn 1:14 cf 1:34, 49; 5:25; 10:36; 11:27; 17:1; 19:7; 20:31; etc).

The christological formulae in the Johannine epistles: 'to confess Jesus *Christ* [who has] come in the flesh' (1 Jn 4:2; 2 Jn 7 cf 1 Jn 2:22), '[to confess] *the Son*' (1 Jn 2:23), 'to confess that Jesus is *the Son of God*' (1 Jn 4:15), have a marked confessional character. John's intention in using these brief and concise christological confessions is not so much to arm his readers against the attacks of an emergent gnosticism which questioned the truth of the incarnation and the universality of redemption but rather to warn them against those 'antichrists' (1 Jn 2:18, 22; 4:3; 2 Jn 7) who, influenced by the pagan milieu, indulged in an insidious materialism, had given way to religious indifference, no longer took their christian calling seriously, and had turned their backs on Jesus Christ. Here as in the fourth gospel we cannot fail to notice the marked christocentricity of the writer.

III. *The Locus.* Though the literary evidence no longer permits us to determine exactly in each case the original situation in which these forms of christological confession arose, we can in a general way designate their *Sitz im Leben* as *the worship of the early church*, the celebration of the eucharist and early christian preaching in particular. This gives these christological statements a distinctly *confessional* character.

In the ordinary divine service of the early church, especially in the *celebration of the eucharist*, the community confessed its faith in Jesus Christ with 'psalms and hymns and spiritual songs' (Eph 5:19; see also Acts 2:47). In Phil 2:6–11 Paul has preserved for us in rhythmic form one of the most ancient confessions of faith. This is a composition which can with reason be called a christian psalm. Its climax comes in the avowal (*exhomologeisthai*, see too Is 45:23) that 'Jesus is the Lord', Lord, that is, over the whole cosmos. We find ancient christological hymns also in 1 Tim 3:16 and, in a fragmentary state, 1 Pet 2: 21–4; perhaps also in the opening verses of Eph, Col, and 1 Pet (see Col 1:15–20).

The many formulae in the Johannine writings which speak of Jesus as Christ and Son of God, as also the post-resurrection formulae 'my lord and my God' (Jn 20:28) and 'it is the lord' (Jn 21:7, 12) reflect the confession of faith in Christ in early christian liturgy.

Praise of Christ in the liturgy probably took on at an early stage the fixed form of a cultic *homologia* (see Heb 3:1; 4:14; 10:23).

In Heb 13:15 the community 'confesses' the name of God, doubtless in the context of a liturgical celebration.

The well-known resurrection confession of 1 Cor 15:3–7 was probably recited and explained in early Christian *preaching* and *catechesis*. As he tells us himself, Paul had taken it from the primitive church and explained it in his preaching to the Corinthians. It held a position of primary importance in his missionary preaching ('as of first importance', v 3): the expiatory death of Jesus, his burial and resurrection according to the scriptures, his appearances after his resurrection. The confession of faith in the risen and exalted lord was the centre of his preaching against the cult of Caesar and the gods (1 Cor 12:3; 2 Cor 4:5) and as such aroused in his hearers both faith and the open confession of faith (Rom 10:8f).

From the earliest times the administration of baptism provided the occasion for confession of faith in Jesus Christ. Even if v 37 in Acts 8:36–8 is generally considered inauthentic, it can still be taken as a very ancient witness to the fact that a confession of faith in Christ followed baptismal catechesis—'I believe that Jesus Christ is the Son of God' (see Mt 28:19; Mk 16:16). Rom 10:9 refers in all probability to a confession of faith in the resurrection which preceded baptism. 1 Pet 3:18–22 has also preserved a confession of faith which was made during baptism, faith in Christ who died for our sins, who 'went and preached to the spirits in prison . . . who has gone into heaven and is at the right hand of God'. This christological confession is interrupted by the parenthesis of vv 20–1 which form a short baptismal instruction.

According to New Testament tradition the christological confession of faith also contains the idea of *judgement*, the context of which is to be sought during the time of persecution when the faithful had to decide clearly either for or against Christ.

According to the entire context of 1 Tim 6:12–16, Timothy is represented as standing at the bar of judgement where he has already made 'the good confession' (of faith) in the presence of many witnesses (v 12). He still has to 'fight the good fight', that is, confess Jesus openly before his judges in imitation of the testimony which Jesus himself gave during his trial. In other words, just as Jesus made 'the good confession' during his trial in the hearing before Pilate by solemnly declaring himself to be the messianic king, so must Timothy testify to the messianic kingdom of Jesus. Perhaps the christological confession 'Jesus is the *kurios*' (Rom 10:9) is referred to indirectly here, in the sense that Timothy boldly declares before the Roman judgement seat for the *kurios* Jesus rather than for the *kurios* Caesar. 1 Cor 12:3; 'No one can say, "Jesus is lord" except by the Holy Spirit', has nothing to do with speaking with tongues but reflects, in the same way, a time of persecution. According to Mt 10:17–20 (see also Lk 12:11–12) Jesus promises his disciples the gift of the Spirit when they are brought to judgement by the synagogue and stand before earthly governors and rulers. This points in the same direction.

The same can be said of the saying of Jesus about confessing him before human judges. This judgement is paralleled by the confessing of the 'Son of Man' at the final judgement (Mt 10:32: *homologein en tini* = 'to confess *in* someone' is an Aramaism for the more normal accusative; Lk 12:8; see too Mk 8:38 = Lk 9:26; 2 Tim 2:12; Rev 3:5). In their difficult confrontation with a hostile world the disciples can count on the assistance of the Holy Spirit (Mk 13:11; Lk 12:11f). The avowal of faith in Christ is therefore given the greatest possible importance since it already decides the ultimate fate of the individual here and now. The primitive form this confession took is continually developed and expanded as time goes on.

The opposite of confession or avowal is *denial* (*arneisthai*: Mt 10:33; Lk 12:9 cf Mk 8:38; Lk 9:26). The opposite of confessing Jesus as Messiah and *Kurios* is quite simply apostasy (1 Cor 12:3).

According to the synoptics and Acts, the form 'Jesus is the Christ' expresses the personal faith of the apostles. This, however, very soon became a kind of slogan or watchword in the struggle against judaism and a confession of public faith appropriate to certain specific occasions in the life of the christian community as, for example, at baptism and in time of persecution (see 1 Tim 6:13).

These christological confessions of faith could also have a polemical tone, for example in the struggle against false teachers (eg 1 Jn 2:23; 4:2–3; 4:15; 2 Jn 7). The formula in 1 Cor 8:6 directed against pagan polytheism also no doubt conceals a polemical note: '*One* God, the Father, from whom are all things and for whom we exist, and *one* lord Jesus Christ, through whom are all things and through whom we exist'. The reference to meat offered to idols in the first verse of the same chapter shows us how polemic against many gods and the many lesser 'lords' could have led to the expansion of the primitive form 'Jesus is lord' into the dual formula we find here which refers also to the Father.

The publicly proclaimed faith of the community gives its answer to the kerygma or gospel by declaring in unison: 'Jesus is the Christ', 'Jesus is the *Kurios*', 'Jesus is the Son of God'. In these brief christological formulae we feel the heartbeat of the early church which on more than one occasion took its witness to the point of martyrdom. It was on the basis of these christological confessions that the great statements of faith were gradually built up.

Bibliography: F. Kattenbusch, *Das apostolische Symbol* (2 vols), Leipzig 1894 and 1900; W. Foerster, *Herr ist Jesus*, Gütersloh 1924; E. Lohmeyer, *Kyrios-Jesus: eine Untersuchung zu Phil 2:5–11*, Heidelberg 1928; F. J. Babcock, *The History of the Creeds*, New York 1930; O. Michel, 'Biblisches Bekennen und Bezeugen', *ET* 2 (1935), 231–45; O. Proksch, *Das Bekenntnis im AT*, Leipzig 1936; G. Bornkamm, 'Homologia', *Hermes* 71 (1938), 377–93; W. Fiedler, *Bekennen und Bekenntnis*, Berne 1943; C. H. Dodd, *The Apostolic Preaching and its Developments*, London 1944²; H. Dörries, *Das Bekenntnis in der Geschichte der Kirche*, Göttingen 1947²; M. Noth, *Überlieferungsgeschichte des Pentateuch*, Stuttgart 1948, 48–67; O. Cullmann, *The Earliest Christian Confessions*, London 1949; J. Jeremias, 'Zwischen Karfreitag und Ostern', *ZNW* 42 (1949), 194–201; C. Crehan, *Early Christian Baptism and the Creed*, London 1949; J. N. D. Kelly, *Early Christian Creeds*, London 1950; O. Cullmann, *Early Christian Worship*, London 1956; O. Michel, *TDNT* v, 199–220; H. A. Blair, *A Creed before the Creeds*, London 1955; E. Schweitzer, *Erhöhung und Erniedrigung bei Jesus und seinen Nachfolgern*, Basle 1955; E. Lichtenstein, 'Die älteste christliche Glaubensformel', *ZKG* 63 (1950/1), 1–74; E. Schweitzer, 'Discipleship and Belief in Jesus as Lord from Jesus to the Hellenistic Church', *NTS* 2 (1955/6), 87–99; C. Westermann, 'Bekenntnis II. Im AT und Judentum', *RGG* I, Tübingen 1957³, 989–91; E. Kamlah, 'Bekenntnis III. Im NT', *RGG* I, 991–3; E. Schweitzer, 'Der Glaube an Jesus den Herrn in seiner Entwicklung von den ersten Nachfolgern bis zur hellenistischen Gemeinde', *ETL* 17 (1957), 7–21; H. Braun, 'Der Sinn der ntl. Christologie', *ZTK* 54 (1957), 341–77; R. Schnackenburg, 'Bekenntnis II. Biblisch', *LTK* II², 143–4; H. Schlier, *Die Verkündigung im Gottesdienst der Kirche*, Cologne 1958²; R. P. Martin, *An Early Christian Confession: Phil 2:5–11 in Recent Interpretation*, London 1960; J. Schreiner, 'Führung—ein Thema der Heilsgeschichte im AT', *BZ* 5 (1961), 2–18; N. Brox, 'Bekenntnis I. Biblisch', *HTG* I, Munich 1962, 151–5; P. Sandevoir, 'Confession', *DBT*, London 1967, 71–2; H. Ott, *Glaube und Bekennen*, Basle 1963; V. H. Neufeld, *The Earliest Christian Confessions*, Leiden 1963 (bibliography 147–54); F. Hahn, *Christologische Hoheitstitel. Ihre Geschichte im frühen Christentum*, Göttingen 1964².

Robert Koch

Conscience

The ancient world was not ignorant of the idea of conscience and of man's responsibility with regard to good and evil, but the word *suneidēsis* (=consciousness, conscience), of Ionian origin, which occurs for the first time in Democritus (fl. c. 430 BC: see frag. 297, H. Diels, *Fragmente der Vorsokratiker*), is very rare in the inscriptions and papyri (W. H. Buckler, W. M. Calder, and W. K. C. Guthrie, *Monumenta Asiae minoris antiqua* IV, Manchester 1933, 648, 10f; *Pap. Osl.* XVII, 10; *Pap. Ryl.* 116, 9; and others, all after the first century AD) and is found only twice in the Old Testament (Sir 10:20; Wis 17:11; see the variants of the Codex Sinaiticus on Sir 42:18). Although the word is not found at all in the gospels—Jn 8:9 is inauthentic—it is used by Paul, Hebrews, and Peter surprisingly often (some thirty times in all), and usually with a qualifying adjective such as 'good', 'bad', 'defiled', or 'pure'. It is just possible that the apostle's use of the word 'conscience' is derived from his compatriot, the Stoic Athenodorus of Canana (near Tarsus), who lived from 74 BC to AD 7 and instructed the Emperor Augustus (see Seneca, *De Tranqu. Anim.* III, 4). It is, however, an established fact that the hellenistic philosophers, and especially the Romans (Cicero, Seneca, and Lucretius), influenced by the teaching of Zeno and the Stoa on *sunkatathesis* (=assent given by the mind to its perceptions), tackled the study of this power of discernment and free choice insofar as it applied to rational human beings (see Philo, *De Spec. Leg.* I, 203; II, 49; *De Virt.* 206). But when it is realised that the word does not appear in Epictetus, Plutarch, Marcus Aurelius, or in the *Onomasticon* of Pollux, and that it occurs only once in Von Arnim's *Stoicorum Veterorum Fragmenta* (Chrysipp., III, 43, 2–5), one is bound to come to the conclusion that Paul's use of the word is not in fact derived from the Stoic philosophers—nor did he borrow it from literary sources, but, coming across the word in everyday speech and in hellenistic moral teaching, he took it and made out of it his detailed and elaborate moral and religious conception of conscience, placing special stress on its autonomy of judgement and its powers of moral responsibility.

It is no longer a question of mythological deities whether of a terrifying or a benevolent kind, such as the Greek Fates or Graces, who personify the moral law and its sanctions, or of the *daimōn*, the individual intellect, which is implanted in each man as a share in the godhead. Nor is it a question of the voice of wisdom which fortifies each individual man in his response to the ideal of the good life. It is, on the contrary, a capacity, situated in the ↗ heart, or, one might almost say, in the interior of the soul, which each man, even the heathen, has at his disposal (Rom 2:15), and which spreads its light so that it can act as a guide to practical conduct or as a law-giver, and sanction such action as a judge. This is above all a judgement based on reflection, which puts man in the position to take stock of the way he is living his life, so that he is able to pass a favourable or unfavourable judgement upon it. The *suneidēsis* distinguishes between right and wrong, good and evil, and in doing so metes out praise or blame (1 Cor 10:28f; Tit 3:11) as an impartial, sovereign judge who pronounces a verdict (2 Cor 1:12). The conscience has authority, as its verdict is guaranteed by Christ (1 Cor 8:12), and is produced in collaboration with the Holy Spirit (Rom 9:1) and by means of divine illumination (2 Cor 1:12; 4:2; Acts 23:1; 24:16). This distinct and well-justified evaluation extends to all basic attitudes and to all good intentions as well as to their translation into action (2 Cor 4:2). This accounts for the summons to examine the conscience (1 Cor 11:28; Gal 6:4; see also 2 Cor 13:5), the chief element of which must be the love of one's neighbour, as this is God's chief commandment to his children. No one is without blame, but whatever other errors he has committed, he can have an easy conscience so long as he can prove that he has loved his neighbour in deed and in truth (1 Jn 3:20–3).

This notion of the conscience which follows the act (*conscientia consequens*) incorporates those elements of Paul's contemporaries with which he was quite familiar. But Paul's great innovation in the history of morals is that he elaborated the idea of an imperative conscience which precedes the act and does not simply state what should be done and what should not be done, but speaks with the authority of God himself, and obliges man to act in a certain way. It is a guide or controlling agent of which man, in his ↗ freedom, has the use. (Philo mentions the reins of conscience, *Quod Deter.*, 23; see also *Decal.*, 87). Hence the phrase 'for conscience's sake', which denotes the individual motive and the immediate moral precept for action (1 Cor 10, 25–9; Rom 13, 5). This subjective orientation is to some extent in contradiction to the directives of an external law, as it is determined by the love of what is good and true, knowing this to be the definite will of God, and is not determined by ↗ fear of any possible sanctions. This notion of conscience presupposes a distinction between speculative knowledge and an evaluation of definite action under given circumstances. In the case of the second, a conscience that is 'weak' or 'sickly' (*asthenēs*, which appears for the first time here with a moral, religious meaning, can be said to correspond more or less to 'immature' or 'undeveloped' in the modern classification) can be deceived in the determination of a duty—as, for example, in the question whether it is permissible to eat flesh sacrificed to a false god or an idol. The conscience is in such cases not sufficiently well informed as to the principles of the new religion and the order of priorities within that religion. It is above all not firm or secure enough to apply these principles in every situation, and it also lacks the powers of discretion and prudence to put them to use in particular and complex situations. This conscience, which is so prone to error, is binding in every contingency, even if, under the impression of doing good, its decision is in favour of wrong. It would be a sin to reverse this decision (1 Cor 8:7, 10, 12). Another kind of pathological weakness is the 'scrupulous' conscience, which is hesitant and doubt-ridden, uncertain and easily swayed, and can never come to a decision—as, for instance, in the case of a man who cannot trust himself to take anything other than a vegetarian diet (Rom 14:2). Everyone must act from personal, independent faith and conviction (Rom 14:5), for 'whatever does not proceed from faith is sin' (14:23).

A 'good conscience' (1 Tim 1:5; 1 Pet 3:21) is one, the intention of which, illuminated by God (1 Tim 1:19; 3:9), is direct—that is to say, fixed upon God and the service of God (see Rom 12:2)—and which is secure and firm enough to carry out its decisions (Acts 23:1; 1 Pet 3:16). A 'pure' (*kathara*, 2 Tim 1:3), 'blameless' (*aproskopos*, Acts 24:16), 'good' (*kalē*, Heb 13:18), or 'perfect' (see Heb 9:9) conscience considers God's will and is intent on good behaviour 'in all things' (Heb 13:18). In contrast to this, a bad or 'defiled' conscience (Tit 1:15) is not capable of making morally right decisions (Tit 1:15) or of putting decisions into action. It is also branded by man's hypocrisy and malevolence (1 Tim 4:2), and at the same time afflicted by the stain of guilt and sin which can be washed away only by the ↗ blood of Christ (Heb 10:2, 22; 9:14). In ↗ baptism the conscience is cleaned and at the same time dedicated to God (Heb 10:22; 1 Pet 3:21). This is why it is so intimately connected with worship (Heb 9:9, 14; 10:2) and with the theological virtues, especially that of brotherly love (1 Cor 8), for, unlike the good heathen, the child of God does not confine himself to ascertaining the rule of the intellect, as far as his emotions and attitude are concerned, and simply to behaving decently and correctly. He is, on the contrary, mindful of his neighbour and intent on what will be profitable and edifying to him (1 Cor 10:23f). A conscience which is properly guided by the demands of faith will also be in a position to relate personal freedom with duty to one's neighbour, and to subordinate the permission to perform mutual acts of brotherly love which are neither good nor bad. Paul leaves delicate decisions of this kind to the conscience, and gives it primary importance in his moral teaching on ↗ love. Peter appeals to integrity of conscience as the most effective defence of christian communities (1 Pet 3:16).

Put in another way, merit is commensurate with the degree of goodness which the conscience has, as the conscience is the source and fountain of morality. The objective will of God is translated by the conscience into the subjective rule applicable to man. The christian is either good or bad, only to the extent that he obeys the promptings of his conscience, bearer of the divine law. This is what the Jew meant when he spoke of the 'inclination of the ↗ heart'. Paul, who denounced the Jewish ↗ law and so roundly condemned a purely preceptive morality, was obliged to replace the directions which were engraved on stone tablets by an 'autonomous' ordinance written in men's hearts (Jer 31:33 was a herald of this; see also Heb 8:10). This interior and personal norm of concrete behaviour is the spirit, not the letter, numbered among the finest things which the New Testament ascribes to the child of God, together with freedom, pride, candour, and frankness. On the ethical plane, the step from the old covenant to the new is made in this way—that is, from the written law to personal conscience.

Bibliography: See especially the bibliography in C. Spicq, *RB* 47 (1938), 50–80; C. Spicq, *Jahresbericht über die Fortschritte der klass. Altertumswissenschaft*, 1943, 169f. See further: R. D. Congdon, 'The Doctrine of Conscience', *Bibliotheca Sacra* (1945), 26–232 and 474–89; B. Reicke, *The Disobedient Spirits and Christian Baptism*, Copenhagen 1946, 174–91; J. Dupont, *Studia Hellenistica* 5 (Louvain 1948), 119–53; Haag, 467–653; H. Clavier, '*Hē Suneidēsis*: Une pierre de touche de l'Héllénisme paulinien', *Symposium*, Athens 1953; O. Seel, 'Zur Vorgeschichte des Gewissensbegriffes im altgriechischen Denken', *Festschrift F. Dornseiff*, Leipzig 1953, 291–319; G. Rudberg, 'Cicero und das Gewissen', *Symbolae Osloenses* (1955), 96–104; C. A. Pierce, *Conscience in the NT*, London 1955; B. Reicke, 'Syneidesis in Rom 2:15', *TZ* (1956), 157–61; W. D. Stacey, *The Pauline View of Man*, London 1956, 206f; J. Stelzenberger, *Syneidesis im NT*, Paderborn 1961; G. Bornkamm, *Studien zu Antike und Christentum* II, Munich 1962, 111–18.

Ceslaus Spicq

Consolation

Though the ancient world spoke and wrote much on the subject of consolation and the art of consoling, it remained, in the deepest sense, characterised by lack of consolation. Indicative of this is the fact that the same epoch which recognised a deity, a *numen*, for each and every thing in the world had no god whose function was to console. Once we enter the world of the bible, however, we find it full of divine consolation.

The bible recognises the multiplicity of earthly needs which make men feel so much the necessity of consolation. It recognises too the human means of achieving this end: friendship (Sir 6:16), a visit from friends (Gen 37:35; Job 2:11; 42:11), embassies (2 Sam 10:1–2; 2 Chron 19:1–2), and letters (Jer 29:1–23; Bar 4:5–9; 6 [=Letter of Jeremiah]; 2 Macc 1:1–2, 18; 2 Cor 1:1–7). It knows too of the consolation which food and drink can bring (Gen 14:18) and which comes from ↗ wine, 'the consoler' (Gen 5:29: the name Noah based on word-play with the vine as a consoling agent; Prov 31:6).

It knows also, of the consolation afforded in sorrow and old age by well-disposed children and posterity (Gen 5:29; Ps 128).

But it knows, too, how soon a merely human consolation can risk being an idle expenditure of energy or turning into the empty social custom of 'consoling'—regarded as a disagreeable task (Job 16:2; Jer 6:14; Zech 10:2; Mk 5:38; Lk 7:12; Jn 11:19, 31). So it is that men are advised to mourn but briefly and then 'to console themselves', since uncontrolled sorrow consumes one's life (Sir 30:21–3; 38:17–23). On the other hand, the bible is not ignorant of the dangers of false consolation (Is 28:14–22; Jer 7:4; Zech 10:2; Job 21:34; 31:24; Lk 6:24).

Over against all this there stands, as the true and, in the last analysis, the only consoler, the Lord God. He consoles the individual in trouble (relevant texts are to be found, in particular, among the psalms where they are too numerous to be noted separately), just as he does the people fallen under the sentence of history. (We find this, for example, in Second Isaiah, eg, Is 40:1; 51:3, 12; 66:11–13, and Ezek 33–48; Jer 14:8 [quoted in Lk 2:25]; 31:9; etc.) This divine consolation comes through God's word and his law (see, for example, Ps 119), but in a special way through the 'scriptures' (1 Macc 12:9; 2 Macc 15:9; Rom 15:4) and the ↗ prophets (2 Pet 1:19) who, despite all the warnings of judgement, have as their dearest task that of consoling. They remain in the memory of later generations above all as consolers (Sir 48:24; 49:10).

A special form of this prophetic consolation is their indication of the one who is to come—messianic and eschatological consolation. This line is taken up by the New Testament (Lk 2:25, 38) and attached to the consolation of God manifest in the person of the redeemer Jesus Christ, in the proclamation of salvation, in the Good News. Also, for the New Testament, every genuine consolation comes in the last resort only from God (Rom 15:5; 2 Cor 1:3–5; 2 Thess 2:16–17), and is ordered to eschatological salvation ('Take heart, your sins are forgiven' [Mt 9:2]; 'Blessed are those who mourn, for they shall be comforted' [Mt 5:4]). Conversely, the absence of consolation consists in the last resort in eschatological ruin (Wis 3:18; Lk 6:24).

At the same time, the New Testament does not in any way deny the need which man feels for consolation even in earthly necessities, and so among those who can in particular hope to obtain consolation it numbers the sick and imprisoned (Mt 25:36, 43), orphans and widows (Lk 1:27; 4:25; 7:12; 1 Tim 5:5; Jas 1:27), the poor (Mt 11:5; Lk 4:18; 7:22), the fainthearted (1 Thess 5:14), and the apostle himself, then in prison (Col 4:11). Here, too, the divine 'christian' consolation is achieved through human means. These are the apostles and the other preachers of the good news of salvation, church leaders and, indeed, all christians with respect to one another (1 Thess 2:11; 2 Cor 1:3; 2:1; 7:2, 6, 13; Acts 20:20; 1 Thess 5:14; Col 1:28; 2:2; 4:8; Eph 6:22; Philem 7).

All this consolation goes back in every case to God who shapes all human destinies and consoles the humble (2 Cor 1:3; 7:6, 13). And so the New Testament stands in the same line as the Old-Testament teaching on human and divine consolation, but adds for the consolation of man in his greatest needs, namely, sorrow and death, two forms which come through Jesus Christ: the reference to the ↗ resurrection—'just as Christ has risen' (1 Cor 15; Jn 11:21–7)—and the encouragement to suffer (↗ suffering) in union with the passion of Christ (2 Cor 1:5; 4:17; 1 Pet 4:13), since man can reach his eschatological salvation only by following this road.

Bibliography: O. Schmitz and G. Stählin, *TDNT* v, 771–98; G. Stählin, *TDNT* v, 815–22; G. M. Behler OP, *Die Abschiedsworte des Herrn (Jn 13–17)*, Salzburg 1962, esp. B I 3b (143–54), III 2a (233–40), and III 3 (245–54); W. Klaas, *Anfechtung und Trost*, Neukirchen 1963.

Suitbert H. Siedl

Contest

Starting out from the experience of human life and human history, of which contest and strife, quarrelling and ↗ war, and even rivalry in sport form a part, the bible attempts to elucidate sacred history in terms of struggle and contest. This sacred history is not something other than or apart from human history, but is essentially part of it, and therefore of the many struggles which go to make it what it is.

A. The *Old Testament* speaks not just of the holy war which Yahweh fought on behalf of his people but also of a contest which God undertakes on behalf of men, together with his anointed and his angels, against the political, cosmic, and demonic powers which are opposed to him (eg, Gen 3:15; Is 24:21; Ps 2:1; 5:6; 83:6–9; 89:10). The contest in which God has been engaged against the powers of evil since the beginning of time (Ps 74:13; 89:11; see also Is 51:9f; Job 27:7f) takes on visible form in the struggle against the enemies of his people (Ex 3:20; 11:4; 14:18; Josh 5:13f; Judg 5:4, 20; 2 Sam 5:24; Ps 2; 20; 21; 83:6–9), as also against the people themselves, who sin by breaking the covenant and therefore must be opposed (Num 14:39–44; Josh 7:1; 1 Sam 2:31; Is 1:4–9; 5:26–30; Jer 4:5–5:17; 6; 25:14–38). For their own eventual salvation Yahweh holds a lawsuit with his people who have fallen away from him (Is 1:18; Mic 6:2).

Under the influence of dualistic tendencies—though there is no genuine dualism in the Old Testament, since Yahweh is always the only sovereign lord (Ps 18:4–20)—the apocalyptic writers understand the war waged by the gentiles against 'the saints' (Dan 7:19–25; 11:40–5) as the final powerful attack of the evil powers (Ezek 38; Zech 14:1–3; Judg 1–7). In this they are the heirs of the great prophets of the earlier period. These powers will be finally destroyed by God in the final ↗judgement (Dan 8:25; 11:45), when God will put an end to all evil (Wis 5:17–23). Men are also involved in the struggle which rages between the angels of God on the one side and the hostile spirits on the other (Ass Moses 10:2; Jub 15:26, 31f).

An important role is given in the Qumran writings to the contest between light and darkness, the angels of light and the demons of darkness (1 QS III; 18–IV:1). The members of the community are set up for battle against the unrighteousness and also against their own weaknesses and temptations (1 QS IV: 15–26). This struggle is an anticipation of the eschatological contest of God against his enemies (1 QH III: 29–36). In this final struggle the righteous men of the congregation form the army of God against sinners and sin. The War Scroll (1 QM) has the purpose precisely of preparing and ordering the eschatological struggle of the community against the gentiles. The very existence of the community forces the individual to decide whether he wishes to fight for or against God. The confidence of the community in ultimate victory is rooted in trust in God and in its unique consciousness of election.

B. According to the witness of the *New Testament*, the christian community is also conscious of being heavily engaged in a cosmic struggle—a struggle, however, which through the contest and ↗victory of Christ (Jn 16:33 etc) has already been decided favourably in advance. Unlike the attitude of hatred characteristic of the Qumran community in its warlike preparations (1 QS 1:9–11), the christian community follows Christ in fighting not *against* those who do not belong to it but rather goes out in missionary enterprise into 'the world' (Eph 6:15, 17b; 1 Thess 2:2) on their behalf (Lk 23:34; Acts 7:60). In the following of Christ there is no longer any room for↗ war and fighting with the weapons of this world (Lk 22:50f; Jn 18:36f)—any kind of *makhesthai* (=fight, do battle) receives a negative verdict in the New Testament and is rejected (Jn 6:52; Acts 7:26; 2 Cor 7:5; 2 Tim 2:23f; Tit 3:9; Jas 4:1f). He who wishes to fight for God as a member of the christian community puts on the armour of God (Eph 6:10ff; see also Rom 6:13; 13:12, 2 Cor 6:7; 1 Thess 5:8; 1 Pet 4:1) and fights in the strength of God which has already overcome all powers and principalities in the resurrection and exaltation of Jesus (1 Cor 15:55–7 etc). The contest of the christian is against sin (2 Pet 2:16; see also 1 Tim 3:16; Heb 12:4) and against Satan and the demons, the rulers of this world. Jesus himself engaged in conflict against these powers (Mt 4:1–11; 12:27ff; Lk 11:18ff) which strove to destroy him (Lk 22:3; Jn 13:2, 27; 14:30; Acts 4:25–8; Rev 12:1–5) but which through the death and resurrection of Jesus were finally overcome (Jn 12:31; Col 2:15). Whoever becomes a follower of Jesus is committed to the struggle against the evil powers, a rearguard action which is fought out with extraordinary ferocity (Rev 12:7). These evil powers launch their attacks from every side. The power of this world is manifested both in temptation to apostasy and disobedience and in the persecutions and sufferings which the christian is called upon to endure (Rom 7:23; 8:35–9; 1 Cor 9:27; 2 Tim 2:3; Heb 10:32; Jas 4:1).

By taking over the Jewish apocalyptic tradition and allying it with the diatribe of the Cynics and Stoics, Paul was able to represent the contest in which the christian is engaged as an *agōn* (=contest, 1 Thess. 2:2) which requires the deployment of all one's powers (1 Cor 9:25f; Phil 1:27; Col 1:29; see also Lk 13:24), has to be sustained by prayer in common (Rom 15:30; Col 4:12) and is put to the extreme test by suffering and martyrdom (1 Tim 6:11; 2 Tim 4:6; see also Heb 10:10ff; 12:1ff). The struggle in which the follower of Christ is engaged is represented by Paul in terms of *strateuesthai*, of undertaking a military campaign for the salvation of men through the preaching of the gospel (1 Tim 1:18; 1 Thess 2:2; 2 Cor 10:3f; Phil 4:3; Col 2:1; 2 Tim 2:3–5; see also 1 Cor 9:7). Relying on the victory which Christ has already obtained, the christian enters the contest for the salvation of the world and for the prize which is set before him, the imperishable crown which is eternal life (Rom 8:18; 1 Cor 9:25; 1 Tim 6:12; 2 Tim 2:5; 4:7f; Heb 9:15).

The Revelation of John, which speaks so much of struggle and contest, stands in the tradition of Jewish apocalyptic. It sets out the drama of the final struggle in symbolic images as the victory of the Lamb which has already been won. In view of this victory which is now being celebrated in heaven, it seeks to encourage the christian reader and hearer and exhort him to steadfastness and faithfulness in the fierce attacks which he still has to endure from the evil Power (12:12) here on earth in the period before the end. The message of the glorified Lord to his community on earth is: 'Be faithful unto death, and I will give you the crown of life' (2:10).

Bibliography: *TDNT* I, 135–40; IV, 533f; *TWNT* VII, 701–13; *BHHW* II, 925f; *DBT*, 560–63; R. Völkl, *Christ und Welt nach dem NT*, Würzburg 1961, 315f, 333, 359, 430, and 451f; H. W. Huppenbauer, *Der Mensch zwischen zwei Welten*, Zurich 1959; H. Schlier, *Der Brief an die Galater*, Düsseldorf 1962³, 288–300; H. Schlier, *Principalities and Powers in the NT*, London and New York 1961; R. Leivestad, *Christ the Conqueror: Ideas of Conflict and Victory in the NT*, London 1954; A. von Harnack, *Militia Christi*, Tübingen 1905; Schnackenburg, 223–30; G. Richter, *Deutsches Wörterbuch zum NT*, Regensburg 1962, 492–6.

Rudolf Pesch

Conversion

The *Old Testament* knows of a cultic-ritual repentance (↗ Atonement) which, to be sure, drew upon itself frequently the criticism of the prophets, since the most important element in it, the interior change of heart and correction, was for the most part left on one side. This *interior* conversion is necessarily implied in the word *šûb* (=to turn about, 'to return to Yahweh'). There is here supposed a deep understanding of the nature of ↗ sin. Such a conversion implies obedience with regard to the will of God (Hos 6:1–6), and trust in God even in the absence of earthly or human help (Hos 14:4; Jer 3:22f; Is 30:15). From the negative point of view, conversion implies a turning away from everything evil, an aspect stressed especially by Jeremiah and Ezekiel. In the post-exilic period there comes to the foreground the turning to the Law and its complete fulfilment (Deut 30:2, 10; 2 Kings 23:25; Neh 9:29; 2 Chron 30:6ff). We find a similar legalistic understanding of conversion at Qumran: a man turns away from sin and separates himself radically from sinners in order to observe the Law in its purest form.

Basic for the *New Testament* is the demand of Jesus: 'Be converted!' (*metanoeite*, Mk 1:15). Before this, the preaching of John the Baptist had linked up with the prophetic insistence on conversion: turning away from sin with baptism and confession (Mk 1:4f) and observance of the commandments of God, together with works of love for a neighbour (Lk 3:8, 10–14). Jesus' call to conversion had, however, a yet more decisive and deeper meaning: he demands ↗ faith as the basic condition for forgiveness and salvation: the wedding garment that had to be brought to the heavenly banquet is nothing other than this interior conversion (Mt 22:11–13). The parables of Jesus illustrate at every turn how ready God is to forgive (Lk 15) and what are the necessary conditions on man's part (Lk 18:10–14; see also 17:10). We can trace a definite development in the preaching of repentance and conversion. Whereas the prophets threatened those who did not accept conversion with a judgement of condemnation within time (see also Is 5:25ff; 8:1ff; 9:8ff etc), John the Baptist speaks of a final judgement which is imminent and which will coincide with the coming of the kingdom of Heaven. The Baptist announces that the axe is laid to the roots of the trees and that he who is to consummate human history in judgement is near (Mt 3:10; Lk 3:9). Jesus, on the other hand, does not hurl condemnations but explains that the rule of God, the ↗ Kingdom of God, has already come (Mk 1:15). The condition for entering this kingdom, however, is conversion. Jesus' call goes out to everyone, sinners and the just alike, but especially to sinners (Lk 5:32).

In order to be able to describe what is essential in conversion we have to bear in mind the Lord's word about being converted and becoming like little children (Mt 18:3). It is not just turning away from evil and from ↗ sin; it is not just ↗ asceticism or ↗ fasting and the like that constitute the essence of conversion, but, first and foremost, the turning of the ↗ heart to God, in the manner of little children who allow themselves to be led without guile and with unlimited trust. There is genuine conversion in the sense in which Jesus understood it, when we no longer try to bring about our salvation relying on ourselves and our own powers, but rather, forgetful of self, look for salvation to God and trust courageously in him.

Different from the Baptist, whose preaching is stamped with sombre earnestness, Jesus speaks constantly of ↗ joy in connection with conversion (Lk 15:7, 10, 32). It is, of course, true that Jesus also announces an unmitigated, hard judgement on those who reject this call to conversion (Mt 11:20–4; 12:41). Nevertheless God comes half way to meet the repentant sinner of good will, as Jesus shows by the example of the rich ruler who had attached his heart to property and possessions: 'For it is easier for a camel to go through the eye of a needle than for a rich man to enter the kingdom of God' (Lk 18:25). The question of the disciples, as to who then could be saved, receives its answer: 'What is impossible with men is possible with God' (v 27). ↗ Grace has a decisive part to play in the conversion of the sinner to God.

The apostles continue the preaching of the Lord on conversion, as can be seen from Acts (2:38; 3:19; 5:31; 8:22; 11:18; 17:30; 20:21; 26:20; see also Heb 6:1). Paul uses the words *metanoia* and *metanoein* seldom (2 Cor 7:9f; 12:21; Rom 2:24), but he puts conversion at the beginning of the christian life which has detached itself from sin (1 Cor 6:11; Rom 6:19ff etc) and crucified the flesh (Gal 5:24).

The word does not appear at all in the Johannine gospel and epistles, since the believer (for whom these were written) has already accepted this call to be converted. Basically, conversion is a unique and decisive event. Falling back into the former state is worse than the primitive, unaltered state of unbelief (Lk 11:24–6 and parallels). Heb 6:4–6 expresses the same point: 'It is impossible to restore again to repentance those who have once been enlightened . . . if they then commit apostasy, since they crucify the Son of God on their own account'. The author is speaking, as a pastor, with a severity destined to drive home the lesson—quite apart from the fact that a second conversion is a rarer and more difficult occurrence than a first—and does not intend to take up a position with regard to a dogmatic problem, namely, whether a second conversion is in fact possible.

In Revelation the call to conversion has to do directly with grievances in the communities. (Cf 2:14f; 2:20ff; 3:1f, 14ff.) Tribulations inflicted by God are meant to induce even the most hardened evildoers to conversion and make possible salvation for them (2:22f). Thus, the communities of Philadelphia and Smyrna, often purified by afflictions, no longer required censure and an invitation to be converted, since poverty and oppression are always a good defence for faith and love.

Bibliography: Behm and Würthwein, *TDNT* IV, 975–1003; W. L. Holladay, *The root šûbh in the OT*, Leiden 1958; Schnackenburg, 10ff (with bibliography and index); B. Poschmann, 'Busse und letzte Ölung', *Handbuch der Dogmengeschichte* IV/3, Freiburg 1951, 3–10; J. Schmid, *RNT* 3 (1955^3), 150–5; A. Kirchgässner, *Erlösung und Sünde im NT*, Freiburg 1950, 130–5; A. van den Born, Haag 278–80; L. de Lorenzi, *Riv. Bibl. It.* 5 (1957), 243–9; R. Koch, 'Die religiöse-sittliche Umkehr nach den drei ältesten Evangelien under der Apostelgeschichte', *Anima* 14 (1959), 296–307 (with bibliography); J. Kosnetter, 'Die Busspredigt in der Verkündigung Jesu', *Der Seelsorger* 29 (1959), 200–5; O. Garcia de la Fuente, 'Sobre la idea de contrición en el AT', *SP* I (1959), 559–79; M. F. Lacan, J. Dupont, M. E. Boismard, and D. Mollat, *LV* 9/47 (1960), 1–114; R. Joly, 'Note sur metanoia', *RHR* 160 (1961), 148–56; W. Pesch, *Der Ruf zur Entscheidung. Die Bekehrungspredigt des NT*, Freiburg 1964.

Johannes B. Bauer

Covenant

In the covenant of God with his people there is resumed the essence of the religion of the Old and the New Testament, so that in Dan 11:28, 30 'the holy covenant' comes to mean the same thing as the religion of Israel. Although the etymology of the Hebrew word for covenant, *b^{e}rîth*, is disputed (compare the Akkadian *birîtu* = chain, and *birît* = between) it derives from the domain of human law. *B^{e}rîth* implies the strongest possible mutual pledge, but the ensuing relationship can be of different kinds. The word *covenant* is therefore an inadequate rendering of *b^{e}rîth*. When a *b^{e}rîth* is made between partners of unequal strength it is natural that the stronger accedes to a *b^{e}rîth* for which he can be petitioned by the less powerful (as the Israelites are petitioned by the Gibeonites [Josh 9], and Nahash, King of the Ammonites, by the Jabeshites [1 Sam 11, 1f]). The relation, however, is only apparently unilateral; for the less powerful must observe the conditions under which he petitioned the *b^{e}rîth* in the first place (in the case of Josh 9 and 1 Sam 11:1f, a position of servitude), or at any rate maintain loyalty in respect to the granter of the *b^{e}rîth*; in other words, he must maintain *ḥesed*, the covenant-obligation, and be guilty of no lack of faith in regard of the other; otherwise the preponderant party is no longer bound by his promise.

When two equal partners enter into a *b^{e}rîth*, it is evident that they contract on equal terms—for example, Hiram and Solomon (1 Kings 5:12). Also the covenant-making that we hear of in Gen 21:23–32 (Abimelek and Abraham) and 31:44–54 (Laban and Jacob) is bilateral. Abner petitions David, already King of Juda, for a *b^{e}rîth*, but he is evidently thinking of mutual obligations (2 Sam 3:12). In the case of the *b^{e}rîth* between Jonathan and David, it would appear that at the outset it is the king's son who gives and the poor shepherd who receives (1 Sam 18:3f);

but later (20:8) it demands *chesed* from David's side in respect of Jonathan and his posterity (20:14f). Then the *b^erîth* entered into (that is, renewed) in 1 Sam 23:18 is quite clearly reciprocal, in view of the prevision that David will become king.

The agreement is voluntary on both sides even though the request for a *b*ᵉ*rîth* comes from one side (Gen 31:44), or a party finds itself obliged to enter into one under unfavourable circumstances (1 Sam 11:1ff). The particular stipulations can be of different kinds (see Gen 21:30; 31:50, 52; 1 Kings 5:7–11; 20:34), though in one way or another *šālôm* must always result (Gen 26:31; 1 Sam 20:42; 2 Sam 3:21ff). 1 Kings 5:12: 'And there was *šālôm* between Hiram and Solomon; and the two of them made a *b*ᵉ*rîth*', shows that *šālôm* must mean more than 'peace', which is the word commonly used to translate it, for Hiram had already had friendly relations with David which Solomon continued right from the start. By means of the *b*ᵉ*rîth* the two partners were bound together in a unity which could not be broken, the kind of unity which can imply anything from the guarantee of life (1 Sam 11:1f) to the most intimate personal relationships (as friendship, 1 Sam 18:3f; marriage, Mal 2:14). There can, at any rate, come into existence as a result of the *b*ᵉ*rîth* a relationship which comes the closest possible to blood-relationship and can sometimes even substitute for it. Thus, partners who are to some extent of equal social standing are called brothers, as David and Jonathan (2 Sam 1:26), Hiram and Solomon (1 Kings 9:13), Ahab—by anticipation—and Benhadad (1 Kings 20:32).

By nature, the *b*ᵉ*rîth* is of limitless duration (1 Sam 20:15). The ceremonies accompanying the making of the covenant witness eloquently to the indissoluble nature of the bond. The swearing of an oath (Gen 21:31; 26:31; 31:53; 1 Sam 20:17, 42) or, alternatively, the pronouncement of a ↗ curse, sometimes mentioned expressly at the making of a covenant (Gen 26:28; Ezek 17:13, 16, 18f)—the Hebrew oath-formula is already an abbreviated or implicit form of self-curse—is symbolised by one or both partners passing in the midst of animals which had been quartered (Jer 34:18f; cf Gen 15:9f, 17f—where God perhaps appears also as the fire which consumes the sacrifice, in the opinion of Henninger). This could be the origin of the usual term used for making a covenant, namely, *kārath b*ᵉ*rîth*, literally, 'to cut a covenant'. In the event of breaking the covenant, the contracting parties take upon themselves the same lot which befell the quartered animals—namely, to suffer death. By means of these oaths the covenant is sealed in the eyes of God (see 1 Sam 23:18), and the deity is solemnly invoked as guardian and avenger of the covenant (Gen 31:49f, 53; cf Mal 2:14). In this way a covenant between two human parties is considered as a 'covenant of Yahweh' (1 Sam 20:8; see also Ezek 17:19). The indissoluble fellowship resulting can also be strengthened by the shaking of hands (Ezek 17:18), even more so by both partners dipping the hand together in a bowl filled with blood or some other liquid (for the custom of the ancient Arabs see Karge, 236f), and especially by means of a meal taken in common (Gen 26:30; 31:54; Josh 9:14; 2 Sam 3:20; Ps 41:9), or the tasting together of salt, the great preservative (a 'covenant of salt', Num 18:19; 2 Chron 13:5; see also Lev 2:13).

The line of conduct corresponding to such an ensuing unity goes by the name of *ḥesed*, namely, 'conduct towards others with regard to whom one stands in a relation of kinship, friendship, hospitality or service; the duty arising out of close bonds with another; community; solidarity (L. Köhler, *Lexikon in VT libros*; see also the basic article by N. Glück, 'Das Wort *chesed*', *BZAW* 47 [1927]; and see 1 Sam 20:14; 2 Sam 9:1, 3, 7; 1 Kings 20:31, 34). Renderings such as 'love', 'favour', 'grace', 'goodwill', or 'mercy' (LXX, Vulgate) are inadequate.

At the heart of the Old Testament there stands the Sinai covenant. This however is preceded by two other covenants, that with Noah (Gen 9:8–17) and that with Abraham (Gen 15 and 17). The spiritual relationship of God with our first parents in paradise is never called a covenant (Hos 6:7 refers to the town of Adam and Sir 17:12 to the Sinaitic covenant), since the relationship existed from the beginning and did not need to come into existence through a covenant. In the covenant with Noah, which applied to all living things on the earth, God pledged himself to the continuation of life on the earth without any corresponding stipulation on man's part, though the making of the covenant is preceded by commandments (Gen 9:4ff). According to Is 24:5f, the breaking of this covenant would have as its effect the eschatological catastrophe.

The covenant with Abraham (which comes to us in two traditions, Gen 15 and 17) guarantees to the latter a numerous posterity, beginning with the birth of Isaac (Gen 17:19) and, for this posterity, the land of Canaan (Gen 15:18ff). The condition for this is ↗ faith (15:6); and in 17:1 the covenant is preceded by a general commandment to walk before God and be blameless (as is said in reference to Noah in Gen 6:9). One entered into the covenant by means of the practice of circumcision, which was the sign of the covenant (17:10–14, 23–7).

As with the covenants with Noah and Abraham, so in the Sinaitic covenant the initiative came from God's side. In view of the exalted nature of the divine partner the granting of a *b^e^rîth* is an unheard-of grace, in particular in the covenant with Abraham and on Sinai, since, as a result of these, an interior union comes into existence: Abraham is the friend of God (Is 41:8; 2 Chron 20:7; Jas 2:23) and Yahweh is his guest (Gen 18); Israel is the People of Yahweh, and he is their God (see Ex 6:7; Lev 26:12; Deut 26:17f; Jer 7:23; 11:4; Ezek 14:11). Israel is attached to him in the closest possible way, more than all other peoples, as his personal possession, a people belonging to him, set aside, a kingdom of priests in which Yahweh is King, and in which all Israelites together assume the office of priesthood on behalf of all other nations, by fulfilling the statutes of the covenant (Ex 19:5f).

This relationship appears as even more intimate when represented as one of father to son (Ex 4:22f; Deut 14:1; 32:6; Is 1:2; Jer 31:20; Hos 2:1; 11:1), or of husband to wife (for the first time in Hos 1–3; then Jer 2:2; 3:4, 12; Ezek 16; Is 50:1; 54:4–10; 62:5; in a particularly frank way in the Song of Solomon). *The foundation of the covenant is in the freely-bestowed divine love* (Deut 7:7f; Jer 31:2f), and it represents the sealing of the divine election (see also Deut 14:2; Ps 33:12; Amos 3:2). As a result of this, Yahweh and Israel do not enter into a covenant in the way human partners do (Gen 21:27, 32), but it is Yahweh who makes the covenant with Israel (Ex 24:8—see Köhler, p. 45; when we read, in Josh 24:25; 2 Kings 23:3; 2 Chron 15:12; 29:10; 34:31, of men making the *bᵉrîth*, it is merely a question of solemn promises and an undertaking to fulfil a covenant which is already in existence; there enters at this point a human agency in mediating the covenant between God and the people—here Joshua, elsewhere the king, which is the way of mediating a covenant which we find in one of the Mari texts; see also Hos 2:20). Even more expressive are the phrases 'to establish a covenant' (Gen 9:9; 17:7; Ex 6:4; Ezek 16:60), 'to make' (Gen 9:12; 17:2; Num 25:12) or 'set up' a covenant (2 Sam 23:5), since the covenant is God's doing and God's gift. The LXX rendering of *bᵉrîth* as *diathēkē* = 'covenant' (not *sunthēkē* = 'agreement', 'compact') also presupposes that the covenant is a divine institution. (The Latin *testamentum* = 'last will and testament' is too one-sided a translation.)

The ceremony of making the covenant is symbolical of Yahweh's inner union with Israel. In this ceremony Moses sprinkles the altar, which represents Yahweh, with half the blood of the sacrificial victim and the people with the other half (Exod 24:6, 8). The revelation of his name, Yahweh, which precedes the granting of a covenant, is a sign that God enters into a truly personal union with Israel in the Sinaitic covenant (Ex 3:14f). It is in this name that the covenant is sealed (Ex 6:2–8) and which corresponds in a concrete way to the reality and proximity of God ('I am he, yes, I am he!'), which are manifested in actions of assistance and salvation. Another way of representing this is by God's dwelling among his people in the holy place above the ark of the covenant (Ex 25:8, 22; 29:45f; Lev 26:11f; Deut 4:7; 12:5). All the earthly gifts which Yahweh gives to the Israelites who remain true to the covenant (in particular, their prosperous existence in Canaan) are the outcome and the expression of his love (Deut 7:13ff). The grateful *ḥesed* of the human partner, which must also be a *personal devotion to Yahweh*, should correspond to the *ḥesed* of Yahweh himself (see Deut 7:9, 12; 1 Kings 8:23 = 2 Chron 6:14; Neh 1:5; 9:32; Dan 9:4 where we find the phrase: '. . . who keepest covenant and *ḥesed*'), which is essentially unmerited grace and mercy. This human attitude is included in the commandment of love (Deut 6:4f; 11:1), though already the Song of Deborah had referred to love of Yahweh (Judg 5:31). In this way the Israelite shows that he is not observing God's commandments through compulsion and slavish fear, since he too has entered into the covenant of his own free decision (Ex 19:8; 24:3, 7; Deut 26:17f; Josh 24:15–24).

The whole institution of ↗ law, which developed in the course of time, has an essential relation to the Sinaitic covenant. Its purpose is to actualise in the human partner of the covenant this loving, personal devotion. Even though the external deed required by God is limited and proportioned to human capabilities, yet considered as an expression of the interior homage of obedience it is reckoned to the Israelite as 'righteousness' in the eyes of God (Deut 6:25). On the other hand, God turns away from the external offering when it does not correspond to the conduct required by God, in particular with respect to a neighbour. Hence the war waged by the prophets against a purely external cult (see Is 1:10–20; Jer 7:21–8; Amos 5:4f, 14f, 21–7). In the practice of ↗ justice and charity towards a ↗ neighbour—especially those who are socially handicapped (see Ex 22:24ff; Lev 19:33f; 25:35–43; Deut 12:12; Ezek 18:7)—the Israelite shows the genuineness of his love for God and how much store he puts by his belonging to the covenant, which is, in any case, a privilege he shares with the poor.

It is also within the context of the covenant that we can understand the nature of sin—namely, as infidelity, apostasy. Hence also the heavy punishments inflicted for violation of the covenant (Lev 26:14–39; Deut 28:15–68), which are, however, intended in the first place as a warning against such an apostasy, which also explains the awe-inspiring appearance of Yahweh on Sinai (Ex 20:20). The fear of God, so often praised in the Old Testament, is in reality awe filled with humility, faith, trust and obedience (see Ps 34:10–15; 112:1; Prov 14:26f; Sir 1:11–21; 2:7–11). To be sure, the punishments threatened for the breaking of the covenant are in fact inflicted, in particular, in the ruin of both the kingdoms of Israel and Judah. Yet God maintains his *chesed* (Jer 31:3; Lev 26:44f), and through Jeremiah (31:31–4) he promises a 'new covenant' which brings forgiveness of sins, and by means of which Yahweh writes his law in the heart of each individual. Ezekiel expresses this even more clearly: Yahweh will give the Israelites a new heart in the innermost part of which he will place his Spirit (Ezek 36:26f). This will be an 'everlasting covenant of peace' (37:26), by means of which all will be taught directly by God (Is 54:10, 12). The songs of the Servant of Yahweh widen the circle beyond Israel to take in all peoples and reveal that the ↗ Servant of the Lord will be made by God 'a covenant to the people' (Is 42:6; 49:8)—that is, to all the peoples of the earth (42:5). He is a light for the nations, and through him the salvation of Yahweh reaches the farthest parts of the earth (42:6; 49:6); yet at the same time he will justify 'the many' through his atoning death (53:10ff).

This 'new covenant' will be sealed in the ↗ blood of Christ, as he himself said when instituting the holy eucharist, with reference to Ex 24:8 and Is 53:11; 'This is my blood of the covenant which is poured out for the many' (Mt 26:28; Mk 14:24; Lk 22:20; see also 1 Cor 11:25). Christ is therefore, in an incomparably higher sense, ↗ 'mediator of a new covenant' (Heb 12:24), as Moses was of the Sinaitic covenant. The new covenant is also 'better', since it assures better promises (Heb 7:22; 8:6). It promises and bestows not material gifts, gifts of this earth, but 'eternal redemption' and 'eternal inheritance' (Heb 9:12, 15), and a share in the eternal life of God as is expressed in the somewhat modified ancient covenant-formula in Rev 21:3 and 6f. At the end of time the tabernacle of God will not be with just one people, from whom in any case he is divided by the double curtain (Ex 26:33, 36; Lev 16:2; Heb 9:6ff), but 'with men'; and he will take up his dwelling with them so that they will be his people and God himself will be among them (Rev 21:3). The union with God is at the same time broader and more interior. In addition, it has passed—as already in Jer 31 and Ezek 36—from the collective to the individual plane: 'He who conquers shall have this heritage, and I will be his God and he shall be my son' (21:7). This is actualised in the highest gift which God can give to a human person: 'They will see [my] face' (22:4) in a way represented in Ex 24:10, 17 only as an anticipatory glimmer. Finally, since already in the old covenant God had entered into a personal relationship, we have in the progressive divine self-revelation, culminating in its most exalted and immanent form, an organic process.

History of the covenant. The covenant with Noah can be understood as a theological interpretation of a real historical datum. The covenant with Abraham fits into the religious genre described by Alt (*Der Gott der Väter*, 1929: now *Kleine Schriften zur Geschichte des Volkes Israel* I, 1–78), according to which the deity appears as connected, not with a locality, but with a social group, represented by the ancestral father. In Yahweh the people of Israel see the God of their fathers (Ex 3:6, 13ff), to whom he has revealed and committed himself. The Sinaitic covenant is deeply anchored in the traditions of Israel and corresponds to his nature, since it does not represent him as united to Israel in the nature of things. The covenant is already presupposed in the ancient Song of Deborah (Judg 5:3, 8, 11). There are references to ceremonies in which the Sinaitic covenant was continually renewed: the account of the renewal by Moses before the entry into Canaan (Deut 29:1), under Joshua (Josh 8:30–5, especially 34); the stipulation that this renewal should take place every seven years at the Feast of the Tabernacles (Deut 31:10–13; see also 29:9–14); the coming together in a common sanctuary before the ark of the Covenant (see Judg 21:19; 1 Sam 1:3); the lapidary formulae of the Ten Commandments (Ex 20:2–17; Deut 5:6–21) with their historical framework of the covenant-making (see Deut 5:1–5); or those of the twelve commandments preserved in the form of a curse (Deut 27:15–26), which were certainly not promulgated solemnly only on *one* occasion; the allusions in the Psalms, as in Ps 50 and Ps 81.

In speaking against the abuse of the covenant-idea—proud reliance on their election and false security in this reliance (see Amos 3:1f; 5:14, 18; 6:1; 9:7)—Amos, Isaiah and Micah do not name the covenant expressly, but presume it; but their contemporary, Hosea, names it expressly (6:7; 8:1). The reforms of Hezekiah (2 Chron 29:10; cf 2 Kings 18:4ff, 22), of Josiah (2 Kings 23:3; 2 Chron 34:31), and of Ezra, provided the occasion for an extraordinary renewal of the covenant. After the Exile, Pentecost became the commemorative day of the making of the covenant (see Kutsch). In the Book of Jubilees all the covenants of the Old Testament are dated from Pentecost, even that made between Jacob and Laban. The connection between the Book of Jubilees and Qumran permits us to place their festival of covenant-renewal at Pentecost. This sect referred to itself as 'the Community [Union] of the New Covenant', since it believed that the predictions of the prophets were fulfilled in it. In reality, the new covenant did come while this sect was still in existence; not with the teacher of righteousness, but in Jesus Christ.

Bibliography: P. Karge, *Geschichte des Bundesgedankens im AT*, Münster 1910; J. Pedersen, *Der Eid bei den Semiten*, Strasburg 1914; J. Pedersen, *Israel* I–II, Oxford 1954², 263–310; L. G. de Fonseca, *Bbl* 8 (1927), 31–50, 161–81, 290–319, 418–41; and 9 (1928), 26–40 and 143–60; A. Alt, *Die Ursprünge der israelitischen Rechts*, 1934 (now *Kleine Schriften* I, Münster 1953, 278–332 esp. 322–32); Quell and Behm in *TDNT* II, 104–34; J. Begrich, *ZAW* 60 (1944), 1–11; P. van Imschoot, Haag 267–74; J. Schildenberger, 'Die Religion des AT', *Christus und die Religionen der Erde*, ed. F. König, Vienna 1951, 439–521; Imschoot I, 237–59; J. Henninger, *Bbl* 34 (1953), 344–53; M. Noth, 'Das atl. Berith-schliessen im Lichte eines Mari-Textes', *Geschichtliche Studien zum AT*, 1957, 142–54; L. Arnaldich, 'La Alianza con Dios, Ideal de la Restauración del Orden religioso destruído según la secta del Mar Muerto', *Secc. de Estudios* I (Barcelona 1954), 341–4; P. E. Mendenhall, *Law and Covenant in Israel and the Ancient Near East*, Pittsburgh 1955; E. Vogt, *Bbl* 36 (1955), 565f; E. Kutsch, 'Das Herbstfest in Israel', *TLZ* 81 (1956), 493ff; H. W. Wolf, 'Jahwe als Bundesvermittler', *VT* 6 (1956), 316–20; M. Buber, *The Kingdom of God*, London 1958; Eichrodt I, 36–69; von Rad I, 129–35, 192ff, and 338ff; T. C. Vriezen, *An Outline of Old Testament Theology*, Oxford 1958, 139–43; Hempel and Goppelt, *RGG* I (1957³), 1512–18; V. Hamp and J. Schmid, 'Bund', *LTK* II², 770–78; H. Wildberger, 'Jahwes Eigentumsvolk', *Abh. z. Theol. d. AT u. NT* 37 (Zurich 1960); K. Baltzer, 'Das Bundesformular', *Wiss. Monographien z. AT u. NT* 4 (Neukirchen 1960); W. Beyerlin, *Herkunft und Geschichte der ältesten Sinaitraditionen*, Tübingen 1961; J. Haspecker, 'Bund', *HTG* I, 197–204; N. Lohfink, 'Das Hauptgebot', *Analecta Biblica* 20 (Rome 1963); N. Lohfink, *Das Siegeslied am Schilfmeer*, Frankfurt 1964, 129–50; W. L. Moran, 'Moses und der Bundesschluss am Sinai', *SZ* 170 (1961/2), 120–33; W. L. Moran, 'The Ancient Near Eastern Background of the Love of God in Deuteronomy', *CBQ* 25 (1963), 77–87; L. Krinetzki, 'Der Bund Gottes mit den Menschen nach dem AT u. NT', *WB* 15 (Düsseldorf 1963).

Johannes Schildenberger

Covetousness

The term *pleonexia*, which Paul so often employs, signifies 'covetousness', not 'avarice' (which would be *philarguria*). In the LXX renderings of the Hebrew *betsa*ᶜ or *bātsa*ᶜ, the word-group signifies 'ill-gotten gains', 'rapacity', and is never employed when the profits referred to are come by honestly. This covetousness, is, according to Paul, 'uncleanness' (Eph 4:19; 5:3), and 'idolatry' (Col 3:5; see also the epistle of Polycarp 11:2), just as 'impurity' is 'uncleanness' and 'idolatry'. While we do not feel compelled to conclude with Trench and Klaar that *pleonexia*, since it is mentioned in connection with sins of impurity, must likewise signify illegitimate *sexual* desire, it is nevertheless clear that a single basic *concept* underlies Paul's use of the term. The ideas of covetousness and impurity serve to define the basic attitude of materialism which is characteristic of the pagan world, and in this sense they are equivalent to idolatry. Christian living in the kingdom of God is diametrically opposed to such an attitude (see Eph 5:3ff). The state of holiness which the redeemed christian receives through the sacraments as a member of Christ and as the temple of God must be made manifest in an existential sense; in other words it must be made real in the actual practice of his life.

Bibliography: J. C. Trench, *Synonyms of the New Testament*, London 1901, 51–3; E. Klaar, *TZ* 10 (1954), 395–7; P. Rossano, *VD* 32 (1954), 257–65; R. Beauvery, *VD* 33 (1955), 78–85; G. Delling, *TDNT* vi, 266–74; H. Schlier, *Der Brief an die Epheser*, Düsseldorf 1957, 41f and 233–6; Maurer, *TDNT* vi, 636f.

Johannes B. Bauer

Creation

A. *In the Old Testament. Introduction.* It is in the light of the concept of *doxa* that the significance of creation in the Old Testament becomes apparent. It is concerned with the manifestation of God in his deeds rather than with the proof of his existence, with the *gesta et facta* of God, the *mirabilia Dei*, rather than with his *esse*. For this reason the Old Testament presents the idea of creation not in the sense, or with the logical precision, of a statement of a philosophical thesis, but rather in the form of a historical narrative. When we encounter the term *creation* we moderns think immediately of the idea of 'creation out of nothing'. But if we enquire of the scriptures for this notion of *creatio ex nihilo* then we encounter it there not as the principal factor in a logically structured argument, but rather as an effect of the ↗ glory and dominion of God, who has revealed himself to his chosen people in a manner that manifests his power.

The Terminology. To describe the activity of the creator the Old Testament employs several terms: *ʿāśâh*, the range of meaning of which is roughly equivalent to that of the German term *machen* (=to make) (Gen 1:7, 31; 2:4; Is 43:7); *qānāh*, to found, to form (Gen 14:19, 22); *yātsar* (=to fashion, shape, form: Gen 2:7, 8, 19; Jer 1:5), and above all *bārāʾ* (Gen 1:1; Num 16:30; Ps 51:12). Further terms, borrowed from the world of ideas of the ancient Near East conjure up vivid images. Such are *nāṭâh* (=to stretch out), *yāsad* (=to found) and *kônēn* (=to set up). Of these terms *bārāʾ* is the one which is richest in meaning to the extent that it is predicated exclusively of God. Admittedly it is not in any sense a specialist term belonging to 'ecclesiology', but it does designate the divine activity in the creation, with man and in the miracles performed by God. The very fact that this range of usage is attached to the word *bārʾā* in itself suggests that we should regard creation and fashioning as conceived of in the Old Testament as belonging to the broader category of divine deeds of power. Apart from this chief characteristic of being used exclusively with God as subject *bārāʾ* is characterised especially by the fact that what results from it is new, unprecedented (eg, Is 41:20; Jer 31:22) and extraordinary (eg, Ex 34:10; Num 16:30), as well as by the fact that the manner in which it takes effect is totally free and uncircumscribed.

The distinctive term which the LXX employs to characterise God's creative activity is *ktizō* and not—though this would have been equally conceivable—*dēmiourgeō*. In the case of this latter term it is the element of manufacturing in the sense of actual craftsmanship that is uppermost. *Ktizō*, on the other hand, denotes the original act of a being endowed with intelligence and will. In its original meaning it is used of the founding of cities and other permanent landmarks. By their choice of the term *ktizō*, LXX authors have to a large extent excluded the idea of creation out of pre-existing matter.

The Idea of Creation in the Old Testament. In order to obtain a correct understanding of the Old Testament idea of creation let us first put the question of what the relationship is between God as he appears in the bible and other being apart from himself. How is he related to the dimension of space and time? In the process of explaining what this relationship consists in a quite definite image emerges, on the basis of which the specific character and the origin of the idea of creation can be unambiguously defined without ascribing any undue primacy of importance to any one passage of scripture.

1. *God is the Absolute Lord.* a. *Matter* belongs inalienably to him. Nothing is impossible to him (Jer 32:17). Viewed from his standpoint the cosmos shrinks to the dimensions of a mere toy. He measures the oceans in the hollow of his hand and marks off the heavens with a span (Is 40:12). Men are as minute as grasshoppers in his sight (Is 40:22). He sets Leviathan, the monster, swimming about in the sea like a goldfish in an aquarium (Ps 104:26). All nature belongs to him: he overthrows mountains, shakes the earth out of its place, commands the sun (Job 9:5–7), and so on.

b. A further characteristic, corresponding to this transcendence of his over material things, is his dominion over *history*. He who fashions light and creates the darkness is the bringer of peace and also of woe (Is 45:7). He it is who brings princes to nought, and makes the rulers of the earth as nothing (Is 40:23). He has formed his people for himself (Is 43:21), and led them down the ages with a mighty hand. From him come riches and honour. Light and power are in his hand, and it lies with him to make great and mighty whomsoever he will (1 Chron 29:11–12).

c. This *omnipotence* is not only confined to factors outside the natural order. Without God things *could not exist*. The song lives by the breath of the singer. As soon as he withdraws his breath the song falls away into silence. 'When thou hidest thy face, they are dismayed; when thou takest away their breath, they die' (Ps 104:29). Natural things cannot even claim the support of permanency, for they are changed like a garment while he remains (Ps 102:27).

2. *God is the creator.* The fact that God is totally and completely transcendent over all beings apart from himself is emphasised again and again in the Old Testament, and it excludes the possibility that any non-divine being can be supported in existence independently of God himself. Pressed to its ultimate logical conclusion the omnipotence of God implies his activity as creator, or more precisely the idea of creation out of nothing.

a. *The fact of the creation.* The creation is the deed of God's power, and created things, by their very existence, proclaim the immensity of that power. The bible contains no reference to any conflict between a power which creates order on the one hand and chaos on the other. No trace whatever is to be discerned in the biblical account of the establishment of the world of the idea of some resistance being offered to God as creator. God himself commands the primordial *tōhûwābōhû*, and this is not capable of setting any obstacle to his will. 'In the beginning God created the heavens and the earth'. Thus Genesis intones that powerful hymn of praise which is carried on and developed in the mighty deeds of God throughout the whole of history. The planets which were objects of adoration to the ancients are set in the firmament to act as lanterns (Gen 1:14ff). God has created the earth itself and men and beast upon the earth by his mighty power and his outstretched arm, and he gives them to whomsoever he wills (Jer 27:5).

b. *Creation by the word.* The scriptures do unquestionably contain images ultimately based on anthropomorphic conceptions. But mythology properly so called plays no part in the biblical narrative. At most it serves to provide embellishment. God utters his word and things exist. It is here that the biblical accounts of creation are, theologically speaking, at their most profound: God creates by his word. 'By the word of the Lord the heavens were made, and all their host by the breath of his mouth' (Ps 33:6). He has created all things by his word, and fashioned man by his wisdom (Wis 9:1). He spoke, and it came to be; he commanded, and it stood forth (Ps 33:9). There was no instrument and no mediator, no compulsion and no process of emanation. As St Ephraem Syrus puts it in his *Discourse Upon Faith* 25 (BKV II., 37, 24). 'His will is his treasure-house. For everything came to be out of nothing.'

c. *Creation out of nothing.* This relationship between total impotence on the one hand and total omnipotence on the other finds its only possible counterpart in terms of philosophy in the idea of *creatio ex nihilo*. In 2 Macc 7:28 we find the mother of the Maccabees saying to her son: '... Look at the heavens and the earth and see everything that is in them, and recognize that God did not make them out of things that existed'. We should not regard this as an expresson of a later theological development which should be considered as secondary and as representing a different mentality from scripture as a whole. Rather it is the ultimate logical conclusion and at the same time the intrinsic and inevitable point of departure for what the Old Testament has to tell us about creation. Whether what is recorded in the first book of scripture is *genesis* in the true and strict sense, or merely the imposition of basic order on things is a matter of dispute. But in any case this would make no difference to the statements about creation in the Old Testament as a whole.

3. *The further implications of the idea of creation.* From this basic conception certain consequences follow with regard to the relationship of the creature to his creator. Of these the following, which in our opinion are the most important, may be mentioned at this point: praise, trust and the solidarity of all created things.

a. *Praise.* The ultimate purpose of creation is the glory of God. 'The heavens are telling the glory of God, and the firmament proclaims his handiwork' (Ps 19:1–2). From its contemplation of the work of creation the Old Testament rises again and again to praise of the Creator, and exhorts its readers to share in this praise: 'All thy works shall give thanks to thee, O Lord, and all thy saints shall bless thee' (Ps 145:10). Man in particular, as an intelligent being, has the duty of responding with words of thanksgiving to the word of God in the creation.

b. *Trust.* God is solicitous for the work of his hands. Man is not left to the mercy of conflicting cosmic powers. The creator lovingly upholds his creatures in existence. He distributes while they gather. He opens his hand, they are abundantly satisfied (Ps 104:27). It is on the basis of this elemental trust that Job can actually call God to justice with the words: 'Thy hands fashioned and made me; and now thou dost turn about and destroy me' (Job 10:8–9). And to this question he will obtain the answer of life.

c. *The solidarity of all creatures.* All men are created by God, and in this fact lies the ultimate and inalienable basis of their equality and their value. 'Have we not all one Father? Has not one God created us? Why then are we faithless to one another, profaning the covenant of our fathers?' (Mal 2:10). An offence against one's brother is accounted a sin against one's creator; service of one's brother is service of one's creator. 'He who oppresses a poor man insults his maker, but he who is kind to the needy honours him' (Prov 14:31). In the New Testament this idea attains its full development. It is an idea which has transformed the whole world and continues to transform it right to the present day, while the underlying truth of it which we seek to suppress is knocking at our door with a hostile fist.

B. *In the New Testament. Introduction.* The theocentric approach of the Old Testament remains in force in the New. Knowledge of the creation is not acquired as the outcome of an increasingly advanced process of speculation, but has its basis rather in God as he manifests his omnipotence and reveals himself to us. The word of the fathers is confirmed, but still more, it is seen in a fresh light and achieves its ultimate depths in the God-man. The basic orientation is the same. We do not start from a multiplicity of geometrical points and so conclude where the central point lies. Rather this central point has acquired a fresh clarity beyond all possibility of confusion, and thereby the whole system of co-ordinates falls under the same illumination. The word which God spoke 'last of all' through his own Son (Heb 1:2) contains within it a further word concerning the essence of creation.

Terminology. The terms most frequently used are *ktizō* (=to create: Mk 13:19; Eph 2:10; Col 1:16; etc) and its derivatives: *ktistēs* (=creator: 1 Pet 4:19), *ktisma* (=creature: 1 Tim 4:4; Jas 1:18; Rev 5:13; 8:9), and *ktisis* (=creation: Mk 10:6; Rom 1:20; 2 Cor 5:17). But in addition to these we also have *poieō* (lit.=to make, do: Acts 4:24; Heb 1:2; 3:2), *poiēma* (lit.=a thing made: Rom 1:20; Eph 2:10), *plassō* (lit.=to form, shape: Rom 9:20; 1 Tim 2:13) together with *plasma* (lit. =a thing formed: Rom 9:20), and *kataskeuazō* (lit.=to prepare, build: Heb 3:4). *Ktizō* is used here only of divine creative activity, while *ktisis* can refer to the act of creation or the result of this act—namely, the created order or the creature. Although everything, including even angels and powers (Col 1:16) has been created, *ktisis* is only applied to that part of creation which is visible and transient, of which man is the representative and the spokesman. In considering the whole range of expressions relating to the creation we ought also to include a number of prepositional usages. For the words *ek*, *pro*, *dia* or *eis* are also used to express the origin and the ultimate purpose of all that exists.

The idea of creation in the New Testament. 1. The taking over and the further development of the Old Testament witness to the creation: a. In the New Testament too the creation is regarded in the context of *the manifestations of God's power*. When the apostles Peter and John were acquitted at the end of their judicial examination by the high priests the early christian community praised their Lord as he who made 'the heaven and the earth and the sea and everything in them', and it entreats the all-powerful God to continuc his mighty deeds in the preaching of the gospel (Acts 4:24–30). Creation is the first—and that too in a logical, not merely in a psychological sense—and fundamental deed of power on God's part. It is the paradigm, as it were, on which all else is based, when it is a question of convincing one's self or others that with God nothing is impossible.

In the confrontation between christianity and the pagan world the fact of the divine origin of the creation is more strongly emphasised, and is sometimes made the central point in the whole discussion. It must be remembered, however, that in this controversy the disputants can no longer find a common basis in the Old Testament. In their reaction against the divinisation of the created order and its forces the relevant doctrinal statements in the New Testament acquire a polemical note. When the inhabitants of Lystra react to a miraculous cure on the part of the missionaries of the gospel by attempting to offer sacrifices to them Paul has to use his utmost resources to turn their minds to the living God 'who made the heaven and the earth and the sea and all that is in them' (Acts 14:15). At the Areopagus the controversy about the cult of idols provides a starting-point for the preaching of Christ: 'The God who made the world and everything in it, being Lord of heaven and earth, does not live in shrines made by man' (Acts 17:24). The inversion of the creator-creature relationship, is in fact, *the* sin and *the* reproach of the pagan world (Rom 1:25), in which every evil has its roots. Paul, therefore, constantly renews his insistence upon the divine origin of the creation (Rom 1:25; 11:26; 1 Cor 8:6; 10:26; Eph 3:9; Col 1:16), although admittedly here, in accordance with the theocentric standpoint which he adopts, it is always God and not the creation as such which occupies the central point in his argument.

b. Similarly we encounter in the New Testament the conception of *creation by the will and the word of God*. God calls into being that which does not exist (Rom 4:17), and upholds all things by the word of his power (Heb 1:3). It is by his word that the ages of the world were established (Heb 11:3), and all that exists had, and still continues to have, existence through the word of God alone. As it was and is, so shall it always be from eternity to eternity, and the twenty-four elders of Revelation lay down their crowns before the omnipotent Lord and acknowledge: 'Worthy art thou, our Lord and God, to receive glory and honour and power, for thou didst create all things, and by thy *will* they existed and were created' (Rev 4:11). It was the will of God that ordained the beginning of being, and it is his will that will bring about its ultimate consummation. In scripture we do not find any speculations about anything taking place prior to the creation, or about how the cosmos came to acquire its form, after the manner of the various mythologies. The 'beginning of the creation' constitutes the absolute horizon of all arguments from tradition, whether these are adduced by Jesus himself (Mt 19:4; Mk 10:6; Mt 24:21; Mk 13:19) or by those who scoff at christian teaching (2 Pet 3:4). There can be no reaching back beyond the beginning. That which was established at the beginning has an absolute quality. The fact that emphasis is so often laid upon the beginning in various connections (Mt 19:8; Rom 1:20; Heb 1:10; see also the combinations so frequently employed of *apo* and *pro katabolēs kosmou* = 'from' and 'before the foundation of the world'—Mt 13:35; 25:34; Lk 11:50; Jn 17:24; Eph 1:4; Heb 4:3; 9:26; 1 Pet 1:20; Rev 13:8; 17:8) ultimately goes back to the idea of creation as a *creatio ex nihilo*, and this in turn is to be understood on the basis of the Old Testament.

c. The New Testament insists in season and out of season on the fact that creation as a whole derives its existence and its meaning utterly from God. 'From him and through him and to him are all things' (Rom 11:36; see also Jn 1:3, 10; 1 Cor 8:6; Heb 2:10). There could be no more concise or more exact way of expressing the fact that God is the source, the maintainer and the ultimate goal of creation. These three points of reference, 'from him, to him, and through him' exclude any kind of intermediary, whether this is conceived of as a demiurge, or as pre-existing matter. In all respects and from first to last creation is something that is God-willed and immediate to God. Hence there is no creature which could be concealed from God (Heb 4:13). Hence too there is no creature which could ever separate us from his love (Rom 8:39), and for the same reason there is no food which man has to abstain from. The very fact that it is the gift of God is enough to make it good (1 Tim 4:3). The creation bears the imprint of God's hand, and for this reason it is possible for man to gain knowledge of God from it: 'Ever since the creation of the world his invisible nature . . . has been clearly perceived in the things that have been made' (Rom 1:20; see also Heb 3:4).

Creation in Christ. The New Testament, however, is not only an interpretation of the Old; it extends beyond it in its message and is its fulfilment. 'In these last days he has spoken to us by a Son' (Heb 1:2). And in this word of his a further message about the creation is contained, one which could not hitherto have been deduced. The more the idea of God becomes clarified the more the idea of the creation is freed from the obscurities surrounding it. The *new factor* is that what has been said about God as the creator and the sacred author of all things is now applied to Christ—often, indeed, in the same words. The result is that we can now speak of a christocentric specification of the creation over and above the theocentric aspect in it which was all that we had hitherto perceived. In the relationship between God and creaturehood the name of Christ can now appear where before there was simply the name of God. Christ is the beginning of the creation (Rev 3:14), the first-born of all creation (Col 1:15), but at the same time he is heir to all things (Heb 1:2). Through him all things were made (Jn 1:3); through him the world came to be (Jn 1:10); in him all things were created, through him and for him (Col 1:15, 16). All things have been made subject to him (Heb 2:8). Passages of the Old Testament which speak of the creation are applied directly to Christ (Heb 1:10), and in setting Christ above Moses Paul gives as his reason that the builder of the house is greater than the house itself, and that God is the builder of all things (Heb 3:4–6). In 1 Cor we encounter two statements set in parallelism (8:6): 'Yet for us there is one God, the Father, from whom are all things and for whom we exist, and one Lord, Jesus Christ, through whom are all things and through whom we exist'. What is the significance of this parallelism which is carried through consistently, and which extends to form and content alike? First Paul's intention is certainly to bring out the fact that Christ is on an equal footing with God. This was necessary precisely in view of the tenets of the Jews. But over and above this, the creation is unreservedly and totally orientated to Christ. The nature and history of the creation can find its ultimate explanation only in its relationship to him. It is the function of creation undeviatingly and irresistibly to make manifest the glory of God through the will of every creature, and that too not at random but precisely through the incarnate love and grace of our Lord Jesus Christ. The plan of creation depends for its meaning upon the plan of salvation or, to put it better, on the plan for the manifestation of God's glory. The one is incomprehensible without the other. 'The order laid down in that mystery which has been hidden throughout the ages of the world in God, who has created all things' contains at its kernel the revelation of God in Christ, and embraces both creation and redemption. 'For he has made known to us . . . the mystery of his will, according to his purpose *which he set forth in Christ*, as a plan for the fullness of time, to unite all things in him, things in heaven and things on earth' (Eph 1:9–10). This is the goal of creation, and this goal is achieved with the resurrection, even though its achievement is visible only to the eye of faith. Viewed in this perspective our conception of man's fall and subsequent redemption is no longer hopelessly distorted, as it is when we envisage it as a catastrophic failure of God's plan followed by a repairing of the damage. Creation as a whole is conceived of in view of Christ, in view of the God-man, and what leads up to him in historical terms is the way to its ultimate consummation. ↗ Rebirth, Restoration.

3. *The New Creation.* Admittedly it is not yet possible to perceive the consummation ushered in by Christ in the

present state of the created order. Man stands in a certain mysterious solidarity with creation in that all creation has an inherent connection with matter; and because his destiny is one with that of the created order as a whole, he has subjected the whole of this order, himself included, to the bondage of transience and eventual annihilation (Rom 8:20, 21) by rebelling against the claims of God. We may conceive of God's plan as a song that flows on uninterrupted, and it has been made manifest in Christ that this song does not end in a discord. But, to retain the terms of this simile, the present state of the creation is like a harmony in which a dominant note can be detected, this being open to its due development and, as it were, reaching out towards that development and, in a certain sense, already containing it. With the incarnation and resurrection of Christ the age of the new creation began in the world, an age in which the earlier discords are resolved into a new harmony: 'Neither circumcision counts for anything, nor uncircumcision, but a new creation' (Gal 6:15; see also Eph 2:15–16): 'If anyone is in Christ, he is a new creation', we are told in 2 Cor 5:17: 'the old has passed away, behold, the new has come'. Here again the concept of creation is most intimately connected with that of salvation. Creation is orientated to that which is 'new': the God-man and man as conformed to him by faith and the sacraments. In this connection it would be wrong to regard 'a new heaven and a new earth' (Rev 21:1) as a restoration of the order of paradise. The New Testament is aware that man originally existed in a state of bliss. But any concept of a cyclic process in world history is foreign to it. Christ is not the restorer but the consummator, and we are told that when it is finally revealed the new creation will be something which 'no eye has seen, nor ear heard, nor the heart of man conceived', something which 'God has prepared for those who love him' (1 Cor 2:9). The creation endures until that point in time when the voice of him who is enthroned says: 'Behold I make all things new', and 'It is done' (Rev 21:5, 6).

A final conclusion may be drawn. Creation is the sphere in which *kharis* and *agapē* in Christ are developed to the praise and glory of his name. In temporal terms its total span is coextensive with that of saving history itself. Thus it is not only the basic manifestation of God's power and the reflection of his 'manifold' wisdom; it is also the work of his love, and hence man must be faithful to 'the faithful Creator', and put his trust in him (1 Pet 4:19). ↗ Grace.

Bibliography: H. Fruhstorfer, *Weltschöpfung und Paradies nach der Bibel*, Linz 1927; F. M. T. Böhl, 'Bara als Terminus der Weltschöpfung im altl. Sprachgebrauch', *Festschrift Kittel*, Stuttgart 1913, 42ff; A. Janssens, 'De scripturae doctrina de Creatione mundi', *Coll. Gandavienes* 30 (1947), 95–9; H. Lehmann, 'Schöpfergott und Heilsgott im Zeugnis der Bibel', *ET* 11 (1951), 97–112; G. Lindeskog, *Studien zum neutestamentlichen Schöpfungsgedanken*, Uppsala 1952; Gerhard Schneider, *Kaine Ktisis. Die Idee der Neuschöpfung beim Apostel Paulus und ihr religionsgeschichtliche Hintergrund*, Trier 1959 (see also *TTZ* 68 [1959], 257–70); V. Warnach, *Agape*, Düsseldorf 1951, 496–504; L. H. Taylor, *A Study of the Biblical Doctrine of 'Kaine Ktisis' in Pauline Theology*, Louisville 1955; P. Humbert, 'Emploi et portée du verbe bara (créer) dans l'AT', *TZ* 3 (1947), 401–22; *A. Hulsbosch, *God's Creation*, London and New York 1965; *P. Schoonenberg, *Covenant and Creation*, London and South Bend (Indiana) 1968; *H. McCabe, *The New Creation*, London and New York 1964.

Gerhard Trenkler

Cross

From the historical point of view the cross is the instrument of the *passion of Christ*. It consisted of a beam driven into the ground on which the condemned man was hanged, nailed, or bound, to a cross-beam. The historical connection with the death of Christ introduced the word *stauros* (=cross) into the field of theological language. This usage is exclusive to the New Testament and is in a special way Pauline. The gospels use the word in the material sense only, with but one exception, to which we shall return. In Paul, the cross stands for the passion of Christ, both as showing forth his humiliation and death, and as an expression of his obedience to the father, reaching as far as absolute self-emptying (Phil 2:8). The cross also expresses the mysterious way of salvation which goes against ordinary human wisdom (1 Cor 1:17f; Gal 5:11). The life of the christian must be conformed to the cross (Phil 3:18; Gal 2:19; 6:14)—in presenting which view Paul follows Is 53.

In addition, we also find the idea of the *cross of* ↗ *glory* as the sign of the victory of the Son of Man which will appear with him at the ↗ *parousia*. Mt 24:30 already presents this sense and it occurs in Judaeo–Christian literature (*Did.*, 16, 6; *Epist. Apost.* 27; *Sib.*, 8, 224; ApocPti). It is in this same sense that we have to interpret the custom of drawing a cross on the eastern wall of houses. Another theme allied to that of the cross of glory is that of the cross which accompanied Christ in his descent into the underworld. (EvPti 42), or his ascent into heaven (Sib 6, 26); in these texts the cross appears as a living person. It stands, in fact, for Christ himself, a point which emerges in particular in the gnostic Acts of Apostles (ActJo 98). The cross stands less for the humiliation of Christ than for his victorious power.

It was not long before people began to look for *types* of the cross in the Old Testament, the most ancient of these being the serpent raised up in the wilderness (Jn 3:14) and Moses praying with uplifted arms (Barn 12, 2). In the oldest collections of *Testimonia* we also find Is 65:2 and Deut 33:3. The apologists look for symbols of the cross also in the natural order. Thus mast and plough point to the cross (Justin, *I Apol*, 55, 1–6). The wood of the cross, as distinct from the shape, brings to mind types such as the Tree of Life and the staff of Moses. The mention of the wood is even given a place in an ancient judaeo–christian *targum* on Ps 96:10.

The cross admits of different *symbolical interpretations*. In the first place, its four dimensions can stand for the universality of redemption, which unites the heavenly and the earthly spheres and bridges the gap between Jew and gentile. This symbolism already appears in Eph 2:16 and Jn 12:32, but not in Eph 3:18. It is also found in PsSol 22, 1f and ActPti 38, and Irenaeus often uses it (*Dem*, 34). Again, the cross is presented as strengthening (*stērizōn*) and upholding the world (Melito, *Hom. Pasch.*, 16, 15; ActAnd 14), which would appear to provide a relationship between the 'word' as creating agent and the redeeming cross (1 Clem 33, 3), emphasises the *dunamis* of the cross. Finally, the cross is interpreted as something which divides (*merizōn*), a view which is developed especially in the Valentinian *gnosis*, in which *stauros* and *horos* (=boundary, border) are more or less identified. But the fundamental idea is evidently the identification of the function of the cross with that of the 'Word'.

What, in conclusion, is the meaning of *the cross signed on the forehead* (*sphragis*)? It is usually connected with the cross of Christ, but this reference is secondary. Its origin must be sought in the letter Tau, with which the members of the eschatological community would, according to Ezek 9:4, be signed on their forehead. The LXX translation is *sēmeion* (=sign). The Sadokite community were acquainted with this sign (*CD*, 19, 19) and Revelation speaks of the seal (7:3, *sphragis*) with which the servants of God would be signed on the forehead. This sign stands for the name of Yahweh, since Tau was the last letter of the alphabet. Thus Revelation speaks indifferently of 'signing with the seal' (7:3) and 'signing with the Name' (14:1). Now, we know that at the beginning of the christian era Tau was written either + or ×.

In judaeo-christian texts the cruciform sign made on the forehead still stands in relation to 'the Name'. The *Shepherd* of Hermas (in Parable 8, 10, 3) speaks in this sense of 'those who bear [*bastazein*] the Name', in which connection we must bear in mind that for Hermas 'name' and 'word' are used as synonymns. Very soon, however, the interpretation of the cross as the instrument of Christ's passion prevailed—it is present, in fact, already in the New Testament.

We have so far prescinded from: 'He who does not take [*lambanein*] his cross and follow me is not worthy of me' (Mt 10:38); in Lk (14:27) we read: 'Whoever does not bear [*bastazein*] his own cross . . .' The similarity to Hermas suggests that it is a question here of a play on the idea of Tau on the forehead. One could also compare Gal 6:17: 'I bear [*bastazein*] on my body the marks [*stigmata*] of Jesus.' Shortly before, the cross had been mentioned in the context of circumcision (Gal 6:12), which would appear to indicate that it was considered the sign of belonging to the new Israel. In these texts, then, the Tau, signed on the forehead and signifying the 'Name', is brought into relation with the cross of Christ's passion.

Bibliography: A. Grillmeier, *Der Logos am Kreuz*, Munich 1956; M. Sulzberger, 'Le symbole de la croix', *Byzantion* 2 (1925), 356–83; H. Rahner, 'Das mystische Tau', *ZKT* 85 (1953), 385–410; E. Peterson, *Das Kreuz und das Gebet nach Osten: Frühkirche, Judentum, und Gnosis*, Freiburg 1959, 15–35; E. Dinkler, 'Zur Geschichte des Kreuzsymbols', *ZTK* 48 (1951), 148–72; E. Dinkler, 'Jesu Worte vom Kreuztragen', *Ntl. Studien für R. Bultmann*, Berlin 1954; 117–23; E. Dinkler, 'Kreuzzeichen und Kreuz', *Jahrbuch für Antike und Christentum* 5 (1962), 93–112; J. Daniélou, *Les symboles chrétiens promitifs*, Paris 1961, 143–51; J. Daniélou, 'La charrue, symbole de la croix', *RSR* 42 (1954), 193–204; J. Daniélou, *Théologei du judéo-christianisme*, Paris 1958, 204–8 and 384–6; W. Michaelis, 'Zeichen, Siegel, Kreuz', *TZ* 12 (1956), 505–26; J. L. Teicher, 'The Christian Interpretation of the Sign X in the Isaiah Scroll', *VT* 5 (1955), 189–98.

Jean Daniélou

Cult

A. *Basic data* (*cult in general*). Cult (compare Latin *colere*) refers to an encounter with the divine generally within the framework of determined forms. The connotation given to the word *encounter* here covers the widest possible range of meaning and the forms which the encounter takes change according to the meaning given to the encounter. The encounter can be realised in different places (either natural such as mountains or man-made such as temples), or at different times (either determined by the natural cycle or by history), by a community or by the individual. The intentions which are brought to the encounter can be of different kinds, as also the results which accrue from it such as reassurance, increase of power, defence against demonic powers, expiation, union with the deity. The functionaries who mediate the encounter can be different though they are generally priests, as can the circle of participants (family, clan, community), and also the degree of *intensity* with which one participates or to which one is committed, which will generally be higher for cultically qualified personnel than for others.

B. *The Old Testament* (*basic characteristics*). Even on the level of vocabulary the Old Testament idea of cult is seen to consist above all in *service* (it contains no word which corresponds exactly to *cult* or *worship*). In keeping with this, cultic actions themselves (eg, Ex 40:15ff), together with everything which leads up to and prepares for them (Num 3:31) and everything related to the place of cult and to cultic functions (Num 3:25f), are described in terms of service.

The Old Testament informs us that the patriarchs frequented Canaanite sanctuaries such as Shechem, Bethel, Mamre, Hebron, and Beersheba. They built altars (Gen 12:6ff; etc), sacrificed (Gen 46:1), and called on the name of Yahweh (Gen 13:4). The most impressive expressions of Old Testament cult can be seen in passover (↗ Easter) and the covenant festival (↗ Covenant), and it is characterised by an exclusive attachment to Yahweh, the absence of images, the building of the temple and concentration of worship in the ↗ temple organised by the priesthood. As a result of the cultic reforms of Josiah the temple was to be the only place of worship. In the post-exilic period the sacrificial system became predominant, and the place of prayer in worship was greatly developed as a result of what had happened during the Exile. It was from this latter that the synagogue service as we know it grew.

C. *Qumran*. It is quite impossible to maintain that the Qumran community was opposed to cult. The liturgy of the temple was not rejected in itself. What was objected to was the current practice of cult which was then in the hands of a (high) priesthood which was regarded as illegitimate and unworthy. The Qumran sectarians awaited the re-establishment of legitimate temple liturgy, one which would be fully in accord with the Torah, in the eschatological age. While, therefore, they maintained the necessity of offering sacrifices at the future eschatological temple as the only legitimate place of worship, in the meantime they practised other forms of worship as, for example, ritual lustrations which were in principle reserved to the priests with reference to similar rites prescribed for temple worship. According to 1 QS 3:4–12 these rites had an expiatory effect and therefore could take the place of sacrifice. We should also mention in this respect the daily cultic meal under the presidency of priests which was associated in their thinking with the cultic meals taken by the priests in Jerusalem. These meals called for a high degree of cultic purity on the part both of the participants (only full members who were in a state of purity could attend them) and of the food which was eaten (1 QS 6:4–6; 1 QSa 2:17–22). Finally, sexual abstinence, either in the form of complete celibacy (1 QS) or in that of occasional abstention from marital relations (CD), has to be understood in terms of the striving for absolute purity of the priestly-cultic kind. With regard to the absence of sacrifice at Qumran which, as we have seen, must be explained in terms of the contemporary situation, we can understand how the community opposed its perfect fulfilment of the law to the sacrificial routine of normative judaism. The superiority of their chosen way of law-observance was supported by the use of cultic terms transferred to their own situation as, for example, when the community describes itself as the true temple (1 QS 8:5–10; 9:3–5). We should not, however, overlook the fact that this spiritualisation of the cultic is obviously limited by the fact that cultic actions carried out outside the Jerusalem temple and apart from the priesthood which served it were considered as a way of observing the law.

D. *The New Testament*. I. *Jesus and Old Testament worship*. 1. *Basic principles*. It must be understood in the first place that we can only approach the question of Jesus' position with regard to Old Testament cult through the witness of New Testament writers and the traditions on which they depended and which they incorporated and edited into their work. Insofar as we are able to identify them, these traditions are to be emphasised with respect to the different contribution which each makes. But we can say of all of them that, despite their distinct qualities, they are characterised by the post-resurrection insight into the understanding of the Christ-event in whatever way we choose to define it. This is also true of those elements in the tradition which betray a historical or quasi-historical interest and which demand, or at least allow for, an interpretation based on this premiss. The historical Jesus can be attained by following the course of his life on earth and the identity of this figure engaged in a saving mission with the exalted Christ can be grasped by faith. This identity entails the necessary conclusion that the earthly life of Jesus is represented for the most part as a reflection backwards of the church's image of the exalted Christ. Moreover, the post-resurrection proclamation of Christ took place in a milieu where various influences were at work on the process of preaching, maintaining, strengthening, forming, and deepening faith in Christ, influences which we cannot discuss in detail here and which are not in every case easy to assess. If in carrying out our investigation we bear in mind the presuppositions necessary for understanding the material which the New

Testament offers on our subject, we will be able to recognise without difficulty that the answer to our question about the *historical* Jesus implies the attempt to identify what Jesus really did and said insofar as the New Testament writings and the traditions which we can perceive behind these writings allow us to do so.

2. *A glance at the relevant texts.* a. Mk 1:40–5 and parallels record the healing of a leper. The text reveals an inner tension, not just between the imposition of silence on the healed man by Jesus and his subsequent conduct (vv 44, 45), but in the very demand of Jesus itself (v 44a, 44b). If no one ever hears about the healing it would be impossible for the man to present himself before the priest as healed, therefore his return into society would be dangerous and difficult to accomplish. He would not be able to avoid answering the question as to *how* he had been healed. This tension or contradiction within the text is open to various solutions. For example, one could suppose that two traditions have been incorporated into the account, in one of which (to take one of the main differences) the healed man is commanded to say nothing about it (v 44a), whereas in the other he is commanded to show himself to the priest (v 44b). A solution might also be attempted by taking account of the editorial work of the evangelist as in the addition of the command to keep silent on what had happened. However we attempt to justify the presence in the narrative of the command to show himself to the priest, the question at issue is whether it can be used to show a respect, however conditional, on the part of Jesus for the priesthood, the office which it represented, and the functions which it fulfilled.

We should note in the first place that the whole point of the command is explained by the phrase 'for a proof to the people'. Even if we suppose that this is an editorial addition of the evangelist we would hardly be wrong in seeing here the explanation why the command was given. In this latter case the phrase could hardly be taken as an explanation of what had already been said. If the phrase *eis marturion autois* (='for a proof to them') does not simply indicate the intention to prove that a miracle has taken place, with even less reason can it be taken as justification for the return of the healed man to life in society. *Rather does it presuppose a definite attitude on the part of the priesthood to what had taken place and to the one responsible, namely, to Jesus himself*, and in the view of the underlying tradition and certainly of the evangelist himself this attitude had taken shape long before this point in the narrative. Viewed from this angle, the main centre of interest which determines the thrust of the narrative and focusses on one point becomes clear. Certainly neither the tradition on which the evangelist drew for his information nor the evangelist himself had any intention of depicting Jesus as taking his inspiration from or being directed by the temple and its functionaries; from which it may be concluded that Jesus himself had never given occasion to anyone to think that he had.

b. The critical position which Jesus took with regard to the cultic prescriptions of the Old Testament can be clearly seen in the dispute-saying about what is ↗ 'clean and unclean', which has to be understood against the background of current views on the law and the traditions of the fathers (Mk 7:1–23; see also Mt 15:1–20). This passage is composed as follows: introduction to the general theme and question of the Pharisees (vv 1–5), Jesus' answer to the question (vv 6–13), instruction of the people (vv 14–15), instruction of the disciples (vv 17–23). With regard to the question of ritual purity the attitude of Jesus was clearly one of *rejection* (vv 1–5; see also 15a, 18). Ritual or apparent impurity is contrasted with what really makes a man impure (vv 15b, 20–3), implying that in the conflict between the duty to love one's parents and that of making a gift to the temple the latter must quite definitely be relativised. It is not, however, easy to determine what the phrase *korban* (='given to God') really refers to (v 11). Does it signify the sacrificial offering for the temple worship and does the saying affect the requirement in the law to make such an offering and, if so, in what sense? Or is it in part or entirely here a question of correcting those abuses which had crept in with the practice of vowing property to the temple? If we take the text as it stands it would seem arbitrary and even perverse to limit the criticism of Jesus to this kind of abuse. The text speaks in a general and unspecified way about ritual purity and impurity. The main point at issue is clearly the highly significant one that any kind of cultic prescription must take second place to the law of love; in the fulfilment of the will of God there can be no conflict of duties! To help one's parents is a sacred duty prescribed by God's law. They must not be left to suffer want. God himself can say: 'Every beast of the forest is mine . . . if I were hungry I would not tell you, for the world and all that is in it is mine' (Ps 50:10, 12). That God does not *need* anything from man is a well-established datum of Old Testament revelation.

c. The purification of the temple (Mk 11:15–17 and parallels; Jn 2:13–17). From the point of view of our theme in general this incident seems to the modern reader to have a very special importance; and the meaning seems to be quite simply that to purify means to make holy, to restore an original holiness which had been lost. Yet this text raises a whole series of very difficult questions which have to be faced, two of which may be mentioned here. The first concerns the historical character of the narrative. How could Jesus, acting alone and a stranger in Jerusalem, have cleared the forecourt of the gentiles of merchants and money-changers without interference from the authorities and the temple police or interruption by these people whose concessions to trade there were guaranteed by the authorities? Then there is the theological difficulty: why should Jesus have objected to what after all was meant to be at the service of the sacrificial liturgy of the temple? The difficulty is even greater if the expression 'house of prayer' taken from the Isaian quotation (56:7) refers in general to 'the house where God is worshipped' and therefore presupposes a positive assessment of the temple and its sacrificial liturgy, as all agree is the case, rather than referring merely to synagogue worship. The original connection between this scene and the question of

Jesus' authority (Mk 11:27–33 and parallels) does not offer a solution to the difficulties raised by this passage, especially since it is redacted in such a way as to reveal no interest in providing an answer to these difficulties but rather raises questions of its own similar to these. But if we cannot get any help towards understanding the episode from this quarter other possibilities lie open. Traditions and evangelists which have influenced the formation of the text and given it the form it now has (the difference is important!) leave us in no doubt as to the real meaning of the event. They understand it as a symbolic anticipation of the judgement which threatens the temple as the centre of cult, a judgement which is soon to come upon it or—seen from a later perspective—which has already been passed on it and, at the same time, as pointing to the theological outcome of this judgement which is that the temple is no longer of any significance as a place of cult and its liturgy no longer represents the true worship of God as God himself wills it. At the same time, the character of the event as implying an eschatological promise for the gentiles has also been built into it. Suffice it to think of where the action takes place (the forecourt of the gentiles) and the phrase 'for all the nations' in Mark. It should be added that we cannot exclude the possibility that for some groups at some stage of the formation of the tradition the event may have been understood in a less progressive way within the context of contemporary Jewish eschatology—a new material temple in which a perfect form of divine worship would be carried out.

d. Those texts require a thorough examination which appear to express a direct and forceful rejection of and enmity towards the temple and its worship on the part of Jesus. Mk 13:1f and parallels relate that Jesus replied to one of his disciples who referred to the architectural glories of the temple with a saying predicting its total destruction. This implies that, *in the view of the evangelists, Jesus attributed little value to the temple and its worship*. On this point at least there can be no doubt at all. At the same time, however, this text has been so over-interpreted that we have to insist that nothing more than the above can be extracted from it as it stands. All connections which have been supposed to exist between Mk 13:2 and 14:58; 15:29; Mt 26:61; 27:40 in order to give sharper edge to Jesus' hostility to the temple expressed in this saying must be deemed hypothetical. No matter how much one may be tempted to accept any of these attempts, one thing can be said against them all, namely, that both the tradition and the evangelists insist on branding as false witness (Mk 14:57) brought by false witnesses (Mt 26:60f) the claim that Jesus' own attitude to the temple was one of personal hostility.

The announcement of Jesus that the herodian temple then standing would be destroyed and the severe relativisation of its cult implied in this must be seen against the background of Old Testament and rabbinical tradition. Passages such as 1 Sam 15:21f; Ps 40:6; 50:9–14; 51:16ff; Is 1:11; Jer 7:21–3; Hos 6:6; Mic 6:6–8 speak out very clearly and unambiguously on the sacrificial system. 1 Kings 8:27 presupposes that the temple as the house of

God has no absolute value in itself; Enoch (Eth) 90:28f refers to the old temple as having been set aside; the talmudic tractate Joma 39b (the Babylonian recension, see JerJoma 43c) knows that the temple will be destroyed and in fact presupposes the expectation that in the eschatological age a more glorious temple would take the place of the present building.

e. Mk 12:41–4 (see also Lk 21:1–4): the two coins of the widow. This narrative is always being used to make room in the evangelists' sketch of the earthly life of Jesus for the importance of temple piety. Taken by itself, however, it gives no support to this view; the interest is focussed on the poor widow who shamed the rich by giving all that she had, little though it was. Her exemplary conduct in doing so has really nothing to do with the temple as a place of worship. Her action which provoked Jesus to say what he did could have taken place elsewhere and have been otherwise motivated. It is conceivable that the place where her good action was performed was named to show the greatness of the gifts being made and introduce a variety of givers in order the more clearly to emphasise the poverty of the widow and the smallness of her gift. The episode is not concerned with the significance of the temple and its worship or whether participation in the temple services was necessary and desirable. We hear no instruction on this occasion from Jesus on this subject nor does the narrative as a whole betray any tendency to express a view on the significance of the temple. These are clear indications that this episode has nothing to do with the theme we are discussing.

f. It is generally taken for granted that the saying in Mt 5:23f was associated in the mind of the evangelist with the text just discussed, though the reasons for affirming this differ in each case. If we accept this supposition, the unity of the saying can be better understood. As is generally admitted, its meaning has to be sought on the level of a general statement prescinding from particularities such as the nature of the gift, the identity of the 'brother', what the nature of the disagreement was and the question of guilt. It is reminiscent of Mk 11:25 in that both can be characterised as general statements from the point of view of both form and content.

As far as our present theme is concerned one thing is clear. *The relationship of each one to his 'brother' is the touchstone of genuine worship of God.* There is nothing here about the intrinsic value or lack of value of sacrifice as such. It is therefore illegitimate to interpret the saying in terms of either sympathy for or hostility towards cult; this would represent in either case imposing on the text a weight which it cannot bear. It does not fit at all into this kind of category.

g. We find an abrogation of Old Testament cultic prescriptions expressed in the account of the calling of Matthew, the descriptions of Jesus' dealings with publicans and sinners (Mt 9:9–13 and parallels) and the account of the disciples picking the ears of wheat on the sabbath (Mt 12:1–8 and parallels) which is supported in Matthew by a quotation from Hosea—'I will have mercy and not sacrifice' (Mt 9:13 = 12:7; see Hos 6:6). The frequent dealings of Jesus with publicans and sinners speak for themselves; anyone associating or eating with them could not possibly observe the prescriptions concerning ritual purity. There is, however, more to it than that. The call of Jesus goes out not to the just but to sinners. In calling sinners (it was understandable that occasion was later taken to add 'to repentance') he fulfilled the prophetic oracle or, to put it more strongly and precisely, *the saying of the Lord in Hos 6:6 is fulfilled in the activity of Jesus* (for the character and content of Hos 6:6 as a 'doctrinal clarification' see H. W. Wolff, *Dodekapropheten* I, *Hosea, Biblische Kommentar zum Alten Testament* 14/I, Neukirchen 1961, 131–67 esp. 132, 152–4, 164–7). Even if we do not accept the supposition that the meaning of the Hosean text is conveyed in all its depth in the quotation in Matthew, we have sufficient grounds for believing that here the old cultic ordinances have been voided of significance. This comes about not so much as the result of any direct statement but indirectly, by reason of the new interpretation of the law which Jesus offers in Matthew.

The account of the disciples eating the ears of corn on the sabbath also raises many problems. We shall refer here only to one or two of these. The disciples violate the law of the sabbath, not just by eating the ears of corn, but also by walking through the cornfields. At the least, we must suppose that this brings them very near to a violation—though if a strict interpretation of the law is presupposed, the violation was complete and unambiguous. According to the way the story is told, we might suppose that the Pharisees also were involved in this violation, but the interest is focussed above all on Jesus. We can see here already how strongly the purpose which inspired the composition of this story has influenced and determined the way it is told. The text makes it impossible for us to think of this walking through the fields as the equivalent of a stroll through the park on Sunday. Yet it is clear that the emphasis is elswhere and hence the walking through the fields does not really constitute a serious problem. In this case Jesus and the Pharisees are not considered to have violated the law if the primary intention of the writer is taken into account, and this is a point which has to be borne in mind. And so Jesus is taken to task by the Pharisees not on account of his own but of his disciples' violation of the law.

If, therefore, the story is concerned only with the eating of the ears of corn and not with the walking, it would appear that a simpler answer would have sufficed and indeed been more effective; but in fact the answer of Jesus is on a different plane from the objection made by the Pharisees. He does not reproach them with having themselves violated one or other of the more important stipulations of the law. Nor can his answer be understood in the context of the contemporary discussion carried on by the scribes with regard to the law of sabbath observance. We have to bear all this in mind in order to realise how inadequate the answer of Jesus is seen in the context of the actual situation. His answer goes well beyond this context in a variety of different ways. The disciples are absolved from any guilt (Mt 12: 7c); the reason why the judgement of the Pharisees is declared false is, in the circumstances, couched in the most general of terms: they do not know the true will of God as to how he is to be honoured since they have not grasped the fact, long ago proclaimed through the prophets (v 7a–b), that the Son of Man is also lord of the sabbath and makes a claim which goes far beyond anything that had been expected (v 8). The same was true of the claim made by Jesus that in him there had appeared 'something greater than the temple' (v 6).

There remain the examples adduced by Jesus in vv 3–5. These fit in perfectly to the episode as here interpreted. Jesus approves of the conduct of David with which many of the scribal interpreters of the Scriptures were decidedly uneasy. We must not, of course, regard the two cases—the eating of the Bread of the Presence and the plucking of the ears of grain—as parallel and then set up a discussion on the resulting similarity or dissimilarity. There is not even a remote resemblance between the two cases with regard either to the action or the situation. By taking not a similar case but one which was one of the most extreme possible—and yet one guaranteed by the scriptures—Jesus replied in effect that since even eating the holy bread could be permitted when it was a question of saving life (even though this was the only reason), provided that nothing was done contrary to the holiness of God and his true worship, *a fortiori* could the disciples pluck ears of grain on the sabbath. There is no special emphasis here on the degree of hunger which they suffered (despite v 1b) as if this were the decisive factor on which the justification of their conduct depended.

One final point concerning priestly worship in the temple. The example adduced by Jesus fails in its purpose if we suppose that its only object was to provide a sharp and decisive justification of the disciples. Cultic actions are contemplated by the law itself and cannot be set in opposition to it. Even if we are to regard the action of the priest in giving the holy bread to David and his men in a casuistic way, as objectively an infraction of the law but one which in the circumstances was free of guilt, it would certainly not provide any justification for what the disciples did. The example would only make sense if it presupposed either that the action was deprived of its cultic character and therefore of its privileged position, or that the disciples had the right, justified on religious (cultic) grounds, to make this kind of exception in the conduct of their (profane) existence. In the final analysis both interpretations of the situation come down to the same thing.

h. Mt 17:24–7: the temple tax. The point made in this episode retains its force irrespective of its historicity in the context of the life of Jesus. According to the information provided by Matthew, Jesus instructs Peter to pay the temple tax but the reasons given are not very encouraging for those who wish to make use of this incident to build up a picture of Jesus as spiritually attached to the temple. Not just Jesus himself as *the Son* but *the sons* are basically free with regard to the payment of this tax, and even though the tax is in fact paid the only reason given is to avoid giving offence (v 27a). There is nothing here about the temple being the house of the Father (Lk 2:49), no distinction made between the temple as the house of God and the unworthiness of those who served it. That from a whole series of possible reasons for paying the tax the only one which is given refers to the temple not as the dwelling of God and the place of cult but only to how others thought of it shows clearly enough how far removed from this episode is the whole idea of temple piety.

i. The parable of the Pharisee and the publican points in the same direction (Lk 18:9–14). The place chosen for the confrontation is the temple as a place of prayer (this, we should note, is how it is considered in Luke) and it is as such that it is important in the context of this parable. But the point which the parable makes has really nothing at all to do with the temple nor does its meaning depend on it being understood as the place of worship; in fact the contrary would be nearer the truth. Drawing on Ps 51:3 the publican represents himself as a sinner. His attitude which, according to what Jesus says (Lk 18:14), leads to his being justified by God, is also stated with reference to this psalm (vv 18–19).

j. Other texts could be adduced which, far from weakening the results of our enquiry so far, would in fact further support them. In Mk 12:33, for example, a scribe declares (with indirect reference to 1 Sam 15:22) that an all-embracing love of God and the neighbour is superior to any kind of sacrifice and is acknowledged by Jesus as not being far from the kingdom of God. Mt 23:16–22 refers to the swearing of oaths but in a very different way from the strong expressions found in Mt 5:34. Distinctions made publicly when vowing are brushed aside as invalid; whoever swears by anything which is considered to belong to God is bound by his vow. Lk 17:14 cannot be adduced as a counter-argument to what we have said so far, much less the first two chapters of this gospel which are stamped with such a strongly original literary and theological character. The question asked in Jn 4:20–4 by the Samaritan woman about the legitimate place of worship is very clearly expressed and so is the answer: *the locus of cult is now 'in the spirit and in truth'*. (We cannot go on to discuss here the theological riches contained in this expression.)

3. *The attitude of Jesus to Old Testament cult.* How then can we characterise the situation of the historical Jesus—insofar as we are able to determine it—with respect to Old Testament cult? The picture which the evangelists give us of Jesus while on earth shows that he regarded the cultic ordinances of the Old Testament as nothing more or less than historical data. It is on this neutral basis that Jesus directs his strong criticism against the cultic ordinances of the Old Testament, relativises them in a radical way, predicts in threatening terms their abrogation, and all this in prophetic words, images, expressions, and actions which take up, intensify, and go beyond the prophets of the Old Testament in their condemnation of contemporary cultic practices. In this respect the picture of Jesus given us by the evangelists is as historically well-founded as we could wish, though we should add that, precisely because the emphasis and interest in the gospels is often centred on the theological elaboration and reproduction of the Christ-event, it is often impossible to

reconstruct historically in any useful way what actually happened.

If this last point is neglected we end up in serious difficulties. We would find it impossible to explain, for example, how the hellenistic christians associated with Stephen (Acts 6–7), Paul, and others in the early church period stand in absolute contradiction to a historical reconstruction of Jesus as a Jew full of reverence and respect for the temple (and also to the view that the gospels describe him as such). It is not a question either of a finely balanced harmony or reconciliation between seemingly irreconcilable differences comparable to those which existed between christians of Jewish and hellenistic backgrounds. But it would not be appropriate to leave in abeyance the solution to the vast range of problems concerning Old Testament cult (and also the law) and simply represent Jesus as protesting against certain abuses and aberrant tendencies in temple worship.

The position of Jesus with regard to the cultic regulations of the Old Testament should not be viewed or investigated apart from his preaching as a whole. To characterise these cultic regulations merely as data implies that they only merit consideration insofar as they come in contact in some way with the aims and intentions of Jesus. And insofar as the evangelists intend to represent the Jesus of history, these points of contact are strengthened by the addition of theological reflection pointing to the deeper meaning of the words or the actions. Unfortunately the attitude of Jesus cannot always be discovered and stated clearly and unambiguously, but some points at least can be stated confidently. It will at least follow from what has been said so far that Jesus is not described (in the purification of the temple scene) as attacking and occupying the temple. This is not in accord with what we know of the historical Jesus and cannot be deduced from what the gospels say. It is equally clear that Jesus was not a reformer of the cult. As with the prophets, his chief concern was with the heart of man. What difference would it have made to the aims which Jesus had in his preaching that he drove a few merchants a couple of yards further away from the temple? If Jesus was concerned at all with the merchants as such it would most probably have been with their rather shady way of doing business.

Once we renounce an 'objective' understanding of the texts which is too little subject to critical control and which often is the result of a false attempt at historical reconstruction, we are able to solve the otherwise insoluble problem of an inner contradiction which affects the person of Jesus and shows itself in his actions: devotion to the temple on the one hand, rejection of the temple on the other.

The prophetic criticism of Jesus directed against the cultic institutions of the Old Testament is part of the picture of the earthly Jesus presented by the gospels, a picture which appears to be firmly grounded in history even though the formulation of the traditions which can be found in the gospels or which lie behind them can be shown to come from communities which already believed in Jesus. This prophetic criticism of Jesus may be taken as one of the essential starting points for the development and elaboration of a new cultic reality proper to the New Testament. Yet the connection between the two cannot simply be represented as a continuum; what we have here is a possible line of development which makes sense but which also contains considerable gaps. In this process we also have to leave room for various tendencies of a more or less judaising nature and can accommodate also those texts which paint an idealistic picture (eg, Acts 2:46; 3:1; 5:12) insofar as they can lay claim to historicity.

That Paul in his theological reasoning did not appeal to the earthly Jesus, Jesus during his life on earth, can be understood from the whole context of the question of *complete* freedom from the law and also, of course, from the fact that in his letters he never refers to the earthly life of Jesus.

II. *Cult in the New Testament*. According to the New Testament there is only only one cultic reality, which is the Christ-event. By means of this the way has been opened to the Father (Eph 2:18).

The Christ-event as the new cultic reality proper to the New Testament is expressed in forms which are ever new, which cannot be contained in any kind of framework, elude any attempt to circumscribe them and can often be subsequently harmonised and systematised only in a purely arbitrary way. Any description of what is implied in these ways of expressing the Christ-event, this continual deepening of insight into the faith, will only be able to touch on one aspect of this complex reality and therefore can never be fully satisfactory. They may, perhaps, best be understood as comprehensive expressions set against the background and the changing horizon of a Christian mission of preaching which was forever moving forward into new milieux. It would be quite irrelevant and inappropriate to make comparisons between the various writings of the New Testament—Mark, John, the Letter to the Hebrews, for example—with respect to the excellence of their presentation of the Christ-event. Each one is in its way unique and evades any such classification. Each one has its own unique way of expressing itself. In this respect no one can take the place of another. In keeping with their different approaches to the understanding of the Christ-event, any one New Testament author can communicate to the right kind of reader all that the Christ-event means to him. Moreover, it would be difficult to think of a more impressive witness to the inner dynamic and the ability to fit every situation characteristic of early Christian preaching than the process we have been describing.

The New Testament cult takes up the Jesus of history into the now exalted Christ who is the high priest (Heb 5; 7; and 8), the mediator of the covenant (Heb 8:6; 9:15; 12:24), who offered himself for a sacrifice and that 'once for all' (Heb 7:27; 9:28; 10:12, 14). In this way the thinking and imagery associated with Old Testament cult are put to use in the service of the Christ-event and New Testament cult is seen to be the eschatological fulfilment of the expectation implicit in that of the Old Testament. The total self-giving of Jesus unto death is the object of continuing theological reflection which works out the universal significance of the Christ-event and emphasises its unique and definitive character. The universal significance of the event is seen above all in connection with the idea of vicarious expiation (Rom 4:25; 8:32; Eph 5:2; 1 Tim 2:6) and in dependence on Is 53. And if the self-offering of Jesus is the true, final, and all-surpassing sacrifice of atonement and of the new covenant, whereas the former sacrifices appear now only as shadows and types, then it must follow that Jesus is himself the true lamb of sacrifice (Jn 1:29, 36; 1 Pet 1:19).

III. *The various forms of New Testament worship.* Seen from our point of view, the Christ-event is an event for *us*, not just an event in itself—it is something in which we participate. This participation is brought about and manifested in the various forms of worship which must, however, in being directed to the totality of human life, lay claim to different dimensions which neither require nor allow for any facile harmonisation. We must therefore beware of schematising New Testament worship in a light-hearted kind of way and of a too easy appraisal of the quality of the various forms it takes.

The 'place' in which this worship is carried out is basically and incontrovertibly the entire life of the believing christian. Leaving aside other purposes which the author may have had in mind, this fact is set out in a doctrinal and programmatic way in the Letter to the Romans which, to judge by the salutation, was addressed to the community in the capital of the Roman Empire. The fact that the Roman community was not founded by Paul gives added strength to the claim of teaching a *doctrine* which had binding force rather than a mere series of edifying admonitions. Also, Paul uses the strongest means at his disposal, both stylistically and theologically, this is most apparent in those passages (Rom 12; 14; and 15) where we find a transposition of the terminology and representations associated with sacrifice and cult to the totality of the life of the believer.

On the basis of this radicalisation of Old Testament cultic ideas we are to understand that the only temple is now the community of those who believe (1 Cor 3:16f; 6:19; 2 Cor 6:16; Eph 2:20–2). The community offers sacrifices and is itself a sacrificial offering (Rom 12:1; 15:16; see also the offering of the firstfruits, 2 Thess 2:13; 1 Cor 16:15; Rom 16:5) and is a holy and royal priesthood (1 Pet 2:5, 9). Paul understands his work of spreading the gospel as sacrificial (Rom 15:15f). Within these comprehensive statements which indicate the end of the old cultic order and nothing less than the complete dissolution of the cultic thinking which was determined by it, there is room for a whole series of actions, attitudes, and points of view which can be regarded as genuine acts of cult, such as acts of love (which is true piety, Jas 1:27) and internal detachment from the world which does not think and act in accord with the divine will (also thought of in terms of piety in Jas 1:27). Finally we arrive at the point of the total offering of one's life (Phil 2:17; Rev 6:9). Prayer may also be regarded as an act of true worship (Acts 13:3; Heb 13:15).

We should not make the mistake of wanting to build up a fixed system of these different forms and acts of christian worship; their number remains open and can be augmented in response to new requirements which may arise. Only one thing remains constant, and that is love (1 Cor 13), for the property of love is to guarantee openness to all possible needs and insights. Finally, the community was consoled at a time when persecution threatened by the thought of the heavenly liturgy (Rev 5; 7; 11; 12; 14; 19).

The fact that the locus of the New Testament cultic reality is the entire life of the believing christian corresponds to a basic datum of the experience of man who lives as an individual in the human community to the extent that the existential reality of community is the locus of the cultic reality of the New Testament. However we may look at it, individual and community are inseparably related, and this is true also for the theme which we are discussing.

That the community is the locus where this new cultic reality is realised is seen clearly in the christian cultic assembly which takes shape around the service of the word and the common meal. The gradual development of these forms of worship arises from an inner necessity of human togetherness and corresponds to the requirement of love and care for the neighbour, the brother. In itself, therefore, it in no way implies a concession to superseded forms of cult which tend to re-emerge, even though it is not immune to a relapse into such forms in its understanding of what it is doing. Initiation into the community takes place in baptism and follows on the faith of the one to be baptised (Acts 8:37 is a later and demonstrably stylised interpretation of baptism while recording faithfully one actual case of baptism). Baptism was already *there* before Paul came on the scene: in his letters it is self-evident that all who believe must be baptised (1 Cor 12:13; Rom 6:3). But even though the sacramental character of baptism is presupposed, there is an emphatic attempt to get rid of false interpretations of baptism as merely a cultic and ritual action (1 Cor 10:1–13).

In the context of the history of the early church, the service of the word—which it is practically impossible for us to reconstruct—must be seen as taking different forms according to the circumstances and must not be separated from the celebration of the eucharist. It was thought of as having its distinct quality through the presence of the Spirit of the risen and exalted Lord. It was composed of scripture reading and interpretation, confessional formulae, the singing or reciting of psalms, hymns, and canticles. It also could include speaking with tongues, acclamations, prayers, and intercession (see 1 Cor 14).

In addition to the service of the word the celebration of the eucharist was also the 'locus' of this new cult-reality of the New Testament. In fact this was true of the eucharist in a unique way in so far as the Christ-event was made present in it in a more palpable way by the proclamation of the salvific death of Jesus, the confirmation of the eternal covenant and the participation of those present in the eschatological meal of fellowship. Understood in this way, it was an invitation and an appeal to the believing community to realise this new cultic reality in practice. In all of this the determinative character of the word was not lost. In terms of the New

Testament understanding of cult it would be the height of folly to set the service of the word over against the eucharist, to play off one against the other or to suppose that the Christ-event was *more* present and active in one than in the other. Basic to both is the one whole and entire Christ-event. Having said this, however, we must add that it is entirely legitimate to attempt to grasp the unique dimension of the eucharistic meal as opening up to man in the totality of his existential reality the experience of the pledge implicit in saving history in terms of objective and bodily reality.

From this understanding of the Christ-event as the new cultic reality and the ways in which it is realised are derived the different ministries mentioned in the New Testament. These are always understood primarily in view of the event-character of the word (apostles, prophets, teachers, but also church leaders) and also comprise the sacramental event insofar as this calls for human ministry. Yet the idea of a distinct personnel qualified only for cultic actions has always been alien to New Testament thinking; it belongs rather to the cultic order of paganism or that of the Old Testament which had now been superseded. This is not contradicted by the understanding of the eucharist as a sacrificial meal which is attested in the New Testament (Mk 14:24; Mt 26:28).

The inadequacy of any attempt to describe what is implied in the new experience of the cultic in the New Testament comes through with particular clarity in the fact that it is practically impossible to give a satisfactory account of the fundamental difference between the content of this new cultic reality and other ways of understanding the cultic, while at the same time doing justice to the concepts which we have at our disposal and preserving the distinct and unique element in New Testament cult. The clear and unambiguous uniqueness and apartness of the reality which constitutes New Testament worship must be established not only with regard to the past, that is, to the cultural and spiritual environment of the New Testament, but also to the present, since here too it must be protected as far as possible from misunderstandings. If we remain insufficiently conscious of the impossibility of fitting New Testament cult into any general pattern it will be very difficult to avoid the danger of thinking of it as simply a new experience and form of worship which supersedes others. And once it is thought of in this way, it could easily happen that a wrongly understood idea and practice of worship supposedly based on New Testament principles could produce once again just those accretions against which Jesus and Paul, to mention no others, had so radically protested.

It would certainly be wrong to overlook the fact that we find in the New Testament writings a primitive christian experience and consciousness with regard to worship which set them apart from other areas of living as, for example, from the experience of living with non-believers. Yet acts of cult, in particular the 'sacraments' of baptism and the eucharist, could not, in New Testament thinking, become independent entities, and therefore there could not be a serious conflict of duties between worship and other aspects of life since cultic duties of a kind which could conflict with other duties simply did not exist. This is a conclusion which is presupposed in all the New Testament writings without exception, despite their great diversity, and one the significance of which it is still impossible to exaggerate. (↗ Prayer ↗ Sacrifice ↗ Priesthood).

Bibliography: H. Menschkewitz, *Die Spiritualisierung der Kultusbegriffe Tempel, Priester und Opfer im Neuen Testament*, Leipzig 1932; J. M. Nielen, *Gebet und Gottesdienst im Neuen Testament*, Freiburg im Br., 1937; E. Lohmeyer, *Kultus und Evangelium*, Göttingen 1942; P. Seidensticker, *Lebendiges Opfer*, Münster 1954; Y. Congar, *The Mystery of the Temple*, London 1960; H. Schlier, 'Die Verkündigung im Gottesdienst der Kirche', *Die Zeit der Kirche*, Freiburg 1959², 244–64; A. Vögtle, 'Der Einzelne und die Gemeinschaft in der Stufenfolge der Christusoffenbarung', *Sentire Ecclesiam* (Hugo Rahner Vol.), Freiburg 1961, 50–91; G. Lanczkowski, H. Haag, H. Schurmann, 'Kult', *LTK* VI², 659–65; L. Bouyer, *Rite and Man*, South Bend (Indiana) 1963; O. Cullmann, *Early Christian Worship*, London 1956; R. de Vaux, *Les Sacrifices de l'Ancien Testament*, Paris 1964; *J. Smith, *A Priest for Ever: A Study of Typology and Eschatology in Hebrews*, London 1969.

Odilo Kaiser

Cup

The Greek *potērion*, which in LXX translates the Hebrew *khôs*, means a drinking vessel made out of stone, earth or metal. We find earthenware drinking vessels (bowl-shaped with stands) as early as the Middle Bronze period (*BRL*, 316f) and a chalice in the true sense of the term, together with its stand, on Maccabean coins.

The word is used in different ways in the New Testament. We refer first of all to the relevant texts:

A. *Cup in the proper sense of the term*, as the drinking vessel in daily use among the people, is mentioned in Mk 9:41 (see also Mt 10:42) and Mt 23:25f (see also Lk 11:39–41).

B. *In the metaphorical sense* it refers either to the cup of suffering or the cup of wrath.

1. *The cup of suffering*. The Saviour refers to this in his question addressed to the sons of Zebedee (Mk 10:38–9; see also Mt 20:22–3): 'Are you able to drink the cup that I drink?'. He is asking in effect whether these apostles are prepared to take on themselves the destiny of suffering, namely martyrdom, which he had proclaimed in advance. The cup of suffering appears as a symbol of martyrdom also in early christian writing outside the New Testament, eg, in the Martyrdom of Polycarp (14:2).

In the prayer of Jesus in the garden of Gethsemane the cup which he asks will pass from him or be taken from him (Mk 14:36; see also Mt 26:39, 42; Lk 22:42) refers to the suffering and death for which he is destined. The metaphor of the chalice offered by God symbolises elsewhere in the bible the happy (Ps 16:5; 23:5) or bitter (Ps 11:6; 75:8) destiny reserved for the individual or the people as a whole. It derives no doubt from the Jewish custom of each guest being handed a cup filled with wine by the head of the family (sharing in the cup).

2. *The chalice of wrath*. The image of the chalice in the hand of God which is filled with his anger or the wine of his wrath and which is given to the nations to drink occurs frequently over a long period of time in the Old Testament. We find it most often in the prophetic oracles of doom, as in Jer 25:17f;

Hab 2:15; Is 51:17; Ps 75:8; see also Ezek 23:33. On account of its intoxicating effect it is sometimes called 'the bowl of staggering' (Is 51:17; Ps 60:3). This highly poetical figure could also derive ultimately from the idea of sharing in the cup passed round at a banquet. Some, however, think in terms of a mythological origin, and refer to Babylonian representations of a cup or bowl held by the gods from which is poured the water of life. In this case the cup would symbolise the fact that the determination of human destiny pertains to them (Goppelt, 152 *n.* 32). In the Old Testament the determination of destiny is associated with the will of a personal God; hence the cup of destiny becomes the cup of judgement, a symbol of 'the power of God as judge in human history, his right to judge'. Whether the agent is God himself or someone commissioned to act for him, the offering of this cup signifies condemnation, and drinking from it subjection to the judgement and punishment of God.

In the *New Testament* we come upon this metaphor of the chalice of wrath only in the Book of Revelation, which is here clearly influenced by the Old Testament. The whore of Babylon holds in her hand a golden chalice full of abominations and the impurities of her fornications (Rev 17:4; see also Jer 51:7). The reference is to the power of perversion exercised on the nations by the world-wide empire of Rome. Blinded by the allure of its power, riches and luxury they are led to take up the idolatry and immorality current in 'Babylon' and so drink 'the wine of her impure passion', as the contents of the cup are elsewhere described (Rev 18:3; see also 14:8). In reality it is God himself who offers the peoples this cup of wrath since it is he who has given Babylon the power to deceive them (13:5). The cup in the hand of the scarlet woman makes it quite clear that the Roman Empire is the means by which God's anger is visited upon the world.

Yet this same world-power which has intoxicated the nations with the wine of its fornication (14:8) will suffer retribution and be paid back in kind for what it has visited upon others. Now it will be the nations themselves who will act as instruments of the divine wrath and mix a double draught for Babylon in the cup she mixed (18:6). A particularly hard punishment is often represented in the bible as a double punishment (see Jer 16:18; 17:18; Is 40:2); it is in this way that the cup of the divine anger will be offered to the great city of Babylon (Rev 16:19).

Finally, every single person who allows himself to be led into idolatry by worshipping the anti-Christian world-power as if it were divine will have to drink of the wine of God's wrath which is prepared unmixed in the cup (Rev 14:9f). This will be when God will proceed to the final judgement and his anger will consign all idolaters to eternal damnation (14:11).

C. *The chalice at the last supper*. 1. *The first cup*. At the outset of the last supper, which—according to the view of most exegetes—must be understood in the context of a passover meal, Jesus took a cup filled with wine, recited the prayer of thanksgiving over it, and gave it to his disciples to drink (Mk 14:25; see also Lk 22:17b). This is not the eucharistic cup over which Jesus spoke the words of institution but the first of the four cups of wine drunk at the passover meal. This emerges clearly from the words which accompany the action as found in the following verse of Luke: 'from now on I shall not drink of the fruit of the vine until the kingdom of God comes' (Lk 22:18; see also Mt 26:29; Mk 14:25). In the kingdom of God the passover, which Jesus was celebrating for the last time with his disciples, would find its fulfilment and completion. This eschatological saying of Jesus is based on the prayer of praise and thanksgiving which the father of the family pronounced over the first cup before the breaking of bread. This prayer runs as follows: 'blessed art thou Lord our God, king of the universe, thou who hast created the fruit of the vine' (SB IV, 61f). The Lukan account which puts vv 15–18 before the actual words of institution (which are spoken by Christ over the third cup) is clearer and fuller than that of Mark, in which the eschatological saying and the words of consecration are not clearly distinguished.

2. *The eucharistic cup* (Mk 14:23; see also Mt 26:27; Lk 22:20; 1 Cor 10:16). Paul calls this cup 'the cup of blessing' (1 Cor 10:16), a technical term taken from the usage governing Jewish meals. At every meal during which wine was drunk the head of the family pronounced in the name of all present the prayer of thanksgiving over the cup filled with wine which he raised in his hands. This took place after the main course was finished. On the occasion of the Lord's passover, this was the third of the four cups of wine commonly drunk during this meal. The account found in the synoptics and in Paul of the consecration of the chalice at the last supper is connected with this custom. After the meal was over (Lk 22:20; 1 Cor 11:25) Jesus took the chalice, 'gave thanks' (*eukharistēsas*, Mk 14:23; see also Mt 26:27), spoke over it the words of institution and passed it around the company of the disciples without tasting it himself—as would normally be the case.

D. *The chalice of the Lord and of demons.* In 1 Cor 10:16–22 Paul speaks of the eucharistic cup of blessing: 'The cup of blessing which *we* bless, is it not a participation on the blood of Christ?' By using this emphatic language he wishes to contrast the eucharistic christian cup with the cup of blessing in use during a Jewish meal. His statement presupposes that this cup gives to those who drink of it a share in the blood of Christ and brings them into a living communion with him. It is 'the cup of the Lord' (1 Cor 10:21) which is contrasted in what follows with the chalice of demons. What Paul means is that it is impossible for the christian to drink from both chalices. By saying this he is showing himself to be decisively opposed to christians taking part in pagan cultic meals involving the worship of false gods. On these occasions a drink-offering was made to the deity from the cup. In opposing these practices Paul follows the Old Testament view that any sacrifice which was not offered to Yahweh must be offered to demons (see Deut 32:17, 37f); hence any cup in pagan sacrificial meals could be called the chalice of demons. This by no means implies that he is contradicting his earlier statement about the non-existence of idols (1 Cor 8:4);

he is only emphasising that in reality pagans do offer sacrifice to demons (1 Cor 10:20). He thereby expresses a belief in the existence not of gods but of demons. Who therefore drinks of this chalice of the pagans places himself in the power of demons and cuts himself off from communion with the Lord. For it is impossible to be at the same time in table-fellowship with Christ and with demons.

Bibliography: Haag, 168; E. Kalt, *BRL* I, Paderborn 1937, 207; D. Forstner OSB, *Die Welt der Symbole*, Innsbruck 1961, 552f; F. J. Dölger, 'Der Kelch der Dämonen', *Antike und Christentum* IV, 266–70; L. Goppelt, *TDNT* VI, 148–58 and Büchsel III, 168, 13f; Stählin V, 438, 17f.

Jakob Obersteiner

Curse

A. *Terminology*. The Hebrew language has several expressions which correspond, more or less, to the English *to curse* or *a curse*.

1. *ʾAlâh* is (a) a curse which the owner pronounces aloud and publicly, when he finds he has lost something, against the thief, dishonest finder, or receiver of the property, with the purpose of inducing the person responsible to give the lost object back (Lev 5:1; Judg 17:2; Prov 29:24); (b) a conditional curse upon oneself to corroborate a promise or an agreement, sometimes to back up an ↗ oath (Num 5:21; 1 Kings 8:31; 2 Chron 6:22; Gen 24:41; 1 Sam 14:24; Neh 10:29; Gen 26:28; Ezek 17:13, 16, 18; perjury, therefore, is known simply as *ʾālâh*: Ps 10:7; 59:12; Job 31:30; Hos 4:2, or *ʾālôth šâw*: Hos 10:4); (c) a curse added by a human or divine legislator to a legal code, also to the Code of the Alliance, as a sanction in the case of infraction of the law (Deut 29:19f; Is 24:6; Jer 23:10; Ezek 16:59; 17:19; 2 Chron 34:24). An *ʾālâh* can be directed only against equals, inferiors or one's own person, never against superiors or against God.

2. Formations from the root *ʾārar*: in *qal*, *piel*, and the noun *meʾērâh*. A curse indicated in this way arises from a specific formula, is connected with certain rites, and serves to render enemies and the wicked powerless to harm. The shortest of these curse-formulae goes: *ʾārûr* [cursed] be N.N.!' As a result, according to the idea of the ancient Near East, happiness and blessing would be destroyed in the one so cursed and evil released upon him. At the same time, the person who pronounces the curse announces that he is breaking off all association with the one cursed. Even inanimate objects can be cursed in this way, and will henceforth bring disaster and bad fortune on those who use them. Such curse formulae could also be abused by people for magical ends since sinister powers were attributed to them (Num 22:6; 23:7; Job 3:8). But they could also be used by those who were legitimately members or functionaries within the community, in order to dissociate themselves from evildoers. Thus a father could cast a curse-formula of this kind upon a badly-disposed son (Gen 9:25; 49:7), or the divinely appointed leader of the people against lawbreakers and evildoers (Deut 28:16–19; Josh 6:26; 9:23; 1 Sam 14:24, 28); or the whole people gathered together against members who had ignored a decision made in

common or violated the Covenant law, which was incumbent on the whole people (Judg 21:18; Deut 27:15–26); or God himself against seducers (Gen 3:14), murderers (Gen 4:11), adversaries of the one chosen by him (Gen 12:3; 27:29; Num 24:9) and the land on account of sinners who live in it or cultivate it (Gen 3:17; 5:29). The destructive power emanating from such a curse burdens the one so cursed with an evil fate and finally brings him to utter ruin, unless its course is checked by God. It is called *m*ᵉ*ērâh* (Deut 28:20; Mal 2:2; Prov 3:33; 28:27).

As a means of imposing trial by ordeal on a woman suspected of marital infidelity, a curse was written on the surface of some writing material; this was washed off with water and the water given to the woman to drink. In the event of her being guilty the curse would produce fatal illness in her, but if innocent it would remain without effect. This water was called 'the water that brings the curse' (Num 5:18–27). A curse-formula with *ʾārar* can never be directed against God.

3. The most common expression for 'curse' is the root *qll*, usually in *piel* or in the form of a noun, *q*ᵉ*lālâh*. According to its etymology, its real meaning in *piel* would be 'to make small of', 'to deal with contemptuously' and therefore also 'to mock', 'to make ridiculous'. Since people in antiquity attributed a very real efficacy to the spoken word, they believed that scoffing at any given person really aroused destructive powers and could diminish his happiness. Hence David calls the mocking directed against him by Shimei a *q*ᵉ*lālâh nimretseth* = 'dangerous mocking' (1 Kings 2:8). It is for this reason that *qallēl* can have the meaning 'to curse', though it is a question here not of a curse with determined formulae and rites but rather of an indeterminate execration, mocking, cursing or slandering. It is therefore not always possible to translate *qll* and its derivates as 'to curse', 'a curse', etc. In order to determine the meaning, we have to note the following contexts: (a) Against the king. Here *qallēl* refers not so much to a curse as to the act of condemning, slighting the king, therefore an act of *lèse-majesté* which comes near to rebellion (Judg 9:27; 2 Sam 16:5, 7, 9–13; 19:22; 1 Kings 2:8). (b) Against parents. *Qallēl* refers here to the refusal of obedience and the undermining of parental authority; this threatens the structure of patriarchal society and so is punishable by death (Ex 21:17; Lev 20:9; Prov 20:20; 30:11). (c) Against God. In this case *qallēl* refers to the attitude of a person who has become disillusioned with God, who no longer takes him seriously, abuses him and tries his luck with other gods—therefore blasphemy (Lev 24:11, 14f, 23; in 1 Kings 21:10, 13 and Job 1:5, 11; 2:5, 9, we have also to read *qll* instead of the euphemism ↗ 'bless'). The sons of Eli by their unworthy conduct incurred the guilt of 'making light' of God (1 Sam 3:13), and we have a good example of how such a *q*ᵉ*lālâh* works out in practice in the abusive language used by the Rabshakeh against Yahweh (2 Kings 18:30–5) and in Is 10:8–11. (d) Against other given persons. Here, too, we can easily recognise the basic meaning of 'making light' of someone. Just like the heroes of the Homeric poems with regard to their opponents, Goliath sets out to 'make light' of the

Israelites, and in particular David, by means of wordy and high sounding insults (1 Sam 17:43f). When this kind of slighting of an opponent takes the form of execration we have a form similar to the curse (Gen 8:21; Deut 23:5; Josh 24:9; Jer 15:10; Ps 37:22; 62:4; Prov 30:10; Neh 13:2, 25 etc).

4. *qbb* and *nqb* also have the primary meaning of insulting, abusing, and therefore blaspheming when they have God for object (Lev 24:11, 16). When persons or things are object there can be present here also the idea of a 'curse' (Num 22:11, 17; 23:8, 11, 13, 25, 27; 24:10; Job 3:8; 5:3; Prov 11:26; 24:24).

5. The Hebrew verb *zā*ᶜ*am* really means 'to threaten' or the like (Is 10:5, 25; Jer 10:10; Ps 7:12 etc). But a threat can be equivalent to a curse, especially when pronounced by God (Num 23:7f; Mal 1:4; Prov 24:24).

6. The nouns *ʾālâh* and *q*ᵉ*lālâh*, as used in the expressions 'to make cursed', 'to become a curse'. When a curse has had devastating effect on a person, a city or a country, then these same are said to be 'a curse' (Num 5:21–7; Deut 21:23; 2 Kings 22:19; Jer 24:9; 25:18; 26:6; 29:18, 22; 42:18; 44:8, 12, 22; 49:13; Zech 8:13; similarly Is 65:15, 'an imprecation'). The precise meaning of this type of expression is disputed, but, on the basis of Is 65:15 and Jer 29:22, the most likely interpretation would be that the person or thing in question is in such a fearful condition that his or its fate is taken proverbially for a curse—that is, when anyone desires to curse another person or pronounce a conditional curse upon himself when making an oath he says, 'May you [I] become as that person!' or 'May it happen to you [to me] as to that person or city!'

In the LXX and New Testament *ara* with its derivatives generally corresponds to the Hebrew terms in 1–4, and sometimes to 5. There occurs also *orismos* for 1, and for 3 *katalogein* or, when God is the object, *blasphēmein*.

B. *The curse in the Old Testament.* As with other peoples in antiquity, so in Israel the curse is connected with the belief in the power of the spoken word. In the ancient Near East curses serve as a defence against enemies, to prevent inscriptions and documents from being falsified, or sacred buildings and graves from being profaned, and as a sanction for contracts and laws. The belief was that the evildoer or the person acting in defiance of the curse would be totally ruined, and with him his whole family and descendants.

Since in Israel God was the guardian of order and supreme lawgiver, the Old Testament ascribes the efficacy of a curse inflicted by him or in his name directly to him, and looks to him also to bring to pass the adversity mentioned in the curse. The degree of efficacy of the curse depends on the proximity of the one cursing to God, the heinousness of the outrage, or the importance of what is defended by the curse. Formal curses or threats of ruin which are equivalent to a curse can be found in the Old Testament in the mouth of patriarchs (Gen 9:25; 49:3–7), men of God (Josh 6:26; 1 Sam 15:26; 2 Sam 12:11f; 2 Kings 5:27), kings (1 Sam 14:24; 2 Sam 3:29f), but also of ordinary pious people in their clashes with their own personal adversaries (in the cursing psalms: 5:10; 6:10; 7:10–16; 10:15; 28:4; 31:17f; 35:4ff; 40:15;

54:7; 58:7–11; 69:23–9; 109:6–19; 139:19; 140:9–12; 141:10; 143:12), or of the community as against the national enemies (Ps 79:6, 12; 83:10–19; 129:5–8; 137:7ff). Cursing the king is expressly forbidden (Ex 22:28).

We ought not to judge the curse in the Old Testament according to our present-day moral and religious sensitivity, but rather attempt to understand it within the context of the situation which then prevailed. The rule of law was not yet guaranteed by the existence of a system of justice which really worked, or of a police force, so that it was possible only in a few cases to discover the criminal and make good the damage done. Rulers and conquerors in battle were not in any way bound by law; but even the transgressor, the warrior, the conqueror and the ruler lived in fear of the hostility of numinous powers and of the curse. And so Israel could not dispense with the curse as a means of defence against evildoers and enemies. God made use of this means in favour of his people and his faithful servants, as a sanction for the law of the alliance which he had granted to them, and as a punishment for evildoers (Gen 3:14, 17; 4:11; 12:3; 27:29; Lev 26; Num 24:9; Deut 28:15–68; 1 Sam 2:30–6; etc). The people of the alliance and its functionaries act in a corresponding way when they dissociate themselves from evildoers (Deut 27:15–26). The vision of the flying scroll inscribed with curses against all kinds of evildoers (Zech 5:2ff) expresses the manner in which the Old Testament believes in the immanent sanction of the moral law: God has so instituted the moral order that any infringement of it works out ill for the transgressor in the form of a curse.

When a good man pronounces a curse against an ↗ enemy or a reprobate he thereby calls on God as defender of the right and prays him to apply the sanctions which he has assigned. The curse in the Old Testament, in distinction to the rest of the ancient Near East, is not a magical tool which can be used to compel the deity to intervene, but rather a prayer addressed to God. An irregular curse recoils on the one making it (Ps 10:7–15; 109:16–19). God can turn an irregular curse into a blessing (2 Sam 16:12; Ps 109:28; cf the Oracles of Balaam and Deut 23:5; Neh 13:2). A pointless or irregular curse is 'like a sparrow in its flitting, like a swallow in its flying' (Prov 26:2), namely, without effect. The blessing, too, is no magical force which brings about good fortune necessarily and in all circumstances. If a person does not deserve it God can also turn it into a curse (Mal 2:2; see also 1 Sam 2:30).

We must be careful not to take the individual expressions, which we usually understand as curses, out of their context. At the same time certain curses here and there do appear to be unalterable and to exercise a fateful influence also on the posterity of the one cursed. But here it is not a question of punishing the innocent posterity but the evildoer in question against whom the curse is directed, understood according to the basic concept of a 'punishment on the father'. In other words, the evildoer in such cases is affected in a particularly hard way, insofar as his family is ruined and his 'name and seed' is taken from him (Ps 109:6–14; 2 Sam 3:29f; 1 Kings

14:8–11; 16:2ff; 21:19–24). This idea was based on the fact of general experience that the children are generally no better than the father. As can be easily understood, the one who cast a curse on his enemy in a highly emotional state would not have reckoned with the possibility of the conversion, either of the one he cursed, or his descendants; but the Old Testament historical outlook does take this possibility into consideration, and so Yahweh removes the curse when the person cursed repents (Deut 4:29ff; 30:1–10; Zech 8:13ff).

Judaism at the time of Christ was familiar with the curse, above all in the form of an anathema which accompanied the expulsion of a transgressor of the Law from the Jewish cultic community (SB IV, 293–333). The rabbis freely resort to curse-formulae if they hear of such a transgressor (SB III, 446). In Qumran, the curse pronounced on the godless takes place within the ritual of the Renewal of the Covenant and at the reception of candidates (1 QS II, 4–18).

C. *The curse in the New Testament.* The New Testament is familiar with the conditional self-curse pronounced on the occasion of making a promise confirmed by an oath (Acts 23:12, 14, 21: Jewish fanatics who bound themselves in this way to take Paul's life), or accompanying an oath by which one clears oneself (Mt 26:74; Mk 14:71: Peter protests that he had had nothing to do with Jesus). It is apparent, however, that the curse had to appear in a new light because of the deepened and modified understanding of retribution brought about by the teaching on an after-life and the christian love of neighbour. A curse against one's personal enemies is incompatible with love; the disciples of Jesus bless their enemies instead of cursing them (Lk 6:28; Rom 12:14; see also Jas 3:9–12). At the same time, the New Testament is familiar with the curse retained as a sanction of the divine law and as a means of promoting justice (Mt 25:41; 2 Peter 2:14). The Law of Moses was guaranteed by the sanction of a curse and really brought the curse into effect (Gal 3:10, 13). If the evangelist narrates in Mt 27:25 that those who took part in the condemnation of Jesus called down a curse upon themselves it is evident that he was convinced that the curse was fulfilled in the history of the Jewish people. By means of the cursing of the fig tree (Mt 21:18f; Mk 11:12ff) Jesus showed his determination to pass irrevocable judgement on all those who do not bear 'fruit'. By means of the authority which they had from God, the apostles and the christian community also had the power to deliver over apostate church members and false teachers to a curse (1 Cor 5:3ff; 16:22; Gal 1:8), thereby excluding them from the community. Such a curse, however, did not imply eternal damnation; the demonic forces of destruction would have their effect on the one concerned until he was moved through suffering to contrition and conversion and so regained salvation (1 Cor 5:5). The only irrevocable curse will be the one Jesus will cast at sinners in the Last Judgement (Mt 25:41).

The meaning of the expression 'Christ having become a curse' (Gal 3:13) is disputed. It certainly does not imply that Christ has become the object of the Father's curse (see O. Kuss, *RNT ad loc*), but rather that Christ has taken upon himself the fate of one who is cursed. According to Is 65:15 and Jer 29:22, one could also give it this explanation: Christ has been overtaken by a terrible affliction similar to that which a man would desire for the one he wanted to curse (see A6 above).

Bibliography: J. Behm, *TDNT* 1, 354f; F. Büchsel, *TDNT* 1, 448–51; F. Steinmetzer, 'Babylon: Parallelen zu d. Fluchpsalmen', *BZ* 10 (1912), 133–42 and 363–9; J. Pedersen, *Der Eid bei den Semiten*, Strassburg 1914; P. Heinisch, *Das Wort im AT u. im Alten Orient*, Münster 1922; S. Mowinckel, *Segen und Fluch in Israels Kult and Psalmendichtung*, Kristiania 1924; J. Hempel, 'Die israelit. Anschauungen von Segen u. Fluch im Lichte oriental. Parallelen', *ZDMG* 79 (1925), 20–110; T. Canaan, 'The Curse in Palestinian Folklore', *JPOS* 15 (1935), 235–79; S. H. Blank, 'The Curse, the Blasphemy, the Spell, and the Oath', *HUCA* 23 (1950/1), 73–95; J. Scharbert, '"Fluchen" und "Segnen" im AT', *Bbl* 39 (1958), 1–26; J. Scharbert, *Solidarität in Segen und Fluch im AT und in seiner Umwelt*, Bonn 1958; M. Noth, 'Die mit des Gesetzes Werken umgehen, die sind unter dem Fluch', *Gesammelte Studien zum AT*, Munich 1960², 155–71; F. C. Fensham, 'Malediction and Benediction in Ancient Near Eastern Vassal-Treaties and the OT', *ZAW* 74 (1962), 1–9; F. C. Fensham, 'Common Trends in Curses of the Near Eastern Treaties and Kudurru-Inscriptions', *ZAW* 75 (1963), 155–75; H. C. Brichto, *The Problem of 'Curse' in the Hebrew Bible*, Philadelphia 1963; H. A. Brongers, 'Die Rache- und Fluchpsalmen im AT', *OTS* 13 (1963), 21–42; D. R. Hillers, *Treaty Curses and the OT Prophets*, Rome 1964; J. Kišš, 'Der Begriff "Fluch" im NT', *CV* 7 (1964), 87–92.

Josef Scharbert

Day of Yahweh

The form criticism and history-of-tradition methods of investigation require that we do not view the idea of the Day of the Lord in isolation on the basis of the relevant texts taken singly, but rather within the framework of the related field of ideas. Hence, it is not correct to exclude the concept from Amos 5:18–20, as is usually done, on the grounds that it is not present there expressly but is rather presented as a familiar reality—as a result of which this text lends itself to different and even conflicting interpretations. Apart from this, we meet the idea of the Day of the Lord in Is 2:12; 13:6–9; 22:5; 34:8; Jer 46:10; Ezek 7:10; 13:5; 30:3; Joel 1:15; 2:1f, 11, 31; 3:14; Obad, 15; Zeph 1:7f, 14–18; Zech 14:1.

On the basis of Is 13:4; Ezek 7; Joel 2, it follows that the idea of the Day of the Lord stands in relationship with the institution of the holy war, revived in the prophets—an institution which goes back to the early days in Israel (see especially Deut, Josh, Judg, Sam) with reference to the conquest of the Holy Land, brought about by God. In it Yahweh himself takes part in the battle, musters his army, leads it into battle against the enemy who at once lose heart. In accordance with this, the Day of the Lord, in the texts referred to, takes on the character of a battle and a complete victory for Yahweh which is achieved under the dreadful signs of darkness and earthquake. Even the metaphor of the plague of locusts on the Day of the Lord which we find in Joel 2—an accessible image taken from the actual experience of Israel—is part of this tradition and refers to the battle of Yahweh. Zeph 1 has to be understood in a similar way. It follows from this that the Day of the Lord refers first and foremost to a warlike episode in which Yahweh breaks the resistance of his enemies in battle and overcomes them. It should be said further that this idea was not borrowed from the surrounding milieu but is of israelitic origin, from the epoch of the holy war, many episodes of which reach their climax in a theophany.

It is a question, then, in the prophetic texts which speak of the Day of the Lord, of an actualization of old revelational material. The holy war dealt originally with a saving deed of God on behalf of his people. The original element in the prophetic preaching consists in this, that instead of salvation Israel can and will encounter judgement and merited punishment on the Day of the Lord—see Amos 5:18–20. (This text, we might add, should not be interpreted on the basis of a supposed but undemonstrable festival of Yahweh's accession to the throne, as maintained by Mowinckel; in general, Amos gives no grounds for thinking of the Day of the Lord in terms of a festival which was already in existence in his day.) Looked at in this way, the fall of Jerusalem, 586 BC, and also of Samaria, 721 BC, would represent, being historical events, the Day of the Lord actualised in the course of human affairs.

Gradually, however, the representation of the Day of the Lord takes on in the prophetic preaching meta-historical and eschatological characteristics. It belongs, as a basic concept, to the essential elements introduced in the process of eschatologising which went on within the Old Testament development of revelation. This can be recognised above all in the use of the idea in both parts of Joel. If the plague of locusts in Joel 1f is a description of the inexorable judgement of God on an historical enemy, Joel 3f would appear to be transposed on to an eschatological level, since there the Day of the Lord takes on the characteristics of the final day of judgement, an event of cosmic proportions concerning all nations. The prophets of the post-exilic period announce that the holy remnant will be saved from judgement (see Obad, 15–21; Joel 3:20f). In accordance with this, the Day of the Lord does not imply a total and definitive annihilation but rather, for the holy remnant at least, a passage through to a new eschatological future in which God will cherish Israel in a special way.

The idea of the Day of the Lord passed into Jewish apocalyptic as the day of judgement. Bar (Syr) 48, 47; 49:2 calls it 'thy day' (=the Day of God); 2 Eschas 13:52 'the day of my son'; Enoch (Eth) 61:5 'the day of the Chosen One [the Servant]'.

It has an even more significant role in the New Testament than in the apocalyptic literature. 2 Pet 3:12 and Rev 16:14 depend, in content and terminology, on the Old-Testament presentation. The announcement in Lk 17:24 of the final appearance of the Son of Man in his glory derives from the same presentation. In Jn 8:56 Christ speaks of his day as the day of the ultimate revelation of his glory.

It is above all in Paul that the Day of the Lord, now changed to the Day of Jesus Christ, stands for the day of the judgement of the world in which Christ appears and acts as judge, eg, 1 Cor 1:8; 2 Cor 1:14; 1 Thess 5:2; 2 Thess 2:2; Phil 1:6, 10; 2:16; Heb 10:25.

The concept of the Day of the Lord is therefore one of the leading ideas in the Old and the New Testament which express and embody the eschatological tension and expectation of the future within revelation. It signifies, at different stages of the development of revelation, a decisive incision in the course of history made by God in order to bring his plan of salvation to a more compact and intense reality, while, on the day itself, he both holds judgement according to merit and inflicts punishment where it has been incurred, and at the same time confers on his own the salvation reserved for them. Understood in this way, the Day of the Lord has enough depth of meaning and elasticity both to express the final judgement and to indicate the inauguration of the eschatological age of salvation which coincides with the definite appearance of the kingdom of God.

Bibliography: G. von Rad and Delling, *TDNT* II, 943–53; L. Černy, *The Day of Yahweh and some Relevant Problems*, Prague 1948; R. Pautrel, *DB(S)* IV, 1321–44; B. J. Alfrink, Haag 1580–82; H. H. Rowley, 'The Day of the Lord', *The Faith of Israel*, London 1956, 177–201; S. Mowinckel, 'Jahves dag', *NTT* 59 (1958), 1–56; J. Bourke, 'Le Jour de Yahvé dans Joël', *RB* 66 (1959), 5–31 and 191–212; G. von Rad II, 119–25; G. von Rad, 'The Origin of the Concept of the Day of Yahweh', *JSS* 4 (1959), 77–108.

Heinrich Gross

Death

Death is the common lot of men (Josh 23:14; 1 Kings 2:2; Eccles 9:5; 12:7). All men must die (Sir 14:17), 'We must all die, we are like water spilt on the ground' (2 Sam 14:14)—this is the basic attitude of the Old Testament. Death was taken as an inevitable necessity, and people considered themselves fortunate if they could die 'old and full of days' (Gen 25:8; 2 Chron 24:15) 'at a good old age' (Gen 15:15; Judg 8:32). In the New Testament, likewise, the fact that men were destined to die was taken for granted (Heb 9:27; Jn 6:49, 58; 8:52f; Heb 7:8). Only the living God is immortal (Deut 5:23; 1 Tim 6:16). Man lives in the fear of death (Sir 40:2; Heb 2:15), which would be thought of as desirable, at the most, only in the last age (Lk 23:30). Death is never glorified, not even by Christ and the apostles (2 Cor 4:11f; Rev 2:10; 12:11).

The scriptures do not contain reflections on the details of death as a physiological process. The separation of soul and body (in the modern sense) is never clearly presented as *the cause* of death, even if it is commonly stated, in accord with external appearances, that 'God takes back the breath of life' (Job 34:14; Ps 104:29; Eccles 12:7; see also Gen 2:7). In a similar way, the New Testament speaks of giving up the spirit (Mt 27:50; Lk 23:46; Jn 19:30), or the soul (Jn 10:11, 15, 17; 13:37; 15:13). As one gets older one sees death as something in the nature of things (Ps 90:10). A sudden or premature death is the result of the divine anger (Job 15:32; Ps 55:23; 90:7; Eccles 7:17.) No-one knows the hour of his death (Lk 12:16ff).

God is the absolute lord over ↗ life and death. 'He has established the number of his [man's] months and the bounds which he cannot pass' (1 Sam 2:6; Job 14:5). Death evidently had no part in God's original plan of creation (Gen 2:17)—on the contrary, death even appears as an evil power in opposition to God (1 Cor 15:26; Rev 6:8; 20:12f) which is subject to the empire of Satan (Heb 2:14).

Already in Wis 2:24 the necessity of death is ascribed to the envy of the devil, with reference certainly to the history of the Fall, in which death was threatened as a punishment for neglecting the divine command (Gen 2:17; cf Sir 25:24). The idea that death was a punishment must also be the reason why it rendered unclean (Num 9:6; 19:16; Deut 21:23). Apart from this, death is simply taken in the Old Testament as the inevitable destiny of mankind. An early or sudden death was often taken as a punishment for personal sins (Num 27:3; Ps 55:23; Prov 2:18; Sir 21:2f; Jer 6:11), but was not necessarily this (Is 57:1f; Wis 4:7–15). Before man 'are death and life and whichever he chooses will be given to him' (Sir 15:17). Life and death are in parallelism with good and evil, blessing and curse (Deut 28:15–20; Jer 21:8). In Paul the causal relationship existing between sin ai d death is quite clear; the latter is the result of, and punishment for, the former; it is 'the wages of sin' (Rom 6:23; 1 Cor 15:56). Death came into the world through Adam's sin (Rom 5:15; 1 Cor 15:21f).

Existence after death, as described in the Old Testament, is a comfortless affair. There is no doubt about the fate of the body: it falls away into dust and will be food for worms (Job 34:15; Sir 19:3). The burial of the dead is a sacred duty (2 Sam 21:12ff; 1 Kings 13:29f), and it is a terrible thing not to be buried (1 Kings 14:11; 16:4; 21:19ff). Pagan rites in connection with the dead were ruled out (Lev 19:28; Deut 14:1f), and there was no attempt to get in touch with the dead (Lev 19:31; 20:6, 27; Deut 18:11; 1 Sam 28). Sadness reigned in the world of the dead (Deut 34:8). Apart from 2 Macc 12:38–46 there is no mention of prayers or sacrifices on their behalf. Cremation was considered as dishonourable (Josh 7:25; 1 Kings 13:2).

For the religious man of the Old Testament, however, *death was not the end of all* (↗ Resurrection). If Job complains (7:8): 'while thy eyes are upon me, I shall be gone', this does not imply the end of existence but the end of life conceived of as activity, for he continues: 'as the cloud fades and vanishes, so he who goes down to the Sheol does not come up' (7:9). The dead man is gathered to his fathers (Gen 15:15; 49:33), an expression which can best be explained with reference to the family grave (1 Kings 13:22; Gen 49:29; 2 Sam 21:14). He arrives at the place where the dead are gathered together (Job 30:23), which is in a dark pit (10:21) beneath the waters (26:5). In the description of this underworld, *še'ôl*, (↗ Hell) sombre representations of little comfort predominate. It is referred to, flatly, as destruction (Job 26:6; 28:22; Prov 15:11). It would appear also, according to the original representation, that the dead man was separated from God (Ps 88:5). At any rate, the tongue of the dead can no longer praise God. (Ps 6:5; 88:10ff; 115:17; Sir 17:27f). It is difficult to determine how Yahweh is connected with *še'ôl* (see Is 38:11, 18f), but it is subjected to him in the end, since the reach of his power knows no limits (Amos 9:2; Ps 139:8).

The Old Testament speaks only very

obscurely of survival after death, full assurance of which came only with the Easter-event. The Israelite could, however, already find some consolation in survival in his descendants (Deut 25:6), since the important thing for him was the continued existence of the people, depositary of the promise (Gen 12:1ff). In the taking up of Enoch (Gen 5:24) and of Elijah (2 Kings 2:11), there appear momentary glimpses of a possible overcoming of death. The hope of the just man remained, even 'in his death' (Prov 14:32), without an explanation if looked at from a this-worldly point of view. The faithful Israelite trusted in God his defender (Job 19:25) that he would not be abandoned, and that the grave would not claim him irrevocably. He already knew that God could, in his omnipotence, snatch him from death (Ps 73:23ff), that he forces death to give up its booty (Is 26:19), that it is he who brings down to the underworld and raises up (1 Sam 2:6). In Daniel we come finally to explicit mention of the general ↗ resurrection of the body (Dan 12:2).

The strongest impulse to revise the gloomy picture of death in the Old Testament came from the problem of ↗ retribution (Ps 73:11f, 26). We must be careful, of course, neither to underestimate nor overestimate these texts.

The whole situation changed with the coming of Christ. Through Christ God had destroyed death (Heb 2:14); his victory over death is the great news which the gospel brings (2 Tim 1:10). The belief in the resurrection is a vital part of the New Testament (1 Cor 15). Death is no longer master in his own house, for ever since Christ went down into the underworld (1 Pet 3:19; 4:6) he has in his hands the keys of the kingdom of death (Rev 1:18). As he was dead so is he now living (Rom 8:34; 14:9; 1 Thess 4:14). Christ is the first that death has not been able to detain (Acts 2:24); freely he takes his life back again (Jn 10:18). Death must give up its booty to him (Mt 9:25; Lk 7:14; Jn 11:44), and even has to give way before his disciples (Mt 10:8; Acts 9:40; 20:7–12).

Since Christ himself has died for us (Rom 5:6, 8; 2 Cor 5:14f; Gal 3:13) he has overcome death, that death from which no man is exempt. His death is the model for our dying (Jn 21:19; Acts 21:13; Phil 1:20; 3:10). The faithful christian lives and dies in the Lord (Rom 14:7f); death for him has been overcome in Christ, the firstborn from among the dead (Col 1:18; Rev 1:5; see also Rom 8:38f).

At the same time, death remains the last enemy which must finally be overcome (1 Cor 15:25f; Rev 20:14), for death as the common lot of mankind has not been removed. The three raisings from the dead in the gospels happen as a result of special circumstances (Mk 5:41f; Lk 7:14; Jn 11:44). Describing death as sleep was understood as a euphemism (Mt 9:24; Mk 5:39; Lk 8:52; Jn 11:11f; 1 Cor 15:18)—only, after sleep one wakes up again!

There will be no more death in the consummated ↗ Kingdom of God (Is 25:8; Rev 21:4), but our true life is as yet hidden (Col 3:3). For the christian, however, death is no longer a frightening reality (Rom 14:7f) and has lost its sting (1 Cor 15:55ff), since the christian possesses the living hope (1 Pet 1:3f).

Those who die in the Lord (1 Cor 15:18; 1 Thess 4:16), and in particular the martyrs (Rev 14:13), are not thereby separated from him (Rom 8:38f).

Through↗ baptism, which is a copy of the death of Christ (Rom 6:5), the christian unites himself with the death of Christ with whom he is buried but only to rise again (Rom 6:3–11; Col 2:11ff, 20; 2 Tim 2:11; 1 Pet 2:24).

Through the↗ Law sin was aroused and with sin death. The letter of the law kills (2 Cor 3:6); whence the believer is dead to the law (Rom 7:7; Gal 2:19; Col 2:20), and anyone trying to bring the law back into force nullifies the effects of Christ's death (Gal 2:19–21).

Through the imitation of Christ, the life of the christian becomes a *daily dying* (2 Cor 4:7–12; 6:9; 11:23), and he must each day mortify his flesh and its works (Rom 6:11ff; Rom 14). This being dead to sin (Rom 8:10) is carried through by a change of life. In this new life the christian must take part in all seriousness in the proclamation of the Lord's death in the eucharist (1 Cor 11:20ff). He who is living in sin is as good as dead (Lk 15:32); but the world which is not in Christ is in sin and therefore in death (Jn 1:4; 8:21–4, 34–7). For those who reject it, the gospel deals out death (2 Cor 2:16; 4:3f; Phil 1:28). Outside of the sphere of the gospel even the living are really dead (Mt 8:22; Jn 5:21–5; Col 2:13; 1 Tim 5:6), whereas in Christ even he who is dead lives and cannot be subject to death (Jn 11:25f; 6:50), since he has passed over into life (Jn 5:24, 1 Jn 3:14).

In these texts we are well past the idea of natural dying when death is mentioned. We can perhaps already find allusions to death, understood *in the spiritual sense*, in the Book of Proverbs (7:27; 13:14; 14:27; 23:13). From this death one is rescued by↗ righteousness and almsgiving (Prov 10:2; 11:4; Tob 4:10; 12:9). In the New Testament this death is the result of infidelity and sin (Rom 7:10; 8:6; Jas 1:15; 1 Jn 5:16). Hence we have the reference to the second death, the only one which has to be feared (Rev 2:11; 20:6; 21:8), which is the lot of sinners after the judgement which follows the death of the body (Heb 9:27). He who does not love, abides in death (1 Jn 3:14).

Bibliography: G. von Rad and R. Bultmann, *TDNT* II, 846–9 and III, 7–21 (=*Life and Death* [*BKW* XIV], London 1965, 8–14 and 85–107); H. Alswede, *BTHW* 585f; Allmen, 79–83; J. B. Alfrink, Haag 1625–7; A. Schulz, *Der Sinn des Todes im AT*, Braunsberg 1919; G. Quell, *Die Auffassung des Todes in Israel*, Leipzig 1925; H. M. Feret, *Das Mysterium des Todes*, Frankfurt 1955, 13–126; J. Guillet, *Leitgedanken der Bibel*, Lucerne 1954, 168–92; Imschoot II, 48–82; Heinisch 244–9; A. Kassing, 'Der Tod im Leben des Christen nach dem Apostel Paulus', *Pro veritate*, Münster-Kassel 1963, 7–21; F. Hoffmann, *HTG* II, 661–70; *K. Rahner, *On the Theology of Death*, London and New York 1961.

Ernst Schmitt

Decalogue

A. *The Decalogue in the Old Testament.*

1. *Form and arrangement of the Decalogue.* The division into sections of this short set of laws depends largely on the translation of the LXX, which renders the Hebrew *ʾaśereth haddᵉbārim* (Ex 34:28) as *tous deka logous*. In both languages this phrase means 'the ten

words', and it is usually expressed in English by 'the ten commandments'. Three facts are thus already established in the original text: the exceptional position and the unity of this set of laws within the body of the Torah as a whole, the fact that the commandments number ten, and that they have been moulded into a formula.

The fact that there are *ten* commandments is not quite so certain as might first be thought, for the first commandments exist on a far greater number of different levels than they do in the catechism form which has been adapted for our purposes, and, what is more, they are not in fact numbered at all. Another factor is that the wording has been handed down in two different forms (in Ex 20:1–17 and in Deut 5:6–21), as well as a third version which is derived from the later Jewish period and has been passed on to us in the so-called Nash papyrus, which, like the Phylacterus in Qumran, contains the decalogue and the so-called *šema*ᶜ with the commandment concerning the love of God (Deut 6:4f).

According to Ex 20, the text is worded in the following way:

> I am Yahweh your God, who brought you out of the land of Egypt, out of the house of bondage.
>
> You shall have no other gods before me. You shall not make for yourself a graven image, or any likeness of anything that is in heaven above, or that is in the earth beneath, or that is in the water under the earth; you shall not bow down to them or serve them; for I Yahweh your God am a jealous God, visiting the iniquity of the fathers upon the children to the third and the fourth generation of those who hate me, but showing steadfast love to thousands of those who love me and keep my commandments.
>
> You shall not take the name of Yahweh your God in vain; for Yahweh will not hold him guiltless who takes his name in vain.
>
> Remember the sabbath day, to keep it holy. Six days you shall labour, and do all your work; but the seventh day is a sabbath to Yahweh your God; in it you shall not do any work, you, or your son, or your daughter, your manservant, or your maidservant, or your cattle, or the sojourner who is within your gates; for in six days Yahweh made heaven and earth, the sea, and all that is in them, and rested the seventh day; therefore Yahweh blessed the sabbath day and hallowed it.
>
> Honour your father and your mother, that your days may be long in the land which Yahweh your God gives you.
>
> You shall not kill.
>
> You shall not commit adultery.
>
> You shall not steal.
>
> You shall not bear false witness against your neighbour.
>
> You shall not covet your neighbour's house; you shall not covet your neighbour's wife, or his manservant, or his maidservant, or his ox, or his ass, or anything that is your neighbour's.

Apart from variants in the text due to transcription, differences of expression etc, the text of Deuteronomy has two essential differences which are of interest to us in our examination of this subject. The commandment to observe the sabbath has this substantiating reason—'You shall remember that you were a servant in the land of Egypt, and Yahweh your God brought you thence with a mighty hand and an outstretched arm'. This addition ought to make the social significance of the sabbath even clearer and more emphatic than the version of the commandment in Exodus. That is why, in Deuteronomy, less stress is placed on the day of creation as the day on which man should rest from his labours, and far more is placed on the servitude of the people and their consequent liberation by God.

The second important difference is that the penultimate commandment reads: 'You shall not covet your neighbour's wife', to which are appended the commandments not to covet the house etc, of one's neighbour. It has not been established how this difference might possibly have come about, though Norbert Peters surmises that the transcriber of Exodus might, in error, have copied out the wrong lines here, while Steuernagel tends to the view that in a later period it was considered desirable to recognise the higher status of woman in society. The only certain thing is that the coveting of one's neighbour's wife as such was soon given considerable emphasis and regarded as definitely taboo.

The arrangement of the decalogue is uniform in both Exodus and Deuteronomy. It is the fundamental norm of the Torah which was made known when God manifested himself on Mount Sinai and which was taken as a basis for the setting up of the Covenant.

2. *The origin and purport of the Decalogue and its importance within the framework of the Old Testament.* These three elements, the origin and purport of the Decalogue and its importance within the framework of the Old Testament, must be considered systematically in relation to one another, as both the purport and the importance of the Decalogue throw light on the period of its formation. The controversy concerning the *origin* of the Decalogue is well known. Wellhausen's verdict on the entire tradition regarding the law is that 'such a living law, which at every point reflects real conditions . . . cannot be the whim or fancy of an idle mind, but has arisen out of historical conditions and is destined to intervene effectively in the course of historical evolution' (in his *Prolegomena*).

The theory that the Decalogue was composed by Moses has, all the same, often found champions among non-Catholic scholars such as A. Alt, and, more recently, E. Auerbach, W. Kessler, and G. von Rad among others. The early origin of the Decalogue is, however, supported by archaeology. The 'two tablets' (Ex 32:15) have not, of course, been discovered. As it is only possible to date these by palaeographical methods, based on comparisons with similar material, there is scarcely a single compelling argument in support of the belief that the decalogue was in fact composed by Moses, since the commandments certainly did not bear Moses' signature. On the other hand, although archaeologists have made numerous finds of images of Canaanite gods and goddesses, they have still not brought a single ↗ image of Yahweh or of a female partner to Yahweh to light.

The dictum: 'Apart from me there is no God', must therefore have dominated the entire history of Israel from its very beginning. The commandment which forbids images had accordingly an importance in itself, and was not only a negative complement to the first commandment made simply to secure Yahweh's pre-eminence over all false gods and idols. It was, on the contrary, a true ban on images of false gods, in that even an image of Yahweh was regarded as a contradiction of his spiritual being. There were thus four commandments in the original version which related to God, and the second of the 'two tablets' contained the commandment against coveting one's neighbour's wife and his home in an undivided form.

Certain 'parallel' instances which exist outside the sphere of the bible can be quoted to support the great age of the decalogue. One section of the Assyrio-Babylonian tablets of exorcisms of the Shurpu series establishes definite points of contact with the decalogue. This ritual was applied when a sick man wished to be cured. A list was read aloud, giving a record of the sick man's innocence, and it was hoped thereby that he would be 'delivered from the spell which had previously bound him', as the final sentence reads. The formula consists of a series of rhetorical questions to which the answer 'No' is expected:

> May N. be delivered, you great gods, from the sickness, fear, care, and affliction which troubles him!
>
> Has he consumed what is atrocious to his God, what is atrocious to his goddess . . .?
>
> Has he despised his father and mother or scorned his elder sister? Has he indulged in small matters and neglected great matters?
>
> Has he said 'it is' instead of 'it is not'?
>
> Has he said 'it is not' instead of 'it is'?
>
> Has he uttered impurities or acted recklessly?
>
> Has he uttered calumny?
>
> Has he used false scales?
>
> Has he broken into his neighbour's house?
>
> Has he offended against his neighbour's wife?
>
> Has he shed his neighbour's blood?
>
> Has he ever let a man go in nakedness?
>
> Has he taken away his neighbour's garments?
>
> Has he abducted a good man away from his family?
>
> Has he disrupted the unity of a tribe?
>
> Has he ever opposed the chief of his tribe?
>
> Was his mouth ever honest while his heart was dishonest?
>
> Did his mouth give consent while his heart dissented?
>
> [*AOT* 324f.]

There are further similarities between the Decalogue and Chapter 125 of the so-called *Book of the Dead* which provide a protestation of innocence, which is in fact the protestation of a man who is already dead and who must testify to his innocence in order to enter the hall in which Osiris is enthroned and where the heart is to be 'weighed in the balance'. The most important sections are as follows:

I have not dealt unfairly with men;
I have not slaughtered cattle set aside for sacrifice . . .
I have done nothing abominable in God's sight;
I have not slandered any servant in his master's hearing;
I have let no man go hungry;
I have brought no man to tears;
I have not killed;
I have given no command to kill;
I have not acted badly towards anyone;
I have not taken away from the sacrificial meals in the temples . . .
I have not committed adultery . . .
I have neither taken away from nor added to the corn-measure;
I have not cheated with the measure of arable land . . .
I have not robbed;
I have not been avaricious;
I have not stolen;
I have not killed men;
I have not uttered lies . . .
I have satisfied God with the things that he loves;
I have given bread to the hungry and water to the thirsty and clothes to the naked and a ferry-boat to those who lack a ship . . .
Only save me and protect me and do not testify against me before the great God!
I have clean lips and clean hands and am one to whom 'welcome' is said by those who see me.

[*AOT* 9ff.]

Neither of these two chapters is the expression of a serious moral decision, but both are connected with the practice of magic and aim either to exorcise sickness or to pave the way to the next world (in this respect, the Babylonian text provides the clearer example). They are thus very clearly distinguished in their spiritual content from the Decalogue. Their purpose is self-assertion and compulsion of the gods, whereas the Decalogue is based, in its essential elements, on obedience to God's command and was made known as a moral imperative demanded by God who had manifested himself expressly as the Lord of morality. The unsystematic arrangement which is not ordered according to the degree of guilt, and in which matters pertaining both to worship and to morals are quite mixed up, is striking from the point of view of the form of the Decalogue. On the other hand, the extra-biblical texts do show that there was in existence, distinct from and independent of the biblical revelation, a moral consciousness which had already achieved a literary expression and had had some influence on the conscience.

Thus the Decalogue is in no way an isolated case in its period, though even this fact tends to prove that its author was Moses. The decisive factor was, however, the close link with the cult of Yahweh. In changing the old order, Moses fashioned a new one which was to reshape the world.

It is now necessary to take a look at *the Decalogue within the framework of the history of the people of the Old Testament.* That it was valid in the spiritual sense is indisputable, but the principal question is: Was it known in its literary form? There is no word-for-word quotation of the 'ten commandments' apart from the versions given in Exodus and Deuteronomy. Many scholars regard this fact as a strong argument in support of the view that it was not Moses but the prophets who were the originators of ethical monotheism. In contradiction to this theory, however, it must be affirmed that once the decalogue was well known an exact quotation was hardly necessary, when one wished to refer to the 'statute of God'. A straightforward memorising of the Decalogue would not have succeeded in establishing the relationship between God's law and the actual sins which the prophets were intent on denouncing. The task of the prophets consisted in showing the people that their conduct, despite their apparent piety, nonetheless contradicted the law of God (Jer 8:8). If, on the other hand, one places too great an emphasis on the tension between the Decalogue and the message of the prophets, it is easy to fall into self-contradiction holding the view that the Decalogue is a result of the prophetic mission.

The two oldest writing prophets provide evidence that they are acquainted with the Book of Exodus. Amos mentions the forty years in the desert (5:25). He knows too of the taking out of Egypt and the closely allied fact that the Hebrews were God's chosen people (3:1f), and he draws certain moral conclusions from these data. Hosea would appear to be quoting the introduction to the Decalogue when he twice emphasises the words of God with the sentence: 'I am the Lord your God from the Land of Egypt' (12:9; 13:4). Furthermore, he gives a list of vices which has certain points of contact with the ten commandments: 'Swearing, lying, killing, stealing and committing adultery' (4:2). Jeremiah has a similar list: 'Will you steal, murder, commit adultery, swear falsely, burn incense to Baal, and go after other gods?' (Jer 7:9). The Hebrew word for 'to murder' or 'to kill' is identical in these instances quoted from Jeremiah and Hosea with the word used in the Decalogue. As for any variation in the order in which the sins are listed, the order in the Nash papyrus, from the fifth commandment onwards, also reads: 'commit adultery, murder, steal, bear false witness'. The order is thus, as far as our problem is concerned, not important. The fact that the oldest prophets were also familiar with the written law of God is stated unambiguously in Hosea (8:12), and all the other prophets know about God's 'precepts' (Amos 2:4; Jer 6:19).

Jeremiah also bears witness to the fact that the commandment regarding the sabbath had already been given to the fathers (22:17), just as it was already regarded at the time of Amos as an obligation under law (8:5). The formulaic principle with which Tamar confronted her half-brother Amnon on the point of raping her, 'such a thing is not done in Israel' (2 Sam 13:12), should be seen as a consequence and an application of the unusual fact that the commandments of the Decalogue are in the indicative: 'Thou shalt not kill, thou shalt not commit adultery' etc. There are features of Psalm 15 and 24 which have certain similarities with the Decalogue, namely, the 'examination of conscience' when a visit is made to the temple.

The sequence, numbering and additions vary from one version of the Decalogue to another. This tends to show that the *original version* is no longer extant and that this must have been much simpler in form and more closely approximating to an apodictic form, which may have had the following wording:

I am the Lord thy God.

1. Thou shalt have no other gods beside me.

2. Thou shalt not make to thyself any graven image in order to worship it.

3. Thou shalt not take the name of God in vain.

4. Remember that thou keep holy the sabbath day.

5. Honour thy father and thy mother.

6. Thou shalt not kill.

7. Thou shalt not commit adultery.

8. Thou shalt not steal.

9. Thou shalt not bear false witness.

10. Thou shalt not be covetous.

B. *The Decalogue in the New Testament.* Christ has also instituted his new order by changing the old. Christ's ethics are therefore not the same as those of Moses, yet despite this he formulates his ethical demands—for example, in what he says to the rich young man (Mt 19:17–19)—in the words of the Decalogue. In this connection it should not be forgotten that in Deuteronomy too the commandments of the 'first tablet' are simplified and dominated by the demand: 'Hear, O Israel: the Lord our God is one Lord; and you shall love the Lord your God with all your heart . . .' (Deut 6:4f). There is also another extant version in which the 'second tablet' might have been worded in another way: 'You shall love your neighbour as yourself' (Lev 19:18). Christ himself has, with deliberate emphasis, pronounced the love of God and one's neighbour to be the root, the measure and the consummation of all moral conduct (Mt 22:36–40). He has also given greater depth and intensity to the positive demands of the Decalogue which he has personally assimilated and has thus made them sound afresh with a new note. They have not been abolished but 'fulfilled' (Mt 5:17–32). If one result of this is that it is impossible to conceive of this 'law of liberty' as existing without any moral content, then both James (2:8–13) and Paul (1 Cor 5:1f) have, for a particular reason in every case, cleared up these and similar misunderstandings (↗ Law NT).

In contrast to those commandments which were assimilated by Christ himself, the commandment to observe the sabbath was so closely bound up with the Old Testament that it had to be replaced when the Old Testament was replaced, and in fact no longer obtained. It is not to be expected, however, that any analogous Christian commandments should come from Christ himself, so long as the saving events in the course of salvation had not been accomplished. In this case it is only the tradition of the apostles and the early church which can give us any idea as to what strictly pertains to the New Testament in this respect, unless Christ's words 'do this in remembrance of me' (Lk 22:19) are regarded as capable of being construed as a commandment. Christian tradition can also assure us that the commandment against the making of images no longer holds force, for Christ certainly had no reason to take any definite attitude with regard to this. It is, however, an established fact, despite the lack of explicit references, that Christ did not wish the commandment that God alone should be worshipped, and that his name should be sanctified, to be overlooked. (It should be noted that the clause 'hallowed be thy name' of the Our Father is different in substance from this.)

Bibliography: A. van den Born and H. Cazelles, Haag 316–20; P. Volz, *Mose und sein Werk*, Tübingen 1932; A. Alt, 'Die Ursprünge des israelitischen Rects', *Kleine Schriften*, Munich 1953, 278–332; H. Reiner, 'Zur Frage "Sittlichkeit und Religion"', *Die Sammlung* II, 1947; A. Schüler, *Werantwortung*, Munich 1948; H. H. Rowley, *Moses and the Decalogue*, Manchester 1951; E. Auerbach, *Moses*, Amsterdam 1953; W. Kessler, 'Die literarische, historische und theologische Problematik des Dekalogs', *VT* 7 (1957); H. Schneider, 'Der Dekalog in den Phylakterien von Qumran', *BZ* 3 (1959), 18–31; G. E. Mendenhall, 'Recht und Bund in Israel und dem vorderen Orient', *TS* 64 (1960).

Othmar Schilling

Demon

A. *In the Old Testament.* The idea of demon, *daimōn* began as a Greek name for gods and beings with divine powers, and especially for unfriendly beings against whom it is necessary to seek protection by means of magic spells and invocations. There are traces too, in the Old Testament, of a similar popular belief in such spirits. Although there is no single, comprehensive name for such beings in the Hebrew version of the bible, the LXX Daimonion invariably has *daimonion* (the adjective derived from *daimōn*) and the New Testament, following LXX, has this also in most cases.

An 'evil spirit', which troubles men or throws them into confusion, is referred to several times, but it is a spirit which comes from God (1 Sam 16:14–16, 23; 18:10; 19:9; see also 1 Kings 22:21). There are also spirits of the dead, which can be conjured up (1 Sam 28:13—here denoted by *ᵓᵉlōhîm*, 'God', 'divine being'). It is true that Saul had driven all the magicians and necromancers from the land (1 Sam 28:9). Such people ought not to be tolerated among the Jews (Lev 19:31; 20:6, 27; Deut 18:11). The *šēdîm* (Deut 32:17; Ps 106:37)—the word is connected with the Akkadian *šedu*, meaning deities—are also true demonic figures, and this is translated in the LXX by *daimonia*, while the *śᵉʿîrim* (Lev 17:7; 2 Chron 11:15; Is 13:21; 34:14—the description, as 'hairy ones' is to be understood in the sense of their having the form of a goat) are translated in the LXX by *mataia* (nothingness, nothing: Lev, 2 Chron, as above), or else rendered by *daimonia* (Is, as above). These *śᵉʿîrim* inhabit ruins (Is, as above—here mentioned only to describe in popular fashion the destruction in store for the people). The Israelites also offered sacrifices to them (Lev, 2 Chron, as above), as well as to the *šedim* (Deut, Ps, as above), although it is questionable whether the sacrifice is really offered to such beings or whether these names do not in fact apply to some strange gods thus described out of scorn (see LXX Is 65:3; Bar 4:7). The Lilith (corresponding to the Assyrian demon of the storm *lilitu*) is one spirit which is the object of popular belief and lives in the ruins (Is 34:14). Azazel is the demon which inhabits the desert and which, on the Day of Atonement, is presented with a goat, to which the high priest has transferred all the sins of the people (Lev 16:8, 10, 26). On one occasion, at least according to the LXX, the just man refers to the need of protection from the noonday demon—although it should be noted that the Hebrew text has 'the plague at noon' here (Ps 91:6). Jewish belief in demons is most strikingly encountered in the popular account which forms the Book of Tobit. The demon Asmodeus (*Asmodaus* or *Asmodaios*, presumably derived from the Iranian *aēsma daēva*, or 'evil demon') slays the seven husbands of Sarah (Tob 3:8). Any demon or evil spirit (*daimonion ē pneuma ponēron*) which haunts a man or woman can only be banished if the heart and the liver of a fish is burnt before that man or woman (6:8). Tobit does this on the advice of the angel Gabriel, when he goes into Sarah's bridal chamber, and, with that, Asmodeus is driven away by the smoke and flees into the desert of upper Egypt where Raphael binds him (6:17f; 8:2f).

B. *In the extra-canonical, later Jewish literature.* There are very many references here to fallen angels who have, as is generally believed to be the case in connection with Gen 6:2, 4, sinned by having sexual intercourse with human women (Jub 4:22; 5:1; 7:21; 10:5; Enoch [Eth] 6f; 12:4; 15; 69:2–4; 84:4; 86:1–6; Test Rub 5:6; Test Naph 3:5; Bar [Syr] 56:12; CD 17f; Josephus, *Antiquitates Judaicae* 1, 3, 1 [73]). These angels are, however, different from demons, though Philo equates the 'angels' of the bible with the 'demons' of the world of Greek mythology (*De Gigantibus*, 6). Elsewhere the demons are considered as the fruit of that union between angels and human beings, as spirits who animated the 'giants' who were the children of those unions and who, after their death, cause mischief among human beings as demons (Jub 10:5f; Enoch [Eth] 15:8–12; 16:1; 19:1; Enoch [Slav] 18:5). Although the name 'demon' occurs relatively infrequently (eg, Enoch [Eth] 19:1; Bar [Gr] 16:3; *Test. Adae* 1:1), these fiends are often simply called 'spirits' (Jub 10:5, 8; 11:5; 19:28; Enoch [Eth] 15:10–12; 19:1; 1 QS 3, 24); also 'evil spirits' (Jub 10:3, 13; 11:4; 12:20; Enoch [Eth] 15:8f; 1 QM 15, 14; 'malicious spirits'); 'unclean spirits' (Enoch [Eth] 99:7; see also Jub 10:1); the spirits of Mastema (Jub 19:28), or Beliar (Test, Iss 7:7; Test Dan 1:7; Test Jos 7:4; 1 QM 13, 2, 4, 11f; CD 12:2; see also Test Rub 2:2). Their prince is Mastema (Jub 10:8; 11:5; 19:28). But, like Beliar (Belial), Mastema is a name for the devil, who thus rules over the evil spirits.

The demons do grievous harm to human beings (Jub 10:1–3, 5, 8; 11:5; Enoch [Eth] 15:11; 16:1; Bar [Gr] 16:3; Test Adae 1:1; 2:10 [Greek fragments in M. R. James, *Apocrypha Anecdota*, Cambridge 1893, 141 (frag 10a) and 142 (frags 1a and 4a)]; *Lives of the Prophets* 16 [P. Riessler, *Altjüdisches* Schrifttum ausserhalb der Bibel, Augsburg 1928, 878]). In particular, they tempt men to bad actions (Jub 7:27; 10:1f, 8; 11:4f; 12:20; Test Dan 5:5; Test Benj 3:3; 1 QS 3, 24; see also 1 QH 14, 11), such as bloodshed (Jub 7:27; 11:5) and sacrifices to demons (Enoch [Eth] 19:1), or to false gods or idols (Jub 11:4). The worship of false gods or idols is nothing but the worship of demons, as false gods and demons are similar (*Jerusalem Targum* 1; see also Deut 32:17). It is [the same as] adoring demons (Jub 22; 17; Enoch [Eth] 99:7).

It was not only feared that demons can do harm to men and tempt them, but it was also believed that they can take possession of men. The belief arose that there was such a thing as demonic ↗ possession, in a form which was not mentioned in the Old Testament (Josephus, *Antiqu Jud* VIII 2, 5 [45–8]; see also many examples in the New Testament and in the rabbinical texts). There are also references to fallen angels who tempt human beings (Enoch [Eth] 9:6–8; 10:8; 64:2).

There is one angel of darkness, apparently Belial, the devil, who reigns over the unjust and makes the just fall into error (1 QS 3, 20–2). This angel has subordinate 'spirits' who attempt to make the 'sons of light' fall (1 QS 3, 24). Whoever does not live according to the law of Moses comes under the sway of an angel of Mastema (*CD* 16:5).

The Satans (Enoch [Eth] 40:7; 65:6) are a group of evil beings on their own and must not be confused with the being who is specifically known as Satan, that is, the devil (Enoch [Eth] 53:3; 54:6).

No more than a tenth of the entire number of demons still remains on earth to the detriment of mankind. The rest are already in the place of damnation (Jub 10:9). The demons lose their power in the messianic age (Test Sim 6:6; Test Lev 18:12; see also Jub 23:29; 50:5), and men rule over them. (Test Sim 6:6; Test Lev 18:12; see also under C). Eventually the demons incur eternal punishment (Test Jud 25:3 [Armenian translation]; see also Enoch [Eth] 16:1), which is also the lot of the evil angels (Enoch [Eth] 21:10; 90:22–5; see also 18:13–16; 21:3–6).

In cases such as these, many primitive beliefs are revived and perpetuated (eg, demons as spirits of the dead). What is of theological importance is, however, that Jewish monotheism avoided an absolute dualism, of which many rudiments might have existed. As far back as our knowledge goes of the history of evil angels and demons, God is always thought of as the creator of all spirits, both those of light and those of darkness (1 QS 3:25).

C. *In the New Testament.* Beside 'demons' (*daimonion*, but in one instance [Mt 8:31] *daimōn*), the New Testament also has the name 'spirit' (Mt 8:16; 9:33; Mk 9:20; Lk 9:39; 10:20; Acts 16:18), 'unclean spirit' (Mk 1:23, 26f; 3:11, 30; 5:2, 8, 13; 6:7; 7:25; 9:25; Mt 10:1; 12:43; Lk 4:36; 6:18; 8:29; 9:42; 11:24; Acts 5:16; 8:7; Rev 16:13; 18:2; cf Lk 4:33), 'evil spirit' (Lk 7:21; 8:2; Acts 19:12f, 15f), 'spirit of a demon' (Lk 4:33; Rev 16:14) and various other names. Though there is one instance of possession of animals (Mk 5:12f and parallels), the most frequent references are to the ↗ possession of men by demons (Mk 1:23–6, 32, 34; 5:2–13 and parallels; 9:17–26 and parallels; Mt 4:24; 8:16; 9:32f; 12:22; Lk 4:33–5, 41; 7:21; 8:2; 11:14; Acts 5:16; 8:7; 16:16–18; 19:12). Such spirits can cause a person to become dumb (Mk 9:17, 25; Mt 9:32); deaf (Mk 9:25; Mt 12:22; Lk 11:14); blind (Mt 12:22); insane (see Lk 7:33; Jn 7:20; 8:48f, 52; 10:20); or diseased

(Lk 13:11). They can also cause a person to prophesy (Acts 16:16). By no means all diseases or physical infirmities can be traced to the influence of demons, even though they are in the last resort the work of the devil (Acts 10:38). It is possible for many demons to dwell in one human being (Mk 5:9; Lk 8:2, 30; see also Mt 12:45; Lk 11:26). Such spirits are able to impart an extraordinary strength to those whom they possess (Mk 5:3f; Lk 8:29; Acts 19:16). They torment those whom they attack (Mk 5:5; 9:18 and parallels), and treat them as tools with no power to resist (Mk 1:26; 5:3–7; 9:18–26 and parallels; Lk 4:35; 8:29). There is, however, no single instance of demons leading the men whom they possess so far astray that they commit morally reprehensible deeds, nor do they ever attempt to lead them into eternal perdition, as Satan does. Satan is the one who rules over the demons (Mk 3:26 and parallels; Eph 6:11f; see also Lk 13:11, 16). The devil is also apparently given the name of Beelzebul (*Beelzeboul*; in the Vulgate and the Syrian the form is Beelzebub [the origin and meaning of the name are uncertain]; Mk 3:22 and parallels; Mt 12:27; Lk 11:18f; see also Mt 9:34). It is above all Jesus who drives demons out of men with his simple but powerful words (Mk 1:25f, 34 and parallels; 5:2–13 and parallels; 7:29; 9:25f and parallels; Mt 4:24; 9:32f; 12:22, 28; 15:28; Lk 4:35; 6:18; 11:14, 20). It is this fact which tells us that the kingdom of God is at hand (Mt 12:28; Lk 11:20 and that the power of Satan is collapsing (Mk 3:27 and parallels; Lk 10:18). When Jesus exorcises them, the demons acknowledge him to be the Messiah (Mk 1:24, 34; 3:11; 5:7 and parallels; Lk 4:34), and this means torment and destruction for them (Mk 1:24; 5:7 and parallels; Lk 4:34). But the disciples of Jesus also have the power to exorcise demons (Mk 6:7 and parallels; 6:13; Lk 10:17–20; Acts 5:16; 8:7; 16:16–18; 19:12). Even Jews who have not joined Jesus's disciples have this power (Mt 12:27; Lk 11:19), although success is sometimes denied to them (Acts 19:13–16). Once having been driven out of a man, the demon seeks rest in the desert (Mt 12:43; Lk 11:24), or enters animals' bodies (Mk 5:12f and parallels). Demons also inhabit ruins (Rev 18:2). Heathen worship is due to demons (1 Cor 10:20f; Rev 9:20), and those who take part in such practices are brought into close association with the demons (1 Cor 10:20f). There are spirits of error who lead men away from the true faith (1 Tim 4:1; 1 Jn 4:6), and there are also the false doctrines of demons (1 Tim 4:1). There is a wisdom which is demonic (Jas 3:15), and the christian has to resist all demonic spirits (Eph 6:12). These spirits will exert a particular influence in the last days, and try to make men forsake the true doctrine of Christ (1 Tim 4:1; see also 1 Jn 4:1–6; Rev 16:13f). But there is a judgement in store for the demons which will punish them with torments (Mt 8:29; see also Jas 2:19).

Certain beings are to be found in the New Testament which are in fact angels of the devil (↗ Angel, C) but these are never formally equated with demons, despite their similarity to them. The one was clearly distinguished from the other in the early christian period, and it was only after this that they gradually came to be grouped together, as the conception of 'angel' began to change and demonology began to be developed as a branch of theology. For the demonic aspect of principalities and powers and similar beings, see ↗ Angel C and ↗ Principalities and Powers.

D. *Theological importance of the biblical evidence concerning demons.* In judging the importance of the biblical evidence in this respect, two extremes should be avoided. It would be wrong to accept everything that is in the bible concerning demons as factual, as a great deal that merely pertains to the ancient world has been done away with today. But, recognising this fact and bearing in mind that much that was formerly attributed to demons can today be explained by natural or psychical causes, it is still not possible simply to deny the existence and the efficacy of the powers of demonic spirits. It stands to reason that an Azazel, a Lilith, or an Asmodeus have never existed. It is also certain that the Jews saw evil spirits at work when in reality this was due to nervous or psychological disorders. The literary style of the specific text in question must also be borne in mind in any examination of the biblical evidence concerning demons or, for that matter, angels as well. There are, for example, poetical descriptions of the destruction of a town (Is 13:21; 34:14; Rev 18:2), and Tobit contains a good deal of pleasant, free narrative. Even when popular views of the ancient world are quite obviously contained in those statements in the bible that concern demons, it is nonetheless striking, taken as a whole, how reserved these statements are in comparison with those of the later Jewish and extra-canonical writings, the rabbinical texts, and the literature of the early christian period.

Since the eighteenth century, the practice has found increasing favour in protestant exegesis to regard the fairly frequent instances of ↗ possession in the New Testament as various manifestations of nervous or psychological disturbances or illnesses, and especially as epilepsy, delirium, schizophrenia, and so on. Apart from the fact that the different accounts cannot be satisfactorily interpreted in this way, the whole problem—and it is admittedly a difficult one—can only be solved if it is seen against the background of Jesus's personality and his work directed against Satan and his kingdom; and thus, in this case, as in all cases of demonology, it is necessary to adhere to the view that there are demonic beings who wish to cause harm to men, but who can be entirely deprived of their power by Jesus. Taken as a whole, the references in the bible to demons do present a real problem which has not yet been satisfactorily settled, and there is a strong case for a more searching and detailed examination.

Bibliography: J. Smit, *De daemoniacis in historia evangelica*, Rome 1913; SB IV, 501–35; H. Kaupel, *Die Dämonen im AT*, Augsburg 1930; K. Prümm, *Der christl. Glaube u. die altheidnische Welt* I, Leipzig 1935, 137–56; W. Foerster, *TDNT* II, 1–20; P. Samain, 'L'Accusation de Magie contre le Christ dans les Evangiles', *ETL* 15 (1938), 449–90; B. Noack, *Satanás und Soteria: Untersuchungen zur ntl. Dämonologie*, Copenhagen 1948; Bruno de J.-M., ODC (ed.), *Satan*, London 1951; E. Langton, *Essentials of Demonology: A Study of Jewish and Christian Doctrine—Its Origin and Development*, London 1949; S. Eitrem, *Some Notes on the Demonology in the New Testament*, Oslo 1950; Haag 305–7;

M. F. Unger, *Biblical Demonology: A Study of the Spiritual Forces behind the present World Unrest*, Wheaton (Ill.) 1952; B. J. Bamberger, *Fallen Angels*, Philadelphia 1952; A. Dupont-Sommer, 'L'Instruction sur les deux Esprits dans le "Manual de Discipline"', *RHR* 142 (1952), 5–35; B. Otzen, 'Die neugefundenen hebräischen Sektenschriften und die Testamente der zwölf Patriarchen', *ST* 7 (1953/4), 125–57; C. H. C. Macgregor, 'Principalities and Powers: the Cosmic Background of St Paul's Thought', *NTS* 1 (1954/5), 17–28; E. von Petersdorff, *Dämonologie: I. Dämonen im Weltplan*, Munich 1956; G. B. Caird, *Principalities and Powers: A Study in Pauline Theology*, Oxford 1956; J. Hempel, *TLZ* 82 (1957), 815–20; M. Ziegler, *Engel und Dämon im Lichte der Bibel*, Zurich 1957; F. Nötscher, 'Geist und Geister in den Texten von Qumran', *Mélanges bibliques A. Robert*, Paris 1957, 305–15; H. Schlier, *Principalities and Powers*, London and New York 1961; J. Henninger, R. Schnackenburg, and A. Darlapp, *LTK* III[2], 139–43; H. W. M. de Jong, *Demonische ziekten in Babylon en Bijbel*, Leiden 1959; E. Dhorme, 'La démonologie biblique', *Hommage W. Fischer*, Montpellier 1960, 46–54; H. Wohlstein, 'Zu den altisraelitischen Vorstellungen von Toten- und Ahnengeistern', *BZ* 5 (1961), 30–8; A. Winklhofer, *Traktat über den Teufel*, Frankfurt 1961; F. J. Schirse and J. Michl, 'Satan', *HTG* II, 465–78.

Johann Michl

Demythologising

The word *demythologising* must be reckoned among the most important keywords in use in recent theoretical writing and discussion. Moreover, its use has spread from biblical theology to philosophy, and from a small circle of specialists to a much wider public—witness the great success of J. A. T. Robinson's book *Honest to God* (London 1963).

By *demythologising* is meant a problem or programme, namely, that of 'abolishing' (*aufheben*) myth. This 'abolition' should, of course, be understood in the Hegelian sense: far from being a completely negative process, it examines mythical modes of thought for their positive truth content.

Theologians currently engaged on the question of demythologising are not usually very much interested in a detailed historical or systematic examination of the *concept* of myth. For some years now philosophers, anthropologists, sociologists, and psychologists who have gone into the matter have been concerned with the *meaning and significance* of mythical modes of thought. There are still problems unsolved, even today. What exactly is myth? What is its role in human life and thought? What is its value? Clearly the answer to these large questions is determined by the programme of demythologisation.

This article could not possibly pretend to provide a survey of the many different aspects and levels of contemporary views on myth, or of the corresponding interpretations of demythologising. Still less could it venture to pass judgement on contemporary research into myth. In an encyclopedia of biblical theology it seems appropriate to confine discussion to an exposition of Rudolf Bultmann's celebrated demythologising of the message of revelation.

In the seventh issue of *Beiträge zur Evangelischen Theologie* (1941) appeared two contributions by Bultmann, the second of which—entitled 'Neues Testament und Mythologie' (quotations will be taken from *Kerygma and Myth: A Theological Debate*, London 1953)—has since given rise to one of the most thorough-going and most passionate theological controversies of modern times. Bultmann attempted to take up a position with regard to the difficulties which bar the way to the acceptance of faith to modern man, formed as he is in the image of science and technology. One of the chief difficulties, as he saw it, was that the churches demand from modern man an unnecessary *sacrificium intellectus*.

According to Bultmann, the New Testament presents the divine kerygma in the form of myth. Bultmann understands myth 'in the sense popularised by the "History of Religions" school. Mythology is the use of imagery to express the otherworldly in terms of this world and the divine in terms of human life, the other side in terms of this side' (*Kerygma and Myth* I, 10, *n* 2).

> The cosmology of the New Testament is essentially mythical in character. The world is viewed as a three-storied structure, with the earth in the centre, the heaven above, and the underworld beneath. Heaven is the abode of God and of celestial beings—the angels. The underworld is hell, the place of torment. Even the earth is more than the scene of natural, everyday events, of the trivial round and common task. It is the scene of the supernatural activity of God and his angels on the one hand, and of Satan and his demons on the other. These supernatural forces intervene in the course of nature and in all that men think and will and do. Miracles are by no means rare. Man is not in control of his own life. Evil spirits may take possession of him. Satan may inspire him with evil thoughts. Alternatively, God may inspire his thought and guide his purposes. He may grant him heavenly visions. He may give him the supernatural power of his Spirit. History does not follow a smooth, unbroken course; it is set in motion and controlled by these supernatural powers. This aeon is held in bondage by Satan, sin, and death (for 'powers' is precisely what they are), and hastens towards its end. That end will come very soon, and will take the form of a cosmic catastrophe. It will be inaugurated by the 'woes' of the last time. Then the Judge will come from heaven, the dead will rise, the Last Judgement will take place, and men will enter into eternal salvation or damnation.
>
> [*Kerygma and Myth*, 1–2.]

The representation of the events of salvation is equated with the mythological view of the world.

> It proclaims in the language of mythology that the last time has now come. 'In the fullness of time' God sent forth his Son, a pre-existent divine Being, who appears on earth as a man. He dies the death of a sinner on the cross and makes atonement for the sins of men. His resurrection marks the beginning of the cosmic catastrophe. Death, the consequence of Adam's sin is abolished, and the daemonic forces are deprived of their power. The risen Christ is exalted to the right hand of God in heaven and made 'Lord' and 'King'. He will come again on the clouds of heaven to complete the work of redemption, and the resurrection and judgement of men will follow. Sin, suffering and death will then be finally abolished. All this is to happen very soon; indeed, St Paul thinks that he himself will live to see it.

> All who belong to Christ's church and are joined to the Lord by baptism and the eucharist are certain of resurrection to salvation, unless they forfeit it by unworthy behaviour. Christian believers already enjoy the first instalment of salvation, for the Spirit is at work within them, bearing witness to their adoption as sons of God, and guaranteeing their final resurrection.
>
> [*Kerygma and Myth*, 2 (textual references omitted).]

'All this is the mythological way of expressing things,' Bultmann goes on, 'and the individual motives for it can easily be traced back to the contemporary mythology of the Jewish apocalyptic period and the gnostic myth of the redemption' (p. 2). But, insofar as it is the language of mythology, then it becomes quite impossible for men of today to believe in it. This is affirmed again and again by Bultmann in various places. For example, he comments on the resurrection:

> It is impossible for modern man to comprehend the *resurrection of Jesus* as an event in history by virtue of which there is set free a life-power which man is able to appropriate for himself by means of the sacraments. This type of language is completely meaningless to the man who has been trained to think in terms of the biological sciences because, for him, the problematic aspect of death does not exist. The idealist too, although he can grasp the significance of a life which is subordinated to death, finds it quite inconceivable that a man who has died may be awakened once again to physical life. . . . But a miraculous natural event such as the revivification of one who is already dead, quite apart from the fact that it is in the first place unworthy of belief, cannot be viewed by him as a divine act which concerns him personally.
>
> [*Kerygma and Myth*, 8.]

Further on (in *Kerygma und Mythos* III, 51—quoted from 'The Case for Demythologising: A Reply to Karl Jaspers', *Myth and Christianity: An Inquiry into the Possibility of Religion without Myth*, New York 1958, 57–71) Bultmann sets out his own position regarding this difficulty of belief in the revivification of the dead: 'He [ie, Jaspers] is as firmly convinced as I am that a body cannot return to life and rise from the grave'.

Thus the New Testament message is presented in a mythical form, and is as such unacceptable to modern man. If this message is to retain its validity, the only course remaining is to demythologise it, not by a process of selection, nor by making deletions, but by interpreting the myth. The question is, however, whether the demythologising would not, if it were in fact carried out under such circumstances, be based on a postulate which is alien to the spirit of the New Testament. Bultmann, speaking both as a historian of comparative religion and as an exegete, is of the opinion that such a demythologising would not go contrary to the spirit of the New Testament.

He has created his theory of myth from the history of religion, and, as a scholar of comparative religion, he includes the New Testament among the mythical modes of thought. Now, in the study of comparative religion, the general laws which are applicable to this type of literature, its significance and the way in which it must be interpreted, have all been carefully worked out.

> The true significance of myth is not to be found in its ability to provide an objective cosmology, but tends rather to be expressed in the sense in which man understands himself in his world. Myth ought not to be interpreted in the cosmological sense, but rather in the anthropological or, even better, in the existential sense. . . . That is why the mythology of the New Testament ought not to be examined with an eye to its objective conceptual content, but rather to the existential perception which is expressed in these concepts. It deals with the question of the truth of this perception and its truth affirms a belief which may not be bound to the conceptual world of the New Testament.
>
> [*Kerygma and Myth*, 8.]

But Bultmann is also an exegete, and as such he points out that the New Testament itself invites criticism by reason of the fact that within its own conceptual world there are individual concepts which cannot be reconciled intellectually with each other, and that indeed concepts which are mutually contradictory are often found in juxtaposition—and that, furthermore, demythologising within the New Testament has in certain places already been carried out.

Bultmann thus attempts to present an existential interpretation of the mythological abstract world in its principal characteristics and by means of a number of examples. Using language which is strongly influenced by that of Heidegger, he outlines the christian apprehension of reality, both external to and within faith. He strives above all to present, in a non-mythological manner, the essential core of the christian message, that is, that Christ's appearance has occurred only once and has not been repeated in the course of history, that God's act in the person of Christ was decisive and that the christian is of necessity closely bound up with this single, unrepeated and unrepeatable, appearance of Christ.

His article 'Heilsgeschehen und Mythologie' has given rise to a spate of books, a great deal of passionate argument, and a veritable storm of indignation within the various protestant communions of the German-speaking countries, and this has all been a matter of considerable surprise to Bultmann himself, who had certainly said nothing more in this single essay than could be extracted quite easily from his exegetical writings, from *The History of the Synoptic Tradition* (1921; English translation, Oxford 1963) and *Jesus and the Word* (1926; ET London 1962).

The controversy over demythologising presents in general a very confused picture, because the struggle to gain an insight into the New Testament message is weighed down by such laborious efforts to understand Bultmann properly. Apart from a general lack of familiarity with Bultmann's historical writings, the main cause of many misunderstandings may have been the literary form of the 1941 article, by means of which the author attempted to give his interpretation of the divine kerygma a more powerful impact, by representing it as the only possible interpretation acceptable to modern man. This pastoral aim, however, conceals the real foundations of Bultmann's attitude to belief. It is probably only in this way that Jaspers' verdict, and other similar judgements, can be explained:

> Bultmann's demand that the New Testament should be demythologised is based on two suppositions, firstly on a view of modern science and of modern man in his world which causes him to deny so many objects of christian belief, and secondly on his view of philosophy itself, which makes it possible for him to adopt those attitudes towards faith which, in his opinion, still hold good, by means of an existential interpretation, the conceptuality of which should be available in a scientific philosophy. These two suppositions form the twin pillars upon which Bultmann has built his thesis. Neither seems to be capable of bearing its weight.
>
> [K. Jaspers, 'The Issues Clarified', *Myth and Christianity*, New York 1958, 72–116.]

Bultmann has, with justice, repeatedly stated his objections to this type of interpretation of his thought. As a protestant and a dialectical theologian, he does not judge faith from the viewpoint of secular science or philosophy. If he came to the question of demythologising already armed with presuppositions, he came also with the experience of an exegete and historian of comparative religion. New Testament exegesis, viewed in the light of comparative religion, does not of itself lead, in Bultmann's opinion, to an acceptance of the power of God to intervene miraculously in the normal course of events in Christ and his church, as is generally taught by the various christian bodies. As a historian, he puts the form of the New Testament message in the same category as the mode of thought which is so well known in the sphere of comparative religion. Bultmann the historian can, it is true, carry out his work of interpretation with a far easier conscience when this is seen as a rationalisation of the views of Bultmann the protestant believer on those aspects of God which are not within our range, and on the principle of *sola fides*, and when it is harmonised with the views of Bultmann the philosopher on the process of understanding in general, and on the value of the concepts contained in the statements concerning God in particular, and when it is regarded as raising Bultmann the pastoral theologian above the level of that clash with the narrow philosophy of man and the world which is considered by so many scientists as their ultimate triumph and achievement. In this sense Bultmann may well be called a systematic thinker, in that such differing elements do not conflict with each other, but rather tend to cohere mutually in his philosophy. He is not, however, a systematic thinker in the sense that he approaches his study of the New Testament with ready-made solutions.

In Bultmann's view, God's act in Christ is decisive in that it makes possible authentic existence, the concept of which is not inaccessible to philosophy, since this existence consists in a willing render to a God, who is invisible and who is not at man's disposal, and in the inner freedom of the world. It is then true to say that Bultmann experiences his greatest difficulties when he strives to preserve the innermost core of the New Testament—in other words, the fact that Christ's appearance has taken place once only and that the christian is of necessity tied in the closest alliance to this single, unrepeated and unrepeatable act of God in Christ. Christ's incarnation and passion remain as little more than an occurrence which, emerging in the person of Jesus and in the earliest christian period, does not become an *event* until the word of grace is actually spoken personally, at a given time, to a man (see *Kerygma und Mythos* III, 57f):

> That words of grace are spoken in this way, and that not the God-idea but God himself appears as *my* God, and speaks personally to *me* here and now, and, what is more, speaks through the mouths of men—this is the 'demythologised' sense of *ho logos sarx egeneto* (= the word became flesh) of the church's doctrine of the incarnation. Moreover, the christian message is to this extent tied to a tradition and looks back to a historical form and an existence in history, insofar as it sees the proof of the identity of these personal words spoken to men in this historical form and existence.
>
> [*Kerygma und Mythos* III, 58.]

In order to form a true assessment of Bultmann's theology, it is important to make a clear distinction between philosophical problems and those of comparative religion. However important they may be in practice, philosophical problems, which concern the fact that God is not available to us and the confusion of our concepts in the evidence that we have of God and the problems concerning the narrow view of man and the world today, remain questions of a purely preliminary nature, or, in Newman's phrase, of antecedent probability. They are, however, the problems with which those catholics who have taken part in the discussion of Bultmann's theology are best acquainted, and it is towards these problems that they have defined their attitude in the most satisfactory manner and in the greatest detail. It would perhaps be as well to give some warning of the risk that is inherent in a certain tendency to use the words 'mythology' and 'mythological' merely in order to stress the transcendence of God and the purely analogous value of human discussion about God, and to represent our statements concerning the existence and ordinances of God as being of necessity mythological.

In any discussion of Bultmann's theology it is not enough, in an attempt to ascertain the orthodox view of the truths of faith, to establish their compatibility with modern scientific thought and a sound philosophy. The problem of demythologisation is essentially a historical problem. To what extent may Holy Scripture, and above all the New Testament, be placed in the category of myth as found in comparative religion, and to what extent, too, should the words of God, spoken personally to men, be interpreted in a purely existential way? The answer to these questions depends on the history of the origins of the New Testament tradition. Before any fruitful discussion of Bultmann's position can take place, it is necessary to make a very careful study of the genesis of this tradition.

Bibliography: The most important contributions to the discussion of the problem of demythologisation have been collected by H. W. Bartsch in the series *Theologische Forschung: Wissenschaftliche Beiträge zur kirklichevangelischen Lehre*, under the general title *Kerygma und Mythos* (five volumes, two of which have been translated into English: *Kerygma and Myth: A Theological Debate*, ed. H. W. Bartsch, London 1953 [vol. I] and 1962 [vol. II]). The most detailed bibliography on Bultmann and the demythologisation debate is to be found in G. Hasenhüttl, *Der Glaubensvollzug: Eine Begegnung mit Rudolf Bultmann aus katholischem Verständnis*, Essen 1963. (There is also a short but useful bibliography of Bultmann's works available in English, and of other books in English dealing with Bultmann's theology, in *Existence and Faith: Shorter Writings of Rudolf Bultmann*, ed. and trans. Schubert M. Ogden, London 1961.) Among recently published works not cited by Hasenhüttl are: R. Bultmann, *Glauben und Verstehen* IV, Tübingen 1965; R. Bultmann, *Jesus Christ and Mythology*, New York 1958 and New York 1960; G. Bornkamm, 'Die Theologie Rudolf Bultmanns in der neueren Diskussion', *TR* 29 (1963), 33–141; R. Marlé, 'Mythos', *HTG* II, 193–201; G. Lanczkowski and H. Fries, 'Mythos', *LTK* VII², 746–52; J. Slok, J. Haekel, S. Mowinckel, R. Bultmann, and H. Meyer, 'Mythus und Mythologie', *RGG* IV³, 1263–84; H. Cazelles, 'Le mythe et l'Ancien Testament', *DB(S)* 1957, 246–61; J. Henninger, 'Le mythe en ethnologie', *DB(S)* 1957, 225–46; R. Marlé, 'Le mythe et le Nouveau Testament', *DB(S)* 1957, 261–8; G. van Riet, *Mythe et Vérité: Problèmes d'Epistémologie*, Paris 1960, 345–422; J. Pépin, *Mythe et Allégorie: Les origines grecques et les contestations judéo-chrétiennes*, Paris 1958.

The proceedings of the conferences which, since 1961, have been held annually on the subject of demythologisation by the International Centre for Humane Studies and the Rome Institute for Philosophical Studies, are as follows: 1. *Il problema della demittizzazione*, 1961 (= *Kerygma und Mythos* VI/1, Hamburg 1963); 2. *Demittizzazione e imagine*, 1962 (= *Kerygma und Mythos* VI/2, Hamburg 1964); 3. *Ermeneutica e Tradizione*, 1963 (= *Herméneutique et Tradition*, Paris 1964); 4. *Tecnical Escatologia, e Casuistica*, Rome 1964; 5. *Démythisation et Morale*, Paris 1965.

Paul Asveld

Descent into hell

The concept of the descent into hell (journey to the underworld), with which important christological and soteriological speculations have been associated from the earliest times (Ignatius of Antioch (?), Justin, Hermas, Irenaeus etc; see also especially the descent into hell which occurs in the apocryphal gospel of Nicodemus), calls to mind at once the time that Jesus spent in the kingdom of the dead between his death and his resurrection. The chief elements which go to build up the idea of what hell or the underworld is like as a place and as a state, are drawn from the contemporary view of the nature of the underworld, and from the way in which late judaism regarded the survival of the soul. Quite apart from numerous Old-Testament references to the underworld or hell itself (1 Sam 2:6; 2 Sam 22:6; Tob 13:2; Job 11:8; 14:13; Ps 49:15f; 86:13; 139:8; Prov 1:12; Sir 21:10; Is 14:11; 38:10, 18 etc), there are also passages which describe a descent into hell, as in the case of the descent into hell of the King of Babylon (Is 14:9–15) and that of Pharaoh and his people (Ezek 32:17–32).

In the New Testament, those passages which indicate or presuppose a descent into hell on the part of Christ are of a predominantly christological interest, since the factual basis of Jesus's death and the reality and the magnitude of his resurrection are illustrated and placed on a firmer footing by his sojourn in hell, which is to be understood in the very widest sense here, as underworld, Hades, or *Sheol.* This resurrection, however, is of great importance in connection with the whole matter of salvation, and Christ's descent into hell must, even from this christological point of view, also have a marked soteriological significance, which will naturally be all the more profound if, in addition to the descent itself, any particular activity on the part of Christ in the underworld can be established. Some evidence of such activity does seem to be provided by the New Testament.

The christological importance of the descent into hell has been expressed since the fourth century in the formula *descendit ad inferos* (var: *infernos*, *inferna*) which occurs between *mortuus et sepultus est* and *tertia die resurrexit* in the Apostles' Creed. It is also apparent in all the passages in the New Testament in which the resurrection of Jesus is described as an *anastasis ek nekrōn* (=resurrection from the dead). The plural form is doubtless intended to denote the kingdom of the dead or the underworld, which is, in accordance with the cosmology of those times, situated in the lower regions of the earth, and where, according to the earliest ideas about hell, the dead dwelt together in a shadowy existence, but where, in the later view which is set out clearly—for example, in Lk 16:19–31—there were separate regions for the just and the unjust. In the remark of the dead rich man (Lk 16:30), Luke already implies that it is possible for someone 'from the dead' (*apo nekrōn*) to be sent back to earth. It is also interesting to note that Herod expresses the view, in Mk 6:14, 17 (see also Mt 14:2; Lk 9:8) that John the Baptist had been raised 'from the dead' (*ek* [*apo*] *nekrōn*). In this way, all similar expressions dealing with Jesus' resurrection presuppose that he had previously spent some time in the kingdom of the dead: see Mt 17:9 (Mk 9:9); 27:64; Lk 24:46; Jn 2:22 (see also 12:1; 9:17, with its reference to the resurrection of Lazarus *ek nekrōn*); 20:9; 21:14. In Acts 2:14–36, where in fact the expression *ek nekrōn* does not occur, the same ideas are stated very clearly when Peter, making use of and interpreting Ps 16:10 in a messianic sense, refers to Jesus' sojourn in Hades (*Sheol*) in the phrase *oute enkataleiphthē eis ha*(*i*)*dēn* (='he was not abandoned to Hades'), and to his body placed in the grave but preserved from corruption in the phrase *oute hē sarx autou eiden diaphthoran* (='nor did his flesh see corruption'). The separate existence of the dead person, in terms of his body and soul, is here vividly represented in the anthropological language of the period and the concept of life after death. Further passages which refer to a resurrection *ek nekrōn* based on the same suppositions are: Acts 3:15; 4:10; 10:41; 13:30, 34, 37; 17:3, 31; Rom 1:4; 4:24; 6:4, 9; 7:4; 8:11; 10:7, 9; 1 Cor 15:12, 20; Gal 1:1; Eph 1:20; Col 1:18 (*prōtotokos ek tōn nekrōn*='first-born from among the dead'; see also Acts 26:23); 2:12; 1 Thess 1:10; 4:13ff; 2 Thess 2:8; Heb 11:19; 13:20; 1 Pet 1:3, 21.

All these passages—and the list could be augmented by others which do not contain the phrase *ek nekrōn*, though referring strictly to the resurrection of Jesus—provide evidence that Jesus spent some time in the underworld, and thus that he must previously have descended into hell. The formula *ek nekrōn*, therefore, does not mean simply that Jesus' body was raised from the sepulchre. Above all, it means that he was also recalled from *Sheol*. The resurrection, furthermore, does not appear only as a personal mark of distinction for Jesus, but also has considerable importance with regard to the salvation of the redeemed. This is illustrated in the description of Jesus as *prōtotokos ek nekrōn* and in evidence such as that provided by Rom 6:4; 1 Cor 15:20–8.

Further evidence of the descent of Jesus into the kingdom of the dead can be drawn from the comparison between the resurrection of Jesus (Mt 12:39ff) and the experience of Jonah, but this is really of no more than secondary importance in this particular passage, as in the case of Mt 16:4 and Lk 11:29, where the principal intention is to call attention to the resurrection as a sign, and the descent into hell is mentioned, as it were, only in parenthesis. It is certainly not necessary to assume that because the peace of the grave is expressed periphrastically by the words 'in the heart of the earth' that this must refer to *Sheol*, as being situated in the interior of the earth (see Jon 2:2f, in which Jonah's prayer is represented as having been uttered 'from the belly of the fish', despite the fact that Jonah 'cried out of the belly of *Sheol*'). A further indirect reference to Christ's descent into hell is also contained in Mt 27:52.

The most obvious instance of the soteriological significance of the descent into hell, or at least the one which is most closely related to Jesus's resurrection, is to be found in Rev 1:18; 'I died, and behold I am alive for evermore, and I have the keys of Death and Hades' (Rev 20:12–15).

From 1 Pet 3:18ff, and possibly also from the evidence in 1 Pet 4:6, which is so difficult to interpret, there emerges a feature which was later developed with the growth of christian tradition and theological speculation. It cannot be established beyond all doubt whether the words: 'being put to death in the flesh but made alive in the spirit; in which he went and preached to the spirits in prison (*en hō*[*i*] [ie, *pneumati*] *kai tois en phulakē*[*i*] *pneumasin poreutheis ekēruxen*), who formerly did not obey, when God's patience waited in the days of Noah, during the building of the ark, . . .'; are to be taken to refer to the descent of Jesus into hell in the sense outlined above, or whether, as many believe to be the case, this is a reference to Jesus's resurrection and exaltation to the right hand of God. It is also not certain whether the 'spirits' who are addressed by Christ refer to the souls of the dead who are waiting in the underworld, either together with, or separated from, their bodies, or angelic beings, rather in the sense of those referred to in Jude 6. In the same way, the intention and the content of the 'sermon' referred to in 1 Pet 3:19 remain obscure.

What stands in the closest relationship to this is the preceding passage in 3:18, which deals with the descent of Jesus after his death, and it is stressed that this death was 'for sins' and 'the righteous for the unrighteous'. For it is particularly striking that what immediately follows the mention of the sermon addressed 'to the spirits in prison' is the reference to the resurrection and exaltation of Jesus to 'the right hand of God . . . swallowing down death [Vulgate], being gone into heaven, the angels and powers and virtues being made subject to him.' In 1 Pet 1:3, 21, the resurrection *ek nekrōn* has already been mentioned. It is therefore permissible to regard the passage in question (1 Pet 3:18ff) as a fairly close representation of the time Jesus spent in the underworld and the 'sermon' may be regarded, not as a severe admonition, but rather as a message of salvation (*ekēruxen*, 'he preached'). True, it is especially the people 'in the days of Noah' who are said to be the recipients of Jesus' sermon, but the particular reason for this may well be that Peter at once leads up to the baptism of Christ which confers salvation and is here symbolised by the flood. The generation of Noah is moreover to be taken as representative of those who are already dead and in the underworld (or perhaps merely of heathens?) and this sermon in Hades is possibly intended to proclaim to them the redemption which the death of Jesus on the cross has brought about, and the incipient dominion of God.

Viewed in this way, 1 Pet 3:18ff is in a direct line with the later controversy and speculation which grew up around the soteriological significance of the descent into hell. In addition, similar themes in the apocryphal tradition of late judaism can readily be called to mind, as, for example, in the first book of Enoch (Eth), after the apocalyptic journey of Enoch through the prisons of the fallen angels (17–20), a visit is made to the 'caves' in which the 'ghosts of the dead are gathered' and 'which are so made that all the souls of human beings can be assembled here' (22:4) in separate chambers or compartments, one of which is reserved for the 'spirits of the just', another for 'sinners', one for the 'souls of mourners', and another for those who are absolutely depraved.

As far as comparative religion is concerned, there is a definite connection between Christ's descent into hell and comparable notions in the ancient Near East and Egypt, as well as in the hellenistic civilisation of Greece and Rome. It is certainly possible to establish many parallels in this respect between the usual external forms of representation and the various ideas of the underworld and the fate of man after death which are common to all. Similarly, the idea of a kingdom of death, inhabited by the dead, and the urgent desire and longing to overcome this power of evil, which gained expression in the form of myth and its related types of worship, is firmly founded in the natural and practical experience of the human race. A close analogy is to be found in the Babylonian myth of the descent of the goddess Inana into the underworld and her consequent re-ascent, the epic of Gilgamesh of Akkad and his unsuccessful attempt to liberate the spirits of the underworld, and the warlike assault on the underworld by Ishtar and Nergal, who conquered the ruler of the kingdom of the dead. The mythology concerning the growth of plants and the phases in the sun's and moon's course play an important part in fashioning man's concept of the next world. Varying examples of this are to be found in the worship of Attis, and of Isis and Osiris, and in the Eleusinian cult. Within hellenistic civilisation, although the descent of Theseus, Orpheus, and Heracles into the underworld are to a certain extent analogous to Christ's descent into hell, it is however not possible to trace any direct influence of an essential kind in this case. Christ's descent into hell is, in fact, unique and distinctive, and the vital truth which lies at the heart of this descent can only be fully understood if it is related to Jesus' incarnation as God-man and his participation in the ordinary lot of mortal man. This implies that the Redeemer had to go down into the realms of death after he had died. But, even more than this, it stood at the time for redemption from death through the power of Christ's resurrection, brought about by God who rules absolutely over life and death, and this power was the condition by means of which all those who have been redeemed in Christ might overcome death.

Bibliography: A. Grillmeier, 'Der Gottessohn im Totenreich', *ZKT* 71 (1949), 1–53 and 184–203; A. Grillmeier, *LTK* v², 450–5, with a full bibliography which includes: K. Gschwind, *Die Niederfahrt Christi in die Unterwelt*, Munich 1911; J. A. MacCulloch, *The Harrowing of Hell*, Edinburgh 1930; B. Reicke, *The Disobedient Spirits and Christian Baptism*, Copenhagen 1946; W. Bieder, *Die Vorstellung von der H.J.Chr.*, Zurich 1949; P. Benoit, 'La descente aux Enfers selon W. Bieder', *RB* (1951). See also: Haag 1206f and the commentaries on 1 Pet, esp. the excursus by J. Michl in his *Der Brief an die Hebr. und die kath. Briefe* (*RNT* 8), Regensburg 1953, 224–6; and K. H. Schelkle, *Die Petrusbriefe, der Judasbrief*, Freiburg 1964², 104–8.

Johannes Kürzinger

Desire

The various words used in the bible to denote the sphere of human striving are, in the main, formations from *ʾāwâh, ḥāmad, epithumos*—see *TDNT* III, 168–70—and cover all shades of meaning—that is, striving which is good, bad, or indifferent. The English word 'desire' can refer to either good or evil striving, and it is in the latter sense that it is discussed here.

Desire can be a sin, and in the form of covetousness it is expressly forbidden in the Decalogue (Ex 20:17; Deut 5:21). Compliance with this commandment is the basis of the more perfect justice demanded by Jesus (Mt 5:27–8).

In the Old Testament the 'wicked man', who is the enemy of the religious man, is characterised in a general way by means of evil desires, wishes, and intentions which are harmful to himself and to others (eg, Prov 11:6; 21:25, 26) but which, however, God is able to thwart (Prov 10:3; Ps 140:9)—though no exact distinction is made here between temptation and sin and between striving in the sexual, sensitive, and spiritual spheres. The piety of a later age, more concerned with the individual's own ethical achievement, will experience all the more painfully this opposition which works in the depth of the soul against the performance of duty. The religious man is acutely conscious of this apparently innate predisposition to sin (Ps 51:7; 130:3; 143:2). The Old Testament contains frequent complaints of man's hardness of heart and obduracy (Ezek 36:26; Ps 81:13), and his lascivious running after evil (Jer 2:23; see also Prov 1:22), and there are also many pleas for self-control and many admonitions and pieces of advice (Prov 23:3; Sir 22:27–23:27). In such cases there is often no clear distinction drawn between the general character of the actual sin committed and the cause which is to be found in man himself, an interior disposition to personal sin (see Ezek 11:19; Zech 7:12; Jer 4:4; Ps 143:2), and there are many references to categories of sins other than those pertaining to desire. It is, however, possible to see, in the later view, that the commandment forbidding evil desire embraces the entire law (4 Macc 2:6; *Vita Adae*, 19; cf Rom 7:7; 13:9), and in the rabbinical doctrine of the 'evil impulse' (see Gen 6:5; 8:21; SB IV 466f) the intersection of the various ideas and terms for one and the same reality, all of which were later grouped by theologians under the common heading of concupiscence (not, incidentally, to be thought of in its exclusively sexual connotation).

In the gospels and the catholic epistles, very much the same picture may be found. Man is defiled by his evil desires (Mt 15:18–20; Mk 7:20–3; see also Gal 5:16–21). They give rise to temptations and sins (Jas 1:13–15; 4:1–4). Man is made a slave to the world by his evil desires, which in any case must perish with the world. Man's evil desires thus exclude him from eternal salvation (1 Jn 2:15–17; see also 1 Tim 5:6; Tit 2:12; Jude 18). In Christ's own interpretation of his parable of the sower, the failure of the word of God to take effect among the third group of people is traceable to the 'cares of the world, and the delight in riches, and the desire for other things' (Mk 4:19; see also Mt 13:22; Lk 8:14). In reality, the same effect is attributed to Satan in the case of the first group of people (Mk 4:15; see also Mt 13:19; Lk 8:12). Thus, it can be assumed that some kind of co-operation exists between the external evil power and man's interior concupiscence. This is quite apparent in 1 Cor 7:5 (see also Jn 8:41–4; Wis 2:24).

In Rom 7:7–8:4, the relationship between desire and salvation is presented with considerable emphasis, although this is merely incidental to the main theme of the passage. Paul devises a whole scheme of salvation-history (see Rom 5:12–17) with unavoidable generalisations and rough outlines, in the form of a drama in which 'sin', 'flesh', 'death', and 'law' enter as personified powers (see R. Benoit, *RB* 47 [1938], 483–5). The 'I' of the narrative is not to be understood as playing an empirically personal or generally human role, but as gathering the unredeemed situation up into a comprehensive entity. Kuhn (*ZTK* 49 [1952], 204–26) points out that an analogous 'I', as narrator, exists in Qumran (1 *QS* 11, 7–6). Although it is certainly difficult to keep 'sin' distinct from evil desire, because the close relationship that exists between them tends to make them appear to be used almost as interchangeable ideas, it would nonetheless be wrong to identify the one completely with the other (Schauf, *Sarx*, 29–32). The desires appear as the object, result, aim or means of the 'sin' which is regarded as the power behind them (Rom 7:8, 11; 6:12, 13). They control the 'flesh'—that is to say, not only the material part of man (see 2 Cor 2:12; Col 2:18), but the entire 'old' man who has not yet become a 'new' man in Christ. The innate tendency of the old man is to oppose God and to incline towards sin (Rom 1:24–5; 6:12–13; 8:6–7; Gal 5:16–24; Eph 2:3), and even to oppose the 'inner', better man, namely his reasoning faculty (Rom 7:22, 23, 25).

The real malice of desire of the 'flesh' is most apparent where it comes into conflict with the Law. The Law is indeed good and holy (Rom 7:12). It certainly does not arouse concupiscence for the first time (Rom 1:24; 2:12, 15), but the very commandment which forbids concupiscence in fact gives it further stimulus (Rom 7:7) and provides occasion for transgression. The Law brings the evil quality of the sin to the forefront and makes the sinner fully responsible for his transgression. The emphasis is thus placed less on the immediate psychological occasion of desire (Rom 7:8, 11; Benoit 487f), than on the fact that desire, acting, as it were, as a kind of fifth column, makes man a slave to sin (Rom 7:14–23; 8:12; Gal 5:17; 1 Pet 2:11; Jas 4:1ff). This is not to say that the law can prevent the tyranny which desire exercises over the flesh from mastering man. In itself the situation is indeed hopeless. (Rom 7:13–25.)

God's intervention in man's affairs through Christ redeems him from sin and death. Salvation consists in the victory of the 'spirit' over the 'flesh' (Rom 8:1–4; see also Gal 5:24; Eph 4:23; Tit 3:3–7; Benoit, 492–502). The situation in which redemption can occur is presented in several contrasting ways—man's one-time evil inclination towards the flesh and its desires and his present inclination towards the life of the spirit; the old man and the new man; death and life; flesh and spirit; the heathen and the redeemed man, and so on. None of these antitheses is purely empirical, but they are valid *de jure*. All these illustrations are accompanied by warnings to christians not to let sins and desires become habitual, and that each individual must develop for himself what has been established as a fundamental principle of redemption (Gal 5:16–24; Eph 4:17–24; Col 3:5–11; Rom 6:11–23; 2 Tim 2:22). Although the Spirit of God has delivered the redeemed from the slavery of their evil desires and sins (Rom 8:1–14), these evil desires have not been physically destroyed. They have, however, certainly been deprived of their power, and the christian is thereby able to renounce sin (Col 3:5; Gal 5:24; 6:14; Rom 8:13). In this way it can be seen that redemption is not simply the realisation of a stoic ideal (see the Coptic Gospel of St Thomas, logion 38 [Leipoldt]: cessation of the sense of shame). For this reason, christians are urged to continue to discipline the flesh (Rom 13:14; see also Sir 22:27–23:27; Behm, *TDNT* IV, 1004).

Only the most obscure indications and hints concerning the origins of evil desire are to be found in indirect references in the bible, which is of course concerned with man in the whole of his afflicted and sinful condition. From a state of general sinfulness which exists from his earliest youth (Ps 51:7; Gen 6:5; 8:21; Deut 31:21; Prov 22:15) it is no more than a step to the acceptance of the idea of his inborn perversity. His condition as a whole is in fact traceable to the original sin of his first parents, but what the bible has in mind is the general state of degenerate man, and here and there this is referred to explicitly (Sir 25:24; Wis 2:23–4; Rom 5:12–21; cf 1 Tim 2:14). It is not possible, however, to gather any unequivocal evidence, as the relative importance of the part played by evil desire as such is nowhere made explicit, though it is indisputable that it was fatally instrumental in preparing the way for the Fall (Gen 3:6).

Bibliography: B. Bartmann, 'Die Konkupiszenz, Herkunft und Wesen', *TG* 24 (1932), 405–46; P. Benoit, 'La Loi et la Croix d'après Saint Paul', *RB* 47 (1938), 481–509; Büchsel, *TDNT* III, 167–72; A. M. Dubarle, 'La condition humaine dans l'Ancien Testament', *RB* 63 (1956), 321–45; A. M. Dubarle, 'Le péché originel dans la Genèse', *RB* 64 (1957), 5–34; A. M. Dubarle, 'Le péché originel dans les suggestions de l'Evangile', *RSPT* 40 (1956), 213–54; K. G. Kuhn, '*Peirasmos-hamartia-sarx* im NT und die damit zusammenhängenden Vorstellungen', *ZTK* 49 (1952), 200–22; R. E. Murphy, '*Bsr* in the Qumran Literature and *Sarx* in the Epistle to the Romans', *SP* II, Paris 1959, 60–76; W. Schauf, '*Sarx*: Der Begriff "Fleisch" beim Apostel Paulus unter bes. Berücksichtigung seiner Erlösungslehre', *NA* 11 (1924), 1–2; Stählin, *TDNT* II, 909–26; R. Storr, 'Das Frömmig keitsideal der Propheten', *BZF* 12/3–4, Münster 1926; SB IV, 466–83; P. Wilpert, *RAC* II, 62–78; S. Lyonnet, '"Tu ne convoiteras pas" (Rom 7:7)', *Neotestamentica et patristica: Eine Freundesgabe, Herrn Professor Dr Oscar Cullman zu sienem 60 Geburtstag überreicht*, Leiden 1962, 157–65; S. Lyonnet, 'Questiones as Rom 7:7–13', *VD* 40 (1962), 163–83.

Johann Gamberoni

Disciple

A. *The Talmid.* The teacher of the Law, or rabbi, was a common sight during the time of our Lord, and he was generally followed at a respectful distance by his pupils, or *talmidim*. At the very commencement of his public life, Jesus gathered disciples round him and these followed him (Mk 1:16f; Jn 1:37–51). At least as far as external appearances are concerned, he resembled a Jewish teacher of the Law, accompanied by his pupils. This is also illustrated by the comparison between the disciples of our Lord and those of John the Baptist and of the pharisees (Mk 2:18; see also Jn 9:28f).

Although the Hebrew verb *lāmad* means in the first place 'to learn a trade', it is in most cases used in the specific sense of being engaged in the study of the Torah. Correctly speaking, the entire people of Israel ought to be, as it were, apprenticed to the Torah and thus be *talmidim*. Even the Messiah was expected to come as pupil and teacher of the Torah. Yet, in practice, it was only comparatively few who could be fully and intensely engaged in the study of the Torah, and those who did specialize in this way became the teachers of the people and, first and foremost, of those specially chosen to be their pupils. These in their turn were also destined, like them, to become teachers of the Law.

The pupil acquired a knowledge of the Law by listening and in debate. He received his initiation in the life-according-to-the-Law by keeping constant company with his teacher. But, although the pupil of the Law was a person who commanded great respect among the more ignorant sections of the community, especially if he was well advanced in his studies, he had a slave-like relationship with the rabbi, who had dedicated his entire life to the study of the Law, and he performed menial duties for him. The attitude of the talmid towards his teacher, the rabbi, was expressed in the respectful distance at which he followed him.

B. *The call of Jesus.* It must be stressed, however, that the resemblance which exists between the pupils of the rabbi and our Lord's disciples is purely external. An important difference was apparent from the very beginning of this discipleship. The pious Jew who wished to become a rabbi singled out one man from among the many who were scholars in the Law and made every attempt, from that time onwards, to be accepted by that teacher as a talmud. Jesus, on the other hand, issued a supreme call to his disciples: 'Follow me!' (Mk 1:17; Jn 1:43), whereas he sent men who tried to force their attentions on him away (Lk 9:61f; Mk 5:18). There was no particular or standard qualification for the vocation of this discipleship. The prophets of the old covenant were not made fit to carry out their task because of certain human facts or data which were already known in advance, but because God himself had made them fit for their work (Ex 3:11f; Is 6:5ff; Jer 1:6ff; Ezek 2:8ff). In just the same way, Jesus called those 'whom he desired' (Mk 3:13) and 'made' them (Mk 3:13; cf Mk 1:17) into what he wanted them to be. He even included the 'sinful man' Peter (Lk 5:8) and Matthew the tax-collector (Mt 9:9).

C. *Those who followed Jesus.* The supreme call of Jesus evoked a corresponding answer from those who were called and they left everything—their parents and their nets or, in the case of Matthew, the custom-house—and at once followed Jesus. There is no parallel between the relationship of the rabbi towards his talmidim and this unreserved obedience in response to Jesus's call, for it is a question of obedience to a master who has the right to demand everything. Jesus is not merely a rabbi. He is the Messiah. It is not a question of choosing between one teacher and another, but of deciding for or against the Messiah—and that is why Jesus did not tolerate consent given to him being qualified in any way at all (see Lk 9:59–62). The Messiah is inseparable from his mission and must give himself to it wholeheartedly and without reserve (see Mk 3:31–5). What applies to the Messiah also applies to his disciples: 'He who loves father or mother more than me is not worthy of me' (Mt 10:37), and, even more pointedly: 'If any one comes to me, and does not hate his own father and mother and wife and children and brothers and sisters, yes, and even his own life, he cannot be my disciple. Whoever does not bear his own cross and come after me, cannot be my disciple' (Lk 14:26f). The pupils of the Hebrew scholars followed their rabbi like servants, out of respect for him and his knowledge of the Hebrew texts, but the disciple of Jesus, in following the Messiah, put his entire existence, his life itself, at the disposal of the Messiah: 'Thomas, called the Twin, said to his fellow disciples, "Let us also go, that we may die with him"' (Jn 11:16).

D. *The Twelve.* Jesus chose twelve from a much larger number of disciples (Mk 3:13–19). These twelve formed what was above all a smaller circle of disciples within the larger circle. From the time of the crisis in Galilee onwards, however, it is more than likely that these two circles overlapped and the 'disciples' and the 'twelve' meant the same thing (compare Mk 14:12ff with 14:17).

What did Jesus intend to do with the Twelve? Mk 3:14 supplies the answer to this question in a nutshell: 'And he appointed twelve, to be [always] with him, and to be sent out [as deputies or plenipotentiaries] to preach.' They were also to be with him and to be initiated into the 'secret of the kingdom of God' (Mk 4:11). They were, however, to be sent out as plenipotentiaries, with full authority. All the twelve disciples whom Jesus had chosen as his ↗ apostles were granted such powers, which were conferred upon them provisionally during his public ministry (Mk 6:7) and definitively—with the exception of Judas Iscariot—after his resurrection (Mt 28:16–20). All twelve—or eleven—were thus apostles, though apostleship was not restricted exclusively to the Twelve, for there were other apostles apart from the Twelve, as for example, Barnabas and Paul. The actual number twelve has nothing to do with the apostolate, although it is not purely coincidental — a fact which emerges clearly from the addition of Matthias to the number of apostles after the defection of Judas (Acts 1:15–26). After its lapse, it was imperative to restore the number twelve, which corresponds to the number of the twelve sons of Israel who formed the basis of God's chosen people. As apostles, it was the function of the Twelve to represent the Messiah (↗ Apostle), but as the Twelve, they represented the New Israel. 'The people of the saints of the Most High' (Dan 7:27) belong to the Son of Man (Dan 7:13ff). The 'kingdom and the dominion and the greatness of the kingdoms under the whole heaven' which is given to the 'people of the saints of the Most High' can be compared with Mt 19:28: 'When the Son of man shall sit on his glorious throne' the Twelve will likewise 'also sit on twelve thrones, judging the twelve tribes of Israel'. Although it would be possible for any arbitrary number of disciples to embody the new people of God, the exact number twelve does unmistakably draw attention to this particular function of Jesus's disciples and at the same time implies a certain compactness. When Jesus 'made' the Twelve (see Mk 3:14: 'He appointed twelve . . .'), he established the basis of the eschatological people of God. This unique and basic function (see also Eph 2:20) is in fact exercised exclusively by the Twelve (among them, Peter has a special role to play [Mt 16:18]), and, what is more, they carry out this function independently from their apostolic mission, as the Twelve. The embodiment of the eschatological people of God is, however, only one part of this basic function that the Twelve have to perform, for they had a particularly active task to fulfil in addition to this more passive one. They accompanied Jesus from the moment that he began his public life to the time of his death. They heard everything that he taught the people and were given special instruction and tuition by him. They shared in the experience of all his miracles and heard all his prophecies. They were eye-witnesses of his passion, death and resurrection and were thus the guarantors of an unbroken continuity between the risen Lord and the Jesus of history. The faith of the church is dependent upon the testimony of these men, who did not happen by chance to be Jesus's witnesses, but were appointed, as authorised witnesses, to exercise this unique function for the church of all ages (see Acts 1:21f). This is why he called upon them to accompany him and to attend upon him constantly and why he appeared to them immediately after his resurrection: 'But God raised him [Jesus] from the dead [on the third day]; and for many days he appeared to those who came up with him from Galilee to Jerusalem, who are now his witnesses to the people' (Paul in Antioch of Pisidia: Acts 13:30f; see also 1 Cor 15:3ff). This double function, then, bestows a unique and supreme importance on the Twelve and puts them in a position of unrivalled distinction with regard to all other members of the embryonic church. It also explains why the death of the last of the Twelve is such a significant date in the history of the church and of revelation.

E. *Discipleship in the widest sense of the word.* The two words *disciple* and *follow* are very closely connected with each other. Used in its fullest sense, and not merely to denote walking aimlessly along behind, 'following' in the New Testament always signifies following Jesus, treading in his footsteps, and implies his physical presence. Thus, apart from the use of the word in Rev 14:4 ('These who follow the Lamb wherever he goes'), it is met with only in the gospels. All the same, it is not always easy to distinguish, in the synoptic gospels, whether the demands which are made on the disciples who follow Jesus are meant to apply only to those disciples who have 'left everything' in obedience to Jesus's call and have given themselves without reserve to the service of the Messiah, or to all men who believe in Jesus. In Jn 8:31, a far wider concept of discipleship comes to light: 'Jesus then said to the Jews who had believed him, 'If you continue in my word, you are my disciples . . .' This concept of discipleship in the wider sense is frequently met with in Acts (Chapters 6–21), but is unknown in the writings of Paul, where a different concept of discipleship, which is only incidental to the text of the synoptic gospels, is to be found. This is the imitation of Jesus. Though the germ of this idea of imitation is contained in the original concept of following Jesus (see Mk 10:45), it does not come into prominence until the time after Easter—that is, subsequent to the Lord's resurrection (1 Cor 11:1; 1 Thess 1:6; see also 1 Jn 2:6; 3:16). These various extensions of the original meaning go to show how the early church strove to preserve, after Easter, the practical significance of the words which Jesus had spoken in connection with discipleship and the need to follow him. It is also possible to perceive in the life of the apostle Paul how he had accepted without any reservation all the demands which Jesus made of his disciples.

Bibliography: G. Kittel, *TDNT* I, 210–16; K. H. Rengstorf, *TDNT* IV, 415–61; P. Gaechter, 'Die Wahl des Matthias', *ZKT* 71 (1949), 318–46; T. Süss, 'Nachfolge Jesu', *TLZ* 78 (1953), 129–40; R. Schnackenburg, *The Moral Teaching of the New Testament*, London and New York 1964; J. Schmid, *Das Evangelium nach Markus* (*RNT*), Regensburg 1954³, 76–9; J. Schmid, *Das Evangelium nach Lukas* (*RNT*), Regensburg 1955³, 178–82; K. H. Schelkle, *Discipleship and Priesthood*, London and New York 1966; P. Gaechter, *Petrus und seine Zeit*, 1958; B. Rigaux, 'Die "Zwölf" in Geschichte und Kerygma', *Der historische Jesus und der kerygmatische Christus*, ed. H. Ristow and K. Matthias, 1960, 468–86; A. Schulz, *Nachfolgen und Nachahmen*, 1962; E. Neuhäusler, *Anspruch und Antwort Gottes*, 1962; H. Kahlefeld, *Der Jünger*, 1962²; A. Schulz, 'Nachfolge', *HTG* II, 202–7; *S. Freyne, *The Twelve: Disciples and Apostles. A Study in the Theology of the First Three Gospels*, London 1968. On the imitation of Christ: W. Michaelis, *TDNT* IV, 659–74.

Elmar M. Kredel

Discipline

A. *The Old Testament.* The Hebrew word *mûsār* (from the root *ysr*) stands indifferently for two distinct concepts, those namely of *discipline* and *chastisement.* The reason for this is that it is through chastisement that one who has neglected the law and tradition, one therefore who is deficient in discipline, must be brought back to a due awareness of them. The concept of discipline carries with it the further connotation of forming one's understanding (see Prov 4:1ff), and for this reason *mûsār* can also signify *education* (*paideia*), *training.* Hebrew contains no term which exactly hits off these ideas. Often it is not easy to distinguish precisely between the various meanings in individual cases. Neither *mûsār* nor the verb *yāsar* is ever used in connection with animals.

The responsibility of maintaining discipline in daily life belonged to the father of the family. He was responsible for bringing up the younger generation in the spirit of the law and of tradition (see Gen 18:19; Ex 12:26; 13:14; Deut 6:7, 20ff). In bringing up his children the father must not spare the rod of chastisement (Prov 13:24; 19:18; 23:13f). It was legitimate for masters to chastise their slaves to a certain limited extent (see Ex 21:20f, 26f; Prov 29:19, 21). In the case of certain specific crimes the judge or the elders of the city had to have the perpetrators chastised (Deut 22:13–19: 25:1–3). In 1 Kings 12:11, 14; 2 Chron 10:11–14 chastisement is mentioned as a method of coercion exercised against subordinates.

Just as a father keeps his son to the right path by chastising him, not in spite of the fact that he loves him but rather because of it, so too the Lord chastises him whom he favours (Prov 3:11f). And just as he acts towards the individual so too he acts towards his people as a whole (Deut 8:5). The whole record of Old Testament history is written from this basic standpoint of the people being educated by God. Disobedience and apostasy from God bring down punishment upon the people (Lev 26:14–33; Jer 2:19), though admittedly these were often unwilling to accept the chastisement (Jer 32:33; Zeph 3:2–7).

Bibliography: L. Dürr, *Das Erziehungswesen im AT und im Antiken Orient*, *MVAG* 36/2, Leipzig 1932; G. Bertram, *TDNT* v, 596ff.

Johannes Gabriel

B. *The New Testament.* The law is the disciplinarian, *paidagōgos*. But when the pupil comes of age there is no further room for this function of the law (Gal 3:24). Christians are no longer under the law, but under grace (Rom 6:14). With Paul the early church took over the ideas of education belonging to the Old Testament, reinterpreting them and developing them further in a christological sense.

The idea of education by God is treated of in Heb 12. When they are chastised christians must take this as a clear sign that they are children of God (12:7f). Sufferings must be regarded as chastisement and so endured, for they admit the sufferer to a share in God's holiness (12:10), and bring him peace and righteousness (12:11).

In Rev 3:19 it is laid down as a principle that God imposes punishments on those men whom he loves in order to educate them and to bring them to ↗ conversion. In Tit 2:12 grace itself 'educates' the community, teaching them to renounce all that is hostile to God, and to live in hope—although in this passage we are told nothing of what means of education are used for the attainment of this. He who does not act as judge towards himself will be judged by the Lord and sentenced to chastisement in order not to be condemned together with the world that is hostile to God (1 Cor 11:32). Sometimes even those who are endowed with grace are chastised in order to make sure that they do not lose it (2 Cor 12:7–9).

In the list of moral precepts in Eph 6:4 the elders are admonished to bring up their children 'in the discipline of the Lord', that is in the discipline which the Lord himself (subjective genitive) exercises through the father, and all the means which are recognised as useful for the purpose in the non-christian world are to be applied here also. The phrase *en paideia(i) kai nouthesia(i)* (='in discipline and instruction') can be taken as a hendiadys, but it is equally possible to find two distinct meanings here, ie, 'discipline' and 'exhortation', and to regard the former as standing for education by means of deeds, while the latter refers to education by means of words.

In the pastoral epistles this basic principle is applied to the community. Scripture itself has an educative value (2 Tim 3:16; see also 1 Cor 10:11). The leaders of the community are responsible for the religious education of their fellow christians (Rom 2:20; 2 Tim 2:25; Heb 12:9). They are also authorised to impose ecclesiastical disciplines (Acts 5:1–11; 13:6–12), and even to deliver individuals over to Satan as a means of chastisement (1 Tim 1:20; see also 1 Cor 5:5 and 2 Cor 12:7).

Bibliography: G. Bertram, *TDNT* v, 619–25; W. Jentsch, *Urchristliches Erziehungsdenken*, Gütersloh 1951; O. Leclerq, *Dict. de la Spiritualité* 3, 1291ff; J. Campos, 'Concepto de la "Disciplina" biblica', *Revista Calasancia*, Madrid 6 (1960), 47–73.

Johannes B. Bauer

Dream

A. *In the Old Testament.* The belief in the significance of dreams was widespread throughout the ancient world. It took a long time to arrive at the rational explanation that in dreaming one's psyche is concerned with the same things which occupy one during the waking hours. This finds expression in the Letter of Aristeas 16 and even earlier in Sir 34:3 'the likeness of a face confronting a face' (see also Ps 126:1). This universal belief in dreams made it possible for God to use the dream as a medium of revelation. This does not imply that the dream as such has any intrinsic capacity for revelation but that it is considered merely as a means whereby God communicates. Hence it is stressed, on the one hand, how transient and ephemeral is what is seen in dream (Is 29:7f; Job 20:8) and, on the other, that God can use even the dreams of pagans as a means of revelation (Gen 20:6; 28:10ff; Dan 2:1ff; 7:1ff). This is shown most clearly by those dreams which require an interpretation since it is only God who can give to whom he pleases the ability to interpret (Gen 40:8; 41:16, 39; Dan 2:17ff).

Both in the ancient world as a whole and in the Old Testament we can distinguish between cultic (Gen 28:11ff), political (Judg 7:13ff), and purely personal dreams (Gen 40:8ff; Job 33:15f). In the early sources of the Pentateuch, the Yahwist is reserved as regards dreams, while the Elohist has—we may say—a strong faith in dreams, even though the latter seems to preserve the distance between man and God much better than the former. In Deut 13:2ff we find a critical position taken up with regard to dream visitations. The criterion for discerning the genuineness of a dream-revelation is whether it confirms fidelity to the God of the covenant. This critical note finds its strongest expression in Jer 23:16ff. Even here, however, it is not dictated by lack of faith. On the contrary, it springs from a genuine faith in Yahweh. Zech 10:2 speaks to much the same effect. It is not until we come to the Wisdom literature that we find a genuinely rational explanation of dreams of the kind referred to earlier (Eccles 5:3, 7; Sir 34:3ff).

B. *In the New Testament.* The line which starts in the Old Testament is continued in the New, and the limits within which one can speak of meaningful dreams are even further restricted. The early christians did not positively disbelieve in dreams but took up a very critical attitude towards them. The dream constituted a marginal phenomenon and there is no case of any central theme of the gospel being based on a dream-revelation. Its significance was restricted to particular cases when God chose this way to guide a certain individual. Paul never refers in his letters to any of the dreams mentioned in Acts (16:9f; 18:9; 23:11; 27:23f), even though they at times touched on decisive points in the life of the church and the apostles. We find accounts of dreams only in Mt (1:20f; 2:12, 13, 19, 22; 27:19), where they clearly are meant to serve an apologetic purpose.

None of the dreams mentioned in the New Testament requires an interpretation. Moreover, biblical dreams in general manifest a striking economy of description and soberness in contrast with the kind of thing found in the cultural milieu of that time. In dreams which we read of in antiquity superstition, idle curiosity and the baser passions generally play a large part. The New Testament dream-narratives, on the other hand, are centred on Christ. God guides those who belong to him (Mt 1:20; 2:13; Acts 16:9) and the Lord consoles and strengthens his disciples (Acts 18:9; 23:11; 27:23f) *even* by means of dreams.

It is only in a later period that we find people reverting to a quite unbiblical propensity to dreams and the interpretation of dreams.

Bibliography: T. Hopfner, *RE* 2/VI (1937), 2233–45; A. Oepke, *TDNT* v (1954), 220–38; E. L. Ehrlich, *Der Traum im Alten Testament*, Berlin 1953; A. Oepke, *ZAW* 67 (1955), 127; A. Caquot, 'Les songes et leur interprétation selon Canaan et Israel', *Les Songes et Leur Interprétation*, Paris 1959; L. Oppenheim, *The Interpretation of Dreams in the Ancient Near East*, Philadelphia 1956; W. Richter, 'Traum und Traumdeutung im Alten Testament', *BZ* 7 (1963), 202–19; A. Resch, *Der Traum im Heilsplan Gottes, Deuting und Bedeuting des Traums im AT*, Freiburg 1964; A. Finkel, 'The pesher of Dreams and Scriptures', *Revue de Qumran*, 15, IV fasc. 3, 357–70; A. Wikenhauser, 'Die Traumgesichte des Neuen Testaments in religionsgeschichtliche Sicht', *Ant. und Christentum* I, Münster 1939, 320–33; A. Wikenhauser, 'Doppelträume', *Bbl* 29 (1948), 100–11.

Johannes B. Bauer

Emotion

A. *Old Testament and judaism.* In the bible no concept is to be found precisely corresponding to what the scholastics called *passio* and *concupiscentia*, and what in the German of the seventeenth century was called *Leidenschaft* (passion). Old Testament man, oriental as he was, and strongly emotional by disposition, was well aware of the reality of passion. Violent desires and sudden changes of mood (Jon 4:2f; see also Gen 30:1; Judg 16:16; 2 Sam 13:2; Prov 17:22) are recorded, and, no less prominently than these, the fear which degenerates into panic. A further phenomenon known to Israel was a kind of uncanny mass excitement which threw whole peoples into enthusiasm, fear, or uproar (Deut 20:8; Ex 23:27; 1 Sam 10:5; 19:20–4; 2 Sam 21f). According to the Old Testament the passions are located not exactly in the body, but in the heart of men (Gen 6:5; 8:21; 1 Kings 3:11f; Hos 4:11; cf Rom 2:29).

All the accounts of ↗ sin and guilt from the sin of paradise (Gen 3:6), the sin of Cain (4:5) and the sin of the generation of Noah (6:5) onwards, and right through the bible to the hatred of the enemies of the Maccabees (1 Macc 7:26; 11:21) either mention passion explicitly, or at any rate presuppose it as an existing fact. Such passion is especially emphasised in the case of two kinds of sin, namely offences against God (Lev 26:19; 2 Kings 19:28; Amos 6:8) especially through idolatry (Ex 32:1–6; Num 25:1–5; 1 Kings 18:26ff; Wis 14:28), and offences against human rights, especially murder and oppression (Gen 4:8, 23f; Job 24:14; see also Is 1:21; Jer 7:9; Hos 4:2) and sexual vices (Gen 39; 2 Kings 13:1f; Dan 13). Instinctive desires of every kind (see Gen 31:30; Deut 12:20f) were considered as in themselves the starting-point and root of every sin (Num 11:4, 34; Deut 9:22; Ps 106:14). Later the formula 'You shall not covet (lust after)' (see Ex 20:17f) came to be regarded, without further qualification, as a summary of all the prohibitions of the Old Testament (4 Macc 2:6; see also Rom 7:7; 13:9).

In the bible Cain is the type of the impulsive and violent man. His passionate nature is explicitly mentioned (Gen 4:5). It is also manifested in the episode in which he builds a city (4:17), which is reminiscent of the Tower of Babel (11:1–9). Most of all it is manifested in his unscrupulous descendant Lamech (4:19, 23f), whose song of victory is a piece of unbridled boasting over his own sense power, and in which he pretends to outdo the power of God without regard to the value of human life (see Judg 11; 1 Jn 3:12).

Passion which is hostile to God in the Old Testament is called drunkenness (Is 29:9). It seals the eyes (29:10f), stops the ears, and makes the heart fat (Is 6:10) or stony (Ezek 11:19). The Old Testament theology of history, unsystematic in character as it is, often represents the effects of passion as coming directly from God and from his Spirit (Judg 9:23; 1 Sam 19:9), without thereby intending to derogate from the ↗ freedom and responsibility of men (Deut 2:30; Josh 11:20; Is 44:18; Jer 7:22ff; Ezek 2:3–7; cf Ezek 12:2 with Is 6:9f; ↗ hardening of heart). It is only in the eschatological age, when God will blot out all the sins of those who are his own, that the vital emotions of the heart will also be cleansed and purified, but not obliterated (Is 57:14–19; Ezek 11:19).

It is not only in excessive sensuality or in a multiplicity of sins that the passionate nature finds expression. On the contrary it is also the prior condition of, and the quality from which proceed many good actions. This is already apparent in natural love; the special intimacy between father and child (Judg 11:35; 2 Sam 19:1), husband and wife (Gen 29:20, 30; 34:2f; Judg 16:4; 1 Sam 1:8; 2 Sam 3:16; esp Song 8:6f), and between two friends (1 Sam 16:21; 18:1, 3; 20:17; 2 Sam 1:26). Again the love of Old Testament man for his God is unrestricted and vehement (Deut 6:5; 30:6; Jer 4:4) because it is based upon an experience of God as Father (Is 1:4; 30:1, 9; Hos 11:1–4) and bridegroom (Hos 1–3; Jer 12:7–9; Is 54:5–8) of his people (↗ love). This love of Old Testament man looks to the end in which God will write another law once and for all in the hearts of men, namely the law of love, and will thereby instill in them an inalienable instinct for God, a purified passion (Jer 31:33; cf Is 57:14–19; Ezek 11:19). In anticipation of this event the devout are already dominated by a passionate hatred of all that is hostile to God. The examples of Phinehas (Num 25:11, 13f; Sir 45:23; 1 Macc 2:26, 54), of Elijah (1 Kings 19:10, 14; 1 Macc 2:58), of Jehu (2 Kings 10:16) and of Mattathias (1 Macc 2:24, 26f, 50) find their echo in prayers and canticles (Ps 69:10; 119:139; ↗ curse), and the good Israelite models his life upon them.

This passion in man is in emulation of the passion of God. Yahweh's ↗ joy is represented as an exuberant rejoicing (Zeph 3:17), Yahweh's aversion as disgust and loathing (Lev 20:23; Ps 106:40), as hatred and ↗ wrath (Deut 12:31; 29:20; 2 Sam 24:1). Conversely Yahweh's love is depicted as boundless jealousy (Ex 20:5; Deut 5:9), and his disappointment as bitter regret (Gen 6:6; Jon 3:10). This anthropomorphism, in which human passions are ascribed to ↗ God is proof of the fact that Yahweh was thought of as existing and reacting as a personal God, that as a holy God he removes all that is unholy far from him, that as a powerful God he intervenes again and again in the course of events. At the same time such anthropomorphisms are used by the preacher to convey a message of penance to sinners, and an exhortation to those who fear God to seek him with a passionate ardour corresponding to his own. Thus the ↗ Spirit of God becomes effective. He comes upon his own and produces effects of incredible power in them (Ex 31:3; Judg 6:34; 13:25; Is 63:11; Ezek 36:27), even to the point of transports and ecstasies (Num 11:25–9; 1 Sam 11:6, 13; 19:20; Joel 2:28f; etc).

In the Wisdom literature of the Old Testament the exhortation to conduct that is without passion, that is without sin, and to moderation in every department of life (↗ wisdom) acquires special significance (Prov 27:4; Wisdom 4:12; see also Job 5:2f). Not the least of the motives adduced for such an exercise of self-discipline are natural ones (Sir 18:33; 30:24; 40:5–7) and specific examples of self-command are held up for emulation (Sir 44:1) as a major element in this moral teaching. This particular kind of moral teaching is in conformity with a Hellenistic influence which was making itself felt at the period in question, although it was at no time absolutely dependent upon this influence. In it a particularly prominent feature is the emphasis on self-restraint in sexual matters (Wis 7:2; Sir 9:1–9; Job 31:1; Dan 13). It finds its finest expression in the prayer for cleanness of heart and for protection from lust and passion (Sir 22:27; 23:6).

Rabbinical judaism evolved the doctrine of the 'evil impulse' by developing earlier sayings (see Sir 15:14; 21:11; TestJud 20), and on the basis of Gen 6:5; 8:21. This impulse, which God inserts afresh into each man, is the cause, so it is held, of all lustful desires and vices, especially unchastity and idolatry. At the same time it impels men to eat, to beget and to strive for happiness. Without the help of God, that is without prayer and fulfilment of the law, no man can bring this impulse under control. This doctrine has nothing to do with the doctrine of the ↗ sin of the first parents as set forth by the apostle Paul (see J. Schmid, *LTK* II [1958[2]], 618–20). It is rather a systematic 'doctrine of the passions external to the bible itself, which is intended to digest theologically and to render comprehensible the statements of scripture and of experienced men.'

B. *New Testament.* The New Testament recognises passion that is holy, and anger that is just (cf Rev 14:10; 16:19; 18:3; 19:15). Of Jesus it records that he was very sorrowful (Lk 19:41–4; Jn 11:33), that he was greatly distressed (Mk 14:33 and parallels) and was stirred up into a holy zeal for God (Mk 11:15–17 and parallels, esp Jn 2:17). The message of the New Testament demands the greatest zeal from all disciples. A passionate ↗ joy shall come upon them (Mt 13:44), so that in a moment, at a sudden inward prompting (↗ vocation) they can abandon all things without a single backward glance to earthly ties and earthly necessities (Mk 8:34–8 parallels; Lk 9:57–62). Their engagement for the Lord is not tempered by any spirit of calculation and human wisdom (2 Cor 11–12), and is to go far beyond the zeal of the Jews, great as this is (see Rom 10:2; Gal 1:14; Phil 3:6; Acts 21:20; 22:3). To be a christian means to become dedicated body and soul to the service of the Lord (Phil 3:12ff), and to remain utterly and unreservedly true to him (2 Cor 8:11f; 9:2; Gal 4:18; Tit 2:14) even to the point of martyrdom (↗ witness). For christians the service of love requires most of all heartfelt compassion (Lk 10:33, 37).

The judgement as described by Jesus (Mt 25:31–46) shows that impulsive acts of compassion are not of little worth, but on the contrary are highly prized (see 2 Cor 7:8–11). The teaching of the New Testament, on this point is stronger than that of the Old. Every good passion, especially if it takes effect in a manner too powerful to be explained in purely human terms (↗ charism) is an act of the Spirit (1 Cor 12–14; ↗ Spirit).

The formula 'Thou shalt not covet' can be taken as a summary of all the particular commandments (Rom 7:7; 13:9). Passion, therefore, is also the root of all sins. In a certain sphere, that namely of the physical in its unconsecrated and 'fleshly' aspect, it takes disastrous effect. It is in such a sphere of unholiness that men who are still unbaptised and men who are heathens live and act (Rom 1:18–32; Tit 3:3; see also Eph 2:3; 1 Pet 1:14). Again in christians who are tepid and not fully committed, men of 'double mind' (Jas 4:8), the passions live on as evil desires, so that the preaching of the sanctifying word has no effect upon them (Mk 4:19 parallels). Teachers of error in particular are often branded in the New Testament as servants of diabolical passions (Phil 3:18f; 2 Tim 3:2–9; 2 Pet 2:12–22). In this connection two powerful expressions of the Old Testament are taken up and repeated. Such teachers of error are like dogs that turn back to their own vomit, and like swine who wallow in the mire (2 Pet 2:22). In the desire for sexual pleasure, which Paul compares to a firebrand (1 Cor 7:9), proneness to passion is a major factor (Rom 1:24–7; 6:13, 19; Jas 4:3f). But in every other kind of sin (catalogue of vices), and above all in apostasy from God and Jesus Christ (↗ blasphemy, sin) a passionate disposition plays a major part.

In the imagery of the New Testament we are clearly told how disastrous passion can be. In the image of the contest it is depicted as the adversary of God (1 Pet 4:2) who tries to kindle the spirit of rebellion against the Lord in man (1 Cor 3:3; 2 Cor 10:4f; Jas 4:1; 1 Pet 2:11), and deprives him of every joy (Gal 5:16ff) and peace (Rom 7:23; 1 Cor 3:3; see Is 57:20f). By means of the image of slavery passion is unveiled as the dangerous enemy of man and of his freedom (Rom 6:17f). He who does not struggle against her, or who submits to her she binds with chains (1 Cor 6:20; 7:23; Tit 3:3). The men thus in bondage are those whose 'God is the belly' (Rom 16:18; Phil 3:19). A third image represents passion as a murderess (1 Jn 3:15), who hands over her slaves to death (Rom 1:32; 6:23; Phil 3:19; Jas 1:15; cf Lk 8:14).

In Paul the essential holiness of believers is emphasised as the opposite to sinful passion (1 Thess 4:3ff). Corresponding to his teaching on this point we find in the later writings of the New Testament that a special emphasis is laid upon one virtue in particular, namely temperance (↗ discipline). Because of the need to strive against the passions (1 Pet 1:13; 5:8) all are bound to practise this virtue, especially the leaders (1 Tim 3:3; Tit 1:7), both men (Tit 2:2) and women (1 Tim 3:11). This virtue is a gift of God (2 Tim 1:7). With its help man subdues his passions for the things of this world (2 Pet 1:4ff) and becomes fruitful in good works (Jas 1:19ff, 26f).

In many passages what the New Testament has to say on the subject of passion corresponds to what it says on↗ flesh and↗ sin. Passion too, like these, drives man into a veritable sphere of the devil, and makes his life a lie (compare Jas 4:1 with 4:2f). Only through the↗ grace of the Lord, and by resolutely becoming the disciple of Jesus (Jas 4:7ff) can he break out of this sphere. His task in this is to belong to Christ, and to crucify the flesh together with its passions and lusts (Gal 5:24; see also Rom 8:13). 'For all that is in the world, the lust of the flesh and the lust of the eyes and the pride of life, is not of the Father but is of the↗ world. And the world passes away, and the lust of it; but he who does the will of God abides for ever' (1 Jn 2:16f).

Bibliography:↗ Asceticism, Body, Joy, Wrath. Bultmann I, 232–43; A. Stumpff, *TDNT* II, 877–88; G. Stählin, *TDNT* II, 909–26; F. Büchsel, *TDNT* III, 167–72; see also L. Köhler. *Der Hebräische Mensch*, Tübingen 1953, 101–10,

Wilhelm Pesch

Enemy

A. *Terminology*. The Hebrew words *ʾôyêb, tsar, śônêʾ*, mean 'enemy', both in the personal and in the national sense. Frequent references are to be found in the Old Testament, and above all in the Psalms, to the enemy of the religious man. Precisely who is meant by this individual enemy has caused lively controversy among exegetes, and the various suggestions which have been put forward as to who the enemy or enemies may be include a personal adversary, an opponent in a lawsuit, a political opponent, rival religious sects, godless fellow-countrymen who have allowed their religion to lapse, Israelite or foreign oppressors, pagans, the enemies of God, or even sorcerers. The question has still not been finally resolved. The notion of this enemy in any case always has a definitely religious flavour, since the enemy of Israel as well as the enemy of the religious man is regarded as the enemy of God. Both in LXX and in the New Testament the enemy is generally rendered by *ekhthros*. The word *polemios*, which is used in Greek for a national enemy or an opponent in war, appears more frequently in 2 Macc (seventeen times in all). In LXX it appears only thirteen times and it is not used at all in the New Testament.

B. *The Enemy in the Old Testament*. 1. *Hostile people*. Alien races living among the Israelites enjoy the protection of the law under the covenant (Lev 19:34; Deut 10:18f; 23:8; 27:19). But races who have severely oppressed Israel in the course of her history or who have tempted her to worship false gods are considered as enemies. The Israelites not only refuse to have anything to do with them (Deut 23:3–6), but also try to exterminate them (Ex 23:31ff; Num 25:1ff, 16ff; Deut 7:1–5; 20:17f; Ps 137; Wis 11:5–20; 16:1–19, 17; Is 34:1–17; Ezek 35). The prophets threaten the enemies of Israel with destruction (Is 13–21; 23; Jer 46–51; Ezek 25–32; 38f; Amos 1:3–2:3). Both individually and collectively Israelites implore God to show no mercy and to take vengeance on their adversaries (Ps 68:22ff; 83:10–19; 129:5–8; Lam 3:64ff), and those who slay the children of the enemy are blessed (Ps 137:9).

To arrive at any understanding or judgement of this attitude towards heathen nations it is necessary to take into account the outlook, still untempered by christian ethics, of a people struggling for its bare existence in a pitiless environment. The Israelites cherished a particular hatred for their semitic neighbours because they had been perfidiously attacked by them again and again despite their blood-ties with each other (Jer 49; Ezek 25:12; Amos 1:11; Obad 8–14; Ps 137:7ff). As each attack on Israel was an attack on Yahweh, the enemies of Israel came to be regarded as the Lord's enemies (Ex 23:22; Num 10:35; Judg 5:31). God was in honour bound to humiliate his enemies (Josh 7:7ff; Jer 46:10; Zeph 2:8; Zech 1:15; Ps 2:1–9; 74; 79; 83; 1 Macc 4:30–3; 2 Macc 14:35ff; 15:22ff). The enemies of Israel will be made to pay in the same coin for the atrocities they have committed, in accordance with the principles of justice expressed in the *Lex Talionis* (Is 13:16; 14:22; Joel 3:4–8; Nahum 3:10; Ps 137:9).

It must not be forgotten, however, in view of the natural temptation to judge Israel's invective against her enemies too harshly, that the prophets were just as harsh in their condemnation of their own people if they broke the covenant which bound them to the Lord (Is 3–5; Jer 18f; Ezek 9; Amos 2:4–8; 4:1–5:3 and many other instances). This desire for judgement to be passed on the heathen nations is in sharp contrast to the confident expectation of Israel that the pagans too will achieve some share in the salvation promised to Israel (Is 19:22ff; Jer 18:7–10; 48:47; 49:6, 39; Zech 8:23; 14:16). Intercession for pagans is a familiar feature of the Old Testament (Gen 18:20–32; 1 Kings 8:41ff; 2 Chron 6:32f; Jer 29:7). It is possible for those who belong to alien races to be considered worthy enough to participate with Israel in the worship of the true God (Ex 18:7–12), to be accepted as members of God's people (Num 10:29–32; Judith 14:10), and to experience special proofs of God's grace (2 Kings 5).

2. *Personal Enemies.* In the Old Testament, the religious man does not hesitate to give frank expression to his hatred of his personal enemies, and he fully expects Yahweh to humiliate or even to destroy them (Ps 5:10; 6:10; 7:9, 16; 10:15; 28:4; 31:19; 35:4ff; 109; 139:19 etc). He wants his opponents to be judged without mercy (Ps 55:15, 23; 140:9ff), and curses them together with their families (Amos 7:17; Jer 17:18; 18:21ff; Ps 17:13; 109:6–14; ↗ Curse). The religious man's joy over the salvation which he receives from the Lord is all the greater if his enemies are witnesses of his good fortune (Ps 5:8; 23:5; 27, 11–14). He gloats over the downfall of his adversaries (Jer 11:20; Ps 37:34; 54:7; 112:8), and most of all wishes to have personal vengeance on them (Ps 41:10). The wise man, however, does not become too upset about the world's injustice, and his attitude towards his enemies is therefore less passionate. All the same, he deems it advisable not to trust his enemies too far, even if they approach him in a friendly and sociable way (Prov 26:24f; Sir 6:13; 12:8–18).

Man in the Old Testament is like every emotional man of the East, and lets his mood or passion of the moment run away with him. Nevertheless, he is inspired with a perfectly fanatical sense of justice which demands that God himself should be relentless in his punishment of injustice. Whoever does an injustice to a pious man must suffer the same evil himself, in accordance with the principles of the *Lex Talionis*. Personal enemies, too, count as enemies of the Lord. This is because the religious man is under Yahweh's protection (Ps 9:3f; 55:22; 139:21), and because the Lord has sanctioned the regulation of justice (Ps 17:6–12; 40:15; 54:5; 55:22f; 59:5). If God were simply to watch the activities of his enemies without taking any action, he would damage his own prestige and strengthen the wicked in their godless deeds (Ps 10:4, 11; 35:25; 64:6; 94:7). Triumph over the enemy is thus the triumph of justice and right, and rejoicing over the downfall of the enemy is rejoicing over the victory of justice (Ps 35:27; 40:14ff).

This attitude towards enemies shows clearly how imperfect the Old Testament is in comparison with the New. Nevertheless, prayers that the enemies should be punished, and the violent outbursts of emotion directed against both national and personal adversaries, do testify to faithfulness to religion, to the constant war which both the individual and the entire race had to wage in order to keep their faith in Yahweh, and to the unshakable trust they had in his justice.

In spite of this hatred of one's enemy which strikes the christian as so strange, the Old Testament is also familiar with the love of enemies, although this love is generally restricted to those of the same race and religion. Joseph forgives his brethren (Gen 45:5, 15). Moses makes intercession on behalf of his people, even though they oppose him (Num 14:10, 13–19). David spares the life of Saul, who is his deadly enemy (1 Sam 24:10), and the wise man advises against taking revenge on one's enemies (Prov 20:22; 24:29).

In Lev 19:17f, the people of Israel are forbidden to entertain feelings of hatred towards their enemies, and are commanded to admonish their adversaries as brothers. The religious man ought not to rejoice over his enemy's misfortune (Prov 24:17), and his enemy should be helped if he gets into difficulties or is in distress (Ex 23:4f; Prov 25:21f). The man who refuses to let God avenge him, but takes his own revenge, will himself be judged (Sir 28:1).

The religious man, knowing that he is a sinner, has therefore to rely on God's mercy. That is why he forgives his enemies (Sir 28:1–9). Not to have rejoiced over the misfortune of an adversary counts as a great merit and is the sign of great piety (Jer 15:11; Job 31:29f).

C. *The Enemy in the Jewish World at the time of Christ.* There was, of course, no formal commandment in the Jewish world to hate one's enemy. Jesus's saying: 'You have heard that it was said: You shall love your neighbour and hate your enemy' (Mt 5:43f) is thus not to be interpreted as referring to one. All the curses in the Old Testament, and especially those contained in the Psalms, the various rabbinical maxims and the utterances in the Qumran texts which sanction the hatred of one's enemy, are sufficient to account for the existence of this saying of Jesus.

Although, generally speaking, the

rabbis condemn hatred of one's enemies (Ab 2:11; SLev 352a; Lev 19:17), they do frequently permit it, when it is directed against the godless (Taan 7b) and pagans (SLev 19:18) and sometimes even command it (Pes 113b). In the Qumran texts, hatred and vengeance against other members of the community are condemned (1 QS 6:25ff; 7:2–9), though, on the other hand, an inexorable hatred is expressly demanded for the 'Sons of Darkness', by whom are probably meant all outsiders (1 QS 1:4, 10; 8:6f; 9:21f). This does not necessarily mean that the godless are to be attacked by force, but rather that they are to be completely ostracised. The 'Sons of Light' will not wage their merciless war of annihilation on the 'Sons of Darkness' until the eschatological time, the messianic age (1 QM).

In the apocryphal writings, the enemy of the human race is quite simply the devil (ApocMos 2; 7; 25; 28; Life of Adam and Eve 17; Bar (Gr) 13; 2).

D. *The Enemy in the New Testament.* Christ's message removes the differences between compatriots and aliens. The disciples of Jesus regard a Samaritan who is, for the Jews, a deadly enemy, as a 'neighbour' (Lk 10:29–37). The only real enemy is the devil, who sows cockle among the wheat in God's field (Mt 13:25ff). The disciples will, however, triumph over him (Lk 10:19). Paul sees death as the enemy which will be conquered by Christ (1 Cor 15:26).

It is, however, true to say that human enemies can be found in the New Testament. These include in particular those who, as allies and instruments of the devil, lie in wait for God's people (Lk 1:71, 74) and his witnesses (Rev 11:5, 12). In this sense even the members of his own family may become the religious man's enemies, if they try to tempt him, as Jesus' disciple, to betray his master or to lose faith in his gospel (Mt 10:36). The man who opposes God or his anointed Son is an enemy of the kingdom of God (Lk 19:27; Acts 13:10; Phil 3:18). But even the man who merely thinks and acts in accordance with the natural law and is continually coming into conflict with God's will is an enemy as well (Rom 5:10; 8:7; 11:28; Col 1:21; Jas 4:4). Jesus too is drastic in his attitude towards his opponents and calls them a brood of vipers (Mt 12:34; 23:33) and sons of the devil (Jn 8:44).

On the other hand, Jesus does realise that his opponents are men who are in need of his mercy and forgives from the cross even those who have condemned him to death (Lk 23:34), in this way making the love of one's enemies a law for christians, not only by his example, but also by means of his explicit commandment (Mt 5:43ff; Mk 11:25; Lk 6:27ff, 35f). His disciples accept this law and follow it in their lives. Stephen, for example, forgives his executioners just as his master forgave his (Acts 7:58ff). The disciples look upon the love of one's enemies as the mark which distinguishes the christian from his heathen counterpart. The christian goes contrary to the custom of the heathen by doing good to those who hate him and by extending his love even to his enemies (1 Thess 5:15; 1 Pet 3:9). He blesses those who persecute him (1 Cor 4:12), and leaves retribution in God's hands (Rom 12:19ff). Because he knows that he is in need of God's pardon, he himself forgives his adversaries (Mt 6:14; 18:13; see also Rom 5:10; Col 1:21f).

Bibliography: J. Nikel, *Das AT und die Nächstenliebe*, Münster 1913; P. Jedzink, *Das Gebot der Nächstenliebe im Evangelium*, Braunsberg 1916; S. Mowinckel, *Psalmenstudien* I, Kristiania 1921; H. Schmidt, *Das Gebet des Angeklagten*, Giessen 1928; W. Foerster, *TDNT* II, 811–16; A. F. Puukko, 'Der Feind in den Psalmen', *OTS* 8 (1950), 47–65; F. Mussner, 'Der Begriff des Nächsten in der Verkündigung Jesu', *TTZ* 64 (1955), 91–9; H. Birkeland, *The Evildoers in the Book of Psalms*, Oslo 1955; J. Ridderbos, *De Psalmen* I, Kampen 1955, 382–408; G. Castellino, *Libro dei Salmi*, Turin 1955, 254–63; J. Gewiess, *LTK* IV², 60–61; B. S. Childe, 'The Enemy from the North and the Chaos Tradition', *JBL* 78 (1959), 187–98; H.-J. Kraus, *Psalmen*, Neukirchen 1960, 40–3; SB I, 353–68.

Josef Scharbert

Epiphany

Apparition (= *epiphaneia*) is a central theme of biblical theology showing only occasional external points of contact with analogous pagan ideas. By this term we understand the intrusion of God into the world which is brought about unexpectedly before men's eyes, either with or without a specific form, which can be of a familiar or mysterious character, and which is withdrawn just as quickly. From the point of view of terminology, we read in the Old Testament of a *theophany*, in the New Testament of an *epiphany*. While there exist in pagan religions what we might call indirect 'epiphanies' by means of which the deity provides proof of its existence through deeds of power, there is in biblical theology a sharp distinction between apparition and miracle. Such apparitions take place, basically, only at crucial points of human history. There are really, therefore, no private revelations since the apparitions granted to individuals are in view of the community as a whole (Gen 18:1ff; Is 6:1ff; Jn 20:11ff; 1 Cor 15:5ff).

We can trace them right back to the beginning of creation insofar as both inanimate and animate nature as well as man himself owe their existence to the apparition of God (Gen 1:1ff), though this belongs to the period of prehistory and can be grasped only in a speculative way. Within the historical period, we have to take account of the various vocation-narratives (of Moses [Ex 3]; of prophets [Is 6:1ff; Ezek 1:1ff]; of Peter near the Sea of Galilee [Jn 21:15ff]; the divine promises of posterity [Gen 18:1ff; Judg 13:3ff]; of a covenant [Gen 17:1ff]; of land [Gen 28:10ff]; of salvation [1 Kings 19:10ff]; the accompanying presence of God in the pillar of cloud and of fire during the wanderings of the Israelites [Ex 13:21f; 40:34ff], sometimes visible appearances during the occupation of the land, at the setting up of an altar [Gen 12:7ff], or the destruction of an enemy city [Josh 5:13ff]; etc). In the Old Testament the climax comes with the occurrence on Mount Sinai with thunder and lightning and other extraordinary phenomena (Ex 19:18ff), an event which lays the foundations of the human order and which, as is stressed throughout the whole of revelation, is unique. In the New Testament the apparitions of Christ are central. They are prepared for by the apparition of angels (Lk 1:11ff; 1:28ff; 2:9ff) which sometimes have the purpose of attesting to an appearance of Jesus (Mt 28:2;

Mk 16:5; Lk 24:4ff; Jn 20:12). In this connection we might mention the occasions when the apostles were miraculously set free from prison (Acts 5:19; 12:7). The theophanies, which are extremely reserved in character, serve the purpose of the divine proclamation of Jesus' messianic status (Mk 9:4). The tongues of fire at Pentecost are described as sent by the Lord (Jn 16:7).

As historical events, these apparitions have a fixed time and place (Ex 19:18ff; Is 6:1; Mk 16:2; Lk 24:1; Jn 20:1). Hence they can never be repeated in the same way—they are unique and isolated events, and there is a complete absence of apparition motifs. There are, at the same time, certain places which are favoured for revelations—mountains (Ex 3; 19:18ff; Mk 9:2); lakes (Mk 6:48); the Ark of the Covenant (Ex 40:34)—these are considered as particularly apt on account of the natural advantages they offer—in particular, solitude.

The apparition, considered in itself, is a complex phenomenon. It is perceptible to the senses, in particular to the eyes and the hearing—assisted in some cases even by the sense of touch (Gen 32:24; Jn 20:27). In the Old Testament the accent is on hearing while in the New Testament sight or vision plays an equally important part, especially in proving the reality of the resurrection. Since the word of God is the essential element, there can be no silent apparitions; it follows that the bearer of the word occupies the centre, and that though he may be hidden it is always a question of a person. His voice can also be heard—from out of the burning thorn bush (Ex 3), in the sighing of the wind (1 Kings 19:13), and in the cloud (Mk 9:7). Every apparition is, therefore, first and foremost an announcement. The divine pronouncements in the Old Testament are promises, in the New Testament they are decisive witnesses of the resurrection, and provide at the same time guidance for the further progress of the kingdom of God, in particular through the confirmation of the office of 'shepherd' (Jn 21:15ff), and the command to baptise and evangelise (Mt 28:16ff).

Thus the biblical apparitions are at the service of the history of salvation and therefore eschatological, unlike their pagan counterparts which serve a momentary purpose only. One can detect already in the historical apparitions characteristics which point to the final goal (Ex 3)—something which comes through even more strongly in the eschatological and prophetic apparition of the day of Yahweh (Amos 5:18; Is 40:3ff), and shines out briefly in the Transfiguration (Mk 9:4ff), reaching its full development in the ↗ parousia. One result of this is that in the pastoral epistles the word *epiphaneia* is used to stand for the second coming of Christ (1 Tim 6:14; 2 Tim 4:1, 8; Tit 2:13). Satanic apparitions (Rev 6; 12:3; 13:1, 11; 2 Thess 2:9) are crude imitations of the parousia of Christ and have the purpose of deceiving the faithful.

Considered as an announcement, the apparition is always addressed to a particular person who has to keep a respectful distance from the holy one who comes to him (delimitation of a place, Ex 19:21; 34:3; of a person, Jn 20:17; taking off one's shoes, Ex 3:5; covering one's face, Ex 3:6;

33:22; 1 Kings 19:13), or to whom God manifests himself but in a hidden way. Smoke, a cloud, also the 'angel of the Lord' (Gen 16:7; 31:11; Judg 6:11; 13:3; accompanied by two others, Gen 18:1ff) and the human form of Christ conceal the true divine being, which, as ↗ glory, will shine forth in its visible splendour only at the end of the world (Is 60:1ff; 62:1f etc; Mk 13:26; Lk 17:24), while in the meantime it is only occasionally discernible (Ex 33:22; Mk 9:3; Acts 9:3). In this connection, angels often appear as messengers of light (Lk 2:9; Acts 12:7), also expressed by their wearing white garments (Lk 9:29; Jn 20:12).

Many obscure points occurring in individual apparition-accounts can be explained by the attempt to conceal the real identity of the person in the apparition (Gen 32:24; Mk 9:2), or as comparisons used as a stylistic procedure (Ezek 1:26; Mt 17:2). This also explains why there were no witnesses present at the ↗ resurrection. The human reaction to the apparition can take different forms. The person concerned can be completely overcome when God lays his hand on him (Is 8:11; Jer 20:7) or, like Paul, be cast to the ground. He can be seized by fear (Gen 28:17; Is 6:4; Mk 6:50; 9:6; Lk 2:9), which explains the frequently used phrase: 'Fear not!' (Mt 28:10; Mk 6:50; Lk 24:38; Jn 6:20). When he is unable to pierce the surrounding obscurity he can be restless and uncertain (Gen 18:12; Jn 20:15), though, on the other hand, once he has understood the profound significance of the experience he can enter fully into it (Gen 32:29f; Mk 9:6f).

In its character of revelation—and to this category the 'It is I' sayings also belong (Mk 6:50; Jn 6:20)—the apparition compels man to a decision and gives him the choice between doubt and faith, refusal or acknowledgement (Jn 20:24ff). It is never just for its own sake, but is an appeal which requires an answer which must show itself in action. The function of the ↗ apostle is, like the mission of the prophets (Is 61:1), intimately bound up with apparition. Thus, only a witness of the resurrection can be chosen to take the place of Judas (Acts 1:22), and Paul explicitly appeals to what happened on the road to Damascus in self-authentication (1 Cor 15:8). In consequence of the close link existing between the members and the head which is Christ, the New Testament apparition has a social character as reflecting the inner and absolute *epiphaneia* of Father, Son, and Holy Spirit (Jn 12:44). That is why apparitions to individuals are less prominent (1 Cor 15:5ff). So Thomas had to learn that the Lord would come to him, not when he was by himself, but only in the company of the brethren (Jn 20:24ff), and it is precisely when they are at table that he allows himself to be recognised (Lk 24:30–41ff; Jn 21:12).

The deepest significance of every apparition is, however, the imparting of salvation in peace and joy (Gen 32:29; Jn 20:19f). This is denied to the unbeliever only if he positively conjures up for himself condemnation and judgement which stand at the opposite pole (Is 2:10ff; 4:4ff; 30:27ff; 2 Thess 1:8); he is then given to see not light but the fire which destroys. He cannot hope to enjoy the final apparition so graphically described in the apocalyptic books (Enoch; Testament of the Twelve Apostles).

The theology of John takes up a special position in this regard, insofar as it views the whole earthly life of the Lord in one broad sweep as *theophaneia* and praises God for it, in hymn form, in the prologue to the gospel (Jn 1:1–18) and in 1 Jn 1:1ff, since from its surrounding mystery the ↗ glory shines forth continually. No certain trace has yet been discovered of a cultic *epiphaneia*, such as some scholars believe they can detect in the Psalms and even in certain texts of the New Testament.

We have to consider this question not just from the religious but also from the *literary* angle. In Ps 29 Ugaritic representations go to make up the outward form only which, however, has been filled with a new substance, since Baal-Hadad, the storm-god as manifested in the elements, is used as a symbol for the showing forth of Yahweh's holiness. In the historical and prophetic books of the Old Testament, the sections in the first person manifest more strongly-emphasised individual characteristics than those in the third person. In the New Testament, Matthew is sober and logical (Mt 17:2), in contrast with the greater originality of Mark, while Luke, bearing in mind the needs of his hellenistic-christian readers, gives prominence to the description of apparitions (Lk 3:21ff; Acts 5:19; 12:7). In Paul the ↗ parousia, the bright rays of which already reach the earth occupies the central position. In the Letter to the Hebrews, there takes place a strong spiritualisation which sees in Sinai and Sion a powerful revelation by word of mouth constituting a divine proclamation. The Apocrypha contain numerous cases of the expansion of the biblical narrative in the form of apparitions (*Protoevangelium Jacobi* 18/20).

The oldest artistic representations of biblical apparitions are to be found in the Museum of Antiquities at Brescia, on the pilgrim bottles of Monza and Bobbio, and in the mosaics at San Vitale and Sant' Apollinare Nuovo in Ravenna. The apparitions of the Risen Christ have been treated by Rembrandt among others.

Bibliography: O. Casel, 'Die Epiphanie im Lichte der Religionsgeschichte', *Benedikt. Monatsschrift* 4 (1922), 13–20; R. Guardini, *Jesus Christus: Das Christusbild in den johanneischen Schriften*, Würzburg 1940; W. Michaelis, *Die Erscheinungen des Auferstandenen*, Basle 1946; C. Mohrmann, *Epiphaneia*, Nijmegen 1953; E. Pax, *Epiphaneia: Ein religionsgeschichtlicher Beitrag zur biblischen Theologie*, Munich 1955; Stauffer 298 *n.* 709; C. Westermann, *Das Leben Gottes in den Psalmen*, Göttingen 1961; H.-P. Müller, 'Die kultische Darstellung der Theophanie', *VT* 14 (1954), 183–91.

Elpidius Pax

Eucharist

A. *Sources*. Three different kinds of text referring to the eucharist are to be found in the New Testament. 1. *Accounts of the institution of the eucharist:* Mt 26:26–9; Mk 14:22–5; Lk 22:15–20; 1 Cor 11:23–5. Luke's account has been handed down in several different forms, but these can be traced back to two original sources—the shorter text of the gospel (15–19a, without 19b–20 in the 'Western' text), and the longer text (15–20), which is generally regarded by present-day scholars as the authentic version, though opinions differ with regard to how it originated. It is possible to look upon Lk 22:15–18 as the fragment of an old account of the feast of the Passover in which the paschal lamb is replaced by the eucharistic offering, as represented by the chalice (this is well brought out in *MTZ* 4 [1953] 223–31). (See H. Schürmann.) The two types which underlie these four accounts are those of Matthew/Mark—that is, Matthew's work of editing, based on Mark's account—and Luke/Paul. It is not that Luke's account depends on 1 Cor, but that both go back to a common tradition. Mark, on the other hand, represents a different line of tradition. The Luke/Paul tradition can be regarded as older than that of Mark's version (H. Schürmann, as against J. Jeremias). Certain features of Luke's version do seem to show that it is closer to the original tradition than Paul's (H. Schürmann, as against J. Betz and others).

These accounts of the institution of the eucharist have been handed down as the standard forms for its celebration in the early christian communities, and their character was to a great extent determined by the current form of worship of the community. (This character bears an imprint which is unchangeable; the liturgical acclamation 'for you' shows a tendency towards parallelism). These accounts are also incomplete—the event taking on a timeless quality in the liturgy. They are concerned first and foremost, not with providing a historical report on what occurred at the last supper, but with setting out the celebration of the eucharist on a basis of Christ's own actions. This is why the words of consecration, as pronounced by Jesus, have not been handed down verbatim, but have been allowed to evolve quite legitimately—without undergoing any essential change or alteration in their meaning.

Paul classes the various accounts of the institution of the eucharist as *paradosis* ('For I received from the Lord what I also delivered to you', 1 Cor 11:23; the rabbis used this term to denote the reception or the passing on of a tradition: see 1 Cor 15:1–3). At the beginning of this chain of tradition is the 'Lord', the historical Jesus, who, having been exalted to the right hand of the Father, directs the life of his church and stands behind the Apostles, who pass on this tradition. The language of the pauline account of the institution of the eucharist is quite uncharacteristic of the writer, and this does tend to confirm the view that the account is 'recitative' and thus traditional. Paul's understanding of the eucharist is thus not due to a revelation which was received direct from God. The form of the words of consecration, which Paul passed on to the Corinthians in the year 49 or 50 AD, was probably received by him in Antioch, round about 40 AD. Whenever he visited Jerusalem, he must have had the opportunity to compare his preaching on the subject of the Eucharist with that of St Peter (Gal 1:18; Acts 9:27; 11:30; Acts 15; Gal 2:1–10). The Semitic influence perceptible in all the accounts of the institution of the eucharist and the peculiar form, found in the Paul/Luke version, of the words spoken over the chalice—due to the fact that the taking of blood was particularly offensive to the Jews—refer to the primitive christian communities as far back as approximately AD 30. These words of consecration contain the 'primeval rock of tradition' (J. Jeremias). As a result of the kerygma of the first apostles, Christ's message is not to be found in its exact form in the various accounts of the institution of the eucharist, but rather in a fragmentary form according to the particular view of each apostle. These, as 'witnesses', passed on the words of Jesus in accordance with their sense and meaning and not with word-for-word accuracy. Any attempt to go behind the words of consecration as they have been handed down to us, and to arrive at the original form which Jesus himself used when he spoke them, can only be in the nature of a reconstruction and can never be based on verifiable historical knowledge. Jesus certainly never merely said: 'This is my body', and: 'This is my blood' (despite what is contained in Justin, *Apol.*, 1, 66, which, contrary to the opinion of R. Bultmann, only hints at this). Jesus undoubtedly gave a much closer interpretation of his gift of the eucharist and of his death (cf the interpretation of the elements in the ritual of the Passover). Thus he would at least have said: 'This is my body (*den bisri*: see J. Bonsirven, *Règne de Dieu*, Paris 1957, *n* 60) which is given for you' (see Mk 10:45; Is 53:12). He must have related the blood to the covenant, for by his death the new people of God were granted a new relationship with regard to the covenant. This may be compared with the eschatological expectation connected with the meals of the Qumran sects (*BZ* and ↗ Mediator).

2. *The promise of the eucharist.* There is no actual account of the institution of the eucharist in John's gospel, although the washing of the disciples' feet (Jn 13:1–17: see *GL* 31 [1958], 25–30) and the 'priestly prayer' of Jesus (Jn 17), neither of which can be said to refer primarily to the eucharist, are in a sense interpretations of Christ's death. Instead, there is a 'lesson on the eucharist' (the 'catechèse eucharistique' of J. Bonsirven, 175). This is composed of material which was handed down and thus already formed before it reached John, but which was arranged and adapted by him. It includes the account of the miraculous feeding of the five thousand and Jesus's walking on the sea (6:1–24). It also includes the discourse on the bread of life (6:25–59), in which two distinct parts stand out in sharp contrast—the sermon on the bread of life as a gift of the Father to men which is received through faith (25–51a), and the sermon on the bread of life as the gift of Jesus himself which will be bestowed only at some future time and will then be taken as food and drink (51b–58). Finally, it includes a repetition of this sermon addressed to the disciples alone (60–71). The individual parts of this lesson on the eucharist are held together by the common theme. Verses 51b–58 are generally understood nowadays of the eucharist, since 'the entire eucharistic terminology' can be found in them (see recently G. Bornkamm, 'Die eucharistische Rede im Johannes-Evangelium', *ZNW* 47 [1956], 161–9). These verses are not the outcome of 'ecclesiastical redaction' and interpolation (contrary to R. Bultmann and G. Bornkamm) since their stylistic quality shows clearly that John composed them on the basis of tradition and adapted them to fit into the gospel

(E. Ruckstuhl, *Die Literarische Einheit des Johannes-Evangelium*, 1951; J. Jeremias, 'Jn 6:51c–58 redaktionell?', *ZNW* 44 [1952/3], 256f). It can be taken as certain that the words about the eucharist were not spoken at the same time as the discourse on the bread of life (27–51a), contrary to the view of E. Ruckstuhl, but were first spoken only at a later period, after Christ had revealed himself as the suffering Messiah (Mk 8:31ff; see also Jn 6:51). This is also the view of M. J. Lagrange. It is quite likely that this is a case of a Johannine *midrash* based on an account of the institution of the eucharist (H. Schürmann, *LTK* III², 1162).

3. *The early christian sacred meal.* Luke uses the expression 'the breaking of bread' (Acts 2:42) or 'breaking bread' (Acts 2:46; 20:7, 11) when, basing himself on early Palestinian sources and his own personal experience (the 'we-sections'), he refers to the communal meals of the early church. This term *the breaking of bread* signifies, in Jewish circles, the rite which inaugurates the meal—the blessing, breaking, and distribution of the bread—and it was regarded as a sacred action (Mk 8:19; though it is questionable whether Lk 24:35 can be viewed in this light: E. von Severus, *RAC*², 620–26). Luke never uses the phrase *share in a meal* (J. Jeremias, *The Eucharistic Words of Jesus*, London 1966). The view is widely held by present-day scholars (eg, E. Haenchen, *Die Apostelgeschichte*, Göttingen 1956, 523ff; Behm, *TDNT* III, 730) that Acts 20:7, 11 refers to the celebration of the 'Lord's Supper' within the context of Paul's mission. The passage in Acts 2:42–6 is clearly meant to refer to the eucharist, since a distinction is made between the 'breaking of bread' and 'taking food'. 'Breaking bread' is, for Luke, a designation for the celebration of the eucharist, and it was, without any doubt, established as such at the beginning of the second century (*Didache* 9, 3f; Ignatius *ad Ephes.* 20:2; *Philad.* 4). Jesus performed the rite of the breaking of bread at the last supper with an unprecedented sense of purpose, as is borne out by his accompanying words of explanation. This new and deeper content is probably the reason for naming this new institution which was set up by Jesus the 'breaking of bread'. The Jewish usage in this christian context was 'narrowed down and made to refer specifically to the eucharistic breaking of bread' (*Bbl* 32 [1951], 526).

In 1 Cor 11:23–33; 10:1–13, 14–22 we find certain and abundant reference to the eucharist. The passage in Heb 13:9f may well be taken to refer to the eucharistic meal, although it is obscure (F. J. Schierse, *Verheissung und Heilsvollendung*, Munich 1955, 184–95). It has been suggested, though without foundation, that 1 Cor 12:13; 1 Pet 2:3; Rev 3:20; Jn 15:1 are closely related, in their subject-matter, to the eucharist.

B. *Setting.* In order to arrive at a true understanding of the eucharist, it is of some importance to consider in what kind of setting it was celebrated.

1. *The setting of the accounts of the institution.* Jesus instituted the eucharist at a festive farewell meal. That this had the character of a feast (see *SB* IV, 611–39) is shown by the fact that it was held in an upper room in Jerusalem Mk 14:15; Lk 22:12), that those present reclined at table according to

the hellenistic custom (Mk 14:18; Jn 13:23, 25), and that wine was used (Mk 14:23ff; Lk 22:17f). That it was also a farewell feast is borne out by the words of farewell (Lk 22:16, 18), the 'testament' of Jesus (Lk 22:28ff) and the parting gift which took the form of the 'institution' of the sacrament, which was bequeathed to the disciples (Lk 22:19; 1 Cor 11:24f).

No complete agreement exists as to whether this festive meal was in fact held on the ritual feast of the Passover (Mk 14:12–17; Lk 22:15 are in support of this; in Jn 18:28; 19:14—see also 19:35—it would appear to have taken place on the day preceding the official feast of the Passover). In the synoptics and in John there can be found numerous unintentional pointers to the fact that this festive meal bore the stamp of the Jewish Passover. In particular the interpretation of the elements of the meal, as expressed by Jesus over the bread and wine, was a stable element, referring to the part played by the head of the family in the Passover celebration (J. Jeremias, *TDNT* v, 896f). Even if Jesus did not celebrate a paschal meal, 'he must certainly have been considerably influenced by the idea of the Passover' (H. Schürmann, *LTK* I^2, 27f).

The eucharist was instituted within the setting of the paschal meal (for this rite see, for example, *RNT* 2, 260ff; A. Stöger, *Brot*, 103–6). The main part of the feast began with the blessing, breaking, and distribution of the soft, round, flat cake of unleavened bread. This was followed by the eating of the paschal lamb, and the feast concluded with what was, in effect, grace after meals, when the father of the family pronounced the prayer of thanksgiving over the cup. Jesus, then, made use of the bread at the beginning of the paschal feast and the wine at the end for the Eucharistic gift (hence the phrase 'after supper' Lk 22:20; 1 Cor 11:25). In the Mark/Matthew version, the two actions of the Eucharist, which are divided in Luke/Paul, are joined together and form a single unity ('while they were at supper' or 'while they were eating'). The celebration of the Eucharist is, as it were, freed from its bond with the Passover in the case of these two evangelists. In Luke's version, the Eucharist is regarded as the new paschal feast (Lk 22:15). Christ is the paschal lamb who has been slain for sacrifice (1 Cor 5:7). According to John's version, Jesus is 'slain' in the same way as the paschal lambs were slain, in the temple sacrifice, and no bone of his body was broken (19:36). This comparison between Jesus and the paschal lamb, which was current in the early church (1 Pet 1:19; Rev 5:6; etc), can indeed be traced directly back to our Lord (J. Jeremias, *TDNT* v, 899). Since 'body-blood' and 'pouring out' are part of sacrificial terminology, Jesus certainly referred to himself as the paschal lamb in the words of institution. The paschal meal was a sacrificial meal (see Deut 16:1–8; Mk 14:12; Lk 22:7). The ancient blood-rite (see Ex 12:7, 22–7), after the reforms which took place in the year 621 BC, under Josias, in the celebration of public worship consisted in the sprinkling of the blood on the altar of sacrifice where the victim was burnt (2 Chron 35:11; Jub 49:20; Pes 5:6). This blood-rite had the character of an atonement. In addition, the sacrificial paschal meal was an act of commemoration which brought both the past and the eschatological future vividly to mind. It was also a communal meal, shared by God's people, which had an exclusive character (Ex 12:43–9) and was binding on all Israelites (Ex 12:6, 43ff; Num 9:10–13). The entire people—in Christ's time no less than ten persons had to be present—was bound to celebrate the meal at the same hour in the square of the temple. From the first century before Christ onwards, the celebration took place within the walls of the temple in Jerusalem.

2. *The setting of the 'breaking of bread'.* It is probable that a picture of the celebration of public worship among the early christians is outlined in Acts 2:42. The faithful listened to the teaching of the apostles, brought their offerings (for the 'poor': see Rom 15:26; Phil 1:5), held a communal feast (the breaking of bread), and said communal prayers together. According to Acts 2:46, Christians continued to take part in the worship in the temple and celebrated the breaking of bread in the houses of their fellow-christians. There they took meals in common and praised God 'with gladness and simplicity of heart'. Although the celebration of the eucharist had been freed from its connection with the paschal feast, it was still associated closely with a meal which was imbued with the joyful hope of the return of the Lord, for he was held to be actually present (1 Cor 16:22: *Maranatha*—'Come, Lord' or 'The Lord is nigh'; see *TDNT* IV, 470f). In Troas, the breaking of bread took place within the setting of the Lord's Supper as celebrated by the Pauline communities. The christian community assembled in the evening of the 'first day of every week' (1 Cor 16:2; Jn 20:19; Rev 1:10; *TDNT* III, 1096, 27f), Paul gave a discourse, broke the bread and ate some of it, not alone, of course, but with the others who were present. The celebration of the eucharist and the delivery of a sermon were inseparable. The place where the community assembled was an upper room, lit by many lamps. (Was this reference to lighting intended to allude to the suspicion that christian religious feasts lent themselves to lewdness?—see Minutius Felix, *Oct.*, 9; Tert., *Apol.*, 8f; E. Haenchen, *Apostelgeschichte*, 524.)

3. *The setting of the Pauline 'Lord's Supper' in Corinth* (1 Cor 11:17–34). The sacramental meal took place as part of a feast at which the participants satisfied their hunger, and Paul was constrained to reproach them on account of abusing this. His censure was not directed against the establishment of these meals as such, in imitation of the Jewish or pagan sacred meals (contrary to the opinion of L. Thomas, *DB*[*s*] I, 145–50 and J. Coppens, *DB*[*s*] II, 1174), since the celebration was already linked to the taking of a meal, but against the lack of fraternal charity which was apparent at such festive meals. This meal, which was later to become an *agapē* (Clem. Al, *Paed.* 2, 1, 4; Tert, *Apol.* 39; etc), was followed by the sacramental meal (1 Cor 11, 27, 34). This account of the setting of the celebration of the eucharist does serve to show that the eucharistic act was regarded as the essential part and was a sacred institution, and, although its setting varied, its essentials remained constant.

C. *Interpretation of the meaning of the eucharist.* 1. *According to the accounts of the institution of the sacrament.* A certain obscurity is bound to persist concerning the implication of the eucharist, as expressed in Jesus' own words, because of the difficulties of reconstructing, with complete accuracy, the original form of the words of consecration, and the fact that a certain amount of revision or consequent touching up must be taken into consideration.

The extant texts go to show that these revisions do not represent any fresh addition, but a development of what is already known from other utterances of Christ himself. The words of consecration constitute a simple and direct pronouncement of salvation.

a. *The meal* which Jesus gives for his own is both a farewell supper (Lk 22:15; 1 Cor 11:23; see also Jn 13:1) and a new paschal meal (Lk 22:15). It anticipates the eschatological meal: that is to say, it looks forward to the feast which will take place in the kingdom of God (Lk 22:16; Mk 14:25; 1 Cor 11:26; see also Lk 22:30).

b. *The presence of Jesus.* Jesus interprets the gifts which he offers. That which is offered (the subject) is identical with his body (the predicate) or blood. (It should be noted that the copula *is* linking subject and predicate is not expressed in Aramaic; that *cup* is a figure of speech by which the contents are represented by the container; and that *covenant* represents the cause by its effect.) It is not the act or actions of the offering, but the gifts themselves, which Jesus interprets, just as the father of the Jewish family interpreted the gifts in the paschal Haggadah. These gifts are not, however, interpreted by Jesus' words merely as symbols, for there is an essential difference between the way in which Jesus interprets the gifts and the way in which this is expressed in the Haggadah. Jesus says, in the case of the bread: 'This is my body', whereas in the Haggadah the words are: 'See the bread of sorrow which our fathers ate when they left the land of Egypt'. Whichever solution to the problem of the originality of either the Luke/Paul or the Matthew/Mark version is accepted (J. Betz, 26–35), the words spoken over the chalice are expressed in discreet and highly individual form which without doubt takes into consideration the Jewish—and pagan—aversion to the taking of blood (Gen 9:3f; Lev 17:10–14; Acts 15:29). The original form of the offering and the emphatic description which accompanies it, as an invitation to eat and drink (Lk 22:17; Mt 26:26; Mk 14:22; Mt 26:27) all serve to stress the unprecedented nature of Christ's gift. It is evident that, in leaving behind a parting gift which is in close harmony with the whole of his mission, Jesus is bound to leave *himself* behind, as the revelation of both the Old and the New Testaments is not a revelation by word alone, but also by deed. All these observations demand a realistic understanding of the words of consecration. They do not simply express a likeness, though a comparison can certainly be drawn between the broken wafer of bread and Jesus' body, the red juice of the grape and his shed blood, and so on. The words are also not just a 'pledge of a spiritual presence' (Behm), nor do they merely imply an activity on the part of Christ within his own community. They are, contrary to the opinion of E. Schweizer, the handing over of a substance. The food and drink which Jesus offers are his 'body' (flesh) and 'blood'. The 'flesh' (body) is the living person of Christ in accordance with his bodily existence. The ↗ blood, as the vehicle of life (Lev 17:11, 14; Deut 12:23), thus denotes the living person of Christ in such a way that attention is drawn first and foremost to the blood. In his body and blood, then, Jesus himself is offered. He presents himself as a gift for salvation (the offering of the chalice is an effective benediction: SB IV, 60). A new depth is thus given to the fellowship at the feast which Jesus keeps with his disciples and which he only succeeds in uniting in a true bond by means of the celebration of the paschal meal, when he offers himself to this company as a saving gift.

c. *Memorial of Christ's death.* In the Luke/Paul version the words: 'which is given [shall be delivered] for you', are added to the words of consecration of the bread. In the Matthew/Mark version, the consecration of the wine contains the phrase: 'which shall be shed for many', and to this Matthew adds, by way of elucidation: 'unto remission of sins' (see Mt 1:21).

All these additions interpret Christ's body and blood in accordance with Is 53:12. Jesus himself represented his death as the propitiatory death of the servant of God (*TDNT* v, 709–13). His is a martyr's death and as such has a propitiatory value. The atonement benefits 'many', which means 'everyone' (*TDNT* VI, 542: the words *for you* do not set a limit to the application, but extend it). Christ's death serves to atone for the world and as such is in a vicarious sense a propitiatory death. His body is 'given' (or 'delivered') and his blood 'poured out' or 'shed'. The logical subject of these passive forms is, in the first place, God (Is 53:6, 10) and in the second, Jesus (Is 53:10b–12). Jesus was destined by God to atone for mankind in suffering and death (Phil 2:8), and he offered himself for this act (Is 53:7, 10). The phrase 'to shed blood' is applied particularly to martyrs (1 Macc 1:37; 7:17), but it also forms part of the accepted language of sacrifice (Ex 29:12; Lev 4:7, 18, 25; etc). In Is 53 too there is a suggestion of the idea of sacrifice (vv 7, 10). It is likely that the words 'flesh' and 'blood' are intended to designate Christ's body and blood as the sacrificial material. 'The life of the flesh is in the blood; and I have given it for you upon the altar to make atonement for your souls' (Lev 17:11). Christ offers himself as a sacrifice of atonement. It is possible that the participle also denotes an action taking place, relatively speaking, in the future (Blass and Debrunner, *Grammatik des neutestamentlichen Griechisch*, Göttingen [1913], 195), but what is more probable is that it has a timeless quality—that is to say, that Christ's blood is sacrificial blood.

d. *The renewal of the covenant.* The words spoken over the chalice refer to the 'covenant' in the Matthew/Mark version and to the 'new covenant' in the Luke/Paul version. The servant of God is the mediator of this covenant (Is 42:6). The Luke/Paul version refers to Jer 31:31–4 (see also Is 54:10; 55:3; 61:8; Ezek 16:60–3; 34:25; 37:21–8). This eschatological promise is, by virtue of the sacrifice of Christ's blood, offered and actually present as a saving possession. The form of the words spoken over the chalice in the Matthew/Mark version are in accordance with the conclusion of the covenant on Mount Sinai (Ex 24:8), while the eucharistic meal is the fulfilment of the meal of the covenant (Ex 24:11). Christ not only announces the eschatological era of salvation, he also inaugurates it, and the kingdom of God is not merely proclaimed by him as a state which is imminent, but is actually inaugurated by his presence and his activity. For this reason it is easy to understand why he does not simply refer to an eschatological meal, but actually anticipates this meal. The contemporary existence of a 'community of the new covenant' (see Qumran and the Damascus Document) helps us to understand this hope and fulfilment. The Eucharistic meal, at the centre of which is Christ himself, contains the fulfilment of all the Old Testament expectations and the dawn of the eschatological hope.

e. *The charge to perpetuate the eucharist.* Both Luke and Paul add, to the words of consecration, the charge: 'Do this for a commemoration of me'. In the case of Luke, these words follow the consecration of the bread. In 1 Cor 11:24, 25, they follow the consecration both of the bread and of the wine. To the latter are also added the words: 'as often as you shall drink'. The Matthew/Mark version does not include this charge, which clearly follows the normal tendency of the traditional Jewish feast, or annual commemoration, especially that of the Passover. It is not in the line of the hellenistic commemoration of death, since Jesus was not regarded as dead by the early church, but as her eternally living *Kyrios*. There is no period in the existence of the church at which this charge to perpetuate the eucharist was not fulfilled. The reason why it is omitted in the Matthew/Mark version is because it is in fact continually put into practice in the celebration of the eucharist. Paul repeats it twice in order to impress forcibly upon the Corinthians that the Lord's supper was instituted by Jesus himself and that it must in fact be treated by them as such. The words of consecration contain Christ's own legacy as well as his charge, and constitute a handing over of his power. 'Commemoration' (*anamnēsis*) must not be regarded as merely a memorial in thought and words alone. The Lord himself is present in the celebration of the eucharistic meal, just as God's act of salvation in the exodus from Egypt is present for each generation of Jews in the feast of the Passover.

All the essential concepts of the Old Testament are gathered up in Christ's words of consecration—the Covenant, the supreme authority of God, atonement and martyrdom, worship and the eschatological message. Everything is centred in Christ and through him God's activity in the matter of salvation is consummated and perfected. Everything that God has done in the past and everything that he wishes to accomplish in the future regarding man's salvation is incorporated in the Eucharist.

2. *The interpretation of the meaning of the eucharist according to Paul* (1 Cor 10:1–4, 14–22; 11:17–23; also Heb 13:9f).

a. *The celebration of the eucharist is the 'Table of the Lord'* (Mal 1:7, 12). In the Greek terminology of worship, the 'table' of a god is a sacrificial table and one on which ritual meals are consumed. The eucharistic celebration is, in striking contrast to the ritual meals of the pagan gods (*TDNT* II, 34f), the Lord's supper (1 Cor 11:20)—a ritual meal which was appointed by the Lord Jesus. For Paul, the celebration of the eucharist incorporates both a sacrifice and a sacrificial meal, and it is the second aspect which predominates. The heathens' sacrifices and sacrificial meals are intended for demons (10:20) and the gods are worthless (Jer 2:5), and demons lie in wait behind them. The sacrifices of the Jews are intended, not for God (1 Cor 10:20) but only for the 'altar'. The 'third race', that is, the Christians, possess the true sacrifice and the true sacrificial meal. The eucharist is the only true form of worship for the new era.

The Lord's supper proclaims the death of the Lord (11:26: note that this is expressed as 'you proclaim . . .'). This is a solemn proclamation to the effect that the death of the Lord is actually happening at the present moment (*TDNT* I, 72). The death of the Lord is actually present because Christ's body, sacrificed for his own in death, and his blood, shed for them in death, are both present (see 11:23f). This commemoration of Christ's death must on no account be understood in the sense of the *dromenon* of the mystery-cults (R. Bultmann, *Mysterientheologie*). Christ's death is given prominence in order to arouse awe, but it is also in complete conformity with the whole of Pauline theology, at the centre of which is Christ's death. The consequence of this death, with all its implications for our salvation, is the glorification, and Paul shows his awareness of this eschatological prospect in the words 'until he come (again)'.

b. *The eucharist is 'food' and 'drink'* (10:1–4). The manna or 'spiritual food' is the type of the eucharistic food. The water out of the rock (Ex 17:1–7) or 'spiritual drink' is the type of the eucharistic drink. Both foreshadow the eucharistic food and drink. The pre-existent Christ—the 'spiritual rock' was Christ (1 Cor 10:4)—was present for the people of God and gave them spiritual or 'pneumatological' drink. Similarly the transfigured Christ, who is present in his church, gives a new food and a new drink for the salvation of its members. They, God's people in exile, are provided for by their Lord. It emerges clearly from Paul's christological appreciation of scripture and of history that he views the eucharist as the nourishment of God's people of the New Testament—as the food for their journey.

A participation or 'communion' (*koinōnia*) in the body and blood of Christ (10:16) is effected by the eating and drinking of the eucharist. This may be contrasted with the sacrificial meals of the heathens, which brought about a communion with demons (10:20) and with the Jewish sacrificial meals, producing a communion 'with the altar'. A communion 'with God' might have been expected in this context (10:13), but this is not expressed, possibly to avoid mentioning the name of God, but more probably because the Old Testament form of worship had already fallen into disuse. There are essential differences between each of these three instances of 'communion'. The communion established by the reception of the eucharist is not merely moral or ecstatic, dependent upon the personal feeling or experience of the recipient, but is a real communion in the sense that it exists independently.

This communion unites those who partake of the eucharistic meal not only with Christ but also with each other (10:17). 'The many are one body'—that is, Christ himself (see Gal 3:27). 'The many—one body' is Paul's definition of the church (Rom 12:5). The concepts of the Covenant, of the servant of God (Is 53:10–12), and of the paschal meal all contain the germ of the idea that it is the eucharist which forms and constitutes the church.

Though the reception of the eucharist brings about man's salvation—his deliverance from God's displeasure (1 Cor 10:5) and from condemnation and destruction (11:32; 10:10f)—it does not do so in every case. To eat and drink 'unworthily' results in 'judgement', which in the first place takes the form of punishment in this world, either by sickness or premature death (11:29f). These, however, can and should lead to a change of heart (see 11:32). The recipient of the Lord's supper partakes 'unworthily' if his moral attitude does not conform to what the eucharist is, in its essence and in its operation. In this context, 'communion' with the Lord and with the other members of his church in mutual charity and sharing of possessions can be contrasted with participation in the sacrificial meals offered to false gods and the complete absence of any sense of communion.

c. It is generally conceded that *Paul conceived the eucharist as a 'sacrament'* and was quite convinced of the real presence of Christ in the eucharist. In his view an essential difference exists between ordinary food and the eucharistic food (11:27, 29). In his teaching, communion with Christ is to be regarded as the effect of reception of the eucharist and this is furthermore an objective occurrence which is fixed in time (*ex opere operato*). At the same time, however, he links this up with an appeal to the will, in order to draw an inference from this effect—namely, to participate in the Lord's supper in the right moral condition, so as not to debar the effect of the sacrament. The effect of reception of the eucharist does not come about in any magical or material way, but is personal and ethical (see 10:1–11).

Paul is at pains to strengthen the attitude of reverence which ought to be present before receiving 'communion', and this is why he stresses that it is 'my' body (cf Luke) and 'my' blood in the words of consecration. This probably also accounts for the interpolation of the phrase: 'as often as you drink' (11:25b), in the commandment to perpetuate the eucharist. Furthermore, he insists that the eucharistic chalice used at the Lord's supper should be the sole wine-cup (11:21; Eph 5:18).

The account which Paul gives of the last supper in his exposition of the abuses which were taking place in Corinth concerning its celebration provides for the regulation ('agenda') of the form of public worship, and the ordering of moral life and of the community (*agapē*). This is even more pronounced in Luke's account of the last supper (22:7–38). The celebration of the eucharist is depicted as an event which is integrally woven into the fabric of the life of the community, and must be completely impenetrated by the moral life of the faithful, so that both the religious worship and the moral life of each individual forms a single entity within the community (H. Schürmann).

d. *Paul takes tradition as his authority for his conception of the eucharist* (11:23). His account of the institution of the sacrament is based firmly on tradition and his conception of the eucharist is derived from the interpretation given by Jesus himself in his words of consecration. Paul brings certain aspects into sharp relief and puts others more into the background, according to his own theological outlook and as a result of coming to grips with the world in which he moved. It is not necessary to resort to the hellenistic communities to understand Paul's view of the eucharist. He remains firmly by the tradition which goes back to the Palestinian communities. The feasts of the hellenistic communities which were 'not properly speaking ritual celebrations, but the expression of a bond of communion in accordance with the tradition of the Jewish world and of the historical Jesus himself' (E. Schweizer, *Gemeinschaftsmahl mit dem Dienen Jesu und eschatologischen Ausblick*) were not remodelled by the Greeks into the form of sacramental feasts, in the manner of mystery-cults (contrary to the claims of Bultmann and others). Rather, they passed on what they too had received and what was already inherited from Jesus himself. All the accounts of the last supper go back to the year 40, and refer to an even earlier period (see above). Is it however possible for such a radical transformation to come about in such a short space of time, a change which was to be such a stumbling-block for the Jews especially? Is it possible that this could have happened under the eyes of the last of the apostles? Can it be that all this escaped his notice, that the hellenistic communities deviated, in a particular matter which St Paul considered essential, from the ancient tradition which he recognised and to which he appealed so strongly, and that these communities consequently drew closer towards the heathen world? (With reference to the question of mystery cults and the eucharist, see *DBs* II, 1194–1210; K. Prümm, *Der christliche Glaube und die altheidnische Welt* II, Leipzig 1935, 81–98.)

Although the Letter to the Hebrews contains no explicit reference to the last supper or to the eucharist, the entire language in which Jesus's mission and work, his high priesthood and his unique sacrifice, is described in the epistle, is derived from eucharistic terminology. In this context, the heavenly gift (Heb 6:4), reminder or *anamnēsis* (10:3), the blood of Jesus (10:19), and Christ's flesh (10:20) should be especially noted, also the particular emphasis placed on the blood of Christ in the work of redemption (C. Spicq, *L'épitre aux Hébreux*, Paris 1952, 316f). Finally, Heb 13:7–16, and in particular v 9, must surely be considered together with these references which emerge from the theology of the Epistle to the Hebrews as pointers to the eucharist. A new type of doctrine was arising in the society to which the epistle was addressed, and this doctrine misconstrued the nature of the life of the Christian community. The balance of christian piety had been shifted to the act of eating the sacrificial food, and 'strengthening of the heart' was expected from this act of eating alone. Anyone expecting grace and salvation —'the strengthening of the heart'— just from the act of eating had fallen back into the old order of salvation which was concerned only with what was imperfect and belonged to this world and had, in fact, been finally done away with. Christians, however, have an 'altar', which is to be thought of in the sense of the heavenly altar of the epistle, namely, as the cross and the eucharistic table in one. Those who continue to serve the things of this world and what is imperfect are not permitted to eat from this table. But eating does not of itself alone lead to communion with Christ. The christian does not achieve this by natural or temporal means, through eating alone, but as the result of a spiritual decision to follow Christ in suffering and death. There are three practical consequences resulting from this: the christian ritual meal should stimulate hunger for the future City of God—in this sense it is an eschatological meal; God must be praised and thanked in connection with it—in this sense it is *eu-kharistia*; lastly, the result of participation in this meal must be works of ↗ love—in this sense it is *agapē*. Its validity is not lost 'despite the excesses, abuses and misinterpretations of the religious attitude of each age towards the sacramental and liturgical life of the church' (F. J. Schierse).

3. *Interpretation of the meaning of the eucharist according to John*. John's conception of the eucharist bears the stamp of the peculiar quality of his theology.

a. He brings out *the realism of Christ's presence* in the sacrament with even greater emphasis than the other evangelists and Paul, almost going so far as to cause scandal, as for example in the use of the word *chew* for eat (6:54, 56, 58) and *flesh* for body. E. Schweizer calls this his 'rough sacramentalism', countering the misconceived spirituality of the Docetic gnosis. On the other hand, it was imperative to overcome any possible scandal of anthropophagy (the 'Capharnaite' or 'Thyestean' meal) and the suggestion, which gave such offence to the gnostics, that 'flesh' and 'blood' were the vehicle of divine life. It was neither dead matter nor matter that was grossly sensual that was consumed in the sacrament, but the flesh and blood of the exalted and transfigured Lord (6:62). Flesh which lacks the life-giving spirit is incapable of leading men to eternal life (6:63). The eucharistic words of promise have to do with flesh and blood, insofar as they contain life which is given by the spirit (see the commentaries on John).

b. John uses the words *flesh* (and not *body*, which is used in the accounts of the institution) and *blood* when he refers to the giving of the eucharist. By using the word *flesh* he portrays the incarnation (1:14). Contrary to the views of the gnostics, the reality of the 'flesh' and the godhead of the *Logos* (=Word) which is latent in it belong to one another. John, who is the 'pre-eminent theologian of the incarnation', succeeds in establishing an intimate connection between the incarnation and the eucharist (see Phil 2:7; 1 Tim 3:16; for a further development of this subject, see also J. Betz, 260–342).

The idea of atonement contained in the sacrifice, as outlined by John (6:51b), harks back to Isaiah (53:12).

The 'many' are replaced by the 'world' and the saving gift of forgiveness of sins is replaced by the Johannine conception of ↗ life. The gift that is offered is the flesh and blood of the 'Son of man' (6:27, 53). The title 'Son of man' is used by John in association with Christ's death and with the glorification so closely connected with it (3:14; 12:34; 12:23; 13:31), with his heavenly origin and his return to heaven (1:51; 3:13; 6:62), and with his office as judge (5:27). Christ's expiatory death recedes into the background as his glorification overshadows it. The effect of the eucharist in atoning for sins, and the idea of sacrifice which goes with this, pale beside the life-giving effects and the resurrection made possible by it. There is clearly a very close connection between 1 Jn 5:8, with its emphasis on the 'water and blood' and the remarkable account given in Jn 19:34 of how 'water and blood' flowed from the wound in Jesus's side. In 1 Jn 5:8, the water and blood point to baptism and the eucharist, and both have a supra-historical function and testify to later generations (1 Jn 5:7). 'God's work of salvation, which can be said to be the result of the mission and death of his Son, is continued uninterruptedly by his church, which makes the divine life available to each and every one of the faithful even in later ages, by means of Christ's message and the sacraments' (R. Schnackenburg, *Die Johannesbriefe*, Freiburg 1954, 234f). Thus it can be seen that the closest possible association exists between the eucharist on the one hand, and the incarnation, death, and glorification (or second coming) of Christ and the descent of the Holy Spirit on the other. The eucharist is the 'representation and application of the whole of christological activity concerning man's salvation' (H. Schürmann). The spirit bears witness to the important role of Jesus in the matter of salvation in the sacraments of baptism and holy eucharist.

c. *The eucharist is food and drink* for the preservation of eternal 'life'. The distinctive quality of the eucharist as food is secondary to its quality as a meal and attention is directed more to the individual than to the community in this respect (R. Schnackenburg, 'Herrenmahl und Lebensbrot', *Amt und Sendung*, Freiburg 1950, 136–60). John's arguments are directed principally against those who are individualistically seeking a purely personal communion with God and eternal life for themselves alone, thus completely disregarding the commandment to love one's brother (1 Jn 2:9–11; 3:10, 14f; 4:8, 20; 5:2).

John emphasises most strongly that reception of the sacrament is necessary to salvation (Jn 6:53f). In the view of the gnostics, with whom John is in conflict, it is possible to make contact with God, to have communion with him, without the aid of any intermediary, whereas the christian faith insists that this communion with God can only be achieved through the unique humanity of Jesus Christ (6:37ff; 1 Jn 1:1–13).

The effect of the eucharistic food and drink is, according to John, a communion with Christ, a sharing in his life (6:56), and this state is expressed by the evangelist in his own characteristic manner—his 'reciprocal expression of Christ's immanence': 'he . . . abides in me and I in him' (15:4–7; 17:1ff; 1 Jn 2:24; 3:24; 4:16). He avoids any expression of identification such as that common to hellenistic mysticism and takes care to keep the individual personalities distinct ('I in him, he in me'). Communion with Christ is a permanent communion and not merely a passing experience. Although an enduring possession, it can, however, be lost, hence the moral admonition which underlies the emphasis on its 'abiding' quality (R. Schnackenburg, *Die Johannesbriefe*, 91–5). Reception of the eucharist makes it possible for the communicant to enter the tide of life which flows from the Father to the Son (6:57). The unity of being and the activity of the Father and the Son form the ideal for the close relationship between Christ and the recipient of the eucharist (Jn 17:20ff). The eucharist bestows life and, at the last judgement, will bring about a resurrection from the dead. Through the eucharist, this eschatological possession becomes the christian's property here and now. The eucharist is superior to manna, because it bestows eternal life and the overriding importance of the messianic age over the Old Testament finds its true expression in the eucharist. The 'peak point' of the call to salvation, which occurred at the time of Moses, is reached and surpassed in the present era. To put it in gnostic terms, the eucharist is 'true' food and 'true' drink (6:56) and fulfils all that is included in the concept of food and drink. It bestows 'everlasting' (divine) life and is the fulfilment of mankind's most powerful desire. The food of the eucharist is not acquired in any mechanically magical way. It is the 'medicine of immortality' (Ignatius on Eph 20:2), but it must be received with faith. (This is particularly stressed in the sermon on the Bread of Life.) It is Christ himself who raises the participant in the sacrament to eternal life (6:54, 57).

An interpretation of the meaning of the eucharist based on the bible alone gives some idea of the inexhaustible profundity of this 'mystery of Faith'. The eucharist appears in a new light in every period of man's history and every generation can illuminate some fresh aspect of this great mystery.

Bibliography: *DB(S)* II, 1164–215 (with bibliography); H. Schürmann, *Der Paschalmahlbericht Lk 22:(7–14,) 15–18* (*NA* XIX, 5), Münster 1953 (with bibliography); E. Ruckstuhl, 'Wesen und Kraft der Eucharistie in der Sicht des Johannesevangeliums', *Opfer der Kirche*, Lucerne 1954, 47–90; H. Schürmann, *Der Einsetzungsbericht Lk 22:19–20* (*NA* XX, 4), Münster 1955; H. Schürmann, 'Die Gestalt der urchristlichen Eucharistiefeier', *MTZ* 6 (1955), 107–31; J. Betz, *Die Eucharistie in der Zeit der griechischen Väter* I/I, Freiburg 1955; A. Stöger, *Brot des Lebens*, Munich 1955; H. Schürmann, *Jesu Abschiedsrede Lk 22:21–38* (*NA* XX, 5), Münster 1957 (with bibliography); H. Schürmann, *Die Abendmahlsbericht Lk 22:7–38*, Paderborn 1957; J. Bonsirven, *Le règne de Dieu*, Paris 1957, 174–81. See also: F. F. J. Leenhardt, *Ceci est mon Corps*, Neuchatel-Paris 1955; 'L'Eucharistie dans le Nouveau Testament', *LV* 31 (1957); W. Marxsen, *Ev. Kirchenlex.* I, 3–6; E. Schweitzer, *RGG* I³, 10–21 (with bibliography); *BTHW* 1–9; J. Jeremias, *The Eucharistic Words of Jesus*, London 1966; H. Schürmann, 'Die Eucharistie als Repräsentation und Applikation nach Jn 6:53–8', *TTZ* 68 (1959), 30–45 and 108–18; R. Schnackenburg, 'Die Sakramente im Johannesevangelium', *SP* 2 (Paris 1959), 239–43; A. Stöger, 'Die Eucharistiefeier des NT', *Eucharistiefeiern in der Christenheit*, 1960, 10–19; J. Betz, *LTK* III², 1143–7; H. Schürmann, *LTK* III², 1159–62; P. Neuenzeit, *Das Herrenmahl*, Munich 1960; J. Betz, *HTG* I, 336–42; *N. Lash, *His Presence in the World: A Study of Eucharistic Worship and Theology*, London and Dayton (Ohio) 1968.

Alois Stöger

Exaltation

According to Mk 14:62, Jesus foresaw and spoke of his exaltation as the Son of Man sitting at the right hand of God and coming with the clouds of heaven. After Easter and Pentecost, christian preaching testified to the fact that this exaltation had taken place and explained it in all the fullness of its significance.

According to Acts 2:33–6 and 5:31, both the term and the concept of the exaltation of Christ are a further stage of the kerygma of his resurrection and ascension (Acts 1:9f). By means of the exaltation, this event is completed insofar as he who rose from the dead is appointed 'Lord and Christ' and enthroned 'at the right hand of God' (Mk 16:19; Rom 8:34; Eph 1:20; Col 3:1; Heb 1:3; 1 Pet 3:22). The hymn in Phil 2:9f, which is probably pre-Pauline, also speaks of the exaltation 'above all'. This implies that Christ receives a new name, which is above all names, namely, the name of Lord. His sovereign power is distinguished as power over heavenly, earthly and infernal beings. At the present and at all times the church experiences the efficacy of this name and the power of the exalted Lord. It is in this name that it receives the Spirit (Acts 2:38), forgiveness of sins (Acts 10:43), and salvation in general (Acts 4:12). It is in this name also that signs and wonders are worked (Acts 4:30).

According to Rom 1:3f, the exaltation means that Jesus, who was already in possession of the divine sonship which had been hidden all along in his human existence, was proclaimed as the Son of God in all the fullness of his power and was established, according to the spirit of holiness and sanctification, in other words, according to his spiritual and divine being. In this sense he is now the Lord of the Church. In another hymn too, the exaltation is described (1 Tim 3:16). Christ is taken up out of the earthly sphere of the flesh into that of the divine and spiritual. He is shown to be justified by means of this, as God acknowledges his faith in him and reveals him who was rejected by the world as the one who is justified (Jn 16:10); so he is invested with divine glory. The canticle goes on to say that the exalted Christ was 'seen by angels' and thus he sees the heavenly triumph over the subjected powers, who pay homage to the one who is exalted (see Phil 2:10; Eph 3:10; Col 2:15; 1 Pet 3:22). It should be noted that Asc Is 11:23 indicates that the New Testament has here taken over certain apocalyptic ideas from the later Jewish world.

On earth too, his dominion is recognised, in that he is 'proclaimed to the heathen and is believed in the world'. In the letter to the Hebrews, the author speaks of the exaltation, using words and images which are both new and old. Jesus is 'crowned with glory and honour' for 'the suffering of death' (Heb 2:9). He was given a new name, that is, the name of Son, which denotes that he has become 'much superior to the angels' (Heb 1:4). He has passed through into the heavens (Heb 4:14) and has received the dignity of high priests for all eternity (Heb 5:5f). He has taken his place at the right hand of God (Heb 1:13). In this way the Epistle declares (as already in Acts

2:34f and elsewhere) that the ancient psalm of coronation (Ps 109:1) has been fulfilled in Christ, following the veiled claim already made for him in Mt 22:44.

The exalted Christ is, however, also the Christ who is to come again. Very often, expressions concerning the exaltation are closely linked with others on the subject of the Second Coming (see Mt 26:64; also Acts 1:2f; Phil 3:20; Col 3:1).

In St John's Gospel, we find statements relating to the exaltation used in the characteristic manner of the evangelist, full of associations and references to other contexts (see John 3:14; 8:28; 12:32–4). Christ's exaltation on the Cross fulfils the foreshadowing of the exaltation in the raising up of the bronze serpent by Moses, and is in itself a foreshadowing and indeed the commencement of his exaltation to divine glory. Since, according to St John's conception, Jesus lives on earth in the closest possible unity with the Father and is always both the Word of God and his Son, the exaltation is simply a return to the glory which he has always possessed and a revelation of this glory which is now, on the occasion of his return to the Father, manifested to the whole world. The christological statement of Jesus's exaltation thus sets out, in figurative and graphic terms, the consummation of God's action and plan for his Christ. In addition, it depicts the eventful beginning, the permanent duration and the awaited consummation of the sovereignty of Christ over the church and the world.

Bibliography: *DB*[*S*] IV, 1068–71; E. Schweizer, *Erniedrigung und Erhöhung bei Jesus und seinen Nachfolgern*, Zurich 1955; A. Vergote, *L'exaltation du Christ en croix selon le 4 évangile*, *ETL* 28 (1952), 5–23; H. Bleienstein, *Der erhöhte Christus*, *GL* 27 (1954), 84–90; G. Bertram, *Der religionsgeschichtliche Hintergrund der Erhöhung in der Septuaginta*, *ZAW* 68 (1956), 57–71; J. Daniélou, *La session à la droite du Père*, Studia evangelica = *TU* 73 (1959), 689–98; W. Thüsing, *Die Erhöhung und Verherrlichung Jesu im Johannesevangelium* (*NA* XXI, 1), Münster 1960.

Karl Hermann Schelkle

Faith

A. *Faith in the Old Testament.* According to the bible, God stands at the midpoint of all history. It is he who directs and guides everything. In the last analysis, everything can be traced back to him; evil itself has no existence if God does not permit it or, in biblical language, 'bring it about'. Faith is, therefore, the attitude which seeks to encounter *him* in all things and in all events, which alone in the last resort can make sense of everything and which shows a way out of present tribulation for a man whose life is based on the bible and who stands in the presence of God and says 'yes' to his summons.

In the Old Testament faith is grounded upon a historical religion—that of the covenant. Faith is, therefore, in the first place, the response of the people to the covenant. Every year, on the occasion of the offering of the first-fruits, the Israelite made his profession of faith: 'A wandering Aramaean was my father; and he went down into Egypt and sojourned there, few in number; and there he became a nation, great, mighty, and populous. And the Egyptians treated us harshly, and afflicted us, and laid upon us hard bondage. Then we cried to the Lord, the God of our fathers, and the Lord heard our voice, and saw our affliction, our toil, and our oppression; and the Lord brought us out of Egypt with a mighty hand and an outstretched arm, with great terror, with signs and wonders; and he brought us into this place and gave us this land, a land flowing with milk and honey. And behold, now I bring the first of the fruit of the ground which thou, O Lord, hast given me' (Deut 26:5–10). This ancient creed praises the freedom, power, fidelity, and love manifest in the gracious choice of God as something which is always new and which must be both recognised and acknowledged anew by each generation. Faith is, then, man's response to this attitude on the part of God.

This faith also expresses the fact that God presides over events and the course of history. What has come to pass in the beginning has been brought about by God and this bestows certainty and assurance on faith and the hope that God will continue his intervention on behalf of his people.

Two Hebrew roots in particular are used to express faith. One (*ʾāman*) stresses the idea of certainty, strength and firmness; the other (*bāṭaḥ*) expresses the energy of faith and trust. The Hebrew word for ↗ truth, authenticity is *ʾemeth*; the Hebrew mind does not contrast truth with error but with nothingness, which is known as vanity or futility (*šeqer*). Thus God is also called the God of *ʾemeth*, of truth, or more accurately, the God of faithfulness or of trustworthiness. Yahweh is a God *neʾemān*, that is to say, a sure God who can be relied upon and trusted (Deut 7:9). Christ himself is called the 'Amen' in this sense (Rev 3:14). It is necessary to go back to Deut 27:15–26, in order to gain some impression of the true significance of the term Amen—the knowledge that one is committed to and involved in the covenant with God. *Heʾemin* therefore refers to that attitude which comprises a complete reliance on what is incapable of disappointing and is absolutely certain and dependable. Indeed, it goes further than this and implies that the believer leaves himself entirely in the hands of the one who on his own merits deserves this unlimited self-commitment.

The other root—*bataḥ*—expresses above all the energy of faith, showing that there is no place in it for any kind of passivity. There is also a certain element of hope and expectation contained in the meaning, and in this way the word occurs about a hundred times in the Psalms and is rendered as 'believe' and frequently also as 'trust' or 'hope'. In Ps 4:5, for example, we find: 'trust in Yahweh'; in Ps 25:2; 'O my God, in thee I trust'; and in Ps 55:23; 'But I will trust in thee'.

The first model for this unlimited faith, this believing and faithful self-abandonment to God based on the covenant, is *Abraham*, the father of those who believe. 'He believed in Yahweh; and he reckoned it to him as righteousness' (Gen 15:6). Literally, everything was demanded of him, so that his faith was tested to the utmost limit (Gen 22:1: 'God tested Abraham'). In the first place, he had to exchange his homeland and family, well-being and security, for the uncertain and unsettled life of a nomad. Then he was obliged to have a son, despite his great age, and finally he had to sacrifice this son, the heir to God's promise. Again and again, these various situations in which he finds himself and which affect him in his inmost being are intended to confront the man as he is, and make him into a 'believer' or an 'unbeliever'. Nonetheless, we read in Heb 11:8f: 'By faith Abraham obeyed when he was called to go out to a place which he was to receive as an inheritance; and he went out, not knowing where he was to go. By faith he sojourned in the land of promise, as in a foreign land, living in tents with Isaac and Jacob, heirs with him of the same promise ... By faith Sara herself received power to conceive, even when she was past the age'. Paul had also to go into the meaning of this faith in Rom 4, as faith is as essential to the New Covenant as it was to the Old.

The *prophetic period* brought these still latent characteristics of such sublime personalities into full relief, in accordance with the religious tendencies which were peculiar to them—Abraham (Gen 20:7) and Moses (Hos 12:13) were explicitly associated with the prophets.

A similar theme of the pre-prophetic period can, however, be found in an ancient royal psalm, and this theme, that the king in Israel, if he wishes to live up to his calling, must acknowledge no other support or source of strength than God, is later even further developed: 'Now I know that the Lord will help his anointed; he will answer him from his holy heaven with mighty victories by his right hand. Some boast of chariots, and some of horses; but we boast of the name of the Lord our God. They will collapse and fall; but we shall rise and stand upright' (Ps 20:6–8).

The extraordinarily graphic and vivid quality of the allegorical language of Israel can often be traced back to concrete historical origins. The horse cannot have originated until the beginning of the second millennium or thereabouts, at the time of the *Hurrite* invasions in the Near East. The Israelites first discovered it when it was used by their enemies and did not know how to defend themselves against it. The Lord had to give them help and instructions as to how they might save themselves (Josh 11:6–9). This gave rise to the theme of 'fallax equus ad salutem'—a theme which recurs frequently, as for example in Hos 14:3; Ps 33:17; 147:10; Deut 17:16. In Zech 9:9f, we read: 'Rejoice greatly, O daughter of Zion ... Lo, your king comes to you; triumphant and victorious is he, humble and riding on an ass, on a colt ... I will cut off the chariot from Ephraim and the war horse from Jerusalem ...' For the messianic king arrays himself again in the archaic uniform and equipment of a desert chieftain; he has appointed a day of judgement over all that is proud and arrogant (see Is 2:12ff). The power of men is to be destroyed and the weakness of man saved. Again in Zech (4:6) we read: 'Not by might, nor by power, but by my Spirit, says Yahweh of hosts'. Ezra (8:21ff) prefers to ask God (for a good journey) after proclaiming a general fast, although he might have asked the king to provide a protective escort. In his revision of the material, the chronicler transforms the hosts of Jehoshaphat into spectators who sing praises to God and at the same time watch while God deals with their enemies (2 Chron 20).

It is *the prophet Isaiah* who teaches and himself fully embodies heroic faith. No more than an indication of this can be given here. On looking at Chapter 7, for example, we find that King Ahaz wants to provide human safeguards, such as the construction of fortifications and alliance with the Assyrians, because he fears the enemy who wishes to overthrow him (Is 7:6). His people too are in a state of panic (7:2). Only Isaiah remains calm and proclaims the word of the Lord: 'It [ie, the sack of Jerusalem] shall not stand, and it shall not come to pass . . . If you will not believe, surely you shall not be established' (Is 7:7, 9). The sign which the Lord gives is none other than the continued existence of the dynasty and this is given at a time and in circumstances which seem to be humanly impossible. The royal house and capital are the tangible signs which guarantee the continued existence of the Covenant (see 2 Sam 7:15f). It is possible to follow the proclamation of the prophet and the reaction of the king in this way throughout the entire book, and Isaiah's utterance is one which again and again demands faith.

A hundred years later Habakkuk preaches on exactly the same theme in his attempt to give support to the hopelessly wavering people at the time of the Babylonian invasion. The prophet listens to God, who commands him: 'Write the vision; make it plain upon tablets, so he may run who reads it. For still the vision awaits its time; it hastens to the end—it will not lie. If it seem slow, wait for it; it will surely come, it will not delay. Behold, he whose soul is not upright in him shall fail, but the righteous shall live by his faith' (Hab 2:2–4). Habakkuk addresses what he says to the whole nation, yet the final sentences could easily refer to the content of the book of Job. The task of the individual is thus the same as that of the nation. If the history of the chosen people is viewed as a movement between these two opposite attitudes—that of believing against all human calculation that God's help will not fail and that of relying on one's own strength, not trusting in God, not believing God since he at times lets his people down—then the life of the individual must also be considered in this light.

The Book of Job sets forth the situation of the believer in the most moving manner. Satan is presented as one of the angels in God's presence and is asked whether he has seen Job on earth and has observed how pious and god-fearing he is. Satan answering said to the Lord: 'Doth Job fear God *for naught*?' (Job 1:9). This is the question which is central to the book. If it were to be proved that the pious man does serve God 'for naught', Satan would have to admit defeat. Job has no idea of this prelude in heaven. His sons and daughters are suddenly taken from him in an accident, he himself is stricken with leprosy and has to withdraw from the town. He is completely misunderstood by his wife and his friends. He is ground down and tormented to the limits of his endurance, all human support is taken away from him and his friends, instead of comforting him, reason thus: 'if you are so afflicted, then you must have offended God in some way'. Satan too speaks through his wife: 'Curse God and die!'

But, in spite of everything, Job cleaves to God. He knows that he is bound to God in faith and even when he has been deprived of everything, including the ultimate guarantees of this faith, he refuses to allow himself to be argued out of it (see 13:15; 16:19f; 19:25).

Thus, in its religious usage, the word *heʾemîn* (in LXX and in the New Testament most frequently translated as *pisteuein*), carried on by its use in the prophets and employed in the vocabulary of individual piety, has come to occupy a prominent place than other roots of similar meaning as the word which best describes the relationship which exists between the people of the covenant and God.

Bibliography: O. S. Virgulin, *Bbl* 31 (1950), 346–64 and 483–503 (on Isaiah); J. C. C. van Drossen, *De derivata van dem staam "mn" in het Hebreeuwsch van het OT*, Amsterdam 1951; A. Weiser, *TDNT* VI, 182–96; P. van Imschoot, Haag 578f; Jacob 148–63; A. Gelin, *LV* 22 (1955), 431–42; J. B. Bauer, *BL* 23 (1955/6), 226–30; E. Pfeiffer, 'Glaube im AT', *ZAW* 71 (1959), 151–64; O. S. Virgulin, *La fede nella profezia d'Isaia*, Milan 1961.

Johannes B. Bauer

B. *Faith in the New Testament*. I. *Belief in the Message of Jesus*. In Mk 1:15, Jesus's message is summarised thus: 'The time is fulfilled, and the kingdom of God is at hand; repent, and believe in the gospel'. 'Faith' can accordingly be described as the acceptance of the kingdom of God as it has been brought about by Jesus's proclamation.

1. *Contrast between the idea of faith in the Old Testament and that contained in the New*. In contrast to the Old Testament, two fresh impulses are given to the idea of faith in the New Testament:

a. 'The time is accomplished', which means that what has been promised in the Old Covenant is fulfilled in the person and in the work of Jesus of Nazareth. That is why the synoptic account is moulded on the life and work of Jesus in accordance with the message of the Old Testament (see especially the story of the Passion) and why the evangelists themselves repeatedly stress that such and such has come to pass 'in order that the Scriptures might be fulfilled'. This evidence of faith occupies a particularly important place in Matthew's gospel (Mt 1:22f; 2:15, 17f, 23; 4:14ff; 8:17; 12:17ff; 13:14f, 35; 21:4f; [26:54]; 26:56; 27:9f).

b. Conversion as a condition of faith now implies—as in the message of St John the Baptist (see Mt 3:2)—not only a turning away from everything that is contrary to God, but also a turning towards God as he has become manifest in Christ, and a radical preparation for the kingdom of God as it has dawned in Christ. 'The conversion and penitence to which he urges the Jews implies at the same time belief in him' (Schmid, *RNT* 2:117). This is why Jesus condemns the cities of Galilee which have failed to believe in him in spite of all the miracles which had taken place in them (Mt 11:20–4; Lk 10:13–15).

2. *Faith and Christ*. What emerges from this is that Christ claims for himself the faith which had been directed to God. It makes no real difference whether this is regarded as belief in God or belief in Christ (cf Mk 9:42 and Mt

18:6), since faith in God is contained in the latter.

a. His miracles demand faith, so that we find many cases where Jesus ascribes his saving acts of curing disease to the power of faith (Mt 9:2, 22, 29; Mk 2:5; 5:34; 10:52; Lk 5:20; 7:50; 8:48; 18:42). Everything is possible to him who believes; he can obtain from God even what is impossible (Mk 9:23; 11:23; cf Mt 17:20; Lk 17:6). If faith is absent, no miracle is possible (Mk 6:5, 6; cf Mt 13:58). Nevertheless, it is not faith which works miracles, but the divine power of Jesus, who makes his working of miracles dependent on the faith of men. It is for this reason that Jesus reproaches his disciples for their unbelief or 'little faith' (Mt 17:20). When he is with them on the boat nothing can happen to them, however violently the storm may rage (Mt 8:23–7; Mk 4:35–41; Lk 8:22–5). Peter is able to walk on the waves in perfect safety at Jesus's command, although he sinks at first because fear overcomes him and he begins to doubt (Mt 14:28–31). Since faith is a condition for the working of a miracle, Jesus rejects the demands of his demonic enemy and his earthly opponents who clamour for 'signs', that is to say, proofs of his power which compel recognition of his messianic mission and his divinity and leave no place for faith (Mt 4:1–11; Lk 4:1–13; Mt 12:38, 39; Lk 11:29, 30; Mt 16:1–4; Mk 8:11–13; Lk 11:16; Mt 27:42; Mk 15:32). It is true that Jesus's miracles have the object of authenticating his messianic mission and his claim to divinity. There is, however, no contradiction here, since Jesus demands of those who wish to experience his power no immediate, complete faith, but rather only a firm trust in his power and his desire to help them; his miracles do not compel faith, but always leave the way open for man to decide of his own free will.

b. *His words demand faith.* It is possible only for the believer to penetrate the secret of Jesus's doctrine and to make it his own. Mk 4:10–12 demonstrates this with frightening clarity (see also Mt 13:10–15; Lk 8:9f). This passage originally referred, probably in an all-embracing sense, to Jesus' activity as a teacher, and its meaning has thus been narrowed down by the evangelist to refer to the sermon on parables. In it, Jesus makes a clear dividing line between 'you'—that is, the apostles—and 'those that are without'. To the latter, everything that he says is mysterious, whereas the secret of the kingdom of God is revealed to the apostles. It is faith, however, which draws this dividing line and causes God to reveal himself to the former and harden the hearts of the latter (passive phrases are used to express periphrastically the activity of God). The outcome of Jesus's message, which offers grace and passes judgement, bestows salvation and life and brings ruin and death, is powerfully exemplified in this Logion (see Lk 2:34; J. Jeremias, *The Parables of Jesus*, London 1954, 11ff). It is faith which brings about grace, salvation and life, and this faith must not be regarded as the meritorious action of man, but as a free gift on the part of God. Since faith implies a distinction between the apostles and those who are outside, this will apply also to the parables—this is, at any rate, how Mark has understood it. Although it is the apostles who are, in accordance with their special position, entrusted with the task of clarifying the teaching of Jesus and making it comprehensible to men, the result of their activity is in fact that only those who believe can be led by them into the mystery of the kingdom of God. Only the believer is able to assimilate the absolute and authoritative claims which Jesus's words make, as in the 'I say to you' of the sermon on the mount (Mt 5:22, 32, 34, 39, 44) or in his full power to forgive sins (Mk 2:1–12; see also Mk 1:27). For the rest this is a stumbling block.

c. *Faith as a decision for Christ.* What emerges from all this is that man is called upon by Christ to make a decision, either for him or against him: 'He who is not with me is against me; and he who does not gather with me scattereth' (Mt 12:30; cf Mk 9:40). This decision takes place in the profession of faith as Peter pronounces it in the name of the disciples (Mk 8:29 and parallels). It is not by chance that Mark places Peter's profession of faith precisely in the middle of his gospel. What is evident here is that the people as a whole do not acknowledge Jesus as the Messiah and that only the small band of his disciples believes in him. The declaration of faith in Jesus, however, decides the attitude of man towards God: 'So every one who acknowledges me before men, I also will acknowledge before my Father who is in heaven; but who ever denies me before men, I also will deny before my Father who is in heaven' (Mt 10:32, 33; Lk 12:8, 9; see also Mk 8:38).

3. *Faith and the kingdom of God.* a. *Faith as grace.* A faith which implies complete self-surrender to God and opens up the kingdom of God must be brought about by God himself. Thus Jesus pronounces Peter to be blessed after he has made his profession of faith: for flesh and blood has not revealed this to you, but my Father who is in heaven' (Mt 16:17). Thus he praises his Father, in his prayer of rejoicing, for hiding his revelation from the 'wise and prudent' and bestowing it upon the 'little ones' (Mt 11:25). It is clear from this that Jesus ascribes both the unbelief to the 'wise and prudent' and the belief of the 'little ones' to the dispensation of his heavenly Father.

b. *Faith is necessary to salvation.* If unbelief precludes salvation (Lk 8:12; Mk 16:14, 16), then belief is necessary to salvation. That is why the worst thing that can be done to the 'little ones who believe' is to cause them scandal, that is to say, lead them astray in their faith. It would be better for any man who does such a thing, if 'a great millstone were hung round his neck and he were thrown into the sea', rather than that he should undergo the punishment which threatens him at the Last Judgement (Mk 9:42).

c. *The new condition.* Faith is the prerequisite for the new condition of being into which the disciple of the Lord enters when he leaves everything behind in order to follow Jesus (Mk 1:18; Lk 5:11; cf Mk 10:28). By this is meant that the believer separates himself from everything and everybody (Mt 10:34–7; Lk 14:26; cf Lk 18:29) in order to unite himself with Jesus in a lifelong communion. He participates in the destiny of his Lord, shares his poverty (Mt 8:19f), takes up his cross with Jesus (Mk 8:34), is scorned and abused, hated and persecuted with him (Mt 10:17–22). 'It is enough for the disciple to be like his teacher, and the servant like his master' (Mt 10:25). But he also has a share in his life, he is permitted to enter the kingdom of God which has dawned with Christ (see Lk 9:61f) and partake of his glory, since the Beatitudes of the sermon on the mount (Mt 5:3–12) and the acknowledgement by the Son of Man when he comes in his glory (Mk 8:38; 9:1) can be referred to him.

II. *Faith in the preaching of Paul.* With 'faith', we are dealing with an idea that springs from the very centre of Paul's theology and message. This can be observed even from a superficial examination of the Pauline epistles, in that the basic noun *pistis* and the verb *pisteuein* not only occur very frequently in all the epistles, but also occupy a central place in them, and especially in those to the Romans and the Galatians. It is an idea which, however, has different levels of meaning. The range of meaning of *pistis* extends from that of 'fidelity' (Rom 3:3; Gal 5:22; 2 Thess 1:4; 2 Tim 4:7) to certainty of belief and conscience (see Rom 14:23) and finally to the idea of faith in the truly religious sense.

1. *The exposition of faith according to Rom 10: 4–17.* It would not be too wide of the mark to assume that Rom 10:4–17 is the passage in which the apostle sets out in general terms his view of faith. Faith presupposes revelation, and this is brought about by the word, either directly, as Paul himself experienced it on the way to Damascus (1 Cor 9:1; 15:7; 2 Cor 4:6; Gal 1:15, 16; Eph 3:3; see also Acts 9:1–19; 22:5–11; 26:12–18), or indirectly, by means of the proclamation of the word of God to men: 'Faith comes from what is heard, and what is heard comes by the preaching of Christ' (Rom 10:17). The proclaimed word, in Paul's view, places Christ firmly in the centre, and, what is more, Christ crucified (1 Cor 1:18, 23; Gal 3:1). By belief is meant—and here Paul explains by means of the example of Abraham, Rom 4—that as Abraham considered his body which was 'as good as dead' and yet remained, despite all human considerations, firmly convinced of the truth of the word of God which had established him as 'father of many nations' (4:18), so should we consider the body of the dead Christ on the cross and remain, here too despite all human considerations to the contrary, firmly convinced that God has established him as 'father of many nations', that is to say, that he was 'raised for our justification' (Rom 4:25). *Hupakoē* comes from *akoē*, 'obeying' comes from 'listening' (see Rom 10:16); and indeed, in Paul 'faith' and 'obedience' are very closely related. In Rom 1:5 and 16:26, he speaks of the 'obedience of faith', which means in all probability the faith which consists in obedience, recognition and acknowledgement of the christian message and subjection to the will of God which is revealed in it. In this way the apostle is able to employ the words 'faith' and 'obedience' almost reciprocally. What is designated in Rom 1:8 as 'your faith' can be called, in Rom 16:19, 'your obedience'.

What occurs in man's inmost heart concerning the complete renunciation of self and subjection to the will of God for the purpose of salvation, is made external in the oral profession of faith.

In Rom 10:9, 10, basing his reasoning on Deut 30:11–14, Paul makes a distinction between 'belief in the heart' and 'belief confessed with the mouth'. Faith 'in the heart' has its counterpart in the statement made in Rom 4:24; 'that God has raised him from the dead' (Rom 10:9; cf 1 Cor 15:12ff), whereas the essence of the external profession of faith is to be found in the primitive christian credo: 'Jesus is the Lord' (Rom 10:9; cf 1 Cor 12:3; Phil 2:11; Acts 18:28). Similarly, the apostle speaks of the *fides qua creditur* and of the *fides quae creditur*. It is possible to assume with complete certainty that he makes use of formal professions of faith which have been handed down to him (see Rom 10:9; 1 Cor 15:3, 4; 1 Tim 3:16). Faith is thus indispensable and must remain indispensable (see 1 Cor 13:13) because it forms the basis of the new existence for the christian and represents the first step towards 'existence in Christ' which is ultimately brought about through ↗ baptism, when the believer receives Christ's act of redemption, his death and resurrection (Rom 6:4, 6, 8; Gal 2:19; 5:24; 6:14; Col 2:12; 2 Tim 2:11).

2. *Faith and justification.* Over and above these general features which characterise the Pauline conception of faith, it is also particularly distinguished by the fact that it stands in complete contrast to the pharasaical and judaistic idea of man's ↗ justification through the operation of the law. The great emphasis on faith which we find in the theology of Paul is doubtless occasioned by his early passionate defence of the ↗ law as the only means to salvation, sustained until he was overcome by the power of grace (see Gal 1:13–16). Christ's atoning death, becomes effective for the individual human being through faith (Rom 3:25), and by faith the individual is justified (Rom 3:28). His justification does not take place by means of the works of the law, but by means of faith. The various arguments of the Letter to the Romans move, as it were, around this central idea. The law has shown itself to be incapable of leading men to salvation. This inability does not arise from the law itself, but from man's failure to fulfil its demands in their entirety. It is true that 'the doers of the law . . . will be justified' (Rom 2:13), but man is incapable of becoming a 'doer' in the fullest sense of the word. Paul recognises the deceptive external lustre that typifies the proud self-confidence of the Jew who strictly obeys the law and who imagines himself to be 'a guide of the blind', 'a light of them that are in darkness', 'an instructor of the foolish', 'a teacher of infants' and who supposes that he possesses 'the form of knowledge and of truth in the law'. The apostle, however, points out to such a man the fatal dichotomy that exists between the demands made by the law and their fulfilment, between the desire to fulfil them and their accomplishment (Rom 2:19ff) and shows that all are 'under the power of sin' (Rom 3:9) and that no human being is justified before God through the works of the law (see Rom 3:20). Sin has indeed made use of the law in order to show up in its true colours, for sin is only imputed where the law is (Rom 5:13). Paul is able to make this idea all the more pointed and precise in his statement: 'Law came in, to increase the trespass' (Rom 5:20). What has been enacted in the

whole of the history of salvation is reiterated in the life of the individual, as experienced personally by Paul himself. At first he lived without the law. Then the law came and he experienced a revival of sin and he himself died. The law, then, forces man into a situation from which there is no way out and no rescue, except through Christ. 'For God has done what the law, weakened by the flesh, could not do', namely sending his Son into the world (Rom 8:3). God's justice has thus been revealed without the law (Rom 3:21). God has brought about, by a free act of grace, what man would never have dared to anticipate, and man cannot attain salvation by his own actions, but has to be given it by God through grace. Now he is 'justified by his grace as a gift', by virtue of the redemption in Christ Jesus (Rom 3:24). Thus the provisional disposition of salvation under the law is contrasted with its final disposition according to grace. Grace has taken the place of the law: 'for Christ is the end of the law' (Rom 10:4). Whereas the law demands works, the indispensable condition for grace is faith: 'for we hold that a man is justified by faith apart from works of law' (Rom 3:28). What the apostle has in mind is the following antithesis:

Without Christ	With Christ
Law	*Grace*
Works	*Faith*

What is contained in this distinction is a clear choice: either with Christ or without him, either grace or the law, either faith or the works of the law. As a way to salvation, the one excludes the other: the way of faith has replaced that of the works of the law.

This is shown with great clarity in Gal 3:23–6. The law is the taskmaster or 'pedagogue', under whose authority men used to stand: 'but now that faith has come, we are no longer under a custodian' (Gal 3:25). 'Faith' is to be understood here simply as the new disposition or order of salvation which has been brought about through Christ and is so closely connected with him that it can in fact almost be identified with him, for the passage, 'now that faith has come ...' could be read as 'now that Christ has come ...' After it has been revealed by Christ, faith has become the only way to salvation.

3. *Faith in Christ.* Paul's statements on the matter of faith are imprinted with his own particular individuality and not only where they point to this antithesis to judaism. The apostle also develops a view of faith which is entirely his own, derived from his passionate 'intimacy with Christ' and for which he has coined the formula 'in Christ'.

Phrases such as *pistis in Khristō(i) Iēsou* (lit = 'faith in Jesus Christ': Gal 3:26; 5:6; Col 1:4; 2:5 [*eis Khriston*]; Eph 1:15; 1 Tim 1:14; 3:13; 2 Tim 1:13; 3:15) or *pisteuein eis Khriston Iēsoun* (lit = 'believe in Jesus Christ': Gal 2:16; Phil 1:29; see also Eph 1:13) occur quite often in Paul's letters, and these can indeed be rendered quite correctly by the literal translations given. Neverthless, it is possible to assume that the phrases *en Khristō(i)* and *eis Khriston* are not used here in the technical sense of the pauline formula. The new existence 'in Christ' in fact grows out of faith (Gal 2:20; 3:26; 2 Cor 4:18; 5:7; 13:5) and faith and communion with Christ belong so closely together that it is possible to say that faith in Christ means that faith is brought about through a life-relationship with Christ.

In addition to this, the word *faith* is frequently met with—as is the case with other important ideas connected with christian existence—in the genitive construction *pistis Khristou* (lit = 'faith of Christ': Rom 3:22, 26; Gal 2:16, 20; 3:22; Eph 3:12; Phil 3:9; 1 Tim 3:13; 2 Tim 3:15). Just as we find references in Paul to 'Christ's afflictions' (Col 1:24), the 'marks of Jesus' (Gal 6:17), the 'steadfastness of Christ' (2 Thess 3:5) and the 'love of Christ' (2 Cor 5:14; Eph 3:19; Phil 1:8), so do we find him speaking of the 'faith of Christ' (see O. Schmitz, *Die Christusgemeinschaft des Paulus im Lichte seines Genetivgebrauches*, Gütersloh 1924, 268; A. Deissmann calls this genitive construction 'genetivus mysticus' in his *Paul*, New York 1957, 161ff; see also E. Wissman, *Das Verhältnis von 'pistis' und Christusfrömmigkeit bei Paulus* (*FRLANT* 40), Göttingen 1926, 68ff; see also Meinertz 2, 136). The apostle is referring here to his own faith which he has in communion with Christ.

4. *Faith in the Letter to the Hebrews.* Important statements are made concerning faith (in the Epistle to the Hebrews) especially in the eleventh chapter. Nevertheless, in considering Heb 11:1, we should guard against thinking in terms of a 'definition' of faith, as the writer's intention here is, strictly speaking, only to give the distinguishing marks of the attitude of faith which he would like to recommend to his readers. In his view, this attitude is characterised by two aspects: 'assurance (*hupostasis*) of things to be hoped for' and 'conviction (*elegkhos*) of things not seen'. The first links faith in the most intimate way with hope and calls it a confident and optimistic approach to what is hoped for, an attitude for which there are countless examples in the history of salvation (Chap. 11), by far the most outstanding being that of Christ himself (12:1–11). The second of these aspects extends the meaning of the first insofar as it sees in faith, the 'proof' for what is of its nature invisible, and recognises in it the essential reality from which the visible reality has emerged (see 11:3). In this way faith has for its object the existence of God and the fact that he is the rewarder of good works (v 6). Without this attitude of faith, which includes confident trust and conviction, it is impossible to please God or to come to him (v 6: cf 6:12; 10:22).

If faith, in accordance with the particular stress which the author here places on it, is the attitude of firm confidence with regard to what is hoped for, then it is scarcely to be wondered at that the word *pistis* is frequently used in the sense of 'constancy in faith'. Thus, the examples of faith mentioned in Chap. 11 are at the same time examples of constancy in faith as well. As Christ himself proved his faithfulness (3:1–6; cf 10:23), so is it necessary for christians to preserve this attitude of commitment and not to betray this trust (10:32–9), so that, after all that God has bestowed upon them, they do not go astray through lack of trust and so apostasise (3:7–4:11). Two things stand in very close relationship to each other here. On the one hand, faith must be demonstrated in patience (10:36; 12:1).

On the other hand, however, it is also coupled with a victorious frankness (*parrhēsia*) with which the christian has confident access to God (4:16; 10:19) and is able to endure all that the world may inflict upon him (10:32–6).

III. *Faith in the Letter of James.* At first sight the comments made on faith in the Letter of James appear to contradict completely Paul's statements on the same subject. In particular, the basic expositions contained in the Letter to the Romans seem to stand in formal contrast to what is stated in Jas 2:14–26 (cf especially Jas 2:24 with Rom 3:28; see also Gal 2:16). It must, however, be taken into account that James envisages a different antithesis from Paul (see above). With him there is no question of discussing the relationship between faith and works in the matter of justification, but of giving practical guidance and impressing on christians that their faith should be a living faith which has a positive result in everyday life (1:3, 6, 21; 2:1–5; 4:7; 5:8–11, 15). The demons believe in the one God and shudder (2:19); a faith without works is dead and barren (2:17, 20). A living faith is shown in patience (1:3), in the love of one's neighbour (2:15–17), in hospitality (see 2:25), in trusting prayer (1:6; 5:15) and, above all, in piety (1:27; 2:22).

Paul's letters demonstrate clearly that such a conception is in no way opposed to the pauline view of faith, and Paul too fundamentally insists on the practical working out of faith in everyday life (Gal 5:6).

IV. *Faith in the writings of John.* When John writes, towards the end of his gospel: 'But these are written that you may believe that Jesus is the Christ, the Son of God, and that believing you may have life in his name' (20:31; see also 1 Jn 5:13), he acknowledges that his entire message is aimed at faith, and it is true to say that 'faith' plays a very important part in his writings, especially in his gospel and in 1 Jn.

He frequently expresses the idea, as is shown in the passage quoted above, in accordance with the general use of the word in the New Testament, that it is necessary to 'believe' in Christ, the Son of God, in order to achieve salvation, or, more simply, that the acceptance of the message of Christ makes one a 'believer' (Jn 3:15, 18; 4:53; 6:47; 8:24; 1 Jn 5:1, 5; see also Acts 2:44; 9:42; 11:17; 14:23; 16:31; 18:8; 19:4; 1 Cor 15:2; Gal 2:16; Phil 1:29). As is the case with other books of the New Testament, the object of faith is often expressed in John in a *hoti*-clause (Jn 8:24; 11:42; 13:19; 14:10f; 16:27, 30; 17:8, 21; see also Rom 10:9; 1 Thess 4:14; Heb 11:6; Jas 2:19).

A rapid examination of John's writings will reveal the particular quality of the Johannine conception of faith, and it is remarkable that whereas the verb *pisteuein* occurs frequently (ninety-six times in the gospel and nine times in 1 Jn), the noun *pistis*, with the exception of 1 Jn 5:4 and Rev 2:19; 13:10, does not appear at all. What undoubtedly seems to emerge from this is that John is more concerned with the reality of faith than with any abstract discussion of a conception of faith.

Another peculiarity of John's writings is that *pisteuein* occurs more frequently with the dative than as *pisteuein eis*. Thus, in John, men believe the word which Jesus says (4:50; cf 2:22), or simply his words (5:47); they believe him (8:31, 45, 46; 10:37, 38; 14:11) or they believe the Father who has sent him (5:24; cf 5:38). A further characteristic of John's texts is that 'to believe' is replaced by various other words and can thus be elucidated to a considerable degree. 'To believe' means 'to hear' (5:25; 6:60; 8:43, 47; 18:37); 'to believe in him' means 'to come to him' (5:40; 6:35, 37, 44f, 65; 7:37); 'to receive him' (1:12; 5:43) or 'to love him' (8:42; 14:15, 21, 23f, 28; 16:27).

1. *The essence of faith.* The manner in which faith is brought about in man, how it originates and is consummated, is set out in many different ways in the writings of John. The faith of the ruler who asks Jesus to cure his son resides in the first place merely in a trust in Jesus's power to work miracles. The Lord says to him: 'Go; your son will live'. The man places his faith in the word of the Lord and makes the long journey home, with nothing more than this word in his possession. Then, when the news is brought to him by his servants that his son is alive, he experiences the truth and the divine power of the word of Christ. It is not until that moment that faith in its fullest sense comes to him: 'And he himself believed, and all his household' (4:46–54). The course of events is similar in the case of the healing of the man who was born blind (Chap. 9). The blind man who has begun to see attains, through the miracle of his cure, a generic faith and believes that Jesus is a prophet (v 17). This faith emerges successfully from the test of the debate with the pharisees which even leads to the man's explusion from the synagogue, and eventually reaches its culmination through Christ's personal revelation (v 37). The healed man says: 'Lord, I believe', and falls down before Jesus in adoration (v 38). At the marriage in Cana (2:1–11), what is revealed by Jesus's miracle of the transformation of water into wine is 'his glory' and, as a result, 'his disciples believed in him' (2:11). When he meets the risen Christ, Thomas falls down before him with the words 'My Lord and my God!' (20:26–8). If the aim of this event of faith—the personal encounter with Christ and the falling down in adoration of his *doxa* or 'glory'—is achieved, then there is no further need of any external sign, whether this takes the form of a miracle or of a word. In this way, the Samaritans believe in the first place on account of the testimony of the woman, but after their personal encounter with Christ they say: 'It is no longer because of your words that we believe, for we have heard for ourselves and we know that this is indeed the Saviour of the world' (4:42). The following factors come together at the same time when the act of faith takes place: on the basis of an external sign—a miracle or a word—there is an encounter, either direct or indirect, with Christ. The outcome of this is that the initial faith reaches its perfection and the man falls down in worship of Christ as the one who reveals the 'glory' of God. Faith must however be able to do without the external sign as well, and be strong enough to be dependent upon Christ alone. The latter emerges from Peter's confession of faith (see 6:68, 69) and from what the Lord says with regard to Thomas's act of faith: 'Blessed are those who have not seen and yet believe' (20:29; see also 4:48).

2. *The effects of faith.* John describes

the effects of faith in various passages: 'He who believes in him is not condemned' (3:18); 'He has eternal life; he does not come into judgement, but has passed from death to life' (5:24); 'He who believes in the Son has eternal life' (3:36; 6:40, 47; 20:31; 1 Jn 5:13; see also 6:35; 11:25ff; 12:36, 46; 1 Jn 5:1, 5). What is common to all these references is the conviction that faith is the means to salvation and that unbelief leads to perdition. It is a particular attribute of John's conception of faith that both faith and unbelief anticipate the end—judgement on lack of faith is already effective and where faith is present everlasting life has already dawned (3:14–21; see also 5:24).

Faith in Christ is thus decisive in the matter of man's salvation, since his relationship with Christ determines his relationship with God: Whoever believes in Christ believes in the Father (12:44); whoever does not believe in Christ neither sees nor hears the Father (5:37, 38). 'To see God' means, in effect, to believe that Christ is in the Father and the Father is in him (10:38; 14:10, 11, 20).

It is clear from this that man cannot produce faith of his own accord. Faith must be bestowed upon him by God: 'No man can come to me unless the Father who sent me draws him' (6:44; cf 6:65; 17:6–8). On the other hand, however, it is man's own fault if he does not come to believe (15:22: cf 40).

3. *Faith and knowledge.* We have noted that other verbs can, in John's writings, be allied with 'to believe'—for example, the verb 'hear' (4:42) or 'see' (20:8, 25). There is, however, a particularly strong link between 'believe' and 'know', and these two verbs are so closely connected that they are almost indistinguishable one from the other. Both have the same object, for it is stated, with reference to the same fact, that it can be 'believed' and 'known' (6:69; 1 Jn 4:16; see also Jn 17:8; 8:24, 28). This does not mean, however, that 'to know' or knowledge is intended to describe a higher status of christian being, the achievement of which leads to the abolition of 'faith'. If this were so, the two expressions would not be so closely related in the text and interchanged so frequently in order of sequence. For example, in Jn 6:69 we read 'We have believed, and have come to know', but in 1 Jn 4:16 'We know and believe'. There is, however, a difference between the two words, and this is clearly expressed in the relationship between the Son and the Father, which can certainly be rendered by 'knowledge', but never by 'faith' (10:14f; 17:25). If, in this instance, 'knowledge' denotes what is usually rendered in the johannine gospel as 'I and the Father are one' (10:30; cf 17:11) or 'the Father is in me and I am in the Father' (10:38; cf 14:20), then it becomes apparent that 'to know' implies the utter self-abandonment of the Son to the Father and the perfect communion between the Father and the Son. A state of 'knowing' is thus possible for the man who believes that God is in Christ and that Christ lives in the most intimate communion with the Father, that is to say, he can also be included in this life-communion as this is expressed in Christ's prayer, as 'high priest' for his apostles (17:21; cf 17:3, 11). All the same, there can be no 'knowing' without 'believing' and this

is why we find the demand: 'Believe the works, that you may know' (10:38). 'Knowing' is thus the result and the aim of 'believing'.

4. *Faith and conduct.* If John holds that faith must be orientated towards God, and that this orientation reaches its objective in 'knowing', then it follows that this orientation must be closely related to the conduct of the christian in the world. It is true that the christian is not 'of the world' (15:19; 17:14, 16; cf 17:6), but he is 'in the world' (13:1; 17:11, 15; 1 Jn 4:17) and his faith is that very power which triumphs over the world (1 Jn 5:4f). The faith of one who is 'in the world' is demonstrated in keeping the commandments (15:10; 1 Jn 2:3f; 3:22ff; 5:2) and especially the commandment to love one another (13:34; 15:12; 1 Jn 2:7f; 4:21). This 'new commandment' of love of one's neighbour arises from the new relationship between man and God which is based on faith (13:34; 15:12). John stresses again and again, especially in 1 Jn, that the love of God which the believer receives must be effective in the love of one's neighbour. This injunction at the same time points out clearly the task of the christian with regard to the 'world'—the 'world' will know christians as the disciples of Christ by their love for each other (13:35).

Bibliography: J. Huby, 'La connaissance de foi dans St Jean', *RSR* 21 (1931), 385–421; T. Soiron, *Glaube, Hoffnung, Liebe,* Regensburg 1934; R. Schnackenburg, *Der Glaube im vierten Evangelium,* Breslau 1937 (dissertation); E. Walter, *Glaube, Hoffnung und Liebe im NT,* Freiburg 1940; O. Kuss, 'Der Glaube nach den paulinischen Hauptbriefen, *TG* 46 (1956), 1–26; P. Morant, 'Der Glaube in der ntl. Theologie, *Anima* 13 (1958), 5–14; A. Schlatter, *Der Glaube im NT*, Stuttgart 1927[4]; E. Grässer, *Der Glaube im Hebräerbrief,* Marburg 1965; P. Valloton, *Le Christ et la foi: Etude de théologie biblique,* 1960; W. G. Kümmel, 'Der Glaube im NT', *TG* 16 (1938), 209–21; P. Antoine, *DB*[*S*] III, 276–310; A. Weiser and R. Bultmann, *TDNT* VI, 174–228; P. van Imschoot, Haag 578–83; Meinertz II.

Heinrich Zimmermann

Fasting

The law commands a fast only on the great Day of Atonement (Lev 16:29–30; 23:27, 32; Num 29:7). The practice of fasting, on the other hand, is very common and takes many different forms, even if the special food laws of the Levites and thc abstinence practised by priests, Nazarites, and Rechabites, which are outside the scope of this article, are not taken into consideration.

Those who fast include men of every class in society, both individuals and the whole people, and even beasts (Jon 3:7). Fasting is carried out either on one's own account or on official instructions and lasts from one to three or seven days, three weeks, fourteen days or even one's entire life (Judith 8:6). Annually repeated and prescribed fasts became more numerous after the exile (Zech 7:3, 5; 8:19) and special fasts, which were not unknown before, were more frequently proclaimed (Ezra 6:16; Neh 9:1). The pious fasted twice a week (Lk 18:12).

In the Old Testament, fasting is scarcely ever practised purely for its own sake. It forms a conspicuous part of the religious life and worship of the individual or of a group within the nation, requiring serious external application, when it is necessary to turn to God in a time of distress. The following are often closely connected with the essential abstinence from food and drink, or the voluntary limitation of these (as, for example, in Dan 10:3): lamentation, wailing, the use of sack-cloth and ashes, dust, the rending of garments, abstinence from marital relationships, neglect of the care of the body such as anointing and bathing, going barefoot, neglect of normal greetings, sleeping on the ground (as in 2 Sam 12:16) and, in the case of public fasts, religious meetings and abstinence from work (Joel 1:14; 2:14–16; 1 Kings 21:9–10, 12; Jer 36:6, 9). Prayer is never out of place during a fast (eg, Neh 1:4), nor are external works of mercy (Is 58:3–7). Fasting is often called, together with these acts, the essence of piety (eg, Tob 12:8). See Fruhstorfer, *TPQ* 69 (1916), 59–72.

The external peculiarities associated with fasting are, in their natural environment, the normal expression of deep sorrow (as with fasting as a means of lamenting for the dead, [1 Sam 31:13; 2 Sam 1:11, 12]; fasting among widows in mourning, [Judith 8:5, 6]). This is why fasting is always incompatible with joy (Judith 8:6; Joel 2:18–27; Zech 7:3; 8:19). The word *tsôm* (=fasting) is often substituted or elucidated by "*ᶜinnâh napšō*' (='to humiliate one's soul', that is, 'oneself': Lev 16:29, 31; 23:27, 29, 32; Num 29:7; 30:13; Is 58:3, 5; Ps 35:13: see also 1 Kings 21:27, 29; Sir 2:17). It is the external expression of a conscious desire to escape from the threatened punishment of God's might, and an inner dissociation from the sin which calls forth this power (see Sir 2:17ff). Even where no sin is involved, fasting is the expression of the same mental attitude or a reminder of it or a means towards achieving it. The man who is conscious of his guilt and his dependence upon God does all within his power to remove the possible cause of God's severe intervention and in a plain and straightforward human way seeks to move God to pity. Fasting is a form of prayer which hopes for everything from God (Is 58:3; Jer 14:2; Mt 6:18). In the Old Testament we find little to remind us of the ascetic aspect of our 'mortification of the flesh'. Any magical conception of fasting is also quite unknown in the bible. The outward aims of fasting are many: remorse for sins (1 Sam 7:6; Sir 34:25–6), the desire to avert misfortune or punishment (1 Kings 21:27, 29; Esther 4:1–3, 16; 9:31), or to appease God's anger (Joel 2:14–17); fasting forms a part of or reinforces vows and adds support to petitions (1 Sam 14:24; 2 Sam 12:15–23; Joel 1:13ff; 2:17; Ezra 8:21; Tob 7:11; see also Acts 23:12, 14), it serves as a reminder of national catastrophes (Zech 7:3; 8:18–20; Esther 9:31), and prepares the way for special encounters with God, for example, revelations (Ex 34:28; Deut 9:9; Judg 20:26, 27; Dan 9:3; 10:2; Acts 13:2; Lk 2:37; 1:80) and other manifestations (Acts 14:22; see also Mt 4:2 and parallels; 9:29). In the case of official acts of public worship, fasting takes the form of a ceremonial penitential preparation (1 Sam 7:6; Judg 20:26). Atonement is peculiar to the ritual actions of the priest (Lev 16:32–4; Num 29:11).

Neither the prophets, the sages nor Jesus himself are opposed to fasting as such, but to fasting which is devoid of true spirit and represents pride and a demanding attitude rather than humility towards God (Zech 7:5–6; Lk 18:12, 14; Mt 6:16–17). What is important is that the essential duties of outward and inner morality, and especially those of justice and charity, are fulfilled (Is 58:3–5; Jer 14:12; Sir 34:25–6; Joel 2:12, 13). Isaiah gives to fasting which is hopeful and pleasing to God the figurative meaning of the practice of justice and active charity (Is 58:6–12). The prophets and sages maintain the ideal of true piety in opposition to the tendency towards spectacular and ostentatious practices which become more and more pronounced with the passage of time (see Mt 6:16–18; StB IV 105–7).

We find two important statements in Zech 7:1–8:23; a negative one to the effect that the fasts undertaken up to that time were worthless, because they have not been related to God (Zech 7:1–3, 4–5; cf 7–14), and at the same time a series of passages which contain promises of salvation in contemporary form (8:1–23) and give an affirmative answer (8:18–19) to the query (7:3) whether or not the periods of fast should be occasions of joy. It is not a question here of material fasting; the author is referring rather to the true sense and meaning of all striving—namely, 'truth and peace', that is, true morality. Thus the real point at issue (that is, fasting) is passed over and attention is directed to a point beyond it, as the interrogators had expected. There is no rejection of contemporary practice in the text; this has already been kept up at least partially for a long time. But this transition is intended to stimulate the people, who have become enslaved to ritual, to intensify their inner life and to reflect about the meaning of fasting.

Jesus's answer to the question put by the pharisees and the disciples of John on the matter of fasting (see especially Mk 2:18–20, 21–2; also Mt 9:14–17; Lk 5:33–9) should be seen in a similar light. Jesus completely dismisses the unreasonable twofold suggestion which is contained in the question, that he includes himself and his disciples among those who are recognised as 'pious' and that fasting according to their particular manner is therefore necessary (Mk 2:19). He bases his answer in the parable of the bridegroom and the 'children of the marriage' on his presence as the Messiah. What emerges from the text and context of both the parables which follow, concerning the fundamental newness of the christian reality and the necessity of new categories in the philosophical sense (Mk 2:21–2), is at least the strong probability that Jesus is not referring to special periods of fast and is neither approving these nor condemning them (Mk 2:20), but is dealing with something more profound which must first be grasped by his interrogators. Their narrow and ritualistic philosophy completely misses the single, decisive fact that Jesus, who is salvation itself, is present. If they could understand that, the irrelevance of their misguided anxiety would dawn on them. Another kind of 'fasting', not self-imposed, is in store for the disciples. They will, after Jesus's death and ascension into heaven, be in a state of mourning, deprived of his visible presence (Mk 2:20; see also Mt 9:15; 2 Cor 5:6–8; Phil 1:23). 'Fasting' is thus, in Mk 2:20, depicted figuratively and symbolically in the allegory of the 'bridegroom'. In this way, Jesus directs attention to salvation. Zechariah (8:18–19) points to the joy of the consummation; Jesus on the other hand points to the distress of man's period of transition on earth. Both make use of 'fasting' to typify different situations within salvation, Zechariah by abolishing it and Jesus by giving it a new and more perfect meaning. Both transcend the normal bounds of authority in respect of the details which had come to the fore in ritual practice (see Logion 28 in the Coptic Gospel of Thomas [Leipoldt] where 'fasting' = to abstain from the world.

Nothing either in favour of or in opposition to the christian practice of fasting can be deduced from Jesus's answer to his questioners; and, in fact, this text has never been seen as providing a valid argument either then or later (Schäfer, *Synoptische Studien*, 124–47).

The ritual decrees concerning 'meat and drink', being but 'shadows of things to come', are in themselves neutral in the 'kingdom of God' (Col 2:16–17; Rom 14:17; 1 Cor 8:8). Jesus does not introduce any new external norms, but the fullness of salvation and of piety. The christian has to fashion such norms in freedom from his own upright mental attitude. In certain circles there was a very keen interest in such matters as fasting which had in earlier times frequently been systematised by the law and various customs. The keenness of this interest and the uncertainty which prevailed are demonstrated by the numerous difficulties associated with the question concerning fasting in Mk 2:18–20 as found in the apocryphal writings and in the works of christian writers (see Arbesmann, 32–3) and at a later stage in practically all the obscure Logia in the Coptic Gospel of Thomas (Log 5; 14; 28; 101 [Leipoldt]) which are concerned in a passive sense with fasting. Some textually uncertain New Testament passages in which the mention of fasting may not be original are, by their very existence, proof of the esteem in which fasting was held in certain circles (Mk 9:29 = Mt 17:21; Acts 10:30; 1 Cor 7:5). Both Jesus's personal example and his teaching positively commend genuine fasting and persevere with what is valuable and lasting in the Jewish practice. When he dismisses prearranged regulations concerning external fasts and in so doing describes the life of christians on earth as 'fasting', he indirectly implies that bodily fasting, correctly conceived, has a place in the new order as well.

Bibliography: R. Arbesmann, 'Fasting and Prophecy in Pagan and Christian Antiquity', *Traditio* 7 (1949–51), 1–72; K. Fruhstorfer, 'Fastenvorschriften und Fastenlehren der Heiligen Schrift des Alten Bundes', *TPQ* 69 (1916), 59–72; K. T. Schaeffer, '. . . und dann werden sie fasten an jenem Tage' (Mk 2:20), *Synoptische Studien: Festschrift A. Wikenhauser*, Munich 1953, 124–47; Behm, *TDNT* IV, 924–35; D. E. Briggs, *Bible Teaching on Fasting*, Dallas 1953; A. Guillaumont, '*Nēsteuein ton kosmon* (P Oxy 1, verso, 1:5–6)', *Bulletin de l'Institut Français d'Archéologie Orientale: Le Caire* 61 (1962), 15–23.

Johann Gamberoni

Father

The Hebrew word for father (*ʾāb*, Aramaic *ʾābba*) is onomatopoeic (compare *pappa*). The concept of father in the bible is determined by the structure of patriarchal society which gives the primacy in the family (or the larger structures based on the family) to the father. He has jurisdiction over the children (Ex 21:7, 9; Gen 38:24 limited by Ex 21:7–11, 26ff; son = servant in 2 Kings 16:7), the son also is dependent on the father's will with regard to marriage (Gen 24:31; 28:1ff; 34:4; 38:6–8; Judg 14:1–2), a daughter's vow has no validity apart from the father's consent (Num 30:4–6), it is the father who decides with regard to legacies (Lk 15:11–32), he even exercises sacerdotal rights (cf Judg 17ff: the ↗ priest is called 'father'; according to Ex 12:1–14, 21–8 the paschal lamb was slaughtered in the family, therefore by the father).

The earthly father. The authority of the father (and the mother) is guaranteed in the ↗ decalogue (Ex 20:12; Deut 5:16; cf Lev 19:3). Rebellion against the father, or the act of cursing or striking him are transgressions punishable by death (Ex 21:15, 17; Deut 21:18–21). The Wisdom literature in particular is concerned to a great extent with the piety of children towards their father (and mother). We find a summary of this teaching in Sir 3:1–16 (cf Prov 1:8; 4:1; 6:20; 10:1; 13:1; 15:20; 19:26; 20:20; 23:22, 24, 25; 28:24; 29:3; 30:11, 17; Sir 7:27; 23:14; Tob 4:3–5).

Jesus confirms the fourth commandment (Mk 10:19 and parallels) and establishes its original meaning as against contemporary rabbinical casuistry (Mk 7:10–13; Mt 15:4–7). He has a tender regard for the relations between father and child (Mk 5:40; Lk 8:51; Mk 9:14–29; Mt 17:14–21; Lk 9:37–43). Moreover, the words of Jesus which seem to go against the duties of filial piety do not in fact oppose piety with regard to one's father but rather express the urgency of the decision which a follower of Christ has to make with relation to the kingdom of God (Mt 8:21ff; Lk 9:59ff; 14:26 where 'to hate' means 'to give second place to' cf Gen 29:31, 33—Mt 10:37; 19:29). In these logia Christ demands from those who wish to share in the kingdom of God nothing more than that implied in contracting ↗ marriage, namely, separation from one's parents (Gen 2:24).

The moral rules which Paul lays down for families (Col 3:18–4:1; Eph 5:22–6:9) include also warnings for both father and son (Eph 6:4; Col 3:21; Eph 6:1–3; Col 3:20). The 'honouring' enjoined in the decalogue is defined as 'obedience', the promise contained in the fourth commandment is spiritualised and the *patria potestas* limited through religious (Eph 6:4) and psychological (Col 3:21) considerations.

In a broader sense, the *ancestors* of the people of Israel are called 'fathers' (Acts 5:30; 13:17, 32; 15:10; 28:25; Heb 1:1). The scribes and pharisees wish to avoid the offences committed by the fathers in going against the prophets sent by God, nevertheless Jesus must reproach them with having, by their attitude towards him, filled up 'the measure of the fathers' (Mt 23:30, 32; cf Lk 6:23, 26; 11:47ff; Acts 7:11–52). The term 'fathers' is used in a special way for the generation which passed through the desert and had experienced the decisive event in the history of salvation in the Old Testament, thus becoming a 'type' for the last age (Jn 6:31, 49, 58; Acts 7:19;

13:17; 1 Cor 10:1; Heb 3:9). All the outstanding men of days gone by are commemorated in Sir 44:1–50:26 under the heading 'Praise of the fathers'.

The period of late judaism refers to ↗ Abraham, Isaac and Jacob as fathers. The God who presides over sacred history is the God of these fathers (Acts 3:13; 5:30; 7:32; 22:14). It was to them that the promises and the ↗ covenant had been given. The promises made to them are fulfilled in Jesus (Lk 1:55, 72ff; Acts 3:25). The ↗ fulfilment and completion of all the promises, namely, the kingdom of God, is described as sharing a meal with these fathers (Mt 8:11; Lk 13:28). The history of salvation begins with father Abraham (Acts 7:2); the promises are directed to him, those promises by which he was to become the ancestor of many peoples (Gen 12:2; 15:5; 17:5). The Jews regard themselves with pride as free sons of Abraham (Jn 8:33, 37, 39) and think that, since they have Abraham as father, they do not stand in need of the ↗ conversion demanded by the Baptist (Mt 3:9; Lk 3:8). Their father Abraham rejoiced that he was to see the day of Christ; he saw it and was glad (Jn 8:56). The promise directed to him finds its fulfilment in Christ (Gal 3:16). Christ and with him all christians are the descendance of Abraham (Gal 3:29)—he is in fact father of all those who believe in Christ (Jn 8:56; Gal 3:7). All christians, of both Jewish and pagan origin, venerate Abraham as their father since they follow him in his faith (Rom 4).

Persons in authority are also known as fathers: priestly officials (Judg 17:10), ↗ prophets (2 Kings 2:12; 6:21), persons holding office (Gen 45:8; Is 22:21; 1 Macc 11:31ff), benefactors (Job 29:16). Rabbis also accept this name as a title of honour (SB 1, 287, 919). Jesus forbade his disciples to accept this title on the grounds that there was only one father, their father in heaven (Mt 23:9). Paul refers to himself as father of the communities which he had founded—but in a metaphorical sense, not as a title, insofar as through his preaching the ↗ gospel the faithful had been given ↗ life (1 Cor 4:15; cf Gal 4:19; Philem 10). He admonishes and consoles his children like a father (1 Thess 2:11). He says of Timothy that he had served him as a child a father in announcing the gospel (Phil 2:22).

↗ *God as Father.* Only rarely is the word *father* used in the Old Testament to describe the relationship between God and ↗ man. This reticence seems to have been imposed through the fear of being misunderstood in a mythological sense. God is not the father of men through procreation or physical descent; the name *father* is thought of and expressed in a metaphorical sense. It is used to represent the idea of election and of the covenant and expresses Israel's belonging to God and his care and ↗ love for his people. God is the father of his chosen people because he made them, gave them their very essence and existence (Deut 32:6ff), is their saviour (Is 63:16ff) and creator (Mal 2:10) and has shown them every sign of his love (Jer 3:19; 31:9; cf 31:18–20). God is father of the offspring of David; God will be his father and he will be God's son (2 Sam 7:14; cf Ps 89:27; 2:7). He is called father of the ↗ poor since he takes care of all the lowly and helpless with solicitous love (Ps 68:5f; cf 27:10; 103:13). Later on, with the advent of a more individualistic way of thinking, he is also called father of the individual religious person (Sir 23:1, 4; 51:10), though this title is used in connection with ↗ 'Lord'.

Jesus often refers in his preaching to 'your father', 'your father in heaven', and addresses God simply as 'father'. He uses the word when he announces the new saving deed of God: the dawn of the rule of God (↗ kingdom of God, Mt 13:43; 20:23; 25:34; Lk 12:32), the mission of the ↗ Spirit (Mt 10:20), the confession of Christ (Mt 16:17), hearing the unanimous ↗ prayer of the disciples (Mt 18:19), ↗ reward (Mt 6:1). The God who sets up his kingdom is also the father. Above all there is contained in the idea of father the thought of God's care for men (Mt 6:26, 32; Lk 12:30; Mt 6:8; 10:29), his generous love that delights to give (Mt 5:45; 7:9–11; Lk 11:11–13) and forgiveness (Mt 6:12, 15; Lk 15). According to Jesus' proclamation, God is therefore father, a fact expressed in an absolute way by the use of this title for God (Mt 11:25; Lk 10:22; Mt 24:36; Mk 13:32; Lk 9:26; 11:2, 13; Mt 5:16). Jesus demands that men fulfil the will of the father (Mt 7:21; 5:45) and that they be perfect (Mt 5:48), merciful (Lk 6:36) and ready to forgive (Mt 6:14) as their father is. He desires that the father mean more to them than anything else and that they seek him in all things (Mt 5:16; 6:14, 18). This preaching about God as father is intimately bound up with the idea of the kingdom of God. Jesus gives great importance to his relation to the father—his knowledge of (that is, association with) the father (Mt 11:27; Lk 10:22) and his invocation of him (Abba, Mt 6:9; Lk 11:2; cf Rom 8:15; Gal 4:6).

According to *Paul*, God is 'our God and Father' (Gal 1:1; Phil 4:2; 1 Thess 1:3; 3:13; 2 Thess 2:16). He speaks almost always of salvation (1 Cor 6:14) and ↗ judgement (1 Thess 3:13) in connection with God the father. God is the father from whom is everything and for whom we exist (1 Cor 8:6)—he is the father of all (Eph 4:6). As father, God is the giver of salvation—the salutation formulae at the beginning of the epistles describe peace as a gift of 'God our father' (1 Cor 1:3; 2 Cor 1:2; Gal 1:3; Eph 1:2; Phil 1:2; Col 1:2; 2 Thess 1:1; 1 Tim 1:2). It is the father who qualifies us to share in the ↗ inheritance of his saints in ↗ light (Col 1:12ff). It is reserved for those who believe to experience what the Old Testament promised, namely, that God will be to them a father and that they will be his sons and daughters (2 Cor 6:18; cf Ezek 37:27). Through the gift of the spirit of adoption (↗ sonship) believers are enabled to invoke God full of confidence with the title abba ('dear father'—Rom 8:15; Gal 4:6).

John deepens this idea of the fathership of God for men in that he speaks of 'being born of God' (or, 'from above'). This is a necessary condition in order to be able to share in the good things of salvation (Jn 3:3), in freedom from sin (1 Jn 3:9) and victory over the ↗ world (1 Jn 5:4). Being born of God is not understood literally but rather in an eschatological sense (1 Jn 3:1, 2). It is given through ↗ baptism (Jn 3:3), through ↗ faith in the ↗ revelation of

Christ (Jn 1:13; 1 Jn 5:1; cf 2:23; 2 Jn 9) and through a morally good life consisting in ↗ justice (1 Jn 2:29; 5:18), ↗ love (1 Jn 4:7) and separation from the world (1 Jn 2:16).

Jesus's revelation of God as his father. In all his prayers which have come down to us Jesus prays to God as his father (Mt 11:25, 26; Lk 10:21; Mk 14:36; Mt 26:39; Lk 22:42; Lk 23:34, 46; Jn 11:41; 12:27, 28; 17:1, 5, 11, 21, 24, 25). Mk 14:36 has also preserved the *ipsissima verba Christi* of this prayer which consists in abba ('dear father'). Judaism did not presume to use this simple, trustful and intimate form of address; even in the popular way of speaking in aramaic the solemn, liturgical Hebrew form *ʾab* was used when it came to addressing God as father.

When Jesus speaks of God as his father, the word takes on a wholly particular tone. He asks that the will of his father be done (Mt 7:21), has it at heart that his father's house be honoured (Jn 2:16), knows the decisions of his father (Mt 15:13; 16:17; 18:35; 20:23; 24:36; Mk 13:32; Mt 25:34; Lk 11:13; 24:49). He must be about his father's business (Lk 2:49), he submits himself to the will of his father (Mt 26:39; Mk 14:36). The father has delivered all things to him (Mt 11:27; Lk 10:21); he has bequeathed his kingdom to him and Jesus now disposes fully of it (Lk 22:29); he acknowledges his own (Mt 10:32; 26:53) and hears the prayers which are addressed to him in the name of Jesus (Mt 18:19). The Son of Man comes in the ↗ glory of his father (Mt 16:27; Mk 8:38; Lk 9:26). Jesus' relation to the father consists in a unique and exclusive knowledge (in the sense of association with him; Mt 11:27; Lk 10:22; cf Jn 10:15). He speaks of God as father and of himself as son. When he speaks of the father, either in prayer or conversation, he does not put himself in the same category with his disciples (Jn 20:17). His consciousness of divine sonship and of a special relationship to the father is not the result of his eschatological ↗ hope but rises rather from his eschatological proclamation; he announces not only the coming of the kingdom of God but also this relationship to his father.

Of the *synoptics* Matthew in particular represents God as father. In *John* 'father' is the common designation for God (115 times); the fatherhood of God in relation to Jesus illustrates for him the whole idea of revelation. The father is the dispenser of revelation, the son is the revealer who lives in intimate union with the dispenser. The union between father and son comes about through love (3:35; 10:17; 15:9; 17:23, 26), ↗ obedience (6:40, 49; 10:18, 37; 14:31; 18:11), knowledge (10:15), unity in work (5:17, 21; 10:25), being in one another—what we can call reciprocal immanence (10:38; 14:10, 11; 16:32; 17:21), being *one* (8:19; 10:30; 14:9; 15:23; 16:3). The father gives everything into his hands (13:3), gives him all (3:35), shows him all (5:20: cf 8:28; 12:50), places a seal upon him (6:27), gives him mankind (10:29), life (6:57), his ↗ name (17:11), and glory (17:22). Jesus is the 'only son' (1:14; 3:16, 18; 1 Jn 4:9); who is in the bosom of the father (Jn 1:18), the only-begotten of God (1:18; cf v 1). This divine sonship is not understood in a merely functional sense (that is, as the perfect revelation of God) but also metaphysically.

Paul, in his solemn formulae of blessing or confession of faith, speaks of 'the God and Father of our Lord Jesus Christ' or 'God the Father of our Lord Jesus Christ' (2 Cor 1:3; Eph 1:3; Col 1:3; Eph 1:17; Rom 15:6; Gal 1:1). The Book of *Revelation* demonstrates the greatness of Christ by referring to God as his father. Christ has made the faithful to be priests for his God and father (1:6), he has received power from his father (2:27), he will confess the name of the victor before his father and the angels (3:5) and grant him to sit on his throne just as his father had placed him upon his throne after his victory (3:21). The chosen ones bear the name of the ↗ Lamb and the name of his father written on their foreheads (14:1).

In *the trinitarian formulae* the father is the 'first person', as can be seen in the baptismal form (Mt 28:19). Such a formula is surely behind the phrase: 'Through Jesus we both have access in one Spirit to the Father' (Eph 2:18). The father is the final goal of sacred history (1 Cor 15:24) and of the confession of Christ in which sacred history is implied (Phil 2:11). In cases like this, the name 'father' can also simply be substituted by 'God' (2 Cor 13:14—a trinitarian formula).

Bibliography: G. Quell and G. Schrenk, *TDNT* v, 945–1014; R. Gyllenberg, 'Gott der Vater im AT und in der Predigt Jesu', *Studia Orientalia* 1 (1926), 3–140; E. Lohmeyer, *Das Vaterunser*, Göttingen 1952³, ch. 2; H. Schürmann, *Das Gebet des Herrn*, 1957, 17–26; W. Marchel, *Abba, Père*, Rome 1964. For further bibliography ↗ Sonship.

Alois Stöger

Fear

A. *The Old Testament*. The beginning of man's fear of God coincides with the first sin committed in Paradise. The consequence of this original sin is the loss of intimate and childlike communion with God (Gen 3:10: Adam is afraid because he realises that he is naked). As soon as this communion with God is restored, man may safely forget all his fear. God is always calling upon those who are dear to him to do this (Abraham in Gen 15:1; Isaac in Gen 26:24; Jacob in Gen 28:13; Hagar in Gen 21:17; Jeremiah in Jer 1:8, 17). All the manifestations of religious fear and fearlessness which occur in scripture lie between these two extremities. Any appearance of God arouses fear, and a striking example of this is the theophany on Mount Sinai (Ex 20:18). Exactly the same phenomenon occurs in the case of any miraculous act on God's part, as for example the destruction of the Egyptians in the Red Sea (Ex 14:31). So long as God is with Israel, his people have nothing to fear from their enemies (eg Num 14:9; Deut 1:29; Josh 1:9, etc). Any reference in ancient times to the fear of God almost always implies a concrete and literal fear, based on the fact of God's prodigious and sovereign might or a reverent awe of the *Mysterium Tremendum* (eg Jacob's fearful awakening with the memory of the heavenly ladder, Gen 28:17). God's intention, in inspiring this fear which is his due, is to provide a motive for moral behaviour (eg Lev 19:32; 25:17). As the man who acknowledges God must of necessity also fear him, the way was open for the term 'to fear God' to develop by abstraction from its proper and original meaning into the generally accepted and widely used sense of religious awe. In the psalter especially this extended meaning is almost always consistently adhered to (to mention a few of the many examples: Ps 22:23; 23:4; 25:12; 61:5, etc). A parallel case is to be found in the sapiential literature. On the one hand, the 'fear of God' is called the 'beginning of wisdom' (eg Prov 1:7; 9:10; Sir 1:13, 14, 16), and in this usage the original meaning is still discernible; on the other hand, however, those who fear God certainly appear to be equated with the 'pious' (eg Sir 1:13; 2:7, 8, 9, 15, 16, 17 etc). The use of the phrase 'those who fear God' in the New Testament (see Acts 13:16, 26) for pagans who are sympathetically inclined towards judaism and its culture, provides a partial view of the line of development of this conception which was already beginning to appear clearly in the Old Testament.

B. *The New Testament.* Here, too, there is frequent reference to the fear of God in the ordinary sense of the word. Christ himself requires that we fear God on account of his fearful punishments (Mt 10:28 and pars.—note the reference to hell; see also Heb 10:27, 31). Man in the New Testament also experiences fear with regard to the *Mysterium Tremendum.* Fear is experienced, for example, in the case of the angelic apparition (to Zachary in Lk 1:12f; to Mary in 1:29f; to the shepherds in 2:9); in the case of extraordinary occurrences which reveal the hand of God (the healing of the man sick of the palsy, Mt 9:8 and pars; the expulsion of the demons from the swine, Lk 8:37 and pars; the healing of the woman with an issue of blood, Mk 5:33 and pars; possibly also Joseph's fear, Mt 1:20; the events which take place at the time of Jesus's death, Mt 27:54; the resurrection of the young man at Naim, Lk 7:16). A sensation of fear was also often present in connection with Christ, not only among those who had to reckon with his superior might when they attacked him (the Synedrium, Mt 21:26, 46 and parallels; Mk 11:18; 12:12 and parallels; a similar case is that of Herod's fear of putting John the Baptist to death, Mt 14:5 and parallels). This fear is also experienced as a religious awe (by Christ's most intimate friends) on account of the mysterious power which is active in him, as, for example, in the case of the Transfiguration in Mt 17:6 and pars, his walking on the lake in Mt 14:27, the miraculous catch of fish in Lk 5:9ff and his foretelling of his own passion in Mk 9:32 and pars, when the apostles do not dare to ask him what this means.

Again and again Christ exhorts his own to fear no more. Many terrifying experiences may be in store for the disciples, as, for example, persecution (Mt 10:26) and physical death (Mt 10:28). There is, however, still no cause for fear, as the soul is incomparably more valuable than the body and is in God's hands (Lk 12:4). They have, moreover, his promise of intercession with the Father (Mt 10:29–31 and pars) and the promised inheritance of the 'kingdom' as his 'little flock' (Lk 12:32). In the case of the miraculous walking on the waters, the disciples ought to have felt no fear as it was Christ himself who performed this miracle (Mt 14:27; Jn 6:20). Peter would not have feared and thus would not have sunk beneath the surface of the lake if he had trusted and believed in the Lord (Mt 14:30). Jairus too ought to have believed, in which case he would have been able to overcome all fear for his daughter's well-being (Mk 16:8; Mt 28:10). It is hardly surprising that the risen Christ inspires fear in the women and in the apostles (Mk 16:8; Mt 28:10), but there is also no cause for them to go on fearing, as he has truly arisen (the message of the angel, Mt 28:5; Christ himself 28:10). In John's gospel we find Christ's own reason for urging his disciples to be fearless: 'Have confidence; I have overcome the world' (Jn 16:33). Christ is simply the fulfilment of the message of the prophets: 'Fear not, daughter of Zion; behold thy king cometh sitting on an ass's colt' (Zech 9:9; Jn 12:15; see Is 40:9). He and he alone provides the reason for our complete fearlessness.

The most significant and characteristic admonition to christians concerning the necessary interrelationship between fear and fearlessness comes from *St Paul.* The redeemed christian who possesses the Spirit of God has the duty to forsake fear (Rom 8:15). All the same, he must work out his salvation in fear and trembling (Phil 2:12). This, then, is the characteristic situation of the christian—he has already attained his salvation, but this salvation must nevertheless be worked out continually during his life in this world. What is interesting here is the reason for this affirmation of St Paul, namely that it is God himself who both conceives and carries out the work of salvation. Thus, here too, there is a close connection between God inspiring fear and taking it away.

The fearlessness which is required of the christian makes no difference to the fact that even the Apostle himself experiences both human fear and apprehensions and misgivings. He was filled with fear when he came to Corinth (1 Cor 2:3). Inner fear, as well as external conflicts, is the constant companion of all apostolic activity (2 Cor 7:5). St Paul too fears the one before whom we must all appear (2 Cor 5:11).

In his teaching, the apostle frequently enjoins fear for human masters and human authority. This injunction holds good for the state as the servant of God (Rom 13:3f) in respect of those who have cause to fear punishment on account of their evildoings, for the masters of servants or slaves, whether these are well disposed or not (1 Pet 2:18; Eph 6:5; slaves are here enjoined to be subject to their masters 'as to Christ') and finally for husbands (Eph 5:33: the husband-wife relationship refers here also to the relationship between Christ and his church). But in all these instances, legitimate fear can be aroused and respect claimed only because those in question have received their authority for the time being from God.

St Paul's own personal example in this respect applies also to the various communities within the church of God which have been entrusted to his care. The christian who has been moved by God's elective grace to forsake heathenism must guard against presumption with regard to the fate of Israel whose people were called upon to believe in the first place; he must have salutary fear (Rom 11:20). The sanctification of the christian will be perfected in the fear of God (2 Cor 7:1). Timothy is to admonish sinners publicly so that the others may feel fear as a motive for prudence and improvement (1 Tim 5:20). Christians are to be subject one to another in the fear of Christ (Eph 5:21).

In his first Letter, Peter lays great stress on fear as the necessary basis for a proper mental attitude on the part of the christian. Christians are exhorted time and again to fear God (1 Pet 2:17) and to conduct themselves in fear so long as they are here on earth (1 Pet 1:17). The chaste and holy conduct of wives is to be grounded on fear (1 Pet 3:2) and the servants of the house are to be subject to their masters in fear (1 Pet 2:18). As a general rule, christians are urged to conduct themselves with modesty and fear (1 Pet 3:16), but, on the other hand, St Peter's first Epistle also recognises the other side of the christian message concerning fear. The christian is not to fear those who act evilly towards him (the state may be implied in this instance: 1 Pet 3:14 = Is 8:12). Similarly, wives who, like Sarah, are upright in their actions (Sarah obeyed Abraham: 1 Pet 3:6), have no cause for fear.

In John's gospel we find many passages in which Christ especially encourages his disciples to be fearless. Though this exhortation is prominent also in all the teaching of Christ in the rest of the johannine writings, we find it said here too that God is to be praised by those who fear him (Rev 19:5 = Ps 115:13). The other angel calls upon the people to fear God and give him the honour that is due to him (Rev 14:7). God will reward those who fear him (Rev 11:18). The way in which this fear which is demanded of men is to be understood is demonstrated in the Book of Revelation itself by the comforting assurance which the Son of Man gives to John: 'Fear not, I am the first and the last, and the living one; I died, and behold I am alive for evermore' (1:17–18). This statement leads directly to the great, and genuinely johannine statement concerning the reason why we should not fear: 'There is no fear in love, but perfect love casts out fear. For fear has to do with punishment, and he who fears is not perfected in love' (1 Jn 4:18). Thus it can be seen that St John has also reached the point where he accepts, as St Paul did before him in his conception of the spirit of adoption, that God has saved us from fear because he wished to make us brothers of his dearly beloved Son.

The biblical pronouncement on the subject of fear can be briefly summarised thus: the man who is completely united with God knows no fear. Separation from God leads to the development of fear as an important element in man's life, and he is then bound to fear his fellows, the principalities and powers of this world and even God himself, who wishes, as far as we are concerned, to be nothing but love. Christ appeared in order to liberate us from the bonds of fear through his presence. And even if fear is still the lot of man who has already been redeemed, so long as he has not reached the point of sharing in a complete and undivided way in God's love, nevertheless he can at the same time already put aside every vestige of servile fear.

Bibliography: W. Lütgert, 'Die Furcht Gottes', *Festschrift für M. Kähler*, 1905, 165ff; S. F. H. J. Berkelbach van der Sprenkel, *Vrees en Religie*, 1920; R. Sander, *Furcht und Liebe im palästinensischen Judentum*, 1935; Köhler 36ff; E. Boularand, *Dict. de la Spiritualité* II, Paris 1953, 2464–775; D. Lys and E. Diserens, Allmen 51–5; R. Borchert, *Ev. Kirchenlex.* I (1956), 1408f; G. van der Leeuw (C. M. Edsman), *RGG* II³, 1180ff (on the comparative religion aspect, with relevant bibliography); Bultmann I, 320ff and II, 213f; Haag 607f; L. Nieder, *LTK* IV², 1107f; K. Romaniuk, 'La crainte de Dieu à Qumran et dans le NT', *RQ* 4 (1963), 3–10; Eichrodt III, 1964, 184–90; P. Auvray and P. Grelot, *DBT* 149–51.

Wolfgang Beilner

Fire

A. *The Old Testament.* The word *fire*—in Hebrew *ʾēš* and in Greek *pur*—often occurs in the bible in its normal meaning and is particularly used in connection with ↗ sacrifice (Lev 1:7ff; 6:9, 15; 10:1 with the appropriate instructions).

Fire, with its consuming power, is used as a symbol or image of calumny (Prov 26:20ff), anger (Sir 28:10ff), bloody deeds and murder (Sir 11:32; 22:24), physical passion and lust (Sir 9:8; 23:16; see also 1 Cor 7:9), adultery (Job 31:12; Prov 6:27f) and sin (Sir 3:30; 8:10). Very often we find the image of fire used with reference to the ↗ law and to the anger or ↗ wrath of God (Jer 4:4; 5:14; Ezek 21:31; Ps 79:5; and elsewhere in the Psalms). Fire also accompanies God's appearances to man (theophanies)—good examples of this are Ex 19; 3:2 and Judg 6:21—and is occasionally a sign of a favourable ↗ visitation, as, for example, when God wishes to show his satisfaction with a sacrifice (Gen 15:17; Lev 9:23f; Judg 6:21, etc), to lead the people in a pillar of fire (Ex 13:21f; 14:24; Num 14:14) or to protect his people by encircling them with a wall of fire (Zech 2:5). Whenever God himself is called a 'consuming fire', it is not really that he wishes to be represented in the form of personified fire, but rather that he seeks to give expression to his just and merciful majesty.

B. In *later judaism* and in the *Qumran texts* we find fire used especially in the eschatological sense, that is, in connection with God's justice (1 QpHab 10:5; 10:13). In 1 QS 2:8 wc find reference to the everlasting fire of ↗ hell, and in 1 QH 3:29–33 to the idea of the universal conflagration (as in the Jewish Sibylline Oracles, 2:186ff; 3:83ff; 4:172ff; 5:158ff, etc).

C. *The New Testament.* As in the Old Testament, fire is often used here to symbolise God's judgement, together with representations taken from the everyday language of a rural society, such as trees which no longer yield fruit (Mt 3:10), chaff (Mt 3:12), cockle and other weeds (Mt 13:40)—these are all to be burnt. In the Apocalypse in particular, fire appears as an omen of the judgement of God (8:7, 8; 11:5; 13:13; 14:18). In the main, however, fire is used in the New Testament in the eschatological sense, as the fire of God's judgement. The baptism by fire is foretold in the sermon of John the Baptist (Mt 3:11; Lk 3:16). The most probable interpretation of the passage in Mk 9:49, 'everyone shall be salted with fire', is that everyone who wishes to enter the Kingdom of God has to pass through the judgement of God. Lang (*TDNT* VI, 944, *n* 82) compares this with 2 Cor 5:17 and Jn 3:3, 4, 7 (which are in a different theological setting). Jn 3:18 has also to be taken into consideration in this connection. Lang gives this striking explanation: for everyone, 'the way to fellowship with God is by judgement of the old man' (*TDNT* VI, 944). In Lk 12:49ff, we find the following comment on the promise of John the Baptist which was brought to fulfilment through Jesus: Jesus himself must also go through the fire, that is to say, through his ↗ passion; he himself has cast fire on the earth (v 49) and with his coming the eschatological judgement has dawned. A remarkable and johannine passage occurs in the Coptic Gospel of Thomas: 'I have cast fire on the *cosmos* and will *maintain* it until the (= the fire?) burns' (Logion 10). In this context we must also include the agraphon (a saying of Jesus that has not been handed down through the medium of the Bible): 'Whoever is close to me is close to the fire; whoever is far from me is far from the kingdom' (in another version, 'far from life'). This passage occurs in the Gospel of Thomas, Logion 82, and should be compared with Origen, Hom lat in Jer 3:3, etc. What is very clearly expressed here is that closeness to Jesus implies closeness to the judgement, and at the same time closeness to the ↗ kingdom of God and to ↗ life, and that life and access to the Kingdom are to be gained through this judgement (see J. B. Bauer, *TZ* 15 [1959], 446–50).

Paul speaks in three places about fire and in each case refers to the eschatological fire of the judgement. In 1 Cor 3:13–15, we read that the fire will try every man's work. The man who works with little success to achieve the kingdom of God will be able to survive only by the skin of his teeth when the Lord comes—this is what is meant by the passage 'he himself will be saved, but only as through fire' (v 15). Paul depicts, in 2 Thess 1:7f, the ↗ parousia of the Lord as the revelation of his miraculous power to all those who believe in him (v 10) and as the ↗ judgement and ↗ retribution he will exact from those who do not acknowledge God. Jesus will reveal himself here 'in flames of fire'. The quotation from Prov 25:21f, which Paul uses in Rom 12:20, is not easy to understand in itself (see O. Michel, *Der Brief an die Römer*, Göttingen 1955, 278f), but it would appear to be associated by Paul himself with God's judgement (see verse 19). The coals heaped upon the head of one's enemy symbolise his humiliation, which will either lead him to conversion or condemn him in the end to perish in God's judgement by fire.

The eschatological fire of God's judgement is also alluded to in Heb 10:27; 12:29, as well as in Rev 20:9 and in 2 Pet 3:7, where it is connected with the wider teaching on the universal conflagration. The fire of ↗ hell (see that article for examples) is mentioned both in the Book of Revelation and in the rest of the New Testament.

Finally, fire and brightness occur frequently as symbols of heavenly glory. The Book of Revelation gives many examples of this usage: the description of Christ triumphant (Rev 1:14f; see also 2:18; 19:12), the description of the angel (10:1), that of the seven spirits who appear before the throne in the form of torches or lamps of fire (4:5), and the description of the 'sea of glass mingled with fire' (15:2). Fire marks out the angels and spirits as important elements of the heavenly world of light. In this connection, rather than in the Stoical sense in which spirit and fire are equated, the fire which appears in the account (given in Acts 2:3) of the descent of the Holy Spirit at Pentecost can be regarded as a sign of the miraculous and heavenly origin of the Holy Spirit—a visible sign of God's invisible revelation.

Bibliography: F. Lang, *Das Feuer im Sprachgebrauch der Bibel, dargestellt auf dem Hintergrund der Feuervorstellungen in der Umwelt*, Tübingen 1950; F. Lang, *TDNT* VI, 928–52 (full bibliography); F. Lang, *Ev. Kirchenlex.* I, 1282f; H. Eising, *LTK* IV², 107f; J. Gaillard, *Catholicisme* IV, 1227–9: on the subject of purgatory, not implied in 1 Cor 3:12–15, see J. Gnilka, *LTK* IV², 50f (bibliography included); S. Cipriani, *Rivista Biblica* 7 (1959), 25–43; G. Rinaldi, 'La preparazione dell'argento e il fuoco purificatore', *Bibbia e Oriente* 5 (1963), 53–9; J. Michl, 'Gerichtsfeuer und Purgatorium, zu 1 Cor 3:12–15', *Stud. Paul.* (Rome 1963), 395–401; P. D. Miller Jr, 'Fire in the Mythology of Canaan and Israel', *CBQ* 17 (1965), 256–61.

Johannes B. Bauer

Firstfruits (firstborn)

Religious ethnology is familiar with the institution of the offering of firstfruits in very many ancient and primitive religions. By means of this practice the deity was acknowledged and thanked as the lord and preserver of life. It could also constitute a recognition of the deity's right to the object in question in that it could be made use of only after payment of an appropriate levy. So, for example, hunting tribes offered the first animal taken at the beginning of the hunting season and shepherds and farmers offered the first produce of the herd or the fields. The Old Testament is no exception to this practice; we find there the terms *bᵉkôr* (the firstborn of men and cattle: Gen 25:13; Ex 11:5; 12:29) and *bikkûrîm* (the first produce of the grain and the fruit trees: Ex 23:16; Lev 23:20; Num 18:13) and to these Yahweh laid special claim. During the first three years the produce of the fruit trees was considered 'uncircumcised' (↗ circumcision), namely, not to be put to common use; it was consecrated to Yahweh in the fourth year and was thus not to be enjoyed until the fifth year (Lev 19:23–5). Similarly one could not eat of the corn harvest until the first sheaf had been offered to Yahweh (Lev 23:14). This offering was associated in the first place with the three great agrarian festivals (see Lev 23:9f; 15ff). In Deut 16:1ff we find preserved the prayer to be recited at the offering of the firstfruit of the land which reveals the deep significance of this act performed at the sanctuary; it was first and foremost the fulfilment of Israel's duty of gratitude to her divine lord for his gracious gift of the land of Canaan.

The firstborn of men had to be offered to Yahweh. The firstborn of unclean domestic animals (the ass) had to be substituted for by the offering of a clean animal (the lamb, Ex 13:2, 12f; 34:19f; Num 3:12f), since they belonged to Yahweh. If they had not already been sacrificed on the eighth day after birth at a local sanctuary

(Ex 22:29) the firstborn of animals were used in the sacrificial meal. This idea seems to be associated with the Passover and the offering of the Passover animal which occurred at the beginning of the year (see Ex 13; 34:19ff; Num 3:13). The fact that the laws concerning firstfruits speak of animals and men together may constitute something of a difficulty, and some have tried to explain it by applying an hypothesis taken from the history of religions to the Old Testament according to which an original practice of human sacrifice was later replaced by the sacrifice of animals. Human sacrifices certainly took place in the ancient Near East—for example, the Phoenician practice of sacrificing children at the dedication of a building—but these were extremely rare. The sacrifice of Isaac (Gen 22:1–19) has always been understood as an exceptional testing of faith rewarded by the renewal of the divine promise to the descendents of Abraham. Its relevance for Israel was that it showed her that she owed her existence to the divine mercy and to the obedience of her ancestors. The sacrifice of Jephthah (Judg 11:30–40) must be thought of as an exceptional case analogous to the sacrifice carried out later by the king of Moab (2 Kings 3:27). The sacrifice carried out at the consecration of a building under king Ahab (1 Kings 16:34) was due doubtless to Phoenician influence. The Israelites never sacrificed children to Yahweh, though some sacrifices to Moloch took place in the eighth and seventh centuries BC. Old Testament religion rejected human sacrifice right from the beginning, it was expressly forbidden in the Law (Deut 12:31; 18:10; Lev 18:21; 20:2–5), and the prophets denounced it as an idolatrous practice (Hos 13:2). The redemption of the firstborn of men found in the oldest sources of the Pentateuch together with the injunction to sacrifice the firstborn of animals (Ex 22:28f; 34:19f) does not by any means imply a mitigation of the cruel practice of child-sacrifice current at an earlier period. All it implies is that the firstborn of both men and animals belong to Yahweh and that the former had to be redeemed and the latter sacrificed. Ezekiel, who condemned child-sacrifice, certainly never thought that this practice was ever positively inculcated by Yahweh (Ezek 16:20; 20:31). He does indeed say on one occasion (20:25f) that Yahweh gave his people, as punishment for their idolatry, ordinances which must have been objectionable to them in so far as they would be rendered unclean by the sacrifice of children. But this only implies that on account of the sin of the people, what had been originally meant as a blessing turned into a curse for them. The stipulation about the consecration of the firstborn could be interpreted by a people whose mind was far from God as if child-sacrifice was required by Yahweh. Moreover Jer 7:31 denies clearly and explicitly that Yahweh had ever commanded the sacrifice of children.

The levites were consecrated to Yahweh in a special manner as a substitute for the firstborn of the people (Num 3:12f; 8:16–18). They certainly received part of their living from the sacrificial offering of firstfruits brought to the sanctuary (Ex 23:19 E; Ex 34:26 J; Deut 12:6f, 11f, 17–19). The first produce of the fields, the trees and the herds was considered as of special value. The firstborn son enjoyed special privileges over the other children during the lifetime of the father (Gen 43:33), received a double portion of inheritance after his death (Deut 21:17) and became head of the family. These privileges could, however, be lost as the result of punishment (Gen 35:22) or waived in favour of another (Gen 25:29–34). ↗ Sacrifice.

Bibliography: A. George, 'Le Sacrifice d'Abraham', *Mélanges Vaganay*, Lyon 1948, 99–110; W. Kornfeld, 'Der Moloch', *WZKM* 51 (1952), 287–313; J. Henninger, 'Menschenopfer bei den Araben', *Anthropos* 53 (1958), 721f and 776f; de Vaux, 490–91.

Walter Kornfeld

Flesh

Flesh may mean simply meat (Rom 14:21; 1 Cor 8:13), but in most places in the bible it is used, together with various other words, in a different sense, to convey a theological meaning.

1. *Flesh and man.* Flesh is the animate substance, the carnal matter which is fashioned into human or animal form. It is man's external substance (Gen 2:21; Ex 4:7; 1 Sam 17:44; 2 Kings 5:10, 14; 9:36; Ezek 37:6; Job 2:5; Lk 24:39—the risen Christ is not a 'spirit' because he has flesh and blood: 1 Cor 15:39). Flesh is also the body, in which usage the idea of an organic unity is disregarded, as this is contained in the term 'body'. Here the idea of vitality is brought more closely into focus. Flesh is used for body in Ex 30:32; Num 8:7; 1 Kings 21:27, and the 'thorn' in the flesh (2 Cor 12:7) and the 'bodily ailment' (Gal 4:13f) are physical frailty, not sexual temptation. 'Tribulation of the flesh' is an abject distress (1 Cor 7:28; see also Col 1:24; 2 Cor 7:5; 1 Pet 4:2). When Paul refers to others seeing his 'face in the flesh' (Col 2:1), he is referring to his physical countenance. The 'destruction of the flesh' (1 Cor 5:5) is of course death. By his flesh, that is to say, by his passion and death, Christ has made peace (Eph 2:14; Col 1:22). Circumcision is performed in the flesh (ie body) (Rom 2:28; Gal 6:12f; Eph 2:11; Col 2:13). Presence in the flesh is physical presence (Col 2:5). The bread of the Eucharist is called flesh (John 6:51–6; it is called 'body' in the synoptic gospels) and it is the living body, the whole of Jesus's being in his physical existence. The phrase 'my flesh' replaces the personal pronoun 'I' in Ps 16:9; 63:1; Acts 2:26; 2 Cor 7:5; Rom 7:18. 'All flesh' is creation as a whole (Gen 6:17; Ps 65:2; 136:25; Sir 40:8), mankind (Is 40:5 = Lk 3:6; Joel 2:28 = Acts 2:17; Jn 17:2). Flesh is the human person, the living man, and the logos, or pre-existent Christ, has become flesh (Jn 1:14; 1 Jn 4:2; 2 Jn 7; 1 Tim 3:16). The boundary which exists between the man as body and the personal 'I' is not always clearly determined, but often remains fluid. Flesh is the living creature, the human person, similar to the 'soul' (cf 1 Cor 2:14 with 3:3; 1 Cor 15:44–6; 'natural' is the same as 'carnal'). According to the Hebrew mode of thought, the elements which comprise the human being are not viewed as static, but as dynamic, not as anatomical units, but as a complete entity and as a living unity. This conception of man remained unchanged

until the influence of Greek philosophy began to be felt (Wis 8:19f; 9:15; in 1 Pet 3:21 flesh is contrasted with the conscience and possibly with the soul already touched by grace).

Flesh also expresses the community of man and his relationship with his fellow-men. Eve, because she is taken from Adam and is part of the same essential being, is 'flesh of his flesh' (Gen 2:23). They are joined to each other in marriage and are thus 'one flesh' (Gen 2:24; quoted in Mt 19:5; Mk 10:7f; 1 Cor 6:16; Eph 5:31; see also 5:29). Blood-relations are (one bone) and one flesh (Gen 29:14; 37:27; Judg 9:2). Fellow citizens are also one flesh (2 Sam 5:1; 19:12; Is 58:7). 'Eating the flesh of my people' (Mic 3:2f) means to destroy the entire people. Physical genealogy is characterised by 'flesh' (Rom 4:1; 9:3, 5; 11:14; 1 Cor 10:18). This is also the probable reason why the genital organs are called 'flesh' (Lev 15:2; Ezek 16:26; 23:20).

The expression 'all flesh' is also used with a collective meaning, in the sense of the unity of mankind. This meaning is to be found in the second part of the book of Isaiah, in which the mode of thought is universal in application (Is 40:5; 49:26; 66:23), as well as in Jer 25:31; Joel 2:28. The promises of salvation are to be extended to the whole of mankind. These ideas are taken up in the New Testament with reference to the Old (Lk 3:6, with reference to Is 40:5; Acts 2:17, with reference to Joel 2:28; Jn 17:2, in which Jesus, in the prayer of the high priest, praises the Father for giving him power over 'all flesh'). The whole of mankind stands in need of salvation, since 'all flesh' is infirm (1 Pet 1:24 = Is 40:6), prone to sinfulness (Rom 3:20; Gal 2:16 = Ps 143:2), unable to glory in itself (1 Cor 1:29) and is subject to pain and tribulation at the end of time (Mt 24:22; Mk 13:20). In certain places, flesh represents the whole of creation, both men and animals (Gen 6:12f; 7:21; 9:11; possibly also Jer 32:27). Man is closely associated with the whole of creation (Rom 8:20f).

2. *Flesh as man's frailty and infirmity.* Flesh is man specifically in his humanity. The bible views man throughout in his relationship with God, and flesh portrays man's situation with regard to God. In the light of God's truth man can discover what he really is—a being that is shortlived (Gen 6:3; Is 40:6), weak (Ps 55:5; Is 31:3), and doomed to death (Ps 78:39; cf Ps 90:5ff: Sir 14:17f). No trust can be placed in the flesh (Jer 17:5). 'Flesh and blood' cannot penetrate the mysteries of the revelation without God's help (Mt 16:17), nor can it resist temptation (Mt 26:41; Mk 14:38). This idea of weakness is generally discernible in the phrase 'flesh and blood'. As examples of this we find that flesh and blood cannot inherit the Kingdom of God (Sir 14:18; cf 17; 17:31; 1 Cor 15:50), that our conflict is not against flesh and blood, but . . . against the evil spirits in high places (Eph 6:12; see Gal 1:16). A further reference to flesh and blood is to be found in Heb 2:14. Flesh and blood are not separate parts of man. The bible views man as an indivisible whole.

Flesh represents the sphere of the earthly and natural, of the purely human in contrast to that of the supramundane, the supernatural and the divine. This contrast is not always explicit but it is always suggested. Above all, no ethical judgement is implied in it. A contrast is made between circumcision of the flesh and that of the heart (Rom 2:28f), earthly (or carnal) things and supernatural (or spiritual) things (1 Cor 9:11), the purely natural mode of thinking and faith (2 Cor 5:16), the wisdom of this world (represented by those who are wise according to the flesh) and that which has been revealed and given to us by the Spirit (1 Cor 2:1–16). To live in the flesh (Gal 2:20; Phil 1:22, 24) or to walk according to the flesh (Rom 8:9) means to live one's life, as a human being, on the purely material and earthly plane, as opposed to living it in the spirit (Rom 8:9), with Christ (Phil 1:23) and in faith (Gal 2:20). Onesimus is to be treated as a brother both in the flesh and in the Lord (Philem 16), as a human being and as a christian. 'According to the flesh' expresses a natural relationship (eg genealogy), in implicit or explicit contrast to a relationship which has been brought about supernaturally by God. Jesus is descended according to the flesh from David (Rom 1:3; cf 9:5), Abraham is the father of the Jews according to the flesh (Rom 4:1), St Paul himself is a brother of the Jews according to the flesh (Rom 9:3). Israel according to the flesh (1 Cor 10:18) is contrasted with the Israel of God (Gal 6:16), Ishmael was Abraham's son according to the flesh (that is, as a result of natural, human procreation), whereas Isaac was his son according to the spirit (that is, he was begotten in a miraculous manner). Similar examples of this usage are to be found in the rest of the New Testament. Flesh and spirit are contrasted in Jn 3:6—a man cannot enter the Kingdom of God purely as a result of his having been born in this world; he must be born again supernaturally (of the spirit, according to Jn 3:7f; according to 1 Pet 1:23, of the word of God). In 1 Pet 3:18 the human body is contrasted with the spirit (as divine essence).

3. *Flesh in contradiction to God.* Whenever man presumes exclusively on the flesh, his purely human status, this attitude would appear to disqualify him (Is 31:3; Jer 17:5). He cannot attain salvation when he places his hopes solely in the flesh, that is, in his descent from the people of Israel (Phil 3:3f), in exclusively human privileges or qualities (2 Cor 11:18), in personal asceticism (Col 2:18, 23) or in his fulfilment of the mosaic law (Gal 3:3). 'Flesh and blood', that is, man alone acting without grace, cannot inherit the kingdom of God (1 Cor 15:50). Flesh is thus man in isolation, seeking his salvation merely by the exercise of his own powers. The Jew does this by fulfilling the law, the Greek by means of his philosophy. Man is always eager to work out his own salvation without God, by his own efforts alone, and this is basically the original sin of man, that he wishes to achieve perfection—to be as God—without God (Gal 3:5). Man's illusion is that he, who is flesh, can be God despite his condition.

Flesh is man in hostility to God and represents that part of man which is not just physically but also morally weak and infirm. St Paul in particular states this with great insistence, particularly in Rom 7–8 and Gal 5. Before Christ, unredeemed man is carnal and sold under sin (Rom 7:14): 'The mind that is set on the flesh is hostile to God' (Rom 8:7), and 'those who are in the flesh cannot please God' (8:8). It is sinful conduct to walk according to the flesh (Rom 8:4; 2 Cor 10:2), to live according to the flesh (Rom 8:12), or to exist according to the flesh (Rom 8:5). Christians are to live no longer according to the flesh (Rom 8:9) but according to the spirit (Rom 8:4f), according to God (2 Cor 11:17) and according to love. Flesh and spirit are completely opposed to each other, as sin and obedience to God, as selfishness and love, or as death and eternal life (Gal 5:17). 'Sarx' is a power or principle to which man is subject and against which he is scarcely able to defend himself successfully (Rom 8:7).

The works of the flesh are the so-called sins of the senses, such as lewdness, impurity, debauchery, drunkenness and gluttony. Among these sins, however, are those which more or less belong to the sphere of spirituality, such as idolatry and sorcery, animosity, enmities and contention, jealousy, quarrels and dissension, selfishness, envy and arrogant pride (Gal 5:19ff; Col 2:18). Only 2 Pet 2:10 calls unchastity the 'licentious passions of the flesh' (see 2:18). In Jude 7f, 'going after other flesh' is called leading an unchaste life. The 'works of the flesh' are evoked by the desires which urge man towards what is morally bad (Rom 7:14; 7:5—here the 'sinful passions' are those passions which lead to the committing of sin: Gal 5:16, 24; Eph 2:3; 2 Pet 2:18; 1 Jn 2:16). These desires are the wisdom of the flesh (Gal 5:24) and are situated in the flesh (Rom 7:5—'nothing good dwells in me, that is, in my flesh').

4. *Flesh and redemption.* According to the theology of St Paul sin (regarded as a personified force) makes use of the Mosaic law to stimulate the desires which are situated in the flesh, law to goad men on to commit sin and to establish all the more firmly the mastery of sin (Rom 7:7–13). The law cannot be fulfilled on account of the 'weakness of the flesh' (Rom 8:3). Unredeemed man serves the law of sin with the flesh (Rom 7:25). He who lives according to the flesh must die. 'While we were living in the flesh (ie unredeemed), our sinful passions, aroused by the law, were at work in our members to bear fruit for death' (Rom 7:5; cf 8:3). Flesh, the ↗ Law (see also ↗ Justification), ↗ sin, and ↗ death are very closely associated. What lies behind Rom 7 is man's proneness to sin. Paul does not really mean here that man's *nous* (=mind) is a power which can, after the manner of the Greek philosophers, master his *sarx* (=flesh), but rather that pre-christian man could only act, despite the best of intentions, in a manner which contradicted God.

Yet God uses this very flesh, which has the ability to lead man to sin and destruction, as his means to save man, by sending his own Son 'in the likeness of sinful flesh' (Rom 8:3). The Son of God accepted and took on the infirm nature of man, which, in our case, is under the sway of sin. Paul refers especially to the 'likeness of sinful flesh' because he is anxious to forestall any possible idea that Christ also might have been subject to sin or have actually sinned, since Jesus 'knew no sin' (2 Cor 5:21). In the death of the flesh God condemned the tyrant Sin and deprived him of his power (Rom 8:3). By means of baptism, christians have crucified the flesh with its passions and desires (Gal 5:24; no asceticism is implied here in the use of the word 'crucify'). Similarly they have put off the old man together with his works (Col 3:9). God has given christians, who were dead by reasons of their sins and their uncircumcised and unredeemed flesh, life together with Christ, by the forgiveness of sins (Col 2:13). Flesh is, as we have already seen, not a part of man which can be put off or 'mortified'. It is man himself. The christian, then, does not live according to the flesh but according to the spirit (Rom 8:4, 9). The sacramental act of baptism calls for a corresponding moral response. Even when the baptised christian has put aside his sinful flesh, the weakness of the flesh remains and continues to exert its influence (Rom 6:12ff; cf 8:9). The flesh is still in revolt against the spirit (Gal 5:17), and this is why the admonition against living according to the flesh is still necessary (Rom 8:5, 12f; 13:14; Col 3:5). It is not until the resurrection that the flesh will be finally and completely overcome (see Rom 8:10f). Paul does not call the transfigured body 'flesh', but 'a spiritual body' (1 Cor 15:44). Flesh and blood cannot possess the Kingdom of God, just as corruption cannot possess incorruption (1 Cor 15:50).

5. *Interpretation of the pauline doctrine of the flesh.* The synoptics tend to use the language of the Old Testament (see Mt 26:41; Mk 14:38). This applies also to James and to the Rabbinical writers and Qumran. In the case of St Paul, St John and St Jude, as well as in 1 and 2 Pet, this Old Testament linguistic usage is overlaid by the new way of thinking, although there are few relevant texts apart from St Paul. The characteristically pauline use of the word 'flesh' to designate a power which can completely control man cannot be traced back to the Old Testament. St Paul views flesh as a personal force, similar to sin—it has its own way of thinking, its own aims (Rom 8:5ff; 13:4; Col 2:18), it is constantly in revolt against the spirit (Gal 5:17, 24), performs works (Gal 5:19) and even appears as a believer (Rom 8:12). This view of the flesh is not based on mythological ideas, but is firmly established in his own thought patterns. St Paul does not think of flesh in the dualistic sense of the Greek philosophers or the gnostics, as something which is directly opposed to the soul—though it is of course possible that he may have been influenced by their terminology. We find, for example, that even the man who is justified and sanctified (1 Cor 6:11) lives in the flesh. He lives in the flesh, but does not fight according to the flesh (2 Cor 10:3; Gal 2:19f). Even Christ himself, who is without sin, lives in the flesh (2 Cor 5:16; Rom 8:3). The association of flesh and sin is neither necessary nor essential. It is not possible to detect any latent traces of the strictly dualistic conception of the antithesis between flesh/body and spirit/soul in the pauline antithesis between sarx and pneuma. St Paul is not hostile to the body and the antithesis between the 'flesh' and the spirit is not physical but ethical. Man is

flesh insofar as he is in a state of disorder as a result of original sin (see Rom 5:1–12) and insofar as he is in the bondage of sin. This condition, in which he is afflicted by original sin, expresses itself in selfish activity. Outwardly man, with his desires and the physical organs which serve them, is given over to the service of these false activities. The disorder in his life can only be overcome by the Spirit of God, by charity and by a new life in Christ. The germs of the church's teaching on original sin and concupiscence can be found in the doctrine of the flesh.

Bibliography: W. Schauf, *Sarx* (*NA* XI), 1–2 (Münster 1924); E. Käsemann, *Leib und Leib Christi*, Tübingen 1933, 100–18; Prat II 1941[28], 59–65 and 487–9; W. Gutbrod, *Die paulinische Anthropologie*, Stuttgart-Berlin 1934; N. Krautwik, 'Der Leib im Kampf des "pneuma" wider die "sarx"', *TG* 39 (1949), 296–311; Bultmann I, 227–46; *BTHW* 139–42; Nötscher, 85f; O. Kuss, *Der Römerbrief*, 1959, 506–40; E. Schweizer, 'Die hellenistische Komponente im neutestamentlichen *Sarx*-Begriff', *ZNW* 48 (1957), 237–53; E. Schweizer, '*Sarx*', *TWNT* VII, 98–151.

Alois Stöger

Foolishness

The concept of foolishness is opposed to wisdom; which means that what is said about foolishness in the scriptures will be the contrary of the descriptions found there of ↗ wisdom (or prudence).

A. The *Old Testament* has a number of words which stand for fool, foolishness, foolish. What constitutes a foolish person as such is the refusal and even the inability to accept instruction or to learn from experience and to regulate his behaviour in accordance with the laws in force in the community.

The fool despises wisdom and discipline (Prov 1:7); he derides warnings (Prov 15:5) and hates reproof (Prov 12:1). He does not listen to good advice (Prov 12:15) and despises instruction (Prov 23:9). It is practically impossible to instruct a foolish person: 'A rebuke goes deeper into a man of understanding than a hundred blows into a fool' (Prov 17:10, cf Sir 21:14). Nor does experience make a fool any the wiser: 'Like a dog that returns to his vomit is a fool that repeats his folly' (Prov 26:11).

Instruction in Israel included religious and moral teaching as well as general rules of prudence. The kind of foolishness that despises instruction is therefore a religious or moral fault though it can also be merely a violation of ordinary worldly wisdom. Israel also is called foolish when she does not live according to the commandments of the Lord her Father and Creator (Deut 32:6) and turns to strange gods (Jer 5:21ff). This also applies to the Samaritans who were considered as fools for having separated themselves from Israel (Sir 50:26). Anyone who has no care for God, who gives the lie to God in his practical, everyday life, is also a fool (Ps 14:1). Sin, therefore, is always foolishness (see Prov 15:21), and sins such as reviling God (Ps 74:18, 22), hardness of heart (1 Sam 25:25), the violation of a virgin (2 Sam 13:12) and adultery (Deut 22:21) are expressly referred to as foolishness.

In his dealings with his fellow-men the fool lacks in prudence. He speaks without deliberation (Prov 10:14; 12:23; 13:16; 14:3) and at the wrong time (Prov 20:19); he gives an answer before he has time to hear the question

(Prov 18:13), and even any infraction against good manners is considered as foolishness (Sir 21:22–4).

Scripture warns against the company of fools since there can come of it only provocation (Prov 27:3; Sir 22:13) and harm (Prov 13:20). There is no real prospect that a fool will correct his ways (Prov 27:22) since his folly sooner or later gets the better of him (Job 5:3–7; Prov 1:32; 5:23). God himself punishes the foolish who, through their immoral conduct, provoke his power to punish (Wis 5:4–14). They will acknowledge their foolishness at the final judgement (Wis 5:4–14).

B. In the *New Testament* there are only a few cases where foolishness refers to ordinary lack of intelligence. Thus, in comparison with the Greeks, the culturally backward barbarians are fools (Rom 1:14). Christians have to avoid giving foolish men (among the heathens) any occasion for slanderous talk (1 Pet 2:15). In his parables, Jesus speaks of the foolish man who built his house upon sand (Mt 7:26ff) and of the foolish virgins who did not prepare themselves for the coming of the bridegroom (Mt 25:1–13). Both parables demand that the believer base his conduct upon the last judgement (cf here the parable of the rich and foolish farmer, Lk 12:16–21; the saying about salt 'becoming foolish'—ie insipid, Mt 5:13; Lk 14:34, and the use of 'fool' as an expression of abuse, Mt 5:22—see the commentaries).

In the remaining cases foolishness gets its meaning with reference to revelation. Thus, the heathens are foolish since they do not know the true God, worship false gods and do not observe God's law (Rom 1:21, 22, 31; 2:20; 10:19; Tit 3:3). Hair-splitting theological speculations which do not help towards salvation (Mt 23:17; Lk 11:40), and indeed all empty talk (Eph 5:4) are described as foolish. Jesus refers to the disciples as without understanding since they do not know how to explain his parables (Mt 15:16; Mk 7:18) and have not grasped the meaning of his death on the cross (Lk 24:25). Christians are foolish who do not know the will of the Lord (Eph (5:17), who wish to observe the Jewish law (Gal 3:1, 3) or who quite simply lack the necessary knowledge of the faith (1 Cor 15:36). Paul describes his self-praise as foolish since it is not done with the Lord's authority (2 Cor 11:17; cf 11:1, 16, 23).

Paul confronts in a most forceful way the christians of Corinth, who consider themselves wise and strong (1 Cor 4:10), with the foolishness of the cross (1 Cor 1:18). God redeemed the world in a way quite different from what they had expected. A crucified Messiah was for Jews quite unacceptable and indeed a stumbling-block, while for Greeks it seemed sheer folly to believe in a crucified man. Hence the preaching of the cross must appear as foolishness to the world (1 Cor 1:23). But since God himself was active in the event of the crucifixion, the wisdom and power of God were revealed precisely in the foolishness and weakness of the cross (1 Cor 1:18ff). The man who is confronted with the word of the cross has to make a decision: either to hold on to his own criteria and expectations, in which case he must reject the word of the cross as foolishness, shut out the wisdom and the power of God ready to help and thus be lost; or give up his natural ideas about God and the divine activity, becoming foolish and believing in the apparently foolish message of the cross, and thus be saved.

Just as Christ is revealed as the crucified wisdom and power of God (1 Cor 1:24), this divine wisdom and power is only communicated to christians when they recognise themselves as foolish and weak, when they realise that they are radically dependent upon God (1 Cor 1:26–31). Hence Paul's warning to the 'wise' Corinthians: 'If any one among you thinks he is wise in this age, let him become a fool that he may become wise. For the wisdom of this world is folly with God' (1 Cor 3:18, 19a).

Bibliography: E. Kalt, *Bibl Reallexikon* II, Paderborn 1939², 882–4; W. Caspari, 'Über den bibl. Begriff der Torheit', *NKZ* 39 (1928), 668–95; *TDNT* IV, 832–47; U. Wilckens, *Weisheit und Torheit: Eine exeget-religionsgeschichtliche Untersuchung zu 1 Kor 1 and 2*, Tübingen 1959; A. Caquot, 'Sur une désignation vétérotestamentaire de "l'insensé"', *RHR* 155 (1959), 1–16.

Georg Ziener

Freedom

A. *External freedom*, that is, the freedom which gives man the opportunity to lead his life according to his own discretion, was regarded by the Greeks as 'a fine and splendid possession, both for the individual and for the state' (Socrates, cited by Xenophon, *Memor.* IV, 5, 2; further references are to be found in *TDNT* II, 487ff, and in Otto Michel, 2–12). A conspicuous mark of this essential freedom is the right of free speech, *parrhēsia*, which the Greeks found by experience could most easily develop in a democracy (see *TDNT* II, 490 and V, 870ff). Almost an earlier form of Jesus' words: 'The truth will make you free' (Jn 8:32), is to be found in one of the truly classic sayings of Anaxagoras (d. 427 BC): *Anaxagoran . . . tēn theōrian phanai tou biou telos einai kai tēn apo tautēs eleutherian legousin* = 'they say Anaxagoras maintained that philosophical contemplation, and the freedom which comes from it, is the purpose and goal of human life' (cited by Clem. Alex, *Str* II, 130, 2 [Diels II, *Anaxagoras* A 29]).

In the Old Testament too, freedom is held in very high esteem. Moses defended a Jew against oppression by his Egyptian overseer (Ex 2:12) and later—although it must be admitted that he did this as a result of God's repeated exhortation (Ex 3:7–4:17)—led the entire people of Israel out of Egypt, the 'house of bondage' (Deut 7:8), to a freedom which was however, to begin with, associated with uncertainty, distress and hunger, with the result that the Hebrews longed to go back to the flesh-pots of Egypt (Ex 16:3). But, in Yahweh's view, it was more important for the people of his Covenant to be free than to be economically secure in Egypt, as he had their future tasks in mind. The people of Israel were certainly permitted to own slaves (see Lev 25:44), but, both socially and legally, their position was essentially better than that of slaves owned by other races. This was laid down in the 'Slavery Decalogue' (Ex 21:2–11). According to these laws, Hebrew slaves or servants had to be set free again after six years, though this regulation was certainly not always followed (see Jer 34:14–18).

When Jerusalem was destroyed in the year 586 BC and the majority of the people led away into captivity in Babylon (2 Kings 25; 2 Chron 36:17–21), this loss of national freedom was powerfully expressed in the Lamentations of Jeremiah. Later, the political independence of Palestine was defended again and again by the Maccabees in heroic battles, as it was feared that if political freedom were lost, religious freedom would be sacrificed also (see 1 Macc 1:41–9; 2:19ff; 14:29; 2 Macc 3:1ff; 6:1ff, etc).

In the New Testament, the political freedom of the Jewish people, or their attempt to regain it, no longer plays any important part. Jesus had made it abundantly clear by his admonition: 'Render to Caesar the things that are Caesar's', that he had no intention of being a political Messiah or one who would liberate them from the political yoke of Rome, but that he had come as the redeemer of the world (Mt 28:19; Lk 24:47; Jn 4:21; 11:52). He was able to admonish the Jews to do this with an easy mind, since they had possessed a great measure of religious freedom and many special privileges since the time of Caesar (see Jos., *Ant.* 14, 10, 5–8) and were thus able to give to God the things that were God's without hindrance. Mere external freedom is moreover not the highest possession, nor the one which the christian should strive at all costs to gain, for he has no lasting dwelling-place here on earth, but should seek the one that is to come (Heb 13:14). 1 Cor 7:21 has probably to be understood in this sense too, on account of the statement made in v 24 (see J. Michl, *Freiheit* 30f; C. Biber 158, No. 3; and H. D. Wendland, *Die Briefe an die Korinther*, 1954, 54: 'religious freedom in Christ is more than civil liberty'). At the same time, Paul himself laid heavy stress on the need for personal freedom to be respected by and among christians. He sent the baptised slave Onesimus back to his master Philemon 'no longer as a slave but . . . as a beloved brother' (Philem 16).

B. Man's *freedom of will* is the basis of all moral responsibility and the prerequisite for all punishment or reward. The very first human beings in paradise, who were created in God's likeness—God's absolute freedom here is stressed in the well-known simile of the potter shaping his vessel (Jer 18:6; Wis 15:7; Rom 9:21)—possessed this freedom of will (Gen 2:7; Sir 15:14ff; 'It was he [God] who created man in the beginning, and he left him in the power of his own inclination. If you will, you can keep the commandments, and to act faithfully is a matter of your own choice'). On Mount Sinai, life and death, blessing and malediction are presented to the people of Israel, with the admonition 'therefore choose life!' (Deut 30:19). Later, the prophets remind the people again and again that they should not abuse this freedom of will (Is 1:19; Jer 11:8, etc) and according to Sir 31:10 praise and glory is assured for the man who might have transgressed but who in fact did not. In Eccles too we find no fundamental denial of man's freedom of will, although many passages (Eccles 2:26; 7:13; 8:10, etc) do give this impression (see Nötscher, *Schicksal*, 460ff).

In the Qumran texts divine predestination is occasionally quite emphatically stressed (eg Hymn Scroll

15:12–20), but this should on no account be taken to mean absolute predestination. The 'elect' had to make their own personal decision to enter the covenant. That is why they were also called 'the Chosen Ones' (*hammithnadbîm*—see 1 QS v, 1, 6, 8, 10, etc). The relatively severe punishments for any transgression of the rules of the community also, without any doubt, imply the possibility of the exercise of free will and personal decision, but precisely how this can be aligned with divine predestination is not yet clear from the Qumran texts which have so far been edited. The compilers of the texts were, generally speaking, not scholarly theologians, but men who were intent on the practice of asceticism (see, in this connection, K. Schubert, *Die Gemeinde vom Toten Meer*, 1958, 55ff; and Nötscher, *Schicksalsglaube* 218).

The heathen philosophers too are convinced of the need for freedom of will and regard victory over desire and passion as possible and worth striving for. Epictetus (*Ench.* 15) compares life to a banquet at which one can and may take part in a civilised way: 'But if of yourself you do not take what is proffered ... you are not merely a worthy guest of the gods; you will also reign with them' (*TDNT* II, 494, 45ff).

Naturally, Philo too never tires of praising this higher, inner freedom as the greatest good of man. No intelligent man, in his view, is ever enslaved, even when others have bought him; and no irrational man is free, be he Craoesus, Midas, or the King of Persia (*Quod omn. prob*, lib. c XIX, sec. 136). God and the natural law are the final guarantees of this freedom (*Quod omn. prob.* X, 62). Simply being able to live as one wants is not in itself freedom; only the man who is pleasing (to God) is prudent in all he does, and so only he is free (*Quod. omn. prob.* IX, 59: *panta phronimōs poiei ho asteios; monos ara estin eleutheros*). Of course, the only one who is in the fullest and truest sense free, and able to make others free, is God himself (*Quis rer. div.* 38, 186: *ho monos apseudōs eleutheros kai eleutheropoios theos*. Further references in H. Leisegang, *Philo-Index*, under '*eleutheros*'.)

The New Testament also takes freedom of will for granted and expresses it clearly: 'How often would I have gathered your children together ... and you would not' (Mt 23:37). So great a respect did Christ have, during the time he spent on earth, for the free will of his people, that he preferred to submit himself to death on the cross, rather than to force Israel to accept his saving message, 'and so freedom became a stumbling block' (Schmaus 83), because the danger exists at all times that man will misuse it for evil purposes. Nevertheless, the decision to accept the new doctrine of salvation is for Paul essentially an act of man's free will ('We beseech you on behalf of Christ, be reconciled to God!' [2 Cor 5:20]). The evangelists may not compel this act (Acts 13:46; 18:6; Tit 3:10), but God is able to bring it about by means of his grace (Acts 9:15; 22:18; Gal 1:19; Phil 1:29) and indeed is even obliged to do so, if conversion is really to take place (Rom 9:16; Phil 2:13). In every case the freedom of the human will is preserved, though how this act is achieved remains a mystery which we should not, according to the admonitions of many of the Fathers of the Church, try to penetrate in our curiosity and presumption (see Schelkle, 195–9).

In the case of fallen men, who are thus 'sold' under sin (Rom 7:14), there are however also many *obstacles*, some more formidable than others, in the way of freedom of will. These may take the form of the↗ world which is hostile to God (1 Jn 2:15), personal weakness (Mt 26:41), the desires and longings of the↗ flesh (Rom 8:7; Eph 2:3) and many other obstacles which can thwart the carrying out of any good intention (Rom 7:19). This was as clearly recognised in the Jewish as in the heathen world (Ovid, *Metam.* 7:19: *aliudque cupido, mens aliud suadet: video meliora . . . deteriora sequor.* Further examples of both can be found in SB III, 234ff; H. Lietzmann, *An die Römer*, 1933, 77; and *TDNT* III, 167ff). All the same, these obstacles are generally surmountable with the help of God's grace (2 Cor 3:5; Phil 2:13; 4:13) and the christian remains in any case responsible for his actions both before and afterwards, and will also be judged according to his works (Mt 7:21; 25:34–46; Rom 2:6; 2 Cor 5:10; Gal 6:7; Heb 6:10; Jas 2:14ff; Rev 22:12). Luther, unlike Melanchthon and Erasmus, tried, as is well known, to escape this extremely serious responsibility by a denial of free-will (see Veit 148). Even modern, post-christian man obviously labours under the difficulty that he has to rely entirely on his own strength for the responsibility of his actions and decisions, as is well expressed by J. P. Sartre: 'L'homme est condamné à être libre' (more on this in Grässer 333).

C. *Christian freedom* is something quite new and unknown before Christ. The necessary condition for christian freedom is faith in Jesus Christ as the Son of God: 'If you continue in my word, . . . you will know the↗ truth, and the truth will make you free . . . so if the Son makes you free, you will be free indeed' (Jn 8:31–6). 'Where the Spirit of the Lord is, there is freedom' (2 Cor 3:17). This freedom is received objectively through baptism—its seed is implanted by the sacrament (see Rom 8:23: *aparkhē*, 2 Cor 1:22; 5:5: *arrabōn*)—and it gradually becomes a personal possession of the child of God in the subjective sense (Rom 8:21). Its effects on the different departments of christian life are many and various.

1. He is *freed from sin*, which had fallen to his share since Adam (Rom 5:12ff; 1 Cor 15:21; Eph 2:3) and to which he had been a slave because of personal transgression as well (Rom 6:17–20)—literally 'sold' under sin (Rom 7:14). The apostle, however, triumphantly proclaims: 'Sin will have no dominion over you' (Rom 6:14) and we are 'freed from sin' (6:18). The result of this is:

2. *Freedom from eternal* (*the 'second'*) *death* (Rev 2:11; 20:6; 21:8), since death is the wages of sin (Rom 6:23) and its inevitable consequence (Rom 7:11) and indeed its child: '. . . and sin when it is full-grown, brings forth death' (Jas 1:15). This applied to Adam's sin (Gen 2:17) and it still applies to ours. The resurrection of the Lord did not only free him from physical death—it also freed us from eternal death (Col 2:12–14). This everlasting death has certainly 'not been conquered once and for all by means of a mark of the Covenant like baptism. On the contrary, it hangs like a

constant threat of danger above the baptised man's head' (O. Michel, *An die Römer*, 1963, 135). The Christian too can be lost, if his faith remains 'without works' (Jas 2:14ff). Death (both in the physical and in the spiritual sense) will only be completely destroyed by God at the end of time (1 Cor 15:26: see also Rev 21:4). God also bestows on the christian:

3. *Freedom from the rule of Satan*, who, although he had already tempted Christ three times without success (Mt 4:1–11 and pars) and was thereby deprived of much of his influence over men (satanic possession, Mt 8:28ff; 12:22; 17:18; Lk 13:16; Jn 12:31), tries again and again to gain mastery over him and thus to regain his dwindling influence in human affairs (Eph 6:12; 1 Pet 5:8). An outstanding example of Satan's success is that of Judas (Jn 13:27). Satan must be overcome by prayer and fasting (Mt 17:21). Before the end of the world he will be first of all bound for 'a thousand years' (Rev 20:3) and then, after a short interval, he will be damned for all eternity (Rev 20:10). A further consequence of the redemption is:

4. *Freedom from the mastery of the↗ flesh*, which fights in us against the spirit (Rom 8:5–9; Gal 5:17ff), which is synonymous with the 'old self' in us (Rom 6:6; Eph 4:22; Col 3:9) and the activity of which, aiming as it does at our ruin, must be mortified by the spirit (Rom 8:13), so that our mortal body, which is in itself good—a temple of the Holy Spirit (1 Cor 9:27)—may at last share in the resurrection (Rom 8:11). Last, but not least, Christ has brought us:

5. *Freedom from the↗ law of the Old Testament*: 'You are not under the law, but under grace' (Rom 6:14; see also Gal 5:18). Christ is the 'end of the law' (Rom 10:4), which was in itself holy, just (Rom 7:12) and good (1 Tim 1:8), because it aimed to preserve men from sin (Gal 3:24). Because of the increasingly strict application of the 'tradition of the elders' (Mk 7:3) however, it developed with the passage of time into an unbearable yoke (Acts 15:10; Gal 2:4), a dungeon in which the Jews were shut up (Gal 3:23), a bondage, from which Christ has liberated us (Rom 7:6). It should be noted, however, that the rabbis also warned that the 'fence around the Torah' should not be built too high in case it should collapse and crush the plants inside; this type of warning did not, however, appear until the second century AD (see H. J. Schoeps, *Paulus* [1959] 302). Man was certainly quite unable, purely on his own account and without the help of grace, to fulfil the Law and thus to achieve↗ justification (Rom 3:28; Gal 2:16).

The christian has been 'called to freedom' (Gal 5:13) by reason of Christ's work of redemption, but the apostle gives the warning in the same sentence that this liberty is not to be conceived as an unbridled licence. Christian freedom from ritual and dietary laws (↗ pure), which were imposed in Old Testament times, was not to be abused as a 'pretext for evil' (1 Pet 2:16). Though it is true that the baptised man is a 'freedman of the Lord', he remains at the same time a 'slave of Christ' (1 Cor 7:22) who has purchased him with his blood, and is thus bound to the law of Christ (1 Cor 9:21). This law has loosened our previous bonds and is truly the 'perfect law of liberty' (Jas 1:25). In this way, christian freedom clearly bears the imprint of a 'dialectical character' (in the phrase of Bultmann) and must be conceived as a 'freedom of service' (J. Michl 26) which not only has a regard for the conscience of each individual among the 'weaker brethren' (1 Cor 8:9; 9:19ff), but also willingly complies with the requirements of public law and order and the demands of the communal good (Rom 13:1–7; Tit 3:1; 1 Pet 2:13). It is thus a freedom in charity, as is proper to the children of God. On the other hand, it is, in the last analysis, all to the advantage of those in authority in the church when they respect the freedom of individuals to express their opinion—even when contrary—in established cases and in the appropriate manner (see Gal 2:11–14; and further, Hirschmann 88ff). Pius XII once drew attention to the fact that there must be a 'public opinion' in the church entitled to scope and tolerance. It is 'the birthright of any normal human society' (*Osservatore Romano*, 18 February 1950). Details in Rahner, *Free Speech in the Church*, 5f.

D. *Religious liberty*, freedom of conscience, or freedom of belief is the right (and duty) of a man to adhere to whatever religion or world-view he in conscience firmly believes to be right (even when, objectively speaking, he may be wrong). Consideration for the misguided consciences of the weak is to be found as early as Paul (1 Cor 10:28ff), in the case of those who regarded eating the food offered to idols as wrong for a christian in any circumstances—provided, that is, that they are fully convinced of their view (Rom 14:5). Tit 3:10 may certainly be regarded as the first christian 'edict of toleration': 'As for a man who is factious (*hairētikos*), after admonishing him once or twice (ie, to no effect), have nothing more to do with him'; he will henceforward have to take on himself the responsibility for his actions. Admittedly, in later times a church which was too often hand-in-glove with the state (*une foi*, *une loi*, *un roi*; further references in Heinzel, 9) frequently forgot the early christian maxim: 'not force but persuasion' (*mē anagkazein, alla peithein*: Athanasius, *Hist. Arian.* 67 [*PG* 25, 773A]). The same is true of the Reformers, who unquestioningly accepted *cuius regio, eius religio*, with the result that Henry VIII, Calvin, and others could equally lightly allow the execution of 'heretics'.

Only with Leo XIII did the early christian attitude to this range of problems really make itself felt once more. Its authoritative echo remains in Canon 1351 of *CIC*: *Ad amplexandam fidem catholicam nemo invitus cogatur* ('no-one is to be compelled to embrace the catholic faith against his will'). But simple tolerance is not adequate for our modern pluralist society, particularly insofar as it is a-catholic. If tolerance were not to lead to indifferentism, it could only be 'relative tolerance' (see Ebneter, 202); that is to say, erroneous consciences, even when in good faith, cannot be given the same status as a religious conviction which corresponds to objective truth, since truth and error of their very nature cannot claim equal protection. On the same grounds E. Melichar has recently explained (*LTK* VIII [1963], 1177) that religious liberty is only 'to be tolerated'—a view which now, however, seems superseded by *Pacem in Terris*. John XXIII was not concerned to protect error as such, but the man in error, since 'he does not cease to be a man and never loses his personal value, which must always be taken into account' (*AAS* 55 [1963], 299).

This view has finally prevailed. In its *Declaration on Religious Liberty* the second Vatican Council declared—after long and heated debates—that religious liberty is an authentic right of the person, rooted in his human dignity, which civil society is obliged to recognise.

Bibliography: H. Schlier, *TDNT* II, 487–502; E. Kalt, *Bibl. Reallexikon* I, 1937, 556f; E. G. Gulin, 'Die Freiheit in der Verkündigung des Paulus', *ZST* 18 (1941), 458–81; O. Michel, *Universitas* I (1946), 1–17; O. Veit, *Die Flucht vor der Freiheit*, Frankfurt 1947; R. Egenter, *Von der Freiheit der Kinder Gottes*, 1949; E. Wolf, *ET* 9 (1949/50), 127–42; J. Michl, *Freiheit und Bindung: Eine zeitgemässe Frage im Lichte des NT*, Munich 1950; K. H. Schelkle, 'Erwählung und Freiheit im Römerbrief nach der Auslegung der Väter', *TQ* 131 (1951), 17–31 and 189–207; H. Ridderbos, 'Vrijheid en wet volgens Paulusbrief aan de Galaten', *Arcana revelata* (Festschrift F. W. Grosheide), Kampen 1951, 89–103; Bultmann I, 330–40; S. Lyonnet, *Liberté chrétienne et loi nouvelle selon S. Paul*, Rome 1954; E. Grässer, *ET* 15 (1955), 333–42; G. Harbsmeier, *ET* 15 (1955), 469–86; C. Biber, Allmen 129ff; M. Schmaus, 'Kirche und Freiheit', *MTZ* 8 (1957), 81–92; R. Guardini, *Freedom, Grace and Destiny*, London 1961; J. B. Hirschmann, 'Die Freiheit in der Kirche', *SZ* (1957), 81–92; B. Ramazzotti, *Riv. bibl. it.* 6 (1958), 50–82; G. Heinzel, 'Kirche und Toleranz' (rectorial address 1958); Campenhausen and Bornkamm, *Bindung und Freiheit in der Ordnung der Kirche*, 1959; F. Nötscher, 'Schicksal und Freiheit', *Bbl* 40 (1959), 446–62; F. Nötscher, 'Schicksals glaube in Qumran und Umwelt', *BZ* 3 (1959), 205–34; P. Bläser, *LTK* IV², 328–31; J. Gnilka, *LTK* IV², 338–40; C. Spicq, *Charité et liberté dans le NT*, Paris 1961; O. Betz, *Gefährliche Freiheit*, Munich 1961; C. Maurer, 'Glaubensbindung und Gewissenfreiheit im NT', *TZ* 17 (1961), 107–17; K. Rahner, 'Freedom in the Church', *Theological Investigations* II, London and Baltimore 1963, 89–107; *K. Rahner, *Free Speech in the Church*, London and New York 1959; L. Roy, *DBT* 532–7; A. Güemes, *El Descubrimiento de la Libertad por san Pablo*, Madrid 1963; B. Häring, 'Die religiöse Freiheit', *Theologie d. Gegenwart* 7 (1964), 187–93; A. Ebneter, 'Von der Toleranz zur religiösen Freiheit', *Orientierung* 28 (1964), 202f; H. Küng, *The Church and Freedom*, 1965; *H. Küng, *Freedom in the World: St Thomas More*, London 1965; *H. Küng, *The Theologian and the Church*, London 1965; J. Leclerq, *Kirche und Freiheit*, 1964; J. C. Murray, *The Problem of Religious Freedom*, London 1965; C. Spicq, *La liberté chrétienne: Théologie morale du NT* II, Paris 1965, 623–64; K. Niederwimmer, *Der Begriff der Freiheit im NT*, 1966.

Johannes Kosnetter

Freedom of speech

Freedom of speech and frankness are terms used to render the Greek *parrhēsia*. This derives originally from the political sphere, and it is only secondarily that it has been transferred from that into the sphere of private life, where it is applied to friends who tell each other everything. It is related to the concept of ↗ freedom. In LXX God endows the people with freedom of speech (Lev 26:13), and wisdom is said to show frankness in this sense (Prov 1:20). In this the biblical term is still wider in its range of meaning than the Hellenistic one, as appears in passages such as Job 27:9f, where frankness means the free and joyful attitude in God's presence of one who has unhindered access to him. In Wis 5:1 we read that the just man will show great frankness or boldness in his dealings with those who have oppressed him (see 5:5, 15f). Such frankness presupposes↗ righteousness. Only the righteous man, not the sinner, possesses frankness (see Prov 13:5f). This frankness is expressed in prayer (Job 27:9; 22:21–7). The philosopher prays in a similar manner (see Epictetus, *Diacr.* 2, 17, 29: as a free man looking up to heaven, as a friend of God who has nothing to fear). The actual idea of friendship with God is mentioned in Job 22:21 (not in LX, where the passage has been brought into conformity with Job 9:4, whereas MT rightly translates: 'Become friends with him').

In Ps 93:1 LXX and 11:6 LXX the verb *parrhēsiazesthai* is used with God as subject. The original Hebrew word which lies behind this is commonly translated: 'to radiate light', 'to appear illumined with light'. There is no doubt that the reference here is to God emerging from his silence and appearing in radiant glory as judge of the wicked and as deliverer of the just.

The *New Testament.* In the Acts of the Apostles *free speaking* (*showing frankness*) is used only in relation to men, and is frequently found in parallelism to terms signifying 'to teach' and 'to speak' (4:29, 31; 9:27f, etc), so that here it is actually possible to translate *parrhēsiazesthai* as 'to preach'. Often it is the Jews (2:29; 13:46 etc), the Jewish authorities (4:13; 26:26), but also Jews and Gentiles together with their authorities (4:29, 31; 14:2f) in whose presence the apostles speak. Here it is always some specific utterance based upon the↗ confession of faith; it has a force which does not derive from rhetorical training but which the Lord imparts to his ministers (see 4:13, and 14:3), and which is made possible through the↗ Spirit (see 4:8, 31; 18:25f). In this way this frankness or free speaking attains the status of a ↗ charism.

The *Pauline literature* yields a similar picture. Free speaking here is no less relevant when applied to the preaching of the gospel (Eph 6:19f) than as used in the sense of openness in relation to God (2 Cor 3:12 and esp Eph 3:12). The freedom of speech which the apostle exercises in his dealings with men (Eph 6:19f; 1 Thess 2:2 etc) is based on his frankness in his relations with God, and is a reflection of the divine↗ authority. The comparison with Moses in 2 Cor 3:12ff makes this clear (On this point van Unnik has rightly pointed out that the words corresponding to *parrhēsia,* in Aramaic and Syrian signify 'unveiled countenance' and 'uncovered head'. This conclusion, moreover, enables us to understand the association of ideas in the mind of the apostle to the gentiles). Eph 3:11f provides a still clearer expression of the idea: in Christ man shows frankness and (what amounts to the same thing) trustful access (to God) through faith in Christ.

In Col 2:15 the *parrhēsia* of Christ himself is spoken of. He has disarmed the principalities and powers, and triumphed over them in his coming in boldness and frankness, that is in power and without fear.

There are four occurrences of the term 'freedom of speech' or 'frankness' in the Letter to the Hebrews. In 3:6 it is associated with the hope which we may truly take pride in, in holding firm to which christianity consists. The same thing is expressed in another way in 3:14, where it is said that we share in Christ if only we hold firm to the end to the position which we adopted in the beginning (*hupostasis* never means confidence, but refers to the state of soul), and avoid being made obdurate by the deceitfulness of sins (3:13). This frankness, like ↗ hope in and expectation of Christ, consists not merely in an interior attitude, but also in the reality to which that attitude is directed, namely the actual fact that we have freedom of access to God. Since however it is always possible to forfeit this (10:35), an exhortation to hold fast to this attitude of frankness and boldness is included. Taken together vv 4:14 and 10:19 tell us how Christ our high priest has opened this new way to us, namely through his blood, through his death. But it is only when our conscience is pure, and when we have been washed in the waters of baptism and are sure in our faith (10:22), that we can follow this way of free speaking and boldness.

The *Johannine Usages*. In Mk 8:32 (the sole occurrence in the synoptics) *parrhēsia* is already used as the opposite of teaching in parables. And in the passage concerned this mode of speaking, precisely in its openness, veils the Messiah from the disciples, as the episode with Peter which follows makes clear. Thus according to Mark also Jesus can appear in 'openness' only to the eyes of faith. It is only in following the way of the Cross that we can understand him (see E. Schweizer, *ZNW* 56, 1965, 7). For John, Jesus' works are indeed performed in public before the eyes of the world (18:20f; cf 7:25f). Yet this openness of Jesus' work is not to be confused with an openness as to his actual nature, a mistake into which the disciples fall because they fail to understand the character of his works as signs (7:4f). As the evangelist understands it, on the other hand, Jesus went up to Jerusalem 'in secret' (7:10). The openness of Jesus' work which is immediately visible for all to see is not the *parrhēsia* of the revealer himself (10:24f). It is the same in 11:11 ('Lazarus *sleeps*') and, by contrast with this, 11:14 ('Then Jesus said to them *openly*, "Lazarus is *dead*"'). The disciples do not understand that the presence of Jesus makes death into a mere sleep from which one arises! Only at his return in the power of the Paraclete is this veil removed. Only in his ↗ glorification will his *parrhēsia* appear. Admittedly the believer can see through the veil, as is shown by 16:29ff as following upon 16:25ff.

The first Letter of John recognizes that man can take up a frank or bold attitude in God's presence by reason of his good conscience (3:21). Those who keep his commandments are assured that this frankness will obtain them the hearing of their ↗ prayers (5:14f), 'if we ask according to his will'.

This attitude of (eschatological) frankness or freedom of speech is the opposite of ↗ fear in that it is maintained in the presence of the judge (2:28; 4:17), cf the adumbration of this in Wis 5:1. The attitude of frankness excludes the possibility that at the end we must be overcome by shame and fear. In fact this attitude of frankness and free speaking is in the last analysis based upon the fact that God loves us and brings his love for us to its perfection. The attitude of abiding in that love that knows no fear because it keeps the commandments manifests itself at the judgement precisely in the fact that man can have access to God freely and without fear.

Bibliography: M. Radin, 'Freedom of Speech in ancient Athens', *Am. Journ. of Philology* 48 (1927), 215–20; E. Peterson, 'Zur Bedeutungsgeschichte von parrhesia', *Festschrift für R. Seeberg* I, 1929, 283–97; P. De Ambroggi, *VD* 9 (1929), 269–76; P. Joüon, 'Divers sens de parrhesia dans le NT', *RSR* 30 (1940), 239–41; C. Spicq, *L'Epître aux Hébreux* II, Paris 1953, 69f; H. Schlier, *TDNT* V, 871–86; H. Jäger, 'Parrhesia et fiducia, Etude spirituelle des mots', *Studia Patristica* I (TU 63) Berlin 1957, 221–39; W. C. Van Unnik, 'De semitische achtergrond von parrhesia in het NT', *Mededelingen Kon. Nederl. Akad. van Wet., Letterk.* 25 (1962); W. C. van Unnik, 'The Christian's Freedom of Speech in the NT', *BSRL* 44 (1961/2), 466–88; H. Holstcin, 'La parrhesia dans le NT', *Bible et Vie Chrétienne* 53 (1963), 45–54; G. Scarpat, *Parrhesia. Storia del termine e delle sue traduzioni in latino*, Brescia 1964; L. Engels, 'Fiducia dans la Vulgate', *Graecitas et Latinitas Christianorum primaeva* (Suppl. I), Nijmegen 1964, 97–141.

Johannes B. Bauer

Fulfilment

1. The original meaning of the word 'fill' (see Ex 8:17: to fill a space) is extended to denote the universal presence of God (Jer 23:24) and of his spirit (Wis 1:7). This should not be taken to mean that God is enclosed by the universe (see 1 Kings 8:27), but that he embraces the universe in his creative power, rules it and preserves it in existence (see Wis 1:7; 7:24, 8:1). In Ex 40:34f, it is Yahweh's presence in the midst of his people (Ex 25:8, 22; 29:45f), which is represented by his glory (*kābôd*) in the cloud filling the tabernacle. In Is 6:3, where we read that all the earth is filled with Yahweh's glory, what is implied is the revelation of God, who is holy (ie, exalted above the earth) and who shows his power in acts of punishment and salvation. This is to be understood within the total context of Isaiah's prophecy (see Num 14:21; Ps 72:19; see also B. Stein, *Der Begriff Kebod Jahweh*, Emsdetten 1939, 171–96).

According to Eph 4:10, Christ has ascended above all the heavens 'that he might fill all things (*ta panta*)', that is, rule them as a sovereign (the opinion of Gewiess, Mussner, Schlier, Schnackenburg). Paul is referring in particular to the beings that are 'in heaven and on earth' who have received the spirit (Eph 1:10; Col 1:16), for with his ascension Christ has 'put all things under his feet', especially the spiritual powers which are hostile to God (Eph 1:21ff; Col 2:15). It is also possible to understand Eph 1:23: 'the fullness of him who fills all in all' (=who fills everything in all parts, universally and intensively) in the light of Eph 1:10, 20ff as well as Eph 4:10. Although it is possible to think of *plēroumenou*, in the middle voice in Greek, as having an active meaning, *plērousthai* is never used in this way in the New Testament. In the Vulgate and in the writings of Origen and St John Chrystostom the sense is always passive. In any case, the meaning that Christ, as Head, receives his fullness through his mystical body, the Church, in all its parts (*ta panta*, in the adverbial sense) and members, is not really appropriate within the context. However suitable the idea is in itself, it is certainly not to be found anywhere in Paul. He does not regard the church as making up what is lacking in Christ, as a fulfilment of Christ (for *plērōma* in this sense, see Mt 9:16; Mk 2:21). According to him, the faithful, therefore the church, are filled by Christ, who is the head of every principality and power (Col 2:10). The parallel with Eph 1:21ff, in which Christ is also seen to appear elevated above all these various powers, is quite clear and is made even clearer when Col 2:9 is taken into consideration. Here the entire pleroma of divinity is seen to dwell corporeally in Christ, that is to say, 'the whole fullness of diety dwells bodily' in Christ and not simply as a shadow of what is to come (see Col 2:17: A. Wikenhauser, *Die Kirche als der mystische Leib Christi nach dem Apostel Paulus*, Münster 1937, 188). The interpretation that this fullness took flesh in Christ is less probable here, although it is grammatically feasible. In Col 2:9f, we find also that christians are filled by Christ in whom the entire fullness of divinity dwells. Col 1:19 should also be considered in connection with Eph 1:23: 'For in him all the fullness of God was pleased to dwell'. According to the usual interpretation, the same is meant here as in Col 2:9, but more correctly, it refers to the fullness of divine and created being (Benoit). But Paul, unlike the Stoics, nevers calls the cosmos *plerōma*. What he is using in this case is a conception taken up by the judaeo-gnostic heretics of Colossae, but he uses it against them. What he is in fact saying is that it is not the angelic powers to which they give worship who represent the *plērōma*, but that the fullness of all power and everything that exists which is great and good is in Christ, with the result that he takes precedence in everything (Col 1:15–18). Thus Eph 1:23 may be understood in the sense of Col 1:19: Christ is filled by everything in every possible way (Benoit and Feuillet, for example, accept the passive meaning here), and may be matched with what is expressed in Eph 1:10: everything (=the universe, *ta panta*) that is in heaven and on earth (the heavenly and terrestrial world which has been disrupted by Adam's sin) will, by God's ordination, in the fullness of time, be gathered up into one (*anakephalaiōsasthai*) in Christ as into one short and ordered heading, an epitomised compendium (*kephalaion*: see also Heb 8:1), so that all things may once again be brought into that peaceful unity through him—the unity that is already present in him by reason of the union of his divine and human nature. The Christ who is filled in this way fills the universe (Eph 4:10), which means that he keeps it together by his power as ruler as he does the church which is his *plērōma* (Eph 1:23) and which is filled by him (Col 2:10) through his being and the power of his grace. Accordingly, christians are to attain the 'measure of the stature (in the Vulgate, measure of the age) of the fullness of Christ' (Eph 4:13), and 'existing truly in charity' ('speaking the truth', see Gal 4:16: 'doing the truth', Vulgate), they may 'in all things (*ta panta*) grow up in him who is the head, even Christ' (4:15). According to the traditional interpretation, *auxēsōmen* is taken here to be intransitive, thus meaning simply to grow, in the same sense as *auxei* in Eph 2:21 (see Eph 4:16; Col 2:19). The transitive meaning used by Schlier, to make grow (see 1 Cor 3:6; 2 Cor 9:10): 'to make everything grow up to him' tends to result in an unusual sense and one which is not strictly appropriate to Eph 4:16 (see Schnackenburg). According to Eph 4:10, Christ fills the universe as a result of his ascension, ruling directly over it (see 1:21f) and not through his church. The faithful, filled with the fullness of Christ (Eph 4:13), are also 'filled with all the fullness of God' (Eph 3:19), for the 'fullness of deity' or divinity 'dwells bodily' in Christ (Col 2:9). It is possible to take *plēroumenou* (Eph 1:23) here either in the sense of the passive or the middle voice, but in either case what is expressed is Christ's fullness of power which he allows to penetrate his church by filling her, his mystical body, with himself. Paul refers to this fullness of power which the church shares with Christ in order to demonstrate to the faithful in Colossae, in opposition to the teaching of the heretics there, that they had no need to worship angels (Col 2:18) and also no need to fear those powers which were hostile to God (Col 2:15), but that they could successfully hold out against them in the power of Christ (Eph 6:10–17). He had already told the Corinthians that they had become rich in all things in Christ and thus lacked none of the gifts of grace, and that Christ would so strengthen them to the end that they might be found without blame on the day of his coming.

When Paul says that he vicariously fills up (*antanaplērō*) for the faithful what is lacking in the suffering of Christ by his own suffering and tribulation (Col 1:24), he does not intend to imply that anything is essentially lacking in the work of redemption on Christ's part—Christ has indeed brought a perfect reconciliation by his death on the cross (Col 1:20). What he is referring to here are the 'sufferings of Christ' which continue to take place, and must thus continue within his mystical body (see also 2 Cor 1:5; 4:10; Gal 6:17). All the members of this body have the task of contributing towards its building up or edification (Eph 4:12, 16) and the first and foremost must be the apostles (Eph 4:11), especially by means of their sufferings (2 Cor 4:12; Eph 3:13; Acts 9:16; 1 Cor 4:9ff; 2 Cor 11:23ff).

Other examples of the verb *to fill*, used in its wider meaning, present few difficulties. Among these we can include the following references: ↗ wisdom (Lk 2:40), ↗ joy (Acts 2:28), sorrow (Jn 16:6), the fruit of ↗ justice (Phil 1:11), the ↗ knowledge of the will of God (Col 1:9). When he refers to the 'fullness' of Israel (Rom 11:12) or the fullness of the gentiles (Rom 11:25), Paul implies their completion with the 'fullness of time' (Gal 4:4; Eph 1:10) and the full measure that has been prepared for them by God and which they will receive with the coming of Christ (cf Mk 1:15: 'the time is fulfilled'). The 'times' will acquire their full meaning in Christ. The 'fullness of the blessing' of Christ's teaching (Rom 15:29) is, similarly, blessing in full measure. The incarnate Son of the Father is 'full of grace' to such an extent that we receive 'from his fullness . . . grace upon grace' (Jn 1:14, 16).

2. *Fill* is also used in the sense of *fulfil*, as for example, fulfilling the law (Rom 8:4; 13:8; Gal 5:14). Christ has to 'fulfil all ↗ righteousness', that is to say, what is right in God's sight and

what he demands (Mt 3:15; cf 6:1; 1 Jn 2:29; Rev 22:11).

3. *Fill* or *fulfil* is moreover used, for example, in Mt 5:17, according to the context (see especially 5:20–48) and, taking into consideration the fact that Christ is here exercising his function as a teacher, with the sense of accomplish. He has, in any case, already fulfilled the law of the Old Testament in the sense that he has adhered to it (see Rom 15:8; Gal 4:4). But in this instance he is referring to his messianic mission to accomplish and perfect everything. This is brought about in the case of the ↗law by his making the will of God which is proclaimed in the law effective in its total purity. Thus he transcends the letter of the ancient law by forbidding the evil motive which leads to evil action as strictly as he forbids the action itself, by prohibiting all temporary concessions in connection with the law (see 'hardness of heart' Mt 19:8) and by assigning to the law the place that is due to it (the commandment to love one's neighbour takes precedence over that concerning the Sabbath). The accomplishment which has come about through Christ also includes the complete abolition of the Old Testament form of worship and the ceremonial laws which are appropriate to the provisional and temporary nature of the Old Testament, since these have lost their sense and purpose with Christ, for whom they were a preparation (see J. Schmid, 1959[4], 87 and 90–94). Since fulfilment is reached with Christ, the 'time is fulfilled' with his appearance (Mk 1:15; Gal 4:4), has acquired its full measure and is brought to a conclusion. Further examples of *fill* or *fulfil* used in the sense of accomplish or bring to an end are: Lk 7:1; 22:16; Jn 3:29; 15:11; 16:24; 17:13; Acts 12:25; 13:25; Rom 15:19 (what is meant here is that Paul's sermon on the gospel is at an end): Col 1:25 (cf 1:28f): 2 Thess 1:11; Rev 3:2.

4. *Fill* or *fulfil* is also found with the sense of realise. This usage is found particularly in connection with the messianic prophecies of the Old Testament, which are fulfilled or realised in Christ and his church. After his resurrection, Christ is at pains to point out to the apostles that everything that was written about him in the Mosaic Law, the Prophets and the Psalms is to be fulfilled (Lk 24:25ff, 44ff). But he does this even before his resurrection: see Mt 11:3ff; Lk 4:17ff; 7:22 and Is 35:5f; 61:1f—Mt 11:10, 14; 17:12f and Mal 3:1; 4:5—Mk 9:12; 14:49; Lk 22:37 and Is 53—Mk 10:45; 14:24 and Is 53:10ff—Jn 10:14, 16 and Ezek 34:23f; 37:24. The apostles and evangelists also point to the fulfilment or realisation of the Old Testament prophecies in Christ, in a general way in Mt 26:56; Acts 3:18, 24; 10:43; 13:27, 29; 17:3, 11; 20:27; 28:23; Rom 1:2; 15:8; 1 Cor 15:3f; 2 Cor 1:20, and with reference to more precise details in the following instances: Christ is the son of Abraham and David (Mt 1:1; cf Gen 22:18; 2 Sam 7:16; Jer 23:5); he is to be born of a virgin (Mt 1:22f; Is 7:14); further examples of this fulfilment are: Is 9:1, 2 (Mt 4:14ff); 11:10 (Rom 15:12); 42:1–4 (Mt 12:17ff); 53:7f (Acts 8:32ff); Jer 31:31–4 (Heb 8:8ff); Mic 5:2 (Mt 2:6); Zech 9:9 (Mt 21:4f); 12:10 (Jn 19:37; Rev 1:7); Ps 2:1 (Acts 4:25f); 2:7 (Acts 13:33;

Heb 5:5); 16:8ff (Acts 2:25ff; 13:35 ff); Ps 22:18 (Mt 27:35; Jn 19:24); 22:22 (Heb 2:12); 45:7f (Heb 1:8f); 110:1 (Acts 2:34f; Heb 1:13); 110:4 (Heb 5:6; 7:1–28). The fulfilment of the Old Testament prophecies in Christ is in particular clearly demonstrated by a review of the relevant texts (↗ messianism). The most sublime and purely religious features of the image of the Messiah, those features which transcend national and political considerations and which are the least easy to explain on the purely natural level, all come together in Christ and his work to form an inner unity which is even less easily explained on the natural level. As early as Gen 3:15 we find reference to the expectation that the disorder brought about by the original sin of man's first parents is to be remedied not simply by God, but by a man who represents the whole of sinful mankind. This man is depicted in the ↗ Servant of God (especially in Is 53) and Jesus has fulfilled this prophecy completely in his atoning death and fulfilled it for all mankind (see Is 49:6; 53:12). The spread of the religion of Israel over the whole world (see Is 2:2ff; 45:22f) is accomplished by Christ and his church. The high quality of this atonement and reconciliation which includes the whole world is based on the union of the human and the divine in Christ's nature which is indicated in Is 9:6; Ps 2:7; 45:7; 110:1, 3; Dan 7:13. Furthermore, the representation of divine ↗ wisdom as a person who proceeds from God and dwells with him in the most intimate communion of life and activity (Prov 8; Wis 7f) provides a preliminary insight into the true relationship which exists between the Father and the Son. What is also demonstrated in Christ is the truthfulness of the promises that God will come to redeem his people and dwell in their midst (see Is 40:3ff; 42:13ff; Ezek 34:11ff; 43:1ff; 48:35; Zeph 3:15; Zech 2:10ff; Mal 3:1ff). As the divine Messiah, Christ is the son of a virgin (Is 7:14) and a 'priest for ever' (Ps 110:4). Even the features of the messianic image which caused the Jewish commentators such difficulties and were so often misinterpreted or falsely understood by them are to be found in Jesus Christ in a state of harmonious unity. One of the basic principles of the plan of salvation, namely, that God is to bring about the salvation of mankind by means which are humanly inadequate (Is 9:3f—the day of Midian; see also Judg 7:2ff) is put into effect in Christ's death on the cross (see 1 Cor 1:23ff). It is, of course, true that the promise concerning the miraculous fertility and transformation of nature, Israel's victory and supremacy over the other races, Jerusalem's glory and the royal sway of the Messiah was not fulfilled in the way in which these things were described, or at least has not yet been fulfilled in this way. But it must be borne in mind in any consideration of these promises, that God had to allow his prophets to present his future kingdom in the various forms which were familiar to them and which they had encountered in the present and in the past, so that what they were promising would both be understood by their contemporaries and be attractive to them, with the result that their religious and moral attitude would be fashioned by their view of the messianic future (see Is

2:5). All this conformed to the way in which God wished to bring about his people's gradual religious development. Thus the messianic period is described as a complete reversal of the present unhappy state of bondage (see Is 14:2; 60:9ff; 61:5f) or as a return to the ideal time of David (Is 11:13f) or to the exodus from Egypt (Is 11:15f; 40:3ff; 41:17ff; 43:16ff). Indeed, everything is depicted as being far more splendid than these happy times of the past. It is in fact the task of the prophets to bring the importance and the happiness of the messianic future powerfully home to the people, and descriptions which attempt to approximate to the truth are sufficient to give a general but vivid picture of this supremely important future. In every consideration of this problem it is necessary to remember the essential and ultimate task of the prophets. When, for example, Jeremiah (33:20ff) or Zechariah (6:13) proclaim the eternal preservation of David's kingdom or the priesthood of the levites, they are not ruling out the possibility that this may be realised in a more sublime form. It is also permissible for the ↗ church of Christ to claim that those passages which deal with Israel and Jerusalem are applicable to herself, since shc rightfully inherits these ancient promises because she is incorporated, by means of her faith and sacraments, into Christ, who inherits them (Gal 3:29). The church has in fact grown organically from the ancient people of God and it is she who perpetuates its life (↗ people of God). The prophecies, moreoever, leave the way clear for the possibility of a gradual fulfilment which can unfold in stages. The first stage in the fulfilment of the prophecies is completed in the return from exile. The first glimpse that the prophets give provides the outlines of the picture, but the prophecies penetrate beyond this and envisage the following stages: the redemption from ↗ sin through Christ, and the glorious consummation with the transfiguration of the whole of nature. The resplendent colours of the picture are provided by this final accomplishment. The intervals of time between the stages generally remain obscure to the prophets. Whenever they speak of an imminent realisation of the prophecies (see Joel 1:15; 2:1; Hag 2:6) it is possible that they are referring to the first stage, though in any case they always have a practical purpose in mind, to exhort the people to a state of constant watchfulness, intense expectation and trusting ↗ hope which will not result in disappointment, even if this 'soon', this imminent coming, is something which has been determined by and is known to God alone (see 2 Pet 3:8ff). It should also be noted that it is possible for the prophecies to imply certain conditions which are not expressly stated (see Jer 18:7ff); thus Jerusalem did not know the day of her visitation (Lk 19:42). And yet the day of mercy is still to come for Israel (Rom 11:23–32; cf Mt 23:39). Whenever words from the Old Testament, which in their immediate context refer to persons or things *of* the Old Testament, are quoted in the New as having been fulfilled or as to be fulfilled in Christ (see Mt 2:15 and Hos 11:1; Jn 13:18 and Ps 41:9; Jn 19:36 and Ex 12:46; Num 9:12), then what we have here are types of Christ and examples of the many ways in which the Old Testament foreshadows the New.

This particular type also shows how Christ fulfilled the Old Testament. He accomplished all the good beginnings that were made by the great and pious figures of the Old Testament, but he had to endure as well all the sorrow, misunderstanding and ingratitude that they suffered and to an even greater degree, and he had to embrace the entire history of Israel and make it his own in order to be the faithful Servant of God and to make up for the debt incurred by the blind and deaf servant of God—Israel (see Is 42:19) and indeed by the whole of mankind, and to fulfil what they had not fulfilled.

Bibliography: G. Delling, *TDNT* vi, 238–309; J. Gewiess, *Festschrift Meinertz: Vom Wort des Lebens*, Münster 1951, 128–41; F. Mussner, *Christus, das All und die Kirche*, Trier 1955; P. Benoit, 'Corps tête et plérôme dans les épîtres de la captivité', *RB* 63 (1956), 5–44; A. Feuillet, 'L'Eglise plérôme du Christ d'après Eph 1:23', *NRT* 78 (1956), 449–72 and 593–610; H. Schlier, *Der Brief an die Epheser*, Düsseldorf 1958²; K. Staab, *Die Gefangenschaftbriefe* (*RNT* 7), 1959; R. Schnackenburg, *God's Rule and Kingdom*, Edinburgh, London and New York 1963; J. Schildenberger, 'Weissagung und Erfüllung', *Bbl* 24 (1943), 107–24 and 205–30; J. Schildenberger, *Vom Geheimnis des Gotteswortes*, Heidelberg 1950, 181–204; P. Bläser, 'Erfüllung der Schrift', *LTK* iii², 983f; Baumgärtel and Kümmel, 'Weissagung und Erfüllung im AT und NT', *RGG* vi³, 1584–8; H. Gross, 'Zum Problem Verheissung und Erfüllung', *BZ* 3 (1959), 3–17; Eichrodt i, 381–7; von Rad ii, 357–87; P. Grelot, *Sens chrétien de l'AT*, Tournai 1962, 388–403; C. Westermann, *Probleme atl. Hermeneutik*, Munich 1960, 28–53; W. Zimmerli, *Verheissung und Erfüllung*.

Johannes Schildenberger

Glory

The Hebrew word *kābôd* is rendered as *doxa* in the Greek bible. Our usual translation is 'glory'.

A. *Extra-biblical usage*. Among ancient writers *doxa*, which is of course connected with the verb *dokeō* (lit = to think), is used with two meanings: 1. 'the opinion which I have', and 2. 'the opinion which others have of me'. In the first case, the meaning is extended to include expectation, perception, doctrine, dogma, axiom, imagination, outward appearance, etc, and in the second to include good reputation. In conjunction with an appropriate adjective, however, it can also mean 'bad reputation'.

Philo also uses the word with the above meanings. In all the two hundred and fifty instances in which it is found in his works, only once does it mean 'brightness', and then obviously as a result of biblical influence. In Josephus, it means splendour or magnificence.

B. *Biblical usage in general*. In the Septuagint and the New Testament, *doxa* is never found with the first meaning, that is, opinion, but can mean (a) fame, reputation or honour, (b) brightness, brilliance or splendour, (c) reflected splendour and (d) when referring to God, heavenly brilliance, sublimity or magnificence. In the last meaning, *doxa* can even be used in parallelism with the name of God, and elsewhere as a substitute for God. This arises from the fact that in LXX *doxa* is equivalent to *kābôd*, and is in fact even used to translate other Hebrew words closely related, in their context, with the idea of *kābôd*.

C. *Old Testament usage*. 1. In the *Masorah*, *kābôd* has the secular Hebrew meaning of 'honour', *what adds to a person's standing, what increases a person's position and influence*. (The basic meaning of the root *kbd* is 'to be heavy'.) In the concrete sense, it means 'wealth' or 'position of honour' (see Gen 31:1; 45:13; Nahum 2:9; Ps 49:17). When it refers to peoples and racial groups, *kābôd* means the prestige or the standing of a given race among others in the world (Is 16:14; 17:4; 21:16). Splendour or glory is the meaning of *kābôd* in Is 10:18; 60:13, used in conjunction with a wood or a hill. *Kābôd* may also be used as parallel with *nepheš* and *ḥayyîm*, with the meaning of 'soul' or 'I', in many of the psalms. This usage is, however, questionable, as the reading may be *kābēd* (liver).

Whenever *kābôd* is used in connection with God—this occurs frequently in the phrase *k^ebôd Yahweh*—it means the 'impact of the divine appearance'. The transcendent God reveals himself on earth in meteorological phenomena, as for example in a dark thunder-cloud (Ex 24:15; Ezek 1:4; Ps 29; 50:2f). In Ex and Num particularly, the *k^ebôd Yahweh* appears in conjunction with *ʾānān* (cloud). This is also the case in 1 Kings 8:10. This cloud, however, only serves to conceal the real apparition of God—the all-consuming fire and light—which would destroy men if it were fully revealed to them (Ex 24:17; 33:18ff). God reveals himself in this way only at important points in the history of salvation, and it is possible to define the *k^ebôd Yahweh* as 'God himself, whenever he reveals himself in a solemn theophany, accompanied by thunder and lightning, storm and earthquake' (Steinheimer, 6). The *k^ebôd Yahweh* is therefore not God himself in his true and unrecognisable essence, but *God insofar as he allows men to recognise him.* What *k^ebôd Yahweh* means in substance, then, is the power, majesty, magnificence, and *glory of God* (Ex 24:16f; Num 16:9ff) and, at the same time, his appearance and heavenly substance of light (Ex 24:15ff; 40:34ff; Ps 50:2; 104:2: and, less obviously, in 1 Kings 8:11). In the vision of Ezekiel, the cloud is replaced by cherubs (eg Ezek 1:4ff; 43:2). In both Ezekiel and Psalms, the *k^ebôd Yahweh* is associated with the temple, the tabernacle or the holy mountain, Sinai—all places which are intimately connected with God's earthly appearances. In Ps 66:2 and 79:9, *kābôd* is used in parallel with *šēm* (name), and stands for the name of God. *Kābôd* is also frequently used in the psalms, with the meaning of greatness and honour, in conjunction with verbs, to imply that man is bound to give this honour to God. 'Giving honour' in this case adds nothing to God's majesty; it is simply a recognition of it (Ps 19:1; 24:7; 66:2; 96:3, 7; 138:5; 145:5, 11). In Is 42:8; 48:11, God makes it clear that he will not share this honour with others. In the case of Ps 57:5, 11; 72:19; Is 40:5, *kābôd* implies the kingdom of God which will appear at the end of time.

2. In LXX, *doxa* occurs 445 times, including 280 times in the protocanonical books. Generally speaking, it translates the Hebrew *kābôd.* As Kittel quite rightly claims, the two words *doxa* and *kābôd* have become identical in meaning. The classical meaning of 'opinion' is completely absent from LXX, whereas that of glory is to be found when it refers to splendour, power, reputation, or honour in the human sense or to power, glory, honour, brightness or, as in the case of *kābôd*, self-revelation in the divine sense.

Doxan didonai tō(i) theō(i) (lit. = to give *doxa* to God) has the same meaning—that is, 'recognition of the glory of God'—as the Hebrew phrase 'to give *kābôd*' (to sing or tell of the glory of God).

3. *Kābôd* in *later Jewish* usage. In the Targums, *kābôd* is usually rendered by *yeqār* (honour). The rabbis tend to use *kābôd* in the sense of human honour, with which God, however, frequently identifies himself. They regard the divine *kābôd* as a foreboding of the advent of the *šekinâ*. Man has no share in this divine *kābôd*, although according to Ex 34:29f Moses, and according to Gen rabba 11, the *ʾādām qādmôn*, who lost this share in the divine *kābôd* through the fall, are apparent exceptions. The rabbis infer from Dan 12:3 that the pious will have a share in the divine *kābôd* at the end of time, though according to Num 3:15 it is only the Messiah who will have a real share in this *kābôd*. Blessedness for the others consists merely in being permitted to behold the divine *kābôd* (b Ber. 34a). The apocryphal books (Apoc Mos 20f; 4 Ezr 7:91–7; Bar (Syr) 51:10; 1 Hen 38:4) reveal a similar attitude towards the *kābôd*.

D. The *New Testament usage* is in accordance with that of LXX: the usual meanings are 'renown', 'power', 'honour', and 'divine revelation'. The brightness which accompanies God's appearance is sometimes stressed; at other times it is little emphasised (Lk 2:9; 9:31ff; 2 Pet 1:17; Acts 22:11; Rev 15:8; 21:23). In the New Testament, too, *doxan didonai* means a recognition of the divine majesty (Acts 12:23; Rom 4:20; Rev 14:7). In the doxologies of the New Testament, the word needed to complete the sense is not *eiē(i)* (lit. = let [it] be), but *esti(n)* (lit. = [it] is)—this is shown very clearly by 1 Pet 4:11: 'To him *belong* glory and dominion for ever and ever. Amen'. The *doxa theou* (= glory of God) of the New Testament is associated with revelations which are of importance in the matter of salvation, as is the case with the *kâbôd Yahweh* of the Old Testament. As, however, these New Testament revelations are always intimately bound up with the person of Jesus, the New Testament goes beyond the Old and makes the *doxa* appear as something new, referring to Jesus as the Christ. It is only in John that such statements are made with reference to Jesus in this world. John is, however, perfectly in accord with the writers of the synoptic gospels, in maintaining that this *doxa* is veiled, and can be recognised only in *pistis* (= ↗ faith; see Jn 1:14). The man who has faith is able to recognise the *doxa* in the *dunameis* (powers) of Jesus (Jn 2:11; 11:4, 40). In Lk 2:9, it shines forth as a final greeting from the heavenly world. In the Transfiguration on Mount Tabor, the presence of *doxa* is clearly indicated in the substance of all three synoptic accounts, although it is only Luke who explicitly refers to it (9:31f). In John, however, Jesus frequently prays for the coming of the *doxa* (Jn 12–17). It is personally revealed in him on the occasion of his passion, death and resurrection. On his ascension, Jesus returns to his heavenly *doxa* (Acts 1:9; Phil 2:9; 1 Tim 3:16). Stephen is permitted to see him in this heavenly glory (Acts 7:55). At his parousia, Jesus will appear in his *doxa* and with his *dunamis* (Mt 19:28; 25:31; Mk

8:38; 10:37; 13:26; Lk 21:27; Tit 2:13; 1 Pet 5:4, 10).

The New Testament presents a far more hopeful picture of the *doxa* of the faithful than the Old. Not only does the New Testament state that the faithful will behold the *doxa* of God (1 Cor 13:12)—it also promises that they are to be led, through their sharing with Christ in suffering, to a share in his *doxa* (Mt 13:43; Phil 3:21; Col 3:4; 1:27; Rom 5:2; 8:17; 2 Thess 2:14). *Aiōnios doxa* (eternal glory) is the aim which they are called to achieve in Christ and the goal to which he is leading them, as members of his body (2 Cor 4:17; 1 Thess 2:12; 2 Tim 2:10; 1 Pet 5:4, 10). The faithful already have, in this life, a share in the *doxa mellousa* (coming glory), in a hidden sense, in the *pneuma* (Spirit). It is the *aparkhē* (=firstfruit: Rom 8:23; 2 Cor 3:7f; 1 Pet 4:14) which will eventually be accomplished. There is no real contradiction here with Jn 17:22, in which Jesus gives the *doxa* to his disciples. The *pneuma* belongs so intimately to him that it can, in fact, be completely identified with him. In the New Testament, the angels too possess this glory, because they are constantly in the company of God (Heb 9:5; Rev 18:1; Jude 8; 2 Pet 2:10).

E. Usage in the *Latin bible*. In the pre-Vulgate Latin translations, *claritas* was used when the emphasis was on the light or brilliance of the apparition (African translation), *gloria* when the idea of light or glory was predominant (Itala), and *maiestas* when God's power was to be stressed. In the Vulgate, which is based upon the Itala, *claritas* does not appear at all in Matthew, Mark, or the catholic epistles, and very rarely in Luke, Revelation, or the letters of Paul. *Maiestas* appears very rarely in the Vulgate translation of Matthew, Luke, Jude, and the Apocalypse. In most cases, the Vulgate translates *doxa* by *gloria*. The church fathers follow the biblical usage, seeing in the *doxa* the divine essence of the Blessed Trinity and also the divine essence of Christ. They tend to speak very often of the *gloria crucis*, *gloria passionis*, and *gloria resurrectionis*. The fact that the divine *Logos* (Word) retained the *gloria* in becoming man was regarded by the fathers as the first step in the incorporation of human nature in the glory of the Father. The Roman meaning of 'renown' or 'honour' is perpetuated in *gloria*, in patristic references to the glory of the martyrs.

Finally, the liturgy continues this biblical usage—in the case of the Roman (Latin) liturgy, that of the Latin translations.

Bibliography: G. Kittel and G. von Rad, *TDNT* II, 232–55; J. Schneider, *Doxa* (Ntl. Forschungen III/3), Gütersloh 1932; G. Kittel, *Der Herrlichkeit Gottes*, Giessen 1934; B. Stein, *Der Begriff kebod Jahwe und seine Bedeutung für die atl. Gotteserkenntnis*, Emsdetten 1939; M. Steinheimer, *Die 'Doxa tou Theou' in der römischen Liturgie*, Munich 1951 (with bibliography). See also: Z. Alszeghy and M. Flick, *Greg* 36 (1955), 361–90; C. Mohrmann, *Festschrift A. Debrunner*, Berne 1954, 321–8; P. de Haes, *Collectanea Mechlinensia* 27 (1957), 485–590; E. Pax, 'Ex Parmenide as Setuaginta: De notione vocabuli *doxa*', *VD* 38 (1960), 92–102; *J. Bourke, 'Encounter with God', *Life of the Spirit* XV (1961), 398–405 and 490–7.

Georg Molin

God

A. *The image of God in the Old Testament*. Not only does the Old Testament recognise no image of Yahweh in the form of a statue or any kind of visual representation, it also contains no fully developed, systematic doctrine in the form of a 'spiritual' image of God. What occupies the most prominent place in Old Testament revelation is not the divine being, but divine activity, although there is no lack of statements in which God is used predicatively with the verb to be. What is more, the activity of God as it appears in the Old Testament provides a good deal of information about his being. Before attempting, however, to fit together the individual details of what we may call the image of God in the Old Testament, it should be noted that Old Testament revelation is intrinsically a 'revelation in process of development' (*revelatio in fieri*). Although Yahwism can scarcely be traced back to any generally accepted form of historical religious development, it is certainly subject, at its own particular level, to certain laws of growth which are ultimately to be found in the teaching concerning the God of revelation. The ebb and flow of time plays an important part in this process, as well as Israel's contact with various spheres of tradition and proximity to various kinds of written and oral testimony and traditions. In any attempt to systematise the Old Testament statements concerning God, different factors such as these must of necessity overlap, but all must be borne in mind.

I. *The one and unique God.* In striking contrast to the other religions of the Ancient East, Israel's monotheism is the crystallisation and the universal postulate determining the structure of all religious teaching. This monotheism has its own historical development in Israel, a development towards greater explicitness and clarity. In the patriarchal age, what is stressed is Israel's commitment to the one God of revelation, without any clear statement being made concerning the non-existence of other divine beings. The God of Moses reveals himself as the God of the Patriarchs (Ex 3:6). He will not tolerate any form of worship for other gods (Ex 20:3). What is more, the question of the existence of any other gods is not raised. The God of the Covenant is, for Moses, without any doubt the God of the whole world, even if the statement 'All the earth is mine' is accepted as a later gloss (Ex 19:5). It is thus possible for us to speak with complete certainty of a monotheism in practice with regard to those who were witnesses to divine revelation even in the early history of Israel. The ordinary people would for a long time also have taken the existence of other gods in foreign lands and among strange people for granted. Evidence of this is to be found in Judg 11:24; 1 Sam 26:19; 2 Kings 3:27. A formal and theoretical monotheism was evidently less important to the God of revelation, at least in the early stages, than the achievement of a single-minded obligation on the part of the people of his Covenant towards him alone. His purpose was to lead them by a progressive enlightenment. It was only later, through the prophets, that he allowed the full truth to be disclosed in all its clarity, that no other associations were possible because no other gods in fact existed. According to the evidence of 1 Kings 18:39, Elijah was able to stir the people to the expression of monotheistic belief: 'The Lord, he is God! The Lord, he is God!' This is the one great theme which is common to all the prophets, however variously they express their message, and it eventually emerges in the sixth century in Deutero–Isaiah in hymn form, as for example in 43:10ff; 'I, I am the Lord, and besides me there is no saviour.' With such an absolute monotheism as the sure foundation of its official religion, Israel stands out on a lonely and isolated prominence in the Ancient Near East, although from the political and cultural point of view it was an insignificant and second-rate people compared with the other peoples of that period. Various finds made in the Middle East indicate, it is true, that monotheistic tendencies existed in individual and private devotion in Egypt and Mesopotamia, but these had no influence on the official religion of the people. The attempt made by the Pharaoh Achnaton in the fourteenth century to establish monotheism failed completely. The religion of Zarathustra is the only phenomenon which is even remotely analogous to the monotheism of Israel, but both spatially and temporally there could have been no contact between the two before 500 BC. Furthermore, the monotheism of Zarathustra was weakened by dualistic elements, which were unknown in the religion of Israel.

II. *The transcendent God.* In the sun-worship of Achnaton, divinity belongs completely to this world and is regarded as immanent. Its being is essentially a 'being in the world', which is a basic conviction common to all the religions of the Ancient East and is in particular the distinguishing feature of all the western Semitic fertility religions against which Yahwism had to try to make headway. Yahweh, on the other hand, appears (despite his close personal relationship with man and his bearing on the world) as the transcendent God who is in his true being and essence raised above all worldly affairs. This transcendence is manifested in many different ways.

1. *Yahweh is transcendent.* Whereas divinity was in the first place always conceived in the ancient Near East as a regional numen or Lord of a particular locality (as an example of this, see 2 Kings 5), the God of the Patriarchs is proved to be one who is in no way limited to a particular land, people or empire. His sovereign power extends over the whole of the so-called 'fertile crescent'—therefore from the estuary of the Euphrates to Egypt. He has control over the land of Baal, that is, Canaan, in the first place by virtue of the promise and later by virtue of the fulfilment of the promise. Although it is true that he appears, at the time of Moses, to be the God of Mount Sinai and, during the period of the monarchy, the God of the city of Jerusalem, this 'localisation' does not imply that his presence was limited to a particular place, but that he had appeared there. The people themselves certainly never thought that they would be able to find him only on Sinai or in Jerusalem. They endeavoured to worship him everywhere in the country where the so-called 'high-places' were to be found. Even Elijah repaired the altar on Mount Carmel (1 Kings 18:30). According to the view of those appointed to bear the revealed word of God, Yahweh could not be contained within the walls of the temple of Jerusalem. In Isaiah's well-known vision of the temple (Is 6), the whole space above the

throne is empty, there is room in the temple only for the royal train of Yahweh, and the Seraphim testify that the whole is filled with the overwhelming glory of the king of the world. The author of Solomon's prayer of dedication of the Temple, belonging to a prophetical movement, puts these words into the mouth of the builder (1 Kings 8:27): 'Behold, heaven and the highest heaven cannot contain thee; how much less this house which I have built?' According to Jer 7:12, Yahweh can thus also allow the Temple to be destroyed. Yahweh's supraspatial aspect is further indicated in Amos in the eighth century: 'Not one of them shall flee away, not one of them shall escape. Though they dig into Sheol, from there shall my hand take them; though they climb up to heaven, from there I will bring them down. Though they hide themselves on the top of Carmel, from there I will search out and take them; and though they hide from my sight at the bottom of the sea, there will I command the serpent, and it shall bite them' (Amos 9:1ff). The author of Ps 139 has taken up this theme and explains the idea of God's action and influence as transcending space with reference to the transcendant nature of his being and essence: 'Whither shall I go from thy Spirit? Or whither shall I flee from thy presence? If I ascend to heaven, thou art there! If I make my bed in Sheol, thou art there! If I take the wings of the morning and dwell in the uttermost parts of the sea, even there thy hand shall lead me, and thy right hand shall hold me' (Ps 139:7–10). Yahweh is in fact Lord of nature and of all space. He is, however, in no way a part of nature. Even the heavenly powers of the cosmos which produce the movement of the stars and planets are not of the same being as he is. According to Genesis 1, the sun and the moon are merely 'lamps', thus material things—mere material elements of the cosmos in the most matter-of-fact sense of the word. All great human powers too are insignificant before him. Considering the mighty empires of the ancient world, whose extent and power impress us so much today, and faced with the presence of the Mediterranean civilisations of Europe, Africa and Asia, Deutero–Isaiah nevertheless says: 'Behold, the nations are like a drop from a bucket, and are accounted as the dust on the scales; behold, he takes up the isles like fine dust. Lebanon would not suffice for fuel, nor are its beasts enough for a burnt offering. All the nations are as nothing before him, they are accounted by him as less than nothing and emptiness. To whom then will you liken God, or what likeness compare with him?' (Is 40:15ff). This transcendence of Yahweh above everything that is visible is firmly rooted in his absolute creativeness concerning everything that is in the process of being. This creativeness did not flow or proceed from his being by emanation, but was brought into existence out of the original power of his creative will, as his word which, so to speak, takes on concrete form (Gen 1:1ff; Is 42:5; 45:18; Ps 33:6, 9; 148:5, etc.).

2. *Yahweh is universal.* Evidence of Yahweh's transcendence is also to be found in his attitude towards the people of God as presented in the Bible. He is not simply the God of the people of Israel, to be thought of in the same way as the other peoples regarded the chief

god of their pantheistic system. In the Ancient Near East, the relationship between a god and his people was conceived in purely natural terms. In Israel too, there was always a tendency to regard the union between Yahweh and Israel as a kind of natural bond—as a mutual dependence upon each other. In contrast to this, the Mosaic tradition testifies from the very beginning that the relationship of the covenant must of necessity be conceived as a relationship based upon free election, with the result that it contains the inherent possibility of rejection. This became a fundamental aspect of the teaching of the prophets. They emphasise again and again that the Covenant depends upon grace and in this way direct attention to the fact that it is possible for Yahweh and Israel to exist at a distance from each other. Amos assumes the role of spokesman for Israel when he proclaims the verdict of God: 'Are you not like the Ethiopians to me, O people of Israel? . . . Did I not bring up Israel from the land of Egypt, and the Philistines from Caphtor and the Syrians from Kir?' (Amos 9:7). Here Yahweh disavows the purely practical use which Israel has made of him, as a God of the people. His special Covenant with Israel is a free one, and can therefore be broken. Indeed, Jeremiah is bound to announce the restoration of Israel by the promise of a 'new Covenant' (Jer 31).

3. *Yahweh is the Lord of time*, though he is not in any way subject to any temporal laws or to any diminution of his being. The Hebrew does not think of eternity simply as another mode of existence, but in his imagination lengthens the line of time both forwards and backwards into the vast obscurity where nothing is visible. Everything that is coming into being or passing out of existence occurs along this imaginary line, with the exception of what is divine. In this way the Old Testament stands in complete contradiction to all the mythological theogonies of neighbouring civilisations. Existence is such an essential part of Yahweh's being that even what we find in the introductory verse of the Johannine gospel (=in the beginning *was* God) is left out of Gen 1:1. Only in Ps 90:2 do we find 'Before the mountains were brought forth, or ever thou hadst formed the earth and the world, from everlasting to everlasting thou art God'. God is thus the fulness of life itself, to which transience is completely unknown. This is why, according to Ps 90:4, a thousand years are as a single day to him, and why Deutero-Isaiah calls him 'the first and last' (44:6; 48:12), and why, according to Hab 1:12, the death referred to in the myths of the vegetation-gods is unknown to him. He is simply the living one in whom every generation can have absolute confidence (Judg 8:19; 1 Sam 14:39, etc.). Nothing is capable of diminishing his life. It can also not be diminished by sin. Job exclaims (7:20; cf 35:6): 'If I sin, what do I do to thee, thou watcher of men?' Yahweh's life is at the same time so abundant that it is incapable of being increased, either by justice (Job 35:7), purity (22:2f), fasting (Zech 7:5) or sacrifice (Is 1:11ff, etc.). The God of Israel has no need of anything from man to sustain his life, as this is far removed from everything that is temporal or in any way tied to the world.

4. *Yahweh transcends every type of sexual*

dimorphism. Sexuality is a phenomenon which pervades the whole of terrestrial life, and which contains the source of life in the animal and human sphere. Life and the origin of life is a divine mystery for the people of the Ancient Near East. They look for the source of all fertility in the womb of divinity and do not think of this in the metaphorical but in the concrete sense, and thus their idea of human sexuality is transferred to the divine sphere. It even takes the form of sexual dualism, and god and goddess are worshipped as a divine couple. In direct contrast to this, Yahweh appears in the Old Testament as a single divine being. The Hebrew word for goddess has not even been handed down to us. Yahweh has no female counterpart, although he is regarded as the source of all life and has been endowed with human characteristics and is always represented as possessing the fullness of life and serene happiness. Even the conception of Yahweh as a Father does not have an exclusively male application in his case (see Is 49:15; 66:13). Indeed, whenever the Covenant is, for the purpose of elucidation, likened to a matrimonial covenant or union, Yahweh appears in the role of bridegroom or husband, although this is always in the form of an allegory and refers to his activity rather than to his being. This transcendent quality with regard to sexuality distinguishes Yahweh from the deities of all the other religions of the period, and it is not possible to find an adequate explanation for it—even if Israel's alleged fear of sex is taken into consideration—on the purely natural level.

5. *Yahweh is intrinsically holy.* The adjective ↗ holy, used predicatively (*qādôš*) has the strictly etymological and objective meaning of being separate and completely different and has a close affinity with the 'taboo' of comparative religion. The notion of holiness is also closely connected with a particular place, as, for example, in Gen 28:17 (Jacob at Bethel) and Ex 3:5 (Moses and the burning bush). But what is behind this is the experience of the 'mysterium tremendum', which is God's way of manifesting himself. God's 'jealousy' and the theophany in the form of fire (Ex 20:5; 34:4) clearly indicate this. That holiness is, from the ontological and the ethical point of view, the essence of Yahweh, is borne out not only by the theology of the priests and levites (see Lev 19:2), but also, even more emphatically, by the prophets. According to Amos 4:2, Yahweh swears by his holiness, which is for him the most sublime and ultimate ideal. In his prophetic vision (Chap. 6), Isaiah sees Yahweh as a king of terrifying sublimity, blinding purity and overwhelming splendour. The only possible reaction that man can experience in the face of such holiness is to feel himself a sinner and the lowest of creatures, and the power of Yahweh's holiness thus forms the principal theme of Isaiah's message (see 10:7 and the constant reference to Yahweh as the 'Holy One of Israel', Is 1:4; 5:19; 10:20; 12:6, etc.). According to Deutero-Isaiah, the mark of Yahweh's holiness is that it bears no comparison with anything belonging to man or the world (see Is 40:13ff, 25; 55:8, etc.). But this quality of being absolutely other also contains the idea that Yahweh is quite different from man in his love (see Hos 11:8 and Is 55:8).

6. *Yahweh is the God who must be worshipped 'differently'*. In all the religions of the ancient civilisations, divinity is visibly apparent in the form of a statue or statues. From the earliest times, the only object or place which visibly represents God for Israel was the sacred Ark of the covenant. The commandment forbidding images, handed down to Israel in the Sinaitic tradition, applied in the first place originally to the making and worshipping of images of other gods, and it was therefore possible for cases of a popular image-worship of Yahweh to crop up occasionally (see Judg 17:4f; 1 Kings 12:28ff). But the true tradition of Israel was, from the very beginning, a worship of Yahweh without images (see Ex 34:17) and this became more and more marked with the passage of time (see Deut 4:15ff) and even more firmly established on the basis of the conception that Yahweh could not be compared with any creature or wordly object (Is 40:12ff). In the matter of sacrifice, however, the worship of Yahweh does appear to approximate very closely to the other religions of Israel's neighbours. It is not difficult to find phenomenological and terminological support for this comparison, but the significance and the spirit of Israel's sacrificial worship are quite different from those of other religions. All magical tendencies are dismissed forthwith (see Ex 20:7 [and the commandment in 20:2]; 22:18; Deut 18:10ff). In this way, sacrifice is conceived as the fruit and the expression of a fundamental moral choice on the part of the people, who share in the covenant. Thus, even at the conclusion of the Covenant on Mount Sinai, what is central to the sacrificial ceremonies is ethical and personal commitment to the will of Yahweh (Ex 24:6ff). The prophets repeatedly point out the overriding importance of moral and personal commitment in the religion of revelation and reject any sacrifice which is not accompanied by the 'spirit' which God desires (Amos 5:21ff; Hos 6:6; Is 1:10ff; Mic 6:6ff; Jer 7:21ff).

It is in the transcendence of God that the religion of Israel differs so completely from all other religions which are known to have existed in that region at that time, and it is this which makes it simply impossible to derive Yahwism from other sources. There are no satisfactory, natural reasons which can explain how it was that the small, politically and culturally insignificant people of Israel arrived at this idea of God, and from this point of view Israel's idea of a transcendent God is quite simply the miracle of the Old Testament. What, nonetheless, is remarkable about this idea is that, despite the transcendence of the divine being and essence, the immanence of the divine activity and influence is demonstrated again and again. In what he does Yahweh is, as it were, present at every single point of time and space. Natural phenomena are all traceable back to him, though no particular notice is taken of what might be termed intermediate causes (see Ps 147:15–18; Job 38:28ff). The principal theme of the Old Testament is that Yahweh is truly the Lord of history. It is true to say that not only does the Old Testament contain, in an unparalleled manner, a fully developed theology of history, but that it is in fact a theology of history in itself, according to which Yahweh, with a definite plan and object in view, yet 'reacting' specifically to human 'action', intervenes in man's history with mercy and justice and is indeed himself the central and leading factor in the history of the chosen people and of mankind in general. The most striking attestation of Yahweh's influence and control over everything that happens is to be found in the practice of giving him the title of king (see Num 23:21; Is 6:5; 24:23; 33:22; 41:21; 43:15; 44:6; 52:7; Jer 10:7, 10; Mal 1:14; Ps 24:7; 47:6; 93:1; 96:10; 97:1, etc). This conception of the kingship of Yahweh incorporates and gradually develops the idea that he is directing the history of the cosmos and of mankind towards the eventual revelation of his royal majesty and glory in a restored world. Thus nature and history do not come into being and evolve as independent and self-contained consequences of what is and what happens. What we could call the established laws of nature or even of history appear in the Old Testament as divine action taking place according to a regular pattern, which is controlled by its own laws but which is always open to God's free intervention. Thus the transcendence of God's essential being is attested in the free immanence of his activity. It must be admitted, however, that the consistent employment of a markedly anthropomorphic mode of expression, which appears throughout the whole of the Old Testament with very few variations from the earliest to the latest texts, seems to be diametrically opposed to this conception of God's transcendence. The main reason for such an anthropomorphic form of writing with regard to divine matters is generally speaking to be found in the innate limitations and the finite quality of the human mind, but it must also be borne in mind that this pronounced anthropomorphism of the Old Testament is intimately connected with the extremely figurative and metaphorical oriental mode of thought and speech. These frequent examples of anthropomorphism do not, however, expose the basic Old Testament image of God's transcendence to any real danger of compromise or diminution, for what they aim to portray is not God's being which is withdrawn from the world, but his activity which is immediately effective within it. It is, in fact, only possible for them to appear in precisely this form and in such abundance against the background of the fundamental transcendence of God. They do, however, fulfil a very important and positive function in enabling the Hebrews to comprehend and to depict Yahweh in the fullness of his total personality.

III. *The personal God.* It should be clearly recognised at the very outset that, contrary to some modern objections concerning the personality of God, the authentic conception of personality does not imply any essential modification or limitation of being as it presupposes any essential independence, in the sense of a relationship with itself, and this applies equally whether this relationship is, in its being, finite or infinite. The Jews, like other oriental people of antiquity did not develop the idea of ↗ spirit and spirituality into a philosophy, but they did firmly grasp the essence of the spirit and conceived it as an element that relates strictly to itself and intimately possesses itself, and succeeded in delineating it in the most sublime manner in their own image of God, which was stamped through and through with the mark of their personal conception of the nature of the spirit. Divinity is thus not represented simply as the creative first cause and the source of all being in the aspect of an indeterminable and all-embracing 'it', nor is it seen merely as being itself (*ipsum esse*). God is quite simply viewed as 'he' or 'I', or as a 'self'. This is most strikingly evident in the principal statements made about him in the Old Testament, that is, in those places where God 'speaks'. In these passages his knowledge and wisdom, his will and his freedom are expressed, not only in the subject-matter, but also in the fact of his speaking. Hence very often this speaking by God takes place after the manner of a dialogue in which God is the subject, the 'I' who is speaking and, in the majority of cases, man is the object, the 'thou' who is addressed by God. It is hardly necessary to quote particular instances of this phenomenon, since almost every page of Holy Scripture provides at least one. Furthermore, what is contained in the representation of man as the 'image of God' (↗ Likeness) is the fundamental statement that God is personality, and the divine elucidation of the name of Yahweh ('I am who I am': Ex 3:14ff) incorporates the personal element as a component of the divine essence. God also makes direct allusions to the fact that he is a person, and in a manner which could not be more directly personal. This is found in books which are principally concerned with the law, in the sapiential literature and above all in the prophetic books. The following two examples have been selected from many: 'I will be gracious to whom I will be gracious and will show mercy on whom I will show mercy." (Ex 33:19) and 'I say: my counsel shall stand, and I will accomplish all my purpose' (Is 46:10). In these two examples alone, God's spirit and freedom appear with unmistakable clarity as essential elements of absolute personality. Finally, the divine being as a person is most conspicuously in evidence in God's freedom and autonomy with regard to his love for man within the Covenant. This love of Yahweh within the Covenant forms the main theme, not just of New Testament revelation, but also of that of the Old Testament (↗ Covenant). Everything that forms part of God's rule [and the government of man] revolves around this axis: ↗ love and ↗ judgement (see also ↗ justification), ↗ wisdom, guidance and faithfulness, promise and threat, admonition and warning. The God of the Covenant shows himself as the Father of the people (Ex 4:22f; Hos 11:1; Is 64:8; Mal 2:10, etc), as a Father in whom the paternal and the maternal elements are intimately interwoven (see Hos 11:1ff; Jer 31:9–20; Is 49:15; 66:13), as the Father of kings (2 Sam 7:13f; Ps 89:26f), as the Father of orphans (Ps 68:5), as the Father of those who fear him (Ps 103:13) and of the just (Wis 2:16). He also reveals himself as a provident shepherd (Mic 4:6; Zeph 3:19; Jer 31:10; Ezek 34; Ps 23:1ff), and as bridegroom and husband (see Hos 2:16; Jer 2:2; Ezek 16:8; Is 54:5 and Song of Sol.). In the same way that the human person is characterised in particular by his heart and his face, the God of the Old Testament too has a heart (see Gen 6:6; 1 Sam 13:14; 1 Kings 9:3; Jer 3:15; Ps 33:11, etc.) and a face (Ex 33:14f, 20; Job 1:11; Ps 80:19, etc). All higher inward impulses can be predicated of him and, what is more, even those which seem to be particularly human, which has at times provided material for indictments against the Old Testament image of God. These human impulses which the Old Testament attributes to God should, however, be understood in relation to the rest of Scripture and in the context of the whole of divine revelation (see 3). Moreover, the very fact of their lack of perfection bears witness to Yahweh's vital personality whose inner decisions and motives are often obscure to man. With regard to the problem of natural theology concerning the existence of evil in the world, the book of Job alludes to the impenetrable mystery of the divine dispensation, but, at the same time, firmly precludes the idea of any form of solution in the nature of a blind or impersonal fate. In Job 38ff Yahweh reveals himself as a person of a unique kind. At the same time, his universal causality is also clearly demonstrated, as indeed it is in almost every book of the Old Testament. The Hebrew mind makes no clear distinction between what God causes to happen and what he permits to happen. Thus it is that the Hebrew is able to express dialectically the objectively identical fact of the Pharaoh's obduracy of heart in the two statements: 'The Lord hardened Pharaoh's heart' (Ex 9:12) and 'Pharaoh . . . sinned yet again . . . and his heart was hardened' (= Pharaoh hardened his heart, Ex 9:34–5). God's personal causality and man's freedom of choice receive an equal emphasis and, as in the thomist formulation of their interrelationship, they are not regarded as antitheses which cancel each other out. In this way, it is possible for Yahweh to appear quite frequently to bring evil about, or for some seemingly demonic attribute to be present in the metaphorical and often hyperbolical delineation of his dispensation over man. In any attempt to arrive at a theological interpretation of passages of this kind, care should be taken not to divorce such texts from the context of the customary Hebrew manner of expression and the question of literary genre, particularly relevant here, and to bear in mind also the imperfection of Old Testament revelation relative to the New.

IV. *God as the source of abundant life.* Although God is transcendent, he is also the vital source of all ↗ life in the human and animal kingdom. In Num 27:16, he is called the 'God of the spirits of all flesh'. Considered in its context, this refers particularly to man. According to the passage dealing with creation, man, unlike the animals, is also essentially constituted by God breathing the breath of life into his nostrils (Gen 2:7). On the other hand, however, according to Ps 104:29ff, animal life is also a form of divine breath. Thus all life on earth is a sharing in the divine life. But what strike us especially in this flowing of the living spirit of God into man are the extraordinary and unusual manifestations of life, such as the special strength of Samson (Judg 14:6), the creative inspiration of artists and craftsmen (Ex 28:3), the ecstasy of the prophets (see 1

Sam 10:5ff) and the understanding of the wise men (see Job 32:8). The more extraordinary and supernatural such phenomena become, the more powerfully is God's vital activity at work in them. Indeed, he manifests himself in them simply as life itself, and the believing Israelite freely acknowledges himself as one who has, at all levels of his existence, been given life by him. This is why the psalmists (and particularly the author of Ps 119) so willingly address the petition 'Give me life!' to Yahweh. What is sought first and foremost here, of course, is deliverance from mortal danger, but closely associated with this is a renewal of the inner life (see Ps 22:20f; 69:33), and finally a joyous experience of the spiritual treasures of life, such as the word of God (Ps 119) and has grace and friendship within the covenant. Thus we find in Ps 16:11: 'Thou dost show me the path of life; in thy presence there is fullness of joy, in thy right hand are pleasures for evermore'. This sentiment is expressed even more powerfully in Ps 36:7: 'How precious is thy steadfast love, O God! The children of men take refuge in the shadow of thy wings. They feast on the abundance of thy house, and thou givest them drink from the river of thy delights. For with thee is the fountain of life; in thy light do we see light.' It is precisely this knowledge of Yahweh's plenitude of light and life which made it possible for the believer to endure the tension which is inherent in his strictly monotheistic conception of God and which may be described by the phrase 'absolute solitude'. It is true that the Israelite knows that the 'heavenly ones', to whom he gives various names including even that of 'sons of God', are with Yahweh, but he is bound to conclude from his knowledge of the transcendence of God that even these cannot, for Yahweh, be perfect associates. The post-exilic books which are concerned with speculation about wisdom certainly intimate that the life of God must, personally and in itself, be abundantly rich. This reflection about the nature of divine wisdom, which claims to rely upon the support of scriptural texts (see A. Robert, 'Les attaches littéraires bibliques de Prov 1–9', *RB* 43 [1934] 42ff) led, in Prov 8, to a personification of ↗ wisdom, the significance of which goes beyond a merely poetical expression of the matter-of-fact truth that Yahweh is wise. What is in fact attained in this personification of God's wisdom is the first clear expression of an inspired knowledge of God's personal plenitude of life, even though there is no explicit indication yet of any kind of authentic plural personality in God. This particular passage has, however, been positively identified as one of the Old Testament bases of the New Testament teaching of the *Logos*. The divine ↗ word was also personified in the Old Testament, though in this case the outline is always fainter and less clearly defined than that which appears in the case of divine wisdom. Nevertheless, we find in Ps 119:89: 'For ever, O Lord, thy word standeth firm in heaven' and the word 'stand' is used in this way in Hebrew with a characteristically personal connotation. The 'word' too is thought of here as a divine herald, standing above all heavenly beings, in which Yahweh's speaking—and at this period the whole of God's connection with the world and with man is contained within the category of divine 'speaking'—acquires precise form and powerful expression. A similar idea is to be found in the following texts: Is 9:7; 55:11; Ps 107:20; 147:15ff; Wis 16:12; 18:14ff. In certain passages, too, Yahweh's ↗ spirit is personified: in Hag 2:5, his spirit dwells as a protector among the people of Israel; according to Neh 9:30, his spirit warns them through the prophets; in Is 63:10, his spirit is afflicted by the people and according to Wis 1:7, the spirit of the Lord which fills the entire world and embraces the universe has knowledge of every voice. These personifications of God's wisdom, word and spirit should on no account be regarded in the philosophical sense of hypostasisation, but they are, on the other hand, much more than poetic or merely exaggerated literary expressions. They demonstrate the wealth and abundance of the divine life and represent, from the point of view of sacred history, the first tentative and anticipatory movements in the direction of the revelation of the plural personality within the fullness of being of the single divine essence which emerges ultimately in the New Testament as the Trinity.

The Old Testament does not present a complete and self-contained reflected-image of the divine being. What St Paul says about the mysterious and fragmentary knowledge of the image of God (1 Cor 13:12) is applicable to that given in the Old Testament. It is, however, in every way greater than any image that could possibly have been achieved by any human process of intuition, reflection or contemplation in the history of the highest religions or philosophies. The Old Testament image not only depicts, but also signifies the presence of the God of revelation himself and thus the direct encounter with the 'God of Abraham, Isaac and Jacob' as in Pascal's phrase and consequently with the God who is the Father of Jesus Christ.

Bibliography: H. Schrade, *Der verborgene Gott, Gottesbild und Gottesvorstellung in Israel und im Alten Orient*, Stuttgart 1949; M. Rehm, *Das Bild Gottes im AT*, Würzburg 1951; W. Eichrodt, *Das Gottesbild des AT*, Stuttgart 1956; A. Gelin, 'Le monthéisme d'Israel', *LV* 29 (1956), 9–26; V. Hamp, 'Montheismus im AT', *SP* 1 (1959), 44–56; M. Buber, 'Die Götter der Völker und Gott', *Festschrift O. Michel*, Cologne 1963, 44–57; O. Eissfeldt, 'Jahwe, der Gott der Väter', *TLZ* 88 (1963), 481–90; *H. Renckens, 'The God of Israel', *The Religion of Israel*, London and New York 1967, 97–139.

Alfons Deissler

B. *The Image of God in the New Testament.* 1. *Jesus and the Image of God in later Judaism.* Jesus and the primitive church did not announce a different God from the God of the Old Testament, but they did proclaim the old God in a new way and in an extended revelation. Nowhere in the New Testament is it possible to find an antithesis to the creator of the world and the God of the covenant (such as the evil demiurge and law-giver of Marcion and other gnostics). It also gives a false and unbalanced picture to portray Jesus's image of God in the soft colours of mildness and pity. Any attempt to tone down the strong and severe aspects of this image results only in a diminution of the background against which the message of God's mercy stands out in brilliant relief.

Jesus presupposes the image of the

God of the Old Testament and judaism in its fullest dimensions. For Jesus God is the creator (Mk 10:6ff; 13:19; see also Jn 17:5–24), the Lord of heaven and earth (Mt 11:25); he is also the God of the patriarchs who spoke to Moses in the burning bush (Mk 12:26; see also Mt 8:11; Lk 16:23ff) and who proclaimed the ten commandments on Mount Sinai (Mk 10:19). It is this same God who must be loved with one's whole heart and one's whole strength (Mk 12:29ff), just as the pious Jew remembered him in his daily recitation of the *šᵉmaʾ* ('Hear, O Israel . . .' Deut 6:4ff). He must be served exclusively (Mt 6:24), with an undivided heart (Mt 6:21), in purity (see Mt 5:8; 6:23) and in sincerity (Mk 7:6ff). His commandments take precedence over human laws and institutions (Mk 7:8–13). In all this, Jesus is, in a sense, stricter than the Pharisees. A sublime and pure idea of God reigns in his soul and this conception cannot be tainted by human thought or dragged down to the human level (see Mk 8:33). In later judaism the notion of God's transcendence was greatly heightened by removing his heavenly dwelling place even farther away from earth into the 'third' or 'seventh' heaven and by surrounding his throne by countless heavenly beings and many categories of angels. The feeling of awe for God was also considerably enhanced not only by the strict avoidance of the use of the holy name of God in speech, but also by the employment of substitutes, such as 'the Name' and 'the Place', for the title 'Lord'. Jesus did not seek to lessen in any way this attitude of religious reverence and even makes use himself of this veiled manner of speaking of God by means of words such as 'heaven' (Mt 18:18; Lk 15:7–18, etc: cf the 'authority of heaven' with the 'authority of God'), or 'angels' (Lk 12:8f; 15:10); sometimes using a passive construction (Mt 5:5; 7:8, etc) or the third person plural (Lk 6:38; 12:20; 16:9, etc). But it should be noted that he avoided all scrupulous anxiety and aimed to teach a true reverence by stressing the absolute holiness of God and everything that is associated with him, as against the punctilious and hair-splitting attitude which characterised the pharasaical approach (see Mt 23:16–22). He goes much further than Moses, who proclaimed the laws of God, and the prophets, who emphasised morality in the worship of God, by giving radically new moral commandments in the authority of his messianic mission: 'But I say to you, do not swear at all, either by heaven, for it is the throne of God, or by the earth, for it is his footstool' (Mt 5:34ff). Thus he seizes upon one of the most sublime images for God's transcendent greatness (see Is 66:1) and draws grave moral inferences from it. By continuing: 'Or by Jerusalem, for it is the city of the great King' (cf Ps 48:2), he shows clearly that he also accepts the fact that God dwells among his people, and particularly in the Temple at Jerusalem, just as he does not hold himself personally aloof from the worship of the Temple (eg festivals connected with pilgrimages to Jerusalem, the Passover, etc). Elsewhere he enhances the true reverence for this place where God is particularly close to his people by refusing to tolerate the presence of buyers and sellers in the forecourt of the Temple, who turn the house of God into a 'den of robbers' (Mk 11:17; cf Jer 7:11). To be sure, he envisages the approach of the end of Jewish worship which was required by God for a definite period in the history of salvation, and indeed sees this end as having already come. He will himself build another Temple, 'not made with hands', thus hinting at the eschatological community of God (see Mk 14:58). This new temple is, according to the profound vision of St John, his own person (Jn 2:21ff). The true adoration of the Father 'in spirit and in truth' (Jn 4:23f) is in no way a devotion of a piously individualistic nature and it will surpass the old form of worship in universality, merit and spiritual content.

One of the most exalted features of Jesus's image of God is that of unlimited divine power, which can bring about salvation for mankind or show itself in the form of justice. What Jesus desires is a wholesome fear of the one who has the power to destroy both soul and body in hell (Mt 10:28) and who is able to claim the life of and call to account a rich man who, in his self-satisfaction and complacency, has forgotten God (Lk 12:20). God does whatever he wishes, but his will is exercised in the direction of salvation and mercy (see Mt 20:15). With him, everything is possible—this, indeed is the answer which Jesus gives to the fearful question of the disciples: 'Who then can be saved?' (Mk 10:27). The power of God is shown in his constant activity, but for Jesus the most urgent aspect of this activity is God's work in curing the most deeply concealed of all human maladies, sin. Jesus feels himself to be personally called to co-operate with the Father in this work and to save man from sin and also from physical infirmities (Jn 5:17; see also 14; Mk 2:1–12 and pars). But God is also the Lord of history and guides it towards the end which he has ordained for it. He has appointed the times and fixed the hours (see Lk 12:56; Acts 1:6f). All that happens is subject to his decree—'This must take place' (Mk 13:7). All that is to happen at the end of time, too, is known only to him and is subject absolutely to his decree: the day and hour are known only to the Father (Mk 13:32). He will, however, shorten the days of eschatological tribulation for the sake of the elect (Mk 13:20). All that can be done is to pray for the coming of God's sovereignty in power and glory (Mt 6:10). It is God alone who bestows positions of honour (Mk 10:40). He has, from the very beginning of the world, 'prepared' the kingdom for his blessed (Mt 25:34) and everlasting fire for Satan and his angels (Mt 25:41). Even in later judaism, this sovereignty of God as the Lord of the world was recognised and humbly submitted to, though the people were still groaning under the rule of Belial (see the Qumran texts). Jesus certainly did not destroy the image of God which was in force at that time, but rather proclaimed the message that the time of God's sovereignty was at hand—the sovereignty which promised salvation and indeed had already brought it (Mk 1:15).

But only those who are converted and who believe in Jesus's saving message are saved. It is not possible to ignore the terrible fate which, according to Jesus's warning, will befall all those who refuse God's offer of grace and mercy in their last hour. With prophetic insight he pronounces judgement on the cities of Galilee that had witnessed so many of his miracles and yet have not been converted. It will be more tolerable for the heathen cities of Tyre and Sidon than for them in the day of judgement (Mt 11:22). Whatever city does not receive his disciples, when they bring his message of the coming of God's sovereignty, will hear the joyous tidings as a threatened judgement: 'I say to you, it shall be more tolerable at that day for Sodom than for that city' (Lk 10:12). The inhabitants of Nineveh will rise up as witnesses for the prosecution against this generation at the last judgement, for they did penance as a result of Jonah's preaching, 'and, behold, something greater than Jonah is here' (Mt 12:41). Indeed, the Son of Man himself will accuse those who did not confess him while he was still on earth (Mk 8:38 and pars).

What is more, the moral obligations of those who wish to participate in God's sovereign rule are related directly to their actions: 'Not every one who says to me, 'Lord, Lord', shall enter the kingdom of heaven; but he who does the will of my Father who is in heaven' (Mt 7:21). The most striking example of the close interrelationship in the New Testament between God's mercy and judgement is provided by the parable of the unforgiving servant (Mt 18:23–35). God is willing to forgive even the greatest debt that man can owe him, and he makes a start by showing boundless mercy. But he expects man to respond to this by showing equal love and pardon towards his fellowmen. Otherwise, his mildness is transformed into a terrible anger. With the same measure that we mete out, God will measure to us (Lk 6:38). In the great scene of judgement (Mt 25:31–46), the question which is asked concerns deeds of charity on behalf of 'the least of the brethren' and those who did not do these will be consigned to the everlasting fire.

All this forms the background to Jesus's message of salvation, but his own personal and essential message is that of a God who is gracious, forgiving and super-abundant in his gifts, and by virtue of this message, Jesus stands out in clear relief against judaism for the first time and presents us with an image of God that had not been revealed up to this point and was indeed almost beyond the understanding of his contemporaries.

2. *The special message of Jesus concerning God.* The word 'father' was frequently applied to God in judaism at the time of Jesus, but he was always thought of as the Father in heaven, or, as in the case of the Jewish prayer, the Eighteen Petitions, in close association with 'our King'. The intention here was to preserve a reverent distance and to avoid any confusion with one's purely physical father here on earth. Jesus, on the other hand, simply took over the word Abba, which was used colloquially by the Jewish child to address his father and 'sounded familiar and disrespectful to His [Jesus's] contemporaries' (G. Kittel), and instructed his disciples to pray to God with an attitude of childlike trust (cf also the form of the Our Father without the words 'in heaven' in Lk 11:2; see also Rom 8:15; Gal 4:6). Elsewhere, too, Jesus speaks in a completely

spontaneous and natural way of 'your' Father, frequently without any direct reference to his own personal relationship with God. These examples show how 'the language of the family circle has been extended to apply to God' (G. Dalman). What Jesus aims to bring home to us by this use of language is the goodness of God and his willingness to forgive us and to grant us a hearing, for in all these respects, God surpasses any human father. Jesus repeatedly makes use of a comparative way of speaking which proceeds from the lesser to the greater: 'If you then, who are evil, know how to give good gifts to your children, how much more will your Father who is in heaven give good things to those who ask him?' (Mt 7:11; see also Lk 11:13). Other examples are the parable of the man who is seeking a hearing with his friend (Lk 11:5–8; the point here is that a hearing is in fact granted) and that of the unjust judge (Lk 18:2–5, and the application of the parable to God, 6–8). Jesus consciously heightens the graphic quality of his parables by drawing boldly on everyday experience, in order to impress upon us the great goodness of God, which is at the same time both human and superhuman. But this father-image of God is not intended simply to help in a general way in religious instruction. It also serves to further Jesus's eschatological message and to clarify the special relationship between Jesus's disciples and God: since we have been called to seek first the kingdom of God, we may safely burden God with all our cares concerning our life and our body, for he knows all our needs (Lk 12:22–31 = Mt 6:25–33). In the Our Father, the petition for our daily bread is subordinate to that which seeks the coming of God's kingdom, and the ceaseless cries of the elect have an effect in bringing about their eventual deliverance from eschatological suffering. Jesus encourages his apostles by telling them that, when they are brought to trial the spirit of their Father will speak through them (Mt 10:20) and that they have no need to fear, for he without whose will not a single sparrow is permitted to fall to the ground, will protect them with his hand (see Mt 10:29–31 = Lk 12:6f).

This close relationship with God is so important for Jesus because it is only when it has been established that real attention will be paid to his message of grace and redemption. God is inconceivably rich in mercy and always ready to call all men, even sinners and 'lost' souls, through Jesus, into his kingdom. The mystery of God's sovereignty is that it is brought closer by Jesus's words and deeds, not in the form of justice, but as saving grace and mercy. To many people of the Jewish world of that time, and in particular to the pharisees, Jesus's message was so outrageous that he was obliged to justify it. Thus he defended his association with publicans and sinners (Mk 2:17 and pars) and, while proclaiming God's mercy in the parables of the Prodigal Son, of the Workers in the Vineyard and of the Pharisee and the Publican, he spoke out against narrow-minded piety. There is a double climax in the parable of the Prodigal Son. In the first part of the parable, Jesus draws a striking and unforgettable picture of the forgiving heavenly Father, who reinstates the son who was 'lost' but who has returned, penitent and converted, to his previous position of privilege. In the second part, the elder son is taught not to criticise his father's attitude (Lk 15:11–24, 25–32). Jesus similarly justifies the goodness of the owner of the vineyard in doing exactly what he likes with regard to the dissatisfied labourers who have toiled throughout the day (Mt 20:1–15). In the parable of the Pharisee and the Publican, he goes even further and launches an attack, and we are told that the penitent publican 'went down . . . justified rather than the other' who bragged so loudly about his works (Lk 18:14; see also Mt 21:31). Jesus is also deliberately harsh in the contrast he makes between the characteristically Jewish attention to literal detail and the approach of the Gentiles who will share in the kingdom of God. Many will come from all over the world and recline at table with the Jewish patriarchs, whereas those who were originally called—the 'sons of the kingdom' —will be cast out into the exterior darkness—excluded, in other words, from the kingdom (Mt 8:11–12 = Lk 13:28ff). The parable of the Marriage Feast too (Mt 22:1–10; cf Lk 14:16–24) contains a polemical climax (the originally intended contrast may have been between the pious and the sinners) which both evangelists who have handed this parable down to us have made clear, each in a different way. In Matthew, we find an allusion to the judgement which will be passed on the Jewish leaders and on Jerusalem (Mt 22:7), whereas St Luke refers to God's call to the Gentiles (Lk 14:23). Jesus's deeds, and especially his forgiveness of sins (see Mk 2:1–12; Lk 7:36–50; Jn 5:14; 8:3–11; also Lk 19:1–10; 23:43), reaffirm his message of salvation and firmly establish as the central teaching of the Gospel God's offer of unlimited grace and his desire to save the whole universe.

Finally, an essential part of God's goodness and magnanimity is the super-abundant reward which he promises to those who believe his Son's message and who follow him with perseverance. It is a recompense (see Lk 17:7–10) which exceeds all expectations (see Mt 20:1–15). God will, in St Luke's image of the corn-measure, pour a good measure, pressed down, shaken together and running over, into the lap of anyone who follows the commandment to love his neighbour and freely gives what he has to others (Lk 6:38). The disciples who have left everything for Jesus's sake will receive a hundred-fold reward (Mk 10:29ff). The fitting summit to the work of redemption of the God of love is the matchless eschatological reward in which he finally gives himself to the blessed in a state of perfect communion (see Mt 5:8–9).

3. *The image of God of the early church deepened through belief in Christ.* The early church received Jesus's image of God and was also able to work it out more fully after he had fully revealed himself and they had begun to believe in him as their risen and exalted Lord. The early christians followed his teaching on the subject of the Father and his instructions concerning prayer in the spirit of adoption, crying Abba, and were thus able to experience the freedom of the sons of God (Gal 4:6ff; Rom 8:15ff). They became joyously sure of the God whom Jesus had proclaimed as merciful and desirous of man's

redemption through their faith in the blood of Christ and by the power of their new life in the Holy Spirit. They praised him at once as 'God the Father' or as 'God the Father of our Lord Jesus Christ', since he had raised Jesus to the state of Kyrios (see Acts 2:34–36) and every hymn to the Lord Jesus Christ ended (as in Phil 2:11) in the praise of God the Father. God's eternal plan of salvation, which was realised in the temporal sphere by Christ's redemption, was now fully disclosed to the christian community and visibly displayed before its members as a testimony of God's incomprehensible wisdom and goodness, and they praised him in splendid eulogies (Eph 1:3–12), doxologies (Rom 16:25–7; Eph 3:20ff; Jude 24f) and hymns of praise (see especially the Apocalypse). With deep emotion Paul speaks of the unsearchable ways of God's salvation (Rom 11:33–6) and John acknowledges God's perfect love, which conforms essentially to his nature and his alone, and which sent the son to a world enslaved by sin, to be the fundamental principle motivating all his actions (Jn 3:16; 1 Jn 4:8–11; 16). This same God gave 'repentance unto life' (Acts 11:18) to the heathens as well, and his saving grace appeared to all men (Tit 2:11). More than any of the contemporary rulers or emperors, God merits the title of *Sōtēr* ('Saviour'), since his goodness and kindness appeared in Jesus Christ (Tit 3:4). This same God also satisfied the profound longing felt in the Greek world for the need to overcome the transience of the world and to become 'partakers of the divine nature' (2 Pet 1:4). Thus, though it was possible for many gods and many lords to be worshipped at that time, there was, for the christian, 'but one God, the Father, from whom are all things and for whom we exist [are created], and one Lord Jesus Christ, through whom are all things and through whom we exist' (1 Cor 8:6).

The cosmic dimensions of this image of God, however, in no way prevent the primitive church from being loved, guided and heard by the Father of Jesus Christ and of being conscious of this love and guidance and of the hearing which God the Father grants her. Jesus' promise that prayer will be heard by the Father (see Mk 11:23ff and pars), a promise which is, according to Jn 16:26ff, founded on the love of the Father for the disciples of Jesus, was a powerful incentive to the early community to ardent prayer for protection and freedom of action (see the oldest prayer of the christian community: Acts 4:24–30). The triumphant spread of the gospel from Jerusalem to Rome, which was at that time the centre of the known world, forms the principle theme of Acts. From it emerges the deep conviction that God is directing the mission and the history of the church according to a carefully prepared plan. The Apocalypse is only one document which testifies to the great confidence which the church in Asia Minor, already shaken by the first storms of persecution, felt that God nonetheless remained all-powerful and would soon grant victory to the oppressed christian community on earth and give the church power to rule in such a way that the violence and might of evil would be destroyed and God's perfect kingdom would be established.

Faith in God the Father, in Jesus

Christ, the Messiah and the Son of God, and in the Paraclete, whom Jesus sent to his own when he had returned to the Father (Jn 16:7) must have finally opened men's eyes to the mystery of the Trinity. There are many indications of the gradual emergence and development of this final divine revelation in the New Testament. The New Testament writers did not define the doctrine of the three persons in one God as such, nor did they reduce it to a doctrinal formula, but they did, however, describe quite clearly the efficacy of the united activity of the three divine persons in the matter of salvation, sometimes in parallel passages (1 Cor 12:4–6; 2 Cor 13:14). Frequently, however, they showed their close co-operation (Jn 14:16ff, 26; 15:26; 16:7–11, 13f) in acts which were directed towards man's salvation and would be realised in the course of the history of salvation: the Father's eternal predestination, the Son's redemption by his blood, the Spirit's gift of life and sanctification (see Eph 1:3–14; 1 Pet 1:2). The Holy Ghost, who is the first fruit of salvation in the eschatological sense and the pledge of the full redemption which is to come (see Rom 8:23; 2 Cor 1:22; 5:5; Eph 1:13ff), is always regarded as the gift of the Father and the life spirit of the risen Son (see Rom 8:9–11; 1 Cor 15:45; 2 Cor 3:17f). Even though the New Testament may lack conceptual clarity, it makes up for this by its remarkable portrayal of the triune God's dynamic action for our salvation. The aim and result of this view of God is a personal, living and constantly developing communion with God and with all those who similarly confess him and are closely associated with him in love (see Eph 3:14–19; 1 Jn 1:3; 3:24; 4:13).

Bibliography: T. Paffrath, *Gott, Herr und Vater*, Paderborn 1930; W. Koester, 'Der Vater-Gott in Jesu Leben und Lehre', *Scholastik* 16 (1941), 481–95; W. G. Kümmel, 'Der Gottesverkündigung Jesu und der Gottesgedanke des Spätjudentums', *Judaica* 1 (1945), 40–68; V. Warnach, *Agape*, Düsseldorf 1951; E. Lohmeyer, *Das Vaterunser*, Göttingen 1952³; K. Rahner, *Theological Investigations* I, London and New York 1961, 79–148; J. Jeremias, *Synoptische Studien* (Festschrift A. Wikenhauser), Munich 1954, 86–9; G. Kittel, *TDNT* I, 5–6; E. Stauffer *TDNT* III, 90–119; G. Schrenk, *TDNT* V, 978–1014; F. J. Schierse, *LTK* IV², 1078–80; E. Neuhäusler, *Anspruch und Antwort Gottes*, Düsseldorf 1962, 17–36; G. Delling, 'Partizipiale Gottesprädikationen in den Briefen des NT', *ST* 17 (1963), 1–59; W. Marchel, *Abba, Vater!*, Düsseldorf 1963. See also: J. Leipoldt, *Das Gotteserlebnis Jesu im Lichte der vergleichenden Religionsgeschichte* (Angelos-Beiheft 2), 1927; R. A. Hoffmann, *Das Gottesbild Jesu*, Hamburg 1934; T. W. Manson, *The Teaching of Jesus*, Cambridge 1935² (reprinted 1951), 89–170; H. F. D. Sparks, *The Doctrine of the Divine Fatherhood in the Gospels: Studies in the Gospels*, Oxford 1955, 241–62; W. Grundmann, *Die Geschichte Jesu Christi*, Berlin 1957, 65–86.

Rudolf Schnackenburg

Good and evil

The combination 'good and evil' (*tôb warā*ᶜ) is often used in the Old Testament, generally in connection with a verb, rarely alone.

We find phrases such as: 'to know good and evil' (with the verb *yāda*ᶜ, Gen 2:9–17; 3:5–22; Deut 1:39); 'to distinguish between good and evil' (2 Sam 19:36 with *yāda*ᶜ; 1 Kings 3:9 with *bîn*; 2 Sam 14:6 cf Deut 1:16 with *šāmēa*ᶜ); 'to refuse the evil and choose the good' (Is 7:15–16); 'to depart from evil and do good' (Ps 34:14; 37:27); 'seek (*dāraš*) good and not evil' (Amos

5:14); 'to hate evil and love good (Amos 5:15; Mic 3:2 the other way round); to do 'good and not harm' (Prov 31:12); to speak neither good nor evil (Gen 24:50); 'to do good or bad' (Num 24:13); 'to speak neither good nor evil' (Gen 31:24–9: 2 Sam 13:22); 'to substitute a good for a bad' (Lev 27:10); 'to value as either good or bad' (Lev 27:12, 14); 'to inquire whether it is good or bad' (Lev 27:33); to return 'evil for good' (1 Sam 25:21; Prov 17:13; see also Jer 18:20; Ps 35:12; 38:20). The two words can also stand by themselves: 'good or evil' (Num 13:19; Jer 42:6); 'not good but evil' (1 Kings 22:8, 18; cf Ps 52:5); 'good and evil' (Deut 30:15; Is 5:20; Jer 39:16; 44:27; Lam 3:38; Job 30:26).

Perhaps the most important use of the combination 'good and evil' occurs in the theological etiology of sin and fallenness where it plays a fundamental and decisive role. The whole account is centred on 'the tree of the knowledge of good and evil' (Gen 2:9–17; 'of good and evil' as object of the infinitive used substantively is syntactically awkward and therefore probably an addition which anticipates the *dénouement*; see also 3:5–22). The fruit of this tree is forbidden under pain of death (Gen 2:17; 3:5–11, 13); 'the knowledge of good and evil' is a rather protean phrase; its purpose is, as Quell puts it, 'rather to conceal than to reveal'. It derives from the theological and psychological reflection of the teachers of wisdom in Israel who had given long thought to the enigma of sin. The cunning serpent dangled before the woman the prospect of a godlike knowledge: 'God knows that when you eat of it your eyes will be opened, and you will be like God, knowing good and evil' (Gen 3:5). After the sin had been committed God exclaimed: 'Behold, the man has become like one of us, *knowing good and evil*' (3:22). By knowing good and evil, therefore, man becomes godlike. This raises a twofold question: (a) what is meant here by *knowledge*; and (b) what are we to understand by 'good and evil?' In order to answer these difficult questions we shall have to refer to the relevant texts which are susceptible of more than one explanation. Hence the difficulty and ambiguity in interpreting the meaning of this combination.

a. *The kind of knowledge implied.* As can be seen from the name of the tree and the context as a whole, eating of its fruit gives knowledge which our first parents actually acquired as a result of their sin (Gen 3:11–13, 22). As is clear from what the Serpent, Eve and God say, it is a divine kind of knowledge. The Serpent tempts them by saying 'you will be like God' (3:5). The beauty of the tree seduces the woman's heart: 'the tree was good for food and a delight to the eyes and to be desired to make one wise (*lehaśkîl*)' (3:6). This verb in the causative means 'to make wise or clever' (cf Deut 32:29; Is 41:20; Jer 9:23; 23:5; Ps 119:98) and is more often than not used in parallelism with the noun *daᶜath* (knowledge). So, for example, Jeremiah promises for the messianic age: 'I will give you shepherds after my own heart, who will feed you with knowledge (*daᶜath* and understanding (*haśkêl*)' (Jer 3:15; cf Dan 1:17; Job 34:35). It follows therefore that 'knowledge' in Gen 2-3 refers first and foremost to an *interior and spiritual process*. This is confirmed in the words spoken by God: 'Behold, the man has become *like one of us*' (3:22). This kind of knowledge is the exclusive privilege of the elohim, those within the divine sphere. By taking of the forbidden fruit man hoped to attain to this higher knowledge and so become like the elohim.

But if the main emphasis is on intellectual knowledge the experiential aspect could hardly be absent for men of that time living in the ancient Near East. Hence it refers also to an experience which irrupted into human life after the fall ('their eyes were opened', 3:5–7) and was to be characteristic of the existential distress in which man now lives. It was this dark aspect of the preferred knowledge which the Serpent withheld from the woman.

It was a rather perverted aberration on the part of liberal exegesis to interpret this knowledge as the awakening of sexual desire and awareness of sexual differentiation which our first parents achieved by having intercourse either in defiance of a divine prohibition (Clement of Alexandria) or before arriving at sexual maturity (H. Gunkel and J. Guitton). The sexual interpretation is excluded purely on the grounds of vocabulary: the verb 'to know' is of course used in some texts as a euphemism for sexual congress (Gen 4:1–17; Judg 11:39; 1 Sam 1:19 etc) but there is all the difference in the world between the man 'knowing' the woman or knowing good and evil. There are no grounds in the text for identifying the two; in fact, there is no specification at all with regard to the object of knowledge.

The attempt was also made to prove the same thing on the basis of interpreting 'good and evil' in terms of the experience of sexual passion (H. Schmidt). Against this is the fact that *tôb* (good) never has a sexual connotation in the Old Testament. Such an interpretation, which held the field for a long time, has 'a far too strong dash of sentimentality about it' (G. Quell in *TDNT* 1, 284). The kind of knowledge referred to here is on the spiritual level. Through these chapters there blows the clean air of faith in Yahweh and we hear a note reminiscent of the Song of Songs and the love between the bridegroom and the spouse.

Whether the internal and spiritual sin was externalised in some sexual way is of purely marginal importance and in any case can no longer be determined. The essence of the first sin is not touched at all by this possibility.

b. '*Good and evil*'. The phrase 'good and evil' points in a different direction from the views discussed above; it points upwards not downwards. Since according to Old Testament usage the combination is susceptible of more than one interpretation we find different views on the kind of spiritual activity referred to. We cannot solve the problem purely on the basis of vocabulary and the meaning of the words; we have to look at the context and at parallel passages in the Old Testament. In any case these differing interpretations have at least one good thing in common, that unlike the sexual interpretation they all start out from specifically scriptural data.

1. According to some exegetes the Yahwist understood 'the knowledge of good and evil' as the awakening of the intellect or of moral consciousness (P. Humbert). These exegetes refer to

certain texts which speak of children arriving at 'the knowledge of good and evil' explained as the ability to differentiate between what is sweet and bitter, pleasant and unpleasant, useful and harmful and above all between what is morally good and evil (cf Deut 1:39; Is 7:15f). The old man, on the contrary, is no longer able to distinguish between good and evil or, in other words, 'taste what he eats and what he drinks' (2 Sam 19:35; cf Lev 27:10, 12, 14, 33 where the reference is to the good and bad qualities of the sacrificial animals).

On the basis of these texts the same meaning is given to the phrase 'good and evil' in Gen 2–3. But this conclusion is quite clearly false. From the fact that the phrase has this meaning in the texts adduced it does not follow at all that it must have the same meaning in Gen 2–3. On the contrary, the immediate and wider context does not support this interpretation. The power of reason and moral consciousness were not first acquired by Adam and Eve after they had eaten the fruit since both are presupposed necessarily for the responsible action which they performed. It would hardly have been reasonable of God to impose on them a prohibition under pain of the most severe penalties if they had been incapable of acting as responsible beings. If they could only grasp the meaning and import of the prohibition *after the fall* he would have been the most cruel of tyrants to impose it in the first place.

The entire narrative reveals that the first parents are represented as anything but immature and innocent children. God put man in the garden so that he might cultivate it (2:15). The man gave to each animal a name corresponding to its properties (2:20a). The bringing together of the animals to the man did not, however, produce the desired result; only in the woman did he recognise a helper fit for him (2:23–4). God then laid upon him the prohibition of eating of the tree of knowledge (2:17). It is clear from all this that the Yahwist is thinking of a grown man in the full possession of his spiritual and moral capacities.

Further, in these two chapters *ʾadam* is correctly translated by 'man' (2:7, 8, 15, 16, 19–23, 25; 3:8, 9, 12, 20–2, 24) and the aetiological explanation of the narrative has recognised correctly that the Yahwist is here expressing something of permanent validity on the nature of man, the close relation between man and woman, sin, evil tendencies, sorrow, the burden of work and the inescapable fact of death. Hence it is clear that in speaking of 'the knowledge of good and evil' he cannot be referring to the development of reason or moral consciousness but rather to sinful knowledge possessed by a grown man.

2. For this reason other exegetes explain 'good and evil' as universal knowledge (eg H. Junker, G. von Rad, P. van Imschoot). They appeal to certain texts where the two opposite terms found in combination refer to a totality in either a positive or negative sense, either 'all' or 'nothing'. So, for example, David seems to the wise woman of Tekoa to be 'like the angel of God to discern good and evil' (2 Sam 14:17) which is further explained in v 20 in that she attributes to David a wisdom 'like the wisdom of the angel of God to know all things that are on

the earth'. The expression: 'to speak neither good nor evil' means to say nothing at all (Gen 24:50) as also 'to say nothing of either good or evil' (Gen 31:24–9; 2 Sam 13:22).

Purely on the grounds of vocabulary one could attribute this meaning of universal knowledge to the expression as used in Gen 2–3. But we must not overlook the fact that the man after his sin really did not attain to such knowledge which the exclamation of God in 3:22 would have led us to expect. Further, the knowledge of good and evil understood as universal knowledge is too exclusively intellectual. The Hebrew verb 'to know' always has the idea of concrete experience of some kind or other. He who knows something or gives a name to something has gained power over it and can exert influence on it. This means that the man did not achieve any effectual knowledge of 'good and evil' since, according to the narrative, nature and the animal kingdom turn against him (3:15, 17–19). Finally, according to the context as a whole, it is not so much a question of universal knowledge as of a knowledge which enables one to distinguish and differentiate.

Other exegetes have taken account of the experiential character of this 'knowledge'. They restrict 'knowledge of good and evil' to what is either useful or harmful, sweet or bitter, healthy or unhealthy or even in a general way to cultural progress (J. Wellhausen and G. Quell). But the general feel of the narrative is quite alien to the question of the progress of civilisation and intends only to describe in dark colours the irruption of evil into the lives of the first parents and the escalation of sin in their descendants. And quite apart from this the expression always takes in the idea of a moral dichotomy especially in those texts which speak of a distinction between good and evil (eg Deut 1:39; 30:15; 2 Sam 19:35; 1 Kings 3:9; Is 7:15f; Amos 5:14f; Mic 3:2; Eccles 12:14). Though it is not stated explicitly, this also applies to Gen 2–3. The man is confronted with a choice between obedience and disobedience, paying attention to the divine prohibition of eating from the tree or neglecting it. The expression 'good and evil' fits this situation very well.

3. This is the direction in which we are to look for a solution. What is at issue is not the gift or talent for differentiating or discernment but the *ability* to do so. The man strives for a *divine* knowledge as the serpent promised the woman: 'you will be like God' (3:5) and as God himself states: 'Behold, the man has become like one of us' (3:22). He was no longer happy to live under the moral guidance of God but wanted to decide autonomously what was for him morally good and morally evil. What he aimed at therefore was *moral autonomy*. Certainly, the man had to decide freely between good and evil but this decision was to be made under divine guidance. When a judge has to make a decision between two parties in a question of law he too decides between good and evil according to the norms of law. He does not make the decision autonomously but in dependence on basic principles laid down by God; he does not act purely on his own initiative, at his own good pleasure, but in accordance with the will of God (see 1 Kings 3:9). By his sinful deed the man

turns the basic principles of good and evil upside down. What is good he calls evil and what is evil he calls good according to his own good pleasure (cf Is 5:20; Amos 5:14–15). Sin is the reversal of basic values. R. de Vaux remarks appositely: 'En se prenant eux-mêmes pour mesure, ils ont commis une faute de démesure' (*RB* 56 [1949], 340), and the same view is expressed in other words by H. Renckens, A-M Dubarle, and other authors.

The striving for moral independence really implies arrogating to oneself a prerogative which is superhuman and divine, one that belongs to God alone. By so striving man usurps to himself a 'knowledge' which lies at the root of all sin. In each evil deed that he commits he grasps at the forbidden fruit *sub specie boni*; but as with the first man bitter disappointment is quick to follow.

The sin of 'knowing good and evil' took place deep in the soul of the first parents. It was an internal and original experience. Instigated by the serpent they attempted to be 'like God' (3:5–22) in a limitless autonomy. They were guilty of the sin of pride, of arrogance beyond measure, of *hubris* as were, later on in the narrative, those who began to build the tower of Babel (11:1–9).

In keeping with the literary genre of this narrative, psychologically perceptive and theologically profound as it is, this teacher of genius presents 'the tree of the knowledge of good and evil' as figurative of a spiritual reality, as we have attempted to demonstrate above. How did he come by this symbol? Though this tree of life is in some respects reminiscent of the 'plant of life' or 'tree of life' found in Mesopotamian mythology (for example, in the Gilgamesh epic) it is really without parallel. We must attribute it to the creative power of the Yahwist himself.

The texts do not allow us to arrive at any certain conclusion as to the external form which this spiritual sin took. We are only told that it was committed by both the man and the woman (3:6b).

Bibliography: H. D. A. Major, 'The Tree of the Knowledge of Good and Evil', *Expository Times* 20 (1909), 427–8; H. Gunkel, *Genesis*, Göttingen 1964[6]; H. Schmidt, *Die Erzählung von Paradies und Sündenfall*, Tübingen 1931; H. Junker, *Die biblische Urgeschichte*, Bonn 1932; P. Humbert, *Etudes sur le récit du Paradis et de la chute dans la Genèse*, Neuchatel 1940, 82–116 (see the review of A. Bea, *Bbl* 25 [1944], 81f); L. J. Kuyper, 'To Know Good and Evil', *Interpr.* 1 (1947), 490–2; J. Coppens, *La Connaissance du bien et du mal et le Péché du Paradis*, Bruges-Paris-Louvain 1948; J. Guitton, *Le Développement des Idées dans l'Ancient Testament*, Aix-en-Provence 1947; M. Buber, *Good and Evil, two Interpretations*, New York 1953: J. Engnell, '"Knowledge" and "Life" in the Creation Story', Suppl. *VT* 3 (1955), 103–19; W. Buchanan, 'The Old Testament Meaning of the Knowledge of Good and Evil', *JBL* 75 (1956), 114–20; Bo Reicke, 'The Knowledge hidden in the Tree of Paradise', *JSS* 1 (1956), 193–201; R. Gordis, 'The Knowledge of Good and Evil in the Old Testament and the Qumran Scrolls', *JBL* 76 (1957), 123–38; I. de Fraine, 'Jeux de mots dans le récit de la chute', *Mélanges Bibliques A. Robert*, Paris 1957, 47–59; H. S. Stern, 'The Knowledge of Good and Evil', *VT* 8 (1958), 407f; H. Renckens, *Urgeschichte und Heilsgeschichte: Israels Schau in die Vergangenheit nach Gen 1–3*, Mainz 1961[2], 240–4; A-M. Dubarle, 'La Tentation dans le jardin d'Eden. Genèse 3:1–6', *LV* 53 (1961), 13–20; Haag 412–13; *DEB* 342–4 (H. Renckens); *DBT* 101–5 (H. de Vaux); G. von Rad I, 154ff; Imschoot II, 288–90.

Robert Koch

Goodness

A. *In the general sense*, Yahweh's goodness was a fact which was always strikingly evident in the history of the Israelites. Whether it goes back to the original revelation made to the Hebrews, or whether its source is to be found in the powerful divine acts which were manifested in the Exodus, what is certain is that all the biblical texts refer to God's goodness, either directly or by implication. Yahweh is the good, kind and benign one who shows his favour and benevolence to his people, and does this by virtue of their election and of the covenant. The full revelation of God's goodness is certainly not finally established in the earliest books—these merely mark the end of the first, preliterary stage in the progressive revelation of the divine nature and the gradual intensification of the collective and individual relationship which was growing up between the people of Israel and their God. In the course of this gradual development, fresh aspects of goodness in the biblical sense are all the time being brought to light, providing an essential contribution towards progress in man's relation to God.

B. *The concept of divine goodness.* No clear or theologically well developed concept of divine goodness can be found in the earliest books of the bible. The word which is most commonly used to include all aspects of goodness is the Hebrew *tôb*. In its original meaning, it was probably used mainly to denote sense perceptions and then, in an extension of meaning, to include higher perceptions. In the historical books of the Old Testament, however, *tôb* is found especially in connection with ethical judgements and aesthetic assessments—even in the account of the creation, God's work is described as *tôb* (see *Mélanges Bibliques A. Robert*, Paris 1957, 22–6). On the one hand, this predicative use of *tôb* usually implies God's beneficent acts, leading to the well-being of the people, while, on the other hand, it can apply to anything which is fitting or morally good (here it is synonymous with the Hebrew *yāšār*: 1 Sam 12:23 etc). The idea of essential goodness underlies all these different shades of meaning, and this basic idea is contrasted with that of evil (raᶜ). *Tôb*—in the sense of a state of absolute goodness—is, of course, applied exclusively to God, and, in the New Testament too, it is to him alone that this absolute quality of goodness can be truthfully applied (Mt 19:17; Mk 10:18; Lk 18:19; see also W. Wagner, *ZNW* 8 [1907], 143–61). The Hebrew word *ḥesed* expresses goodness in a more concrete form, in the sense of divine favour and God's loyal readiness to give help, particularly in connection with the covenant made on Mount Sinai. Whenever Yahweh is powerfully affected by his people's distress—or by the distress of a single individual—he exercises his *raḥᵃmîm* (*raḥûm*), or mercy, and this appears as his divine favour and finds expression in concrete acts of beneficence. Even when the Israelites are forgetful of God's goodwill (*ḥēn*) and turn away from their benefactor, God does not resort to judgement and punishment, but waits with patient forbearing (*ᵓerek appîm*) until they are converted.

The earliest Greek translators of the Old Testament seem to have set themselves the special task of determining the many shades of meaning contained in the generalised use of the word *tôb*, and they must take the credit for having established the bases of a real theology of goodness by employing the word *khrēstotēs* (goodness) in the context of revelation. *Khrēstos* (good) is derived from *khraomai* (to use, to be of use, to refer to, to have relations with), and its original meaning was certainly that of usefulness or sociability. But, from the very beginning, the word also conveyed the sense of moral excellence, with the result that *khrēstotēs*, which was coined at a later stage and had a meaning which was distinct from that of the original *khrēstos*, managed to combine the idea of moral perfection and sublimity with that of friendliness and loving kindness. As an honorary title and as an epithet used to describe a sovereign ruler—though probably never in the profane sense—*khrēstotēs* was particularly suitable for the purpose of conveying the fullness of divine *tôb* towards men. To convey God's absolute state of goodness, however, the early Greek translators naturally had recourse to the word *agathos*. In addition, however, they also introduced a second, purely biblical word, *agathōsunē*. This word contains the same subtle shades of meaning as *khrēstotēs*, but points rather more clearly in the direction of God's quality of goodness and uprightness (see Jerome, *PL* 26,420). In contrast to this, *philanthrōpia* (human kindness in general) and *epieikeia*, which signifies a lenient and forbearing attitude of mind, were introduced into the bible, but played only an insignificant part in it, because of their close associations with the whole heathen way of life.

Although *benignitas* as used in the Vetus Latina corresponds exactly to the Greek *khrēstotēs*, the Latin tradition nevertheless preferred 'sweetness' (*dulcedo* or *suavitas*: see Jerome's definition, *PL* 26,420) to emphasise the intimate nature of man's experience of God's goodness (perhaps with reference to Ps 34:8; see also 1 Pet 2:2–3). Nowadays we tend to think of *khrēstotēs* as having lost much of its original and deeply theological significance, and as having become to some extent debased in meaning—this false conception of a sweet and sentimental bearing on the part of God can be traced back to the use, in the Vulgate and elsewhere, of the word *sweetness*. Jerome's later translation of the psalms—'Versio Piana'—was far more sober in this respect and, going back to the original Hebrew, has replaced these traditional shades of meaning by the more consistent use of the words *bonus* (good) and *bonitas* (goodness) and, in a few instances, by *benignus* (kind) and *benefaciens* (beneficent).

C. *The theology of goodness.* 1. *In the Old Testament and in later judaism.* Theological speculation concerning the nature of Yahweh's goodness began at a very early date. This is demonstrated, for example, in the formula used in the worship of Yahweh in Ex 34:6: 'The Lord, the Lord, a God merciful and gracious, slow to anger, and abounding in steadfast love and faithfulness' (see also *Bbl* 38 [1957], 130–50). Frequent use is made of technical formulae of this kind in later texts (see Ps 86:15; 103:8; 145:8; Joel 2:13; Jonah 4:2; Neh 9:17). God's mercy and his faithful readiness to help his people are, however, forcefully stressed in the earlier biblical texts, and are regarded as that particular form of goodness which the people of God clearly remembered from the time of the Exodus and the birth of the nation of Israel. The historical books of the Old Testament, with their particular literary form, were also, of course, less well suited to the function of detailed theological speculation on the subject of Yahweh's goodness.

It is in the *Psalms* that the first true theology of divine goodness appears. It is possible to make a general statement to the effect that divine goodness is present in the psalms as a *basic law of God's providence*. At the one extreme, it appears in the most general form, promising mercy to all creatures (Ps 145:9), while at the other extreme it appears in a more concrete form, giving an assurance of positive help in every necessity. When God shows his goodness, all living creatures are overwhelmed with gifts, but when he turns his face away from them, their well-being is transformed into affliction and even into ruin (Ps 104:28–9). It is, however, the proofs of God's goodness towards men which provide the most common motive for thanksgiving in the psalms. With the passage of time, an appropriate formula was perfected, and this may have played a very important part in the worship of the people: 'Give thanks to the Lord, for he is good; for his steadfast love endures for ever' (Ps 106:1; 107:1; 136:1, etc). These proofs of Yahweh's goodness were, of course, shown particularly to the chosen people. The fullness of divine goodness was reserved for them, even though, in Ps 100:1–5, all the earth is called upon to praise God for his goodness.

It is in Yahweh's glorious acts, during his people's wanderings in the desert, in which he showed his great power, that we find the essence of divine goodness in the Old Testament and, at the same time, the most frequent motive for his people's praise of him. These divine acts reveal the superabundance of Yahweh's goodness. He shows his omnipotence, together with his goodness, in preserving his chosen people. Divine goodness is often portrayed as the favour and compassion of a king or ruler—in Ps 65:11, Yahweh is seen as a king who travels throughout the land in his chariot, dispensing blessings upon it. Divine goodness has this special attribute—it cares particularly for the weak and the persecuted, and, in so doing, it assumes the quality of a protective grace which first of all delivers the subject from a desperate situation and then grants protection from further persecution (Ps 31:20). An angel of God pitches his camp round about those who fear the Lord in order to protect them from danger of any kind. This causes the psalmist to cry out enthusiastically: 'O taste, and see that the Lord is good!' (Ps 34:8–9). The religious man is so certain of God's goodness that his thanksgiving follows directly upon his prayer of petition, as if he had already experienced the effects of divine goodness (Ps 31:18–20, and elsewhere).

Even the *sinner* is not excluded from God's goodness, so long as he is ready to repent and places his trust in God's mercy. Because of his goodness, God is not only willing to forget the sins and misdeeds committed earlier in life (Ps 25:6f); he is also ready to set the sinner, by means of the Law, which is a particular gift of divine goodness, on the right path (Ps 119:41–72).

In the psalms, the two poles between which the goodness of God is operative are his immense mercy and his justice, though no tension exists between these two divine attributes, nor are they placed in antithesis. Despite Yahweh's goodwill towards man, it is always upright, and would seem, in fact, to be a special work of divine ↗ justice, through which God fulfils his promise, made under the covenant, in so magnanimous a way.

It is in the *later books of the Old Testament*, however, that a *change of mood with regard to divine goodness* is, for the first time, clearly perceptible. Captivity and the loss of independence led to a tension between God's power and his goodness which was previously quite unknown. What is expressed with increasing frequency in these last books is the inaccessibility of God: 'O Lord God, Creator of all things, dreadful and strong, just and merciful, who alone art the good king' (2 Macc 1:24). Divine goodness is also praised indirectly as ↗ wisdom (Wis 7:30).

If we leave on one side the biblical texts which were influenced by hellenistic thought, it becomes obvious that the idea of *human goodness*, as opposed to divine goodness, is relatively little developed in the Old Testament. Yahweh is essentially good. Man, on the other hand, is good only in a very limited sense. Ps 14:3 expresses this conviction clearly: 'They are all alike corrupt; there is none that does good, no, not one'. The same thought is even more clearly expressed in the apocryphal Psalms of Solomon: 'the goodness of man is grudging and is shown only for the sake of reward and it is an admirable thing when man shows his goodness again and again without murmuring' (Ps Sol 5:13 [15]). Human goodness is, in fact, overshadowed by the all-embracing favour and compassion of God, which is too sublime for man to imitate. It calls for recognition—and this plays a decisive part in man's moral formation. The Qumran texts provide a fairly well-developed theology of goodness, in the form of instructions concerning human conduct, and the whole bears a striking resemblance to the Pauline notion of *khrēstotēs*. In the list of the attributes of the Spirit of Light, which is part of the teaching on the Two Spirits, in addition to mercy (*raḥ^a^mîm*) and patience (*ʾerek ʾappayîm*), there is also 'eternal goodness' (*ṭôb ʿôlāmîm*) (1 QS IV, 3), which is closely connected with a humble attitude. The communal life of the sect obviously also required this of its members. This 'eternal goodness' should also be compared with the frequently recurring phrase 'merciful love' (*ʾâhābat ḥesed*). But the feeling of 'eternal hatred' for the sons of injustice (1 QS 4:17) certainly indicates that the spiritual delineation of goodness given in the Qumran texts shows distinctly Old Testament features and a colouring which is peculiar to later judaism.

2. *The New Testament*. The great advance in the concept of goodness shown in the New Testament is intimately connected with the deeper penetration into the nature and essence of God given us in Jesus Christ. In the New Testament, the effects of divine goodness are no longer to be found in good actions, blessings or as protective graces—God's goodness is entirely concentrated upon man's salvation and the events connected with it. The gospels outline the close relationship between divine goodness and the new

life in Christ, whereas the letters of Peter and Paul tend rather to portray the part played by God's goodness in the history of salvation.

It is almost possible to state that divine goodness can now be applied to those who were excluded from God's love in the Old Testament. Those who are hostile to God, those who are ungrateful, hardened sinners—all such people have a special, prior claim to God's goodness in the New Testament. The commandment to hate, which was clearly formulated in the law of the Qumran sect (1 QS 1:9ff, and elsewhere), and which is continually inculcated in the Old Testament, is finally overcome in the New Testament by the Father's *khrēstotēs* and the new relation of *agapē* (love: Lk 6:35). The 'easy' yoke of Christ, which Jesus calls upon all who are weary from the burden of the law to bear (Mt 11:30) expresses the same idea. Only one condition is imposed upon those who wish to be able to experience the full goodness of this new yoke, and that is that they must take it up in the same attitude of humility and gentleness as Jesus, when he took it from his father.

The *crowning biblical-theological definition of goodness is to be found in Paul's letters.* The Old Testament conception of God's goodness is still clearly perceptible in the Letter to the Romans, although it appears in quite new proportions, in view of the now completed work of redemption. In a vigorous diatribe, Paul strikes out at the typical Jew who, in his self-righteousness, mistakenly interprets the most shining examples of God's goodness as a reluctance to punish. A similar attitude arising from a wrong way of thinking about divine goodness or a scornful attitude towards it is a basic sin against goodness (Rom 2:4). The consequences of such an attitude may well be disastrous for the sinner—in his severity, God may ultimately reject him (Rom 11:22).

It is only in his later epistles that Paul has fully embodied goodness into the organic whole of the plan of salvation, and he achieves this by presenting the entire plan of divine redemption in function of God's goodness. The two most important historical moments in this plan are the manifestation of divine goodness (Tit 3:4), that is, the moment of Christ's birth, and the perfection of divine goodness in the time which is to come (Eph 2:7). Human life flows between these two points of time and undergoes a process of maturation within the context of the goodness which is revealed in Jesus Christ.

A harmonious relationship has already been established between God and man in the preaching of Jesus, in that the new man seeks to imitate the goodness of God. Paul is obviously convinced that it is quite within the reach of every christian, by virtue of his union with his Lord and Master, to realise this goodness to a high degree in his own life. This idea underlies all Paul's lists of virtues in which he recommends goodness, although the contexts, in which occur also humility, gentleness, mercy and patience, are still reminiscent of what we find in the Old Testament, and, above all, in later judaism. This goodness is frequently given a more concrete form by being placed in close proximity to agape; the clearest example is to be found in Paul's hymn to love, in which goodness appears as an essential attribute of charity (1 Cor 13:4; cf Eph 4:32; Col 3:12). The position of goodness among the fruits of the Spirit testifies to the importance which Paul attaches to it (Gal 5:22; see also 1 QS IV, 2f—although, from the theological point of view, there are basic differences here). It is the new vital principle, brought about by the Holy Spirit.

In Paul's view, then, goodness is an essential part of the christian way of life. It provides the new man, the man of Christ, with the sensitivity and delicacy of feeling with which he is able to enter into the mind and spirit of others. Its possession of course presupposes a high degree of moral maturity in man. While the Greek and gentile world held that this quality was apparent above all in rulers and outstanding personalities, it is clear from the New Testament that from this time onwards all men were called to share in the sublimity of the divine life and thus to practise goodness in the full, christian sense. It is possible to do full justice to the quality of goodness only when its chief function is regarded as a radiation of charity. Viewed in this way, not only does the active and utterly spontaneous nature of goodness become at once apparent—it is also possible to perceive its intimate relationship with ↗ agape.

D. *Systematic theology of goodness.* In the bible, the theology of goodness is developed progressively. This line of development can be traced without a break from the earliest stages of divine revelation, through the culminating point of Christ's revelation and onwards to its effects on the whole of human life. In the first place, God's paternal goodness was responsible for the creation of the universe. Man himself, and all the gifts with which he was endowed in his original state, resulted from this goodness, and God's plan of salvation was carried out, after man's first fall, above all as a direct consequence of God's goodness. It is to God's initial impulse to save mankind and to all the various concrete forms of his goodness which subsequently came into being—the law, the mission of the prophets, his assistance in every kind of distress—that we owe his mercy, which constitutes the principal form of divine goodness towards fallen man. Even in the Old Testament, goodness, although it reveals itself only gradually, already points clearly to Christ—the fullness of time coincides with that moment in history when divine goodness is bestowed upon mankind in its most perfect form. Christ undertook to offer the sacrifice of goodness to the Father in order to set a seal upon the new covenant of love. The way of Christ's goodness leads from the mystery of the Incarnation—that vital decision of the Trinity—through the goodness of his earthly life up to his death on the Cross and his glorification. In his act of salvation, Christ has revealed the meaning of goodness, as it is progressively revealed in the bible, by realising in his own life its every single feature, both divine and human. Furthermore, the fact that goodness prevails within the Trinity is disclosed in the person of Jesus Christ. That Christ's goodness is the mark of his communion with the Father is forcibly demonstrated in the theology of Paul, who points out how this goodness is derived from the Father who is its source and how it was realised in history, so that it might be conferred on men by the Holy Spirit. The spirit of Christ's goodness guides the life of the church and is renewed in her members. This will continue until the mystery of salvation is consummated at the end of time.

Bibliography: R. C. Trench, *Synonyms of the New Testament*, London 1901; A. Vögtle, *Die Tugend- und Laster-Kataloge im Neuen Testament* (*NA* XVI, 4/5), Münster 1936; J. Ziegler, *Dulcedo Dei* (*AA* XIII/2), Münster 1937; C. Spicq, 'Bénignité, mansuétude, douceur, clémence', *RB* 54 (1947), 321–39; C. L. Mitton, 'Motives for goodness in the New Testament', *Expository Times* 63 (1951/2), 360–4; J. B. Bauer, *BL* 19 (1951/2), 73–5; L. R. Stachowiak, *Chrestotes, ihre biblisch-theologische Entwicklung und Eigenart* (Studia Friburgensia NF 17), Freiburg/Schwaben 1957; A. I. Mennessier, 'Douceur', *Dictionnaire de la Spiritualité* III, 1674–85 (Volume XXIV, 1957); J. Chatillon, 'Dulcedo', *Dictionnaire de la Spiritualité*, III, 1777–95 (Volume XXIV, 1957); Eichrodt 232ff; S. Wibbing, *Die Tugend- und Laste-kataloge im NT* (*ZNW* 25), Berlin 1959, esp. 46–105; C. Spicq, *Agape* II, Paris 1959, 379–91; W. Barclay, *Flesh and Spirit*, London 1962, 97–102; K. Winkler, 'Clementia', *RAC* III, 206–31; Suitbert H. Siedl, *Qumran—eine Mönchsgemeinde im Alten Bund*, Rome 1963, 195–209.

F. L. R. Stachowiak

Gospel

A. *The meaning of the word.* In classical Greek, *euangelion* signified everything connected with a *euangelos*, or bearer of good news (Aeschylus, *Agamemnon*, 646ff), whose *euangelion* could apply both to the glad tidings which he carried to other people or to the reward which he received for performing his task (Homer, *Odyssey* 14, 152ff; 166ff). The word was especially used to denote a message announcing a victory. Its religious connotation was derived from its oracular usage, in which connection it signified a divine utterance (Plutarch, *Sert* 11), and from its use in emperor-worship. As the emperor was regarded as a divine being and the bearer of salvation (*sōtēr*), everything which referred in any way to him was included in the category of *euangelion*. The news of his birth, of his ascension to the throne and even of his imperial decrees were all joyous messages.

Hellenistic Jewish writers such as Philo and Josephus, also used the word in this sense (Schniewind 78–112) and it is even found in the Septuagint with the same profane meaning (2 Sam 18:20, 25, 27; 2 Kings 7:9; Jer 20:15, and elsewhere). Whenever it is found in the New Testament, however, it is used neither in the pagan, hellenistic sense, nor with the meaning with which it is associated in LXX. The New Testament uses the word in the sense in which it, or its Hebrew equivalent (*bāśar*, and the noun *b*ᵉ*śôrâh*), is employed in Deutero–Isaiah and texts depending on him (Nahum 1:15; Ps 68:11; 96:2; Ps Sol 11:2)—thus signifying the news that the time of salvation is at hand. The bearer of glad tidings is the herald who speeds on ahead of Yahweh's triumphal procession, proclaiming his victory and announcing to Sion: 'Your God reigns' (Is 52:7). The time of salvation is actually made present by the very fact of its proclamation. This conception of the bearer of good tidings and his message of salvation persisted as a vital reality also in Palestinian judaism (see the targum on Is 40:9; SB III, 8–11).

B. *The gospel as an eschatological message of joy in the New Testament.* Jesus claimed for himself the office of bearer of the eschatological message of joy when he replied to John the Baptist's question: 'Art you he who is to come?' (Mt 11:3; see also Lk 1:22) and when he preached in the synagogue in Nazareth (Lk 4:16–21). Whereas in the case of emperor-worship in the Greco-Roman world the joyous tidings look back to an event which has already taken place, the gospel looks forward to something which is still to come. The message of Jesus is of this type (see Mk 1:14ff). The underlying theme of his preaching is the coming of the ↗ kingdom of God (see Lk 4:43; Mk 1:38; Mt 4:23; 9:35; 24:14). In the rest of the New Testament, however, the word 'gospel' is generally not used in this original, 'biblical' sense (one exception is Acts 8:12; the word does not occur at all in John). This may be attributed to the fact that the early christians were fully conversant with the idea of Jesus not simply as the herald of the kingdom of God, but also as the embodiment of the gospel itself. This idea was, of course, based on their knowledge of his manifest work of salvation, and the word itself underwent a change of meaning—'gospel' no longer implied a proclamation of salvation to come, but an announcement of salvation already present. The central theme, then, of the preaching of the apostles is Jesus himself and his work of redemption (Acts 5:42; 8:35; 11:20). This is particularly so in the case of Paul, who uses the word far more frequently than any of the other New Testament writers (eg Rom 1:9; 15:20; 1 Cor 9:12, 18; 2 Cor 2:12; Gal 1:6, 7). That the 'gospel' concept has become by this time quite firmly established is shown by the fact that Paul uses the word in an absolute sense and usually without any qualifying adjective (see Rom 1:16; 11:28; 1 Cor 9:14 and elsewhere; similarly Mk 8:35; 10:29; 13:10; 14:9). In Paul, the word has the double meaning of the act of proclamation, preaching activity (Rom 1:1; 2 Cor 2:12; Phil 4:3, 15) and of the content of this preaching (1 Cor 15:1; 2 Cor 11:4; Gal 1:6, 11f; Col 1:23 and elsewhere). The actual content of the gospel is found in Rom 1:3f; 1 Cor 15:3–11; 2:16. Paul sometimes calls it the 'gospel of God', because it proceeds from God (Rom 1:1; 15:16; 2 Cor 11:7, etc), and sometimes the 'gospel of Christ', both because it is derived from Christ and because it deals with him (1 Cor 9:12; 2 Cor 2:12; 9:13; 10:14; Gal 1:7, etc). He also calls it 'my' or 'our' gospel (Rom 2:16; 16:25; 2 Cor 4:3; 1 Thess 1:5; 2 Thess 2:14), not in order to contrast it with the gospel of Peter, but because he has received it himself from Christ (Gal 1:12; 1 Cor 15:3) and because he, as the 'minister' of the gospel (Col 1:23), has the task of proclaiming it. Since the gospel is the gospel of God, the 'power of God' is given to everyone who accepts it in faith (Rom 1:16; Eph 1:13). The meaning of the gospel is not 'reasonable' to man, but 'hidden' (2 Cor 4:3)—it is a stumbling block and foolishness for many, but for those who are called it is the power of God and the wisdom of God (1 Cor 1:18–25). At the judgement, the fate of man depends upon his acceptance or his rejection of the gospel (2 Thess 2:14). Paul also calls it the word of God, prec[illegible]ecause it is the gospel of God (Col [illegible] When the apostle proclaims the gospel, the words which are heard are those of God, who speaks through the mouth of the preacher (1 Thess 2:13). It is the 'word of truth' (2 Cor 6:7; Eph 1:13) and cannot be 'bound' by men because it comes from God (2 Tim 2:9). The essential meaning and content of the gospel is, for Paul, always Christ's death and resurrection. He passes over the preaching and miracles of Jesus, not, however, simply due to the fact that he himself was never personally acquainted with the 'historical' Jesus, but because Christ's work of redemption, rather than any historical account of his earthly life formed the real theme of the message of salvation. Obedience to the faith is not the only demand made by the gospel (Rom 1:5; 16:26)—it also supplies the norm for all moral behaviour (Phil 1:27). The proclamation of the gospel message initiates a new order in the history of salvation.

Throughout the New Testament, 'gospel' means the *living, spoken word of Christ's saving message*, and is thus never a literary concept. Also, since there is only *one* saving message, the word is consistently used only in the singular. Even in the second century, this primary meaning predominates (Polycarp, *Philad* 9:2; *Did* 15:3, 4). The individual gospels, too, are referred to as *to euangelion kata Matthaion, kata Markon*, etc (='the gospel according to Matthew, according to Mark', etc). In the second century, however, it is also used for the titles of books (Justinian, *Apol* I, 66; *Dial* 10:2; 2 Clem 8:5; Theophilus, *Ad Autol* 3:14). Used thus, it may also refer to the *whole* of the New Testament, with the result that its content and meaning are brought to mind (Iren, *Adv Haer* II, 27:2).

C. *The gospels of the New Testament.* The transference of the name 'gospel', originally referring to the oral missionary preaching of the joyous message, to the *written* gospels bears witness to the important fact that these texts were recognised as having the same missionary value as oral preaching, and as serving the same purpose, namely, that of awakening men to faith and of confirming them in that faith (Jn 20:31). In their content and meaning, therefore, the gospels refer back to the *euangelion* in its original sense, since, in handing down the words and acts of Jesus Christ, they clearly reveal his mission and his absolute power, including that over human disease and demons. In this way, they visibly demonstrate who he is—the Messiah, the Son of God and the Saviour of mankind, who proclaims in his preaching the will of God and the moral demands which God makes upon man. This, and not the history of Christ's life on earth in the biographical sense, forms the basic content of the gospels. The material of the gospels is derived from that tradition which goes back directly to the oral preaching of the apostles who were eye-witnesses and the first 'ministers of the word' (Lk 1:2). The apostles certainly never intended to provide their hearers with a complete, coherent and fully rounded picture either of the life of Jesus or simply of his public ministry. Their 'proclamation' consisted rather of the sayings and parables of Jesus and of his various controversies. Above all, however, they were concerned to proclaim his death and resurrection. All these various details were gathered up into a whole within a single framework—which is nevertheless strikingly different in the case of each individual evangelist—and, when this was done, the total result was a written record vividly illustrating the message of Jesus Christ. The origin of the gospels is quite clearly discernible in the form in which they have been handed down to us. Their literary style, which cannot be placed in the same category as any of the Jewish or Greek writings of the same period, was determined by the manner in which they originated. The historical and biographical interest of the gospels is completely subordinated to their religious and kerygmatic content. It is clear that little attempt was made either to produce a complete account, or to set out the events in chronological order. Generally speaking, the gospel events are strung together very loosely—this is especially evident in Mark, which is the earliest of the gospels—or according to purely practical criteria, and the order varies widely in the case of each evangelist. The only exception to this is the account of the Passion, but even here the gospels differ markedly from every other historical account, for they view the events of the Passion not as the result of human will, but as the outcome of the expression of God's will. In the gospel accounts of the Passion, it is not the Jewish opponents of Jesus who are at work, but God. When the apocryphal writers attempted to fill in the gaps left by the canonical gospels, they evinced an interest in the person of Jesus which was different from and alien to that of the evangelists. But since the canonical gospels are, to all intents and purposes, the only real sources of the knowledge we have of the life of Jesus, we can safely say that a modern 'life of Jesus', offering only what has been historically handed down to us, can in fact never be written. Not only would such an undertaking be impracticable, but it would be without religious significance from the point of view which the evangelists themselves intended to present, namely, the significance of the person of Jesus within the context of salvation history.

The written gospels originate in the preaching or kerygma of the first christian community. They also reflect the situation of the communities in which and for which they were written. Finally, there is the literary and—most important—theological purpose of each individual evangelist. These various factors allow us to understand the many, often significant differences between the texts, and even in the renderings of the words of Christ. Examples of the tendency at work in such cases to rearrange, or sometimes even to rewrite, are the interpretations added to the parables of the sower (Mk 4:1–9, 13–20) and of the weeds (Mt 13:24–30, 36–43). Matthew in chapter 18 has put together various sayings of Christ to make a 'community code' aimed at the situation of a community and its problems, and passages such as Mt 7:15–23 (parallel Lk 6:43–6) and Mt 24:10–12 reflect the unsatisfactory state of such communities. The conversation between John the Baptist and Jesus which precedes the account of the baptism of Jesus in Matthew (3:13–15) clearly betrays an apologetic purpose. It was a puzzling question for early christian circles how Jesus, the sinless one, could come to the Baptist to receive the baptism of repentence—and by doing so subordinate himself to the

Baptist. It is Matthew's intention to answer this question. The more radical reorganisation of the parousia speech in Lk 21:5–36 (contrast Mk 13:1–33) becomes intelligible once one takes into account the way the expectation of an imminent second coming recedes in the third gospel, and once one notes in addition that Luke clearly looks back to the destruction of Jerusalem as an event in the past. It is only a careful consideration of the obvious differences between the gospels and the individual tendencies they bring to light which enables us to appreciate the true character of the gospels, and also to see how the fourth gospel, so different not simply in literary form but also in theological content, can occupy a place beside the synoptics. The question of how far the picture of Jesus given by the gospels draws on the characteristics of the historical Jesus is, however, the central problem of contemporary gospel studies.

Bibliography: J. Schniewind, *Euangelion*, Gütersloh 1937–41; E. Molland, *Das paulinische Euangelion*, Oslo 1934; K. L. Schmidt, 'Die Stellung der Evangelien in der allgemeinen Literaturgeschichte', *Eucharisterion* II (dedicated to H. Gunkel), Göttingen 1925, 50–134; R. Asting, *Die Verkündigung des Wortes im Urchristentum*, Stuttgart 1939; M. Albertz, *Die Botschaft des NT* I/I, Zurich 1947; J. Huby, *L'Evangile et les Evangiles*, Paris 1954[3]; Bultmann I, 87–92; *TDNT* II, 707–37; H. Ristow and K. Matthiae (edd.), *Der historische Jesus und der kerygmatische Christus*, Berlin 1961[2]; X. Léon-Dufour, *Les évangiles et l'histoire de Jésus*, Paris 1963.

Josef Schmid

Government

The Greek word *exousia*, can signify 'controlling power' (eg Rev 17:12f) and 'area of jurisdiction' (eg Lk 23:7), but is normally applied to those *persons* who, or *institutions* which, are vested with such controlling power. The bible has no fixed term for what we call 'the state'. To express the reality underlying this term it not only speaks of 'controlling power' or 'authority' but uses such terms as 'king', 'kingdom', 'caesar', 'ruler', 'potentate', etc. Moreover in questions connected with authority its interest is restricted almost entirely to the aspect of man's practical attitude to authority. Even such expressions as do appear to carry more fundamental implications normally envisage the concrete situation, so that in themselves they do not admit of any universally applicable rules being deduced from them. At the same time the New Testament does contain certain fundamental statements of principle, which can serve as starting-points for the working out of a theory in terms of natural law.

A. *Old Testament and judaism.* To understand the attitude of the Old Testament to political authority it must be noticed that Yahweh was accounted the Creator and Lord of Israel his people, and also as their sole king: 'I am the Lord, your Holy One, the Creator of Israel, your King' (Is 43:15; see also 33:22; Num 23:21; Deut 33:5; Judg 8:23; 1 Sam 12:12). Hence the demand of the people for a king was at first considered as a rejection of Yahweh (1 Sam 8:6f; 10:19; 12:12, 17, 19). But when the people had overcome all opposition and obtained a king, those who had opposed them came to terms with the altered situation by explaining that the king was Yahweh's representative or vizier

(1 Chron 28:5; 29:11f, 23; 2 Chron 9:8; Ps 72:1), that he had been chosen by him (1 Sam 10:24; 16:12; Wis 9:7), instituted by him (1 Sam 12:12; 15:17, 28, 35), and guided by him (Prov 21:1) as his anointed one (1 Sam 15:17; 24:6, 10; 16:6; 26:9, 11, 23). And if the king depended for his position upon God, this meant that men could not institute and depose kings at their own discretion (Hos 7:3; 8:4, 10), and it also meant that those who opposed him were in a real sense opposing Yahweh himself (2 Chron 13:8). By reason of his close connection with Yahweh, a closeness which finds its most pregnant expression in the description 'son of God' (2 Sam 7:14; Ps 89:27; 2:7), the king was also considered to be, in a special sense, the bestower of blessings (2 Sam 6:18; 1 Kings 8:14, 55f; 1 Chron 16:2; 2 Chron 6:3), and a powerful intercessor on his people's behalf (1 Kings 8:22–53; 2 Kings 19:15–19; 2 Chron 6:12–33; 30:18f). And this in turn was one of the reasons why he was particularly remembered in the prayers of the cultic community (1 Kings 8:66; Ps 20:9; 61:6–9; 84:9). But however exalted a conception of the king men might entertain they never forgot the fact that the power of God sets a limit to all political power (Ps 33:16–18; see also Rev 17:12f). Thus in Israel we never find a divine status ascribed to the king, as it is in writings emanating from other royal courts of the ancient Near East. Nor was there any lack of criticism of the monarchy as experienced in concrete fact (Hos 10:3; Jer 10:21; 21:11–23, 8; Ezek 34:5). It is significant how easily the people dispensed with any return to the monarchical form of government after the exile. The rebellion instigated in certain pious circles against Alexander Jannaeus (Josephus, *Ant* 13:372, 376; *Bell* 1:70, 88) probably originated from the fact that this potentate, like Aristobulus (*Ant* 13:301; 14:41), had laid claim to the title of king. Now precisely in a community which—to use a formulation first coined by Josephus—wished to be a 'theocracy' there was no lawful place for a king: 'The government of states had been entrusted here to monarchs, there to a few powerful families, elsewhere to the people; our lawgiver, on the contrary, refused to entertain any such form of government, but—to sum the matter up in a single pregnant word—made the state into a theocracy in that he submitted it to the power and dominion of God.' [*Apol* 2:164.] Now if God is the head of his people it follows that its leaders are by vocation the priests. 'Where could a more sublime or a wiser dispensation be found than that which makes God the director of the universe, the head, and makes over the whole administration of government in the state to the priests?' [Josephus, *Apol* 2:185]. According to Josephus the authority of the high priest is, in a certain sense, quasi-divine: 'He who does not hearken to the high priest must do penance in exactly the same way as if he had sinned against God himself (*Apol* 2:194). But if in spite of this a king ever rules in the land he may not do this without the priests: 'The king shall undertake nothing without the high priest and the council of the elders' (*Ant* 4:224). In his letter to Caligula, Agrippa I maintains that his forebears would have thought of themselves first as priests and only

secondarily as kings because the dignity of the high priest is greater than that of the king, just as God is greater than man (Philo, *Leg ad Caium*, 278). Yahweh, however, is Creator and Lord not only of Israel but of the whole earth (Jer 27:5; see also Ex 15:18; 19:5; Josephus, *Ant* 14:24), and as such 'king of the nations' too (Jer 10:7, 10f; Ps 22:28; 99:1) and over their rulers, 'Lord of kings' (Dan 2:47) or 'king of kings' (3 Macc 5:35; Enoch [Eth] 9:4; Jub 8:26; 23:1), in fact 'king of the kings of kings' (Sir 51:14). He institutes and deposes the kings of the peoples at will (Dan 2:21; 4:22; cf 2:37; 2 Kings 19:15; Jer 27:5–11; Is 37:16; 45:1; Sir 10:4). All kings, even gentile ones, have received their power from God (Wis 6:3; Enoch [Eth] 46:5; Barn [Syr] 82:9; Letter of Aristeas, 219, 224), and are therefore merely vassals of God, 'ministers of his kingdom' (Wis 6:4). Among the rabbis too there were hardly any differences of opinion on this point (instances in SB III, 303f). The Essenes had to swear an oath that they would keep faith with everyone, and especially with the rulers, for it fell to no-one to have dominion except by God's will (Josephus, *Bell* 2:140). Therefore the people were exhorted to pray for the ruling body in power at the time even when these were gentiles as in Babylon (Jer 29:14; Bar 1:11). According to Ezra 6:9f Darius provided the materials for public sacrifices in Jerusalem, directing that at these sacrifices prayers should be offered 'for the life of the king and his sons'. Again sacrifices seem regularly to have been offered in the temple at Jerusalem for Antiochus the Great, for he made notable provisions for the sacrificial cult at Jerusalem (Josephus, *Ant* 12:140) and there is reliable evidence of a sacrifice at least being offered for him from the time of the Maccabee wars (1 Macc 7:33). In the Letter of Aristeas forty-five sacrifices and prayers offered by the Jews for the Egyptian king and his family are spoken of. From the time of Augustus two lambs and an ox were offered daily in the temple at Jerusalem 'for Caesar and the Roman people' (Philo, *Leg ad Caium*, 157, 317; Josephus, *Bell* 2:197; *Apol* 2:77), and these sacrifices, paid for according to Philo by Caesar, according to Josephus by the Jewish people, but in reality probably out of Jewish taxes, were continued up to the outbreak of the revolution in the year AD 66 (Josephus, *Bell* 2:409f, 415f). In addition to these, supplementary sacrifices for Caesar were also offered on special occasions: thus under Caligula at his accession to power (Philo, *Leg ad Caium*, 232), at his recovery from a serious illness and before the beginning of his campaign against the Teutons (*ibid*, 356; see also *In Flaccum*, 48f). The fact that the Roman authority could be valued as a regulating force is attested by the following statement of Rabbi Ḥananiah from the period of about AD 70: 'Pray for the wellbeing of the [gentile] government. For if it were not for the fear of this we would already have swallowed one another up alive' (Mischna, Abot 3:2). When the demands of the ruling body are in conflict with the law then admittedly one must refuse to obey them. As early a ruler as Saul was forced to experience the fact that his people were 'more afraid of offending God than of refusing to obey the king' (Josephus, *Ant* 6:259).

The reply of the priest Mathias to the emissaries of the Syrian king was: 'Far be it from us to desert the law and the ordinances. We will not obey the king's words by turning aside from our religion to the right or to the left' (1 Macc 2:21f). Similarly the youngest of the Maccabee brothers said: 'I will not obey the king's command but I will obey the commandment of the law which was given to our fathers from Moses' (2 Macc 7:30). A tendency is apparent in the apocalyptic writings to discern behind the great empires of the world powers hostile to God which are to be annihilated in the final age (Is 27:1; Dan 7:2–12; Hen eth 89:59–90, 25; see also 1 QM 15:2f), and cut off from the eternal kingdom of God (Dan 7:13–18). The authority of Rome was rejected root and branch by the Zealots, who recognised no-one save Yahweh alone as king and Lord (Josephus, *Ant* 18:23f; *Bell* 2:118, 433; 7:323, 410, 418), and hence proclaimed and unleashed the holy war against Rome.

B. *New Testament*. We may commence with the saying of Jesus which runs: 'Render to Caesar the things that are Caesar's and to God the things that are God's' (Mk 12:17 and parallels). Manifestly this is quite different from the demand of the Zealots that their compatriots should refuse to pay taxes to Caesar. At the same time, however, it does not in any sense set Caesar on an equal footing with God, but rather throws all the emphasis upon the exhortation to render to God the things that are God's. The will of God is the sole standard for Jesus, and in cases of conflict the will of the earthly lord goes unheeded, as is shown from Jesus' reply to the veiled attempt to banish him from the territory of Herod Antipas (Lk 13:31f). He is aware of how in concrete fact the ruling body tends to misuse its power (Mk 10:42f; 13:9–11 etc), but he still refuses to rebel against it (though not to speak against it, Jn 18:22f; see also Acts 23:3) even when he has to endure injustice at its hands. This appears from the manner in which he bore himself in the passion (see especially Mk 14:48f; Mt 26:52–4; Jn 18:11). He has no political aims to pursue (Mt 4:8–10 and parallels). His kingdom is not of this world (Jn 18:36), and anyone who denies this will be disappointed in his expectations (Jn 6:14f; see also Lk 19:11; 24:21; Acts 1:6). The primitive church is in accord with the Old Testament and judaism in adopting a fundamentally positive attitude towards the ruling authorities, if, indeed, we may not go so far as to maintain that in 2 Thess 2:6f an actual function in salvific history is ascribed to the Roman government. The existing order derives its power from God (Rom 13:1; Jesus's answer to Pilate in Jn 19:11 has a different meaning). It must protect and reward the good and punish the wicked (Rom 13:3f; 1 Pet 2:13f). All have to give it their obedience (Rom 13:1; Tit 3:1; 1 Pet 2:13), and that too not under compulsion but on grounds of conscience (Rom 13:5) or for the sake of God (1 Pet 2:13). So true is this that any disobedience would actually amount to a resisting of what God has appointed (Rom 13:2). The way of the christian is not to reject the authority of the pagan ruling body, but to pray for it (1 Tim 2:1f; see also Lk 23:34; Acts 7:60; 1 Clem 60f; Polyc

12:3; Justinus, *Apol*, I, 17:3; Theophilus, *Ad Autol*, I, 11; Tertullian, *Apol* 30:39). Just as the secular authority has its source in the will of God, so too it has its limits there: 'We must obey God rather than men' (Acts 5:29; see also 4:19). The exhortation in 1 Pet 2:17: 'Fear God. Honour the emperor' is perhaps an intentional corrective to the Old Testament exhortation: 'My son, fear the Lord and the king' (Prov 24:21). Paul's attitude towards the Roman authorities, which is on the whole (in spite of 1 Cor 6:1–6) an affirmative one, is to be explained primarily by his Jewish origins (see above under A), but his basic eschatological orientation (see Rom 13:11–13; Phil 3:20; also 1 Pet 2:11) and his relatively favourable experiences of the workings of Roman authority are also factors which have to be taken into account. In the case of the Book of Revelation the situation is quite different. Here the Roman authority, claiming divine honour for Caesar as it does, figures explicitly as a Satanic power (13:2–4), against which the church summons its members, not indeed to rebellion, but certainly to a refusal of obedience even at the cost of martyrdom. Lk 4:6 might represent an anomaly if we do not follow Irenaeus (*Haer* 5, 22:2; 24:1) in taking this saying of Satan as empty boasting. The idea that the world as a whole is under the dominion of Satan might represent, to some extent, a parallel to this (Jn 12:31; 13:2, 27; 14:30 etc).

Bibliography: General: F. G. Dölger, 'Zur antiken und frühchristl. Auffassung der Herrschergewalt von Gottes Gnaden', *Antike und Christ*, 3 (1932), 117–27; 5 (1936), 142ff; K. L. Schmidt, *TDNT* I, 564–93; *TDNT* VI, 516–35 (see *Basileia* [*BKW* VII], London 1957); C. H. Powell, *The Biblical Concept of Power*, London 1963. On A: K. Galling, *Die israelitische Staatsverfassung in ihrer vorderorientalischen Umwelt*, Leipzig 1929; C. R. North, 'The OT Estimate of the Monarchy', *Am. Journ. of Semitic Languages* 48 (1931/2), 1–19; O. Procksch, *Der Staatsgedanke in der Prophetie*, Gütersloh 1933; W. Rudolph, 'Volk und Staat im AT', *Volk, Staat, Kirche. Ein Lehrgang der theol. Fak. Giessen*, Giessen 1933, 21–33; E. R. Goodenough, *The Politics of Philo Judaeus*, New Haven 1938; B. Balscheit, *Gottesbund und Staat. Der Staat im AT*, Zürich 1940; M. Noth, 'Gott, König, Volk im AT', *ZTK* 47 (1950), 157–91; A. Seeger, *Staatsgott oder Gottesstaat im alten Israel und Hellas*, Göttingen 1951; H. J. Kraus, *Die Königsherrschaft Gottes im AT*, Tübingen 1951; H. J. Kraus, *Prophetie und Politik*, Munich 1952; A. Alt, 'Das Königtum in den Reichen Israel und Juda', *VT* 1 (1951), 2–22; A. Alt, 'Die Staatenbildung der Israeliten in Palästina', *Kleine Schriften* II, Munich 1953, 1–65; H. Gross, *Weltherrschaft als religiöse Idee im AT*, Bonn 1953; I. Mendelsohn, 'Samuel's Denunciation of Kingship', *BASOR* 143 (1956), 17–22; A. Weiser, 'Samuel und die Vorgeschichte des israelit. Königtums', *ZTK* 57 (1960), 141–61; L. Rost, 'Königsherrschaft Jahwes in vorköniglicher Zeit?', *TLZ* 85 (1960), 721–4; W. Schmidt, *Königtum Gottes in Ugarit und Israel*, Berlin 1961; T. Blatter, *Macht und Herrschaft Gottes*, Fribourg 1962; G. Wallis, 'Die Anfänge des Königtums in Israel', *Wiss. Zschr. d. M. Luther- Univ. Halle-Wittenberg* 12 (1963), Gesellsch. und sprachwiss. Reihe, 239–47; E. Lipinsky, 'Jahwe malakh', *Bbl* 44 (1963), 405–60; H. Donner, *Israel unter den Völkern*, Leiden 1964. On B: W. Stählin, 'Das Reich Gottes und der Staat', *TB* 6 (1927), 141f; H. Windisch, *Imperium und Evangelium im NT*, Kiel 1931; F. Delekat, *Die Kirche Jesu Christi und der Staat*, Berlin 1933, G. Bertram, 'Volk und Staat im NT', *Volk, Staat, Kirche. Ein Lehrgang der theol. Fak. Giesse*, Giessen 1933, 35–52; K. Pieper, *Urkirche und Staat*, Paderborn 1935; E. Stauffer, *Gott und Kaiser im NT*, Bonn 1935; G. Kittel, 'Das Urteil des NT über den Staat', *ZST* 14 (1937), 651–80; K. L. Schmidt, *Die Polis in Kirche und Staat*, Basle 1939; F. J. Leenhardt, *Le chrétien doit-il servir l'État?*, Geneva 1939; G. Kittel, *Christus und Imperator*, Stuttgart 1939; W. Bieder, *Ecclesia und Polis im NT*, Zürich 1941; W. G. Kümmel, *Theol. Rundschau* 17 (1948), 133–42; W. Schweitzer, *Die Herrschaft Christi und der Staat im NT*, Zürich 1948; L. Hick, *Die Staatsgewalt im Lichte des NT*, Aachen 1948; K. H. Schelkle, 'Jerusalem und

Rom im NT', *TG* 41 (1950), 77–119; E. Gaugler, 'Der Christ und die staatlichen Gewalten nach dem NT', *Intern. Kirchl. Zschr.* 40 (1950), 133–53; J. Hering, *A Good and a Bad Government according to the NT*, Springfield (Illinois) 1954; R. Schnackenburg, *The Moral Teaching of the New Testament*, London 1964; M. Dibelius, 'Rom und die Christen im 1 Jh.', *Botschaft und Geschichte* II, Tübingen 1956, 177–228; H. Schlier, 'Die Beurteilung des Staates im NT', *Die Zeit der Kirche*, Freiburg 1956, 1–16. See also *Catholica* 13 (1959), 241–59; L. Goppelt, *Der Staat im NT*, Tübingen 1961[2]; O. Michel, 'Das Problem des Staates in ntl. Sicht', *TLZ* 83 (1958), 161–6; W. Schmauch and E. Wolf, *Königsherrschaft Christi. Der Christ im Staat*, Munich 1959; H. W. Bartsch, 'Die ntl. Aussagen über den Staat', *ET* 19 (1959), 375–90; A. Penner, *The Christian, the State and the NT*, Scottdale (Penn.) 1959; R. Völkl, *Christ und Welt nach dem NT*, Würzburg 1961; H. von Campenhausen, 'Die Christen und das bürgerliche Leben nach den Aussagen des NT', *Tradition und Leben*, Tübingen 1961, 180–202; C. E. B. Cranfield, 'The Christian's Political Responsibility according to the NT', *SJT* 15 (1962), 176–92; W. Böld, *Obrigkeit vor Gott?*, Hamburg 1962; H. U. Instinsky, *Die Alte Kirche und das Heil des Staates*, Munich 1963; C. J. Mans, 'De owerheid in die NT en by die reformatore', *Hervormde Teologiese Studiese* (Pretoria) 18 (1962), 90–115; H. R. Schlette, 'Die Aussagen des NT über "den Staat"', *Der Anspruch der Freiheit*, Munich 1963, 21–52; H. R. Schlette, 'Staat', *HTG* II, 551–5; A. M. Ferrando, *Christianisme et Pouvoir civil* (dissertation), Fribourg 1961; M. L. Ricketts, 'Christians and the State—the New Testament View', *Religion and Life* 33 (1963/4), 74–9. On Mk 12:17: E. Stauffer, *Christus und die Cäsaren*, Hamburg 1954[4], 121–49; E. Stauffer, *Die Botschaft Jesu*, Bern 1959, 95–118; A. Bea, *CC* 109 (1958), 572–83; P. Vanbergen, *LV* 50 (1960), 12–22; L. Goppelt, *Ecclesia und Respublica*, Göttingen 1961, 40ff; J. W. Doeve, *Vox Theol.* 32 (1961/2), 69–83; J. N. Sevenster, *Nederl. Theol. Tijdschr.* 17 (1962), 21–31. On Jn 19:11. H. von Campenhausen, *TLZ* 73 (1948), 387–92. On Rom 13: W., Bauer, *Jedermann sei untertan der Ordnung, Gött. Universitätsreden*, Göttingen 1930; L. Gaugusch, *TG* 26 (1934), 529–50; G. Dehn, *Festschr. K. Barth*, Munich 1936, 90–109; J. E. Uitman, *Onder Eig. Vaandel* 15 (1940), 102–21; W. Parsons, *Theol. Studies* 1 (1940), 337–64; 2 (1941), 325–46; J. Koch-Mehrin, *ET* 7 (1947/8), 378–401; H. von Campenhausen, *Festschr. A. Bertholet*, Tübingen 1950, 97–112; K. H. Schelkle, *ZNW* 44 (1952/3), 223–36; A. Weithaas, *TG* 45 (1955), 433–41; A. Strobel. *ZNW* 47 (1956), 67–93; R. Morgenthaler, *TZ* 12 (1956), 289–304; E. Käsemann, *ZTK* 56 (1959), 316–76; C. E. B. Cranfield, *NTS* 6 (1960), 241–9; P. Meinhold, *Römer 13*, Stuttgart 1960; E. Bemmel, *TLZ* 85 (1960), 837–40; C. D. Morrison, *The Powers that Be*, London 1960; E. Käsemann, *Beitrag z. EvT* 32 (1961), 37–55; E. Barnikol, *Studien z. NT und z. Patristik* (=*TU* 77), Berlin 1961, 65–134; F. Neugebauer, *Kerygma und Dogma* 8 (1962), 151–72; G. Delling, *Römer 13:1–7 innerhalb der Briefe des NT*, Berlin 1962; O. Kuss, *Auslegung und Verkündigung* I, Regensburg 1963, 246–59; J. Kosnetter, *Sud. Paulin. Congr. Intern. Cath.* I, Rome 1963, 347–55; G. Hillerdahl, *Luth, Rundschau* 13 (1963), 17–34; A. Strobel, *ZNW* 55 (1964), 58–62; V. Zsifkovits, *Der Staatsgedanke nach Paulus in Röm 13*, Vienna 1964. On 1 Tim 2:1f. A. Bludau, *Der katholische Seelsorger* (Vienna) 18 (1906), 295–300, 349–55, and 391–5; L. Biehl, *Das liturgische Gebet für Kaiser und Reich*, Paderborn 1937. On Rev 13. P. Ketter, *TTZ* 1 (1941), 70–93; H. Schlier, *Die Zeit der Kirche*, Freiburg 1956, 16–29; L. Cerfaux, *The Sacral Kingship*, (=*Studies in the History of Religion* IV), Leiden 1959, 459–70.

Josef Blinzler

Grace

A. *In the Old Testament.* No special word is used in the Old Testament to convey what is understood by grace in the christian, and particularly in the Pauline sense. The Old Testament did, however, prepare the way for an understanding of the nature of grace, and displays an inherent recognition of it. *Kharis* is the usual translation in LXX of the Hebrew *ḥēn*, which in the first place means affection, goodwill, favour, or friendliness (particularly on the part of someone in a high place) (see Ps 45:2). The meaning of *ḥēn* is extended to the object of this special goodwill or favour, to imply charm, graciousness, comeliness or beauty (see Prov 4:9; 5:19; 11:16; 31:30; Nahum 3:4). Thus *ḥēn* and *kharis* have basically the same meanings, though the meaning of *kharis* developed from that of charm, beauty, etc, to that of goodwill or favour. The meaning of *ḥēn* is to be found especially in the phrase: 'to find favour in the sight of God, or of man' (in the sight of God, see Gen 6:8; 18:3; 19:19; Ex 33:12f, 16f; 34:9; in the sight of man, see Gen 39:4; 47:29; Ex 3:21; 12:36). The adverb *ḥinnām*, in vain, which is formed from the same root as *ḥēn*, and the two instances of the use of the word in Gen 18:3 and Ex 33:12, suggest a favour which the recipient does not deserve. The word *ḥesed*—translated by *kharis* in LXX (Esther 2:9, 17), but elsewhere generally by *eleos* (=pity: *misericordia* in the Vulgate translations of Psalms) means the attitude of mind and individual behaviour appropriate to life in the community, and in particular the mutual loyalty of those who share in the covenant (see 1 Sam 20:8, 14ff; 2 Sam 9:1, 3:8) and their duty towards one another within the community. The ↗ covenant, which God entered into with man, proceeded from his freely-given love, and was therefore grace. For this reason, his attitude towards the covenant (*ḥesed*) was also grace, and in a very special sense, his attitude towards his people when they broke the covenant. The translation of *ḥesed* as 'mercy' is thus factually correct. (For *ḥesed* in connection with the covenant, see Deut 7:9; 1 Kings 8:23; Neh 9:32; Dan 9:4; Ps 89:28; Is 55:3.)

The Old Testament certainly foreshadows the idea of grace which helps men—again and again we find explicit references to the need for Yahweh's help. Israel was freed from bondage in Egypt, led through the wilderness and given the land of Canaan (see Ex 6:6ff; 13:21f; Deut 7:17–24; 8:2ff, 7–18; Josh 21:43f). The land was, indeed, always under the special care of God (Deut 11:10ff, 14ff). The Israelites had always to remember that they could do nothing of their own accord (Deut 8:17f; Judg 7:2; Ps 44:3–9). The prophets constantly censured the people for relying arrogantly upon themselves and neglecting to trust in God, and for presuming upon worldly means to gain power (see Is 2:7–17; 28:15; 30:16; 39:2–7; Amos 6:8, 13; see also 2 Sam 24), as well as for allowing themselves to be deluded into thinking that the fruits of the land came from the fertility gods or goddesses (Hos 2:5, 8, 12). God's way of making his people realise that they owed everything to him was invariably to withdraw his gifts and his help (see the schematic outline in Judg 3:7ff, 12ff; 4:1ff; also Hos 2:9, 12; 5:13ff; 13:9ff; 14:4–9; Mic 5:9f; Zeph 3:11f). The strength of Israel is completely dependent upon the people's trust in Yahweh (see Ps 20:7ff: Is 7:9; 30:15). No man was to glory in his wisdom, his strength or his riches, but in his understanding and knowledge of Yahweh, who exercises mercy and ↗ goodness (*ḥesed*), judgement, and ↗ justice on earth (Jer 9:24; cf 1 Cor 1:31). The prosperity of every single person depends upon the ↗ blessing of Yahweh (see Num 6:22–7). This conviction is at the heart of the faith of every religious Israelite. Whenever Yahweh turns away his face, every being is confounded and destroyed and all security is lost (see Ps 30:7; 31:15ff; 104:27–30; 121; 127; 145:15ff; 146; 147:9ff). It should be noted, in this context, that the word of blessing which comes from Yahweh is efficacious and accomplishes that which he purposes (Is 55:11), as, indeed, is true of his↗ word in general. This confident faith and trust in Yahweh (see also Prov 18:10f) corresponds closely to the belief that he was the creator of the universe and its first mover (see Prov 16:1, 4, 7, 9; 19:14; 20:24; 21:1; Sir 11:14).

The Old Testament also recognises that divine grace, in the form either of goodwill or of a gift, is both *freely bestowed* on God's part and *undeserved* on man's part. This is clearly so in the case of man's state of original blessedness in Paradise. The name *hā'ādām* (man) indicates that man is destined, by his very nature, to cultivate the soil (*hā'adāmāh*: see Gen 2:5). God, however, assigns a much more pleasant task to him by putting him in a garden full of splendid trees (Gen 2:8–15). Man, fashioned from clay, is by nature mortal, but God ordained not only that he should labour at tilling the soil, but also that he should die only as a punishment for his transgression of the divine commandment (Gen 2:17; 3:17ff). In this context, man's intimate relationship with God in Paradise (see Gen 2:19, 22; 3:8f) is shown to be a grace which is quite independent of any merit on his part. But an even more striking example is that of God's treatment of fallen man within his plan of salvation. He does not carry out the sentence of death on the day of his sin, as he had threatened to do, but rather makes it possible for the human race to perpetuate itself and eventually to triumph over the seducer, the serpent, whose head will be crushed underfoot (Gen 3:15). Adam, in grateful recognition of this action, calls his wife Eve, mother of all the living, that is, *life* (Gen 3:20). Moreover, as the further history of man's salvation clearly shows, God did not forsake man after the fall (see Wis 10:1). Another instance of his grace is the covenant which he made with Noah—although he recognised that man was incorrigible, he nevertheless guaranteed his continued existence (Gen 8:21). By far the most striking example of this grace, however, is God's Covenant with Israel. It is impressed upon the minds of the Israelites that Yahweh has chosen them and has entered into the covenant with them from motives of pure love, and without any merit at all on their part (Deut 7:6ff; see also Ezek 16:4–14). God's predestination is made especially clear in his choice of Isaac (Gen 17:18–21; 21:12f) and of Jacob (Gen 25:23) for the continuity of the patriarchal line and the furtherance of the covenant. (Paul has a penetrating comment on this in Rom 9:7–13.) God himself is emphatic about the absolute nature of his choice—he will have mercy on whom he will (Ex 33:19; see also Rom 9:15). The fact that God's grace is not dependent upon human merit emerges very clearly in the attitude of Yahweh towards his people when they have not been faithful to the covenant (see Ex 34:6–10; Lev 26:44f; Is 43:22–44:5; Jer 31:3, 20; Hos 11:8f; Mic 7:18ff). There are, furthermore, two culminating points within the whole of the messianic prophecy which indicate the *necessity* of divine grace as new nature and as the present help of God. In Jer 31:31–4, a distinction is made between the 'new covenant' and that made on

Mount Sinai. Under this 'new covenant', Yahweh will not simply present his law externally to his people on stone tablets or in his word, but will rather present it interiorly to each individual man, writing it in his heart, with the result that it will become, as it were, his second nature. God will give to each man an inner understanding of himself, and to the Hebrew mind, which sees everything as a single whole, this would imply a corresponding attitude and moral behaviour on the part of the recipient (see Jer 22:15ff; 1 Jn 2:4). The negative aspect of this transformation is the overcoming of sin through God's forgiveness. Ezek 36:25–28 gives clear evidence of this change, and shows even more strikingly how God's grace is both habitual and actual. Yahweh will cleanse those from their sins who have been delivered from exile, give them a new heart and a new↗ spirit by putting his own spirit into them, thus causing them to keep his commandments. But Yahweh does not do this for their sakes—he does it for the sake of his holy name (Ezek 36:22, 32; see also Is 48:9, 11). It is thus evident that there is no question at all of any merit on the part of Israel. A close parallel exists between Ezek 36:25ff and Ps 51:9–14—the psalmist speaks of being cleansed of his sins, of being given a clean heart and a new, firm and willing spirit and of being informed by the holy, divine spirit. It is clearly stated in this psalm that this transformation can only come about by means of God's creative power. Is 6:7f shows too that the↗justification of a sinner really implies the eradication of his sin and grants him a new life which may enable him to become God's herald or prophet. The justification of Israel, as expressed, for example, in Is 45:25, does not imply that Israel has an automatic claim to justification, which would be in direct contradiction to what is stated in Is 43:22ff and elsewhere. On the other hand, however, it should be noted that this is not simply a declaration of God's justice, as Is 44:22 shows (see also, for example, Mic 7:19).

Finally, the fact that divine grace, in its choice of persons for special purposes and offices, is not dependent upon the merit of the man chosen, is exemplified in Num 16:3–11; 18:7 (the gift of priesthood): 1 Sam 9:21; 15:17; 2 Sam 7:18ff, etc.

Bibliography: J. Ziegler, *Die Liebe Gottes bei den Propheten* (*AA* 11, 3), Münster 1930; J. Köberle, *Sünde und Gnade im religiösen Leben des Volkes Israel*, Munich 1905; J. Hempel, *Gott und Mensch im Alten Testament*, Stuttgart 1936²; W. F. Lofthouse, 'Chen and Chesed in the Old Testament', *ZAW* 51 (1933), 29–35; N. Glueck, 'Das Wort chesed im alttestamentlichen Sprachgebrauch' (*BZAW* 47), Giessen 1927; F. Asensio, *Misericordia et Veritas: E, Hèsed y 'Emet Divinos*, Rome 1949; R. Bultmann, *TDNT* II, 477–82; P. van Imschoot, Haag, 589f; J. Guillet, *Leitgedanken der Bibel*, Lucerne 1954, 29–111; D. R. Ap-Thomas, 'Some Aspects of the Root "chen" in the OT', *JSS* 2 (1957), 128–48; G. Farr, 'The Concept of Grace in the Book of Hosea', *ZAW* 70 (1958), 98–107; J. Haspecker, 'Gnade', *LTK* IV², 977–80; I. Hermann, *HTG* 1, 548–53; H J. Stoebe, 'Die Bedeutung des Worted ḥäsäd im AT', *VT* 2 (1952), 244–54; A. Jepsen, 'Gnade und Barmherzigkeit im AT', *KD* 7 (1961), 261–71; E. Würthwein, 'Gnade im AT und Judentum', *RGG* II³, 1632ff.

Johannes Schildenberger

B. '*Kharis*' *in the Greek-speaking world.* 1. In the Greek-speaking world, *kharis* (grace) was a commonly used word, and one with very many shades of meaning. On the one hand, it was used to denote certain aesthetic qualities and had the meaning of charm, loveliness, or graciousness; in the sphere of personal relationships, on the other hand, it was used in the sense of favour, goodwill, beneficence, gift, thanks and gratitude. In the language of hellenistic Emperor-worship it expressed condescension on the part of the ruler. At a lower level, in the spells and charms of the religion of the people, it implied secret power. Aristotle defines the word according to the sense in which it was used in the New Testament, that is to say, something which was bestowed, not as wages or as a reward, but as a freely offered gift, without any implication of debt (see *Ars Rhet.*, lib. B, cap. 7, 1385a).

2. In the writings of Philo, the word *kharis* has a decidedly theological significance. The original divine powers or moving forces are designated by Philo as the *kharistikē dunamis* (lit. = gracious power) and the *kolastikē kharis* (lit. = chastising power) (*Quis rerum div.* 34, 166). Not-being attains to being by means of the *kharites* (graces: *De migr. Abr.* 32, 183), and it is only by virtue of *kharis* that it is possible 'to leave the kingdom of mortals or to remain immortal' (*De ebrietate* 36, 145–6).

3. LXX translates the Hebrew *ḥēn* fairly adequately by *kharis*, but does not use it in the strictly religious sense. The Hebrew *ḥesed* better conveys the idea of grace in the New Testament sense, though this is only translated twice in LXX by *kharis* (Esther 2:9, 17). (See ↗ Grace in the Old Testament.)

C. *In the New Testament.* In the New Testament *kharis* still bears distinct traces of the original meaning with which it was used in secular Greek literature—Luke employs it quite frequently in the current sense—but in general it is certainly not possible to claim that the New Testament has preserved the word according to its original linguistic usage. Although a number of overtones, traceable to its original secular usage, are certainly present in the theological concept of *kharis* in the New Testament, its application to man's salvation gives the word a unique quality which has no etymological derivation. An entirely new meaning is added to *kharis* by its use in a soteriological sense.

The unique position which this word occupies in the New Testament and the supreme importance of the concept of *kharis* in the theology of the New Testament is due above all to Paul. It is, in fact, a Pauline concept. The word occurs most frequently in his writings and in those texts which were written under his influence (Luke and the Petrine letters).

1. *God's will to save.* The translation of *kharis* as 'favour' or 'goodwill' (*favor, benevolentia*) certainly has its merits, though grace does not mean the divine goodwill which God, as creator, bestows upon all his creatures. In the New Testament, the word grace has a definitely soteriological connotation. With the exception of a few passages, grace always refers to the redemption. 'According to his grace'—a phrase which occurs frequently in Paul—implies the absolute supremacy of God in the work of redemption. We are saved according to his free will and by his free choice. In theological controversy with the Jews, grace goes beyond the meaning of the origin of the

redemption, or God's will and decision, to save man, and takes on the meaning of a principle which permeates the whole history of man's salvation. It is not used to imply that a display of leniency on the part of the judge will make up for any deficiency in divine justice in the judgement of man. (The phrase 'to show mercy rather than justice' is not to be found.) It means rather that justification according to works is cancelled out by a spontaneous act of will on the part of God, in other words, that the law is invalidated by divine grace. It is 'according to grace' that we have been called before the origin of the world (2 Tim 1:9) and that the promise was made (Rom 4:16). It is 'according to the riches of his grace' that we have redemption (Eph 1:7) and 'according to the election of grace' that there was, at the time of Paul, a remnant of Jews who were saved (Rom 11:5).

2. *God's decision to save and the fact of salvation.* God's will to save did not, however, remain an abstract entity. His decision was taken once and for all time in Christ (see 2 Tim 1:9). It is possible to state that all references to grace are ultimately references to Christ. *Kharis* is thus *hē kharis hē en Khristō(i) Iēsou* ('the grace that is in Christ Jesus': 2 Tim 2:1) and *kharis hē tou henos anthrōpou Iēsou Khristou* ('the grace of that one man Jesus Christ: Rom 5:15). Grace came by Christ (Jn 1:17). The passion appointed for Christ and the glory which was to follow this passion are the grace of which the prophets spoke (1 Pet 1:10–11). The work of redemption itself is sometimes referred to as grace (2 Cor 8:9). In Gal 2:21, grace and Christ's sacrificial death are understood as interchangeable terms.

3. *The gift of salvation.* The grace which was revealed in Christ is in no sense a historically isolated manifestation of God's attitude towards salvation. On the contrary, this grace brings the christian into communion with God. The benedictions at the beginning and the end of most of the epistles must be considered with this in mind. God has bestowed his beloved Son upon us with his grace (Eph 1:6). The christian 'stands' in this grace (Rom 5:2; 1 Pet 5:12) and must continue in it (Acts 13:43).

This communion which the christian shares with God is certainly not an abstract or intellectual relationship. It is a soteriological gift. The word *kharis* has the unique quality of being able to stand both for gift and for mental attitude, but whereas these are two separate entities at the human level, they are, in God's eyes, identical. Divine grace is not simply effective in bringing about man's salvation by means of the redemption through Christ's death on the cross—it is at the same time salvation itself and causes a new reality to come into existence. Grace and ↗justice are often found together in the epistles and are clearly complementary terms. To be made 'void of Christ', that is, to be separated from him, means that the Christian is outside of grace (Gal 5:4). The 'abundance of grace' and the 'free gift of righteousness' (Rom 5:17) are two aspects of the same reality seen, in the case of the first, from the point of view of the giver, and in the case of the second, from the point of view of the recipient. Grace 'reigns' now (Rom

5:21), having broken the power of sin (Rom 6:14). We are instructed by grace (Tit 2:11f) and if we are lacking in grace, evil may grow and flourish in us (Heb 12:15). We should feed our hearts with grace (Heb 13:9) and strengthen ourselves with it (2 Tim 2:1). Grace is also the origin of the various gifts of the Spirit which are given to every christian (Rom 12:6; 1 Cor 1:4–7). It is in fact impossible to grasp the full meaning of grace so long as it is regarded simply as an intention to save upon which man can confidently rely; it is rather *the* sustaining power in the life of the Christian, as will be brought out more clearly in what follows.

4. *The power of grace.* Grace is very closely associated with the idea of 'power' and that of the 'apostolate'. To think of the recipient of grace as being simply brought into intimate contact with God, as being in communion with him in a purely static way, is to underestimate the vital importance of grace in the christian life. Grace is an active agent, and as such is not simply effective in the interior life of the christian as a power which overcomes the sins of the recipient; it goes further than this and has a powerful external effect. We learn that Stephen was 'full of grace and power'—the power of the grace that was in him enabled him to lead a most effective christian life among the people (Acts 6:8). Barnabas rejoiced to see the effects of divine grace—the conversion of a great number of gentiles (Acts 11:23). This dynamic aspect of grace is especially noticeable in Paul's references to himself. When he asked God to take away the cause of his temptation, he received the answer: 'My grace is sufficient for you', and further, 'for my power is made perfect in weakness' (2 Cor 12:9). This divine strength which was given to Paul was not without fruit (1 Cor 15:10)—its outcome was his apostolate among the gentiles. He was made a minister of the gospel 'according to the gift of God's grace which was given' him (Eph 3:7). Also 'according to the commission of God given' to him he was the wise architect who laid the foundations (1 Cor 3:10). It should be noted in this context that *sophia* (wisdom) and *kharis* are closely related concepts (see also, for example, 2 Cor 1:12; 2 Pet 3:18). But grace is not a gift or endowment, which can be separated from the giver—it is most important not to lose sight of the fact that grace means essentially that God is at work. In the case of the free gifts of the Spirit (see ↗ Charisma), we read that 'all these are inspired by one and the same Spirit' (1 Cor 12:11). There is, in fact, no such thing as a power which is separate from God. Paul says, in Gal 2:8f: *ho gar energēsas Petrō(i) eis apostolēn tēs peritomēs energēsen kai eis ta ethnē* ('for he who worked through Peter for the mission to the circumcised worked through me also for the gentiles'), and continues thus: *kai gnontes tēn kharin tēn dotheisan moi . . . dexias edōkan emoi . . . koinōnias* ('and when they perceived the grace that was given to me . . . [they] gave to me . . . the right hand of fellowship'). What is meant by 'they perceived the grace that was given' to him is that they recognised that the one who had been at work in Peter was also at work in Paul. *Grace thus is a name for the activity of God with and through men, for the purpose of salvation.*

We may conclude this very brief examination of the concept of grace in the New Testament by summarising it as follows: grace is the soteriological activity of God, decreed from eternity, which is made manifest to man and effective in his salvation in Christ's act of redemption and which continues and perfects the work of redemption in us and in the world. The New Testament does not acknowledge two separate concepts of grace—that of a divine gift and that of a disposition on the part of God, though it does happen that at times the one aspect of grace and at other times the other emerges more clearly. They are, however, integrally part of each other—God's benevolence and goodwill towards man is a gift, and whenever God gives, he gives himself. Grace includes the redeeming God and redeemed man. In connection with the subject of grace, see also ↗ justification, ↗ goodness, ↗ love.

Bibliography: P. Bonnetain, *DB(S)* III, 701–1319; O. Loew, *Kharis*, Marburg 1908 (this work is concerned only with an examination of the word in its secular Greek sense); J. Moffat, *Grace in the New Testament*, London 1931; J. Morson, *The Gift of God*, Cork 1952; A. Pujol, 'De salutatione Apostolica "Gratia vobis et Pax"', *VD* 12 (1932), 38–40, and 76–82; H. Rondet, *Gratia Christi*, Paris 1948; T. Torrance, *The Doctrine of Grace in the Apostolic Fathers*, London 1948; R. Vömel, *Der Begriff der Gnade im NT*, Leipzig 1913; G. P. Wetter, *Charis*, Leipzig 1913; R. Winkler, 'Die Gnade im Neuen Testament', *ZST* 10 (1933), 642–80; J. Wobbe, *Der Charisgedanke bei Paulus*, Münster 1932.

Gerhard Trenkler

Hardness of heart

1. *The concept.* Hardness of heart can be defined as 'persistent refusal when faced with the divine call' (see Hesse, 6). The subject can be either an individual or the people of Israel. God's call can take the form of either an invitation or a demand.

2. *Hardness of heart in the New Testament.* In the New Testament hardness of heart refers particularly to the persistent refusal when faced with the divine reality which has appeared on earth in the person of Jesus Christ. The New Testament is not, however, familiar with a relevant term which is immediately recognisable. It uses rather metaphorical expressions such as the verbs *pōroun* (to harden), *sklērunein*, which has roughly the same meaning, and *pakhunein* (to 'make fat'); the nouns *pērōsis* (hardening) and *sklērotēs* (hardness, stubbornness); and their derivatives *sklērokardia* (hardness of heart) and *sklērotrakhēlos* (obstinate). The centre of all this is the *kardia* (heart) regarded as the source of the moral and religious life of a person. Hence unbelief can occur as parallel with hardness of heart (Mt 16:14). We also read, however, of eyes and ears being hardened (or blinded), that is, disturbed in their function of perceiving and recognising. The recognition in question here is not just an act of the intellect but an obedient and thankful acceptance of the activity of God and his demands upon us. In every case hardness of heart is presented as a condition which has become so far advanced through long duration that only God can take it away.

The disciples are censured for this characteristic of *sklērokardia* in Mt 16:14 while Mk 6:4–6 = Mt 19:8 attributes it to the people of Israel and traces it back to the time of Moses. In

Acts 7:51 Stephen characterises Israel and its leaders right back to the time of the prophets as *sklērotrakhēloi* in parallelism with *aperitmētoi tē(i) kardia(i)* (uncircumcised in heart). Paul sees *sklērotēs*, used in parallelism with *ametanoētos kardia* (impenitent heart, Rom 2:5), as in general a recognisable characteristic of human existence, as can be seen from v 9. Mk 3:5 uses *pōrōsis tēs kardias* (hardness of heart) as characteristic of the attitude of those in the synagogue confronted with a healing on the sabbath carried out by Jesus, while Paul in Rom 11:25 uses the same expression for the relation of Israel to Jesus, and finally, in Eph 4:18, for the obtuseness of the heathens in their relations with God. With regard to the verbs, *sklērunō* is used in Heb 3:8, 13, 15; 4:7 in a quotation from Ps 95:7–11; in Acts 19:9 with reference to the Jews of Ephesus and in Rom 9:18 as a reminiscence of its use in the story of the Exodus. This is particularly significant since Paul here wishes to testify to the sovereignty of God which stands out with special clarity in the Exodus, the God who has mercy upon whomever he wills and hardens the heart of whomever he wills.

Pōroun is used in Mk 6:52 of the disciples (passive participle) as in Mk 8:17. Rom 11:7f takes us back to the Old Testament (Deut 29:4; Is 29:10) as well as to 2 Cor 3:14 and Acts 28:27 (*pakhunō*). Is 6:9f is explicitly quoted in this last text. This quotation takes on a very particular significance in the mouth of Jesus—see Mt 13:15 (see Mk 4:12; Lk 8:10). Since the quotation in the Marcan version corresponds to the form it has in the Palestinian Targum we certainly have here an actual saying of Jesus which goes straight back to Is 6:9ff. According to J. Jeremias (*The Parables of Jesus*, London 1954, 11ff) it did not originally belong to the context of the question about the reason for speaking in parables but was meant to provide an explanation of why Jesus gave esoteric teaching to his disciples which had to be withheld from those who, through hardness of heart, refused his message. In this respect, *mēpote* presents a problem since it can mean not only 'lest' (I should heal them) but also 'so that' (I might heal them). Jeremias suggests translating 'so that' in Mark, as corresponding to *dilema* in the targum, and, on the other hand, 'lest' in Matthew as corresponding to *pen* in the Massoretic text. This would be in agreement with the fact that the use of the imperative in Matthew gives his version a more peremptory form than Mark. There would, therefore, according to this explanation, be quite a different point of view as regards the real nature of the hardness of hearts referred to in the Isaian text as interpreted on the one hand as a hardening brought about positively by God (in Matthew) and on the other as brought about by man himself for which he alone is responsible (in Mark) and after which he can still do penance, though indeed this might be considered an improbable eventuality. Both viewpoints can be found in the Old Testament. In Lk 8:10 and Jn 12:40 God seems to be clearly considered as the original agent of this hardening of hearts.

J. Gnilka, however (*Die Verstockung Israels*), comes to quite different conclusions. He would prefer also to translate the *mēpote* of Mk 4:12 as 'lest' (cf the *dilema* of the targum). Therefore, according to Mark's point of view, Jesus would be speaking to the people in parables *so that* their hearts might be hardened, and according to Matthew, *since* they were already hardened. Therefore the point of view represented by Jeremias would be completely reversed. According to Gnilka, the Lukan version expresses in the strongest possible form the idea of predestination. In Acts 28:26ff Luke uses the Isaian quotation in order to provide a justification for the changeover to the mission of the gentiles. The connection of the logion in Mark 4:11 with the parable of the sower, Gnilka continues, is not original but comes from a different synoptic source; but he takes it to be an authentic saying of Jesus the original form of which is best preserved in Mark despite later editing and which in the Markan setting shows clear evidence of its antiquity. The connection with the Isaian context also goes back to Jesus, for he sees this text fulfilled in the attitude of the people in his regard and reads it as an expression of the will of God. He does not seek to mitigate this divine decision to punish, as is the case with the form adapted in the targum, but sees in it a pinpoint of light in the surrounding darkness, namely, that the 'holy Remnant', now constituted by the community of his disciples, would become the nucleus of a new People of God.

3. *Hardness of heart in the Old Testament.* The fact that the New Testament texts which refer to the hardening of hearts are found, in the great majority of cases, connected with Old Testament quotations or allusions, shows clearly that the New Testament seizes on Old Testament lines of thought—whether it is a question of the sayings of Jesus or a text in Paul or an occurrence elsewhere. The idea of the hardening of hearts in the Old Testament is closely allied with the theology of the covenant, and only against this background does it become fully intelligible.

We can state at once that the terms used in the New Testament are taken from the Old since the verbs, adjectives and nouns used there (to harden, hardening, to be stubborn, stubbornness, 'to make fat') go back to the literary usage of LXX. What is common to them all, as also to the Hebrew words from which they derive, is a strong graphic character capable of representing and objectivising an inner event of the human heart. This, together with the ability of the Hebrew to express a wide range of shades of meaning, really proves to be necessary since the Old Testament shows concern to present the idea according to its different aspects, while the New Testament takes over the expressions of the Old.

As regards verbs, the Old Testament uses: *kābēd* in Qal occurring only in Exodus; in Hiphil in Exodus, Isaiah, and Zecharias; and in Piel in 1 Samuel; *ḥāsaq* in Qal only in Exodus; in Piel in Exodus and Joshua; and in Hiphil in Jeremiah 5:3; *qāšâh* occurs only twice without an object, but elsewhere with *lēb* (heart), *rûaḥ* (breath, spirit), *pānîm* (face), *ᶜorep* (neck), and once with *derek* (way). In Hiphil it occurs twice, and the relative adjective *qāšeh* six times, with *ᶜorep*. *šāᶜaᶜ* (cry out) occurs only seldom —twice in Isaiah, in Qal and Hithpalpel; *šāman* (make fat)—once in Hiphil, with *lēb* (Is 6:10); *ʾāmats* (strengthen) thirty-three times with *lēbāb* (heart) or *lēb*; and, finally, *qāšâḥ* (harden) in Is 63:17. The idea of hardness, stubbornness, and heaviness therefore predominates. As one can see from the frequent connection with *leb*, the Old Testament has already laid down the essential lines for the New. The heart, seat of the moral and religious life, is hardened, made obdurate, made 'fat', namely, insensitive and unwilling to act. Side by side with this usage, we also find as objects of this process, the eyes, ears, face, forehead and neck. The end-result of the hardening can be a 'stiff-necked people', an uncircumcised (*ᶜārēl*) heart, a heart of stone (Ezek 11:19; 36:26), dullness of heart (*mᵉginnath lēb*, Lam 3:65) or obstinacy of heart (*šerirûth lēb*), which latter is frequent in Jeremiah and Deuteronomy.

This usage continues in post-biblical terminology and occurs frequently in 1 QS and 1 QH. It is striking how often the Old Testament causative usage (Hiphil of *kābēd* and Piel of *ḥāzaq*) occurs, expressing the idea that this condition of hardness is the result of an action freely willed. In the J strata of the Pentateuch and in Jeremiah, Ezekiel, and Deutero-Isaiah the subject is often a human agent or Israel itself. In a particular case, this subject refuses to pay attention to the word of God and hardens his (its) heart. While on the one hand Deutero-Isaiah and as far as can be seen also Jeremiah and Deuteronomy contemplate the possibility that a man can remove this condition of a hardened heart and turn to God again, it would appear on the other hand that in Ezekiel and the J strata of the Pentateuch the hardening is so deeply implanted and so far progressed that the one concerned is irretrievably lost, for he has passed from a personal decision to a permanent state, a habit which no conversion can get rid of and which in fact excludes the idea of conversion. It is quite different in Isaiah, Trito-Isaiah, and the P strata of the Pentateuch. In this last God hardens the heart of the Pharaoh in order to place him in a state of guilt and therefore to punish him, just as is the case in Joshua 11:17 with the kings of Canaan. In Isaiah this applies to Israel as a whole and in Trito-Isaiah to the sum total of the godless within Israel. We should not suppose that it is a question here of demonic characteristics in the nature of Yahweh; rather what is implied in these hard expressions which savour of predestination is that, in the last resort, no other will has any force except the will of God, that God's designs are to be fulfilled when the kingdom of God, the final end of all history, becomes a reality. The God whom the prophets encounter is the God whose will is omnipotent, while the priestly tradition knows a God who unfolds his plan for the world in spite of the opposition of the enemies of Israel and the godless. This priestly tradition is continued in the thinking of the Qumran community, characterised as it is by predestination and dualism (1 QS, 1 QH).

As for the object of the hardening of hearts, it is in the first place Israel on which God has a special claim as a result of the Covenant. Israel repudiates this claim and consequently its heart is hardened by God and it becomes liable to be punished by him. It becomes ripe for judgement, only beyond this judgement it is possible for it once more to receive the covenant-gift of salvation. This view is expressed most clearly in Is 6:9ff where the prophet receives the mission from God to harden the heart of the people through his announcing the judgement merited by the continual repudiation of the divine claim upon her. This fate can, however, also overtake the individual Israelite insofar as he refuses God's call expressed in the law and the preaching of the prophets. According to Jeremiah, Deuteronomy, and Deutero-Isaiah, hardening of the heart is simply the result of a wrong decision which is at the same time sinful in itself and brings other sins in its wake. If this chain of sin is not broken in time through conversion to God (*šûb*) it will become a vicious circle from which there is no escape. In this case, judgement is not left over to an eschatological event even if represented as imminent, but comes in the course of historical events, so that there is still at times room for the saving action of God. Isaiah seems to represent the hardening itself as judgement, while in Trito-Isaiah it is a sign of the divine anger which the evildoer brings upon himself. The emphasis placed on the guilt of the individual confronted with the divine will permits of no mitigation of the teaching on predestination and therefore of no exoneration of the evildoer.

When the Old Testament mentions foreigners (non-Israelites) as the objects of this process of hardening of the heart, they are defeated by God after being presented with a concrete demand on the part of God—as, for example, the Pharaoh who must allow the people of Israel to leave—a demand which they refuse to recognise and so, through their hearts being hardened, are led on to judgement. They must encounter this judgement because they stand in the way of the saving action of God on behalf of his people and so obstruct the coming of the Kingdom of God. In this respect the New Testament goes even further. In his epistle to the Romans, Paul places the pagans also under the obligation of knowing God in which respect he refers to the possibility of arriving at a knowledge of God starting from created things.

Throughout the different statements on the hardening of hearts in the Old and the New Testaments there is present a certain strange and almost unnatural element which can be detected very strongly in Is 6:9ff. No wonder, then, that this text has had such considerable influence on both Old and New Testaments. This element alluded to is, however, softened somewhat by the references to the fidelity of God in keeping his promise so that even the most severe expressions of the prophets undergo a certain correction of perspective through this hope that God himself will resolve the vicious circle and that, on the other side of judgement, the redeemed 'holy remnant' will be able to experience the grace of God. By means of this grace God will change the dispositions of the heart and lead it to such a joyful and voluntary obedience that any hardness of heart will be unknown in this new world. Sometimes however, judgement and hope stand in unreconcilable opposition—a sign that God is not rationally comprehensible and free of mystery for us, that he is not at our disposal but at all times his will remains sovereign.

Bibliography: J. Jeremias, *The Parables of Jesus*, London 1954; K. L. Schmidt, 'Die Verstockung der Menschen durch Gott', *TZ* I (1945), 1ff; F. Hesse, *Das Verstockungsproblem im AT* (*BZAW* 74), Berlin 1955; J. Gnilka, *Die Verstockung Israels*, Munich 1961; Eichrodt II/III[4] (Index); Hesse and Gnilka give further bibliography.

Georg Molin

Harvest

A. *In the literal sense*. 1. Every harvest comes from God who gave vitality to the seed and fruitfulness to the earth (Gen 1:11), who gave the fruits of the earth to man, for his sustenance (Gen 1:29; 9:3) and solemnly guaranteed that the cycle of seed-time and harvest would not cease (Gen 8:22; Jer 5:24). God also gives a fruitful land to his people, as their inheritance (Ex 3:8; Num 13:17–27, etc). To those whom he loves, he gives to reap a hundredfold (Gen 26:12; Ps 128:2), but to those who disobey him and are hostile, he sends bad harvests and famine (2 Sam 21:1; 1 Kings 17:1; 2 Kings 8:1; Mic 6:15; Amos 4:7; Jer 5:17; 12:10–13; Joel 1, etc). The pronouncement of a blessing or a curse upon the harvest was an important form of parenesis in the Old Testament (Deut 28; Lev 26, etc). One of the most frequently occurring elements constituting the hope of Israel was an abundant yield in the harvest (Mic 4:4; Zech 3:10; see also 1 Kings 42:5). This element is also to be found in the prophetic and apocalyptic promises (see below). In the New Testament period too, there are references to God's blessing on (Mt 6:26) and his care for the seed (Mk 4:27f; 1 Cor 15:36ff) and the fruit of the earth (Jas 5:18).

2. The harvest was always an occasion for great joy (Is 9:3; Ps 4:7; 126:5; Hos 9:1), for charitable actions (Lev 19:9f; 23:22; Deut 24:19–21; see also Deut 25:4) and also to praise God, especially at the great harvest feasts of the year—Easter, Whitsun and the Feast of the Tabernacles (Ex 23:16–19; 34:22; Lev 23:9–21). These feasts were marked by an offering of the first fruits, the first loaves (Num 15:17–21; Deut 26:1–11) and various other gifts. The seventh year, when the land was to lie fallow, was designated as a sabbatical year in honour of Yahweh (Lev 25:2–5). There are frequent references in later Jewish writings and in the New Testament to such festivals of the harvest accompanied by the payment of honour to God and charitable works, and to such offerings of the first fruits and of tithes.

B. *In the figurative sense*. 1. The image of the harvest is used in a proverbial saying to denote literary activity (Sir 33:16f) and man's death (Job 5:26). The seed and the harvest, sowing and reaping, are images which occur frequently in many different proverbial sayings, especially of course in the sapiential literature (Prov 6:8; 10:5; 22:8; Job 4:8; Sir 7:3) and in the prophets (Hos 8:7; 10:12f). The same image is used by Philo to illustrate his ethic of immanence (*Conf. Ling.* 152); it can be used also in strictly legalistic teaching (4 Esdras 2:28–39; 7:17–19), as a figure of eschatological promise (Midrash on the Song of Songs 8:14), and finally in the New Testament message. Paul also applies the image of the harvest to the spiritual seed of the preaching of the gospel, from which he expects to receive the fruit, for his own sustenance (1 Cor 9:7–11; Phil 4:17) and for Jerusalem (Rom 15:28; 2 Cor 9:6). He uses the image too in his teaching on the resurrection (1 Cor 15:35–58) and in terse, aphoristic form in the phrase: 'Whatever a man sows, that he will also reap' (Gal 6:7). Closely related to the image of the seed and the harvest, sowing, and reaping, is that of the tree and its fruit (SB 1, 466f, 638f; Mt 7:16–20; 12:33). The bible makes frequent use of such proverbial utterances to stress a law which is of great importance in the doctrine of retribution, namely that man's actions are closely connected with his salvation, both in time and in eternity.

2. *God's judgement* is often described in the bible by the image of the harvest. This takes three forms:

The chastisement of God. There are biblical references to the harvest as God's judgement on the enemies of the people (Is 24:13; Jer 51:33), on his people themselves in times of national calamities (Hos 13:3; Amos 8:2; Is 17:5f; Jer 6:9) and at the final, eschatological judgement (Is 63:1–6; Joel 3:13). John the Baptist refers to the one who is to come as him who will gather in the harvest (Mt 3:12). John, in the Book of Revelation, speaks of the harvest of the earth as the judgement on the world. Christ's allegorical interpretation of the parable of the cockle is also distinctly apocalyptic in manner (Mt 13:37–43).

The *beginning of the time of salvation.* The image of the harvest, based on the pattern of the ancient sayings on the subject of abundant harvests, is found in the promises occurring in contexts probably dating from after the Exile (Amos 9:13–15; Mic 4:4). The day of God's judgement on the enemies of his people will be one of great joy for Israel (Joel 2:19–24; Is 27:12f). On that day the eternal harvest will begin (Joel 3:18), and Israel will be comparable to a luxuriant plantation (Is 60:21; 61:3; cf 5:1–7). This image of the rich eschatological harvest was developed in great detail by the Jews (P. Volz, *Die Eschatologie der jüdischen Gemeinde*, Tübingen 1934, 387f), and the idea of the eschatological community as God's plantation plays a very important part in rabbinical teaching (SB 1, 666; see also 4 Esdras 6:41), in the literature of Qumran (1 QS 8, 5:12f; 11:8; see also 1 QH 6:25; 8:6) and in the New Testament (Mt 15:13; 1 Cor 3:6f; Heb 12:15; Rev 22:2).

The *individual retribution imposed by God.* The Old Testament seldom refers to the retribution which God demands from man, according to his 'fruit' (see Sir 27:6), but there is frequent mention of it in later judaism (SB 1, 466f, 638f). At the last judgement God will 'harvest' the deeds of every man (Volz, 305f)—both John the Baptist (Mt 3:8–10) and Jesus (Mt 7:16–20) also refer to this harvest. The same idea is further developed in the missionary preaching of the New Testament, often in the form of lists of virtues and vices, accompanied by pointed references to God's judgement (Gal 5:19–23, etc). The same idea is also made available to the apostles in the missionary field (see Mk 4:14–20).

3. Two further important aspects of the image of the harvest are to be found in the New Testament:

The *kingdom of God* is a harvest. The parables of Jesus which speak in terms of contrasting situations do not emphasise the phase of development and ripening (this is alien to the biblical mode of thought), but rather draw a contrast between the beginning and the end. Thus, despite everything that happened to prevent it, the sower's harvest is plentiful (the parable of the sower: Mk 4:3–8); despite the smallness of the grain of mustard seed, the significance of the fully grown tree is world-wide (the parable of the mustard seed: Mk 4:30–32) and without any human assistance, the seed grows of its own accord and the harvest is suddenly there (the parable of the seed growing secretly: Mk 4:26–9). Finally, it is necessary for man to wait patiently for the day which God appoints for the harvest (the parable of the good seed and the cockle: Mt 13:24–30). But, in Jesus' opinion, it is already time for the harvest and for this reason he tells his disciples to pray for labourers to be sent to reap this great harvest of the kingdom of God (Mt 9:37f). Those who are to proclaim the gospel of Christ are not the sowers of the seed, but the reapers (Jn 4:35–8) and their mission is the beginning of the eschatological harvest (Rom 1:13). It is this which gives the 'harvest' its judicial and decisive aspect, as part of the final fulfilment.

The second important aspect of the harvest image in the New Testament is that *Jesus is both the sower and the seed.* This emerges from the allegorical interpretations which Jesus provides for the parables of the sower (Mk 4:14–20) and of the cockle in the field (Mt 13:37–43). What we have here is Jesus himself, his word and the christian message. Paul applies the image to the christian message (1 Cor 3:6–9; Col 1:5f)—he who sows in the Lord and in the Spirit reaps everlasting life (Rom 6:21f; 7:4f; Gal 6:8). In the same way, John stresses the importance of communion with Christ in order to yield fruit (Jn 15:1–8). Most important of all in this context is the word of Jesus, when he compares himself to a grain of wheat (Jn 12:24f). By its death, this seed yields a rich harvest to the world.

Bibliography: F. Hauck, *TDNT* III, 132f and 614f; H. Traub, *BTHW* 120; J. P. Ramseyer, Allmen 182; H. Sahlin, 'Die Früchte der Umkehr', *Studia Theologica* I (1947, Lund 1948), 54–68. See also G. Dalman, *Arbeit und Sitte in Palästina* III; F. Nötscher, *Altertumskunde* 173–82.

Wilhelm Pesch

Hatred

One of the most striking manifestations of the inner division within man is mutual antipathy between individuals. Gen 4:2–8 represents hatred, which appears with the first descendants of Adam and Eve, as one of the direct consequences of the fall. Though this depends on the point of view of the Yahwist author in his survey of primitive history it corresponds to an understanding of human nature which is found throughout the bible. In the Old Testament hatred is above all a datum of experience in both public and private life. The earliest writings simply state it as a fact of experience without attempting to explain it by going more deeply into it.

In order to designate this whole complex process which goes on in the will and the feelings, biblical Hebrew disposes only of the one word *šānēʾ* which LXX translates almost invariably by *misein*. This must be explained not only by the fact that Hebrew has a limited vocabulary for expressing concepts but also by the unique characteristic of Hebrew in expressing reality in antithetical terms. In general the Semite prefers to express a relationship of sympathy or antipathy in polarized terms rather than distinguish with psychological nicety between different spiritual states. Thus the language of the Old Testament prefers to speak directly of love or hatred rather than of a preference for or antipathy towards a certain person or thing; hence the frequency with which we come across polarized concepts in relation to this theme. In divorce proceedings, for example, the texts refer to the man 'hating' the woman but this simply means that they failed to get along together (see Deut 21:15; 22:13–16 with Gen 29:33 where the 'hatred' of Jacob merely signifies that he was less pleased with her than previously).

This, however, does not at all imply that the existence of real hate testified to in the Old Testament is to be questioned; it merely implies that caution is in order in explaining the terms used. Hatred in the Old Testament takes in every degree of intensity of bad will from lack of love (Ex 20:5; Deut 7:10) or omission of friendly relations through occasional hostilities and speaking in hostile terms (Gen 26:27; Judg 11:7; 2 Sam 5:8; 13:22; 22:18, 41; 1 Kings 22:8) to a permanently hostile state which can end in murder (Gen 4:2–8; 27:41; 2 Sam 13:22, 28–9). The decisive factor in deciding punishment for a murderer is whether the killing resulted from hatred (Deut 19:4, 6, 11; Josh 20:5). Only in this case was the death penalty inflicted on the guilty party even when he had fled to a city of refuge (Deut 19:11ff).

Although hatred is essentially a human characteristic Yahweh is, by analogy, represented as harbouring feelings of hatred which find expression in opposition to the sinful deeds of men. This divine antipathy applies in the first case to any kind of idolatry (Deut 12:31; 16:22; Ps 31:6; Jer 44:4), to false oaths (Zech 8:17) and to a great number of moral lapses (Ps 5:5ff; 11:5; Prov 8:13; Sir 10:7; 27:24 etc). This way of speaking is, of course, metaphorical; it would be quite impossible in view of the loving assent of Yahweh to his creation to transfer to him human hatred in the real sense of the term (Wis 11:24). What is expressed in speaking of God hating is the incommensurability between his holiness and any kind of unrighteousness in which man remains obdurate. On account of its infidelity even the chosen people can provoke Yahweh to hatred (Hos 9:15; Jer 12:8) until such time as it finds again the way of truth.

The true Israelite must not hate his fellow-men but must, on the contrary, show them brotherly love (Lev 19:17f). Although the basis of the so-called Law of Holiness is clearly formulated it has in the course of time been interpreted and put into practice in very different ways. In practice, the law of love was restricted to Israelites; those outside the covenant merited hatred insofar as they proved themselves to be the enemies of Yahweh or of his people (Num 10:35; Ps 83:2ff). Within the community evil-doers, those who persecuted the righteous and pious devotees of Yahweh (Ps 34:21; 35:19; 38:19f; 86:17), were to be regarded as hating God (Ex 20:5; Deut 5:9; 7:10 etc). The hatred of the godless against those closely united with God is found throughout the whole length of salvation history. It reaches its climax in the crucifixion of Christ for which hate was responsible even though it was through the cross that the eternal enmity of the Evil One was overcome.

In the Old Testament it is expressly forbidden to the pious Israelite to enter into league with the evil-doer or show him love (2 Chron 19:2); on the contrary, he must be hated as Yahweh hates him (Ps 26:4f; 101:3f; 139:21 etc). This is closely connected with the demand of unconditional self-giving to Yahweh encumbent on every Israelite. According to the anthropomorphic way of speaking common in the Old Testament, God is jealous for the love of his people. Understandably hatred has for its first object evil and wickedness but for Old Testament man no real distinction was made between hating evil and hating the evil-doer.

The idea of the ↗ covenant played a large part in emphasising the polarity between hatred and love. In connection with the feast of covenant-renewal formulae of cursing and blessing were developed which were applied respectively to the transgression and observance of the covenant stipulations. At any rate, by the inter-testamentary period we find stereotype liturgical formulae of curse and blessing as those, for example, in use in the Qumran community (1 QS 2:4–18; 1 QM 13:1–6). It we take these into account we will be better able to interpret the law of love: not only was the neighbour to be loved but the evil-doer was to be hated. As is well known, the Old Testament not only does not contain such a commandment but several expressions appear to contradict it (Ex 23:4; Prov 25:21). Yet the words attributed to Jesus in Matthew's gospel (5:43) and those found in the Manual of Discipline of the Qumran sectarians (1 QS 1:9f; 9:16, 21f; cf 4:17) prove that this was in fact the practice in Old Testament times.

The Zadokite community of Qumran thought of itself as the only true people of God; hence it became more and more imbued with a sense of the distinction between its members and those who did not form part of it. But whether all of these latter were to be hated without distinction is not so certain. The stipulation in 1 QS 1:10 clearly speaks in a restrictive way: the true member of the community must hate 'the sons of darkness each one according to the extent that he has incurred the vengeance of God'. The basic criterion is here the same as in the Old Testament: in their dealings with one another men must follow the example of God himself. At the same time, however, the obligation to hate is expressed in even more precise and stringent terms than is the case in the Old Testament. Judgement is passed on the 'spirit' of each member, that is, on the degree of perfection which he has attained, with reference not only to how he loves but how he hates (1 QS 9:15–16). Yet the devout member of the community postpones the wrath of God on those to be hated until 'the day of visitation' (1 QS 10:17–18). This obligation to hate expresses the radical demand made on the member to segregate himself from any kind of evil; an obligation made necessary by the imminence of the world-end. By keeping clear of unrighteousness (understood dualistically), expressed in terms of hatred, these sectarians hoped to make their contribution to the ultimate victory of God over the forces of evil.

It is quite another question, however, when we ask how this basic postulate of hating the enemy was worked out in the practical everyday living of Old Testament man and the member of the Qumran community. There was obviously the constant danger of identifying the enemy of God with one's personal enemies which could at least have the result of excluding these from the category of 'neighbour' to whom love was due. 'Who is my enemy?' was a question as obscure and ambiguous to Old Testament man as that other asked of the Lord: 'who is my neighbour?' (Lk 10:29).

Christ dissolved any possible misunderstanding by absolutely forbidding any kind of hatred. The Old Testament prohibition of hating one's brother (fellow-Israelite) was now applied universally and given a new meaning by being displaced by the command to love one's enemy (Mt 5:43–4; Lk 6:27f). The unconditional love of the Father is activated by acceptance of the neighbour and the putting aside of any kind of hostility towards him. By means of the saving activity of Christ those who had been re-created in him learned to overcome hate by love, even though the tension between these two opposing attitudes was not thereby removed. The authors of the most recent books of the Old Testament are already beginning to reflect on the roots of hatred and traced its cause to Satan, the old enemy of the human race (Wis 2:24, cf Jn 8:44). According to the apocalyptic writers the present age was subordinate to him, and the world which had fallen prey to hatred lay in his power. By keeping clear of hatred which had been overcome in principle by Christ (Tit 3:3f) the Christian hastened the coming of the future age. But at the same time he continued to live in the world where hatred is an ever-present reality. He should therefore not be surprised if the world hates (Mt 10:22; Jn 15:19; 17:14; 1 Jn 3:13) or persecutes him (Mt 5:10; Lk 6:22). On the contrary, he has to rejoice that it is given him to follow in the footsteps of the Master (Lk 6:22f; Mt 27:18; Jn 5:18; 7:7; 15:24; Eph 2:14, 16).

In the fourth gospel hatred is presented within the context of the author's 'theology' of light. As the essence of darkness (1 Jn 2:9, 11), hate reveals itself as to all intents and purposes a satanic force which is violently active in opposition to the fulfilment of God's saving design. In the opposition between love and hate we recognise the definitive distinction between the kingdom of light and the kingdom of darkness (1 Jn 2:9–11) and the appearance of a judgement within history (cf Jn 3:19). Hatred of the brethren is likened to murder (1 Jn 3:15; cf Mt 5:22) and excludes the one who hates from eternal life (see Jn 15:23–5).

In addition to this we should note that Old Testament usage also lies behind much of what we find on the subject of hatred in the New Testament.

The admonition of Jesus addressed to the disciples to hate their relatives (Mt 10:37; Lk 14:26) or even themselves (Lk 14:26) signifies a radical rupture of natural ties which could compromise their absolute dedication to the Saviour and his saving mission (see Jude 23 on the need to keep away from those who are fickle and inconstant). To the same way of speaking belong what Paul has to say in Rom 7:15 where hatred is to be understood as the opposite of the will to do good in man delivered up to the power of sin; also Lk 19:14 (see Rev 17:16) which refers to political malice. ↗ Vengeance. ↗ Love.

Bibliography: A. Carr, 'The Meaning of "Hatred" in the New Testament', *The Expositor* VI, 12 (1905), 153–60; J. Denney, 'The word "Hate" in Lk 14:26', *Expository Times* 20 (1909), 41f; W. Bleibtreu, *Paradoxe Aussprüche Jesu*, 1926, 15–35; O. Michel, *TDNT* IV, 683–94; Haag 649–51; M. Smith, 'Mt V, 43. Hate thine enemy', *Harv. Theol. Review* 45 (1952), 71–3; R. Schnackenburg, *Die Johannesbriefe*, Freiburg 1953, 174–6; H. Braun, *Spätjüdisch-häretischer und frühchristlicher Radikalismus* II, Tübingen 1957, 57–9 (esp. *n.* 1); C. Spicq, *Agapè* I, Paris 1958, 17–20; E. F. Sutcliffe, 'Hatred at Qumran', *Revue de Qumran* 2 (1959/60), 345–56; J. Brière, 'Hate', *DBT* 198–200; M. Weise, *Kultzeiten und kultischer Bundesschluss in der Ordensregel vom Toten Meer*, Leiden 1961; B. Renaud, *Je suis un Dieu jaloux*, Paris 1963; A. Dihle, *Die goldene Regel*, Göttingen 1962, 114–16.

F. L. R. Stachowiak

Head

In the literal sense of the word, head stands of course for the head of a living creature, and especially for the head of a human being. Jesus's head is also mentioned occasionally (Mt 8:20 and pars; Jn 19:30). As the head is the most important part of the body, it is customary to swear by one's head (Mt 5:36). Various movements of the head are used to express a person's thoughts, feelings, and reactions. An uplifted head expresses self-confidence and justifiable pride (Sir 11:1). It can also express haughtiness, arrogance, and boundless presumption (Ps 83:3; Job 20:6). On the other hand, it can also be the expression of justified hope and joy (Lk 21:28). The opposite movement—bowing of the head—may indicate either submission, humility, and reverence (Sir 4:7), or fear and timidity (Job 32:6 Vulg). Jesus bowed his head when he died (Jn 19:30). Shaking the head is a gesture of incomprehension, disdain, scorn or mockery (Job 16:4f; Ps 22:7; Lam 2:15; Mt 27:39). Covering the head is a sign of affliction, disappointment or shame (2 Sam 15:30; Esther 6:12; Jer 14:3f; Mic 3:7). Paul regarded it as a disgrace for a man to cover his head while praying or at public worship, whereas for a woman it was disgraceful to pray with uncovered head (1 Cor 11:4–7). The hairs of the head are all numbered (Mt 10:30) because God's providence is concerned even with such relatively unimportant things as this. Even their colour is determined by God (Mt 5:36). The head was shaved after the Nazaritic vow had been taken (Acts 21:23f). The Israelite was bound by the law to honour those whose hair had become grey with age by standing up (Lev 19:32). Finally, baskets, are carried on the head (Gen 40:16).

Certain symbolic acts are associated with the head. Dust or ashes are put on the head as a sign of affliction or grief (Josh 7:6; Lam 2:10). Hands are placed upon the head to bestow a blessing (Gen 48:14; Mk 10:16) or to transfer responsibility to another person (↗ laying on of Hands). In the consecration of priests or kings, the head is anointed with oil (Ex 29:7; 1 Sam 10:1). The expression 'to heap hot coals of fire upon the head of an enemy' by doing good to him (Prov 25:21f; Rom 12:20) undoubtedly means that good actions will result in causing the recipient to feel shame and humiliation.

The head is the noblest part of the human body and as such it frequently stands for the whole person and in particular for the individual as against a large number of people (see Ex 16:16). In this way, when people are numbered in the bible, they are counted by heads (see, for example, Num 1:18), that is to say, a count is made of individual persons. To raise up the head of a person means that this person is honoured (Gen 40:13) and the guardian of someone's head is the guardian of the whole person and of his life (1 Sam 28:2). A curse pronounced upon another person or upon other people, or the delegation of responsibility to another or to other persons is spoken of as being upon his head or upon their heads (2 Sam 1:16; Acts 18:6). But a person who wishes to take on himself a very heavy responsibility expresses this readiness by declaring that he is prepared that the blood of another be on his own head (Josh 2:19; cf Mt 27:25). In Ezek 17:19, however, God reserves for himself the right to take the appropriate action against the person who has failed him when he says: 'I will lay upon his head the oath he has despised and the covenant he has broken'.

The bible also contains references to the head of superterrestrial beings and to the head of God himself, since celestial beings and God are both described in human forms. In the Apocalypse, for example, the head and the hair of the Son of Man appear as snow-white wool (Rev 1:14). The Son of Man also has a golden crown on his head (14:14). The angel's head is adorned with a rainbow (10:1) and the twenty-four ancients also wear crowns of gold (4:4).

There are also frequent references to the heads of animals, as in their case, too, the head is the most important part of the body. The head of the serpent is to be crushed (Gen 3:15) and the head of the Paschal lamb is to be eaten (Ex 12:9). In the case of the 'dog's head' used as a term of abuse (2 Sam 3:8), it is clear that the head is, as with man, referred to as *pars pro toto*.

The word *head* is also frequently used in the *figurative sense*. The position of the head in relation to the rest of the human body results in an extension of meaning, in which the word is applied figuratively to denote, for example, a topographical or architectural feature which is elevated. In this sense, the Hebrew word head is used for the top of a mountain (Gen 8:5; Is 2:2) and elsewhere for a whole mountain range rising above a plain ('the head of the valley': Is 28:1, 4). In the same way, the Hebrew word for head is used to denote the top of a tree (Is 17:6) or the capital of a pillar (1 Kings 7:16). The highest stone forming the top of a building is also called its head (Zech 4:7) and the lintel of a gate is known as the head (Ps 24:7, 9). The word is also used figuratively in Hebrew for the upper end or top of an object such as Jacob's ladder (Gen 28:12), a sceptre (Esther 5:2) or an ear of corn (Job 24:24).

The meaning is further logically extended to denote what is qualitatively superior to everything else. The 'head' of balsam is the best and finest sort of this spice (Ezek 27:22) and the word for head is similarly used in Ex 30:23 and Song 4:14 to designate the best kinds of various spices. The greatest joy, superior to all other kinds of joy is the 'head', or summit of joy (Ps 137:6).

Since, in the case of animals, the head is the foremost part of the body, we have the extended meaning of 'head' as the first in time, the beginning. Thus we find the word *head* used to indicate the beginning of the night-watch (Judg 7:19), the first days of a month (Num 10:10; 28:11) or the first month of a year (Ex 12:2). It can also mean the beginning of a series of actions (1 Chron 16:7), the beginning of a road (Is 51:20; Ezek 16:25, 31) or the source of a river (Gen 2:10). The beginning of a paragraph or book is called its head (Ps 40:8 in LXX; Heb 10:7). It is also used for the capital in the sense of the first and main instalment of a payment due (Lev 6:5). The word is used also to convey the idea of primary or basic elements in nature (Prov 8:26).

The word is extended even further in meaning to include the idea of priority over others. Thus, the ruling classes of Israelite society are referred to as the 'head' of the people, in contrast to the 'tail'—the mass of the people which follows them and is subordinate to them (Is 9:14). This idea is, however, not restricted solely to Israel. The prophet Isaiah also calls Damascus the 'head' of the Syrian Empire (7:8). What is meant here is that Damascus is the leading city of Syria. According to Jer 31:7, a people which has gained ascendancy over other races is their 'head'.

The conception of priority, precedence or superiority conveyed by the word *head* and particularly the closely associated idea of gaining and retaining the ascendancy and hegemony over others led to the further meaning of authority, especially that of the head of a family, tribe and so on. Thus the family (Ex 6:14), the tribe (Num 30:1) and even the Galaadite army (Judg 11:8f) has its authoritative leader or head. In the same way, the Syrian king (Is 7:8) and the government of Juda and Israel (Hos 1:11) are called the 'head'. According to 1 Cor 11:3; Eph 5:23, the man is not only the head of the family, but also the head of his wife, that is, as head of the family, he has authority over his wife.

Finally, the New Testament also contains frequent references to *Christ as head.* Here, the various elements common to the figurative use of the word in the Bible come together to form a single, total image, though this image has a certain distinct colouring. As the Head of all things (Eph 1:22), Christ is not simply the uppermost part, the crown of all things, but at the same time the one who is in his very being and essence above the universe, since he himself created all things (Col 1:16) and is the source and origin of all being. As the creator of the universe, he is invested with supreme authority as its Lord right from the moment of his incarnation (Eph 1:20–22). As Head of the universe, the incarnate creator is also Head of every cosmic principality and power (Eph 1:21f; Col 2:10). For this reason the entire universe, including the demonic powers, is subject to the Son of Man since he is exalted to God's throne, that is, he shares in the sovereign supremacy of God's rule (Eph 1:20f). He fills all things—the entire universe which is at his feet (Eph 4:10). He is able to do this by allowing the universe to become entirely permeated by his sovereign power. The demonic powers which succeeded at least for a time in disturbing the unity of the universe, are no exceptions to Christ's sway (Eph 2:2; 6:11f). The original unity of the universe was, however, restored by the exalted God-man, who conferred upon it a new, single principle of government which re-established unity and brought about the subjugation of the demonic powers (Eph 1:21f). The entire universe was gathered up into a single whole under Christ as its Head (Eph 1:10). The first step was taken in establishing this universal unity when the Son of Man was exalted to the right hand of the Father so that he might share in the Father's sovereign rule (Eph 1:20). This single universal unity under one Head will not, however, be finally consummated until the end of time, when the demonic powers will also ultimately be subdued and at the same time completely eliminated (1 Cor 15:24f). This does not imply that these demonic powers are included in the atonement. They are unredeemable (see Rev 20:10). It is only through their submission to the exalted Christ (Eph 1:22) that they are made to realise that the original plan of creation, which was thrown into disorder by them, has ultimately been restored throughout the universe (Mussner).

In a very special sense Christ is also the *head of the church* as his Body (Eph 5:23; Col 1:18, 24). What is new in this aspect of Paul's christology, in contrast to the theology of his earlier epistles, is due principally to his controversy with those who taught false doctrine in Colossae. He realised that what the situation demanded was that he should lay particular emphasis on Christ's sovereignty. In the church too, Christ occupies a sovereign position, as the church is his body. He is also, in a very special sense, the head of the church. The head belongs essentially to the human body, it guides and directs the body and conditions its growth within the essential unity existing between the head and the body. In the same way and with similar functions, Christ as head belongs essentially to the church as his body. The church is subject in obedience to its head, since Christ is also its Lord, just as a wife is bound in obedience to her husband as her head (Eph 5:22–4). This subjection of the church to Christ as its head is complete, total, and unconditional (Eph 5:24). The entire human body is joined and held together by its various muscles and ligaments which proceed from and are controlled by the head—Christ is similarly, as head of his church, the unifying and central principle of the church (Eph 4:15ff). As its head, Christ is also the source from which the church gains sustenance and the means by which it continues to grow (Eph 4:16; Col 2:19). He nourishes and cherishes it (Eph 5:29). Christ is also the ultimate goal to which the church is moving, until all its members achieve full maturity and perfect manhood—'to the measure of the stature of the fullness of Christ' (Eph 4:13). It is in this way that the body of Christ is built up and this process of growth is accomplished in charity (Eph 4:16). It is through this building up of the church, as a result of its growth which proceeds from Christ, that the ultimate stage is reached when Christ becomes, in the fullest and most perfect sense, the head of the universe (Eph 1:10). The entire universe grows, in the church, with and through it, towards Christ as its head (Eph 1:23).

This does not, however, mean (even according to Col 1:20) that the cosmic principalities and powers are for this reason included in the church as the body of Christ. The church is the community of the redeemed (↗ church). The good angels have no need of redemption and the demonic powers cannot be redeemed (see Rev 20:10f). Christ is undeniably their head, but his headship of the demonic powers is totally different from his headship of the church. He is the head of the church in that it is his body, kept alive and nourished by him (Eph 5:29) and enabled to grow by him (Eph 4:13). Christ, the head, and the church, his body, form one single living organism. This does not apply to the demonic powers, which explains why they are never referred to in the New Testament as the body of Christ or as members of that body (cf Eph 1:22a with 22b). Christ is their head only by virtue of the fact that they are—either voluntarily or reluctantly—subject to him as the exalted Son of Man, raised up into heaven and sharing in the sovereign rule of the eternal Father (Eph 1:20–22; Col 2:10).

This truth, that Christ is the head of the church his body, marks the highest stage in the development of the concept of 'head' and, as such, has no parallel in any non-christian religion. Even the Qumran sect can offer nothing which is even remotely comparable to this.

Bibliography: *DB* v, 2100f; E. Kalt, *Bibl. Reallex.* I², 761f; *TDNT* III, 673–82; Haag 651f; W. Bauer, *Wörterbuch zum Neuen Testament*, 1958⁵, 850f; T. Schmidt, *Der Leib Christi*, Leipzig 1919, 166–91; P. Dhorme, 'L'emploi métaphorique des noms de parties du corps en hébreu et en akkadien', *RB* 29 (1920), 465–506; H. Schlier, *Christus und die Kirche im Epheserbrief*, Tübingen 1930; J. Gewiess, *Christus und das Heil nach dem Kolosserbrief*, Breslau 1932 (dissertation); E. Käsemann, *Leib und Leib Christi*, Tübingen 1933; P. Benoit, 'L'horizon paulinien de l'Epître aux Ephésiens', *RB* 46 (1937), 342–61 and 506–25; A. Wikenhauser, *Die Kirche als der mystische Leib Christi nach dem Apostel Paulus*, Münster 1940², 197–224; E. Percy, *Der Leib Christi ('sōma Khristou') in den paulinischen Homologumena und Antilogumena*, Lund 1942; J. Michl, 'Die "Versöhnung" (Col 1:20)', *TQ* 128 (1948), 442–62; B. N. Wambacq, '"*Per eum reconciliare . . . quae in caelis sunt*" (Col 1:20)', *RB* 55 (1948), 35–42; H. Schlier and V. Warnach, *Die Kirche im Epheserbrief*, Münster 1949; O. Cullmann, *Königsherrschaft Christi und Kirche im NT*, Zollikon-Zürich 1950; T. Soiron, *Die Kirche als der Leib Christi*, Düsseldorf 1951; J. Gewiess, 'Die Begriffe *plēroun* und *plērōma* im Kolosser- und Epheserbrief', *Vom Wort des Lebens* (Festschrift Max Meinertz), ed. N. Adler, Münster 1951, 128–41; J. M. Gonzalez Ruiz, 'Sentido soteriológico de "Kefalé" en la cristologia de S. Pablo', *Anthologia Annua*, Rome 1953, 185–225; S. Bedale, 'The Meaning of *kephalē* in the Pauline Epistles', *JTS* 5 (1954), 211–15; C. Maurer, 'Die Begründung der Herrschaft Christi über die Mächte nach Col 1:15–20', *Wort und Dienst* 4 (1955), 79–93; F. Mussner, *Christus, das All und die Kirche*, Trier 1955; J. A. T. Robinson, *The Body: A Study in Pauline Theology*, London 1952; P. Benoit, 'Corps, tête et plérôme dans les épîtres de la captivité', *RB* 63 (1956), 5–44; H. Schlier,

Die Zeit der Kirche, Freiburg 1956, 159–86; E. Schweizer, 'Jesus Christus, Herr über Kirche und Welt', *Libertas christiana* (Festschrift F. Delekat), Munich 1957, 175–87; G. Rinaldi, 'Capo', *Bibbia e Oriente* 1 (1959), 14; E. Schweizer, 'Die Kirche als Leib Christi in den paulinischen Antilogumena', *TLZ* 86 (1961), 241–56.

Nikolaus Adler

Heart

The primary meaning of the Hebrew *lēb* and *lēbāb* and of the Greek *kardia* is heart in the purely physical sense. In the figurative sense, however, these words have a theological significance (see also ↗ conscience, ↗ life, ↗ man).

A. *In the Old Testament.* The heart is the inward, spiritual part of man, into which God is able to see (1 Sam 16:7; Jer 31:33; here 'heart' and 'bowels' are analogous). It is the seat of man's spiritual strength and faculties and of his intelligence.

The heart is also the seat of man's feelings, such as courage (2 Chron 17:6; 2 Sam 7:27; the Hebrew phrase corresponds to the English 'to take heart'), joy (Deut 28:47; Judg 19:9; Zech 10:7; Job 29:13; Ps 45:1), sorrow and grief (Jer 4:19; Is 65:14), arrogance and pride (Jer 48:29; 49:16, etc), goodwill (2 Sam 15:13; Ezra 6:22; Mal 4:6), care (1 Sam 9:20), sympathy or pity (Hos 11:8), excitement (Deut 19:6; Prov 23:17), composure (Prov 14:30), and desire (Ps 21:2; Job 31:7).

We find in the Old Testament a counterpart to the Latin *cordatus*, meaning literally 'man of heart', thus an intelligent, wise, and understanding man (cf Job 34:10 with 37:24; see also 1 Kings 5:7). The man who denies (Hebrew *ḥ^a^sar*) his heart, in this case his intelligence, is a fool (↗ foolishness: Prov 6:32; 10:21; Eccles 10:3). ↗ Wine takes away a man's heart, or intelligence (Hos 4:11). Men's thoughts dwell in the heart (Judg 5:15ff); to 'come into' the heart means to come to mind (Is 65:17).

It is in the heart that intentions and plans are formed (Jer 23:20; Is 10:7; 1 Chron 22:19; Dan 1:8, etc). The heart is the inward impulse causing man to act (Ex 36:2; Num 16:28). The phrase 'with all ones heart' is parallel to 'with all one's soul' (Josh 22:5). Thus it can be seen that the whole man is inwardly under the influence of his *leb*, and especially so where his will and actions are concerned, and from this point it is not difficult to understand how the word 'heart', through its connection with the human will and intelligence, came to have a religious and moral significance. The heart of the upright, pious man trusts in God (Ps 7:10) and accepts his teaching (Prov 7:3). The heart can also be faithless (Is 29:13; Ezek 6:9, etc) and harden itself against God (Ex 4:21; 9:7, etc: ↗ hardness of heart). The heart of the sinner is 'uncircumcised' (Jer 9:25) and must be circumcised, that is to say, it must be converted (↗ conversion) (see Deut 10:16; Joel 2:12). The religious man has a clean heart, meaning that his attitude of mind is pure (Ps 24:4; 51:10). The evil man, on the other hand, has a perverse heart (Prov 11:20, etc).

H. Brunner has drawn attention to the particular usage of the word 'heart' as the secret source of man's life, of his fate and destiny. In Judg 16:15ff, Samuel reveals his entire heart to Delilah—not simply his love for her, but also the ultimate secret of his inner life. We may interpret similarly the words of Samuel to Saul: 'I will tell you all that is on your mind (heart)' (1 Sam 9:19)—in other words, reveal what God has in mind for you, the secret of your life. In this context Dan 2:29ff should also be quoted, where we find the following correspondence: future thoughts = the mysteries of God = the thoughts of the heart, providing evidence for the interpretation in the sense of the secret of man's fate or destiny.

B. *The Qumran texts* reveal a similar picture in their use of the word 'heart'. It is most frequently used for 'courage', as the seat of man's feelings (1 QM 1:14; 8:10; 10:3; 16:14; 18:13; 1 QH 7:16). Those who are 'willing in heart' (1 QM 10:5) are contrasted with those who lose heart (1 QM 10:6; 11:9). In this sense, the heart, that is to say, courage, 'melts' (1 QM 14:6; 1 QH 2:6; 2:28; 4 QpIs[a] 3:4), 'trembles' (1 QH 10:33), 'shudders' (1 QH 7:3) or is 'restless' (1 QH 7:5). On the other hand, the heart rejoices in the ↗ covenant and in the ↗ truth (1 QG 10:30) and is strong in this ↗ joy and superior to the children of the world (CD 20:33).

The rational aspect of the 'heart' (1 QS 11:3) and, even more particularly, the religious and moral aspect is very forcibly expressed in the Qumran texts. The 'integrity of heart' (1 QS 11:2) is contrasted with falsehood ('with a double heart', that is, duplicity, 'not in thy truth' 1 QH 4:14), pride (1 QS 4:9; 1 Q 22:2, 4; 1 QpHab 8:10), hardness of heart (1 QS 1:6; 2:3; 2:26; 3:3; 4:11; 5:4; 7:19, 24; 1 QM 14:7; CD 2:17f; 3:5; 3:11f; 8:8; 8:19; 19:20, 33; 20:10) and perversity of heart (1 QS 11:9; 1 QH 7:27; 17:19). Such a heart is 'foolish' (1 QH 1:37), 'stony' (1 QH 18:26), 'troubled' (1 QH 18:20) or uncircumcised (1 QpHab 11:13); it has idols and false gods (CD 20:9; 1 QS 2:11) and in following its inclinations man is led astray (1 QS 5:4). The members of the community are therefore constantly urged to be converted 'with their whole heart' (1 QS 5:8f; CD 15:9, 12; 1 QH 16:17), to seek God and to love him with their whole heart (1 QH 14:26; 15:10; CD 1:10) and to serve him with their whole heart (1 QH 16:7).

Man is, however, not alone in this struggle, for God opens his servant's heart (1 QS 11:15f; see also 1 QH 2:18; 4:10; 5:33; 7:13; 12:34; 14:8; 17:22, 26; 18:24, 27). Belial, too, holds council in the heart of man (1 QH 6:21f), and the 'spirits of truth and falsehood wage war in the heart of man' (1 QS 4:23; cf 4:2).

Even the 'heart of God' is referred to in the Qumran texts. It is clear from the parallelism in 1 QH 10:2 that what is meant by this is the divine plan, God's will. This use of the word also occurs in 1 Sam 13:14 (God sought 'a man according to his own heart': cf Jer 3:15). The plan of God's heart is established for ever (1 QH 4:18). Evildoers take no heed of God's deeds and do not hearken to his word, but rather say that these are not a revelation of knowledge and the way of his heart (1 QH 4:17f). But, on the contrary, there is no falsehood in God's works and no guile in the plan of his heart (1 QH 4:21) and those who walk in the way of his heart will live for ever, because they hearken to him (1 QH 4:24). The upright man walks without wickedness in the way of God's heart (1 QH 6:7). God leads him on this way by means of the teacher of righteousness (CD 1:11) and no uncircumcised, impure or violent man may walk in God's way with the purpose of tempting the upright man to stray from it (1 QH 6:20f).

C. *In the New Testament*, the Greek word *kardia* is used with the same wide range of meaning as in the Old Testament Greek translation, where it corresponds to leb or lebâb. The Hebrew *leb*, *lebâb* is, however, sometimes translated in LXX by *nous* (lit = mind), and this is of some significance. The essential difference between *kardia* and *nous* is that *nous* places emphasis on the idea of knowledge, whereas *kardia* does not stress this. In *kardia* the emphasis is rather on intention, endeavour and feeling.

The heart feels joy (Jn 16:22; Acts 2:26; 14:17), fear (Jn 14:1), sorrow (Jn 16:6; Rom 9:2; 2 Cor 2:4; Acts 2:37), love (2 Cor 7:3; 6:11; Phil 1:7), longing (Rom 10:1; Lk 24:32), desire (Rom 1:24; Jas 3:14; Mt 5:28; 6:21). Similarly, thoughts, understanding and the intellect are associated with the heart (Mk 7:21; Mt 12:34; Jn 12:40; Acts 8:22, etc). 'To say in one's heart' means to think (Mt 24:48) and 'to come into one's heart' means to come to mind (Acts 7:23).

Decisions have their origin in the heart (Lk 21:14; 2 Cor 9:7; Acts 11:23; sometimes it is God who puts this decision into man's heart, as in Rev 17:17, sometimes it is the devil, as in Jn 13:2). Sometimes the heart is synonymous with ↗ conscience (1 Jn 3:20ff; Test Gad 5:3).

The heart is man's ego, his inward self, his personality (the 'hidden man' of 1 Pet 3:4), in contrast to the outward man (Mk 7:6; Rom 10:8). According to Paul, it is this inward, spiritual man who stands in need of circumcision. This is more important than the outward, visible circumcision of the foreskin (Rom 2:28f).

It is in the heart that God first approaches man, in order to influence him; he searches out man's heart and puts it to the test (Lk 16:15; Rom 8:27; 1 Thess 2:4). God writes his ↗ law in the hearts of man (Rom 2:15; 2 Cor 3:2; Heb 8:10). There is either ↗ faith in the heart (Mk 11:23; Acts 8:37; Rom 10:8–10; Heb 3:12), or else doubt (Lk 24:38; Mk 11:23) or ↗ hardness (Mt 13:15; Rom 1:21; 2 Cor 3:14).

God opens the heart of man (Lk 24:45; Acts 16:14, cf 2 Macc 1:4). He shines into our hearts, to give us the light of the knowledge of his ↗ glory (2 Cor 4:6). The eyes of the baptised christian's heart are enlightened so that he is able to know ↗ hope and the ↗ inheritance stored up for him (Eph 1:18; see also H. Schlier on this subject). The peace of God keeps our hearts and minds in Christ (Phil 4:7). The spirit of God is poured into our hearts (Rom 5:5; 2 Cor 1:22; Gal 4:6) and Christ dwells in our hearts and is active in them by means of ↗ faith (Eph 4:17ff). The christian's heart is purified and sanctified through faith and ↗ baptism (Acts 15:9; Heb 10:22); it is made clean (Mt 5:8);

it is blameless and strengthened by God (1 Thess 3:13). In such a heart it is possible for the christian virtues of ↗ humility, modelled on the example given to us by our Lord (Mt 11:29), simplicity and ↗ obedience (Eph 6:5; Col 3:22) and, above all love of God and of ones neighbour (↗ love: Mk 12:30; Lk 10:27; Mt 22:37) to grow to perfection.

Bibliography: P. Jouon, *Bbl* 5 (1924), 49–53; P. Dhorme, *RB* 31 (1922), 489–508; H. Cazelles, *Catholicisme* 2 (1949), 1280; F. H. van Meyenfeldt, *Het Hart in het Oud Testament*, Leiden 1950; F. Baumgärtel, *TDNT* III, 605–7; J. Behm, *TDNT* III, 608–14; H. Brunner, *Archiv für Orientforschung* 17 (1954/5), 140f; J. Doresse, *Etudes Carmélitaines* 29 (1950), 82–97; B. de Gerardon, 'Le coeur, la bouche, les mains. Essai sur un schème biblique', *Bible et Vie Chrétienne* 1/4 (1953), 7–24; Haag 704; Bultmann I, 220–27; Jacob, 132–5; C. Tresmontant, *Études de metaphysique biblique*, Paris 1955; F. Nötscher, *Gotteswege und Menschenwege in der Bibel und in Qumran* (*BBB* 15), 1958 (indexed under 'heart'); N. Adler, *LTK* v², 285f; N. Schmidt, 'Anthropologische Begriffe im AT', *ET* 24 (1964), 374–88; G. E. Closen, 'Das Herz des Erlösers in den heiligen Schriften des Alten Bundes', *Zeitschrift für Aszese und Mystik* 18 (1943), 17–30 (those passages in scripture which refer to the 'heart of the Redeemer' are mentioned here, as well as in the same author's book, *Wege in die Heilige Schrift*); J. M. Bover, 'Das Heilige Herz Jesu im NT', *Zeitschrift für Aszese und Mystik* 13 (1938), 285–301; J. B. Bauer, 'Das Herz des Erlösers in der Heiligen Schrift', *BL* 19 (1951/2), 291–4; H. Rahner, *Cor Salvatoris*, Freiburg 1954, 19–45; D. M. Stanley, '"From his heart will flow rivers of living water" (Jn 7:38)', *Cor Jesu* I (Rome 1959), 507–42; S. Garofalo, 'Il Cuore del Redentore in San Paolo,' *Cor Jesu* I (Rome 1959), 543–67; J. B. Bauer, *VD* 40 (1962), 27–32.

Johannes B. Bauer

Heathen (gentiles)

In modern usage the word *heathen* has no precise and objective connotation, but carries with it pejorative associations resulting from a tradition which can be traced back to the Old Testament. The pejorative connotation of the word has been further accentuated by the fact that what we have today is a new kind of paganism which really has no right to this name at all. This new paganism is made up to a very high degree of either atheism or pseudo-religious sentiment whereas genuine paganism, in the sense in which the term was used in antiquity, could take in a very deep sense of religious piety. The negative way in which the word is used springs from a christian sense of reality and of the insurmountable opposition between that reality and those who do not share it; and this no doubt contains an element of genuine biblical truth. Karl Barth characterises all non-christian religions as *Unglaube*, the absence of faith, since they represent attempts on man's part to effect his own salvation. Schlink holds that the pagans know that there is a God but do not know *who* he is. Aquinas contrasts christian revelation with the use of unaided reason on the part of pagans. The experience of this opposition between christian faith and paganism finds these and similar expressions in all christian confessions both in ancient and modern times. Behind all of these we find biblical statements which clearly and unequivocally express the distinction between the people of God and the pagans on the grounds that the latter are not within God's covenant.

Biblical usage supports this distinction. Though there are exceptions, the distinction beween *ʿām* and *gôyîm* is clear-cut in the Old Testament and becomes even clearer with the passage of time. The *gôyîm* are the pagan peoples who are outside the covenant or the individuals who belong to such peoples. LXX translate these terms by *laos*, always in the singular, and *ethnē*.

The *gôyîm* have no part in the covenant and the law. They live in sin, the folly of idolatry (Is 44:9–20; Jer 16:18) and pride (Ps 2:1); hence they stand under the anger and judgement of God (Jer 10:25). Whoever makes light of or seeks to oppose God and his chosen people is subject to divine judgement (Ps 137; Is 14; Jer 51:64). Gen 11:1–9 and Deut 32:8 (also Jub 10:22 based on this last) express the idea that the world of the nations comes into existence as the result of a divine judgement for the arrogance of mankind. The judgement expected to come on the pagans is seen, in the first place, in concrete events following on particularly flagrant examples of pride and arrogance (eg Is 37:36ff). As time goes on, however, a more profoundly theological view is taken of this question. So, for example, Daniel (chapter 7) sees judgement coming on the proud and tyrannical world-empires which can have no share in God's kingdom. In keeping with this view it was understandable that the pagans or gentiles had to be avoided (Ex 34:15).

In addition to this line of thought, however, there is another which stresses that the pagan nations have also been created by God and that therefore they too are under his rule and providence (Amos 9:12; Jer 10:7). Their origin is not seen as the result of punishment by God but of the natural spread of humanity on the earth (2[4] Esd 37:12). And if they are created by God they must in the last resort come under his dispensation of grace (Jn 4:10). Many of them acknowledge Yahweh's activity (Ps 126:2; Dan 2:47), he uses them as his instruments (Is 7:1; 45:1; 25:9) and they are promised a share in eschatological salvation (Is 2:2–4; 25:6–8; 44:3; 51:4f; 55:5; 66:18ff; Mic 4:1ff; Zech 2:11; 8:20; 14:16). They too, therefore, have the duty of honouring and praising God (Ps 67:3; 117:1).

The LXX terms *laos* and *ethnē*, which in general correspond with *ᶜam* and *gôyîm* respectively, are taken over and used in the New Testament. Here *ethnē* is often indeterminate and generalised in connotation (Mt 25:32; Mk 13:10) and can sometimes refer to Israel (Lk 7:5; 23:2; Jn 11:48; 18:35). On a few occasions it can be referred to gentile christians on account of their pagan origins. But for the most part it corresponds to the *gôyîm* of the Old Testament and the adjectival form—also used as a substantive—is *ethnikoi*. The most frequently attested paraphrase of *ethnē* is *Hellēnes* (lit. = Greeks) and, the Johannine writings, *kosmos* (lit. = world).

Despite all this, the situation in the New Testament is radically different from that in the Old. The church knows that Christ has died for all men (Rom 5:18; 2 Cor 5:14; 1 Cor 15:3ff; Rev 22:2f) even though he himself had very little contact with pagans (Mt 10:5; 15:24). Hence she preached the good news about Jesus not only to Israel but to all nations (Mt 24:14; 28:19) since Jesus is the light of the nations (Lk 2:32). How persuasive and convincing this preaching was can be seen from the account of the conversion and baptism of Cornelius in Acts 10–11. This was not a case of one of those who 'feared God', a proselyte who could in some way be considered as belonging to the people of God, but of a pious pagan, a pagan in the real sense of the term.

The line of division now runs not between those who belong by descent and faith to the community of Israel and those who do not, nor between those who observe the law and those who do not, those who belong to the old covenant and those who do not, but is determined with reference to Christ and membership of the new covenant. Rom 3:9, 27ff and 1:18f show clearly how those who belong to the old people of God can now be classed with the *ethnē*. Christ is necessary for all and all can through him receive redemption and aggregation to the 'household of God' (Eph 2:12, 19f; 3:6). Those who have not been baptised are, in spite of all their striving, without God and his justification, though Paul himself recognises the value of Israel's obedience to the law and contrasts it with the disobedience and immorality of the pagans (Rom 1:21; 1 Cor 6:9ff; 5:1; 12:2; Gal 2:15; Col 3:5; 1 Thess 1:9; 4:5). They still belong to the old creation which is given up to the things of this world (Mt 6:32) and is doomed to transitoriness, damnation and death. They are far distant from God or, in other words, in sin (Rom 6:1, 16; Eph 2:1ff; 4:17). On the other side of the dividing line constituted by baptism is the new creation initiated by the death and resurrection of Christ and to this belong life, salvation and grace. Baptism means a break with the past and conversion; in other words, dying in order to enter a new life (Acts 11:1, 18; 14:27; 17:30ff; Rom 6:3–11). The anger of God is no longer directed at those who have through Christ returned to the living God. In this state one can see the happy fulfilment of the prophetic utterances (Acts 4:25; Gal 3:8, 14; 1 Pet 2:9).

Paul is the chief representative in the New Testament of this theology of conversion. For him it is the foundation and justification of his life's work. His purpose is to recall the gentiles to Christ so that, together with those members of the old people of God who have believed in Christ, they may come together to form a new people of God and possess one Spirit, one baptism and one eucharist (1 Cor 12:13; Gal 3:27f; Col 3:11; Eph 4:4–6). On the basis of the old people of God there comes into existence, by the grace of God, a new people, the beginnings of a new humanity reconciled with God, all the members of which can now inherit the promise.

The need for such a theology and its outcome in the mission to the gentiles grew out of the universal significance of the death and resurrection of Christ. We know very little of the formation of gentile–christian communities before Paul. According to Acts 11:21 the mission to the gentiles started with individual christians speaking the word to those they met, following on the Jewish mission to the diaspora. In this process the Jewish proselytes (*phoboumenoi ton theon* = 'those who fear God') played an important part. It appears that very soon a great number of small communities came into existence (Acts 21:4ff; 21:13). The sending of Barnabas to Antioch (Acts 11:22) was in effect a legitimation of this mission by the primitive Jerusalem community which remained in contact with it (Acts 24:17;

Gal 2:10; 1 Cor 16:2; 2 Cor 8:4; 9:1, 12). The activity of the apostle Paul was of decisive importance in this movement not only because of its extent but also from the point of view of its theological significance. Only the substitution of Christ for the Torah as the one means of salvation (Rom 3:21f; 10:4; 15:8ff) made it possible to solve the problems raised by the mission to the gentiles (Acts 15:6; Gal 2:1ff) and freed the church from the hold of the synagogue. Now the way to the nations of the world was open and the ground prepared for a confrontation with their laws and way of life which was to be one of the principal tasks of the church fathers. This confrontation has continued throughout the history of the church and has in our day entered a new phase.

Bibliography: C. G. Diehl, *RGG* II³, 141ff (with a full bibliography); Bertram and K. L. Schmidt, *TDNT* II, 364–72; T. W. Manson, *Jesus and the Non Jesus*, London 1955; J. Jeremias, *Jesus' Promise to the Nations*, London 1958.

Georg Molin

Heaven

The Hebrew word for heaven, *šāmayim*, is always found in the plural. The Greek word, *ouranos*, used in LXX and the New Testament, is found sometimes in the singular and sometimes in the plural.

A. *Heaven as part of the universe*. The phrase 'heaven and earth' is of very frequent occurrence, and is used to denote the world as a whole (Gen 1:1; 2:1; 14:19, 22; 24:3; Ps 102:25 [v 10 in the Hebrew]; 136:5ff; Is 1:2; 65:17; 66:22; Hag 2:6 [cf Heb 12:26]; Joel 3:16 [cf Acts 2:19]; Tob 7:18; Judith 9:17; 1 Macc 2:37; Mk 13:31; Mt 5:18; 6:10; 11:25; 28:18; Lk 10:21; 16:17; Acts 17:24; 1 Cor 8:5; Eph 1:10; 3:15; Col 1:16; Jas 5:12; 2 Pet 3:5, 7, 10, 13; Rev 20:11; 21:1). The tripartite formula 'heaven, earth, and sea' also occurs frequently (Ex 20:11; Acts 4:24; 14:15; Rev 10:6; 14:7; see also Ex 20:4; Judith 9:17; Rev 5:13). In this sense, heaven is very much the same as the so-called firmament (Gen 1:6–8), which was thought of as a hollow hemisphere above the earth, bearing above it the ocean of heaven, the 'waters above the heavens' (Ps 148:4: Dan 3:60). Heaven is 'stretched out' (Ps 104:2; Is 40:22; 44:24; 45:12; 48:13; 51:13, 16; Jer 10:12; 51:15; Zech 12:1); it has 'flood-gates' (Gen 7:11; Mal 3:10; see also 2 Kings 7:2, 19); it is supported by pillars (Job 26:11) or rests on foundations (2 Sam 22:8). The sun, the moon, and the stars move in this heaven (Gen 1:14–17; Mk 13:24f; Mt 24:29; Heb 11:12). Man cannot ascend to heaven (Deut 30:12; Prov 30:4; Jn 3:13). Thus by heaven is implied the space of air between the firmament and earth. The frequently used phrase 'birds (fowls) of the air' shows this clearly (Gen 1:26, 28, 30; 2:19ff; 6:7; 7:3, etc; Mk 4:32; Mt 6:26; 8:20; Lk 8:5; 9:58; Acts 10:12; 11:6).

Several *heavenly spheres* are recognised in ancient cosmology. The phrase 'the heaven of heavens' (Deut 10:14; 1 Kings 8:27; 2 Chron 2:6; 6:18; Neh 9:6; Ps 148:4) would certainly seem to reflect this view; it is, however, merely a rhetorical exaggeration, employed to express the sublimity of heaven. It was not until the later Jewish period that several heavens were referred to (Test Lev 2:7–9; 3:1–8; ApocMos 37; ApocAbr 19:5–9; Bar [Gr] 2:2; 3:1; 10:1; 11:1; Enoch [Slav] 3:1; 7:1; 8:1; 11:1; 18:1; 19:1; 20:1; SB III, 531–3; Traub 511f). Paul also refers to heaven in this way (2 Cor 12:2; Eph 4:10).

Heaven, as a part of the structure of the world, will be destroyed in God's judgement (Is 13:13; 34:4; 51:6; Job 14:12; Mk 13:24f; 2 Pet 3:7, 10, 12; Rev 20:11; see also Ps 102:26f; Jer 4:23–6; Joel 3:3f; Hag 2:7, 22; Mk 13:31; Mt 5:18; Lk 16:17; Heb 1:10–12; 12:26). In its place a new heaven will be created, together with a new earth (Is 65:17; 66:22; 2 Pet 3:13; Rev 21:1; see also Rom 8:21f).

B. *Heaven as a space above the world.* 1. *Heaven is the dwelling place of God* (1 Kings 8:30, 32, 34, 36, 39, etc; Ps 2:4; 14:2; 115:3; Mk 11:25; Mt 5:16, 45; 6:1, 9; 7:11, 21; 10:32f; 16:17; 23:9; Lk 11:13; Eph 6:9; Col 4:1; see also Gen 11:5, 7; 19:24; 24:3, 7; 28:12f; 1 Kings 22:19; Job 1:6–12; 22:12; Ps 29:10; Rom 1:18; Rev 21:2, 10). Heaven is also God's throne (Is 66:1; see also Acts 7:49; Mt 5:34; 23:22), in contrast to the earth, which is his footstool (Is 66:1; see also Acts 7:49; Mt 5:34). God's throne is, however, sometimes represented as being situated in heaven (Ps 11:4; 103:19; Wis 18:15; Heb 8:1; Rev 4:2; 5:1; 21:5). God, therefore, is frequently referred to as the God of heaven (Gen 24:7; 2 Chron 36:23; Ezra 1:2; Neh 1:4f; 2:4, 20; Ps 136:26; Jonah 1:9; Rev 11:13; 16:11). Sometimes the word 'heaven' is used for God (Dan 4:23; 1 Macc 3:18; 4:10, 24, 55; 12:15; 2 Macc 7:11; Lk 15:18, 21). Similarly, 'in heaven' means very much the same as 'with God' (Mt 16:19; 18:18) and 'from heaven' means 'from God' (Mk 8:11; 11:30; Jn 3:27). Thus, in place of the 'Kingdom of God', we often find the 'Kingdom of heaven' in the New Testament, although only in the semitically coloured Gospel of Matthew (Mt 3:2; 4:17; 5:3, 10, 19f; 7:21; 8:11, etc). The nearness of God is frequently indicated by the heavens opening (Mk 1:10f; Jn 1:51; Acts 7:55f; 10:11; Rev 4:1; 19:11; see also Is 64:1; Ezek 1:1). The voice of God (Mk 1:11; Jn 12:28; 2 Pet 1:18) and the light which brings divine grace (Acts 9:3; 22:6; 26:13) also come from heaven.

2. *Heaven as the dwelling place of the angels* (Gen 21:17; 22:11; 1 Kings 22:19; Lk 2:15; Heb 12:22; Rev 1:4; 4:5f; 5:11; 7:11; 8:2, etc: see also Job 1:6–12; Ps 89:6f; Tob 12:15). Reference is made to the angels of heaven (Mt 24:36) or in heaven (Mk 12:25; 13:32; Mt 18:10; 22:30) who always see the face of God (Mt 18:10). The angels form the heavenly army (1 Kings 22:19; 2 Chron 18:18; Lk 2:13; Rev 19:14). It is even possible in the bible to use the term 'heaven' when 'the angels of heaven' is meant (Lk 15:7; cf 15:10). The angels call from heaven (Gen 21:17; 22:15) or actually come down from heaven to earth (Mt 28:2; Lk 22:43; Gal 1:8; Rev 10:1; 18:1; 20:1; see also Lk 1:19,26). There are also evil spirits in heaven (Eph 6:12; Rev 12:7f) and even Satan has access to God, and therefore clearly to heaven (Job 1:6–12; 2:1–7; see also Rev 12:8, 10). He falls from heaven, however, as a result of what Christ has done (Lk 10:18; Rev 12:8–10:13).

Many of these statements, it must be admitted, give us cause to ask what is really meant by 'heaven' (see Eph 2:2 with 6:12).

3. *Heaven as the dwelling place of Christ.* From the very beginning, Jesus was with God (Jn 1:1; 17:5). He came down from heaven to earth (Jn 1:9, 11; 3:13, 31; 6:38, 41f, 51; 16:28; 17:8; Eph 4:9; see also Dan 7:13f; Jn 6:33; 13:3; Rom 10:6) and, as the God-man, returned to God in heaven in his ascension (Mk 16:19; Acts 1:9–11; Eph 4:10; Heb 4:14; 7:26; see also Jn 6:62ff; 7:33; 13:3; 16:5, 28; 17:13f; Acts 2:33f; Heb 9:11f, 24). In heaven, Christ sits at the right hand of God (Mk 16:19; Acts 2:33f; 5:31; 7:55f; Rom 8:34; Eph 1:20; Col 3:1; Heb 1:3, 13; 8:1; 10:12; 12:2; 1 Pet 3:22; see also Mk 14:62; Rev 3:21; 5:6). He has once and for all entered into the Holy of Holies of heaven (Heb 9:11f, 24), where he is the intercessor, mediator, and advocate for his church (Rom 8:34; Heb 9:24; 12:24; 1 Jn 2:1). Heaven had to receive him until the time when the world is to be renewed (Acts 3:21); then, at the end of time, he will come again from heaven (Acts 1:11; Phil 3:20; 1 Thess 1:10; 4:16; 2 Thess 1:7; see also Dan 7:13; Mk 8:38; 13:26; 14:62; Mt 26:64; Acts 3:20; 1 Cor 15:47; Heb 9:28; Rev 1:7). At his second coming, he will take his disciples with him into heaven (see 1 Thess 4:16f).

4. *Heaven as the place of salvation.* Heaven is the source of God's blessing (Gen 49:25; Deut 33:13), and God's word stands firm for ever in heaven, because he is there (Ps 119:89). God's mercy and truth are established in heaven (Ps 89:2). It is from heaven that the Holy Ghost comes (Mk 1:10; Jn 1:32; Acts 2:2–4, 33; 1 Pet 1:12; see also Jn 14:16, 26; 15:26; 16:7; Acts 1:8). ↗ Paradise (2 Cor 12:4; see also Lk 23:43; Rev 2:7) and the pattern of the tabernacle established on earth (Ex 25:9, 40; Heb 8:5; 9:23; see also Rev 15:5) are to be found in heaven. The temple of God (Rev 3:12; 11:19; 14:15, 17; 15:5f; 16:17), with the altar of incense (Rev 8:3, 5; 14:18) and the Ark of the Covenant (Rev 11:19) are also in heaven. It is in heaven too that the true Jerusalem is situated (Gal 4:26; Heb 12:22; Rev 3:12). This new Jerusalem will come down on earth when the world is renewed (Rev 21:2, 10). Salvation is preserved in heaven for christians (Col 1:5; 1 Pet 1:4; see also Col 1:12).

5. *Heaven as the abode of the blessed.* In the Old Testament we find occasional examples of men being taken up into heaven (2 Kings 2:11; see also Gen 5:24; Ps 73:24). It was the expectation of later judaism that the just would live for ever with God (Wis 5:15f; 6:18f; see also 3:1–9; Ps 49:15). In the New Testament, the pious store up treasures for themselves in heaven (Mk 10:21; Mt 6:20; Lk 12:33) and it is there that they receive their reward (Mt 5:12; Lk 6:23). The true home of christians who are still on earth is really in heaven (Phil 3:20; Heb 12:22–4; see also 2 Cor 5:6; Heb 13:14), and the names of Jesus' disciples are written in heaven (Lk 10:20; see also Ex 32:32; Ps 69:28; Dan 12:1; Heb 12:23; Rev 21:27). The souls of the just who have died are already in heaven (Heb 12:23), and Jesus' disciples will also eventually go to heaven (Jn 14:2f; 2 Cor 5:1)

immediately after their death (Phil 1:23; see also Lk 23:43; 2 Cor 5:1ff). They will sit with Christ in heaven (Eph 2:6; Rev 3:21), or stand before God's throne (Rev 7:9). They will no longer experience any earthly tribulation or hardship (Rev 7:16; 21:4), but will be protected by God and Christ (Rev 7:17; 21:3f; 22:1–5). In their resurrection, their new form of existence will be from heaven, in contrast to their previous form of existence, which is from earth (1 Cor 15:47–9).

C. *The theological importance of the biblical statements concerning heaven.* The cosmology of antiquity, now completely outdated by the advance of modern scientific knowledge, underlies all these biblical utterances concerning heaven. It is clear that there is no single passage in the bible referring to heaven which is aimed at providing scientific instruction. All these passages, however, do make use of the ancient view of the universe and the linguistic usage of the period to express religious ideas. To appreciate these ideas, it is necessary to peel away the surrounding husk of ancient language and concept—if this is done, the idea of heaven which emerges can be seen to have, in many cases, a definitely qualitative content which, even remaining within the text as it is, predominates over the purely local content. In this sense, then, heaven is seen as *the sphere of God, his angels and saints—the sphere of perfection and salvation.* The word *sphere* is, of course, quite inadequate in this context, and open to misinterpretation, but inadequate and easily misinterpreted language is all that we have when we need to speak of this absolute mystery. In the bible we find an attempt on the part of men to depict heaven in its perfection, beauty and blessedness. The language used is, of necessity, figurative, and we must take this into account in our examination of the subject.

Bibliography: A. Klawek, 'Der Himmel als Wohnung der Seligen im ntl. Zeitalter', *Collecteana Theologica* 13 (1932), 111–24; T. Flügge, *Die Vorstellung über den Himmel im AT*, Borna-Leipzig 1937; H. Bietenhard, *Die himmlische Welt im Urchristentum und Spätjudentum*, Tübingen 1951; H. Traub and G. von Rad, *TDNT* v, 497–538; U. Simon, *Heaven in the Christian Tradition*, London 1958; J. Haecke, J. Schmid and J. Ratzinger, *LTK* v, 352–8.

Johann Michl

Hell

Hell (Old English *hel*, cognate with the Old High German *hêlan*, to conceal; Hel—in Norse mythology, the goddess of the underworld) is the name used in scripture, with various shades of meaning, to denote the place of punishment of the damned after death.

A. In the *Old Testament*, *šᵉʾôl* is the place, believed to be situated under the earth, to which both good and bad go after death (Gen 37:35; Deut 32:22; 1 Kings 2:6; Prov 9:18; 15:11; Job 10:21f; Ps 9:17; 31:17; 49:15; 55:15; 88:3–7, 11–13; 94:17; 115:17; Is 38:10, 18; Wis 1:14). The fate of the dead is, however, gradually seen in a different light in the Old Testament, and good and bad are judged according to their merits. The good are awakened after death to a new, eternal life (Dan 12:2; 2 Macc 7:9, 11, 14, 23; see also Is 26:19) and are received by God (Ps 49:15; Wis 5:15f; 6:18ff; see also 3:1–9). The wicked and godless, however, will be punished (Is 50:11; 66:24;

Judith 16:17; Wis 4:19; Sir 7:17f; see also Wis 3:10, 18) and will rise again to reproach and dishonour (Dan 12:2; see also 2 Macc 7:14). Their punishment will be by fire (Is 50:11; 66:24; Judith 16:21; Sir 7:17f) and worms (Is 66:24; Judith 16:17; Sir 7:17f). In this context, it is important not to overlook the element of imagery contained in these ideas—fire representing destruction and the worm corruption—although in themselves these two elements are scarcely reconcilable.

B. In the *New Testament*, hell is conceived according to the view prevalent in later judaism (with the exception of the canonical books, and especially Enoch [Eth] 22, etc). After death the sinner is taken to Hades (*ha*(*i*)*dēs* is the usual translation of *še'ôl* in LXX), where he is tormented by fire (Lk 16:23f). This place of punishment is often called Gehenna (Mk 9:42f; Mt 5:29f; 10:28; 23:15, 33; Lk 12:5; Jas 3:6), or Gehenna of fire—'hell fire' (Mt 5:22; 18:9). Sometimes it is described as an everlasting or inextinguishable fire (Mk 9:42f; see also Mt 18:8), where the worms and fire torment the damned (Mk 9:47f; cf Is 66:24). The word *Gehenna* (used thus in the Vulgate; in Greek *geenna*) is derived from the Hebrew *gê-hinnōm*, the 'valley of Hinnom' (Joshua 15:8b; 18:16b; Neh 11:30), which is an abbreviation of *gê-ben-hinnōm*, or the 'valley of the son of Hinnom' (Joshua 15:8a; 18:16a; 2 Chron 28:3; 33:6; Jer 7:31f; 19:2, 6). This was the valley or ravine to the south of Jerusalem where children were burnt as sacrifices during the reigns of Ahaz and Manasseh (2 Chron 28:3; 33:6;; Jer 7:31). It was in this valley too, that the Israelites would be punished (Jer 7:32; 19:6). It is in the New Testament and the texts of later judaism (4 Esdras 7:36; Bar [Syr] 59:10; 85:13) that the name first occurs with the meaning of a place of punishment after death. This place of punishment is already in existence, and the human body is corrupted by its influence (Jas 3:6). Other passages refer to various aspects of hell as a place of punishment—eternal fire (Mt 18:8; 25:41; see also Mt 3:12; Lk 3:17; Jude 7), the 'fury of fire' (Heb 10:27), the 'furnace of fire' (Mt 13:42, 50), the outer darkness (Mt 8:12; 22:13; 25:30; see also 2 Pet 2:17), where there is weeping and gnashing of teeth—thus signifying the most extreme agony and the greatest anger (Mt 8:12; 13:42, 50; 22:13; 24:51; 25:30; Lk 13:28) by which hypocrites are punished (Mt 24:51; see also Lk 12:46). This fire is prepared for the devil and his angels, and those who do not show mercy on others will be punished in it (Mt 25:41). In the Apocalypse, it is characterised as the 'lake of fire that burns with brimstone' (Rev 19:20; see also 14:10; 20:9, 14). Into this pool of fire are cast first of all the two beasts, representing the Antichrist (19:20; 20:9f), then the devil (20:9), the kingdom of Death (*ha*[*i*]*dēs*), Death itself (*thanatos*: 20:14) and finally all sinners (21:8). The punishment in this place of fire is final and everlasting (Mt 18:8; 25:41, 46; Rev 19:20; 20:9f; 21:8), but it varies according to the guilt of each individual sinner (Lk 12:47f; see also Mt 10:15; 11:22; Lk 10:12, 14).

In other passages of the New Testament, this ultimate punishment of sinners is not characterised in figurative language or in imagery, but simply as

God's wrath and anger (Rom 2:8; see also 2 Thess 1:8; Rev 16:19), as evil (2 Cor 5:10), as death (Jn 8:51f; Rom 6:21, 23; see also 5:21), as the second death (Rev 2:11; 20:6, 14; 21:8), as judgement (Jn 5:24, 29; see also 1 Cor 11:29), as destruction (Mt 7:13; Gal 6:8; Phil 3:19; Heb 10:39; see also Jn 17:12), as eternal destruction (2 Thess 1:9) or as exclusion from the kingdom of God (Lk 13:28; 1 Cor 6:9f; Gal 5:19–21; Eph 5:5; see also Mt 8:12; Lk 14:24; Col 3:5f). The wicked too will be resurrected (Jn 5:29; Acts 24:15; see also Mt 25:31–46), but to the resurrection of judgement (Jn 5:29; see also Mt 25:31–46).

The New Testament also recognises a temporary state of punishment, which corresponds to the ideas current in later judaism (Jub 5:6, 10; Hen [eth] 10:4–6, 11–14). Thus the sinful angels are kept in chains and in darkness until the last judgement (Jude 6), or in Tartarus, or the lowest part of hell (2 Pet 2:4). What is more, Hades is also regarded as a temporary place of punishment—hell will not only have to give up its dead for judgement at the resurrection (Rev 20:13), but will also be replaced by the everlasting Gehenna (Rev 20:14; hell, together with death, will be cast into the pool of fire). In Hades the sinner's soul is separated from his body. In Gehenna, on the other hand, he will be punished, after the resurrection, both in his body and his soul (Mk 9:43, 45, 47; Mt 5:29f; 18:8f).

C. *The theological importance of the biblical references to hell.* The bible uses words such as fire, worm, and darkness which, in their literal sense, are irreconcilable. Used figuratively, however, such words aim to express, by their associations with terrible experiences undergone in this life, the inexpressible torments of the damned. 'Weeping', for example, is used to express the pain which the damned suffer, 'gnashing of teeth' their anger and despair. Language of this kind, wherever it is found in the New Testament, however, is always extremely restrained and sober, compared with the cruel and fantastic descriptions of hell in the apocryphal books. Its main purpose is, of course, to stir the conscience and to instil a healthy fear of God as heavenly judge. God's anger, which strikes the sinner and, excluding him from the kingdom of heaven, sentences him to eternal perdition, is expressed in the New Testament without recourse to imagery. It is true that certain words—fire, darkness, weeping and so on—are used in an attempt to convey something of the terrible nature of the punishment of the damned, but exactly what this punishment is really like remains a mystery which is not revealed anywhere in the bible. However, any attempt to mitigate the grave and terrible implications of the reality of hell, by appealing, for example, to 1 Cor 15:29, or to some similar passage, is bound to fail, in view of the absolute clarity of scripture on this subject.

Bibliography: J. Felten, *Neutestamentliche Zeitgeschichte* II, Regensburg 1925[3], 227–42 and 258–63; SB IV 2, 1016–118; J. Jeremias, *TDNT* I, 146–9 and 657–8; P. Volz, *Die Eschatologie der jüdische Gemeinde im ntl. Zeitalter*, Tübingen 1934, 256–72 and 309–32; C. Spicq, *Le révélation de l'enfer dans la sainte Ecriture: L'Enfer*, Paris 1950, 91–143; H. Bietenhard, *Die himmlische Welt im Urchristentum und Spätjudentum*, Tübingen 1951, 205–9; J. Gnilka and J. Ratzinger, *LTK* v[2], 445–9.

Johann Michl

Holy

Holiness is a primordial religious phenomenon which can be grasped in full only in objective experience (see Is 6:3ff). Any attempt to analyse holiness is bound to be piecemeal and there is always the danger that its homogeneous nature will be destroyed in the analytic process and that a one-sided interpretation may result from an overemphasis of certain elements at the expense of others. Another risk inherent in such analysis is that of regarding many aspects of holiness as the consequence of a tendency or development, when in fact these aspects are traceable to a gradual deepening of man's understanding of the nature of holiness. It is essentially something different from and alien to our normal empirical knowledge, something which intrudes into this known world and remains in it. No close parallel to the phenomenon of holiness can, in fact, be found.

Holiness is above all connected with material things in Old Testament worship. Certain places (Jerusalem, Is 52:1; Sion, Is 27:13; the tabernacle, Ex 28:43; the temple, 1 Kings 9:3; the Holy of Holies, Lev 16:2; the altar, Ex 29:37), certain objects (the Ark of the Covenant, 2 Chron 35:3), certain vestments (Ex 29:29), sacrifices (Ex 28:38), holy days (Gen 2:3)—all are called holy. Such things are, however, not static in themselves. Frequently they possess a strange dynamic force of their own. Examples of this are Uzzah's death as a result of touching the Ark (2 Sam 6:6f), what happened in Bethel (Gen 28:17) or in connection with the burning bush (Ex 3:5). These instances show quite clearly that a place is called holy when God reveals himself there. That the name of God is, at quite an early stage, used instead of the Ark (Deut 26:2)—it is preferable to regard this less as a spiritualisation than as the emergence of the reality concealed in the Ark itself—is evidence of the fact that holiness in the Old Testament is not abstract or connected purely with material things, as in the case of the pagan religions, but personal. God is, in fact, the three times Holy One (Is 6:3), the Holy One, quite different from men, who is in the midst of men (Hos 11:9). He is the one to whom no man can compare himself (Is 40:25), since he cannot be either approached or touched and thus is able even to swear by his own holiness (Ps 89:35). Although he is unique, he is nonetheless not isolated. In him there is a vital force which is constantly directed outwards and wishes to possess everything in the world by invoking his name upon his people (Amos 9:12), by revealing himself as the Holy One (Ezek 20:41) or by glorifying himself (Ex 14:18). He claims the whole of history as his own (Ezek 20:41; 38:16), until the whole earth is ultimately filled with his glory and fulfilled in him (Num 14:21). On that day every sacrificial vessel in Jerusalem and Judea will be sanctified to the Lord of hosts (Zech 14:21). Ps 29 provides a most impressive description of this dynamic power of God, symbolised here as a thunderstorm which will overcome everything that attempts to stand up against it. His zeal is directed especially towards men, who are to be holy because he is holy (Lev 11:44). From this no one is exempt. The entire people has been chosen by him, the Holy One of Israel (Is 1:4) and is consequently incorporated into his process of sanctification (Lev 20:26). Everyone whose name is written in the book of life forms a part of this plan (Is 4:3). Special leaders are chosen to prepare the way for this sanctification (Ex 19:14; Joshua 7:13), and among these the priests play a very special part (Lev 21:7). Among these consecrated priests, the high priest is to bear the visible mark of dedication to God on his forehead (Ex 28:36).

God's intrusion into the world causes a marked division between what is holy and what is profane. The completely distinct character of holiness prevents any fusion here. The profane element even attempts to protect itself from the power of holiness as it draws near (Ex 3:5; 19:12). Correspondingly, man's reaction to the holiness of God is amazement at its magnitude (Ex 15:11; 1 Sam 2:2), awe which prevents man from uttering the name of God, fear, and even terror (Gen 28:17; Ex 3:6). Together with this goes a feeling of surrender, a sense of dependence, which causes the man who is faced with God's holiness to feel impotent (Gen 18:27) and guilty (Is 6:5). This gulf can be bridged only by God (Is 6:3). The distance does not, however, imply a separation. On the contrary, it serves rather as a bond, as it enables holiness to be recognised as such. The special quality of holiness and its particular relationship with the creature are brought out by this distance.

It is impossible for man to escape God's holiness. He has to come to grips with it in every sphere of his daily life. The giving of a law of holiness (Lev 17–26), which contains so many elements which appear so strange to us and which covered every detail of human life, must be seen in this light. It cannot, in itself, be related to any form of theoretical casuistry. It has to do rather with the requirements of a concrete, but constantly changing situation (see Num 9:15ff). As the individual, however, has not yet reached a sufficiently mature stage to be able to deal with the complications of this situation, he has need of the authority of the priest, whose position consequently becomes increasingly more powerful. Since holiness reveals itself with such incomparable force in the bible, too little serious attention has been paid to the origin and nature of the opposite element, the profane. The tendency has been to see this as the purely negative aspect—the unholy and unclean—and the result has been that the laws concerning public worship were restricted principally to the sphere of consecration and atonement. But since holiness lays a claim to the whole of man, it must at the same time be the moral norm, as expressed in various ways in the decalogue (Ex 19:5f) and in the prophetic books. There is bound to be a sharp clash whenever man sets himself up against what is holy and is thereby exposed to God's justice and punishment (Is 5:16), which descends upon him in judgement (Gen 19:24; 1 Sam 6:19; Ps 18:8f). This was the experience of Adam and Eve when they they were banished by the cherubim from the holy Garden of Eden (Gen 3:23f). Here, however, God reveals himself as the one who is completely different and who shows mercy and grace and gives protection (or asylum,

Obad 1:17) to his people, despite their unworthiness and their persistence in sin. What is more, he does not begin to do this just at a later stage, in Israel's history, but from the very beginning (Gen 3:15–21). Similarly, he is the saviour and redeemer of the 'holy remnant' (Is 41:14; 43:5; 45:22), because he is God and not man (Hos 11:9). Thus we see that in the last resort it is God's love which bridges the gulf between the sacred and the profane and at the same time reveals the innermost heart of holiness, before which man can only fall down in worship, as he does in the presence of the angels (1 Sam 2:2; Is 6:1ff).

The power of God's holiness impressed itself deeply upon all the thoughts and actions of Old Testament man. Nevertheless, the close connection with material things, which in themselves had a deeply religious significance, and the dominant position of the hereditary priesthood, whose members frequently acted as officials and sophisticated theologians rather than as ministers of God, led to a debasement of the idea of holiness. It was the prophets (Is 1:11f; Hos 6:6) who first took up the cudgels against this distortion of the meaning of holiness. The struggle was continued in the New Testament.

With the passage of time, God's holiness was to such an extent regarded as the normal expression of his inner being that it was not particularly emphasised in the New Testament, and, when it is mentioned it refers back for the most part, to the Old Testament (see Rev 4:8; cf Is 6:3). Christ is more often called holy, but always when the intention is to stress the contrast between the holy and the profane, as, for example, in the case of the casting out of the unclean spirits (Mk 1:24) or of Peter's confession (Jn 6:69), or else when Christ's hidden divinity is visible through the outer covering of his humanity, as his ↗ glory (Jn 2:11, etc). For the rest, the emphasis throughout is on the dynamic aspect of divine holiness. Christ expressed this aspect in the first Our Father (Mt 6:9). In its absolute formulation, this Our Father embodies in a most impressive way, without any explicit reference to the creature, this elemental power which will not come to rest until the end of time, as the close bond between the Our Father and the ensuing prayer demonstrates. A decisive part is played here by the Holy ↗ Spirit, who is closely associated with the Lord as the one who announces the glad message (Mt 3:11; Lk 1:35; Jn 20:22) and is sent down with tongues of fire (Acts 2:4) to confirm the new people of God (Rom 15:16; Eph 3:16) which, transcending all national boundaries, includes all men who are sanctified in Christ (1 Cor 1:2), the Lord himself preparing the way for this (Eph 3:5). Luke, in the Acts of the Apostles, has expressed the eschatological restlessness of the Holy Spirit (Acts 1:5, 8). Man, however, no longer feels himself to be exposed to holiness as an incalculable primordial force, but realises that the bridging of the gulf which exists between the holy and the profane is the ultimate aim of his life. It is even possible for him to pray for the fulfilment of this aim, as a child of the father who is holy (Jn 17:11). This does not, however, imply that he should lose sight of the distance between the holy and the profane—the name of God is, for example, avoided in Mt 6:9, and man's consciousness of sin is indicated in Lk 5:4ff. With very few exceptions (Lk 5:6f), the process of sanctification is accomplished essentially within man—in striking contrast to the externalism which prevailed in later judaism—by a deeper penetration into man's being. In this way, human sanctification progresses from the stage where man's sinfulness is expiated by the seraph's touching of his lips (Is 6:7) to the stage where this expiation is brought about by the circumcision of his heart (Rom 2:29). The 'holiness' of Mount Sinai (Lev 11:44) corresponds to the 'perfection' of the Sermon on the Mount (Mt 5:48), which finds its final expression in man's deliverance from ↗ sin, darkness, and the bondage of Satan (Acts 26:18)—in which the essence of unholiness is clearly manifest. The christian, however, is able by virtue of his faith to enter the sphere of holiness through the word of God and above all through ↗ baptism (Eph 5:26). He is thus a man who is set apart for God (Eph 1:1), whose glory shines in him (2 Cor 3:18). The holiness which he possesses in this way is, however, by no means static. It is, of necessity, dynamic, and the christian is above all concerned with the need to preserve it intact. So great is the danger of its loss through the unholy element that the help and power of God the Father himself is invoked (Jn 17:11). Christ's mission (Jn 10:36), culminating in his sacrificial death (Jn 17:18ff), is, however, intimately associated with this process of sanctification, as it is only he who is personally within the sphere of holiness who is able to 'sanctify' others (Heb 2:11). This gradual extension of the range and scope of holiness may, of course, lead to serious conflict with the profane element. Examples of this are Christ's expulsion of the money-lenders from the temple (Mt 21:12), his curse on the fig-tree (Mt 21:19) and his ↗ judgement passed on the 'goats' at his left hand (Mt 25:41). This judgement is firmly established on the principle of holiness (1 Cor 6:2), the marks of which are ↗ truth and ↗ justice (Rev 6:10). But all this is transcended by the love of God which is unique in that he did not spare his own Son in order to draw the whole world to himself. In this context, the 'foolishness' and 'weakness' of God clearly reveal his holiness as otherness, as being totally distinct (1 Cor 1:25).

The early church was unable to prevent a certain debasement of the concept of holiness. As soon as everyone who was touched by God or Christ became known as a 'saint', the word 'holy' was bound to lose its particular significance and become more general and universal in application, and thus to take on all too easily a commonplace and everyday meaning. Acts 3:21 and Eph 3:5 give an indication of the beginning of this process.

Bibliography: J. Dillerberger, *Das Heilige im NT*, Kufstein 1926; Eichrodt I, 107–77; Haag 674–80; B. Häring, *Das Heilige und das Gute*, Tübingen 1948; E. Lohmeyer, *Das Vaterunser*, Göttingen 1952², 41–59; O. Procksch and K. G. Kuhn, *TDNT* I, 88–115; von Rad I, 203–7 and 271–9; O. Schilling, *Das Heilige und Gute im AT*, Leipzig 1956; see also R. Otto, *The Idea of the Holy*, London 1923.

Elpidius Pax

Hope

A. *In the Old Testament.* Hope plays a less important part in the Old Testament than in the New. It is normally expressed by the root *qwh*, meaning to remain, to wait, to look forward, to hope, usually in the sense of waiting or hoping for, or looking forward to, something or someone. In the first place, it refers to something which is expected, but which does not materialise (Is 5:2, 4, 7; 59:9, 11, etc). Frequently, however, it expresses an expectation which is fulfilled (Job 7:2; 17:13, etc). God is often the object of hope (Ps 25:2, 4, 21; 27:14; Is 8:17; Jer 14:22, etc). The noun *miqweh*, formed from the root *qwh*, also usually refers to God (Jer 14:8; 17:13; 50:7; see also 1 Chron 29:15), whereas the other noun formation, *tiqwâh*, which is found frequently in Job, Proverbs, and Sirach, tends to refer to worldly happiness and good fortune. In the religious sense, *qiweh* and *tiqwâh* refer especially to things which God bestows on man in this life and which the just expect to receive from him alone. (In the Psalms, *qiweh* is translated by *hupomenō* or by *menō* and its compounds and *thiqwah* as *hupomonē*; in Job and in Proverbs, however, they are translated by *elpis.*) *Elpizō* denotes a state of expectation in the soul of something either greatly desired or else greatly feared. *Hupomenō*, on the other hand, preserves the basic meaning of remaining behind, thus waiting, looking forward to. Both words are used to translate *qiweh*, with the same meaning. A verb which is less commonly used is *ḥâkâh* (Is 8:17; 30:18; Dan 12:12; Ps 33:22; 106:13, etc). It implies especially an expectation of an event, a turning towards God, the idea that God will do something. The word *śābar* is used when something is expected of somebody (Ps 104:27; 119:116, 166, etc), *Yāḥal*, and its noun derivative *tôḥeleth*, is used in a specifically religious sense, and refers to Yahweh and to his grace, favour, judgements, and word (Ps 33:18; 119:43, 74, 81, 114, 147; 130:5, etc). *Bāṭaḥ* is a static verb, used to express a state of the soul. It means to have trust or confidence, to hope confidently (sec various parallel passages with equivalent verbs, Judg 18:7, 27; Ps 78:22; Job 24:22). It is frequently found without an object and often refers to Yahweh (Ps 4:5; 9:10; 21:7, etc) or to his grace or mercy (Ps 13:6; 52:9). According to this sense man ought not to trust in his own justice (Ezek 33:13), in Egypt (Is 36:6, 9; Jer 46:25), in princes (Ps 146:3), in his own strength (Ps 10), in riches (Prov 11:28; Ps 52:7; Jer 48:7) or in vanities and lying words (Jer 7:4, 8; Is 59:4, etc). *Ḥāsâh*, meaning to seek refuge, to conceal oneself (Ps 2:13; 5:11; 7:1; 11:1; 16:1; 17:7, etc) always has God as its object, or the shadow of Yahweh's wings (Ps 36:6). The noun *maḥseh* is also used in many places. It denotes a refuge, a place of refuge or a fortress. God will save his own if they take refuge in him (Ps 7:1; 17:7, etc), since he is just (Ps 31:1f) and good (Ps 25:8) (in LXX this is translated by *elpis*, *elpizō*, etc). ᵓ*âman* can also be included under this head. In the Niphal and the Hiphil, LXX translates this word by *pisteuō* and *pistis* and occasionally by *alētheia* (↗ faith, ↗ truth). The root ᵓ*âman* tends here to approach the sphere of faith, although strictly speaking it belongs more closely to the verbs which have already been discussed, and bears a special affinity to *bāṭaḥ*.

The Old Testament idea of hope is, however, not so closely related to the conception we have of it. We tend more or less to think of hope as an attitude of the soul, a turning towards something, in itself difficult to attain, with the aim of possessing it. In the Old Testament, however, and particularly in LXX, hope is closely connected with trust; it clings, in its expectation, to Yahweh's faithfulness, although the element of uncertainty, which is part of this hope, is never absent, for the man who hopes submits himself utterly to the mysterious will of God, knowing that he may often be put to the test for a long time, and that God is not necessarily bound to act (see also ↗ resurrection, ↗ messianism, ↗ prophecy).

B. *In the New Testament*, hope is expressed especially by *elpis* and *elpizō*. In the secular Greek world, these words had the meaning of anticipation, expectation, apprehension, supposition, or conjecture. In the New Testament, this anticipation or expectation was always directed towards a good, and never towards an evil object, and, as in LXX, included an additional shade of meaning, which implies trust and taking refuge. In 1 Tim 4:10, the implication is not that the christian hopes to possess God (in the beatific vision), but that he should place his hope in him and expect his salvation from him—as in LXX, *elpizō* has come closer in meaning to *pepoitha* and *pisteuō*.

The formula 'faith, hope and charity' (1 Cor 13:13) is of the greatest significance here. It may have developed from a bipartite formula—'faith, charity'—to which the third virtue, hope, was added on account of its close proximity to and intimate association with faith (see 1 Thess 1:3; 5:8; Gal 5:5f; Col 1:4f; 2 Thess 1:3f; Tit 2:2; Rev 2:19). The words 'now there remain . . .' (1 Cor 13:13) are not intended to affirm the continuation of the three theological virtues into the eschatological age; they serve rather as an introductory formula, in the sense of 'now what are important are . . .' (see Plato, *Crit.* 48b).

Unshakable trust in God is expressed in those formulae, such as 'to hope in God' (Rom 15:12; 1 Cor 15:19, etc), which are derived from the Old Testament. The man who hopes is prevented from experiencing disgrace or ignominy (*aiskhunē*) (see Ps 22:6; 25:3, 20), which is not the same as shame or a sense of shame. 'To put to shame', or 'confound' (*kataiskhunein*) is more accurately an act of God which places man in a disgraceful or ignominious situation or leads him to judgement or destruction (see Ps 35:26, etc). When it is put to shame or confounded, hope is thus much more than just disappointment. It is not just that what was hoped for is not accomplished. Indeed the very opposite result is achieved, and this, what is more, is brought about by divine ordinance. Christian hope is, in this sense, not brought into disgrace or 'confounded' (Rom 5:5). The opposite situation is that of *doxazesthai* and *kaukhasthai* (see Ps 91:15; Is 45:24f), of 'glorification'.

Paul, in his contribution to the theology of hope, has made it clear that the object of hope is the *doxa*, or ↗ glory, of God and Christ. Man has been deprived of this glory (Rom 3:23). The christian, however, is able to 'rejoice in the hope of sharing the glory of God' (Rom 5:2; see also 8:18; Eph 1:18).

The same object of christian hope is also called ↗ salvation (Rom 5:9f; 1 Thess 2:13), ↗ life or life everlasting (Rom 5:17; 6:22; 1 Cor 15:22; Gal 6:8; Tit 1:2; 3:7), the resurrection (see 1 Cor 15:19; Phil 3:21), the redemption of our body (Rom 8:23), ultimate justification (Gal 5:5), the ↗ inheritance (Rom 8:17; Eph 1:18; Tit 3:7; 1 Pet 1:3f), the ↗ kingdom, or the kingdom of God (Rom 5:17; 1 Cor 6:19; 15:50; 2 Thess 1:5; 2 Tim 4:18), the things which 'no eye has seen' (1 Cor 2:9; see also 2 Cor 4:17f), and 'the hope laid up for you in heaven' (Col 1:5). *The expectation of 'what we do not see'* (Rom 8:24f) can be taken as a kind of popular and rough definition of hope, referring to things over which we have no control, and no doubt meant as an admonishment to perseverance. In 2 Cor 4:18 and Heb 11:1, however, the contrast is between what is visible and what is invisible in order to indicate the glory of Christ and of christians, at present still concealed, but to be revealed in the future. Thus it is clear that *christian hope is definitely eschatological* and refers to the final fulfilment of the already 'realised eschatology'.

The main motive of hope is *God's promise* (Gen 15:6; see also Rom 4; Gal 3), the *divine mystery*—God's plan of salvation (Col 1:25–7; see also Eph 1:3–14; 3:1–21). Closely connected with this are two other motives, namely that a beginning has already been made in the realisation of the divine work of salvation in the first place through Christ—in his mission, death, and resurrection—and secondly through the gift of the ↗ Spirit (Rom 5:5). In this connection, the two important Pauline texts on hope (Rom 5:1–11; 8:17ff) should be consulted.

With regard to the *attitude of the soul* within christian existence, the relationship between *hope* and *faith* consists in the fact that hope arises from faith in the divine promises and, like faith, is directed towards the future (Gal 3:11; 5:5).

The relationship between *hope* and ↗ *love* (*agapē*) is to be found in the eschatological character of the latter. The work of God's 'love' has already begun; his charity has been poured out into our hearts to strengthen them in preparation for the ↗ parousia (see Rom 5:5; 1 Thess 3:12f; 2 Thess 2:16f; Phil 1:9f).

The relationship between *hope* and *patience* (*hupomonē*): Stoic philosophy excludes hope and is sufficient in itself (see Boethius, *Cons.* 1, m. 7:25ff; 'gaudia pelle, pelle timorem, spemque fugato nec dolor adsit!'). The patience of the Stoic is not expectation. It is rather self-mastery with regard to the world and to destiny. In the New Testament, however, patience is an auxiliary virtue to hope. It is always used in an eschatological context (Rom 5:3f; 2 Tim 2:12; sec also Mk 13:13). If hope is always directed towards the aim of eschatological perfection, patience consists in putting up with ↗ suffering. This attitude of patience, perseverance and endurance enables man to share not only in the Lord's patient and persevering attitude, but also in the fruits of his suffering (Rom 8:17; 2 Cor 4:7ff; Col 1:24).

Finally, there is a close relationship between *hope and fear*. Like patience, fear is an essential characteristic of christian hope, since it is possible that, in great tribulation, a christian may not persevere to the very end (1 Cor 10:12). So long as the christian hopes, in faith, for the↗ grace of God, he is safe (1 Cor 2:5; 1 Pet 1:21). If, however, he lives in the↗ flesh, he is exposed to↗ temptations and must 'fear', not with anxious fear, but with a salutary fear which is inseparably bound up with christian existence—an existence which remains constantly in faith and hope and can never depend upon itself (Rom 11:20–22). What is of importance concerning the attitude of hope in the individual soul is not necessarily of importance with regard to the hope of the christian community as a whole. The church awaits the parousia of the Lord and the revelation of his glory with unerring certainty, whereas each individual christian is not necessarily justified (1 Cor 4:4; Phil 3:12). This is why hope is always accompanied by trust—the basic meaning of *pistis* and *elpis* shows this, and Paul also mentions this fact (2 Cor 3:12f; Eph 3:12).

According to Paul, then, christian existence is characterised by hope. In contrast, the pagan world is marked by an existence without hope (Eph 2:12; see also 1 Thess 4:13; Marcus Aurelius, *De Seipso* 3:14).

Bibliography: J. de Guibert, *RSR* 4 (1913), 565–96; A. Pott, *Das Hoffen im NT*, Leipzig 1915; A. Lesky, *Gnomon* 9 (1933), 173ff; R. Bultmann and K. H. Rengstorff, *TDNT* II, 517–35 (=*BKW* XII); T. C. Vriezen, *TLZ* 78 (1953), 577–86; C. Westerman, *Theologia Viatorum* 4 (Berlin 1952), 19–70; E. Wolf, *ET* 13 (1953), 157–69. See especially: J. van der Ploeg, *RB* 61 (1954), 481–507; W. Grossouw, *RB* 61 (1954), 508–32; W. Grossouw, *NKS* 51 (1955) 265–76; S. Pinckaers, *NRT* 77 (1955), 785–99; F. Urtiz de Urtaran, 'Esperanza y Caridad en el NT', *Scriptorium Victorense* 1 (Vitoria 1954), 1–50; E. Schweizer, *Studies C. H. Dodd*, Cambridge 1956, 482–508; J. P. Ramseyer, Allmen 172–4; Bultmann 1, 319–23 and 344–7; P. A. H. de Boer, 'Études sur le sens de la racine QWH', *OTS* 10 (1954), 225–46; H. Haag, *Anima* 12 (1958), 111–18; G. Bertram, *ZNW* 49 (1958), 264–70; A. Gelin, *LV* 8 (1959), 3–16; E. Neuhäusler, *LTK* v², 416–18; H. Schlier, 'Über die Hoffnung', *GL* 33 (1960), 16–24; L. Fedele, 'La speranza cristiana nelle lettere di S. Paolo', *Aloisiana* 1 (Naples 1960), 21–67; J.-H. Nicolas, 'Valeur de l'espérance enseignée par l'Ecriture', *Dict. de la Spiritualité*, 1960, 1209–16; G. Bornkamm, 'Die Hoffnung in Col', *TU* 77 (1961), 56–64; C. F. D. Moule, *The Meaning of Hope*, Philadelphia 1963.

Johannes B. Bauer

Hour

In the bible *hour* does not simply refer to a unit of time into which the day (see Jn 11:9; the day has twelve hours) or the night is divided (the Jews divided the night into three watches of four hours each: Judg 7:19; Lk 12:38; the Romans into four watches of three hours each: Mk 13:35). Corresponding to the Hebrew *ʿēth* it also commonly stands for the period of time during which an action takes place (eg the phrase 'in that hour'). The Semitic experience of time is less of the spatial-temporal order than dynamic, determined by the experience of the event which fills or takes up time (eg 'in a single hour', Rev 18:10, 17–19 = very quickly; and phrases such as 'the hour of the harvest, of temptation, for taking a meal', etc). Hence there are special 'hours' in which, following on the divine decision, some specific event will take place which will have significance for the salvation of the world.

1. *Jewish apocalyptic.* Jewish apocalyptic writers refer to particular 'hours' in a way which is of special theological significance. In Old Testament prophecy 'the day of Yahweh' or 'that day' played an important part, sometimes referring to an event within history, sometimes having an eschatological connotation. But this way of speaking did not imply that the last age was thought of as divided into discrete periods, into 'hours'. This tendency is peculiar to apocalyptic writing and we find it for the first time in Daniel (chapter 9: the seventy weeks of years). In this chapter LXX translates 'the final age' (Hebrew: *ʿēth qes*) by 'an hour of the fixed time' (for the end, that is = *hōra kairou*; 8:17, 19; cf 11:40, 45). The 'fixed times' determined by God which the apocalyptic writers refer to are called 'hours' in the Apocrypha: 'but now your time is passing quickly and your hours are upon you' (Bar [Syr] 36:9); 'he has measured the hours by measure and numbered the times by number' (4 Esd 4:37); 'he governs the hours and whatever things come to pass in the hours' (4 Esdras 13:58). We also find reference to 'the twelve hours of the age of the world' Apoc Abr 29:1f) and especially to 'the twelfth hour of the godless age of the world' (ApocAbr 29:8; cf 13). Attempts were made to calculate the time of 'the end' by means of various signs and it was believed that God would, for the sake of the righteous, shorten the last terrible age (see Volz, *Eschatologie* 137f; 141–6).

2. *In early christianity.* Jesus had nothing to do with such apocalyptic speculations and attempts to predict the end of the world (see Lk 17:20; Mk 13:32). His eschatological message concerned the time of fulfilment, the approaching kingdom of God (Mk 1:15), the time of God's gracious visitation (Lk 19:44). To express all of this another concept was used, that of the *kairos* or appointed time. The *kairos* is the eschatological time of salvation determined by God and inaugurated by Jesus. It is a time when salvation is offered to men, a time of decision and crisis in which men must acknowledge the power of God and decide to accept the offer in conversion and faith (cf Lk 12:56). This *kairos* which brings on a state of crisis is not at all to be understood as an 'hour' in the sense of a discrete unit of time measured along a line of temporal succession. It is determined uniquely by the events which take place, events which are brought about by God and impinge on the life of men. The apocalyptic writers speak not only of 'times or seasons' (*kairoi*; Acts 1:7; see also 1 Thess 5:1) but also of 'the day' and 'the hour'. It is categorically denied in Mk 13:32 that anyone apart from the father knows anything about 'that day or the hour'. There are, indeed, comparable statements in the apocalyptic literature about God reserving such knowledge to himself, but here it is emphasised that even Jesus, who is 'the Son', can say nothing about the time of the end and that therefore such speculations are pointless and all that is demanded is vigilance (vv 33–7). In this logion it is not a question of determining a specific hour in a day which is deemed imminent; 'hour' is

just another way of expressing the same thing as 'that day'. The Son of Man will come 'at an hour you do not expect' (Lk 12:40; see also v 46 = Mt 24:44, 50).

Any attempt to calculate 'the hour' is therefore rejected (see Lk 12:38; Mk 13:35). Paul only appears to do this when he speaks metaphorically of 'the hour' to arise from sleep and states that the night is far gone and the day draws nigh (Rom 13:11f). Objectively considered, we have here an eschatological appeal and 'the hour' is nothing else but the *kairos* of salvation (see 2 Cor 6:2, and for this metaphor also 1 Thess 5:1–6). We have to interpret in much the same way the 'last hour' in 1 Jn 2:18, the coming of which can be recognised by the appearance of false teachers. This 'hour' is not to be understood as the last hour which strikes before the end but rather as a way of characterising the last age (that is, the period of time before the end) in general. The decisive factor, even for the Apocalyptics, is not the end of a temporal succession but the way in which fulfilment takes place. In spite of the proximity of the end (understood as the *kairos* of eschatological fulfilment; see 1:3 and 22:10) the community does not know at what hour the Lord will come (3:3: cf 16:15). There is 'the hour of judgement' and 'the hour of the harvest' (14:7, 15); the emphasis is on the fact of divine judgement rather than the time when it will take place (18:10, 17, 19).

In Mk 14:41 the 'dark hour' in which Jesus will be 'delivered up', the hour of the Messiah's death foreordained by God, corresponds to the 'hour' of the coming of the Son of Man in glory. In Gethsemani Jesus is afraid of this hour and prays that it may pass from him (14:35) even while accepting it from his Father's hand. This has to be understood within the 'Son of Man theology' of Mark's gospel. According to Lk 22:53 this is the hour of his enemies ('your hour') and of 'the powers of darkness'.

3. *The Gospel of John.* 'The hour' or 'the hour of Jesus' is given most importance theologically in John's gospel. Though its significance is expressed in different ways there is an underlying unity. This gospel makes use of eschatological terminology as when it speaks of the 'hour to come' when the dead in their graves will hear the voice of the Son of God (5:28), or when it refers to persecutions which will come upon the disciples (16:2, 4), or when it records Jesus as saying that he will speak to them no longer in figures (16:25). But the genuinely johannine view is that the hour which is to come has already come in Jesus, that the true worshippers of the Father worship him in spirit and truth (4:23) and that 'the dead' hear the voice of the Son of God and that they who hear it will live (5:25). The eschatological turning-point is already present in Jesus and therefore the eschatological 'hour' has already been accomplished.

In view of this context, which understands salvation as already present in Christ, hardly any difference is made between the time of Jesus's life on earth and that of his exaltation when he dispenses salvation to makind. It is another matter, however, when the author has in view his death and subsequent return to the glory which is his in heaven. Here he speaks of 'his hour' which is the hour of the decisive turning-point (13:1). This is the hour of his exaltation on the cross (3:14; 8:28; 12:32, 34) which is also the hour of his glorification (12:23; 17:1). According to the johannine point of view, the cross is no longer the nadir of the humiliation of Christ (see Phil 2:8) but rather a lifting up (symbolically of the lifting up of the cross: see 12:34), the beginning of his glorification and of the salvific activity of the exalted Christ (12:32; 17:1f). His 'hour' on the Mount of Olives (12:27f) must also be taken into account in this perspective. This decisive hour in the redemptive mission of Jesus is entirely dependent on the will and the power of the Father for its fulfilment. Hence we are told on more than one occasion that the Jews did not lay hands on him since 'his hour had not yet come' (7:30; 8:20). Immediately before the Passover of his death, at the Last Supper, Jesus knows that the hour of his return to the Father has come (13:1), and after the traitor has left the room he says that the Son of Man is 'now' glorified (13:31; cf also the 'now' in 12:31). The 'little while' which must pass before that hour is really at hand (16:16ff) disappears as far as Jesus is concerned (see the tenses in 12:23, 31; 13:31; 16:32; 17:1) but signifies for the disciples a time of tribulation (16:20ff—comparison with 'the hour' of the woman in travail) and temptation.

It is clear, therefore, that 'the hour of Jesus' has its meaning more from what happens than from its significance as a unit of time. What is decisive is that both as regards what happens and when it happens it is within the salvific design and the will of God. This is important for the interpretation of the most difficult passage which we have to consider, namely, the words of Jesus at the marriage feast of Cana (2:4). There are many catholic exegetes who attempt to interpret the hour of which Jesus speaks on this occasion ('my hour') as referring to the hour of his exaltation and glorification and therefore as revealing his glory of which the miracle of changing water into wine is a sign or symbol. Others recognise here only the expression of the messianic consciousness of Jesus whose entire activity, right from the beginning of his self-revelation on earth, results from the mission given him by the Father and is manifested by 'signs'. In this case 'the hour' cannot be understood in a purely temporal sense since Jesus goes on at once to work the miracle.

The attentive expectation of the Jesus of the fourth gospel for the striking of the eschatological hour of salvation in which the will of the Father is revealed serves as an admonition to his disciples to recognise the eschatological hour which has come with him and is still to be completed and, at the same time, to take cognizance of their situation within the history of salvation and the task which awaits them (see 16:1–4, suffering and persecution; 16:22–7, joy and confidence; 16:33, peace and the assurance of victory).

Bibliography: P. Volz, *Die Eschatologie der jüdischen Gemeinde*, Tübingen 1934²; G. Delling, *Das Zeitverständnis des NT*, Gütersloh 1940; O. Cullmann, *Christ and Time*, London 1951; J. Barr, *Biblical Words for Time*, London 1962; R. Motte, 'Hour', *DBT*, 439ff; P. Neuenzeit, '"Als die Fülle der Zeit gekommen war . . ." (Gal 4:4): Gedanken zum biblischen Zeitverständnis', *Bibel und Leben* 4 (1963), 223–39.

Rudolf Schnackenburg